SQL Server 2017 Deve
Guide

A professional guide to designing and developing enterprise database applications

Dejan Sarka
Miloš Radivojević
William Durkin

BIRMINGHAM - MUMBAI

SQL Server 2017 Developer's Guide

Copyright © 2018 Packt Publishing

Commissioning Editor: Amey Varangaonkar
Acquisition Editor: Vinay Argekar
Content Development Editor: Snehal Kolte
Technical Editor: Sayli Nikalje
Copy Editor: Safis Editing
Project Coordinator: Manthan Patel
Proofreader: Safis Editing
Indexer: Rekha Nair
Graphics: Tania Dutta
Production Coordinator: Nilesh Mohite

First published: March 2018

Production reference: 1140318

Published by Packt Publishing Ltd.
Livery Place
35 Livery Street
Birmingham
B3 2PB, UK.

ISBN 978-1-78847-619-5

www.packtpub.com

To my son, Dejan, and to the love of my life, Milena.

– Dejan Sarka

To my wife, Nataša, and my children, Mila and Vasilije.

– Miloš Radivojević

To my wife Birgit, and son Liam. You make it all possible

– William Durkin

`mapt.io`

Mapt is an online digital library that gives you full access to over 5,000 books and videos, as well as industry leading tools to help you plan your personal development and advance your career. For more information, please visit our website.

Why subscribe?

- Spend less time learning and more time coding with practical eBooks and Videos from over 4,000 industry professionals

- Improve your learning with Skill Plans built especially for you

- Get a free eBook or video every month

- Mapt is fully searchable

- Copy and paste, print, and bookmark content

PacktPub.com

Did you know that Packt offers eBook versions of every book published, with PDF and ePub files available? You can upgrade to the eBook version at `www.PacktPub.com` and as a print book customer, you are entitled to a discount on the eBook copy. Get in touch with us at `service@packtpub.com` for more details.

At `www.PacktPub.com`, you can also read a collection of free technical articles, sign up for a range of free newsletters, and receive exclusive discounts and offers on Packt books and eBooks.

Contributors

About the authors

Dejan Sarka, MCT and Data Platform MVP, is an independent trainer and consultant focusing on the development of database and business intelligence applications. Besides working on projects, he spends about half of his time training and mentoring. He is the founder of the Slovenian SQL Server and .NET Users Group. He is the main author or co-author of 16 books on databases and SQL Server. He has also developed many courses and seminars for Microsoft, SolidQ, and Pluralsight.

Thanks to my family and friends for their patience!

Miloš Radivojević is a database consultant in Vienna, Austria. He is a Data Platform MVP and specializes in SQL Server for application developers and performance/query tuning. He works as a principal database consultant in bwin (GVC Holdings). He is a cofounder of PASS Austria and speaks regularly at international conferences.

I would like to thank my wife, Nataša, my daughter, Mila, and my son, Vasilije, for all their sacrifice, patience, and understanding while I worked on this book.

William Durkin is the co-founder of Data Masterminds, a Microsoft Data Platform consultancy. William is a UK born Data Platform MVP, now living in Germany. William speaks at SQL Server focused events across the globe and is the founder and organizer of the small, but popular, SQLGrillen.

A big thank you goes to my wife Birgit and son Liam—both have put up with my grumpiness and late nights for far too long. I love you up to the sky and the bits!

About the reviewer

Tomaž Kaštrun is an SQL Server developer and data analyst with more than 15 years experience in business warehousing, development, ETL, database administration, and query tuning. He also has more than 15 years experience in data analysis, data mining, statistical research, and machine learning.

He is a Microsoft SQL Server MVP for Data Platform and has been working with Microsoft SQL Server since version 2000. He is a blogger, the author of many articles, the co-author of a statistical analysis book, a speaker at community and Microsoft events, and an avid coffee drinker.

Packt is searching for authors like you

If you're interested in becoming an author for Packt, please visit `authors.packtpub.com` and apply today. We have worked with thousands of developers and tech professionals, just like you, to help them share their insight with the global tech community. You can make a general application, apply for a specific hot topic that we are recruiting an author for, or submit your own idea.

Table of Contents

Preface

Microsoft SQL Server is developing faster than ever before in its almost 30-year history. The latest versions, SQL Server 2016 and 2017, bring with them many important new features. Some of these new features just extend or improve features that were introduced in the previous versions of SQL Server, and some of them open a completely new set of possibilities for a database developer.

This book prepares its readers for more advanced topics by starting with a quick introduction to SQL Server 2016 and 2017's new features and a recapitulation of the possibilities database developers already had in previous versions of SQL Server. It then goes on to, the new tools are introduced. The next part introduces small delights in the Transact-SQL language. The book then switches to a completely new technology inside SQL Server—JSON support. This is where the basic chapters end and the more complex chapters begin. Stretch Database, security enhancements, and temporal tables are medium-level topics. The latter chapters of the book cover advanced topics, including Query Store, columnstore indexes, and In-Memory OLTP. The next two chapters introduce R and R support in SQL Server, and show how to use the R language for data exploration and analysis beyond what a developer can achieve with Transact-SQL. Python language support is then introduced. The next chapter deals with new possibilities for using data structures called *graphs* in SQL Server 2017. The final chapter introduces SQL Server on Linux and in containers.

By reading this book, you will explore all of the new features added to SQL Server 2016 and 2017. You will become capable of identifying opportunities for using the In-Memory OLTP technology. You will also learn how to use columnstore indexes to get significant storage and performance improvements for analytical applications. You will also be able to extend database design using temporal tables. You will learn how to exchange JSON data between applications and SQL Server in a more efficient way. For very large tables with some historical data, you will be able to migrate the historical data transparently and securely to Microsoft Azure by using Stretch Database. You will tighten security using the new security features to encrypt data or to get more granular control over access to rows in a table. You will be able to tune workload performance more efficiently than ever with Query Store, and use SQL Server on Linux platforms and in containers. Finally, you will discover the potential of R and Python integration with SQL Server.

Who this book is for

Database developers and solution architects looking to design efficient database applications using SQL Server 2017 will find this book very useful. Some basic understanding of database concepts and T-SQL is required to get the best out of this book.

What this book covers

Chapter 1, *Introduction to SQL Server 2017*, very briefly covers the most important features and enhancements, not just those for developers. The chapter shows the whole picture and point readers in the direction of where things are moving.

Chapter 2, *Review of SQL Server Features for Developers*, brief recapitulates the features available for developers in previous versions of SQL Server and serves as a foundation for an explanation of the many new features in SQL Server 2016. Some best practices are covered as well.

Chapter 3, *SQL Server Tools*, helps you understand the changes in the release management of SQL Server tools and explores small and handy enhancements in **SQL Server Management Studio** (**SSMS**). It also introduces RStudio IDE, a very popular tool for developing R code, and briefly covers **SQL Server Data Tools** (**SSDT**), including the new **R Tools for Visual Studio** (**RTVS**), a plugin for Visual Studio, which enables you to develop R code in an IDE that is popular among developers using Microsoft products and languages. The chapter introduces Visual Studio 2017 and shows how it can be used it for data science applications with Python.

Chapter 4, *Transact-SQL Engine Enhancements*, explores small Transact-SQL enhancements: new functions and syntax extensions, ALTER TABLE improvements for online operations, and new query hints for query tuning.

Chapter 5, *JSON Support in SQL Server*, explores the JSON support built into SQL Server. This support should make it easier for applications to exchange JSON data with SQL Server.

Chapter 6, *Stretch Databases*, helps you understand how to migrate historical or less frequently/infrequently accessed data transparently and securely to Microsoft Azure using the **Stretch Database** (**Stretch DB**) feature.

Chapter 7, *Temporal Tables*, introduces support for system-versioned temporal tables based on the SQL:2011 standard. We explain how this is implemented in SQL Server and demonstrate some use cases for it (for example, a time-travel application).

Chapter 8, *Tightening Security*, introduces three new security features. With Always Encrypted, SQL Server finally enables full data encryption. Row-level security on the other hand, restricts which data in a table can be seen by a specific user. Dynamic data masking is a soft feature that limits the exposure of sensitive data by masking it to non-privileged users.

Chapter 9, *Query Store*, guides you through Query Store and helps you troubleshoot and fix performance problems related to execution plan changes.

Chapter 10, *Columnstore Indexes*, revises columnar storage and then explores the huge improvements relating to columnstore indexes in SQL Server 2016: updatable non-clustered columnstore indexes, columnstore indexes on in-memory tables, and many other new features for operational analytics.

Chapter 11, *Introducing SQL Server In-Memory OLTP*, describes a feature introduced in SQL Server 2014 that is still underused: the In-Memory database engine. This provides significant performance gains for OLTP workloads.

Chapter 12, *In-Memory OLTP Improvements in SQL Server 2017*, describes all the improvements to the In-Memory OLTP technology in SQL Server 2017. These improvements extend the number of potential use cases and allow implementation with less development effort and risk.

Chapter 13, *Supporting R in SQL Server*, introduces R Services and the R language. The chapter explains how SQL Server R Services combine the power and flexibility of the open source R language with enterprise-level tools for data storage and management, workflow development, and reporting and visualization.

Chapter 14, *Data Exploration and Predictive Modeling*, with R in SQL Server, shows how you can use R for advanced data exploration and manipulation, statistical analysis, and predictive modeling. All this is way beyond what is possible when using the T-SQL language.

Chapter 15, *Introducing Python*, teaches the Python basics and how to use the language inside SQL Server.

Chapter 16, *Graph Databases*, provides an overview of graph database architecture and how to create database objects in SQL Server 2017.

Chapter 17, *Containers and SQL on Linux*, introduces the two technologies mentioned in the chapter title and provides an overview of how to get started using them both.

To get the most out of this book

1. In order to run all of the demo code in this book, you will need SQL Server 2017 Developer or Enterprise Edition. In addition, you will extensively use SQL Server Management Studio.
2. You will also need the RStudio IDE and/or SQL Server Data Tools with R Tools for Visual Studio plug-in

Download the example code files

You can download the example code files for this book from your account at www.packtpub.com. If you purchased this book elsewhere, you can visit www.packtpub.com/support and register to have the files emailed directly to you.

You can download the code files by following these steps:

1. Log in or register at www.packtpub.com.
2. Select the **SUPPORT** tab.
3. Click on **Code Downloads & Errata**.
4. Enter the name of the book in the **Search** box and follow the onscreen instructions.

Once the file is downloaded, please make sure that you unzip or extract the folder using the latest version of:

- WinRAR/7-Zip for Windows
- Zipeg/iZip/UnRarX for Mac
- 7-Zip/PeaZip for Linux

The code bundle for the book is also hosted on GitHub at https://github.com/PacktPublishing/SQLServer2017Developer'sGuide. In case there's an update to the code, it will be updated on the existing GitHub repository.

We also have other code bundles from our rich catalog of books and videos available at https://github.com/PacktPublishing/. Check them out!

Download the color images

We also provide a PDF file that has color images of the screenshots/diagrams used in this book. You can download it here: `https://www.packtpub.com/sites/default/files/downloads/https://github.com/PacktPublishing/SQLServer2017Developer'sGuide_ColorImages.pdf`.

Conventions used

There are a number of text conventions used throughout this book.

`CodeInText`: Indicates code words in text, database table names, folder names, filenames, file extensions, pathnames, dummy URLs, user input, and Twitter handles. Here is an example: "The simplest query to retrieve the data that you can write includes the `SELECT` and the `FROM` clauses. In the `SELECT` clause, you can use the star character (`*`), literally `SELECT *`, to denote that you need all columns from a table in the result set."

A block of code is set as follows:

```
USE WideWorldImportersDW;
SELECT *
FROM Dimension.Customer;
```

When we wish to draw your attention to a particular part of a code block, the relevant lines or items are set in bold:

```
USE WideWorldImporters;
CREATE TABLE dbo.Product
(
    ProductId INT NOT NULL CONSTRAINT PK_Product PRIMARY KEY,
    ProductName NVARCHAR(50) NOT NULL,
    Price MONEY NOT NULL,
    ValidFrom DATETIME2 GENERATED ALWAYS AS ROW START NOT NULL,
    ValidTo DATETIME2 GENERATED ALWAYS AS ROW END NOT NULL,
    PERIOD FOR SYSTEM_TIME (ValidFrom, ValidTo)
)
WITH (SYSTEM_VERSIONING = ON);
```

Any command-line input or output is written as follows:

```
Customer                        SaleKey  Quantity
------------------------------- -------- -----------
Tailspin Toys (Aceitunas, PR)   36964    288
Tailspin Toys (Aceitunas, PR)   126253   250
Tailspin Toys (Aceitunas, PR)   79272    250
```

Bold: Indicates a new term, an important word, or words that you see onscreen. For example, words in menus or dialog boxes appear in the text like this. Here is an example: "Go to **Tools | Options** and you are then able to type your search string in the textbox in the top-left of the **Options** window."

 Warnings or important notes appear like this.

 Tips and tricks appear like this.

Get in touch

Feedback from our readers is always welcome.

General feedback: Email `feedback@packtpub.com` and mention the book title in the subject of your message. If you have questions about any aspect of this book, please email us at `questions@packtpub.com`.

Errata: Although we have taken every care to ensure the accuracy of our content, mistakes do happen. If you have found a mistake in this book, we would be grateful if you would report this to us. Please visit `www.packtpub.com/submit-errata`, selecting your book, clicking on the Errata Submission Form link, and entering the details.

Piracy: If you come across any illegal copies of our works in any form on the Internet, we would be grateful if you would provide us with the location address or website name. Please contact us at copyright@packtpub.com with a link to the material.

If you are interested in becoming an author: If there is a topic that you have expertise in and you are interested in either writing or contributing to a book, please visit authors.packtpub.com.

Reviews

Please leave a review. Once you have read and used this book, why not leave a review on the site that you purchased it from? Potential readers can then see and use your unbiased opinion to make purchase decisions, we at Packt can understand what you think about our products, and our authors can see your feedback on their book. Thank you!

For more information about Packt, please visit packtpub.com.

1
Introduction to SQL Server 2017

SQL Server is the main relational database management system product from Microsoft. It has been around in one form or another since the late 80s (developed in partnership with Sybase), but as a standalone Microsoft product, it's here since the early 90s. In the last 20 years, SQL Server has changed and evolved, gaining newer features and functionality along the way.

The SQL Server we know today is based on what was arguably the most significant (r)evolutionary step in its history: the release of SQL Server 2005. The changes that were introduced, allowed the versions that followed the 2005 release to take advantage of newer hardware and software improvements, such as: 64-bit memory architecture, better multi-CPU and multi-core support, better alignment with the .NET framework, and many more modernization's in general system architecture.

The incremental changes introduced in each subsequent version of SQL Server have continued to improve upon this solid new foundation. Fortunately, Microsoft has changed the release cycle for multiple products, including SQL Server, resulting in shorter time frames between releases. This has, in part, been due to Microsoft's focus on their much reported Mobile first, Cloud first strategy. This strategy, together with the development of the cloud version of SQL Server Azure SQL Database, has forced Microsoft into a drastically shorter release cycle. The advantage of this strategy is that we are no longer required to wait 3 to 5 years for a new release (and new features). There have been releases every 2 years since SQL Server 2012 was introduced, with multiple releases of Azure SQL Database in between the *real* versions.

While we can be pleased that we no longer need to wait for new releases, we are also at a distinct disadvantage. The rapid release of new versions and features leaves us developers with ever-decreasing periods of time to get to grips with the shiny new features. Prior versions had multiple years between releases, allowing us to build up a deeper knowledge and understanding of the available features, before having to consume new information.

Following on from the release of SQL Server 2016 was the release of SQL Server 2017, barely a year after 2016 was released. Many features were merely more polished/updated versions of the 2016 release, while there were some notable additions in the 2017 release.

In this chapter (and book), we will introduce what is new inside SQL Server 2017. Due to the short release cycle, we will outline features that are brand new in this release of the product and look at features that have been extended or improved upon since SQL Server 2016.

We will be outlining the new features in the following areas:

- Security
- Engine features
- Programming
- Business intelligence

Security

The last few years have made the importance of security in IT extremely apparent, particularly when we consider the repercussions of the Edward Snowden data leaks or multiple cases of data theft via hacking. While no system is completely impenetrable, we should always be considering how we can improve the security of the systems we build. These considerations are wide ranging and sometimes even dictated via rules, regulations, and laws. Microsoft has responded to the increased focus on security by delivering new features to assist developers and DBAs in their search for more secure systems.

Row-Level Security

The first technology that was introduced in SQL Server 2016 to address the need for increased/improved security is **Row-Level Security** (**RLS**). RLS provides the ability to control access to rows in a table based on the user executing a query. With RLS it is possible to implement a filtering mechanism on any table in a database, completely transparently to any external application or direct T-SQL access. The ability to implement such filtering without having to redesign a data access layer allows system administrators to control access to data at an even more granular level than before. The fact that this control can be achieved without any application logic redesign makes this feature potentially even more attractive to certain use-cases. RLS also makes it possible, in conjunction with the necessary auditing features, to lock down a SQL Server database so that even the traditional *god-mode* sysadmin cannot access the underlying data.

> Further details of Row-Level Security can be found in `Chapter 8`, *Tightening Security*.

Dynamic data masking

The second security feature that we will be covering is **Dynamic Data Masking** (**DDM**). DDM allows the system administrator to define column level data masking algorithms that prevent users from reading the contents of columns, while still being able to query the rows themselves. This feature was initially aimed at allowing developers to work with a copy of production data without having the ability to actually *see* the underlying data. This can be particularly useful in environments where data protection laws are enforced (for example, credit card processing systems and medical record storage). Data masking occurs only at query runtime and does not affect the stored data of a table. This means that it is possible to mask a multi-terabyte database through a simple DDL statement, rather than resorting to the previous solution of physically masking the underlying data in the table we want to mask. The current implementation of DDM provides the ability to define a fixed set of functions to columns of a table, which will mask data when a masked table is queried. If a user has the permission to view the masked data, then the masking functions are not run, whereas a user who may not see masked data will be provided with the data as seen through the defined masking functions.

> Further details of Dynamic Data Masking can be found in `Chapter 8`, *Tightening Security*.

Always Encrypted

The third major security feature to be introduced in SQL Server 2016 is Always Encrypted. Encryption with SQL Server was previously a (mainly) server-based solution. Databases were either protected with encryption at the database level (the entire database was encrypted) or at the column level (single columns had an encryption algorithm defined). While this encryption was/is fully functional and *safe*, crucial portions of the encryption process (for example, encryption certificates) are stored inside SQL Server. This effectively gave the owner of a SQL Server instance the ability to potentially gain access to this encrypted data—if not directly, there was at least an increased surface area for a potential malicious access attempt. As ever more companies moved into hosted service and cloud solutions (for example, Microsoft Azure), the previous encryption solutions no longer provided the required level of control/security. Always Encrypted was designed to bridge this security gap by removing the ability of an instance owner to gain access to the encryption components. The entirety of the encryption process was moved outside of SQL Server and resides on the client side. While a similar effect was possible using homebrew solutions, Always Encrypted provides a fully integrated encryption suite into both the .Net Framework and SQL Server. Whenever data is defined as requiring encryption, the data is encrypted within the .NET framework and only sent to SQL Server after encryption has occurred. This means that a malicious user (or even system administrator) will only ever be able to access encrypted information should they attempt to query data stored via Always Encrypted.

 Further details of Always Encrypted can be found in Chapter 8, *Tightening Security*.

Microsoft has made some positive progress in this area of the product. While no system is completely safe and no single feature can provide an all-encompassing solution, all three features provide a further option in building up, or improving upon, any system's current security level. As mentioned for each feature, please visit the dedicated chapter (Chapter 8, *Tightening Security*) to explore how each feature functions and how they may be used in your environments.

Engine features

The Engine features section is traditionally the most important, or interesting, for most DBAs or system administrators when a new version of SQL Server is released. However, there are also numerous engine feature improvements that have tangential meanings for developers too. So, if you are a developer, don't skip this section—or you may miss some improvements that could save you some trouble later on!

Query Store

The Query Store is possibly the biggest new engine feature to come with the release of SQL Server 2016. DBAs and developers should be more than familiar with the situation of a query behaving reliably for a long period, which suddenly changed into a slow-running, resource-killing monster. Some readers may identify the cause of the issue as the phenomenon of *parameter sniffing* or similarly through *stale statistics*. Either way, when troubleshooting to find out why one unchanging query suddenly becomes slow, knowing the query execution plan(s) that SQL Server has created and used can be very helpful. A major issue when investigating these types of problems is the transient nature of query plans and their execution statistics. This is where Query Store comes into play; SQL Server collects and permanently stores information on query compilation and execution on a per-database basis. This information is then persisted inside each database that is being **monitored** by the Query Store functionality, allowing a DBA or developer to investigate performance issues after the fact. It is even possible to perform longer term query analysis, providing an insight into how query execution plans change over a longer time frame. This sort of insight was previously only possible via handwritten solutions or third-party monitoring solutions, which may still not allow the same insights as the Query Store does.

 Further details of Query Store can be found in `Chapter 9`, *Query Store*.

Live query statistics

When we are developing inside SQL Server, each developer creates a mental model of how data flows inside SQL Server. Microsoft has provided a multitude of ways to display this concept when working with query execution. The most obvious visual aid is the graphical execution plan. There are endless explanations in books, articles, and training seminars that attempt to make *reading* these graphical representations easier. Depending upon how your mind works, these descriptions can help or hinder your ability to understand the data flow concepts—fully blocking iterators, pipeline iterators, semi-blocking iterators, nested loop joins... the list goes on. When we look at an actual graphical execution plan, we are seeing a representation of how SQL Server processed a query: which data retrieval methods were used, which join types were chosen to join multiple data sets, what sorting was required, and so on. However, this is a representation after the query has completed execution. Live Query Statistics offers us the ability to observe during query execution and identify how, when, and where data moves through the query plan. This live representation is a huge improvement in making the concepts behind query execution clearer and is a great tool to allow developers to better design their query and index strategies to improve query performance.

 Further details of Live Query Statistics can be found in `Chapter 3`, *SQL Server Tools*.

Stretch Database

Microsoft has worked a lot in the past few years on their Mobile First, Cloud First strategy. We have seen a huge investment in their cloud offering, Azure, with the line between on-premises IT and cloud-based IT being continually blurred. The features being released in the newest products from Microsoft continue this approach and SQL Server is taking steps to bridge the divide between running SQL Server as a fully on-premises solution and storing/processing relational data in the cloud. One big step in achieving this approach is the new Stretch Database feature with SQL Server 2016. Stretch Database allows a DBA to categorize the data inside a database, defining which data is *hot* and which is *cold*. This categorization allows Stretch Database to then move the *cold* data out of the on-premises database and into Azure Cloud Storage. The segmentation of data remains transparent to any user/application that queries the data, which now resides in two different locations. The idea behind this technology is to reduce storage requirements for the on-premises system by offloading large amounts of archive data onto cheaper, slower storage in the cloud.

This reduction should then allow the smaller *hot* data to be placed on smaller capacity, higher performance storage. The *magic* of Stretch Database is the fact that this separation of data requires no changes at the application or database query level. This is a purely storage-level change, which means the potential ROI of segmenting a database is quite large.

 Further details of Stretch Database can be found in Chapter 6, *Stretch Databases*.

Database scoped configuration

Many DBAs who support multiple third-party applications running on SQL Server can experience the difficulty of setting up their SQL Server instances per the application requirements or best practices. Many third-party applications have prerequisites that dictate how the actual instance of SQL Server must be configured. A common occurrence is a requirement of configuring the *Max Degree of Parallelism* to force only one CPU to be used for query execution. As this is an instance-wide setting, this can affect all other databases/applications in a multi-tenant SQL Server instance (which is generally the case). With Database Scoped Configuration in SQL Server 2016, several previously instance-level settings have been moved to a database level configuration option. This greatly improves multi-tenant SQL Server instances, as the decision of, for example, how many CPUs can be used for query execution can be made at the database-level, rather than for the entire instance. This will allow DBAs to host databases with differing CPU usage requirements on the same instance, rather than having to either impact the entire instance with a setting or be forced to run multiple instances of SQL Server and possibly incur higher licensing costs.

Temporal Tables

There are many instances where DBAs or developers are required to implement a change tracking solution, allowing future analysis or assessment of data changes for certain business entities. A readily accessible example is the change history on a customer account in a CRM system. The options for implementing such a change tracking system are varied and have strengths and weaknesses. One such implementation that has seen wide adoption is the use of triggers, to capture data changes and store historical values in an archive table. Regardless of the implementation chosen, it was often cumbersome to be able to develop and maintain these solutions.

One of the challenges was in being able to incorporate table structure changes in the table being tracked. It was equally challenging creating solutions to allow for querying both the base table and the archive table belonging to it. The intelligence of deciding whether to query the *live* and/or *archive* data can require some complex query logic.

With the advent of Temporal Tables, this entire process has been simplified for both developers and DBAs. It is now possible to activate this *change tracking* on a table and push changes into an archive table with a simple change on a table's structure. Querying the base table and including a temporal attribute to the query is also a simple T-SQL syntax addition. As such, it is now possible for a developer to submit temporal analysis queries, and SQL Server takes care of splitting the query between the live and archive data and returning the data in a single result set.

Further details of Temporal Tables can be found in Chapter 7, *Temporal Tables*.

Columnstore indexes

Traditional data storage inside SQL Server has used the row-storage format, where the data for an entire row is stored together on the data pages inside the database. SQL Server 2012 introduced a new storage format: columnstore. This format *pivots* the data storage, combining the data from a single column and storing the data together on the data pages. This storage format provides the ability of massive compression of data; it's orders of magnitude better than traditional row storage. Initially only non-clustered columnstore indexes were possible. With SQL Server 2014, clustered columnstore indexes were introduced, expanding the usability of the feature greatly. Finally, with SQL Server 2016, updateable columnstore indexes and support for In-Memory columnstore indexes have been introduced. The potential performance improvements through these improvements are huge.

Further details of columnstore indexes can be found in Chapter 10, *Columnstore Indexes*.

Containers and SQL Server on Linux

For the longest time, SQL Server has run solely on the Windows operating system. This was a major roadblock for adoption in traditionally Unix/Linux based companies that used alternative RDBM systems instead. Containers have been around in IT for over a decade and have made a major impression in the application development world. The ability to now host SQL Server in a container provides developers with the ability to adopt the development and deployment methodologies associated with containers into database development. A second major breakthrough (and surprise) around SQL Server 2017 was the announcement of SQL Server being **ported** to Linux. The IT world was shocked at this revelation and what it meant for the other RDBM systems on the market. There is practically no other system with the same feature-set and support network available at the same price point. As such, SQL Server on Linux will open a new market and allow for growth in previously unreachable areas of the IT world.

 Further details of columnstore indexes can be found in `Chapter 17`, *Containers and SQL Server on Linux*.

This concludes the section outlining the engine features. Through Microsoft's heavy move into cloud computing and their Azure offerings, they have had increased need to improve their internal systems for themselves. Microsoft has been famous for their *dogfooding* approach of using their own software to run their own business and Azure is arguably their largest foray into this area. The main improvements in the database engine have been fueled by the need to improve their own ability to continue offering Azure database solutions at a scale, and provide features to allow databases of differing sizes and loads to be hosted together.

Programming

Without programming, a SQL Server isn't very useful. The programming landscape of SQL Server has continued to improve to adopt newer technologies over the years. SQL Server 2017 is no exception in this area. There have been some long-awaited general improvements and also some rather revolutionary additions to the product that change the way SQL Server can be used in future projects. This section will outline what programming improvements have been included in SQL Server 2017.

Transact-SQL enhancements

The last major improvements in the T-SQL language allowed for better processing of running totals and other similar window functions. This was already a boon and allowed developers to replace arcane cursors with high performance T-SQL. These improvements are never enough for the most performance conscious developers among us, and as such there were still voices requesting further incorporation of the ANSI SQL standards into the T-SQL implementation.

Notable additions to the T-SQL syntax include the ability to finally split comma-separated strings using a single function call, STRING_SPLIT(), instead of the previous *hacky* implementations using loops or the **Common Language Runtime (CLR)**.

The sensible opposing syntax for splitting strings is a function to aggregate values together, STRING_AGG(), which returns a set of values in a comma-separated string. This replaces similarly *hacky* solutions using the XML data type of one of a multitude of looping solutions.

Each improvement in the T-SQL language further extends the toolbox that we, as developers, possess to be able to manipulate data inside SQL Server. The ANSI SQL standards provide a solid basis to work from and further additions of these standards are always welcome.

Further details of T-SQL Enhancements can be found in Chapter 4, *Transact-SQL and Database Engine Enhancements*.

JSON

It is quite common to meet developers outside of the Microsoft stack who look down on products from Redmond. Web developers in particular have been critical of the access to *modern* data exchange structures, or rather the lack of it. JSON has become the de facto data exchange method for the application development world. It is similar in structure to the previous *cool-kid* XML, but for reasons beyond the scope of this book, JSON has overtaken XML and is the expected payload for application and database communications. Microsoft has included JSON as a native data type in SQL Server 2016 and provided a set of functions to accompany the data type.

Further details of JSON can be found in Chapter 5, *JSON Support in SQL Server*.

In-Memory OLTP

In-Memory OLTP (codename Hekaton) was introduced in SQL Server 2014. The promise of ultra-high performance data processing inside SQL Server was a major feature when SQL Server 2014 was released. As expected with version-1 features, there were a wide range of limitations in the initial release and this prevented many customers from being able to adopt the technology. With SQL Server 2017, a great number of these limitations have been either raised to a higher threshold or completely removed. In-Memory OLTP has received the required maturity and extension in feature set to make it viable for prime production deployment. Chapter 11, *Introducing SQL Server In-Memory OLTP* will show an introduction to In-Memory OLTP, explaining how the technology works under the hood and how the initial release of the feature works in SQL Server 2014. Chapter 12, *In-Memory OLTP Improvements in SQL Server 2017* will build on top of the introduction and explain how the feature has matured and improved with the release of SQL Server 2016 and 2017.

 Further details of In-Memory OLTP can be found in Chapter 11, *Introducing SQL Server In-Memory OLTP* and Chapter 12, *In-Memory OLTP Improvements in SQL Server 2017*.

SQL Server Tools

Accessing or managing data inside SQL Server and developing data solutions are two separate disciplines, each with their own specific focus on SQL Server. As such, Microsoft has created two different tools, each tailored towards the processes and facets of these disciplines.

SQL Server Management Studio (**SSMS**), as the name suggests, is the main management interface between DBAs/developers and SQL Server. The studio was originally released with SQL Server 2005 as a replacement and consolidation of the old Query Analyzer and Enterprise Manager tools. As with any non-revenue-generating software, SSMS only received minimal attention over the years, with limitations and missing tooling for many of the newer features in SQL Server. With SQL Server 2016, the focus of Microsoft has shifted and SSMS has been de-coupled from the release cycle of SQL Server itself. This decoupling allows both SSMS and SQL Server to be developed without having to wait for each other or for release windows. New releases of SSMS are created on top of more recent versions of Visual Studio, and have seen almost monthly update releases since SQL Server 2016 was released into the market.

SQL Server Data Tools (**SSDT**) is also an application based on the Visual Studio framework. SSDT is focused on the application/data development discipline. SSDT is much more closely aligned with Visual Studio in its structure and the features offered. This focus includes the ability to create entire database projects and solution files, easier integration into source control systems, the ability to connect projects into automated build processes, and generally offering a developer-centric development environment with a familiarity with Visual Studio. It is possible to design and create solutions in SSDT for SQL Server using the Relational Engine, Analysis Services, Integration Services, Reporting Services, and of course the Azure SQL database.

 Further details of SQL Server Tools can be found in `Chapter 3`, *SQL Server Tools*.

This concludes the overview of programming enhancements inside SQL Server 2016. The improvements outlined are all solid evolutionary steps in their respective areas. New features are very welcome and allow us to achieve more while requiring less effort on our side. The In-memory OLTP enhancements are especially positive, as they now expand on the groundwork laid down in the release of SQL Server 2014. Please read the respective chapters to gain deeper insight into how these enhancements can help you.

Business intelligence

Business intelligence is a huge area of IT and has been a cornerstone of the SQL Server product since at least SQL Server 2005. As the market and technologies in the business intelligence space improve, so must SQL Server. The advent of cloud-based data analysis systems as well as the recent buzz around *big data* are driving forces for all data platform providers, and Microsoft is no exception here. While there are multiple enhancements in the business intelligence portion of SQL Server 2016, we will be concentrating on the feature that has a wider audience than just data analysts: the R language in SQL Server.

R in SQL server

Data analytics has been the hottest topic in IT for the past few years, with new niches being crowned as the pinnacles of information science almost as fast as technology can progress. However, IT does have a few resolute *classics* that have stood the test of time and are still in widespread use. SQL (in its many permutations) is a language we are well aware of in the SQL Server world. Another such language is the succinctly titled **R**. The R language is a data mining, machine learning, and statistical analysis language that has existed since 1993. Many professionals such as data scientists, data analysts, or statisticians have been using the R language and tools that belong in that domain for a similarly long time. Microsoft has identified that although they may want all of the world's data inside SQL Server, this is just not feasible or sensible. External data sources and languages like R exist and they need to be accessible in an integrated manner.

For this to work, Microsoft made the decision to purchase Revolution Analytics (a commercial entity producing the forked *Revolution R*) in 2015 and was then able to integrate the language and server process into SQL Server 2016. This integration allows a *normal* T-SQL developer to interact with the extremely powerful R service in a native manner, and allows more advanced data analysis to be performed on their data.

> Further details of R in SQL Server can be found in Chapter 13, *Supporting R in SQL Server* and Chapter 14, *Data Exploration and Predictive Modeling with R in SQL Server*.

Release cycles

Microsoft has made a few major public-facing changes in the past 5 years. These changes include a departure from longer release cycles in their main products and a transition towards subscription-based services (for example, Office 365 and Azure services). The ideas surrounding continuous delivery and agile software development have also shaped the way that Microsoft has been delivering on their flagship integrated development environment Visual Studio, with releases occurring approximately every six months. This change in philosophy is now flowing into the development cycle of SQL Server. Due to the similarly constant release cycle of the cloud-version of SQL Server (Azure SQL Database), there is a desire to keep both the cloud and on-premises versions of the product as close to each other as possible. As such, it is unsurprising to see that the previous release cycle of every three to 5 years is being replaced with much shorter intervals. A clear example of this is that SQL Server 2016 released to the market in June of 2016, with a **Community Technology Preview** (**CTP**) of SQL Server 2017 being released in November of 2016 and the **Release To Market** (**RTM**) of SQL Server 2017 happening in October 2017. The wave of technology progress stops for no one. This is very clearly true in the case of SQL Server!

Summary

In this introductory chapter, we saw a brief outline of what will be covered in this book. Each version of SQL Server has hundreds of improvements and enhancements, both through new features and through extensions on previous versions. The outlines for each chapter provide an insight into the main topics covered in this book, and allow you to identify which areas you may like to dive into and where to find them.

So let's get going with the rest of the book and see what SQL Server 2017 has to offer.

2

Review of SQL Server Features for Developers

Before delving into the new features in SQL Server 2016 and 2017, let's have a quick recapitulation of the SQL Server features for developers that are already available in the previous versions of SQL Server. Please note that this chapter is not a comprehensive development guide; covering all features would be out of the scope of this book. Recapitulating the most important features will help you remember what you already have in your development toolbox, and also understand the need for and the benefits of the new or improved features in SQL Server 2016 and 2017.

This chapter has a lot of code. As this is not a book for beginners, the intention of this chapter is not to teach you the basics of database development. It is rather a reminder for the powerful and efficient **Transact-SQL (T-SQL)** and other elements included in SQL Server version 2014 and even earlier.

The recapitulation starts with the mighty T-SQL SELECT statement. Besides the basic clauses, advanced techniques such as window functions, common table expressions, and the APPLY operator are explained. Then you will pass quickly through creating and altering database objects, including tables and programmable objects, such as triggers, views, user-defined functions, and stored procedures. You will also review the data modification language statements. Of course, errors might appear, so you have to know how to handle them. In addition, data integrity rules might require that two or more statements are executed as an atomic, indivisible block. You can achieve this with the help of transactions.

The last section of this chapter deals with parts of the SQL Server Database Engine that is marketed with the common name *Beyond Relational*. This is nothing beyond the relational model; *beyond relational* is really just a marketing term. Nevertheless, you will review how SQL Server supports spatial data, how you can enhance the T-SQL language with **Common Language Runtime** (**CLR**) elements written in some .NET language such as Visual C#, and how SQL Server supports XML data.

The code in this chapter uses the WideWorldImportersDW demo database. In order to test the code, this database must be present in your SQL Server instance you are using for testing, and you must also have **SQL Server Management Studio** (**SSMS**) as the client tool.

This chapter will cover the following points:

- Core Transact-SQL SELECT statement elements
- Advanced SELECT techniques
- Data definition language statements
- Data modification language statements
- Triggers
- Data abstraction—views, functions, and stored procedures
- Error handling
- Using transactions
- Spatial data
- CLR integration
- XML support in SQL Server

The mighty Transact-SQL SELECT

You probably already know that the most important SQL statement is the mighty SELECT statement you use to retrieve data from your databases. Every database developer knows the basic clauses and their usage:

- SELECT to define the columns returned, or a projection of all table columns
- FROM to list the tables used in the query and how they are associated, or joined
- WHERE to filter the data to return only the rows that satisfy the condition in the predicate

- GROUP BY to define the groups over which the data is aggregated
- HAVING to filter the data after the grouping with conditions that refer to aggregations
- ORDER BY to sort the rows returned to the client application

Besides these basic clauses, SELECT offers a variety of advanced possibilities as well. These advanced techniques are unfortunately less exploited by developers, although they are really powerful and efficient. Therefore, I urge you to review them and potentially use them in your applications. The advanced query techniques presented here include:

- Queries inside queries, or shortly subqueries
- Window functions
- TOP and OFFSET, FETCH expressions
- APPLY operator
- **Common tables expressions (CTEs)**

Core Transact-SQL SELECT statement elements

The simplest query to retrieve the data that you can write includes the SELECT and the FROM clauses. In the SELECT clause, you can use the star character (*), literally SELECT *, to denote that you need all columns from a table in the result set. The following code switches to the WideWorldImportersDW database context and selects all data from the Dimension.Customer table:

```
USE WideWorldImportersDW;
SELECT *
FROM Dimension.Customer;
```

The code returns 403 rows, all customers with all columns.

 Using SELECT * is not recommended in production. Such queries can return an unexpected result when the table structure changes, and is also not suitable for good optimization.

Better than using `SELECT *` is to explicitly list only the columns you need. This means you are returning only a **projection** on the table. The following example selects only four columns from the table:

```
SELECT [Customer Key], [WWI Customer ID],
  [Customer], [Buying Group]
FROM Dimension.Customer;
```

Here is the shortened result, limited to the first three rows only:

Customer Key	WWI Customer ID	Customer	Buying Group
0	0	Unknown	N/A
1	1	Tailspin Toys (Head Office)	Tailspin Toys
2	2	Tailspin Toys (Sylvanite, MT)	Tailspin Toys

You can see that the column names in the `WideWorldImportersDW` database include spaces. Names that include spaces are called **delimited identifiers**. In order to make SQL Server properly understand them as column names, you must enclose delimited identifiers in parentheses. However, if you prefer to have names without spaces, or if you use computed expressions in the column list, you can add **column aliases**. The following query returns completely the same data as the previous one, just with columns renamed by aliases to avoid delimited names:

```
SELECT [Customer Key] AS CustomerKey,
  [WWI Customer ID] AS CustomerId,
  [Customer],
  [Buying Group] AS BuyingGroup
FROM Dimension.Customer;
```

You might have noticed in the result set returned from the last two queries that there is also a row in the table for an unknown customer. You can *filter* this row with the `WHERE` clause:

```
SELECT [Customer Key] AS CustomerKey,
  [WWI Customer ID] AS CustomerId,
  [Customer],
  [Buying Group] AS BuyingGroup
FROM Dimension.Customer
WHERE [Customer Key] <> 0;
```

In a relational database, you typically have data spread in multiple tables. Each table represents a *set of entities* of the same kind, such as customers in the examples you have seen so far. In order to get result sets that are meaningful for the business your database supports, most of the time you need to retrieve data from multiple tables in the same query. You need to *join* two or more tables based on some conditions. The most frequent kind of a join is the *inner join*. Rows returned are those for which the condition in the join predicate for the two tables joined evaluates to *true*. Note that in a relational database, you have three-valued logic, because there is always a possibility that a piece of data is unknown. You mark the unknown with the NULL keyword. A predicate can thus evaluate to true, false, or NULL. For an inner join, the order of the tables involved in the join is not important. In the following example, you can see the Fact.Sale table joined with an INNER JOIN to the Dimension.Customer table:

```
SELECT c.[Customer Key] AS CustomerKey,
   c.[WWI Customer ID] AS CustomerId,
   c.[Customer],
   c.[Buying Group] AS BuyingGroup,
   f.Quantity,
   f.[Total Excluding Tax] AS Amount,
   f.Profit
FROM Fact.Sale AS f
   INNER JOIN Dimension.Customer AS c
     ON f.[Customer Key] = c.[Customer Key];
```

In the query, you can see that *table aliases* are used. If a column's name is unique across all tables in the query, then you can use it without the table name. If not, you need to use the table name in front of the column, to avoid ambiguous column names, in the format table.column. In the previous query, the [Customer Key] column appears in both tables. Therefore, you need to precede this column name with the table name of its origin to avoid ambiguity. You can shorten the two-part column names by using table aliases. You specify table aliases in the FROM clause. Once you specify table aliases, you must always use the aliases; you can't refer to the original table names in that query anymore. Please note that a column name might be unique in the query at the moment when you write the query. However, somebody could add a column later with the same name in another table involved in the query. If the column name is not preceded by an alias or by the table name, you would get an error when executing the query because of the ambiguous column name. In order to make the code more stable and more readable, you should always use table aliases for each column in the query.

The previous query returns 228,265 rows. It is always recommended that you know, at least approximately, the number of rows your query should return. This number is the first control of the correctness of the result set, or in other words, whether the query is written in a logically correct way. The query returns the unknown customer and the orders associated with this customer—or, more precisely, associated to this placeholder for an unknown customer. Of course, you can use the WHERE clause to filter the rows in a query that joins multiple tables, as you would for a single table query. The following query filters the unknown customer rows:

```
SELECT c.[Customer Key] AS CustomerKey,
   c.[WWI Customer ID] AS CustomerId,
   c.[Customer],
   c.[Buying Group] AS BuyingGroup,
   f.Quantity,
   f.[Total Excluding Tax] AS Amount,
   f.Profit
FROM Fact.Sale AS f
   INNER JOIN Dimension.Customer AS c
     ON f.[Customer Key] = c.[Customer Key]
WHERE c.[Customer Key] <> 0;
```

The query returns 143,968 rows. You can see that a lot of sales are associated with the unknown customer.

Of course, the Fact.Sale table cannot be joined to the Dimension.Customer table. The following query joins it to the Dimension.Date table. Again, the join performed is an inner join:

```
SELECT d.Date, f.[Total Excluding Tax],
   f.[Delivery Date Key]
FROM Fact.Sale AS f
   INNER JOIN Dimension.Date AS d
     ON f.[Delivery Date Key] = d.Date;
```

The query returns 227,981 rows. The query that joined the Fact.Sale table to the Dimension.Customer table returned 228,265 rows. It looks as if not all Fact.Sale table rows have a known delivery date, and not all rows can match the Dimension.Date table rows. You can use an **outer join** to check this.

With an outer join, you preserve the rows from one or both tables, even if they don't have a match in the other table. The result set returned includes all of the matched rows like you get from an inner join plus the preserved rows. Within an outer join, the order of the tables involved in the join might be important. If you use LEFT OUTER JOIN, then the rows from the left table are preserved. If you use RIGHT OUTER JOIN, then the rows from the right table are preserved. Of course, in both cases, the order of the tables involved in the join is important. With a FULL OUTER JOIN, you preserve the rows from both tables, and the order of the tables is not important. The following query preserves the rows from the Fact.Sale table, which is on the left side of the join to the Dimension.Date table. In addition, the query *sorts* the result set by the invoice date descending using the ORDER BY clause:

```
SELECT d.Date, f.[Total Excluding Tax],
  f.[Delivery Date Key], f.[Invoice Date Key]
FROM Fact.Sale AS f
  LEFT OUTER JOIN Dimension.Date AS d
    ON f.[Delivery Date Key] = d.Date
ORDER BY f.[Invoice Date Key] DESC;
```

The query returns 228,265 rows. Here is the partial result of the query:

Date	Total Excluding Tax	Delivery Date Key	Invoice Date Key
NULL	180.00	NULL	2016-05-31
NULL	120.00	NULL	2016-05-31
NULL	160.00	NULL	2016-05-31
...	...	...	...
2016-05-31	2565.00	2016-05-31	2016-05-30
2016-05-31	88.80	2016-05-31	2016-05-30
2016-05-31	50.00	2016-05-31	2016-05-30

For the last invoice date (2016-05-31), the delivery date is NULL. The NULL in the Date column from the Dimension.Date table is there because the data from this table is unknown for the rows with an unknown delivery date in the Fact.Sale table.

Joining more than two tables is not tricky if all of the joins are inner joins. The order of joins is not important. However, you might want to execute an outer join after all of the inner joins. If you don't control the join order with the outer joins, it might happen that a subsequent inner join filters out the preserved rows of an outer join. You can control the join order with parentheses. The following query joins the `Fact.Sale` table with an inner join to the `Dimension.Customer, Dimension.City, Dimension.[Stock Item]`, and `Dimension.Employee` tables, and with a left outer join to the `Dimension.Date` table:

```
SELECT cu.[Customer Key] AS CustomerKey, cu.Customer,
   ci.[City Key] AS CityKey, ci.City,
   ci.[State Province] AS StateProvince, ci.[Sales Territory] AS
SalesTeritory,
   d.Date, d.[Calendar Month Label] AS CalendarMonth,
   d.[Calendar Year] AS CalendarYear,
   s.[Stock Item Key] AS StockItemKey, s.[Stock Item] AS Product, s.Color,
   e.[Employee Key] AS EmployeeKey, e.Employee,
   f.Quantity, f.[Total Excluding Tax] AS TotalAmount, f.Profit
FROM (Fact.Sale AS f
   INNER JOIN Dimension.Customer AS cu
     ON f.[Customer Key] = cu.[Customer Key]
   INNER JOIN Dimension.City AS ci
     ON f.[City Key] = ci.[City Key]
   INNER JOIN Dimension.[Stock Item] AS s
     ON f.[Stock Item Key] = s.[Stock Item Key]
   INNER JOIN Dimension.Employee AS e
     ON f.[Salesperson Key] = e.[Employee Key])
   LEFT OUTER JOIN Dimension.Date AS d
     ON f.[Delivery Date Key] = d.Date;
```

The query returns 228,265 rows. Note that with the usage of the parentheses, the order of joins is defined in the following way:

- Perform all inner joins, with an arbitrary order among them
- Execute the left outer join after all of the inner joins

So far, I have tacitly assumed that the `Fact.Sale` table has 228,265 rows, and that the previous query needed only one outer join of the `Fact.Sale` table with the `Dimension.Date` to return all of the rows. It would be good to check this number in advance. You can check the number of rows by *aggregating* them using the COUNT(*) aggregate function. The following query introduces that function:

```
SELECT COUNT(*) AS SalesCount
FROM Fact.Sale;
```

Now you can be sure that the `Fact.Sale` table has exactly 228,265 rows.

You will often need to aggregate data in *groups*. This is the point where the GROUP BY clause becomes handy. The following query aggregates the sales data for each customer:

```
SELECT c.Customer,
  SUM(f.Quantity) AS TotalQuantity,
  SUM(f.[Total Excluding Tax]) AS TotalAmount,
  COUNT(*) AS SalesCount
FROM Fact.Sale AS f
  INNER JOIN Dimension.Customer AS c
    ON f.[Customer Key] = c.[Customer Key]
WHERE c.[Customer Key] <> 0
GROUP BY c.Customer;
```

The query returns 402 rows, one for each known customer. In the SELECT clause, you can have only the columns used for grouping, or aggregated columns. You need to get a scalar, a single aggregated value for each row and for each column not included in the GROUP BY list.

Sometimes you need to *filter aggregated data*. For example, you might need to find only frequent customers, defined as customers with more than 400 rows in the `Fact.Sale` table. You can filter the result set on the aggregated data by using the HAVING clause, as the following query shows:

```
SELECT c.Customer,
  SUM(f.Quantity) AS TotalQuantity,
  SUM(f.[Total Excluding Tax]) AS TotalAmount,
  COUNT(*) AS SalesCount
FROM Fact.Sale AS f
  INNER JOIN Dimension.Customer AS c
    ON f.[Customer Key] = c.[Customer Key]
WHERE c.[Customer Key] <> 0
GROUP BY c.Customer
HAVING COUNT(*) > 400;
```

The query returns 45 rows for 45 most frequent known customers. Note that you can't use column aliases from the SELECT clause in any other clause introduced in the previous query. The SELECT clause logically executes after all other clauses from the query, and the aliases are not known yet. However, the ORDER BY clause executes after the SELECT clause, and therefore the columns aliases are already known and you can refer to them. The following query shows all of the basic SELECT statement clauses used together to aggregate the sales data over the known customers, filters the data to include the frequent customers only, and sorts the result set descending by the number of rows of each customer in the Fact.Sale table:

```
-- Note: can use column aliases in ORDER BY
SELECT c.Customer,
  SUM(f.Quantity) AS TotalQuantity,
  SUM(f.[Total Excluding Tax]) AS TotalAmount,
  COUNT(*) AS SalesCount
FROM Fact.Sale AS f
  INNER JOIN Dimension.Customer AS c
    ON f.[Customer Key] = c.[Customer Key]
WHERE c.[Customer Key] <> 0
GROUP BY c.Customer
HAVING COUNT(*) > 400
ORDER BY SalesCount DESC;
```

The query returns 45 rows. Here is the shortened result set:

Customer	Quantity	CustomerOrderPosition	TotalOrderPosition
Tailspin Toys (Absecon, NJ)	360	1	129
Tailspin Toys (Absecon, NJ)	324	2	162
Tailspin Toys (Absecon, NJ)	288	3	374
...	...	...	...
Tailspin Toys (Aceitunas, PR)	288	1	392
Tailspin Toys (Aceitunas, PR)	250	4	1331
Tailspin Toys (Aceitunas, PR)	250	3	1315
Tailspin Toys (Aceitunas, PR)	250	2	1313
Tailspin Toys (Aceitunas, PR)	240	5	1478

Advanced SELECT techniques

Aggregating data over the complete input rowset or aggregating in groups produces aggregated rows only—either one row for the whole input rowset or one row per group. Sometimes you need to return aggregates together with the detail data. One way to achieve this is by using subqueries, queries inside queries.

The following query shows an example of using two subqueries in a single query. In the SELECT clause, a subquery calculates the sum of quantity for each customer; it returns a scalar value. The subquery refers to the customer key from the outer query. The subquery can't execute without the outer query; this is a **correlated subquery**. There is another subquery in the FROM clause that calculates the overall quantity for all customers. This query returns a table, although it is a table with a single row and a single column. This query is a **self-contained subquery**, independent of the outer query. A subquery in the FROM clause is also called a **derived table**.

Another type of join is used to add the overall total to each detail row. A **cross join** is a Cartesian product of two input rowsets—each row from one side is associated with every single row from the other side. No join condition is needed. A cross join can produce an unwanted huge result set. For example, if you cross join just 1,000 rows from the left side of the join with 1,000 rows from the right side, you get 1,000,000 rows in the output. Therefore, typically, you want to avoid a cross join in production. However, in the example in the following query, 143,968 from the left side rows is cross joined to a single row from the subquery, therefore producing 143,968 only. Effectively, this means that the overall total column is added to each detail row:

```
 SELECT c.Customer,
    f.Quantity,
    (SELECT SUM(f1.Quantity) FROM Fact.Sale AS f1
     WHERE f1.[Customer Key] = c.[Customer Key]) AS TotalCustomerQuantity,
    f2.TotalQuantity
 FROM (Fact.Sale AS f
    INNER JOIN Dimension.Customer AS c
      ON f.[Customer Key] = c.[Customer Key])
    CROSS JOIN
      (SELECT SUM(f2.Quantity) FROM Fact.Sale AS f2
      WHERE f2.[Customer Key] <> 0) AS f2(TotalQuantity)
 WHERE c.[Customer Key] <> 0
 ORDER BY c.Customer, f.Quantity DESC;
```

Here is an abbreviated output of the query:

Customer	Quantity	TotalCustomerQuantity	TotalQuantity
Tailspin Toys (Absecon, NJ)	360	12415	5667611
Tailspin Toys (Absecon, NJ)	324	12415	5667611
Tailspin Toys (Absecon, NJ)	288	12415	5667611

In the previous example, the correlated subquery in the SELECT clause has to logically execute once per row of the outer query. The query was partially optimized by moving the self-contained subquery for the overall total in the FROM clause, where it logically executes only once. Although SQL Server can optimize correlated subqueries many times and convert them to joins, there also exists a much better and more efficient way to achieve the same result as the previous query returned. You can do this by using the **window functions**.

The following query is using the window aggregate function SUM to calculate the total over each customer and the overall total. The OVER clause defines the partitions, or the windows of the calculation. The first calculation is partitioned over each customer, meaning that the total quantity per customer is reset to zero for each new customer. The second calculation uses an OVER clause without specifying partitions, thus meaning the calculation is done over all the input rowset. This query produces exactly the same result as the previous one:

```
SELECT c.Customer,
  f.Quantity,
  SUM(f.Quantity)
   OVER(PARTITION BY c.Customer) AS TotalCustomerQuantity,
  SUM(f.Quantity)
   OVER() AS TotalQuantity
FROM Fact.Sale AS f
  INNER JOIN Dimension.Customer AS c
    ON f.[Customer Key] = c.[Customer Key]
WHERE c.[Customer Key] <> 0
ORDER BY c.Customer, f.Quantity DESC;
```

You can use many other functions for window calculations. For example, you can use the **ranking functions**, such as ROW_NUMBER(), to calculate some rank in the window or in the overall rowset. However, rank can be defined only over some order. You can specify the order of the calculation in the ORDER BY sub-clause inside the OVER clause. Please note that this ORDER BY clause defines only the logical order of the calculation, and not the order of the rows returned. A standalone, outer ORDER BY at the end of the query defines the order of the result.

The following query calculates a sequential number, the row number of each row in the output, for each detail row of the input rowset. The row number is calculated once in partitions for each customer and once over the whole input rowset. The logical order of the calculation is over quantity descending, meaning that row number one gets the largest quantity—either the largest for each customer or the largest in the whole input rowset:

```
SELECT c.Customer,
  f.Quantity,
  ROW_NUMBER()
```

```
    OVER(PARTITION BY c.Customer
         ORDER BY f.Quantity DESC) AS CustomerOrderPosition,
    ROW_NUMBER()
     OVER(ORDER BY f.Quantity DESC) AS TotalOrderPosition
  FROM Fact.Sale AS f
    INNER JOIN Dimension.Customer AS c
      ON f.[Customer Key] = c.[Customer Key]
  WHERE c.[Customer Key] <> 0
  ORDER BY c.Customer, f.Quantity DESC;
```

The query produces the following result, again abbreviated to a couple of rows only:

Customer	Quantity	CustomerOrderPosition	TotalOrderPosition
Tailspin Toys (Absecon, NJ)	360	1	129
Tailspin Toys (Absecon, NJ)	324	2	162
Tailspin Toys (Absecon, NJ)	288	3	374
...	...	...	...
Tailspin Toys (Aceitunas, PR)	288	1	392
Tailspin Toys (Aceitunas, PR)	250	4	1331
Tailspin Toys (Aceitunas, PR)	250	3	1315
Tailspin Toys (Aceitunas, PR)	250	2	1313
Tailspin Toys (Aceitunas, PR)	240	5	1478

Note the position, or the row number, for the second customer. The order does not look to be completely correct—it is 1, 4, 3, 2, 5, and not 1, 2, 3, 4, 5, as you might expect. This is due to repeating the value for the second largest quantity—for the quantity 250. The quantity is not unique, and thus the order is not deterministic. The order of the result is defined over the quantity, and not over the row number. You can't know in advance which row will get which row number when the order of the calculation is not defined on unique values. Please also note that you might get a different order when you execute the same query on your SQL Server instance.

Window functions are useful for some advanced calculations, such as running totals and moving averages as well. However, the calculation of these values can't be performed over the complete partition. You can additionally frame the calculation to a subset of rows of each partition only.

The following query calculates the running total of the quantity per customer ordered by the sale key and framed differently for each row. The frame is defined from the first row in the partition to the current row. Therefore, the running total is calculated over one row for the first row, over two rows for the second row, and so on. Additionally, the query calculates the moving average of the quantity for the last three rows:

```
SELECT c.Customer,
  f.[Sale Key] AS SaleKey,
  f.Quantity,
  SUM(f.Quantity)
   OVER(PARTITION BY c.Customer
        ORDER BY [Sale Key]
        ROWS BETWEEN UNBOUNDED PRECEDING
                AND CURRENT ROW) AS Q_RT,
  AVG(f.Quantity)
   OVER(PARTITION BY c.Customer
        ORDER BY [Sale Key]
        ROWS BETWEEN 2 PRECEDING
                AND CURRENT ROW) AS Q_MA
FROM Fact.Sale AS f
  INNER JOIN Dimension.Customer AS c
    ON f.[Customer Key] = c.[Customer Key]
WHERE c.[Customer Key] <> 0
ORDER BY c.Customer, f.[Sale Key];
```

The query returns the following (abbreviated) result:

Customer	SaleKey	Quantity	Q_RT	Q_M
Tailspin Toys (Absecon, NJ)	2869	216	216	216
Tailspin Toys (Absecon, NJ)	2870	2	218	109
Tailspin Toys (Absecon, NJ)	2871	2	220	73

Let's find the top three orders by quantity for the Tailspin Toys (Aceitunas, PR) customer! You can do this by using the OFFSET...FETCH clause after the ORDER BY clause, as the following query shows:

```
SELECT c.Customer,
  f.[Sale Key] AS SaleKey,
  f.Quantity
FROM Fact.Sale AS f
  INNER JOIN Dimension.Customer AS c
    ON f.[Customer Key] = c.[Customer Key]
WHERE c.Customer = N'Tailspin Toys (Aceitunas, PR)'
ORDER BY f.Quantity DESC
OFFSET 0 ROWS FETCH NEXT 3 ROWS ONLY;
```

This is the complete result of the query:

```
Customer                          SaleKey   Quantity
------------------------------    -------   -----------
Tailspin Toys (Aceitunas, PR)     36964     288
Tailspin Toys (Aceitunas, PR)     126253    250
Tailspin Toys (Aceitunas, PR)     79272     250
```

But wait, didn't the second largest quantity, the value 250, repeat three times? Which two rows were selected in the output? Again, because the calculation is done over a non-unique column, the result is somehow non-deterministic. SQL Server offers another possibility, the TOP clause. You can specify TOP n WITH TIES, meaning you can get all of the rows with ties on the last value in the output. However, this way you don't know the number of the rows in the output in advance. The following query shows this approach:

```
SELECT TOP 3 WITH TIES
  c.Customer,
  f.[Sale Key] AS SaleKey,
  f.Quantity
FROM Fact.Sale AS f
  INNER JOIN Dimension.Customer AS c
    ON f.[Customer Key] = c.[Customer Key]
WHERE c.Customer = N'Tailspin Toys (Aceitunas, PR)'
ORDER BY f.Quantity DESC;
```

This is the complete result of the previous query—this time it is four rows:

```
Customer                          SaleKey   Quantity
------------------------------    -------   -----------
Tailspin Toys (Aceitunas, PR)     36964     288
Tailspin Toys (Aceitunas, PR)     223106    250
Tailspin Toys (Aceitunas, PR)     126253    250
Tailspin Toys (Aceitunas, PR)     79272     250
```

The next task is to get the top three orders by quantity for each customer. You need to perform the calculation for each customer. The APPLY Transact-SQL operator comes in handy here. You use it in the FROM clause. You apply, or execute, a table expression defined on the right side of the operator once for each row of the input rowset from the left side of the operator. There are two flavors of this operator. The CROSS APPLY version filters out the rows from the left rowset, if the tabular expression on the right side does not return any row. The OUTER APPLY version preserves the row from the left side, even if the tabular expression on the right side does not return any row, just as the LEFT OUTER JOIN does. Of course, columns for the preserved rows do not have known values from the right-side tabular expression. The following query uses the CROSS APPLY operator to calculate the top three orders by quantity for each customer that actually does have some orders:

```
SELECT c.Customer,
    t3.SaleKey, t3.Quantity
FROM Dimension.Customer AS c
  CROSS APPLY (SELECT TOP (3)
                  f.[Sale Key] AS SaleKey,
                  f.Quantity
                FROM Fact.Sale AS f
                WHERE f.[Customer Key] = c.[Customer Key]
                ORDER BY f.Quantity DESC) AS t3
WHERE c.[Customer Key] <> 0
ORDER BY c.Customer, t3.Quantity DESC;
```

Here is the result of this query, shortened to the first nine rows:

Customer	SaleKey	Quantity
Tailspin Toys (Absecon, NJ)	5620	360
Tailspin Toys (Absecon, NJ)	114397	324
Tailspin Toys (Absecon, NJ)	82868	288
Tailspin Toys (Aceitunas, PR)	36964	288
Tailspin Toys (Aceitunas, PR)	126253	250
Tailspin Toys (Aceitunas, PR)	79272	250
Tailspin Toys (Airport Drive, MO)	43184	250
Tailspin Toys (Airport Drive, MO)	70842	240
Tailspin Toys (Airport Drive, MO)	630	225

For the final task in this section, assume that you need to calculate some statistics over totals of customers' orders. You need to calculate the average total amount for all customers, the standard deviation of this total amount, and the average count of total count of orders per customer. This means you need to calculate the totals over customers in advance, and then use aggregate functions AVG() and STDEV() on these aggregates. You could do aggregations over customers in advance in a derived table. However, there is another way to achieve this. You can define the derived table in advance, in the WITH clause of the SELECT statement. Such a subquery is called a **CTE**.

CTEs are more readable than derived tables, and might be also more efficient. You could use the result of the same CTE multiple times in the outer query. If you use derived tables, then you need to define them multiple times if you want to use them multiple times in the outer query. The following query shows the usage of a CTE to calculate the average total amount for all customers, the standard deviation of this total amount, and the average count of total count of orders per customer:

```
WITH CustomerSalesCTE AS
(
SELECT c.Customer,
  SUM(f.[Total Excluding Tax]) AS TotalAmount,
  COUNT(*) AS SalesCount
FROM Fact.Sale AS f
  INNER JOIN Dimension.Customer AS c
    ON f.[Customer Key] = c.[Customer Key]
WHERE c.[Customer Key] <> 0
GROUP BY c.Customer
)
SELECT ROUND(AVG(TotalAmount), 6) AS AvgAmountPerCustomer,
  ROUND(STDEV(TotalAmount), 6) AS StDevAmountPerCustomer,
  AVG(SalesCount) AS AvgCountPerCustomer
FROM CustomerSalesCTE;
```

It returns the following result:

AvgAmountPerCustomer	StDevAmountPerCustomer	AvgCountPerCustomer
270479.217661	38586.082621	358

DDL, DML, and programmable objects

As a developer, you are often also responsible for creating the database objects. Of course, in an application, you need also to insert, update, and delete the data. In order to maintain **data integrity**, meaning enforcing data to comply with business rules, you need to implement constraints. In our quick review of the **data definition language** (DDL) and **data modification language** (DML) elements, we will look at the following statements:

- CREATE for creating tables and programmatic objects
- ALTER to add constraints to a table
- DROP to drop an object
- INSERT to insert new data
- UPDATE to change existing data
- DELETE to delete the data

In a SQL Server database, you can also use programmatic objects. You can use triggers for advanced constraints or to maintain some redundant data such as aggregated data. You can use other programmatic objects for data abstraction, for an intermediate layer between the actual data and an application. The following programmatic objects are introduced here:

- Triggers
- Stored procedures
- Views
- User-defined functions

It is worth mentioning again that this chapter is just a reminder of the features SQL Server gives to developers. Therefore, this section is also not a comprehensive database logical and physical design guide.

Data definition language statements

Let's start with data definition language statements. The following code shows how to create a simple table. This table represents customers' orders. For this demonstration of the DDL and DML statements, only a couple of columns are created in the table. The OrderId column uniquely identifies each row in this table, and is a **primary key** for the table, as the PRIMARY KEY constraint specifies. Finally, the code checks first if a table with the name SimpleOrders in the dbo schema already exists, and drops it if true:

```
IF OBJECT_ID(N'dbo.SimpleOrders', N'U') IS NOT NULL
   DROP TABLE dbo.SimpleOrders;
CREATE TABLE dbo.SimpleOrders
(
  OrderId   INT        NOT NULL,
  OrderDate DATE       NOT NULL,
  Customer  NVARCHAR(5) NOT NULL,
  CONSTRAINT PK_SimpleOrders PRIMARY KEY (OrderId)
);
```

For further examples, another table is needed. The following code creates the dbo.SimpleOrderDetails table, created in a very similar way to the previous table, by checking for its existence and dropping it if it exists first. The OrderId and ProductId columns form a composite primary key. In addition, a CHECK constraint on the Quantity column prevents inserts or updates of this column to value zero:

```
IF OBJECT_ID(N'dbo.SimpleOrderDetails', N'U') IS NOT NULL
   DROP TABLE dbo.SimpleOrderDetails;
CREATE TABLE dbo.SimpleOrderDetails
(
  OrderId   INT NOT NULL,
  ProductId INT NOT NULL,
  Quantity  INT NOT NULL
   CHECK(Quantity <> 0),
  CONSTRAINT PK_SimpleOrderDetails
   PRIMARY KEY (OrderId, ProductId)
);
```

The previous two examples show how to add constraints when you create a table. It is also always possible to add constraints later, by using the ALTER TABLE statement. The tables created in the previous two examples are associated through a **foreign key.** The primary key of the dbo.SimpleOrders table is associating the order details in the dbo.SimpleOrders table with their correspondent order. The code in the following example defines this association:

```
ALTER TABLE dbo.SimpleOrderDetails ADD CONSTRAINT FK_Details_Orders
FOREIGN KEY (OrderId) REFERENCES dbo.SimpleOrders(OrderId);
```

Data modification language statements

The two demo tables are empty at the moment. You add data to them with the INSERT statement and you can specify the data values in the VALUES clause. You can insert more than one row in a single statement, as the following code shows, by inserting two rows into the dbo.SimpleOrderDetails table in a single statement. You can omit the column names in the INSERT part. However, this is not a good practice. Your insert depends on the order of the columns, if you don't specify the column names explicitly. Imagine what could happen if somebody later changes the structure of the table. In a bad outcome, the insert would fail. However, you would at least have the information that something went wrong. In a worse outcome, the insert into the altered table could even succeed. However, now you can finish with wrong data in wrong columns, without even noticing this problem, like the following code example shows:

```
INSERT INTO dbo.SimpleOrders
  (OrderId, OrderDate, Customer)
VALUES
  (1, '20160701', N'CustA');
INSERT INTO dbo.SimpleOrderDetails
  (OrderId, ProductId, Quantity)
VALUES
  (1, 7, 100),
  (1, 3, 200);
```

The following query checks the recently inserted data. As you probably expected, it returns two rows:

```
SELECT o.OrderId, o.OrderDate, o.Customer,
  od.ProductId, od.Quantity
FROM dbo.SimpleOrderDetails AS od
  INNER JOIN dbo.SimpleOrders AS o
    ON od.OrderId = o.OrderId
ORDER BY o.OrderId, od.ProductId;
```

Here is the result:

```
OrderId      OrderDate  Customer ProductId  Quantity
-----------  ---------- -------- ---------- -----------
1            2016-07-01 CustA    3          200
1            2016-07-01 CustA    7          100
```

The next example shows how to update a row. It updates the Quantity column in the dbo.SimpleOrderDetails table for the order with OrderId equal to 1 and for the product with ProductId equal to 3:

```
UPDATE dbo.SimpleOrderDetails
   SET Quantity = 150
WHERE OrderId = 1
  AND ProductId = 3;
```

You can use the same SELECT statement to check the data—whether it is updated correctly, as introduced right after the inserts.

You really need to check the data often, right after a modification. For example, you might use the IDENTITY property or the SEQUENCE object to generate the identification numbers automatically. When you insert an order, you need to check the generated value of the OrderId column, to insert the correct value to the order details table. You can use the OUTPUT clause for this task, as the following code shows:

```
INSERT INTO dbo.SimpleOrders
  (OrderId, OrderDate, Customer)
OUTPUT inserted.*
VALUES
  (2, '20160701', N'CustB');
INSERT INTO dbo.SimpleOrderDetails
  (OrderId, ProductId, Quantity)
OUTPUT inserted.*
VALUES
  (2, 4, 200);
```

The output of the two inserts is shown as follows:

```
OrderId      OrderDate  Customer
-----------  ---------- --------
2            2016-07-01 CustB
OrderId      ProductId  Quantity
-----------  ---------- -----------
2            4          200
```

Triggers

The code for creating the `dbo.SimpleOrders` table doesn't check the order date value when inserting or updating the data. The following `INSERT` statement, for example, inserts an order with a pretty old and probably wrong date:

```
INSERT INTO dbo.SimpleOrders
  (OrderId, OrderDate, Customer)
VALUES
  (3, '20100701', N'CustC');
```

You can check that the incorrect date is in the table with the following query:

```
SELECT o.OrderId, o.OrderDate, o.Customer
FROM dbo.SimpleOrders AS o
ORDER BY o.OrderId;
```

Of course, it is possible to prevent inserting an order date too far in the past, or updating it to a too old value, with a check constraint. However, imagine that you don't want to just reject inserts and updates with the order date value in the past; imagine you need to correct the value to some predefined minimal value—for example, January 1, 2016. You can achieve this with a trigger.

SQL Server supports two different kinds of **DML** triggers and one kind of **DDL** trigger. DML triggers can fire after or instead of a DML action, and DDL triggers can fire only after a DDL action. For a database developer, the after DML triggers are the most useful. As you already know, you can use them for advanced constraints, for maintaining redundant data, and more. A **database administrator (DBA)** might use DDL triggers, instead of DML triggers, for example, to check and reject inappropriate altering of an object, to make a view updateable. Of course, very often there is no such strict role separation in place. DDL triggers, instead of DML triggers, are not forbidden for database developers. The following code shows a trigger created on the `dbo.SimpleOrders` table that fires after an `INSERT` or an `UPDATE` to this table. It checks the `OrderDate` column value. If the date is far much in the past, it replaces it with the default minimal value:

```
CREATE TRIGGER trg_SimpleOrders_OrdereDate
  ON dbo.SimpleOrders AFTER INSERT, UPDATE
AS
  UPDATE dbo.SimpleOrders
    SET OrderDate = '20160101'
  WHERE OrderDate < '20160101';
```

Let's try to insert a low order date, and update an existing value to a value too far, in the past:

```
INSERT INTO dbo.SimpleOrders
  (OrderId, OrderDate, Customer)
VALUES
  (4, '20100701', N'CustD');
UPDATE dbo.SimpleOrders
    SET OrderDate = '20110101'
  WHERE OrderId = 3;
```

You can check the data after the updates with the following query:

```
SELECT o.OrderId, o.OrderDate, o.Customer,
    od.ProductId, od.Quantity
FROM dbo.SimpleOrderDetails AS od
  RIGHT OUTER JOIN dbo.SimpleOrders AS o
    ON od.OrderId = o.OrderId
ORDER BY o.OrderId, od.ProductId;
```

Here is the result. As you can see, the trigger changed the incorrect dates to the predefined minimal date:

OrderId	OrderDate	Customer	ProductId	Quantity
1	2016-07-01	CustA	3	150
1	2016-07-01	CustA	7	100
2	2016-07-01	CustB	4	200
3	2016-01-01	CustC	NULL	NULL
4	2016-01-01	CustD	NULL	NULL

Note that the query used an OUTER JOIN to include the orders without the details in the result set.

Data abstraction—views, functions, and stored procedures

A very good practice is to use SQL Server stored procedures for data modification and data retrieval. Stored procedures provide many benefits. Some of the benefits include:

- **Data abstraction**: Client applications don't need to work with the data directly; they rather call the stored procedures. Underlying schema might even get modified without an impact on an application, as long as you change the stored procedures that work with the objects with modified schema appropriately.

- **Security**: Client applications can access data through stored procedures and other programmatic objects only. For example, even if an end user uses their own SQL Server Management Studio instead of the client application that the user should use, the user still cannot modify the data in an uncontrolled way, directly in the tables.
- **Performance**: Stored procedures can reduce network traffic, because you can execute many statements inside the procedure within a single call to a stored procedure. In addition, SQL Server has a lot of work with the optimization and compilation of the code an application is sending. SQL Server optimizes this by storing the optimized and compiled code in memory. The compiled execution plans for stored procedures are typically held longer in memory than the execution plans for ad hoc queries, and thus get more frequently reused.
- **Usage**: Stored procedures accept input and can return output parameters, so they can be easily coded to serve multiple users.

The code in the following example creates a stored procedure to insert a row into the dbo.SimpleOrders table. The procedure accepts one input parameter for each column of the table:

```
CREATE PROCEDURE dbo.InsertSimpleOrder
(@OrderId AS INT, @OrderDate AS DATE, @Customer AS NVARCHAR(5))
AS
INSERT INTO dbo.SimpleOrders
  (OrderId, OrderDate, Customer)
VALUES
  (@OrderId, @OrderDate, @Customer);
```

Here is a similar procedure for inserting data into the dbo.SimpleOrderDetails table:

```
CREATE PROCEDURE dbo.InsertSimpleOrderDetail
(@OrderId AS INT, @ProductId AS INT, @Quantity AS INT)
AS
INSERT INTO dbo.SimpleOrderDetails
  (OrderId, ProductId, Quantity)
VALUES
  (@OrderId, @ProductId, @Quantity);
```

Let's test the procedures. In the first part, the two calls to the dbo.InsertSimpleOrder procedure insert two new orders:

```
EXEC dbo.InsertSimpleOrder
  @OrderId = 5, @OrderDate = '20160702', @Customer = N'CustA';
EXEC dbo.InsertSimpleOrderDetail
  @OrderId = 5, @ProductId = 1, @Quantity = 50;
```

The following code calls the `dbo.InsertSimpleOrderDetail` procedure four times to insert four order details rows:

```
EXEC dbo.InsertSimpleOrderDetail
  @OrderId = 2, @ProductId = 5, @Quantity = 150;
EXEC dbo.InsertSimpleOrderDetail
  @OrderId = 2, @ProductId = 6, @Quantity = 250;
EXEC dbo.InsertSimpleOrderDetail
  @OrderId = 1, @ProductId = 5, @Quantity = 50;
EXEC dbo.InsertSimpleOrderDetail
  @OrderId = 1, @ProductId = 6, @Quantity = 200;
```

The following query checks the state of the two tables after these calls:

```
SELECT o.OrderId, o.OrderDate, o.Customer,
  od.ProductId, od.Quantity
FROM dbo.SimpleOrderDetails AS od
  RIGHT OUTER JOIN dbo.SimpleOrders AS o
    ON od.OrderId = o.OrderId
ORDER BY o.OrderId, od.ProductId;
```

Here is the result after the inserts through the stored procedures:

OrderId	OrderDate	Customer	ProductId	Quantity
1	2016-07-01	CustA	3	150
1	2016-07-01	CustA	5	50
1	2016-07-01	CustA	6	200
1	2016-07-01	CustA	7	100
2	2016-07-01	CustB	4	200
2	2016-07-01	CustB	5	150
2	2016-07-01	CustB	6	250
3	2016-01-01	CustC	NULL	NULL
4	2016-01-01	CustD	NULL	NULL
5	2016-07-02	CustA	1	50

You can see in the result of the previous query that there are still some orders without order details in your data. Although this might be unwanted, it could happen quite frequently. Your end users might often need to quickly find orders without details. Instead of executing the same complex query over and over again, you can create a view which encapsulates this complex query. Besides simplifying the code, views are also useful for tightening security. Just like stored procedures, views are **securables** as well. A DBA can revoke the direct access to tables from end users, and give them access to the views only.

The following example creates a view that finds the orders without details. Note that a view in SQL Server can consist of a single SELECT statement only, and that it does not accept parameters:

```
CREATE VIEW dbo.OrdersWithoutDetails
AS
SELECT o.OrderId, o.OrderDate, o.Customer
FROM dbo.SimpleOrderDetails AS od
  RIGHT OUTER JOIN dbo.SimpleOrders AS o
    ON od.OrderId = o.OrderId
WHERE od.OrderId IS NULL;
```

Now the query that finds the orders without details becomes extremely simple—it just uses the view:

```
SELECT OrderId, OrderDate, Customer
FROM dbo.OrdersWithoutDetails;
```

Here is the result, the two orders without order details:

```
OrderId      OrderDate   Customer
-----------  ----------  --------
3            2016-01-01  CustC
4            2016-01-01  CustD
```

If you need to parameterize a view, you have to use an **inline table-valued function** instead. Such a function serves as a parameterized view. SQL Server also supports **multi-statement table-valued functions** and **scalar functions**. The following example shows an inline table-valued function that retrieves the top two order details ordered by quantity for an order, where the OrderID is a parameter:

```
CREATE FUNCTION dbo.Top2OrderDetails
(@OrderId AS INT)
RETURNS TABLE
AS RETURN
SELECT TOP 2 ProductId, Quantity
FROM dbo.SimpleOrderDetails
WHERE OrderId = @OrderId
ORDER BY Quantity DESC;
```

The following example uses this function to retrieve the top two details for each order with the help of the APPLY operator:

```
SELECT o.OrderId, o.OrderDate, o.Customer,
  t2.ProductId, t2.Quantity
FROM dbo.SimpleOrders AS o
  OUTER APPLY dbo.Top2OrderDetails(o.OrderId) AS t2
```

```
ORDER BY o.OrderId, t2.Quantity DESC;
```

Note that another form of the APPLY operator is used, the OUTER APPLY. This form preserves the rows from the left table. As you can see from the following result, the query returns two rows for orders with two or more order details, one for orders with a single order detail, and one with NULL values in the place of the order details columns for orders without an order detail:

```
OrderId     OrderDate    Customer ProductId     Quantity
----------- ----------- -------- ------------- -----------
1           2016-07-01  CustA    6             200
1           2016-07-01  CustA    3             150
2           2016-07-01  CustB    6             250
2           2016-07-01  CustB    4             200
3           2016-01-01  CustC    NULL          NULL
4           2016-01-01  CustD    NULL          NULL
5           2016-07-02  CustA    1             50
```

Transactions and error handling

In a real-world application, errors always appear. Syntax or even logical errors can be in the code, the database design might be incorrect, there might even be a bug in the database management system you are using. Even if everything works correctly, you might get an error because the users insert wrong data. With Transact-SQL error handling you can catch such user errors and decide what to do upon them. Typically, you want to log the errors, inform the users about the errors, and sometimes even correct them in the error handling code.

Error handling for user errors works on the statement level. If you send SQL Server a batch of two or more statements and the error is in the last statement, the previous statements execute successfully. This might not be what you desire. Often, you need to execute a batch of statements as a unit, and fail all of the statements if one of the statements fails. You can achieve this by using transactions. In this section, you will learn about:

- Error handling
- Transaction management

Error handling

You can see there is a need for error handling by producing an error. The following code tries to insert an order and a detail row for this order:

```
EXEC dbo.InsertSimpleOrder
  @OrderId = 6, @OrderDate = '20160706', @Customer = N'CustE';
EXEC dbo.InsertSimpleOrderDetail
  @OrderId = 6, @ProductId = 2, @Quantity = 0;
```

In SQL Server Management Studio, you can see that an error has happened. You should get a message that error 547 has occurred, that the INSERT statement conflicted with the CHECK constraint. If you remember, in order details, only rows where the value for the quantity is not equal to zero are allowed. The error occurred in the second statement, in the call of the procedure that inserts an order detail. The procedure that inserted an order executed without an error. Therefore, an order with an ID equal to six must be in the dbo.SimpleOrders table. The following code tries to insert order 6 again:

```
EXEC dbo.InsertSimpleOrder
  @OrderId = 6, @OrderDate = '20160706', @Customer = N'CustE';
```

Of course, another error occurred. This time it should be error 2627, a violation of the PRIMARY KEY constraint. The values of the OrderId column must be unique. Let's check the state of the data after these successful and unsuccessful inserts:

```
SELECT o.OrderId, o.OrderDate, o.Customer,
  od.ProductId, od.Quantity
FROM dbo.SimpleOrderDetails AS od
  RIGHT OUTER JOIN dbo.SimpleOrders AS o
    ON od.OrderId = o.OrderId
WHERE o.OrderId > 5
ORDER BY o.OrderId, od.ProductId;
```

The previous query checks only orders and their associated details where the OrderID value is greater than five. The query returns the following result set:

OrderId	OrderDate	Customer	ProductId	Quantity
6	2016-07-06	CustE	NULL	NULL

You can see that only the first insert of the order with the ID 6 succeeded. The second insert of an order with the same ID and the insert of the detail row for order 6 did not succeed.

You start handling errors by enclosing the statements in the batch you are executing in the BEGIN TRY ... END TRY block. You can catch the errors in the BEGIN CATCH ... END CATCH block. The BEGIN CATCH statement must be immediately after the END TRY statement. The control of the execution is passed from the try part to the catch part immediately after the first error occurs.

In the catch part, you can decide how to handle the errors. If you want to log the data about the error or inform an end user about the details of the error, the following functions might be very handy:

- ERROR_NUMBER(): This function returns the number of the error.
- ERROR_SEVERITY(): This function returns the severity level. The severity of the error indicates the type of problem encountered. Severity levels 11 to 16 can be corrected by the user.
- ERROR_STATE(): This function returns the error state number. Error state gives more details about a specific error. You might want to use this number together with the error number to search the Microsoft knowledge base for the specific details of the error you encountered.
- ERROR_PROCEDURE(): This returns the name of the stored procedure or trigger where the error occurred, or NULL if the error did not occur within a stored procedure or trigger.
- ERROR_LINE(): This returns the line number at which the error occurred. This might be the line number in a routine if the error occurred within a stored procedure or trigger, or the line number in the batch.
- ERROR_MESSAGE(): This function returns the text of the error message.

The following code uses the TRY...CATCH block to handle possible errors in the batch of statements, and returns the information about the error using the aforementioned functions. Note that the error happens in the first statement of the batch:

```
BEGIN TRY
 EXEC dbo.InsertSimpleOrder
  @OrderId = 6, @OrderDate = '20160706', @Customer = N'CustF';
 EXEC dbo.InsertSimpleOrderDetail
  @OrderId = 6, @ProductId = 2, @Quantity = 5;
END TRY
BEGIN CATCH
 SELECT ERROR_NUMBER(),
   ERROR_MESSAGE(),
   ERROR_LINE();
END CATCH
```

There was a violation of the PRIMARY KEY constraint again, because the code tried to insert an order with ID 6 again. The second statement would succeed if you executed it in its own batch, without error handling. However, because of the error handling, the control was passed to the catch block immediately after the error in the first statement, and the second statement never executed. You can check the data with the following query:

```
SELECT o.OrderId, o.OrderDate, o.Customer,
  od.ProductId, od.Quantity
FROM dbo.SimpleOrderDetails AS od
  RIGHT OUTER JOIN dbo.SimpleOrders AS o
    ON od.OrderId = o.OrderId
WHERE o.OrderId > 5
ORDER BY o.OrderId, od.ProductId;
```

The result set should be the same as the results set of the last check of the orders with an ID greater than five—a single order without details. The following code produces an error in the second statement:

```
BEGIN TRY
 EXEC dbo.InsertSimpleOrder
  @OrderId = 7, @OrderDate = '20160706', @Customer = N'CustF';
 EXEC dbo.InsertSimpleOrderDetail
  @OrderId = 7, @ProductId = 2, @Quantity = 0;
END TRY
BEGIN CATCH
 SELECT ERROR_NUMBER(),
   ERROR_MESSAGE(),
   ERROR_LINE();
END CATCH
```

You can see that the insert of the order detail violates the CHECK constraint for the quantity. If you check the data with the same query as last time again, you would see that there are orders with ID 6 and 7 in the data, both without order details.

Using transactions

Your business logic might request that the insert of the first statement fails when the second statement fails. You might need to repeal the changes of the first statement on the failure of the second statement. You can define that a batch of statements executes as a unit by using transactions. The following code shows how to use transactions. Again, the second statement in the batch in the TRY block is the one that produces an error:

```
BEGIN TRY
 BEGIN TRANSACTION
```

```
   EXEC dbo.InsertSimpleOrder
     @OrderId = 8, @OrderDate = '20160706', @Customer = N'CustG';
   EXEC dbo.InsertSimpleOrderDetail
     @OrderId = 8, @ProductId = 2, @Quantity = 0;
  COMMIT TRANSACTION
END TRY
BEGIN CATCH
  SELECT ERROR_NUMBER(),
    ERROR_MESSAGE(),
    ERROR_LINE();
  IF XACT_STATE() <> 0
     ROLLBACK TRANSACTION;
END CATCH
```

You can check the data again:

```
SELECT o.OrderId, o.OrderDate, o.Customer,
   od.ProductId, od.Quantity
FROM dbo.SimpleOrderDetails AS od
   RIGHT OUTER JOIN dbo.SimpleOrders AS o
     ON od.OrderId = o.OrderId
WHERE o.OrderId > 5
ORDER BY o.OrderId, od.ProductId;
```

Here is the result of the check:

OrderId	OrderDate	Customer	ProductId	Quantity
6	2016-07-06	CustE	NULL	NULL
7	2016-07-06	CustF	NULL	NULL

You can see that the order with ID 8 does not exist in your data. Because the insert of the detail row for this order failed, the insert of the order was rolled back as well. Note that in the CATCH block, the XACT_STATE() function was used to check whether the transaction still exists. If the transaction was rolled back automatically by SQL Server, then the ROLLBACK TRANSACTION would produce a new error.

The following code drops the objects created for the explanation of the DDL and DML statements, programmatic objects, error handling, and transactions:

```
DROP FUNCTION dbo.Top2OrderDetails;
DROP VIEW dbo.OrdersWithoutDetails;
DROP PROCEDURE dbo.InsertSimpleOrderDetail;
DROP PROCEDURE dbo.InsertSimpleOrder;
DROP TABLE dbo.SimpleOrderDetails;
DROP TABLE dbo.SimpleOrders;
```

Beyond relational

Beyond relational is actually only a marketing term. The relational model, used in the relational database management system, is nowhere limited to specific data types, or specific languages only. However, with the term beyond relational, we typically mean using specialized and complex data types that might include spatial and temporal data, and XML or JSON data, and extending the capabilities of the Transact-SQL language with CLR languages like Visual C#, or statistical languages like R. SQL Server, in versions before 2016, already supports some of the features mentioned. Here is a quick review of this support, which includes:

- Spatial data
- CLR support
- XML data

Spatial data

In modern applications, often you want to show your data on a map, using the physical location. You might also want to show the shape of the objects that your data describes. You can use spatial data for tasks like these. You can represent the objects with points, lines, or polygons. From the simple shapes you can create complex geometrical objects or geographical objects—for example, cities and roads. Spatial data appears in many contemporary databases. Acquiring spatial data has become quite simple with the **Global Positioning System** (**GPS**) and other technologies. In addition, many software packages and database management systems help you work with spatial data. SQL Server supports two spatial data types from version 2008:

- The `geometry` type represents data in a **Euclidean (flat) coordinate system**.
- The `geography` type represents data in a **round-earth coordinate system**.

We need two different spatial data types because of some important differences between them. These differences include units of measurement and orientation.

In the planar, or flat-earth, system, you define the units of measurements. The length of a distance and the surface of an area are given in the same unit of measurement as you use for the coordinates of your coordinate system. You, as the database developer, know what the coordinates mean and what the unit of measure is. In geometry, the distance between the points described with the coordinates (1, 3) and (4, 7) is 5 units, regardless of the units used. You, as the database developer who created the database where you are storing this data, know the context. You know what these 5 units mean, whether it is 5 kilometers, or 5 inches.

When talking about locations on earth, coordinates are given in degrees of latitude and longitude. This is the round-earth, or ellipsoidal system. Lengths and areas are usually measured in the metric system, in meters and square meters. However, the metric system is not used everywhere in the world for spatial data. The **spatial reference identifier** (SRID) of the geography instance defines the unit of measurement. Therefore, whenever measuring some distance or area in the ellipsoidal system, you should also always quote the SRID used, which defines the units.

In the planar system, the ring orientation of a polygon is not an important factor. For example, a polygon described by the points ((0, 0), (10, 0), (0, 5), (0, 0)) is the same as a polygon described by ((0, 0), (5, 0), (0, 10), (0, 0)). You can always rotate the coordinates appropriately to get the same feeling of the orientation. However, in geography, the orientation is needed to completely describe a polygon. Just think of the equator, which divides the earth into two hemispheres. Is your spatial data describing the northern or southern hemisphere?

The `Wide World Importers` data warehouse includes the city location in the `Dimension.City` table. The following query retrieves it for cities in the main part of the USA:

```
SELECT City,
  [Sales Territory] AS SalesTerritory,
  Location AS LocationBinary,
  Location.ToString() AS LocationLongLat
FROM Dimension.City
WHERE [City Key] <> 0
  AND [Sales Territory] NOT IN
      (N'External', N'Far West');
```

Here is the partial result of the query:

City	SalesTerritory	LocationBinary	LocationLongLat
Carrollton	Mideast	0xE6100000010C70...	POINT (-78.651695 42.1083969)

```
Carrollton   Southeast        0xE6100000010C88...   POINT (-76.5605078
36.9468152)
Carrollton   Great Lakes      0xE6100000010CDB...   POINT (-90.4070632
39.3022693)
```

You can see that the location is actually stored as a binary string. When you use the `ToString()` method of the location, you get the default string representation of the geographical point, which is the degrees of longitude and latitude.

In SSMS, you send the results of the previous query to a grid, and in the results pane, you get an additional representation for the spatial data. Click the **spatial results** tab, and you can see the points represented in the longitude-latitude coordinate system, as you can see in the following screenshot:

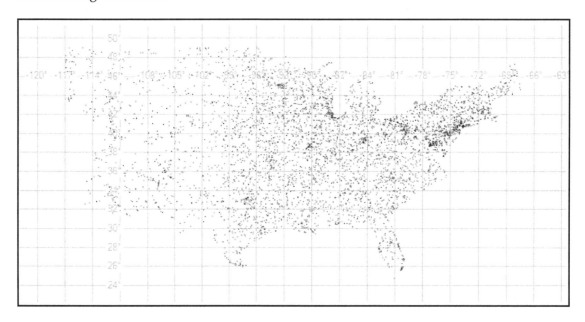

Spatial results showing customers' locations

If you executed the query, you might have noticed that the spatial data representation control in SSMS has some limitations. It can show only 5,000 objects. The result displays only the first 5,000 locations. Nevertheless, as you can see from the previous figure, this is enough to realize that these points form a contour of the main part of the USA. Therefore, the points represent the customers' locations for customers from the USA.

The following query gives you the details, such as location and population, for Denver, Colorado:

```
SELECT [City Key] AS CityKey, City,
   [State Province] AS State,
   [Latest Recorded Population] AS Population,
   Location.ToString() AS LocationLongLat
FROM Dimension.City
WHERE [City Key] = 114129
   AND [Valid To] = '9999-12-31 23:59:59.9999999';
```

Spatial data types have many useful methods. For example, the STDistance() method returns the shortest line between two geography types. This is a close approximate to the geodesic distance, defined as the shortest route between two points on the Earth's surface. The following code calculates this distance between Denver, Colorado, and Seattle, Washington:

```
DECLARE @g AS GEOGRAPHY;
DECLARE @h AS GEOGRAPHY;
DECLARE @unit AS NVARCHAR(50);
SET @g = (SELECT Location FROM Dimension.City
         WHERE [City Key] = 114129);
SET @h = (SELECT Location FROM Dimension.City
         WHERE [City Key] = 108657);
SET @unit = (SELECT unit_of_measure
            FROM sys.spatial_reference_systems
            WHERE spatial_reference_id = @g.STSrid);
SELECT FORMAT(@g.STDistance(@h), 'N', 'en-us') AS Distance,
 @unit AS Unit;
```

The result of the previous batch is shown here:

```
Distance          Unit
--------------    ------
1,643,936.69      metre
```

Note that the code uses the sys.spatial_reference_system catalog view to get the unit of measurement for the distance of the SRID used to store the geographical instances of data. The unit is a meter. You can see that the distance between Denver, Colorado, and Seattle, Washington, is more than 1,600 kms.

The following query finds the major cities within a circle of 1,000 kms around Denver, Colorado. Major cities are defined as the cities with a population larger than 200,000:

```
DECLARE @g AS GEOGRAPHY;
SET @g = (SELECT Location FROM Dimension.City
```

```
            WHERE [City Key] = 114129);
SELECT DISTINCT City,
   [State Province] AS State,
   FORMAT([Latest Recorded Population], '000,000') AS Population,
   FORMAT(@g.STDistance(Location), '000,000.00') AS Distance
FROM Dimension.City
WHERE Location.STIntersects(@g.STBuffer(1000000)) = 1
   AND [Latest Recorded Population] > 200000
   AND [City Key] <> 114129
   AND [Valid To] = '9999-12-31 23:59:59.9999999'
ORDER BY Distance;
```

Here is the result abbreviated to the twelve closest cities to `Denver, Colorado`:

```
City                State         Population  Distance
-----------------   -----------   ----------  ----------
Aurora              Colorado      325,078     013,141.64
Colorado Springs    Colorado      416,427     101,487.28
Albuquerque         New Mexico    545,852     537,221.38
Wichita             Kansas        382,368     702,553.01
Lincoln             Nebraska      258,379     716,934.90
Lubbock             Texas         229,573     738,625.38
Omaha               Nebraska      408,958     784,842.10
Oklahoma City       Oklahoma      579,999     809,747.65
Tulsa               Oklahoma      391,906     882,203.51
El Paso             Texas         649,121     895,789.96
Kansas City         Missouri      459,787     898,397.45
Scottsdale          Arizona       217,385     926,980.71
```

There are many more useful methods and properties implemented in the two spatial data types. In addition, you can improve the performance of spatial queries with the help of specialized spatial indexes.

CLR integration

You probably noticed that the two spatial data types are implemented as CLR data types. The spatial data types are shipped with SQL Server; therefore, Microsoft developers created them. However, you can also create your own CLR data types. SQL Server featured CLR inside the database engine for the first time in the 2005 version.

You can create the following CLR objects in a SQL Server database:

- User-defined functions
- Stored procedures

- Triggers
- User-defined aggregate functions
- User-defined data types

You can use CLR objects to extend the functionality of the Transact-SQL language. You should use CLR for objects that you can't create in Transact-SQL, such as user-defined aggregates or user-defined data types. For objects that you can also create in Transact-SQL, such as functions, stored procedures, and triggers, you should use Transact-SQL for manipulating the data, and CLR only in the areas where CLR languages such as Visual C# are faster than Transact-SQL—such as complex calculations, and string manipulations.

For example, Transact-SQL language includes only a fistful of aggregate functions. To describe a distribution of a continuous variable, you use the first four population moments in the **descriptive statistics**, namely the following:

- Mean, or average value
- Standard deviation
- Skewness
- Kurtosis, or peakedness

Transact-SQL includes only aggregate functions for calculating the mean and the standard deviation. These two measures might be descriptors good enough to describe the regular normal, or Gaussian distribution, as the following figure shows:

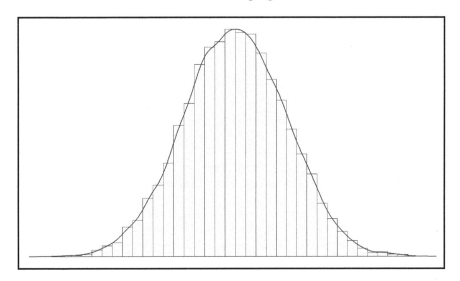

Normal or Gaussian distribution

However, a distribution in the real world might not follow the normal curve exactly. Often it is skewed. A typical example is income, which is usually highly skewed to the right. The following figure shows a positively skewed distribution, where you have a long tail on the right side of the distribution:

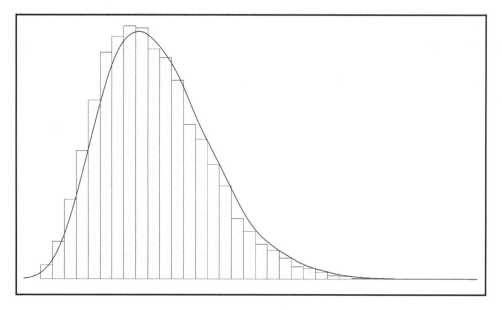

Positively skewed distribution

Here is the formula for the skewness:

$$Skew = \frac{n}{(n-1) * (n-2)} * \sum_{i=1}^{n} \left(\frac{v_i - \mu}{\sigma}\right)^3$$

Where, n = *number of cases*, v_i = *ith value*, μ = *mean*, and σ = *standard deviation*

The formula for the skewness uses the mean value and the standard deviation. I don't want to calculate these values in advance. If I calculated these values in advance, I would need to scan through the data twice. I want to have a more efficient algorithm, an algorithm that would scan the data only once.

I use a bit of mathematics for this optimization. First, I expand the formula for the subtraction of the mean from the *ith* value on the third degree:

$$(v_i - \mu)^3 = v_i^3 - 3v_i^2\mu + 3v_i\mu^2 - \mu^3$$

Then I use the fact that the sum is distributive over the product, as shown in the formula for two values only:

$$3v_1\mu^2 + 3v_2\mu^2 = 3\mu^2(v_1 + v_2)$$

This formula can be generalized for all values:

$$\sum_{i=1}^{n}(3v_i\mu^2) = 3\mu^2\sum_{i=1}^{n}(v_i)$$

Of course, I can do the same mathematics for the remaining elements of the expanded formula for the subtraction, and calculate all the aggregates I need with a single pass through the data, as shown in the following C# code for the user-defined aggregate function that calculates the skewness.

The first part of the code declares the namespaces used:

```
-- C# code for skewness
using System;
using System.Data;
using System.Data.SqlClient;
using System.Data.SqlTypes;
using Microsoft.SqlServer.Server;
```

You represent a **user-defined aggregate** (**UDA**) with a class or a structure in CLR. First, you decorate it with attributes that give some information about the UDA's behavior and information for potential optimization of the queries that use it:

```
[Serializable]
[SqlUserDefinedAggregate(
    Format.Native,
    IsInvariantToDuplicates = false,
    IsInvariantToNulls = true,
    IsInvariantToOrder = true,
    IsNullIfEmpty = false)]
```

The next part of the code for the UDA defines the structure and internal variables used to hold the intermediate results for the elements of the calculation, as I explained in the formula reorganization:

```
public struct Skew
{
    private double rx;
    private double rx2;
    private double r2x;
```

```
private double rx3;
private double r3x2;
private double r3x;
private Int64 rn;
```

Structures or classes that represent UDAs must implement four methods. The `Init()` method initializes the internal variables:

```
public void Init()
{
        rx = 0;
        rx2 = 0;
        r2x = 0;
        rx3 = 0;
        r3x2 = 0;
        r3x = 0;
        rn = 0;
}
```

The `Accumulate()` method does the actual work of aggregating:

```
public void Accumulate(SqlDouble inpVal)
{
        if (inpVal.IsNull)
        {
            return;
        }
        rx = rx + inpVal.Value;
        rx2 = rx2 + Math.Pow(inpVal.Value, 2);
        r2x = r2x + 2 * inpVal.Value;
        rx3 = rx3 + Math.Pow(inpVal.Value, 3);
        r3x2 = r3x2 + 3 * Math.Pow(inpVal.Value, 2);
        r3x = r3x + 3 * inpVal.Value;
        rn = rn + 1;
}
```

The `Merge()` method accepts another aggregate as the input. It merges two aggregates. Where do two or more aggregates come from? SQL Server might decide to execute the aggregating query in parallel, store the intermediate aggregate results internally, and then merge them by using the `Merge()` method:

```
public void Merge(Skew Group)
{
        this.rx = this.rx + Group.rx;
        this.rx2 = this.rx2 + Group.rx2;
        this.r2x = this.r2x + Group.r2x;
        this.rx3 = this.rx3 + Group.rx3;
```

```
        this.r3x2 = this.r3x2 + Group.r3x2;
        this.r3x = this.r3x + Group.r3x;
        this.rn = this.rn + Group.rn;
    }
```

The `Terminate()` method does the final calculations and returns the aggregated value to the calling query:

```
    public SqlDouble Terminate()
    {
        double myAvg = (rx / rn);
        double myStDev = Math.Pow((rx2 - r2x * myAvg + rn *
Math.Pow(myAvg, 2))
                        / (rn - 1), 1d / 2d);
        double mySkew = (rx3 - r3x2 * myAvg + r3x * Math.Pow(myAvg, 2)
                        - rn * Math.Pow(myAvg, 3)) /
                        Math.Pow(myStDev,3) * rn / (rn - 1) / (rn - 2);
        return (SqlDouble)mySkew;
    }

}
```

You can use the C# compiler to compile the code for the UDA. However, in the associated code for the book, a compiled assembly, the `.dll` file, is provided for your convenience. The code also includes the function that calculates the kurtosis; for the sake of brevity, this code is not explained in detail here.

In order to use CLR objects, you need to enable CLR for your instance. The following code enables the CLR for your SQL Server instance, and then checks the CLR configuration options:

```
EXEC sp_configure 'clr enabled', 1;
RECONFIGURE WITH OVERRIDE;
-- Check the CLR options
SELECT name, value, minimum, maximum, value_in_use
FROM sys.configurations
WHERE name LIKE N'clr %';
```

The query returns two rows in SQL Server 2017:

name	value	minimum	maximum	value_in_use
clr enabled	1	0	1	1
clr strict security	1	0	1	1

Note the second option, the `clr strict security` option, which is new in SQL Server 2017, and also available with the latest updates for SQL Server 2016. So what is this option about?

In .NET (or CLR) code, you could traditionally use **Code Access Security** (**CAS**) as a security boundary to protect the system resources. With CAS, you could narrow down the permissions of the user executing the CLR code. For each assembly you imported to SQL Server, you could define a set of CAS permissions, named permission sets. There were three permission sets: SAFE, EXTERNAL_ACCESS, and UNSAFE. With the SAFE set, the CLR code could not perform any action that T-SQL code could not perform, and therefore it was safe to use the assembly. With EXTERNAL_ACCESS, you could access some external resources, like local disks and network shares. With the UNSAFE set, you could do nearly anything with the CLR code, including crashing SQL Server. There were some prerequisites for using unsafe CLR code in SQL Server.

In recent versions of .NET Framework, CAS is not a security boundary anymore. This is not a good piece of news for CLR code in SQL Server. Now SQL Server treats any CLR assembly as UNSAFE.

If the `clr strict security` option is not set to 1 on your SQL Server instance, please execute the following code:

```
EXEC sys.sp_configure 'show advanced options', 1;
RECONFIGURE WITH OVERRIDE;
EXEC sys.sp_configure 'clr strict security', 1;
RECONFIGURE WITH OVERRIDE;
```

In order to use a CLR assembly, you need to catalog, or deploy the assembly in the database with the CREATE ASSEMBLY statement. So, let's try to import the DescriptiveStatistics CLR assembly with permission set to SAFE. The code assumes that the assembly is stored in the C:\SQL207DevGuide folder:

```
CREATE ASSEMBLY DescriptiveStatistics
FROM 'C:\SQL2017DevGuide\DescriptiveStatistics.dll'
WITH PERMISSION_SET = SAFE;
```

You should get error 10343, and import of the assembly should fail. You can get the assembly in the database in one of the following ways:

- Alter the database to set the TRUSTWORTHY option on (which is not the recommended way)

- Sign the assembly with a certificate or an asymmetric key that has a corresponding login with the UNSAFE ASSEMBLY permission
- Add an assembly to the list of trusted assemblies for the server with the sys.sp_add_trusted_assembly system stored procedure

Although this is not a recommended option, I am showing you here how to set the database option TRUSTWORTHY on, because this is the simplest and the shortest way. However, in production, you should sign your assemblies with a certificate. The following code sets the TRUSTWORTHY option on for the WideWorldImportersDW database. In order to change this option, the owner of the database should be the sa login:

```
ALTER AUTHORIZATION ON database::WideWorldImportersDW TO sa;
ALTER DATABASE WideWorldImportersDW SET TRUSTWORTHY ON;
```

Now you can import the assembly. Then you create the aggregate functions with the CREATE AGGREGATE statement. The following code enables CLR, deploys the assembly provided with the book, and then creates the two aggregate functions:

```
CREATE ASSEMBLY DescriptiveStatistics
FROM 'C:\SQL2017DevGuide\DescriptiveStatistics.dll'
WITH PERMISSION_SET = SAFE;

CREATE AGGREGATE dbo.Skew(@s float)
RETURNS float
EXTERNAL NAME DescriptiveStatistics.Skew;

CREATE AGGREGATE dbo.Kurt(@s float)
RETURNS float
EXTERNAL NAME DescriptiveStatistics.Kurt;
```

Once the assembly is cataloged and the UDAs are created, you can use them just like the built-in aggregate functions. The following query calculates the four moments for the sum over customers of the amount ordered without tax. In a CTE, it calculates the sum of the amount per customer, and then in the outer query the average, the standard deviation, the skewness, and the kurtosis for this total:

```
WITH CustomerSalesCTE AS
(
SELECT c.Customer,
  SUM(f.[Total Excluding Tax]) AS TotalAmount
FROM Fact.Sale AS f
  INNER JOIN Dimension.Customer AS c
    ON f.[Customer Key] = c.[Customer Key]
WHERE c.[Customer Key] <> 0
GROUP BY c.Customer
```

```
)
SELECT ROUND(AVG(TotalAmount), 2) AS Average,
   ROUND(STDEV(TotalAmount), 2) AS StandardDeviation,
   ROUND(dbo.Skew(TotalAmount), 6) AS Skewness,
   ROUND(dbo.Kurt(TotalAmount), 6) AS Kurtosis
FROM CustomerSalesCTE;
```

Here is the result:

Average	StandardDeviation	Skewness	Kurtosis
270479.220000	38586.08	0.005943	-0.263897

After you have tested the UDAs, you can execute the following code to clean up your database, and potentially disable CLR. Do not forget to set the TRUSTWORTHY option for the database to off:

```
DROP AGGREGATE dbo.Skew;
DROP AGGREGATE dbo.Kurt;
DROP ASSEMBLY DescriptiveStatistics;
ALTER DATABASE WideWorldImportersDW SET TRUSTWORTHY OFF;
GO
/*
EXEC sp_configure 'clr enabled', 0;
RECONFIGURE WITH OVERRIDE;
EXEC sys.sp_configure 'show advanced options', 0;
RECONFIGURE WITH OVERRIDE;
GO
*/
```

XML support in SQL Server

SQL Server in version 2005 also started to feature extended support for **XML data** inside the database engine, although some basic support was already included in version 2000. The support starts by generating XML data from tabular results. You can use the FOR XML clause of the SELECT statement for this task.

The first option for creating XML from a query result is the RAW option. The XML created is quite close to the relational (tabular) presentation of the data. In raw mode, every row from returned rowsets converts to a single element named row, and columns translate to the attributes of this element.

The FOR XML AUTO option gives you nice XML documents with nested elements, and it is not complicated to use. In auto and raw modes, you can use the keyword ELEMENTS to produce element-centric XML. The WITH NAMESPACES clause, preceding the SELECT part of the query, defines namespaces and aliases in the returned XML.

With the last two flavors of the FOR XML clause—the EXPLICIT and PATH option—you can manually define the XML returned. With these two options, you have total control of the XML document returned. The explicit mode is included for backward compatibility only; it uses proprietary T-SQL syntax for formatting XML. The path mode uses standard **XML XPath** expressions to define the elements and attributes of the XML you are creating.

In raw and auto modes, you can also return the **XSD schema** of the document you are creating. This schema is included inside XML returned, before the actual XML data; therefore, it is called inline schema. You return XSD with the XMLSCHEMA directive. This directive accepts a parameter that defines a target namespace. If you need schema only, without data, simply include a WHERE condition in your query with a predicate that no row can satisfy.

The following query generates an XML document from the regular tabular result set by using the FOR XML clause with AUTO option, to generate element-centric XML instance, with namespace and inline schema included:

```
SELECT c.[Customer Key] AS CustomerKey,
  c.[WWI Customer ID] AS CustomerId,
  c.[Customer],
  c.[Buying Group] AS BuyingGroup,
  f.Quantity,
  f.[Total Excluding Tax] AS Amount,
  f.Profit
FROM Dimension.Customer AS c
  INNER JOIN Fact.Sale AS f
    ON c.[Customer Key] = f.[Customer Key]
WHERE c.[Customer Key] IN (127, 128)
FOR XML AUTO, ELEMENTS,
  ROOT('CustomersOrders'),
  XMLSCHEMA('CustomersOrdersSchema');
GO
```

Here is the partial result of this query. The first part of the result is the inline schema:

```
<CustomersOrders>
  <xsd:schema targetNamespace="CustomersOrdersSchema" ...
    <xsd:import
namespace="http://schemas.microsoft.com/sqlserver/2004/sqltypes" ...
      <xsd:element name="c">
```

```
                <xsd:complexType>
                  <xsd:sequence>
                    <xsd:element name="CustomerKey" type="sqltypes:int" />
                    <xsd:element name="CustomerId" type="sqltypes:int" />
                    <xsd:element name="Customer">
                      <xsd:simpleType>
                        <xsd:restriction base="sqltypes:nvarchar" ...
                          <xsd:maxLength value="100" />
                        </xsd:restriction>
                      </xsd:simpleType>
                    </xsd:element>
                    ...
                  </xsd:sequence>
                </xsd:complexType>
              </xsd:element>
            </xsd:schema>
            <c xmlns="CustomersOrdersSchema">
              <CustomerKey>127</CustomerKey>
              <CustomerId>127</CustomerId>
              <Customer>Tailspin Toys (Point Roberts, WA)</Customer>
              <BuyingGroup>Tailspin Toys</BuyingGroup>
              <f>
                <Quantity>3</Quantity>
                <Amount>48.00</Amount>
                <Profit>31.50</Profit>
              </f>
              <f>
                <Quantity>9</Quantity>
                <Amount>2160.00</Amount>
                <Profit>1363.50</Profit>
              </f>
            </c>
            <c xmlns="CustomersOrdersSchema">
              <CustomerKey>128</CustomerKey>
              <CustomerId>128</CustomerId>
              <Customer>Tailspin Toys (East Portal, CO)</Customer>
              <BuyingGroup>Tailspin Toys</BuyingGroup>
              <f>
                <Quantity>84</Quantity>
                <Amount>420.00</Amount>
                <Profit>294.00</Profit>
              </f>
            </c>
            ...
          </CustomersOrders>
```

You can also do the opposite process: convert XML to tables. Converting XML to relational tables is known as shredding XML. You can do this by using the `nodes()` method of the XML data type, or with the `OPENXML()` rowset function.

Inside SQL Server, you can also query the XML data from Transact-SQL to find specific elements, attributes, or XML fragments. **XQuery** is a standard language for browsing XML instances and returning XML. It is much richer than **XPath** expressions, an older standard, which you can use for simple navigation only. With XQuery, you can navigate as with XPath; however, you can also loop over nodes, shape the returned XML instance, and much more.

For a query language, you need a query-processing engine. The SQL Server database engine processes XQuery inside T-SQL statements through XML data type methods. Not all XQuery features are supported in SQL Server. For example, XQuery user-defined functions are not supported in SQL Server because you already have T-SQL and CLR functions available. Additionally, T-SQL supports nonstandard extensions to XQuery, called XML DML, that you can use to modify elements and attributes in XML data. Because an XML data type is a large object, it could be a huge performance bottleneck if the only way to modify an XML value were to replace the entire value.

The real power of XQuery lies in so-called **FLWOR** expressions. FLWOR is the acronym for **for**, **let**, **where**, **order by**, and **return**. A FLWOR expression is actually a `for each` loop. You can use it to iterate through a sequence returned by an XPath expression. Although you typically iterate through a sequence of nodes, you can use FLWOR expressions to iterate through any sequence. You can limit the nodes to be processed with a predicate, sort the nodes, and format the returned XML. The parts of a FLWOR statement are:

- `For`: With a `for` clause, you bind iterator variables to input sequences. Input sequences are either sequences of nodes or sequences of atomic values. You create atomic value sequences using literals or functions.
- `Let`: With the optional `let` clause, you assign a value to a variable for a specific iteration. The expression used for an assignment can return a sequence of nodes or a sequence of atomic values.
- `Where`: With the optional `where` clause, you filter the iteration.
- `Order by`: Using the `order by` clause, you can control the order in which the elements of the input sequence are processed. You control the order based on atomic values.
- `Return`: The `return` clause is evaluated once per iteration, and the results are returned to the client in the iteration order. With this clause, you format the resulting XML.

You can store XML instances inside SQL Server database in a column of the XML data type. An XML data type includes five methods that accept XQuery as a parameter. The methods support querying (the query() method), retrieving atomic values (the value() method), existence checks (the exist() method), modifying sections within the XML data (the modify() method) as opposed to overriding the whole thing, and shredding XML data into multiple rows in a result set (the nodes() method).

The following code creates a variable of the XML data type to store an XML instance in it. Then it uses the query() method to return XML fragments from the XML instance. This method accepts XQuery query as a parameter. The XQuery query uses the FLWOR expressions to define and shape the XML returned:

```
DECLARE @x AS XML;
SET @x = N'
<CustomersOrders>
  <Customer custid="1">
    <!-- Comment 111 -->
    <companyname>CustA</companyname>
    <Order orderid="1">
      <orderdate>2016-07-01T00:00:00</orderdate>
    </Order>
    <Order orderid="9">
      <orderdate>2016-07-03T00:00:00</orderdate>
    </Order>
    <Order orderid="12">
      <orderdate>2016-07-12T00:00:00</orderdate>
    </Order>
  </Customer>
  <Customer custid="2">
    <!-- Comment 222 -->
    <companyname>CustB</companyname>
    <Order orderid="3">
      <orderdate>2016-07-01T00:00:00</orderdate>
    </Order>
    <Order orderid="10">
      <orderdate>2016-07-05T00:00:00</orderdate>
    </Order>
  </Customer>
</CustomersOrders>';
SELECT @x.query('for $i in CustomersOrders/Customer/Order
                let $j := $i/orderdate
                where $i/@orderid < 10900
                order by ($j)[1]
                return
                <Order-orderid-element>
                 <orderid>{data($i/@orderid)}</orderid>
```

```
                    {$j}
                </Order-orderid-element>')
       AS [Filtered, sorted and reformatted orders with let clause];
```

Here is the result of the previous query:

```
<Order-orderid-element>
  <orderid>1</orderid>
  <orderdate>2016-07-01T00:00:00</orderdate>
</Order-orderid-element>
<Order-orderid-element>
  <orderid>3</orderid>
  <orderdate>2016-07-01T00:00:00</orderdate>
</Order-orderid-element>
<Order-orderid-element>
  <orderid>9</orderid>
  <orderdate>2016-07-03T00:00:00</orderdate&gt;
</Order-orderid-element>
<Order-orderid-element>
  <orderid>10</orderid>
  <orderdate>2016-07-05T00:00:00</orderdate>
</Order-orderid-element>
<Order-orderid-element>
  <orderid>12</orderid>
  <orderdate>2016-07-12T00:00:00</orderdate>
</Order-orderid-element>
```

XML data type is actually a large object type. Scanning through the XML data sequentially is not a very efficient way of retrieving a simple scalar value. With relational data, you can create an index on a filtering column, allowing an index seek operation instead of a table scan. Similarly, you can index XML columns with specialized XML indexes. The first index you create on an XML column is the **primary XML index**. This index contains a shredded persisted representation of the XML values. For each XML value in the column, the index creates several rows of data. The number of rows in the index is approximately the number of nodes in the XML value. Such an index alone can speed up searches for a specific element by using the exist() method. After creating the primary XML index, you can create up to three other types of secondary XML indexes:

- PATH: This secondary XML index is especially useful if your queries specify path expressions. It speeds up the exist() method better than the primary XML index. Such an index also speeds up queries that use value() for a fully specified path.

- VALUE: This secondary XML index is useful if queries are value-based and the path is not fully specified, or it includes a wildcard.
- PROPERTY: This secondary XML index is very useful for queries that retrieve one or more values from individual XML instances using the value() method. The primary XML index has to be created first. It can be created only on tables with a clustered primary key.

Summary

In this chapter, we reviewed the SQL Server features for developers that already exist in the previous versions. You can see that this support goes well beyond basic SQL statements, and also beyond pure Transact-SQL.

The features recapitulation in this chapter is also useful as an introduction to new features in SQL Server 2016 and 2017, introduced in the following chapters, especially in Chapter 4, *Transact-SQL Enhancement;* Chapter 5, *JSON Support;* Chapter 7, *Temporal Tables;* and Chapter 13, *Supporting R in SQL Server.*

3
SQL Server Tools

As developers, we are accustomed to using **Integrated Development Environments (IDEs)** in our software projects. Visual Studio has been a major player in the IDE space for many years, if not decades, and it has allowed developers to use the latest software development processes to further improve quality and efficiency in software projects. Server management, on the other hand, has generally been a second-class citizen for many products in the past. In general, this fact can be understood, if not agreed with. IDEs are tools that design and create software that can generate revenue for a business, whereas management tools generally only offer the benefit of some sort of cost saving, rather than direct revenue generation.

The SQL Server Tools of the past (pre-SQL 2005) were very much focused on fulfilling the requirements of being able to manage and query SQL Server instances and databases, but received no great investments in making the tools *comfortable* or even enjoyable to use. Advanced IDEs were firmly in the application development domain and application developers know that databases are a storage system at best and therefore require no elegant tooling to be worked with.

Luckily for us, the advent of SQL Server 2005, along with the release of the .NET Framework, encouraged some people at Microsoft to invest a little more time and resources in providing an improved interface for both developers and DBAs for database and data management purposes. The **SQL Server Management Studio (SSMS)** was born and unified the functionality of two legacy tools: **Query Analyzer** and **Enterprise Manager**. Anyone who has worked with SQL Server since the 2005 release will recognize the application regardless of whether they are using the 2005 release or the latest 2016 build.

There have been several different names and releases of the second tool in this chapter, **SQL Server Data Tools** (**SSDT**), going back to SQL Server 2005/2008 where the tool was known under the name **Visual Studio Database Projects** (that is, **Data Dude**). The many incarnations of this tool since SQL Server 2005 have been focused on the development of database projects. The SSDT has many of the tools and interfaces known to Visual Studio users and allows a seasoned Visual Studio user to quickly familiarize themselves with the tool. Particularly interesting is the improved ability to integrate database and business intelligence projects into source control and continuous integration and automated deployment processes.

In this chapter, we will be exploring:

- Installing and updating SQL Server Tools
- New SSMS features and enhancements
- SQL Server Data Tools
- Tools for developing R and Python code

Installing and updating SQL Server Tools

The very beginning of our journey with SQL Server is the installation process. In previous versions of SQL Server, the data management and development tools were delivered together with the SQL Server installation image. As such, if a developer wanted to install SSMS, the setup of SQL Server had to be used to facilitate the installation.

As of SQL Server 2016, Microsoft made the very smart decision to separate the management tools from the server installation. This is not only a separation of the installation medium, but also a separation of the release process. This separation means that both products can be developed and released without having to wait for the other team to be ready. Let's take a look at how this change affects us at installation time.

In the following screenshot, given as follows, we see the **SQL Server Installation Center** screen. This is the first screen we will encounter when running the SQL Server setup.exe shown in the installation screenshot. After choosing the **Installation** menu point on the left, we are confronted with the generic installation options of SQL Server, which have only minimally changed in the last releases. The second and third options presented on this screen are **Install SQL Server Management Tools** and **Install SQL Server Data Tools**. If we read the descriptions of these options, we note that both links will redirect us to the **Downloads** page for either SSMS or SSDT. This is the first clear indication that the delivery of these tools has now been decoupled from the server installation:

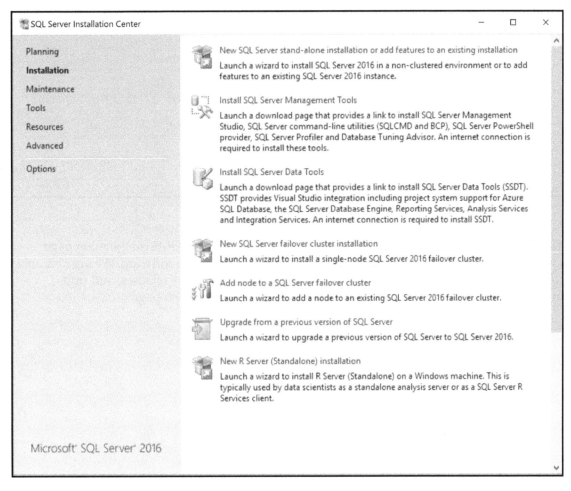

SQL Server Installation Center

After clicking **Install SQL Server Management Studio**, you should be redirected to the **Downloads** page, which should look like the following screenshot:

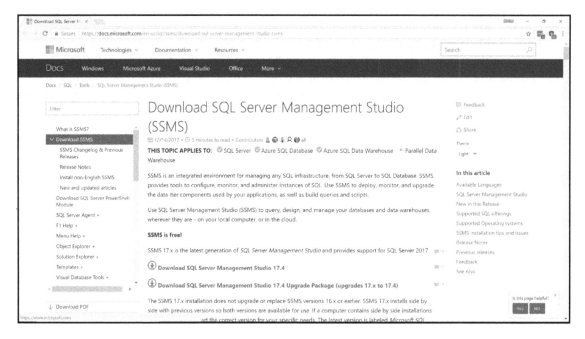

SQL Server Management Studio download page

The **Downloads** page offers us the latest production version of SSMS on the main page, together with any upgrade packages for previous versions of the software. We are also able to see details on the current release and view, download previous releases, and find information on change logs and release notes on the left of the web page:

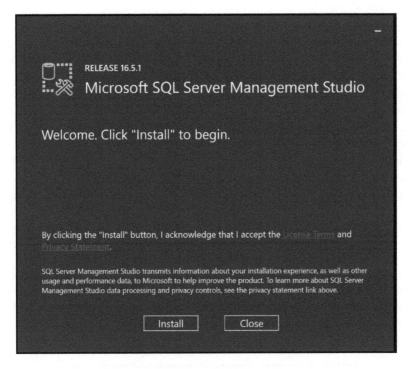

SQL Server Management Studio setup dialogue

After downloading the desired version of SSMS, we can run the installation just the same way as with previous versions of the tool. The next immediately noticeable difference to previous versions is the installation program itself. SSMS 2016.x and higher is based on Visual Studio 2015 Isolated Shell, and as such uses similar color schemes and iconography to Visual Studio 2015.

Once the installation has completed, we can start SSMS and are greeted with a familiar starting screen as in all previous versions of SSMS. The subtle differences in the application is exactly that, subtle. The splash-screen at application start shows that the SSMS is now *powered by Visual Studio*; otherwise there are no major indications that we are working with a tool based on Visual Studio. The interface may feel familiar, but the menus and options available are solely concentrated on working with SQL Server.

Previously, SQL Server and the SQL Server Tools were packaged together. This led to bug fixes and featured additions to the tools having to be bundled with **Cumulative Updates (CU)** and **Service Packs (SP)**, or general version releases of the SQL Server product. Through the decoupling of the applications SSMS and SSDT from SQL Server, we no longer have to wait for CUs and SPs, or version releases of SQL Server, before we can receive the required/requested features and fixes for SSMS and SSDT. The SQL Server Tools team has taken immediate advantage of this and has made regular releases for both SSMS and SSDT since the general release of SQL Server 2016. The initial release of SSMS 2016.x was in June 2016 and there have been subsequent update releases in July 2016, August 2016, September 2016, and December 2016. The change to version 17.x followed in 2017 and the releases were less rapid, as the port from SQL Server releases and integration into the Visual Studio 2015 shell matured and the preparations for the release of SQL Server 2017 were ramping up. Each release has included a range of bug fixes and featured additions which are much more rapidly deployable when compared to the previous versions of SQL Server and SSMS.

A further advantage of the separation of the data tools from the server product is the reduced overhead of managing the installation and updating the tools in a network. The process of updating an already installed SSMS installation is demonstrated in the following screenshot, where we see that a **Check for Updates** option has been included in the **Tools** menu of SSMS:

Checking for updates in SQL Server Management Studio

Further to this, the separation of the tools as a standalone installer will reduce the administrative overhead in larger organizations where software is deployed using centralized management software. Where previously the larger ISO image of an SQL Server installation was required, now a smaller standalone installer is available for distribution.

We also have the option to request that SSMS automatically checks for updates at application start. This will create a notification balloon message in Windows if a new version is available. A sample notification on a Windows 10 machine can be seen in the following screenshot:

Update notification for SQL Server Management Studio

Once the update check has been opened, SSMS connects to the update systems of Microsoft and performs checks against the currently installed version and the latest downloadable release of the software. If updates have been found, these will be offered using the update mechanism, as shown in the following screenshot. We are also able to decide if the automated update check should be performed or not:

SQL Server Management Studio Update Checker

These enhancements to the installation and update process are not mind-blowing, especially considering that these features have been available in other products for years or even decades. However, these are the first main improvements that have to do with the switch from a standalone application to an application based on the extremely successful Visual Studio Framework.

New SSMS features and enhancements

As we saw with the installation process, there are already a few enhancements in the installation and updating process for SSMS. Through the migration of the SSMS application to the Visual Studio 2015 Isolated Shell, there are a number of additions into SSMS that will be familiar to application developers that use Visual Studio 2015 (or one of its derivatives). While some of these are simple improvements, these additions can be of help to many SQL developers who have been isolated inside SSMS 16.x and higher.

Autosave open tabs

The first improvement is the option to choose whether SSMS should prompt to save unsaved tabs when you decide to close SSMS. This is a simple change, but if you use SSMS to run many ad hoc queries and do not want to constantly close out and save each tab, this is now an option. The default is for SSMS to prompt when closing a window, but by unchecking the checkbox marked as shown in the following screenshot you can force SSMS to silently close these windows:

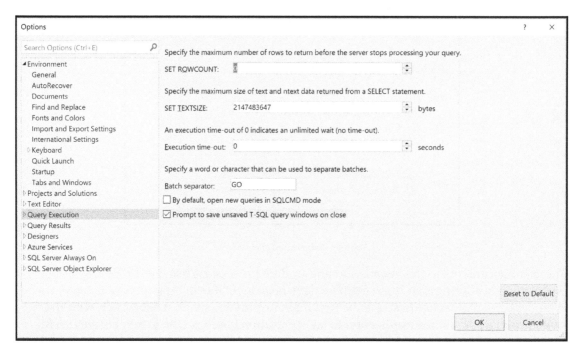

Options window in SQL Server Management Studio—prompt to save unsaved work

Searchable options

The next usability or productivity enhancement comes with the Visual Studio 2015 Isolated Shell features. The **Options** menu inside Visual Studio, and SSMS, are jam-packed with features and functionalities that can be configured. Unfortunately, these options are so numerous that it can be difficult to navigate and find the option you are interested in. To aid us in the search for the settings we are interested in, we are now able to quickly search and filter in the **Options** menu. The following screenshot explains the ability to quickly search through the options for settings using text search without having to memorize where the settings are hidden. Go to **Tools | Options** and you are then able to type your search string in the textbox in the top-left of the **Options** window. In the following screenshot, the search term execution has been entered, the results filtered as the word is typed into the search form:

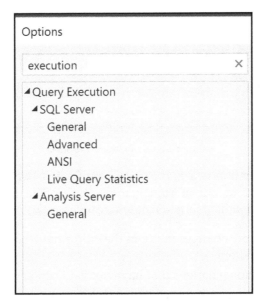

Options window—search/filter

Enhanced scroll bar

A further improvement that will be used on a much more regular basis is the enhanced scroll bar in the **T-SQL editor** tab. In the following screenshot, we can see an example of a T-SQL stored procedure that has been opened for editing:

```
ALTER PROCEDURE [Integration].[GetOrderUpdates]
    @LastCutoff datetime2(7),
    @NewCutoff datetime2(7)
WITH EXECUTE AS OWNER
AS
BEGIN
    SET NOCOUNT ON;
    SET XACT_ABORT ON;
    -- Added comment, not saved
    SELECT CAST(o.OrderDate AS date) AS [Order Date Key],
           CAST(ol.PickingCompletedWhen AS date) AS [Picked Date Key],
           o.OrderID AS [WWI Order ID],
           o.BackorderOrderID AS [WWI Backorder ID],
           ol.[Description],
           pt.PackageTypeName AS Package,
           ol.Quantity AS Quantity,
           ol.UnitPrice AS [Unit Price],
           ol.TaxRate AS [Tax Rate],
           ROUND(ol.Quantity * ol.UnitPrice, 2) AS [Total Excluding Tax],
           ROUND(ol.Quantity * ol.UnitPrice * ol.TaxRate / 100.0, 2) AS [Tax Amount],
           ROUND(ol.Quantity * ol.UnitPrice, 2) + ROUND(ol.Quantity * ol.UnitPrice * ol.TaxRate / 100.0, 2) AS [Total Including Tax],
           c.DeliveryCityID AS [WWI City ID],
           c.CustomerID AS [WWI Customer ID],
           ol.StockItemID AS [WWI Stock Item ID],
           o.SalespersonPersonID AS [WWI Salesperson ID],
           o.PickedByPersonID AS [WWI Picker ID],
           CASE WHEN ol.LastEditedWhen > o.LastEditedWhen THEN ol.LastEditedWhen ELSE o.LastEditedWhen END AS [Last Modified When]
```

SQL Server Management Studio scroll bar enhancements

The main points to pay attention to are: the margin on the left-hand side of the screen and the scroll bar on the right-hand side of Management Studio. The enhancement here allows us to easily identify a few details in our script window, namely:

- **Green blocks** show changes made in the editor have been saved to the file currently being edited
- **Yellow blocks** show changes that have not yet been saved
- **Red blocks** show code that is invalid or has syntax errors (native IntelliSense must be enabled for this feature to work)
- The **blue marker** on the scroll bar shows the location of the cursor

These subtle changes are further examples of the Visual Studio base providing us with further enhancements to make working inside SSMS easier. Knowing what code has been changed or is defective at a syntax level allows us to quickly navigate through our code inside SSMS.

Execution plan comparison

Refactoring and improving the performance of code is a regular occurrence in the working day of a developer. Being able to identify if a particular query refactoring has helped improve an execution plan can sometimes be difficult. To help us identify plan changes, SSMS 16.x and higher now offers the option to compare execution plans.

By saving the execution plan and the T-SQL of our initial query as a `.sqlplan` file, we can then run our redesigned query and compare the two plans. In the following screenshot we see how to initiate a plan comparison:

Activating a plan comparison session

Upon activation, we must choose which `.sqlplan` file we would like to use for the comparison session. The two execution plans are loaded into a separate **Compare Showplan** tab in SSMS and we can evaluate how the plans differ or how they are similar. In the following screenshot we see a plan comparison where there are only slight differences between the plans:

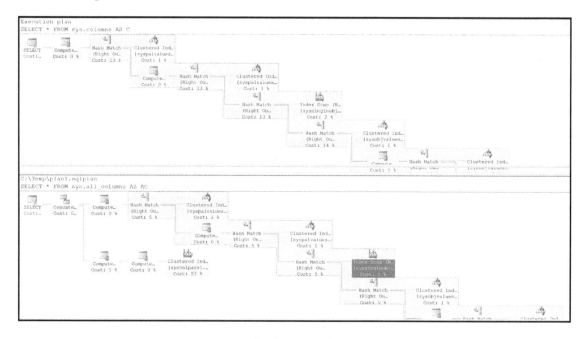

Showplan comparison tab

The nodes of the execution plans in the preceding screenshot that are similar have a red background, while nodes that are different have a yellow background.

If we click the nodes inside one of the plans, the matching node in the comparison plan will be highlighted and we can then investigate how they are similar and how they differ.

Once we have chosen the node in our execution plan, we will be able to view the properties of the node we wish to compare, similar to the details shown as follows:

Showplan comparison—node properties

The **Properties** tab shows clearly which parts of the node are different. In the preceding screenshot we can ignore the lower inequality, which is stating the Node ID is different; this will occur wherever our query has a slightly changed plan. Of interest in this case is the **Estimated Operator Cost** property, which is showing a difference. This example is very simple and the differences are minimal, but we are able to identify differences in a very similar plan with a few simple clicks. This sort of support is invaluable and a huge time saver, especially where plans are larger and more complex.

Live query statistics

Following on from the plan comparison feature, we have one of the more powerful features for a developer. **Live Query Statistics (LQS)** does exactly what the name says—it provides us with a live view of a query execution so that we can see exactly how data is flowing through the query plan. In previous versions of SQL Server and SSMS we have been able to request a static graphical representation of a query execution plan. There have been multiple books, blogposts, videos, and training seminars designed and delivered to thousands of developers and DBAs around the world in an attempt to improve people's abilities to understand these static execution plans. The ability of a developer to read and interpret the contents of these plans rests largely on these resources. With LQS we have an additional tool at our disposal to be able to more easily identify how SQL Server is consuming and processing the T-SQL query that we have submitted to it.

The *special sauce* in LQS is that we don't get a static graphical representation, but rather an animation of the execution. The execution plan is displayed in SSMS and the arrows between the plan nodes move to show the data flowing between the nodes. In the following screenshot we see how to activate LQS inside SSMS for a particular **Query** tab:

Activating Live Query Statistics

As LQS shows a moving image, we are at a distinct disadvantage in a book! However, when we run a query with LQS activated, it is still possible to see an example of how LQS looks while running, as we can see in the following screenshot:

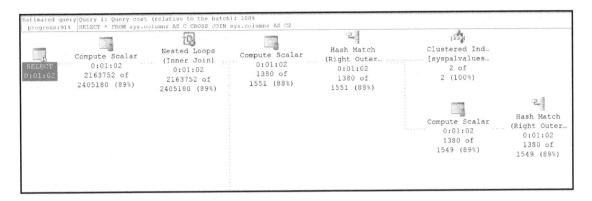

Live Query Statistics—query execution

In the preceding screenshot, we can see that the execution plan image that we are used to has been extended slightly. We now see a few extra details. Starting in the top left of this image, we see the **Estimated query progress** in percent. As with anything to do with query execution and statistics, SQL Server is always working with estimations. Estimations that are based on table and index statistics, which is a topic worthy of an entire book! We also see an execution time displayed beneath each node that is still actively processing data. Also, beneath each node is a display of how many rows are still left to be processed (these are also based on estimations through statistics). Finally, we see the arrows connecting each node; solid lines are where execution has completed, dotted lines (which also move during execution) show where data is still flowing and being processed.

You can try out the same query shown in the preceding screenshot and see how LQS looks. This is a long-running query against sys.objects to produce a large enough result set that LQS has time to capture execution information. The following code shows a sample query function:

```
SELECT * FROM
SYS.OBJECTS AS o1
CROSS JOIN sys.objects AS o2
CROSS JOIN sys.objects AS o3
```

This sample query should run long enough to allow LQS to display an animated query plan long enough to understand how LQS makes a query plan easier to understand. It should also be clear that LQS can only display a useful animation for queries that run longer than a few seconds, as the animation only runs for the duration of the query.

This moving display of data flow allows us as developers to understand how SQL Server is processing our query. We are able to get a better insight into where execution is spending the most time and resources and also where we may need to consider rewriting a query or applying different indexing to achieve better results. LQS, coupled with query plan comparisons, will allow us as developers to design better database solutions and better understand how SQL Server processes our queries. In particular, how SQL Server must wait for certain nodes in an execution plan to complete before continuing onto the next node.

However, we must not forget that running LQS is similar to running a trace, and it requires a certain set of permissions and also consumes resources on the server. We should be approaching our queries with LQS at a development stage and attempting to write optimal code before we deploy into production. LQS should therefore be used primarily in your development work on a test environment and *not* on your production environment.

Importing flat file Wizard

SSMS was designed to make regular tasks of DBAs and developers easier. Wizards were built for many different tasks to guide users to a quicker solution. There was one area that remained frustrating: the simple task of importing a flat file (CSV or TXT file). This seemingly basic functionality was mired by a clumsy and irritating **Import and Export Wizard**, which often made the task of importing data *more* difficult rather than easier.

With SSMS 17.3 came some relief! The **Import Flat File Wizard** removes much of the earlier unnecessary complexities of importing flat files into SQL Server. The wizard can be found using a right-click on a desired database name, then under the menu **Tasks**, as shown in the following screenshot:

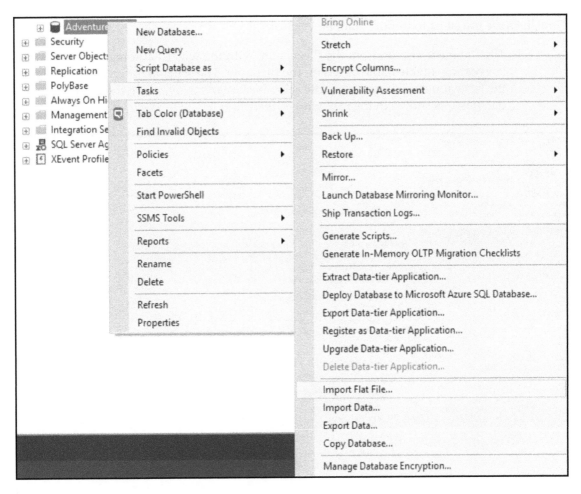

Import Flat File Wizard

The wizard that appears guides the user through a handful of steps to easily import flat files into a target table inside SQL Server.

Now, let's see the steps to import Flat File Wizard:

1. The flat file is chosen from the filesystem, with the wizard automatically suggesting a table name based on the filename. The schema for creating/storing the table must be chosen from the schemas already available in the target database, as shown in the following screenshot:

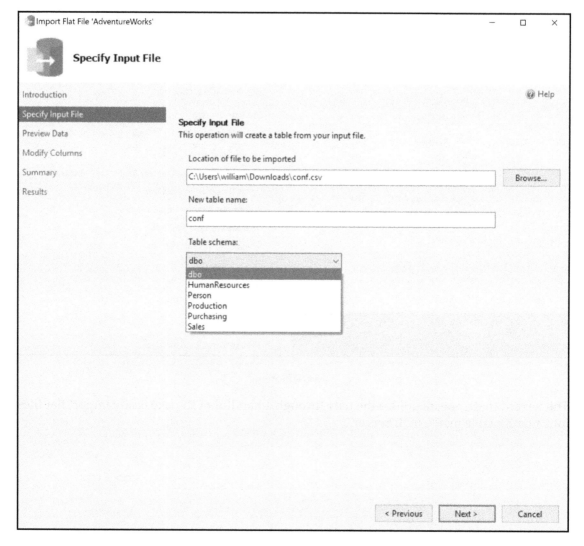

Import Flat File Wizard

2. The next step of the wizard provides a preview of the first 50 rows of data in the
flat file. The wizard parses the data and shows the columns that have been
identified in the file, as shown in the following screenshot:

Import Flat File—data preview

3. The data preview shows how the wizard has interpreted the rows and columns; if this analysis is incorrect, the schema of the new target table can be altered in the next step of the wizard, as shown in the following screenshot:

Import Flat File—Modify Columns

Once we are happy with the target schema, the import is summarized and then started by the wizard. The flat file data is rapidly imported into the new table and the import process completes. This is a big step forward from the previous incarnation of an import wizard and should make it easier to import data into SQL Server with much less hassle.

Vulnerability assessment

The regular headlines of security breaches, along with increasing pressure from governments to hold companies accountable for the breaches, are making more developers (and their managers) pay more attention to security in their IT solutions.

Automated code analysis for application code is nothing new, but database code analysis has been behind the curve for many years.

Microsoft introduced the SQL **Vulnerability Assessment** (**VA**) feature in SSMS 17.4 in December 2017. The idea behind the feature is to easily scan your database(s) for standardized security best practices. The rules of the scan are supplied by Microsoft and (at the time of writing) don't allow for user-designed rules to be implemented. Microsoft states that they are working on multiple improvements, as well as adding to the number of security checks that the tool performs.

In its current state, the tool runs from the SSMS installation and requires no internet connection. The rules that are used for the scan are installed locally to the SSMS installation and are only updated when an update for SSMS is installed.

A vulnerability scan can be performed on any database (including system databases) on any instance from SQL Server 2012 and higher (including Azure SQL Database). The scan is extremely lightweight and generally runs in seconds. The scan is also completely read-only and does not make any changes to a scanned database.

Starting a vulnerability scan is simple. Right-click on a desired database, choose the **Task** menu, and navigate to **Vulnerability Scan**. The options available are to run a new scan or open the report from a previous scan. A scan that is run will store the results in a user-defined location, but it defaults to the user's default documents location. The following screenshot illustrates the process:

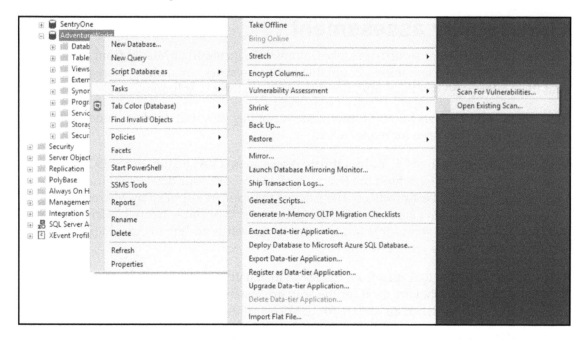

Vulnerability scan

Once a scan is completed, SSMS will automatically open the generated report and display it inside SSMS. At the time of writing, it is not possible to automatically export the results in a different format (for example, Word or Excel). The basis of the report is a JSON file, so any further processing would require waiting for an export functionality from Microsoft or require your ingenuity in parsing the JSON file.

The resulting report displayed in SSMS allows for further analysis of the security threats that may have been found. In the following screenshot, we can see an example scan of an `AdventureWorks` database:

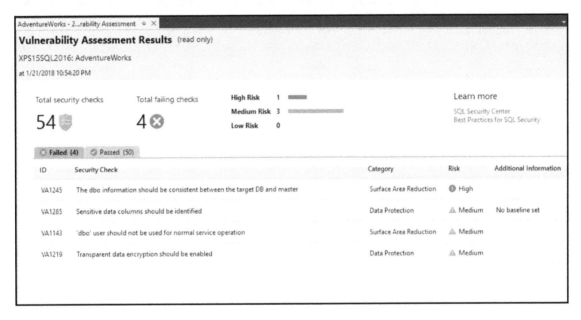

Vulnerability scan results

The scan indicates that the database has passed **50** tests and failed **4**. By clicking on one of the tests we can see more details about the failure/pass.

The following screenshot shows the details of the failed check ID **VA1219**, which states that a database should have **Transparent data encryption** activated:

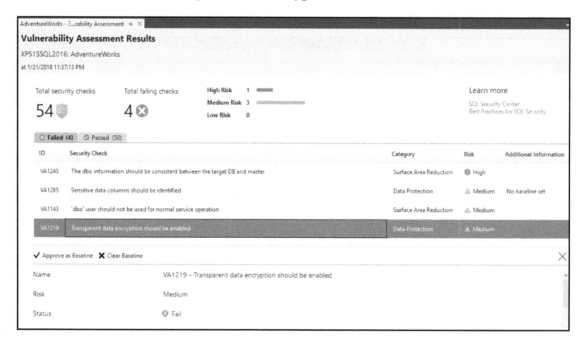

Vulnerability scan—failed TDE

Each check is accompanied with a range of information, including the query that was run against the scanned database. This allows us to see whether the check is correct for our database/environment.

Should a certain check be irrelevant for a database/environment, the **Approve as Baseline** button can be clicked. This will override the check outcome to ensure that a future scan against this database will deem the overridden check to be a pass rather than a failure.

Upon marking the failing TDE check as an acceptable value, a second scan of the AdventureWorks database provides us with **51** passes and **3** failures. The TDE check is now listed as a passing check, with the extra information being set as a custom baseline value. The following screenshot illustrates the baseline:

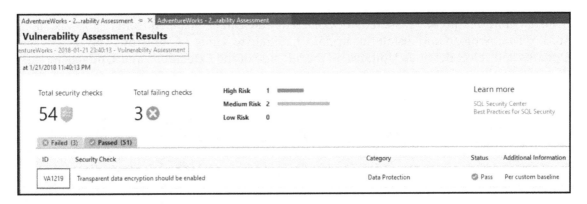

Vulnerability scan custom baseline

The Vulnerability Assessment is by no means a perfect tool, currently *only* covering a limited set of scenarios. It does, however, provide a good start to assessing the security threats inside a database. The tool will continue to receive updates (especially to the rules that are checked against). A further tool to help improve the security of database systems should always be welcomed.

SQL Server Data Tools

As with the installation of SSMS, SQL Server Data Tools is also offered as a separate download. This can be found using the SQL Server setup screen shown at the beginning of the chapter. Clicking on **Install SQL Server Data Tools** will launch a web browser, directing you to the **Downloads** page for SSDT. This **Downloads** page offers the latest stable build and also the latest release candidate of the next version of SSDT (with the usual warning of a release candidate not being production ready). SSDT is delivered with the same Visual Studio Integrated Shell as SSMS, and can be installed as a standalone tool. However, SSDT is aimed at developers and the workflows associated with developing database solutions as a team member. This includes the processes of source control and the packaging of project deployments. With this in mind, it is also possible to install SSDT on a machine that has the full Visual Studio environment installed. Doing so will integrate SSDT into Visual Studio and incorporate the database development templates and workflows, allowing Visual Studio to remain in the development environment, instead of adding a separate environment just for database development.

If Visual Studio is already installed, the SSDTs update can be installed from inside Visual Studio. To download and install this update, navigate to **Tools | Extensions and Updates** and select the node **Updates** on the left side of the **Extensions and Updates** modal window, as shown in the following screenshot:

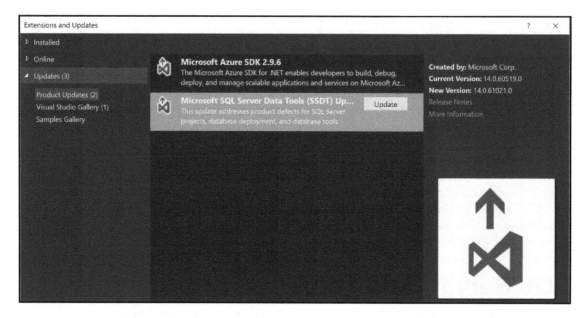

SSDT—extensions and updates

Once installed, SSDT (whether installed as a standalone tool or integrated into Visual Studio) provides four separate project templates to help jump-start development of SQL Server projects:

- **Relational databases**: This is a template designed for traditional relational database development and it supports SQL Server versions 2005 through to 2016 (although SQL Server 2005 is now a deprecated version). SSDT also supports on-premises installations and also Azure SQL Database projects (the Database as a Service solution hosted in Microsoft Azure). It is also possible to design queries (but not full projects) for Azure SQL Data Warehouse (the cloud-based data warehouse solution, hosted in Microsoft Azure).
- **Analysis Services models**: This template is designed to assist in the design and deployment of Analysis Services projects and it supports SQL Server versions 2008 through to 2016.

- **Reporting Services reports**: This template is designed to assist in the design and deployment of Reporting Services projects and it supports SQL Server versions 2008 through to 2016.
- **Integration Services packages**: This template is designed to assist in the design and deployment of Integration Services projects and it supports SQL Server versions 2012 through to 2016.

The template choice dictates what files and folders are automatically prepared at project creation time. Choosing **File** | **New Project** presents the new project dialogue shown in the following screenshot. There are two additions to the project type navigation tree. **Business Intelligence** groups **Analysis Services**, **Reporting Services**, and **Integration Services** projects together. The relational database project type is found under the **SQL Server** navigation node, as shown in the following screenshot:

SSDT—new project dialogue

As shown in the preceding screenshot, a project folder is created and the option to add the project to a source control system is available. Visual Studio offers the option to natively access the source control system's Visual Studio Team Services (a hosted source control system from Microsoft) or alternatively to use a local source control system such as Git. Furthermore, source control systems can be added through the extensive extensions library offered through Visual Studio and they can be accessed through the **Tools** | **Extensions and Updates** menu described earlier in this section.

Working with SSDT and the aforementioned templates should be familiar to any developer that has used Visual Studio before. Upon creating a project, the next step is to begin by adding new items (tables, view, stored procedures, and so on). The dialogue for this is filtered down to the project type, and for an SQL Server database project, we have the option of creating items ranging from Application Roles to XML Schema Collections. Of note is the ability to create **SQL CLR** objects (C# based common language runtime objects), which provide the ability to create more complex calculations that are otherwise not possible (or perform poorly) in the T-SQL language:

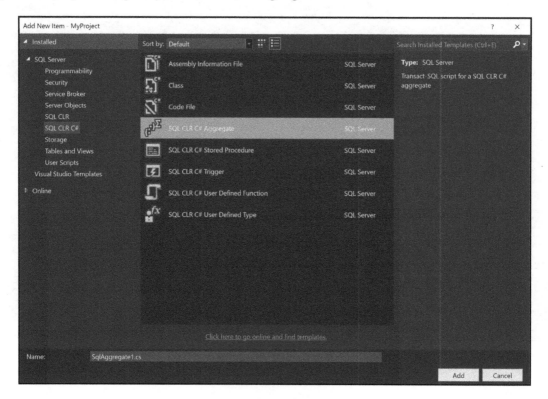

Adding new SQL CLR C# aggregate

The advantages of using SSDT over SSMS for developers is the focus on development workflows and the integrations in the program: source control integration, project structuring, and object templates. This developer focus is further strengthened through the possibility of connecting the source control system to a build system and the option to extend the build system to include **continuous integration/deployment (CI/CD)**. Both automated builds and CI/CD have become ubiquitous in application development circles in the past decade. This area has only seen limited support for database development until now, because databases also permanently store data. Now that application development environments have matured, the ability to introduce CI/CD to database projects has become a reality. Luckily, the foundation for CI/CD has long been laid for application development and so the work to implement CI/CD into a database project is greatly reduced. SSDT is therefore fully capable of integrating SQL Server database projects into a source control system and to extend those projects into automated build, test, and deployment workflows.

There is now a wealth of options to cover CI/CD in the SQL Server world. The tools TeamCity for continuous integration and Octopus Deploy are two products that have been proven to work well in conjunction with SSDT to provide a smooth process for CI/CD in SQL Server projects.

 An interesting and useful website to visit for more information on topics on SSDT is the Microsoft *SQL Server Data Tools Team Blog* at `https://blogs.msdn.microsoft.com/ssdt/`.

Tools for developing R and Python code

As you probably already know, SQL Server 2016 brings the support for the R language, and SQL Server 2017 adds support for the Python language. Of course, you need to have a development tool for the R code. There is a free version of the IDE tool called **RStudio IDE** that has been on the market for quite a long time. This is probably the most popular R tool. In addition, Microsoft is developing **R Tools for Visual Studio** (**RTVS**), a plug-in for Visual Studio, which enables you to also develop R code in an IDE that is common and well known among developers that use Microsoft products and languages.

In this section, you will learn about:

- RStudio IDE
- R Tools for Visual Studio
- Using Visual Studio for data science applications

RStudio IDE

The first tool you get to write and execute the R code in is the **R Console**. The console presents the greater than (>) sign as the prompt to the user. In the console, you write commands line by line, and execute them by pressing the *Enter* key. You have some limited editing capabilities in the console. For example, you can use the up and down arrow keys to retrieve the previous or the next command in the buffer. The following screenshot shows the console, with the demo() command executed, which opens an Explorer window with a list of demo packages.

Because R is a functional package, you close the R Console with the q() function call. Anyway, you probably want to use a nicer, graphical environment. Therefore, it is time to introduce the RStudio IDE. The following screenshot shows the R console:

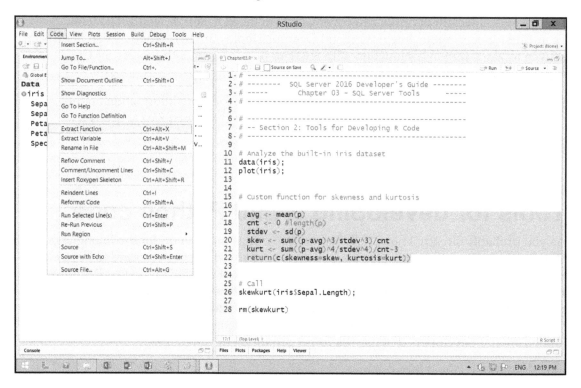

R Console

RStudio is a company that is dedicated to helping the R community with its free and payable products (https://www.rstudio.com/). Their most popular product is the RStudio IDE, or as most R developers used to say, just RStudio. RStudio is available in open source and commercial editions, in both cases for desktop computers or for servers https://www.rstudio.com/products/rstudio/. The open source desktop edition, which is described in this section, is very suitable for starting developing in R. Already this edition has the majority of features built-in for smooth and efficient coding. This edition is described in this section.

You can download the RStudio IDE from the RStudio company site. The IDE supports Windows, macOS, and Linux. Once you install it, you can open it through a desktop shortcut, which points to the C:\Program Files\RStudio\bin\rstudio.exe file, if you used the defaults during the installation.

The RStudio screen is usually split into four panes if you open an R script file, as shown in the following figure. The open script file is showing the R script used for the demos in Chapter 14, *Supporting R in SQL Server R*, of this book:

RStudio IDE

The bottom left pane is the **Console** pane. It works similarly to the R Console Command Prompt utility shipped with the R engine. You can write statements and execute them one by one, by pressing the *Enter* key. However, in RStudio, you have many additional keyboard shortcuts available. One of the most important keyboard shortcuts is the *Tab* key, which provides you with the code complete option. You can press the Tab key nearly anywhere in the code. For example, if you press it when you are writing function arguments, it gives you the list of the possible arguments, or if you already started to write a name of an object, all objects that start with the letters you have already written.

The top-left pane is the **Source** pane, the pane that is by default settings used for the R code script; therefore, this is your basic R code editor. Writing R code line by line in a console is simple, but not very efficient for developing a script with thousands of lines. The **Source** pane does not execute your R code line by line. You highlight portions of your code and you execute it by pressing the *Ctrl* and *Enter* keys simultaneously.

The top-right pane is the **Environment** pane. It shows you the objects in your current environment, the objects currently loaded in memory. However, this pane has more than one function. You may notice additional tabs at the top of the pane. By default, you see the **History** tab, the tab that leads you to the **History** pane, where you can see the history of the commands. The history goes beyond the commands in the current session and in the current console or script.

The bottom-right pane is also a multi-purpose pane. It includes the **Help** pane, **Plots** pane, **Files** pane, **Packages** pane, and **Viewer** pane by default. You can use the **Files** tab to check the files you saved in your RStudio account. With the help of the **Packages** tab you can get a list of all R packages you have access to in the current session. The **Help** tab brings you, of course, to R documentation and a help system. You can use the **Viewer** tab to get to the **Viewer** pane where you can see local web content that you can create with some graphical packages. The **Plots** pane shows you the plots you created by executing R code either in the **Console** or in the **Script** pane.

The following screenshot shows you all the four panes in action. You can see the usage of the *Tab* key in the **Source** pane to auto-complete the name of the dataset used in the plot() function. The dataset used is the iris dataset, a very well-known demo dataset in R. You can see the command echoed in the **Console** pane. The **Environment** pane shows the details about the iris dataset that is loaded in memory. The **Plots** pane shows the plots for all of the variables in the demo iris dataset:

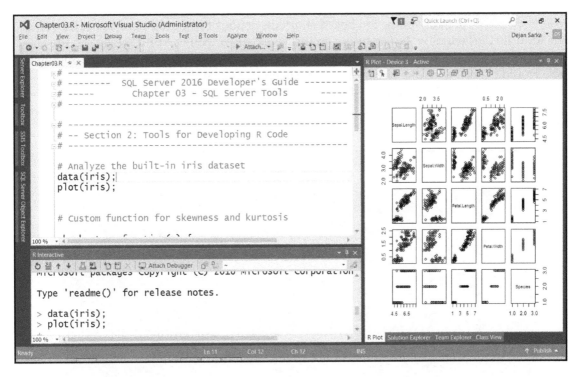

RStudio IDE in action

Note that you can zoom the plot and save it in different graphical formats from the **Plots** pane.

There are literally dozens of keyboard shortcuts. It is impossible to memorize all of them. You memorize them by using them. Nevertheless, you don't need to know all of the shortcuts before you start writing R code. You can always get a quick reference of the keyboard shortcuts by pressing the *Alt*, *Shift*, and *K* keys at the same time. The keyboard **Shortcut Quick Reference** cheat sheet appears, as shown in the following screenshot. You can get rid of this cheat sheet by pressing the *Esc* key.

Please note that, although exhaustive, even this cheat sheet is not complete. In the top-right corner of the cheat sheet you can notice a link to even more shortcuts. Finally, it is worth mentioning that you can modify the pre-defined shortcuts and replace them with your own ones.

You have access to many of the keyboard shortcuts actions through the menus at the top of the RStudio IDE window. For example, in the Tools menu, you can find the link to the keyboard shortcuts cheat sheet. In the Help menu, you can find, besides the help options you would expect, the links to various cheat sheets, for example to the complete RStudio IDE cheat sheet, a PDF document you can download from `https://www.rstudio.com/wp-content/uploads/2016/01/rstudio-IDE-cheatsheet.pdf` at the RStudio site. The following screenshot illustrates the keyboard shortcuts cheat sheet:

RStudio IDE keyboard shortcuts cheat sheet

Using the **Panes** menu, you can change the default layout of the panes. There are numerous options in the **Code** menu. For example, you can extract a function from the code. Figure *Extracting a function* shows an example where the **Source** pane is enlarged at the right side of the RStudio IDE window to show the path to the **Extract Function** option in the **Code** menu. The highlighted code is calculating the third and the fourth population moments for a continuous variable, the skewness and the kurtosis, as known from the descriptive statistics. When you extract a function from the code, you need to provide the name for the function, and RStudio extracts the necessary parameters from the code.

If you extract the function with the name **skewkurt** and test it using the `iris` dataset `Sepal.Length` variable, you get an infinite number for both skewness and kurtosis. Apparently, there is a bug in the code (you can see the bug from the inline comments in the code in the following screenshot). Fortunately, RStudio provides a debugger. You can just click at the left border of the **Source** pane at the line where you want the execution to stop, meaning to set a breakpoint at that line. Then you highlight the code and start debugging by clicking the **Source** button at the top right of the **Source** pane, or by using the keyboard shortcut *Ctrl*, *Shift*, and *S*:

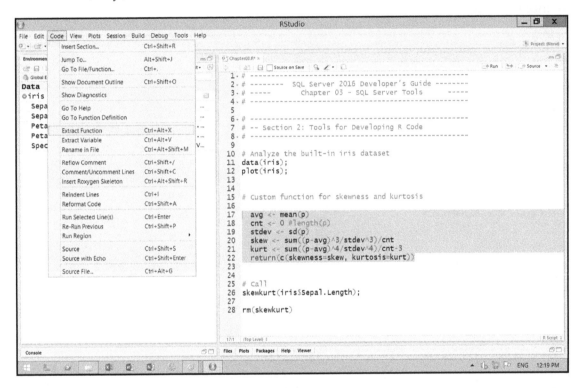

Extracting a function

When you execute the code in the debugging mode, the execution stops at the breakpoint. You can use the buttons in the **Console** pane to execute the code line by line, step into a function, execute the remainder of a function, and more. You can use the Traceback pane to see the full call stack to the code you are currently executing. In the **Environment** pane, you can watch the current values of the objects you are using.

The following screenshot shows a debugging session in RStudio IDE. In the **Source** pane at the right of the window, you can see a breakpoint in **line 19**, near the `cnt <- 0` code. You can see also the line that is just about to execute, in this case **line 22**, with the code `kurt <- sum((p-avg)^4/stdev^4)/cnt-3`. In the **Console** pane at the bottom-left of the screen, you can see the **Next** button highlighted. This button executes the next line of the code. In the middle-left of the screen you see the **Trackback** pane, and at the top left the **Environment** pane. You can see that the value of the variable `cnt` is 0, and because this variable is used in the denominator when calculating the `skewness`, the skew variable has an infinite value:

Debugging in RStudio IDE

After you find the error, you can stop debugging either from the **Debug** menu or with the *Shift* and *F8* keyboard shortcut. Correct the code and run it to test it.

R Tools for Visual Studio 2015

Microsoft is developing **RTVS** for those developers that are used to developing code in the most popular Microsoft IDE, Visual Studio. RTVS comes in two versions: as a free download for Visual Studio 2015 and already included in Visual Studio 2017. You can download RTVS for Visual Studio 2015 from `https://www.visualstudio.com/vs/rtvs/`. Visual Studio 2017 is covered in the next section of this chapter.

Once you install the RTVS you open the Visual Studio like you would open it for any other project. Of course, since SSDT is not a separate product-it is just another shortcut to the Visual Studio IDE-you can also open SSDT and get the R Tools menu besides other common Visual Studio menus.

With RTVS, you get most of the useful common panes of the RStudio IDE. You get the **Source** pane, the **Console** pane- which is called **R Interactive** in RTVS-and the **Plots** pane. The following figure shows the RTVS window with the **Source**, **R Interactive**, and the **Plots** pane open, showing the same plots for the variables from the `iris` demo dataset, shown in the figure *RStudio IDE in action* earlier in this section:

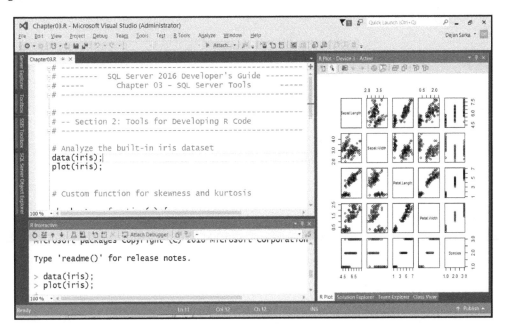

R Tools for Visual Studio

If you are familiar with the Visual Studio IDE, then you might want to test RTVS.

Setting up Visual Studio 2017 for data science applications

Installing **SQL Server 2017 Machine Learning Services** is covered in `Chapter 15`, *Introducing Python*. Here, Visual Studio 2017 is introduced. You can use either the Professional or free Community Edition (`https://www.visualstudio.com/downloads/`) to develop Python and R code.

When installing Visual Studio 2017, be sure to select Python development workload, and then data science and analytical applications, as the following screenshot shows. This will install Python language templates, including data science templates, and also R Tools for Visual Studio 2017:

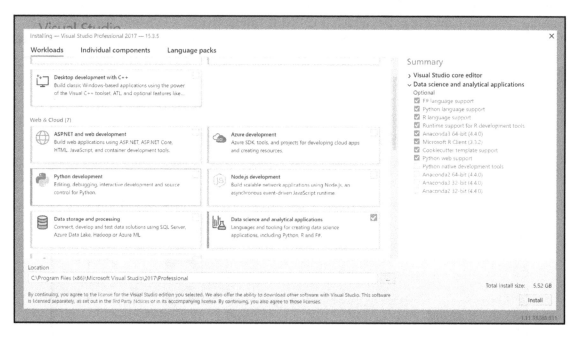

Visual Studio 2017 setup for data science

There you go, you are nearly ready. There is a small trick here. VS 2017 also installs its own Python interpreter. In order to use the scalable one installed with SQL Server, the one that enables executing code in the Database Engine context and includes Microsoft scalable libraries, you need to set up an additional Python environment, pointing to the scalable version of the interpreter. The path for this scalable interpreter is, if you installed the default instance of SQL Server, `C:\Program Files\Microsoft SQL Server\MSSQL14.MSSQLSERVER\PYTHON_SERVICES\python.exe`. You can see how to set up this environment in the following screenshot. Note that there is no need for any additional step for developing R code, because VS 2017 also installs the Microsoft R Client, the open R engine that includes the Microsoft scalable libraries:

Setting up Python environments

That's it. You are ready to start Python programming. Just start a new project and select the **Python Application** template from the Python folder. You can also explore the **Python Machine Learning** templates, which include **Classifier, Clustering**, and **Regression** projects. If you selected the **Python Application** template, you should have open the first empty Python script with a default name, the same as the project name, and the default extension .py, waiting for you to write and interactively execute Python code.

Summary

In this chapter, we have taken a look at the new additions in the developer toolset for SQL Server 2017. There have been some long-awaited improvements made, especially the separation of SQL Server Management Studio from the release cycle of SQL Server itself. The accelerated release cycle of SSMS has brought a breadth of new features and support that will help developers in their daily work with SQL Server.

Some of the featured additions to SSMS are quite powerful and will allow us as developers to be more efficient. Live Query Statistics provides us with excellent insights into how our queries are *actually* processed, removing parts of the guessing game when trying to refactor or tune our queries. The Vulnerability Assessment tool should allow for quicker identification of potential security threats inside our databases. A safer database means a safer business!

For SQL Server developers, there are two new development environments for developing the R code. Of course, one of them, the RStudio IDE, is well-known among R developers. Because it is so widely used, it will probably be the first choice when developing R code,and also for SQL Server developers. Nevertheless, if you are used to and love the Visual Studio IDE, you might give R Tools for Visual Studio a try.

After this short excursion into the tools that are delivered with SQL Server 2017, we will continue our journey through the new features and technologies in SQL Server 2017 in the next chapter.

4

Transact-SQL and Database Engine Enhancements

Each new SQL Server version brings numerous extensions and improvements to the Transact-SQL language. Most of them are used to support newly added database engine features, but some of them address missing functionalities and limitations in previous versions. SQL Server 2016 and SQL Server 2017 come up with many features that require extensions in Transact-SQL: temporal tables, JSON support, improvements for memory-optimized tables, columnstore tables and indexes, new security enhancements, graph databases, and more. They will be explored in detail in the chapters dedicated to the appropriate features.

This chapter covers Transact-SQL features that can make a developer's work more productive and enhancements that can increase the availability of database objects and enlarge the scope of existing functionalities, limited in the previous SQL Server versions. In addition, it will cover how the execution plans in SQL Server 2017 are improved during compilation and after query execution.

This chapter is divided into the following four sections:

- New and enhanced Transact-SQL functions and expressions
- Enhanced DML and DDL statements
- New query hints
- Adaptive query processing in SQL Server 2017

In the first section, you will see new, out-of-the-box functions and expressions that allow developers to manipulate with strings more efficiently, to compress text by using the GZIP algorithm, and play with session-scoped variables.

The second section covers enhancements in data manipulation and data definition statements. The most important one will let you change the data type or other attributes of a table column, while the table remains available for querying and modifications. This is a very important feature for systems where continuous availability is required. You will also be aware of other improvements that let you perform some actions faster or with less written code.

The third section brings a demonstration of how to use newly added query hints to improve query execution and avoid problems caused by the Spool operator or inappropriate memory grants.

Finally, SQL Server 2017 introduces the *adaptive query processing* feature, which breaks the barrier between query plan optimization and actual execution, improves overall performance, and addresses issues that cause suboptimal execution plans.

New and enhanced functions and expressions

SQL Server 2016 and SQL Server 2017 introduce several new functions that can help developers to be more productive and efficient. Additionally, by removing limitations in some existing functions, their scope of usage has been enlarged. SQL Server now contains more than 300 built-in functions. Here is the list of new or changed functions and expressions in SQL Server 2016:

- Two new string functions: `STRING_SPLIT` and `STRING_ESCAPE`
- New date function and new expression: `DATEFDIFF_BIG` and `AT TIME ZONE`
- Four new system functions: `COMPRESS`, `DECOMPRESS`, `SESSION_CONTEXT`, and `CURRENT_TRANSACTION_ID`
- Enhancements to the `HASHBYTES` cryptographic function
- Four JSON related functions: `ISSJON`, `JSON_VALUE`, `JSON_QUERY`, and `JSON_MODIFY`, and one new rowset function, `OPENJSON`

SQL Server 2017 has introduced these string functions: `STRING_AGG`, `TRIM`, `CONCATE_WS`, and `TRANSLATE`.

Using STRING_SPLIT

Since SQL Server does not support arrays, when multiple values need to be sent to it, developers use a list of values (usually comma-separated ones).

SQL Server 2008 introduced an excellent feature called **table-valued parameters** (**TVP**), which allows you to pack values in a table and transfer them to SQL Server in table format. On the server, stored procedures or queries use this parameter as a table variable and can leverage set-based operations to improve performance, compared to separate executions per single parameter value. Thus, in all editions of SQL Server 2008 onwards it is strongly recommended to use TVP instead of a list of values in such cases.

However, lists of values as parameters for stored procedures are still widely used, mainly for the following two reasons:

- **Missing support for TVP in JDBC drivers**: Java applications and services still have to use comma-separated lists or XML to transfer a list of values to SQL Server
- **Legacy code**: Significant amounts of Transact-SQL code from the previous SQL Server versions, where TVP was not supported.

You might ask yourself why companies still have legacy code in their production systems and why they don't migrate the old code so that they can benefit from new features and enhancements. For instance, why are old implementations with comma-separated lists not replaced by the recommended TVPs? The migration steps are not complex and every developer can perform them. However, in a medium or large company, developers cannot decide what should be done. Their responsibility scope is related to *how* and not to *what*. Therefore, in such cases, developers can suggest the migration to project managers or product owners and the decision about the priority of the action is made on the business side. To migrate a comma-separated list to TVP, you need to change not only the body of stored procedures, but also their parameters and their interface. You also need to change the data access layer to touch the application code, to adjust unit tests, to compile the project, and to deploy it. Even if your tests are fully automated, this is not a trivial effort. On the other hand, the migration does not bring significant improvements for customers. Nowadays, development processes are mostly based on the agile methodology and features mostly wanted and appreciated by customers have the highest priority. Therefore, such migration actions usually remain at the bottom of the to-do list.

When a list of values is transferred to SQL Server as a stored procedure parameter, in the stored procedure body this list has to be converted to a table. Until SQL Server 2016, there was no built-in function that could perform this action. Developers had to write **user-defined functions** (**UDF**) or play with the FOR XML PATH extension for that purpose. An excellent overview and performance comparison of existing UDFs for converting a string to a table can be found in the article *Split strings the right way – or the next best way*, written by Aaron Bertrand. The article is available at the following address: http://sqlperformance. com/2012/07/t-sql-queries/split-strings.

Finally, the SQL Server development team added the STRING_SPLIT function into the latest release. This is a table-valued function and converts a delimited string into a single-column table. The function accepts two input arguments:

- **String**: An expression of any non-deprecated string data type that needs to be split
- **Separator**: Single character used as a separator in the input string

Since it is a table-valued function, it returns a table. The returned table contains only one column with the name value and with a data type and length that are the same as those of the input string.

Here is an example showing how this function can be used to produce a three-row table for a comma-separated list as input. Execute this code:

```
USE tempdb;
SELECT value FROM STRING_SPLIT(N'Rapid Wien,Benfica Lisboa,Seattle
Seahawks',',');
```

The preceding query produces the following output:

```
value
-------------------
Rapid Wien
Benfica Lisboa
Seattle Seahawks
```

The actual execution plan for the preceding query looks as follows:

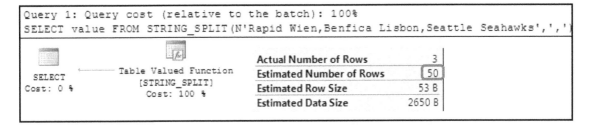

Query 1: Query cost (relative to the batch): 100%
SELECT value FROM STRING_SPLIT(N'Rapid Wien,Benfica Lisbon,Seattle Seahawks',',')

SELECT Cost: 0 %	Table Valued Function [STRING_SPLIT] Cost: 100 %		
		Actual Number of Rows	3
		Estimated Number of Rows	50
		Estimated Row Size	53 B
		Estimated Data Size	2650 B

Estimated Number of Rows for the STRING_SPLIT function

Notice that the **Estimated Number of Rows** is **50**. This is always the case with this function: the estimated output is **50** rows and it does not depend on the number of string elements. Even when you specify the OPTION (RECOMPILE) query hint, the estimation remains the same. In the case of user-defined table-valued functions, the **Estimated Number of Rows** is 100.

As a table-valued function, STRING_SPLIT can be used not only in the SELECT clause, but also in FROM, WHERE, and wherever a table expression is supported. To demonstrate its usage, you will use the new SQL Server sample database: WideWorldImporters. The database is available for download at
https://github.com/Microsoft/sql-server-samples/releases/tag/wide-world-importers-v1.0. The following query extracts stock items with the 16GB tag in the Tags attribute:

```
USE WideWorldImporters;
SELECT StockItemID, StockItemName, Tags
FROM Warehouse.StockItems
WHERE '"16GB"' IN (SELECT value FROM
STRING_SPLIT(REPLACE(REPLACE(Tags,'[',''), ']',''), ','));
```

This query produces the following result:

StockItemID	StockItemName	Tags
5	USB food flash drive - hamburger	["16GB","USB Powered"]
7	USB food flash drive - pizza slice	["16GB","USB Powered"]
9	USB food flash drive - banana	["16GB","USB Powered"]
11	USB food flash drive - cookie	["16GB","USB Powered"]
13	USB food flash drive - shrimp cocktail	["16GB","USB Powered"]
15	USB food flash drive - dessert 10 drive variety pack	["16GB","USB Powered"]

The following code example demonstrates how this function can be used to return details about orders for IDs provided in a comma-separated list:

```
USE WideWorldImporters;
DECLARE @orderIds AS VARCHAR(100) = '1,3,7,8,9,11';
SELECT o.OrderID, o.CustomerID, o.OrderDate FROM Sales.Orders AS o
INNER JOIN STRING_SPLIT(@orderIds,',') AS x ON x.value= o.OrderID;
```

This produces the following output:

```
OrderID       CustomerID   OrderDate
-----------   -----------  ----------
1             832          2013-01-01
3             105          2013-01-01
7             575          2013-01-01
8             964          2013-01-01
9             77           2013-01-01
11            586          2013-01-01
```

Note that, since the function returns a column of STRING data type, there is an implicit conversion between the columns involved in the JOIN clause:

```
DECLARE @input AS NVARCHAR(20) = NULL;
SELECT * FROM STRING_SPLIT(@input,',');
```

This is the output produced by the preceding command:

```
value
--------
```

The STRING_SPLIT function requires that the database is at least in compatibility level 130. If this is not the case, you will get an error. The next code example demonstrates an attempt to use this function under compatibility level 120:

```
USE WideWorldImporters;
ALTER DATABASE WideWorldImporters SET COMPATIBILITY_LEVEL = 120;
GO
SELECT value FROM STRING_SPLIT('1,2,3',',');
/*Result:
Msg 208, Level 16, State 1, Line 65
Invalid object name 'STRING_SPLIT'.
*/
--back to the original compatibility level
ALTER DATABASE WideWorldImporters SET COMPATIBILITY_LEVEL = 130;
```

This is a handy function and will definitely have its use cases. However, as you will have already noticed, there are some limitations:

- **Single character separator**: The function accepts only a single character separator; if you had a separator with more characters, you would still need to write your own user-defined function.
- **Single output column**: The output is a single column table, without the position of the string element within the delimited string. Thus, you can only sort the output by the element name.
- **String data type**: When you use this function to delimit a string of numbers, although all the values in the output column are numbers, their data type is string, and when you join them to numeric columns in other tables, data type conversion is required.

If these limitations are acceptable to you, you should use the STRING_SPLIT function in future developments. I would always suggest a built-in function rather than a user-defined one if they are similar from a performance point of view. It is always pre-deployed and available in all databases. Once again, take note that the database must be at least in compatibility level 130.

Using STRING_ESCAPE

The STRING_ESCAPE function is a scalar function and escapes special characters in input text according to the given formatting rules. It returns input text with escaped characters. The function accepts the following two input arguments:

- **Text**: This is an expression of any non-deprecated string data type.
- **Type**: This argument must have the JSON value, since SQL Server 2016 currently supports only JSON as the formatting type.

The return type of the function is `nvarchar(max)`. The `STRING_ESCAPE` function is a deterministic function; it always returns the same result for the same input parameters.

 The data types text, ntext, and image are marked as deprecated features in SQL Server 2005. This means they can be removed in any of the later versions. The fact that they are still deprecated could mean that they will still be supported, because of legacy code. Microsoft does not want to take risks with actions that could cause damaging changes in customer applications. However, as you can see, with these two functions, all new features, functions, and expressions dealing with strings don't accept these data types. This is an implicit way to force you to use the recommended data types, `varchar(max)`, `nvarchar(max)`, and `varbinary(max)`, instead of their deprecated counterparts.

JSON's escaping rules are defined in the ECMA 404 standard specification. The following table provides the list of characters that must be escaped according to this specification and their JSON conform representation:

JSON escaping rules

Special character	JSON conform character
Double quote	\"
Backspace	\b
Solidus	\/
Reverse solidus	\\
Form feed	\f
Tabulation	\t
Carriage return	\r
New line	\n

In addition to this, all control characters with character codes in the range 0–31 need to be escaped too. In JSON output, they are represented in the following format: `\u<code>`. Thus, the control character `CHAR(0)` is escaped as `\u0000`, while `CHAR(31)` is represented by `\u001f`.

The following several examples will be used to demonstrate how this function works. Suppose you need to escape the following string: a\bc/de"f. According to JSON's escaping rules, three characters should be escaped: back slash, solidus, and double quote. You can check it by calling the STRING_ESCAPE function for this string as the input argument:

```
SELECT STRING_ESCAPE('a\bc/de"f','JSON') AS escaped_input;
```

Here is the result returned by the function:

```
escaped_input
-------------
a\\bc\/de"f
```

The following example demonstrates the escape of the control characters with the code 0, 4, and 31:

```
SELECT
  STRING_ESCAPE(CHAR(0),  'JSON') AS escaped_char0,
  STRING_ESCAPE(CHAR(4),  'JSON') AS escaped_char4,
  STRING_ESCAPE(CHAR(31), 'JSON') AS escaped_char31;
```

This function call produces the following output:

```
escaped_char0     escaped_char4     escaped_char31
-------------     -------------     ---------------
\u0000            \u0004            \u001f
```

The next example shows that the horizontal tab represented by the string and code is escaped with the same sequence:

```
SELECT
  STRING_ESCAPE(CHAR(9), 'JSON') AS escaped_tab1,
  STRING_ESCAPE('    ', 'JSON') AS escaped_tab2;
```

Both statements resulted in a \t sequence:

```
escaped_tab1     escaped_tab2
-------------    ---------------
\t               \t
```

The function returns a NULL value if the input string is not provided. To check this, run the following code:

```
DECLARE @input AS NVARCHAR(20) = NULL;
SELECT STRING_ESCAPE(@input, 'JSON') AS escaped_input;
```

You will get the expected result:

```
escaped_input
--------------
NULL
```

Escaping occurs both in the names of properties and in their values. Consider the following example, where one of the keys in the JSON input string contains a special character:

```
SELECT STRING_ESCAPE(N'key:1, i\d:4', 'JSON') AS escaped_input;
```

Here is the output:

```
escaped_input
--------------
key:1, i\\d:4
```

The STRING_ESCAPE function is internally used by the FOR JSON clause to automatically escape special characters and represents control characters in the JSON output. It can also be used for formatting paths, especially if you need to run it on UNIX systems (which is happening with R integration and SQL Server on Linux). Sometimes, a forward slash or backslash needs to be doubled, and this function is perfect when preparing code for Unix or CMD commands; a backslash needs to be doubled and converted to a forward slash. Unlike the STRING_SPLIT function, this function is available in a SQL Server 2016 database, even in old database compatibility levels.

Using STRING_AGG

This function, introduced in SQL Server 2017, concatenates the values of string expressions and places separator values between them. It accepts three input arguments:

- **String**: This is an expression (usually a column name).
- **Separator**: This is a list of characters used as separators for concatenated strings (with a maximum size of 8,000 bytes).
- **Order clause**: Optionally, you can specify the order of concatenated results by using the WITHIN GROUP clause.

The function returns a string, but the exact return type depends on the input string expression (first function argument). The following table shows the return type of the function for a given input argument:

Input expression data type	Return type
`int`, `bigint`, `smallint`, `tinyint`, `numeric`, `float`, `real`, `bit`, `decimal`, `smallmoney`, `money`, `datetime`, `datetime2`	`NVARCHAR(4000)`
`NVARCHAR`	`NVARCHAR(4000)`
`VARCHAR`	`VARCHAR(8000)`
`NVARCHAR(MAX)`	`NVARCHAR(MAX)`

Return types of the STRING_AGG function

So, this function is opposite to `STRING_SPLIT`. It concatenates table rows into a single string. Expression values (columns) are implicitly converted to string types and then concatenated.

To see this function in action, use this code to generate a comma-separated list of database names from a test server. Run this code against a SQL Server 2017 instance hosting Microsoft sample databases:

```
SELECT name FROM sys.databases;
```

Here is the list of databases on a freshly installed server with the sample databases:

```
name
-------------------
master
tempdb
model
msdb
WideWorldImporters
WideWorldImportersDW
```

To get a comma-separated list of database names, use the following code:

```
SELECT STRING_AGG (name, ',') AS dbs_as_csv FROM sys.databases;
```

As expected, the result is a string:

```
dbs_as_csv
-----------------------------------------------------------------
master,tempdb,model,msdb,WideWorldImporters,WideWorldImportersDW
```

The column does not need to be of string type. You can use a non-string column; data is automatically converted to string, as in the following example:

```
SELECT STRING_AGG (database_id, ',') AS dbiss_as_csv FROM sys.databases;
```

The result is again a comma-separated string of database IDs:

```
dbids_as_csv
--------------
1,2,3,4,5,6
```

Since the input column is a sysname data type (which is equivalent to nvarchar(128) according to the table *Return type of the STRING_AGG function*), the function returns a value of the nvarchar(4000) data type. That means that you can have up to 2,000 characters in the resulting string, including separators.

Therefore, this code, showing all columns in the WideWorldImporters database, will fail:

```
USE WideWorldImporters;
SELECT STRING_AGG (name, ',') AS cols FROM sys.syscolumns;
```

Instead of a comma-separated list, you will see the following error message:

```
Msg 9829, Level 16, State 1, Line 1
STRING_AGG aggregation result exceeded the limit of 8000 bytes. Use LOB
types to avoid result truncation.
```

To show a comma-separated list of all database columns, you need to convert the data type of the name column:

```
USE WideWorldImporters;
SELECT STRING_AGG (CAST(name AS NVARCHAR(MAX)), ',') AS cols FROM
sys.syscolumns;
```

This will produce the expected output—a comma-separated list of all column names in a given database:

```
cols
-----------------------------------
bitpos,cid,colguid,hbcolid,maxinrowlen,nullbit,offset,ordkey,rcmodified,rsc
olid,rsid...
```

The list is, of course, abbreviated, since there are almost 1,700 columns in this database.

Handling NULLs in the STRING_AGG function

The STRING_AGG function ignores NULL values; in the result, they are represented by an empty string. Therefore, the following two statements involved in the UNION ALL operator return the same output:

```
SELECT STRING_AGG(c,',') AS fav_city FROM (VALUES('Vienna'),('Lisbon')) AS
T(c)
UNION ALL
SELECT STRING_AGG(c,',') AS fav_city FROM
(VALUES('Vienna'),(NULL),('Lisbon')) AS T(c);
```

Here is the output:

```
fav_city
-----------------------------------
Vienna,Lisbon
Vienna,Lisbon
```

If you want to represent NULLs in the outputted string, you need to replace them with a desired value by using the ISNULL or COALESCE functions:

```
SELECT STRING_AGG(c,',') AS fav_city FROM (VALUES('Vienna'),('Lisbon')) AS
T(c)
UNION ALL
SELECT STRING_AGG(COALESCE(c,'N/A'),',') AS fav_city FROM
(VALUES('Vienna'),(NULL),('Lisbon')) AS T(c);
```

Now the output is different, NULL is represented with N/A:

```
fav_city
-----------------------------------
Vienna,Lisbon
Vienna,N/A,Lisbon
```

The WITHIN GROUP clause

By using the WITHIN GROUP clause, you can define the order for concatenated values. The following code returns order IDs for three given customers from the Sales.Orders table:

```
DECLARE @input VARCHAR(20) = '1059,1060,1061';
SELECT CustomerID, STRING_AGG(OrderID, ',') AS OrderIDs
FROM Sales.Orders o
INNER JOIN STRING_SPLIT(@input,',') x ON x.value = o.CustomerID
GROUP BY CustomerID
ORDER BY CustomerID;
```

Here is the result:

```
CustomerID  OrderIDs
----------  --------------------------------------------------------
1059        68716,69684,70534,71100,71720,71888,73260,73453
1060        72646,72738,72916,73081
1061        72637,72669,72671,72713,72770,72787,73340,73350,7335
```

You can see that the OrderIDs are sorted in ascending order. However, there is no guarantee that they will be sorted; the database engine will try to generate the result as fast as possible and does not care about the order of IDs. If you want to be sure that the comma-separated list is in a specific order, use the WITHIN GROUP clause. In this example, you use the same statement as in the preceding one, but this time you ensure that OrderIDs are stored in descending order:

```
DECLARE @input VARCHAR(20) = '1059,1060,1061';
SELECT CustomerID, STRING_AGG(OrderID, ',') WITHIN GROUP (ORDER BY OrderID
DESC) AS orderids
FROM Sales.Orders o
INNER JOIN STRING_SPLIT(@input,',') x ON x.value = o.CustomerID
GROUP BY CustomerID
ORDER BY CustomerID;
```

You can see the expected result, but this time the order is guaranteed:

```
CustomerID  OrderIDs
----------  --------------------------------------------------------
1059        73453,73260,71888,71720,71100,70534,69684,68716
1060        73081,72916,72738,72646
1061        73356,73350,73340,72787,72770,72713,72671,72669,72637
```

Use the standard option WITHIN GROUP clause if you want to specify the order for the concatenation.

The functions in SQL Server 2017 are very useful and practical. You can achieve the same result with significantly less code. For instance, if you want to return a list of order IDs for customers given in a comma-separated list in the `WideWorldImporters` database prior to SQL Server 2016, you need to perform two steps. First, you need to create a user-defined function to handle values from a comma-separated list, and then you need to create a comma-separated list of order IDs for output by using XML:

```
CREATE FUNCTION dbo.SplitStrings
(
    @input NVARCHAR(MAX),
    @delimiter CHAR(1)
)
RETURNS @output TABLE(item NVARCHAR(MAX)
)
BEGIN
    DECLARE @start INT, @end INT;
    SELECT @start = 1, @end = CHARINDEX(@delimiter, @input);
    WHILE @start < LEN(@input) + 1 BEGIN
        IF @end = 0
            SET @end = LEN(@input) + 1;
        INSERT INTO @output (item)
        VALUES(SUBSTRING(@input, @start, @end - @start));
        SET @start = @end + 1;
        SET @end = CHARINDEX(@delimiter, @input, @start);
    END
    RETURN
END
GO
SET NOCOUNT ON;
SET STATISTICS IO ON;
SET STATISTICS TIME ON;
DECLARE @input VARCHAR(20) = '1059,1060,1061';
SELECT C.CustomerID,
 STUFF( (SELECT ',' + CAST(OrderId AS VARCHAR(10)) AS [text()]
 FROM Sales.Orders AS O
 WHERE O.CustomerID = C.CustomerID
 ORDER BY OrderID ASC
 FOR XML PATH('')), 1, 1, NULL) AS OrderIDs
FROM Sales.Customers AS C
 INNER JOIN dbo.SplitStrings(@input,',') AS F ON F.item = C.CustomerID
ORDER BY CustomerID;
```

In SQL Server 2017, you can use two built-in functions for that purpose and the code looks simple and clear, and even runs faster than the one from the previous SQL Server versions:

```
SET NOCOUNT ON;
SET STATISTICS IO ON;
SET STATISTICS TIME ON;
DECLARE @input VARCHAR(20) = '1059,1060,1061';
SELECT CustomerID, STRING_AGG(OrderID, ',') WITHIN GROUP(ORDER BY OrderID
ASC) AS OrderIDs
FROM Sales.Orders o
INNER JOIN STRING_SPLIT(@input,',') x ON x.value = o.CustomerID
GROUP BY CustomerID
ORDER BY CustomerID;
```

Note that both queries have set statistics IO and time flags in order to compare their execution parameters. Here is the output of the previous two executions:

```
SQL Server parse and compile time:
   CPU time = 0 ms, elapsed time = 0 ms.

 SQL Server Execution Times:
   CPU time = 0 ms,  elapsed time = 0 ms.
Table 'Worktable'. Scan count 0, logical reads 0, physical reads 0, read-
ahead reads 0, lob logical reads 0, lob physical reads 0, lob read-ahead
reads 0.
Table 'Workfile'. Scan count 0, logical reads 0, physical reads 0, read-
ahead reads 0, lob logical reads 0, lob physical reads 0, lob read-ahead
reads 0.
Table 'Orders'. Scan count 663, logical reads 1549, physical reads 0, read-
ahead reads 0, lob logical reads 0, lob physical reads 0, lob read-ahead
reads 0.
Table 'Worktable'. Scan count 0, logical reads 0, physical reads 0, read-
ahead reads 0, lob logical reads 0, lob physical reads 0, lob read-ahead
reads 0.
Table 'Customers'. Scan count 1, logical reads 4, physical reads 0, read-
ahead reads 0, lob logical reads 0, lob physical reads 0, lob read-ahead
reads 0.
Table '#B12AC5B5'. Scan count 1, logical reads 1, physical reads 0, read-
ahead reads 0, lob logical reads 0, lob physical reads 0, lob read-ahead
reads 0.

 SQL Server Execution Times:
   CPU time = 78 ms,  elapsed time = 87 ms.


SQL Server parse and compile time:
   CPU time = 0 ms, elapsed time = 0 ms.
```

```
SQL Server Execution Times:
   CPU time = 0 ms,  elapsed time = 0 ms.
Table 'Worktable'. Scan count 0, logical reads 0, physical reads 0, read-
ahead reads 0, lob logical reads 0, lob physical reads 0, lob read-ahead
reads 0.
Table 'Orders'. Scan count 3, logical reads 8, physical reads 0, read-ahead
reads 0, lob logical reads 0, lob physical reads 0, lob read-ahead reads 0.

SQL Server Execution Times:
   CPU time = 0 ms,  elapsed time = 0 ms.
```

As you can see, new string functions are not only handy, but they perform better (sometimes significantly better) than the workarounds prior to SQL Server 2017.

Using CONCAT_WS

The CONCAT_WS function is similar to the CONCAT function. It also concatenates a given expression, but unlike with the CONCAT function, here you can specify a separator. The separator is any string type and the number of characters for the separator is not limited (you can even use more than 8,000 characters).

The following query illustrates the usage of the CONCAT_WS function:

```
SELECT CONCAT_WS(' / ',name, compatibility_level, collation_name) FROM
sys.databases WHERE database_id < 5;
```

Here is the output returned by the previous query:

```
db
-----------------------------------------------
master / 140 / SQL_Latin1_General_CP1_CI_AS
tempdb / 140 / SQL_Latin1_General_CP1_CI_AS
model / 140 / SQL_Latin1_General_CP1_CI_AS
msdb / 130 / SQL_Latin1_General_CP1_CI_AS
```

For the same output with the CONCAT function, you would need to put the separator after each input string:

```
SELECT CONCAT(name, ' / ', compatibility_level, ' / ', collation_name) AS
db FROM sys.databases WHERE database_id < 5;
```

Using TRIM

The TRIM function, as in many other programing languages, removes the space character CHAR(32) from both sides of a given string. There is nothing special with this function, except the fact that implementation did not come until SQL Server 2017, although the LTRIM and RTRIM functions had existed for almost 10 years. Prior to this version, if you wanted to remove white spaces, you had to use the LTRIM(RTRIM(<string>)) expression.

Using TRANSLATE

Contrary to expectations, the TRANSLATE function has nothing to do with translations. It lets you specify multiple string replacements within a single function. It accepts three input arguments:

- input_string: A string expression that needs to be changed
- characters: A string expression representing characters that should be replaced
- translations: A string expression representing characters that will replace characters specified with a second argument

The function returns a string expression of the same type as the first input argument.

In the following example, the TRANSLATE function is used to replace square brackets with parentheses:

```
SELECT TRANSLATE('[Sales].[SalesOrderHeader]','[]','()');
```

Here is the output:

(Sales).(SalesOrderHeader)

With the REPLACE function, the same output can be done with a more complex query:

```
SELECT REPLACE(REPLACE('[Sales].[SalesOrderHeader]','[','('),']',')');
```

As you can see, the TRANSLATE function lets you define more replacement characters at once. However, the third argument of the function must have the same length as the second. In other words, you cannot use the TRANSLATE function to replace characters with an empty string (as in, to remove characters). Therefore, the following code won't work:

```
SELECT TRANSLATE('[Sales].[SalesOrderHeader]','[]','');
```

Instead of the table name formatted with parentheses, you will get the following error message:

```
Msg 9828, Level 16, State 1, Line 1
The second and third arguments of the TRANSLATE built-in function must
contain an equal number of characters.
```

Using COMPRESS

The COMPRESS function is a scalar function and compresses the input variable, column, or expression using the GZIP algorithm. The function accepts an expression, which can be either string or binary, but again, the deprecated data types text, ntext, and image are not supported.

The return type of the function is VARBINARY(MAX).

Use this function with wide text columns, especially when you do not plan to query them often. For large strings, the compression rate can be significant, particularly when the original string is XML. Here is an example of significant compression. The example uses the output of the system Extended Event session system_health to check the compression rate when you use the COMPRESS function for the target_data column. Here is the code:

```
SELECT
  target_name,
  DATALENGTH(xet.target_data) AS original_size,
  DATALENGTH(COMPRESS(xet.target_data)) AS compressed_size,
  CAST((DATALENGTH(xet.target_data) -
DATALENGTH(COMPRESS(xet.target_data)))*100.0/DATALENGTH(xet.target_data) AS
DECIMAL(5,2)) AS compression_rate_in_percent
FROM sys.dm_xe_session_targets xet
INNER JOIN sys.dm_xe_sessions xe ON xe.address = xet.event_session_address
WHERE xe.name = 'system_health';
```

The following is the output generated by this query on my test server. You might get a different output, but similar results:

```
target_name   original_size   compressed_size   compression_rate_in_pct
-----------   -------------   ---------------   ------------------------
ring_buffer   8386188         349846            95.83
event_file    410             235               42.68
```

You can see a quite impressive compression rate of 96%. On the other hand, the compressed representation of a short string can be even longer than the original. Consider the following example, where a short string with a size of 30 bytes is used as input:

```
DECLARE @input AS NVARCHAR(15) = N'SQL Server 2017';
SELECT @input AS input, DATALENGTH(@input) AS input_size, COMPRESS(@input)
AS compressed, DATALENGTH(COMPRESS(@input)) AS comp_size;
```

The result of this query (with abbreviated compressed value) is:

```
input           input_size  compressed                              comp_size
-------------   ----------- ----------------------------------      -------
SQL Server 2017  30         0x1F8B08000000000000004000B660864F061...  46
```

The COMPRESS function is not a replacement for row or page compression. It is invoked for a single expression and additional optimizations are not possible (exactly the same string tokens exist in another row or column).

To compare compression rates for the Row and Page compressions on one side and the compression by the COMPRESS function on the other side, I have created four clone tables of the system table sys.messages. I have left one uncompressed and have compressed the other three with ROW, PAGE, and COMPRESS functions, respectively. The complete code for creating and populating tables, as well as for comparing compression methods, can be found in the code accompanying this book. The following screenshot displays the result of this comparison:

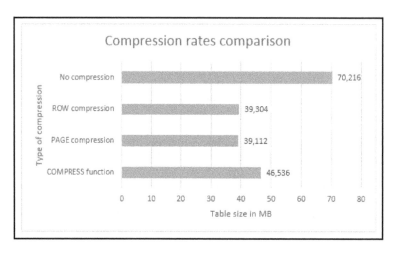

Comparing compression rates between Row, Page, and Compress

You can see that (slightly) more compression can be achieved using Row and Page compression, but a notable compression is also obtained using the COMPRESS function.

Use this function when you want to save some storage space or to compress data that needs to be archived or logged and is thus rarely queried. Since it uses a common and well-known GZIP algorithm, you can compress/decompress data not only in SQL Server but also in client applications and tools communicating with SQL Server.

Using DECOMPRESS

The DECOMPRESS function decompresses the compressed input data in binary format (variable, column, or expression) using the GZIP algorithm.

The return type of the function is VARBINARY(MAX). Yes, you read it right—the result of the decompression is still a VARBINARY data type and if you want to get the original data type, you need to cast the result explicitly.

Consider the following example, where the input string is first compressed and then decompressed with the same algorithm:

```
DECLARE @input AS NVARCHAR(100) = N'SQL Server 2017 Developer''s Guide';
SELECT DECOMPRESS(COMPRESS(@input));
```

Since the function DECOMPRESS is logically complementary to the COMPRESS function, you would expect to get the original input string as the result. The result is, however, in the binary format:

```
input
-----------------------------------------------------------------
0x530051004C00200053006500720076006500720020002000320030003100370020004400650007
60065006C006F00700065007200270073002000470075006900640065000
```

To get the input string back, you need to convert the resulting data type to the initial data type:

```
DECLARE @input AS NVARCHAR(100) = N'SQL Server 2017 Developer''s Guide';
SELECT CAST(DECOMPRESS(COMPRESS(@input)) AS NVARCHAR(100)) AS input;
```

Now you will get the expected result:

```
input
-----------------------------------
SQL Server 2017 Developer's Guide
```

The input parameter for the DECOMPRESS function must have previously been with the GZIP algorithm-compressed binary value. If you provide any other binary data, the function will return NULL.

Notice an interesting phenomenon if you miss the correct original type and cast to VARCHAR instead of NVARCHAR:

```
DECLARE @input AS NVARCHAR(100) = N'SQL Server 2017 Developer''s Guide';
SELECT CAST(DECOMPRESS(COMPRESS(@input)) AS VARCHAR(100)) AS input;
```

When you use the **Results to Text** option to display query results, the following result is shown in SSMS:

```
input
-------------------------------------------------------------------
S Q L   S e r v e r   2 0 1 7   D e v e l o p e r ' s   G u i d e
```

However, when the **Results to Grid** option is your choice, the output looks different, as shown in the following screenshot:

Side effect of an incorrect data type casting

Moreover, if you change the original type and cast to the Unicode data type, the result is very strange. When you swap the data types in the input string and the casted result (input—VARCHAR, result—NVARCHAR), the query will work as follows:

```
DECLARE @input AS VARCHAR(100) = 'SQL Server 2017 Developer''s Guide';
SELECT CAST(DECOMPRESS(COMPRESS(@input)) AS NVARCHAR(100)) AS input;
```

The output looks strange and the same in all display modes:

```
input
---------------------------------
                e
```

To comment on this bizarre behavior: keep in mind that it is always good to cast to the original data type and not to rely on the conversion internals.

Using CURRENT_TRANSACTION_ID

The CURRENT_TRANSACTION_ID function, as its name suggests, returns the transaction ID of the current transaction. The scope of the transaction is the current session. It has the same value as the transaction_id column in the **Dynamic Management Views** (**DMV**) sys.dm_tran_current_transaction. The function has no input arguments and the returned value is of type bigint.

Multiple calls of this function will result in different transaction numbers, since every single call is interpreted as an implicit transaction:

```
SELECT CURRENT_TRANSACTION_ID();
SELECT CURRENT_TRANSACTION_ID();
BEGIN TRAN
SELECT CURRENT_TRANSACTION_ID();
SELECT CURRENT_TRANSACTION_ID();
COMMIT
```

The result on my machine is as follows (you will definitely get different numbers, but with the same pattern):

```
-------------
921170382
921170383
921170384
921170384
```

There is also the SESSION_ID function, which returns the current session ID, but it works only in Azure SQL Data Warehouse and in Parallel Data Warehouse. When you call it in an on-premises instance of SQL Server 2017, instead of the current session ID, you will see the following error message:

```
Msg 195, Level 15, State 10, Line 1
'SESSION_ID' is not a recognized built-in function name.
```

You can use the CURRENT_TRANSACTION_ID function to check your transaction in the active transactions as follows:

```
SELECT * FROM sys.dm_tran_active_transactions WHERE transaction_id =
CURRENT_TRANSACTION_ID();
```

Using SESSION_CONTEXT

Using and maintaining session variables or data within a user session in SQL Server is not so straightforward. With the SET CONTEXT_INFO statement, you can set a 128-bytes long binary value and you can read it with the CONTEXT_INFO function. However, having one single value within the scope of the session is a huge limitation. SQL Server 2017 brings more functionality for playing with session scope-related data.

The SESSION_CONTEXT function returns the value of the specified key in the current session context. This value was previously set using the sys.sp_set_session_context procedure. It accepts the nvarchar data type as an input parameter. Interestingly, the function returns a value with the sql_variant data type.

Use the following code to set the value for the language key and then call the SESSION_CONTEXT function to read the value of the session key:

```
EXEC sys.sp_set_session_context @key = N'language', @value = N'German';
SELECT SESSION_CONTEXT(N'language');
```

The result of this action is shown as follows:

```
-------------
German
```

As mentioned earlier, the input data type must be nvarchar. An attempt to call the function with a different data type (including varchar and nchar!) results in an exception:

```
SELECT SESSION_CONTEXT('language');
```

You get the following message:

```
Msg 8116, Level 16, State 1, Line 51
Argument data type varchar is invalid for argument 1 of session_context
function.
```

The function argument does not need to be a literal; you can put it in a variable, as shown in the following code example:

```
DECLARE @lng AS NVARCHAR(50) = N'language';
SELECT SESSION_CONTEXT(@lng);
```

The size of the key cannot exceed 256 bytes and the limit for the total size of keys and values in the session context is 256 KB.

The system-stored procedure `sys.sp_set_session_context` and the function `SESSION_CONTEXT` allow you to create and maintain session variables within SQL Server and overcome limitations from previous SQL Server versions. The `SESSION_CONTEXT` function is used as a part of the Row-Level Security feature, and it will be explored in more detail in `Chapter 8`, *Tightening the Security*.

Using DATEDIFF_BIG

The `DATEDIFF` function returns a number of time units crossed between two specified dates. The function accepts the following three input arguments:

- `datepart`: This is the time unit (`year`, `quarter`, `month`, `second`, `millisecond`, `microsecond`, and `nanosecond`)
- `startdate`: This is an expression of any date data type (`date`, `time`, `smalldatetime`, `datetime`, `datetime2`, and `datetimeoffset`)
- `enddate`: This is also an expression of any date data type (`date`, `time`, `smalldatetime`, `datetime`, `datetime2`, and `datetimeoffset`)

The return type of the function is `int`. This means that the maximum returned value is 2,147,483,647. Therefore, if you specify minor units (milliseconds, microseconds, or nanoseconds) as the first parameters of the function, you can get an overflow exception for huge date ranges. For instance, this function call will still work, as follows:

```
SELECT DATEDIFF(SECOND, '19480101', '20160101') AS diff;
```

It returns this result:

```
diff
-----------
2145916800
```

However, the following example will not work:

```
SELECT DATEDIFF(SECOND,'19470101','20160101') AS diff;
```

The result of this call is the following error message:

```
Msg 535, Level 16, State 0, Line 1
The datediff function resulted in an overflow. The number of dateparts
separating two date/time instances is too large. Try to use datediff with a
less precise datepart.
```

Due to the mentioned data type limit, the maximal date difference that DATEDIFF can calculate when the second is used as date part parameter is about 68 years only. In the following table, you can find a list of date part units and the maximal-supported date differences for them:

Maximal supported date difference per date part for the function DATEDIFF

Date part	Maximal supported date difference
Hour	250,000 years
Minute	4,086 years
Second	68 years
Millisecond	25 days
Microsecond	36 minutes
Nanosecond	2.15 seconds

In order to cover a greater date range for short date parts, the SQL Server development team has added a new function in SQL Server 2016: DATEDIFF_BIG.

It has exactly the same interface as DATEDIFF; the only difference is its return type—bigint. This means that the maximal returned value is 9,223,372,036,854,775,807. With this function, you will not get any overflow even when you specify a huge date range and choose a minor date part. The following code calculates the difference between the minimal and maximal value supported by the datetime2 data type in MICROSECOND:

```
SELECT DATEDIFF_BIG(MICROSECOND,'010101','99991231 23:59:59.999999999') AS
diff;
```

The following is the very large number representing this difference:

```
diff
--------------------
25242393559999999999
```

However, even with the DATEDIFF_BIG function, you can get an exception if you call it for the same dates and choose the date part NANOSECOND:

```
SELECT DATEDIFF_BIG(NANOSECOND,'010101','99991231 23:59:59.999999999') AS
diff;
```

The maximal value of the bigint data type is not enough to host this difference and to avoid an overflow:

```
Msg 535, Level 16, State 0, Line 1
The datediff_big function resulted in an overflow. The number of dateparts
separating two date/time instances is too large. Try to use datediff_big
with a less precise datepart.
```

Of course, the last two statements are listed just for demonstration purposes; I cannot imagine a reasonable use case where you will need to represent 10,000 years in microseconds or nanoseconds. Therefore, you can say that DATEDIFF_BIG meets all the reasonable requirements related to date difference calculations.

Using AT TIME ZONE

The AT TIME ZONE expression can be used to represent time in a given time zone. It converts an input date to the corresponding datetimeoffset value in the target time zone. It has the following two arguments:

- inputdate: This is an expression of the following date data types: smalldatetime, datetime, datetime2, and datetimeoffset.
- timezone: This is the name of the target time zone. The allowed zone names are listed in the sys.time_zone_info catalog view.

The return type of the expression is datetimeoffset in the target time zone.

Use the following code to display local UTC time, and the local time in New York and Vienna:

```
SELECT
    CONVERT(DATETIME, SYSDATETIMEOFFSET()) AS UTCTime,
```

```
   CONVERT(DATETIME, SYSDATETIMEOFFSET() AT TIME ZONE 'Eastern Standard
Time') AS NewYork_Local,
   CONVERT(DATETIME, SYSDATETIMEOFFSET() AT TIME ZONE 'Central European
Standard Time') AS Vienna_Local;
```

This query generates the following result:

UTCTime	NewYork_Local	Vienna_Local
2018-02-04 22:58:57.440	2018-02-04 16:58:57.440	2018-02-04 22:58:57.440

As mentioned earlier, the values supported for time zones can be found in a new system catalog, sys.time_zone_info. This is exactly the same list as in the registry KEY_LOCAL_MACHINE\SOFTWARE\Microsoft\Windows NT\CurrentVersion\Time Zones.

The target time zone does not need to be a literal; it can be wrapped in a variable and parameterized. The following code displays the time in four different time zones:

```
SELECT name, CONVERT(DATETIME, SYSDATETIMEOFFSET() AT TIME ZONE name) AS
local_time
FROM sys.time_zone_info
WHERE name IN (SELECT value FROM STRING_SPLIT('UTC,Eastern Standard
Time,Central European Standard Time,Russian Standard Time',','));
```

Note that another new function, STRING_SPLIT, is used in this query. The result of the previous query is as follows:

```
name                               local_time
----------------------------------  ------------------------
Eastern Standard Time              2018-02-04 11:27:50.193
UTC                                2018-02-04 15:27:50.193
Central European Standard Time     2018-02-04 17:27:50.193
Russian Standard Time              2018-02-04 18:27:50.193
```

By using AT TIME ZONE, you can convert a simple DATETIME value without a time zone offset to any time zone by using its name. What time is it in Seattle, when a clock in Vienna shows 22:33 today, on *Super Bowl Sunday* (4th February 2018)? Here is the answer:

```
SELECT CAST('20180204 22:33' AS DATETIME)
AT TIME ZONE 'Central European Standard Time'
AT TIME ZONE 'Pacific Standard Time' AS Seattle_Time;
```

In Seattle, it is half past two in the afternoon:

```
Seattle_Time
--------------------------------
2018-02-04 14:33:00.000 -07:00
```

Note that you must convert the string value to datetime. Usually, a string literal formatted as YYYMMDD HH:ss is interpreted as a valid datetime value, but in this case, you need to cast it explicitly to the datetime data type.

Using HASHBYTES

The HASHBYTES built-in function is used to hash the string of characters using one of the seven supported hashing algorithms. The function accepts the following two input arguments:

- algorithm: This is a hashing algorithm for hashing the input. The possible values are MD2, MD4, MD5, SHA, SHA1, SHA2_256, and SHA2_512, but only the last two are recommended in SQL Server 2017.
- input: This is an input variable, column, or expression that needs to be hashed. The data types that are allowed are varchar, nvarchar, and varbinary.

The return type of the function is varbinary (8000). This function has been available in SQL Server since 2005, but it is enhanced in SQL Server 2016. The most important enhancement is removing the limit for the input size. Prior to SQL Server 2016, the allowed input values were limited to 8,000 bytes; now no limit is defined. In addition to this significant enhancement, five old algorithms, MD2, MD4, MD5, SHA, and SHA1, are marked for deprecation. The SHA2_256 and SHA2_512 algorithms are stronger, require more storage space, and the hash calculation is slower, but the collision probability is very low.

To demonstrate the importance of the removed input limit, the former standard sample AdventureWorks database will be used. Execute the following code in a SQL Server 2014 instance with this sample database installed to calculate a hash value for the XML representation of the first six orders in the SalesOrderHeader table:

```
USE AdventureWorks2014;
SELECT HASHBYTES('SHA2_256',(SELECT TOP (6) * FROM Sales.SalesOrderHeader
FOR XML AUTO)) AS hashed_value;
```

The following hashed value is produced by the previous command:

```
hashed_value
------------------------------------------------------------------
0x26C8A739DB7BE2B27BCE757105E159647F70E02F45E56C563BBC3669BEF49AAF
```

However, when you want to include the seventh row in the hash calculation, use the following code:

```
USE AdventureWorks2014;
SELECT HASHBYTES('SHA2_256',(SELECT TOP (7) * FROM Sales.SalesOrderHeader
FOR XML AUTO)) AS hashed_value;
```

Instead of the hashed value, this query, executed in an SQL Server 2014 instance, generates a very well-known and very frustrating SQL Server error message:

```
Msg 8152, Level 16, State 10, Line 2
String or binary data would be truncated.
```

Clearly, the reason for this error is the size of the input string which exceeds the limit of 8,000 bytes. You can confirm this by executing the following query:

```
SELECT DATALENGTH(CAST((SELECT TOP (7) * FROM Sales.SalesOrderHeader FOR
XML AUTO) AS NVARCHAR(MAX))) AS input_length;
```

Indeed, the size of the input argument for the HASHBYTES function exceeds 8,000 bytes:

```
input_length
--------------------
8754
```

Since SQL Server 2017, this limitation has been removed:

```
USE AdventureWorks2017;
SELECT HASHBYTES('SHA2_256',(SELECT TOP (7) * FROM Sales.SalesOrderHeader
FOR XML AUTO)) AS hashed_value;
```

The preceding hash query returns the following result:

```
hashed_value
------------------------------------------------------------------
0x864E9FE792E0E99165B46F43DB43E659CDAD56F80369FD6D2C58AD2E8386CBF3
```

Prior to SQL Server 2016, if you wanted to hash more than 8 KB of data, you had to split input data to 8 KB chunks and then combine them to get a final hash for the input entry. Since the limit does not exist anymore, you can use the entire table as an input parameter now. You can slightly modify the initial query to calculate the hash value for the entire order table:

```
USE AdventureWorks2017;
SELECT HASHBYTES('SHA2_256',(SELECT * FROM Sales.SalesOrderHeader FOR XML
AUTO)) AS hashed_value;
```

This generates the following output:

```
hashed_value
---------------------------------------------------------------
0x2930C226E613EC838F88D821203221344BA93701D39A72813ABC7C936A8BEACA
```

I played around with it and could successfully generate a hash value, even for an expression with a size of 2 GB. It was slow, of course, but it did not break. I just want to check the limit; it does not make much sense to use HASHBYTES to detect changes in a large table.

 AdventureWorks has long been one of the most used SQL Server sample databases. After introducing the WideWorldImporter database, it was not supported in the SQL Server 2016 RTM, but the AdventureWorks is back in SQL Server 2017. You can download it at https://github.com/Microsoft/sql-server-samples/releases/tag/adventureworks.

This function can be very useful to check whether relative static tables are changed or to compare the same database tables in two instances. With the following query, you can check the status of products in the AdventureWorks2017 database:

```
USE AdventureWorks2017;
SELECT HASHBYTES('SHA2_256',(SELECT *
 FROM
  Production.Product p
  INNER JOIN Production.ProductSubcategory sc ON p.ProductSubcategoryID =
sc.ProductSubcategoryID
  INNER JOIN Production.ProductCategory c ON sc.ProductCategoryID =
c.ProductCategoryID
  INNER JOIN Production.ProductListPriceHistory ph ON ph.ProductID =
p.ProductID
  FOR XML AUTO)) AS hashed_value;
```

The following is the output generated by this query:

```
hashed_value
------------------------------------------------------------------------
0xAFC05E912DC6742B085AFCC2619F158B823B4FE53ED1ABD500B017D7A899D99D
```

If you want to check whether any of the product attributes defined by the previous statement are different for two or more instances, you can execute the same query against the other instances and compare the values only, without loading and comparing the entire datasets.

With no limit for the input string, you do not need to implement workarounds for large inputs anymore, and the fact that you can easily generate a hash value for multiple joined tables can increase the number of use cases for the HASHBYTES function.

Using JSON functions

SQL Server 2016 introduces JSON data support, and in order to implement this support, four JSON functions have been added to allow the manipulation of JSON data:

- ISJSON: This checks whether an input string represents valid JSON data.
- JSON_VALUE: This extracts a scalar value from a JSON string.
- JSON_QUERY: This extracts a JSON fragment from the input JSON string for the specified JSON path.
- JSON_MODIFY: This modifies JSON data, updates the value of an existing property, adds a new element to an existing array, inserts a new property and its value, and deletes a property.
- OPENJSON: This provides a row set view over a JSON document. This table-value function converts JSON text into tabular data.

These functions will be explored in more detail in Chapter 5, *JSON Support in SQL Server*.

Enhanced DML and DDL statements

In this section, you will explore enhancements in **Data Manipulation Language** (**DML**) and **Data Definition Language** (**DDL**) that are not part of new features or improved features from previous SQL Server versions.

The section starts with a small syntax extension that you will use often in the code examples in this book.

The conditional DROP statement (DROP IF EXISTS)

With a conditional DROP statement, you can avoid getting an exception if the object you want to drop does not exist. If, for instance, the T1 table has already been removed or it was not created at all, the following statement will fail:

```
DROP TABLE dbo.T1;
```

Here is the error message:

```
Msg 3701, Level 11, State 5, Line 5
Cannot drop the table 'dbo.T1', because it does not exist or you do not
have permission.
```

SQL Server 2016 introduces the conditional DROP statement for most of the database objects. The conditional DROP statement is a DROP statement extended with the IF EXISTS part. Repeat the preceding command with this extended syntax:

```
DROP TABLE IF EXISTS dbo.T1;
```

You can execute this statement any number of times and you will not get an error. To achieve this prior to SQL Server 2016, you had to check the existence of the object before you removed it, as shown in this code example:

```
IF OBJECT_ID('dbo.T1','U') IS NOT NULL
   DROP TABLE dbo.T1;
```

You had to write one more code line and, in addition, it was also error prone—you had to write the name of the object twice. It's not a big deal, but this new form is shorter and is not error prone.

You can use the following code to remove the stored procedure dbo.P1 from the system:

```
DROP PROCEDURE IF EXISTS dbo.P1;
```

As mentioned earlier, you could use the conditional DROP statement in SQL Server 2016 to remove most of the database objects. The following objects are supported: AGGREGATE, ASSEMBLY, COLUMN, CONSTRAINT, DATABASE, DEFAULT, FUNCTION, INDEX, PROCEDURE, ROLE, RULE, SCHEMA, SECURITY POLICY, SEQUENCE, SYNONYM, TABLE, TRIGGER, TYPE, USER, and VIEW.

If you want, for instance, to remove a partitioned function or schema, DROP IF EXISTS won't work. The following command will fail:

```
DROP PARTITION FUNCTION IF EXISTS PartFunc1;
```

And here is the error message:

```
Msg 156, Level 15, State 1, Line 1
Incorrect syntax near the keyword 'IF'
```

To (conditionally) remove a partitioned function, you still need to write your own code to check the existence of the object.

How does IF EXISTS work? It simply suppresses the error message. This is exactly what you need if the reason for the error is the nonexistence of the object. However, if the user who wants to drop the object does not have appropriate permission, you would expect an error message. The command is executed successfully and the caller does not get an error regardless of the object's existence and user permissions! Here are the results when a user wants to drop an object using the conditional DROP statement:

- **The object exists; user has permissions**: When the object is removed, everything is fine.
- **The object does not exist; user has permissions**: There are no error messages displayed.
- **The object exists; user does not have permissions**: When the object is not removed, no error messages are displayed. The caller does not get the information that the object still exists; its DROP command has been executed successfully!
- **The object does not exist; user does not have permissions**: There are no error messages displayed.

You can read more about this inconsistency in the blog post *DROP IF EXISTS aka D.I.E.* at https://milossql.wordpress.com/2016/07/04/drop-if-exists-aka-d-i-e/.

This enhancement is handy; it helps you to abbreviate your code and it is intensively used by consultants, trainers, and conference speakers. They usually create database objects to demonstrate a feature, code technique, or behavior and then drop them from the system. And they do this again and again. However, conditional DROP statements will not be used so often in production systems. How often do you remove database objects from SQL Server? Very rarely, right? You sometimes drop them, when you perform a cleanup or remove some intermediate database objects. However, in most cases, you change existing or add new objects to a database.

More often, you use conditional DROP statements to create or alter objects rather than to remove them from a production system; therefore, the feature in the next section is more important and useful.

Using CREATE OR ALTER

SQL Server 2017 supports the creating or altering of database objects in a single statement. This is also one of the features that has been requested for years and it is introduced in Service Pack 1 of SQL Server 2016. Use the CREATE OR ALTER statement to create an object if it does not exist, or alter it if it is already there. You can use it for stored procedures, functions, views, and triggers. Here is an example of creating or altering a scalar user-defined function:

```
CREATE OR ALTER FUNCTION dbo.GetWorldsBestCityToLiveIn()
RETURNS NVARCHAR(10)
AS
BEGIN
    RETURN N'Vienna';
END
```

This is most probably the first feature you will adopt in SQL Server 2017 and it is very useful for script deployment; you don't need to check whether the object exists. Prior to SQL Server 2016 SP1, if you wanted to update a stored procedure with the latest version and you didn't know whether the previous version had been installed or not, or you simply executed the same script twice without errors, the following code was used:

```
IF OBJECT_ID(N'dbo.uspMyStoredProc','P') IS NULL
  EXEC('CREATE PROCEDURE dbo.uspMyStoredProc AS SELECT NULL');
GO
ALTER PROCEDURE dbo.uspMyStoredProc
AS...
```

This piece of code is error prone, awkward, and even uses dynamic SQL because CREATE PROC needs to be the first statement in a batch. Therefore, I am glad that SLQ Server finally supports a more flexible syntax for object creation and altering.

Resumable online index rebuild

As you might have guessed, this feature allows you to pause and resume an index rebuild operation. Rebuilding an index on very large tables requires a lot of system resources and log space. Sometimes, a rebuild operation is still running when you are at the end of the maintenance window. That usually means, you have to cancel the operation and restart it later from the beginning. The same happens in case of a database failover or when you are running out of disk space.

In SQL Server 2017, you can solve these problems so that you can arbitrarily pause and resume index rebuild operations. To see how this feature works, open a connection to an SQL Server 2017 instance in SSMS and create an index in the WideWorldImporters sample database:

```
USE WideWorldImporters;
CREATE INDEX IX1 ON Sales.OrderLines (OrderId, StockItemId, UnitPrice);
GO
```

Now, put the following code in the same SSMS session, but do not execute it yet:

```
--Connection 1
ALTER INDEX IX ON Sales.OrderLines
REBUILD WITH (RESUMABLE = ON, ONLINE = ON)
GO
```

The RESUMABLE = ON option instructs SQL Server that the operation is intended to be resumable. Now, it is time to open another connection where, as you might have guessed, you will pause the rebuild operation. So, open another connection and put in the following code:

```
--Connection 2
USE WideWorldImporters;
ALTER INDEX IX1 ON Sales.OrderLines PAUSE;
GO
```

Now it is time to execute the commands. First, you need to execute the index rebuild command from the first window and a few seconds later execute from the second connection. Note that the index is not so large, therefore you have to execute the command from the second connection fast, before the rebuild is done. After you have executed the commands from both windows as described, in the first window, you will see the following message:

```
Msg 1219, Level 16, State 1, Line 4
Your session has been disconnected because of a high priority DDL
operation.
Msg 1219, Level 16, State 1, Line 4
Your session has been disconnected because of a high priority DDL
operation.
Msg 596, Level 21, State 1, Line 3
Cannot continue the execution because the session is in the kill state.
Msg 0, Level 20, State 0, Line 3
A severe error occurred on the current command.  The results, if any,
should be discarded.
```

Because the rebuilding index operation is paused with a command from the second window, the session in the first window is disconnected. Although the error message indicates that something failed, in this case, everything is saved to the point of pause. You can check this by querying the sys.index_resumable_operations view:

```
SELECT name, sql_text, state_desc, percent_complete, start_time,
last_pause_time
FROM sys.index_resumable_operations;
```

This query returns the following output:

name	state_desc	percent_complete	start_time	last_pause_time
IX1	PAUSED	23,4927315783105	2017-12-11 13:08:14.223	2017-12-11 13:08:16.203

To continue with the rebuild operation, you should execute the following command in the second connection:

```
USE WideWorldImporters;
ALTER INDEX IX1 ON Sales.OrderLines RESUME;
GO
```

After the rebuild operation is done, when you query the
`sys.index_resumable_operations` view, there will be no entry for the index that you
rebuilt.

 Ever since SQL Server 2016 Service Pack 1, Microsoft has supported the
Consistent Programming Surface Area across all editions of SQL Server. This
means that the most powerful features in previous versions, available in
Enterprise Edition only, can be used now in Standard and even Express
Edition. However, there are still a few features available in Enterprise
Edition only. Resumable online index rebuild is one of them.

Note than when you specify the `RESUMABLE` = `ON` option, you need to specify the `ONLINE`
= `ON` option too, otherwise the command will fail:

```
ALTER INDEX IX1 ON Sales.Orderlines
REBUILD WITH (RESUMABLE = ON);
GO
```

Instead of starting to rebuild the index, you'll get this error message:

```
Msg 11438, Level 15, State 1, Line 58
The RESUMABLE option cannot be set to 'ON' when the ONLINE option is set to
'OFF'.
```

Resumable online index rebuild is a very useful feature; you can pause the index rebuild
when you need to free up resources for something else and resume the rebuild process later
from the saved point. You might also want to perform a rebuild of a very large index in
several smaller transactions, instead of in long-running ones that could block other
processes.

Online ALTER COLUMN

Sometimes you might need to change the attributes of a table column, for instance to
increase the column capacity due to changed requirements, increased data amount, or lack
of data capacity planning. Here are the typical actions for altering a column in an SQL
Server table:

- **Change the data type**: This is usually when you come close to the maximum
  value supported by the actual data type (typically from `smallint` to `int`, or from
  `int` to `bigint`).

- **Change the size**: This is a common case for poorly planned string columns; the current column size cannot accept all the required data.
- **Change the precision**: This is when you need to store more precise data, usually due to changed requirements.
- **Change the collation**: This is when you have to use a different (usually case-sensitive) collation for a column due to changed requirements.
- **Change the null-ability**: This is when the requirements are changed.

To demonstrate what happens when you perform an ALTER column action, you first need to create a sample table. Run the following code to accomplish this:

```
USE WideWorldImporters;
DROP TABLE IF EXISTS dbo.Orders;
CREATE TABLE dbo.Orders(
id INT IDENTITY(1,1) NOT NULL,
custid INT NOT NULL,
orderdate DATETIME NOT NULL,
amount MONEY NOT NULL,
rest CHAR(100) NOT NULL DEFAULT 'test',
CONSTRAINT PK_Orders PRIMARY KEY CLUSTERED (id ASC)
);
GO
```

To populate the table efficiently, you can use the GetNums function created by Itzik Ben-Gan. The function is available at http://tsql.solidq.com/SourceCodes/GetNums.txt. Here is the function definition:

```
CREATE OR ALTER FUNCTION dbo.GetNums(@low AS BIGINT, @high AS BIGINT)
RETURNS TABLE
AS
RETURN
  WITH
    L0   AS (SELECT c FROM (SELECT 1 UNION ALL SELECT 1) AS D(c)),
    L1   AS (SELECT 1 AS c FROM L0 AS A CROSS JOIN L0 AS B),
    L2   AS (SELECT 1 AS c FROM L1 AS A CROSS JOIN L1 AS B),
    L3   AS (SELECT 1 AS c FROM L2 AS A CROSS JOIN L2 AS B),
    L4   AS (SELECT 1 AS c FROM L3 AS A CROSS JOIN L3 AS B),
    L5   AS (SELECT 1 AS c FROM L4 AS A CROSS JOIN L4 AS B),
    Nums AS (SELECT ROW_NUMBER() OVER(ORDER BY (SELECT NULL)) AS rownum
             FROM L5)
  SELECT TOP(@high - @low + 1) @low + rownum - 1 AS n
  FROM Nums
  ORDER BY rownum;
```

Now you can run the following code to populate the table with 10 million rows:

```
INSERT INTO dbo.Orders(custid,orderdate,amount)
SELECT
  1 + ABS(CHECKSUM(NEWID())) % 1000 AS custid,
  DATEADD(minute,  -ABS(CHECKSUM(NEWID())) % 5000000, '20160630') AS
orderdate,
  50 + ABS(CHECKSUM(NEWID())) % 1000 AS amount
FROM dbo.GetNums(1,10000000);
```

Now, once you have created and populated the table, suppose you need to change the data type for the column `amount` to `decimal`. To see what happens during the alter-column action, you need to open two connections. In the first connection, you will have the code to change the data type of the column:

```
ALTER TABLE dbo.Orders ALTER COLUMN amount DECIMAL(10,2) NOT NULL;
```

In the second one, you simply try to return the last two rows from the table just to check whether the table is available for querying. Use the following code for the query in the second connection:

```
USE WideWorldImporters;
SELECT TOP (2) id, custid, orderdate, amount
FROM dbo.Orders ORDER BY id DESC;
```

Now, execute the code from the first connection and then from the second. You can see that both commands are running. Actually, the `ALTER COLUMN` command is running, while the second query is simply waiting—it is blocked by the `ALTER` command. During the changing of the data type, the table is not available for querying. You can see additional details. You would need to establish a third connection and put the following code there (you need to replace 66 with the session ID from the second connection) and repeat the previous two steps by changing the data type of the `amount` column to `money`:

```
SELECT request_mode, request_type, request_status, request_owner_type
FROM sys.dm_tran_locks WHERE request_session_id = 66;
```

The following is the result of this command:

request_mode	request_type	request_status	request_owner_type
S	LOCK	GRANT	SHARED_TRANSACTION_WORKSPACE
IS	LOCK	WAIT	TRANSACTION

You can see that the query could not get IS lock because the ALTER column action is performed as a transaction. Therefore, the table is not available for querying and the query from the second connection has to wait until the ALTER command is done.

You might think that a query with the NOLOCK hint would return results even when an ALTER column action is performed, because NOLOCK obviously means there is no lock on the table. This is not completely true. It is true that a shared lock or intentional shared lock is not acquired, but even with NOLOCK statements we need to acquire a stability schema lock. You can repeat all the three steps with a small modification to the second query to include the NOLOCK hint and the actions will end up with the same results and behavior. The only difference is that in the result set of the third connection, instead of IS the mentioned Sch-S appears.

This behavior is analogous to creating nonclustered indexes offline. While creating an index online has been achievable since 2005, ALTER column was the only operation that was offline until SQL Server 2016.

When you specify the ONLINE = ON option, SQL Server 2016 creates a new shadow table with the requested change, and when it's finished, it swaps metadata with very short schema locks. This leaves the table available, even for changes, except those that could create a dependency for the altering column.

Now you will repeat the three steps from the preceding example (assuming the column amount has the money data type), but this time with the ONLINE = ON option. You need to modify the command from the first connection to the following code:

```
USE WideWorldImporters;
ALTER TABLE dbo.Orders ALTER COLUMN amount DECIMAL(10,2) NOT NULL WITH
(ONLINE = ON);
```

The code in the second connection does not need to be changed:

```
SELECT TOP (2) id, custid, orderdate, amount
FROM dbo.Orders ORDER BY id DESC;
```

Now, execute the command all over again and then run the query from the second connection. You can see that the first command is running, and that the query from the second connection instantly returns results. The table is available for querying, although the data type for one column is being changed. This is a very important feature for systems that need to be continually available.

Altering online capabilities does not remove the usual limitations for changing column attributes. If a column is used in an index, or an expression in a filtered index or filtered statistics, you still cannot change its data type.

However, with the ONLINE = ON option, you can alter a column even if user-created statistics on this column exist. This was not possible prior to SQL Server 2016 (and it is still not possible in the offline mode). To demonstrate this, you will create a user statistic object on the amount column:

```
USE WideWorldImporters;
CREATE STATISTICS MyStat ON dbo.Orders(amount);
```

An attempt to change the data type of the column amount should fail:

```
ALTER TABLE dbo.Orders ALTER COLUMN amount DECIMAL(10,3) NOT NULL;
```

This command immediately generates the following error message:

```
Msg 5074, Level 16, State 1, Line 76
The statistics 'MyStat' is dependent on column 'amount'.
Msg 4922, Level 16, State 9, Line 76
ALTER TABLE ALTER COLUMN amount failed because one or more objects access
this column.
```

However, when you specify the ONLINE = ON option, the same command will work:

```
ALTER TABLE dbo.Orders ALTER COLUMN amount DECIMAL(10,3) NOT NULL WITH
(ONLINE = ON);
```

The statistics are available to the Query Optimizer during the command execution; it is invalidated after the change is done and it must be updated manually.

Like the online index (re)build option, this excellent feature is available in the Enterprise Edition only.

Using TRUNCATE TABLE

The TRUNCATE TABLE statement is the most efficient way to remove all rows from a table. Logically, this statement is identical to the DELETE statement without the WHERE clause, but unlike the DELETE statement, when TRUNCATE TABLE has been issued, SQL Server does not log individual row deletion in the transaction log. Therefore, the TRUNCATE TABLE statement is significantly faster. This performance difference can be very important with large tables. However, if you want to enjoy its efficiency, you have to remove all rows from a table. Even if the table is partitioned, you still need to remove all rows from all the partitions. Well, unless you have SQL Server 2016.

In SQL Server 2016, the TRUNCATE TABLE statement has been extended so that you can specify the partitions from which rows have to be removed. You can specify the comma-separated list or the range of partition numbers. Here is a code example showing how to remove all rows from the partitions 1, 2, and 4:

```
TRUNCATE TABLE dbo.T1 WITH (PARTITIONS (1, 2, 4));
```

In the next example, you will see how to specify the range of partition numbers. From a table with the maximum number of supported partitions, you want to remove a lot of data, but not all of it—you want to leave data in partitions 1 and 2. Here is the code that implements this request:

```
TRUNCATE TABLE dbo.T2 WITH (PARTITIONS (3 TO 15000));
```

You can also combine two input formats in one expression. The following code removes all rows from a table with eight partitions, except from the partitions 1 and 3:

```
TRUNCATE TABLE dbo.T1 WITH (PARTITIONS (2, 4 TO 8));
```

Specifying partitions in the TRUNCATE TABLE statement is possible even if the database is not in compatibility level 130.

To simulate a TRUNCATE TABLE for a specific partition in previous SQL Server versions, you need to perform the following steps:

1. Create a staging table with the same indexes as in a partitioned table.
2. Use the SWITCH PARTITION statement to move data from the partitioned to the staging table.
3. Remove the staging table from the system.

Now you need a single and very efficient statement—a nice and handy feature.

Maximum key size for nonclustered indexes

In previous SQL Server versions, the total size of all index keys could not exceed the limit of 900 bytes. You were actually allowed to create a nonclustered index, even if the sum of the maximum length of all its key columns exceeded this limit. The limit affects only columns used as index keys; you can use very large columns in a nonclustered index as included columns.

To demonstrate this, we will create a sample table. Note that this code should be executed in a SQL Server 2014/2012/2008 instance:

```
USE tempdb;
CREATE TABLE dbo.T1(id INT NOT NULL PRIMARY KEY CLUSTERED, c1 NVARCHAR(500)
NULL, c2 NVARCHAR(851) NULL);
```

As you can see in the code, the maximal data length of the column `c1` is 1,000 bytes. Let's now try to create a nonclustered index on this column:

```
CREATE INDEX ix1 ON dbo.T1(c1);
```

Since the table is empty, the command has been executed successfully with no errors, but with the following warning message:

Warning! The maximum key length is 900 bytes. The index 'ix1' has maximum length of 1000 bytes. For some combination of large values, the insert/update operation will fail

As the message says, you can live with the index in harmony if the size of the actual data in the index columns does not exceed the limit of 900 bytes. The Query Optimizer will even use it in execution plans and it will behave as a *normal* index. Adding a row with data within the maximum key length will be successful, as shown in the following code:

```
INSERT INTO dbo.T1(id,c1, c2) VALUES(1, N'Mila', N'Vasilije');
```

However, when you try to insert or update a row with data longer than the key size limit, the statement will fail:

```
INSERT INTO dbo.T1(id,c1, c2) VALUES(2,REPLICATE('Mila',113), NULL);
```

This action in SQL Server 2014 results in an error message and the INSERT statement fails, as follows:

**Msg 1946, Level 16, State 3, Line 7
Operation failed. The index entry of length 904 bytes for the index 'ix1' exceeds the maximum length of 900 bytes.**

In SQL Server 2016, the behavior remains the same with the difference that the maximum index key size for nonclustered indexes has been increased from 900 to 1,700 bytes. Let's repeat the previous steps, but this time in an instance running SQL Server 2016:

```
DROP TABLE IF EXISTS dbo.T1;
CREATE TABLE dbo.T1(id INT NOT NULL PRIMARY KEY CLUSTERED, c1 NVARCHAR(500)
NULL, c2 NVARCHAR(851) NULL);
GO
CREATE INDEX ix1 ON dbo.T1(c1);
```

There is no warning after this action, since the new limit is 1,700 bytes. However, when you add an index on the c2 column, this won't work:

```
CREATE INDEX ix2 ON dbo.T1(c2);
```

You get the well-known warning message, but with a different limit:

Warning! The maximum key length for a nonclustered index is 1700 bytes. The index 'ix2' has maximum length of 1702 bytes. For some combination of large values, the insert/update operation will fail.

As you can see, the only difference is the different maximum number of bytes.

 The maximum key size for clustered indexes remains at 900 bytes. For memory-optimized tables, the limit is 2,500 bytes.

Now, you can index wider columns than you could in previous versions. For instance, a text column with 500 Unicode characters can be used as a key in a nonclustered index in SQL Server 2016.

New query hints

The SQL Server Query Optimizer does an amazing job of execution plan generation. Most of the time, for most of the queries, it generates an optimal execution plan. And this is not easy at all. There is a lot of potential to get a suboptimal plan: wrong server configuration, poorly designed databases, missing and suboptimal indexes, suboptimal written queries, nonscalable solutions, and more. And the Query Optimizer should work for all those workloads, all over the world, all the time.

Depending on data constellation, Query optimizer generates suboptimal execution plans sometimes. If the execution of the queries is very important from a business point of view, you have to do something to try to achieve at least an acceptable execution plan. One of the weapons you have for this is hints to the Query Optimizer. With hints, which are actually instructions, you instruct the Query Optimizer on how to generate the execution plan. You take responsibility or you take part of the responsibility for the execution plan generation.

There are three types of hints: table, join, and query hints. You use them if you cannot enforce the required execution plan with other actions. Hints should be considered a last resort in query tuning. You should use them if you don't know another way to get a desired plan, when you have tried all that you know, or when you are under time pressure and have to fix a query as soon as possible. For instance, if you suddenly encounter a problem in the production system on the weekend or during the night, you can use the hint as a temporary solution or a workaround and then look for a definitive solution without time or operative pressures. You can use query hints if you know what you are doing. However, you should not forget that the hint and the plan remain forever and you need to periodically evaluate whether the plan is still adequate. In most cases, developers forget about plans and hints as soon as the performance problem is gone.

SQL Server 2016 brings three new query hints to address problems related to memory grants and performance spools:

- `NO_PERFORMANCE_SPOOL`
- `MAX_GRANT_PERCENT`
- `MIN_GRANT_PERCENT`

Using NO_PERFORMANCE_SPOOL

The new query hint `NO_PERFORMANCE_SPOOL` has been added to SQL Server 2016 to allow users to enforce an execution plan that does not contain a spool operator.

A spool operator in an execution plan does not mean that the plan is suboptimal; it is usually a good choice of Query Optimizer. However, in some cases, it can reduce the overall performance. This happens, for instance, when a query or a stored procedure whose execution plan contains a spool operator is executed by numerous parallel connections. Since the Spool operator uses `tempdb`, this can lead to `tempdb` contention when many queries are running at the same time. Using this hint, you can avoid this issue.

To demonstrate the use of this query hint, you will once again use the new `WideWorldImporters` sample database. Assume that you need to display order details for orders picked up by the sales people provided in an input list. To ensure that the execution plan contains a spool operator, this example uses a user-defined function and not the new SQL Server 2016 function `STRING_SPLIT`. Use the following code to create the function and filter orders with the salespeople from the list:

```
USE WideWorldImporters;
GO
CREATE OR ALTER FUNCTION dbo.ParseInt
(
    @List       VARCHAR(MAX),
    @Delimiter  CHAR(1)
)
RETURNS @Items TABLE
(
    Item INT
)
AS
BEGIN
    DECLARE @Item VARCHAR(30), @Pos  INT;
    WHILE LEN(@List)>0
    BEGIN
        SET @Pos = CHARINDEX(@Delimiter, @List);
        IF @Pos = 0 SET @Pos = LEN(@List)+1;
        SET @Item = LEFT(@List, @Pos-1);
        INSERT @Items SELECT CONVERT(INT, LTRIM(RTRIM(@Item)));
        SET @List = SUBSTRING(@List, @Pos + LEN(@Delimiter), LEN(@List));
        IF LEN(@List) = 0 BREAK;
    END
    RETURN;
END
GO
DECLARE @SalesPersonList VARCHAR(MAX) = '3,6,8';
SELECT o.*
FROM Sales.Orders o
INNER JOIN dbo.ParseInt(@SalesPersonList,',') a ON a.Item =
o.SalespersonPersonID
ORDER BY o.OrderID;
```

When you observe the execution plan for this query, you can see the `Table Spool` operator in it, as shown in the following screenshot:

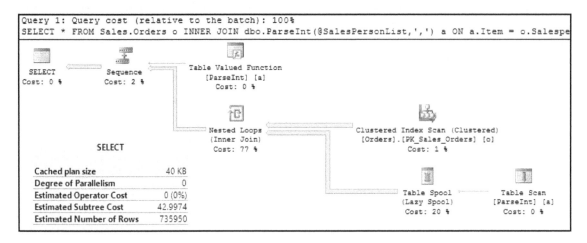

Execution plan with the Table Spool operator

When you execute exactly the same query, but with the query hint `OPTION (NO_PERFORMANCE_SPOOL)`, you get a different execution plan, without the `Spool` operator, as shown in the following screenshot:

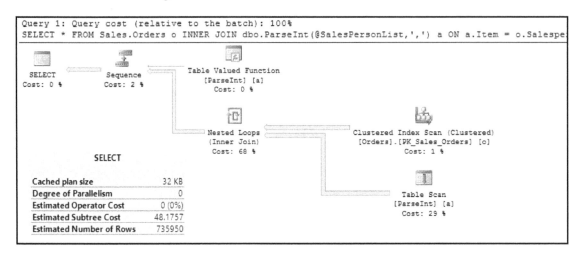

Execution plan without the table spool operator

By observing the execution plan, you can see that the Spool operator has disappeared from it. You can also see that the **Estimated Subtree Cost** is about 10% higher for the plan without the hint (by comparing the yellow SELECT property boxes). Therefore, the Query Optimizer has chosen the original plan with the Spool operator. Here, we used the hint just for demonstration purposes to show that you can enforce another plan, without the Spool operator.

 You have to create a user-defined function in this example because this query with a new STRING_SPLIT function has an execution plan without the Spool operator.

However, if the Spool operator is required in an execution plan to enforce the validity and correctness, the hint will be ignored. To demonstrate this behavior, you will use the next example. First, you need to create a sample table and insert two rows into it:

```
USE WideWorldImporters;
DROP TABLE IF EXISTS dbo.T1
CREATE TABLE dbo.T1(
id INT NOT NULL,
c1 INT NOT NULL,
);
GO
INSERT INTO dbo.T1(id, c1) VALUES(1, 5),(1, 10);
```

Now, assume that you want to add some of the existing rows into the table, say the rows where the ID has a value of less than 10. At this point, only one row qualifies for this insertion. The following query implements this requirement:

```
INSERT INTO dbo.T1(id, c1)
SELECT id, c1 FROM dbo.T1
WHERE id < 10;
```

The execution plan for this query is shown as follows:

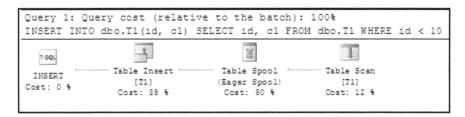

Execution plan for INSERT statement with the table spool operator

When you observe it, you can see the `Table Spool` operator proudly staying in the middle of the execution plan. However, when you execute the same statement with the `NO_PERFORMANCE_SPOOL` hint, you get an identical execution plan; the query hint is simply ignored. The reason for this decision by the Query Optimizer is that the spool operator in this plan is used not for optimization, but to guarantee the correctness of the result. To demonstrate this, execute these two statements:

```
INSERT INTO dbo.T1(id, c1)
SELECT id, c1 FROM dbo.T1
WHERE id < 10;

INSERT INTO dbo.T1(id, c1)
SELECT id, c1 FROM dbo.T1
WHERE id < 10
OPTION (NO_PERFORMANCE_SPOOL);
```

The following screenshot shows both plans and it is obvious that this is the same execution plan:

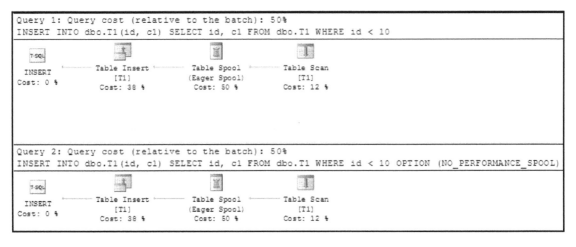

Execution plans showing that the hint NO_PERFORMANCE_SPOOL is ignored

Use the query hint `NO_SPOOL_OPERATOR` when:

- You want to avoid the spool operator in the execution object
- You know that this is a good idea (performance issue is caused by the `Spool` operator)
- You cannot achieve this with reasonable effort otherwise

Using MAX_GRANT_PERCENT

The MIN_GRANT_PERCENT and MAX_GRANT_PERCENT hints were first introduced in SQL Server 2012 SP3 and are now in SQL Server 2016 RTM (they are still not available in SQL Server 2014). They address the problem of inappropriate memory grant for query execution.

Memory grant is a memory associated with the execution of queries whose execution plan contains operators that need to store temporary row data while sorting and joining rows (Sort, Hash Join, and others). The value for memory grant depends on SQL Server's Estimated Number of Rows that should be processed by memory operators. If the Estimated Number of Rows significantly differs from the actual number, the memory grant is overestimated or underestimated.

To demonstrate an overestimated memory grant, use the following query:

```
USE WideWorldImporters;
DECLARE @now DATETIME = GETDATE();
SELECT * FROM dbo.Orders
WHERE orderdate >= @now
ORDER BY amount DESC;
```

The query returns no rows. The execution plan is simple too: Clustered Index Scan followed by the Sort operator. The plan is shown in the following screenshot:

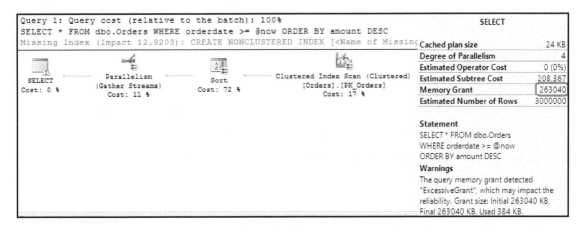

Execution plan with an overestimated memory grant

You can see that the Query Optimizer has significantly overestimated the number of rows for the `Sort` operator. Therefore, it is the most expensive part of the execution plan. Actually, the result of the query is an empty set, but SQL Server *thinks* that 3 million rows from the table will be returned. Since the `Sort` operator requires memory, this query needs a memory grant. With the mouse over the `Select` operator, you can see that the memory granted for this query is 263 MB. More details about memory grant are available in the XML representation of the execution plan, as shown in the following screenshot:

```xml
<?xml version="1.0" encoding="utf-16"?>
<ShowPlanXML xmlns:xsi="http://www.w3.org/2001/XMLSchema-instance" xmlns:xsd="http
  <BatchSequence>
    <Batch>
      <Statements>
        <StmtSimple StatementCompId="2" StatementEstRows="3000000" StatementId="1"
          <StatementSetOptions ANSI_NULLS="true" ANSI_PADDING="true" ANSI_WARNINGS
          <QueryPlan DegreeOfParallelism="4" MemoryGrant="263040" CachedPlanSize="
            <ThreadStat Branches="1" UsedThreads="4">...</ThreadStat>
            <MissingIndexes>...</MissingIndexes>
          <Warnings>
            <MemoryGrantWarning GrantWarningKind="Excessive Grant" RequestedMemo
          </Warnings>
          <MemoryGrantInfo
                  SerialRequiredMemory="512"
                  SerialDesiredMemory="261096"
                  RequiredMemory="2432"
                  DesiredMemory="263040"
                  RequestedMemory="263040"
                  GrantWaitTime="0"
                  GrantedMemory="263040"
                  MaxUsedMemory="384"
                  MaxQueryMemory="702608" />
```

Memory grant information in the XML representation of the execution plan

For the execution of a single query that returns no rows, 260 MB of memory is granted! If this query was executed by 100 concurrent sessions, almost 26 GB of memory would be granted for its execution.

As mentioned earlier, query hints should be used as a last resort for performance tuning. For demonstration purposes, you will use the MAX_GRANT_PERCENT query hint to limit the amount of memory granted.

The MAX_GRANT_PERCENT query hint defines the maximum memory grant size as a percentage of available memory. It accepts float values between 0.0 and 100.0. Granted memory cannot exceed this limit, but can be lower if the resource governor setting is lower than this. Since you know that you have no rows in the output, you can use a very low value in the query hint:

```
DECLARE @now DATETIME = GETDATE();
SELECT * FROM dbo.Orders
WHERE orderdate >= @now
ORDER BY amount DESC
OPTION (MAX_GRANT_PERCENT=0.001);
```

When you observe the execution plan, shown in the following screenshot, you can see that the plan remains the same, only the memory grant value has dropped to 2 MB:

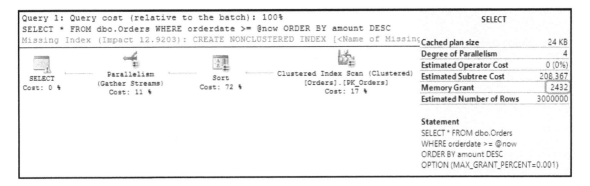

Execution plan with the query hint MAX_GRANT_PERCENT

With the memory grant hint, you cannot change the execution plan, but you can significantly reduce the amount of memory granted.

 All execution plans shown in this section were generated by a database engine with the SQL Server 2016 RTM installed on it. If you have installed SQL Server 2016 Service Pack 1, you will see a new **Excessive Grant warning** in the SELECT property box, indicating a discrepancy between granted and used memory for the query execution. You can find more details about this warning
at: https://support.microsoft.com/en-us/help/3172997.

You can see that the applied query hint saved 2 GB of memory. The query hint
MAX_GRANT_PERCENT should be used when:

- You don't know how to trick the optimizer into coming up with the appropriate
  memory grant
- You want to fix the problem immediately and buy time to search for a final
  solution

Here, you have used the query hint just for demonstration purposes; the correct way to fix a
query is to understand why the estimated and actual number of rows are so discrepant and
to then try to rewrite the query. To help the Query Optimizer to make a better estimation,
you need to avoid local variables and write directly in the WHERE clause:

```
SELECT * FROM dbo.Orders
WHERE orderdate >=  GETDATE()
ORDER BY amount DESC;
```

This generates the execution plan displayed in the following screenshot:

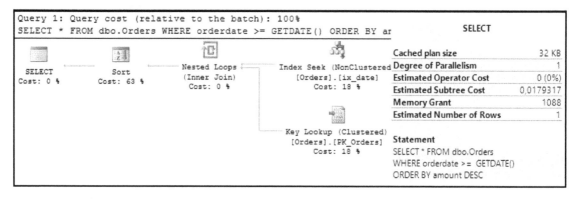

Execution plan where the old cardinality estimator is enforced

You can see the expected Nested Loop Join operator and a symbolic **Memory Grant** of **1
MB**.

Using MIN_GRANT_PERCENT

Similar to the previous example, in the event of a memory underestimation, you can force the optimizer to guarantee a minimum memory grant for a query execution using the `MIN_GRANT_PERCENT` query hint. It also accepts float values between 0.0 and 100.0. Be very careful with this hint, since if you specify 100% as the minimum grant, the whole resource governor memory will be granted to a single query execution. If you specify more memory than is available, the query will simply wait for the memory grant.

Adaptive query processing in SQL Server 2017

SQL Server Query Optimizer performs a very good job in the generation of execution plans. However, due to query complexity, skewed data distribution, suboptimal database design and badly written code, it makes sometimes very bad cardinality estimations that lead to slow performing execution plans. Because of wrong estimations, it can choose inappropriate plan operators (for instance *Nested Loop Join* instead of *Hash Join*), or a query can get significantly more or less memory granted for the execution than it is required. Sometimes, it simply assumes a fixed cardinality of 100 or 1.

SQL Server 2017 introduces query processing improvements that will adapt optimization and address the aforementioned issues. These improvements break the pipeline between query optimization and execution. For the first time, SQL Server 2017 executes a part of the query during the optimization process (without the OPTION (RECOMPILE) clause) and replaces a part of the execution plan that is stored in cache. The improvements are included in the feature and consist of three parts:

- Interleaved execution
- Batch mode adaptive memory grant feedback
- Batch mode adaptive joins

Interleaved execution

Interleaved execution changes the unidirectional pipeline between the optimization and execution phases for a single-query execution and allows plans to adapt during the optimization. This approach solves cardinality estimation issues by executing the applicable subtree and capturing accurate cardinality estimates. The optimization process is then resumed for downstream operations.

If a query references an **MSTVF**, especially if the query is complex, a suboptimal execution plan is not rare. The reason for this is that the estimated output from an MSTVF is fixed to 100 (prior to SQL Server 2014, it was fixed to 1). This can lead to the wrong choice of join operator, under- or overestimated memory grants, and thus result in poorly performing queries.

The new SQL Server 2017 feature allows Query Optimizer to adjust the execution plan by executing a part of the query with the MSTVF call in order to get the exact number of outputted rows. This leads to a much better plan, which is created and adjusted while the query is executing. That means during the plan generation, SQL Server executes a part of the code to improve the execution plan. This optimization is called **interleaved execution**.

To demonstrate the change, you will create a simple MSTVF in the `WideWorldImporters` database that (intentionally) returns order IDs of all orders from the `Sales.Orders` table:

```
USE WideWorldImporters;
GO
CREATE OR ALTER FUNCTION dbo.SignificantOrders()
RETURNS @T TABLE
(ID INT NOT NULL)
AS
BEGIN
    INSERT INTO @T
    SELECT OrderId FROM Sales.Orders
    RETURN
END
GO
```

Now, you will use this function in a sample statement in the same database under the compatibility levels 130 and 140 respectively. Run this code to simulate the execution under SQL Server 2016 and observe the execution plan:

```
ALTER DATABASE WideWorldImporters SET COMPATIBILITY_LEVEL = 130;
GO
SET STATISTICS IO ON;
SET STATISTICS TIME ON;
SELECT ol.OrderID,  ol.UnitPrice, ol.StockItemID
```

```
FROM Sales.Orderlines ol
INNER JOIN dbo.SignificantOrders() f1 ON f1.Id = ol.OrderID
WHERE PackageTypeID = 7;
SET STATISTICS IO OFF;
SET STATISTICS TIME OFF;
GO
```

This query has the execution plan shown in the following screenshot:

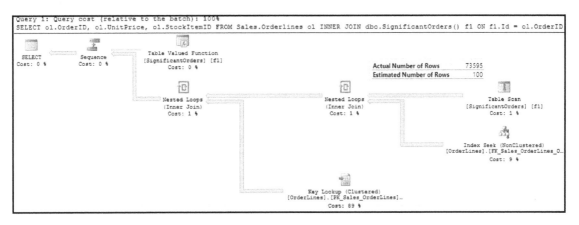

Execution plan for a query with MSTVF in compatibility level 130

You can see the Query Optimizer decided to use `Nested Loop Operator`, since only **100** outputted rows are expected. You can also see that the **Actual Number of Rows** is 73,595 and, due to this fixed estimation, the execution plan is not optimal. Here is the output that you get when you set the `STATISTICS IO ON` and `STATISTTCS TIME ON` options:

```
Table 'OrderLines'. Scan count 73595, logical reads 866031, physical reads
47,...
Table '#AFCC5499'. Scan count 1, logical reads 119, physical reads 0, read-
ahead...
SQL Server Execution Times:
   CPU time = 1093 ms,   elapsed time = 2189 ms.
```

Run this code in the latest compatibility level (140) in SQL Server 2017 and observe the execution plan:

```
ALTER DATABASE WideWorldImporters SET COMPATIBILITY_LEVEL = 140;
GO
SET STATISTICS IO ON;
SET STATISTICS TIME ON;
SELECT ol.OrderID,  ol.UnitPrice, ol.StockItemID
FROM Sales.Orderlines ol
```

```
INNER JOIN dbo.SignificantOrders() f1 ON f1.Id = ol.OrderID
WHERE PackageTypeID = 7;
SET STATISTICS IO OFF;
SET STATISTICS TIME OFF;
GO
```

The execution plan is shown in the following screenshot:

Execution plan for a query with MSTVF in compatibility level 140

The plan with the `Hash Match Join` operator is more appropriate for this cardinality. The execution parameters look better:

```
Table 'OrderLines'. Scan count 4, logical reads 391, physical reads 0,
read-ahead reads 0, lob logical reads 163...
Table 'OrderLines'. Segment reads 1, segment skipped 0.
Table 'Workfile'. Scan count 0, logical reads 0, physical reads 0, read-
ahead reads 0...
Table 'Worktable'. Scan count 0, logical reads 0, physical reads 0, read-
ahead reads 0...
Table '#B2A8C144'. Scan count 1, logical reads 119, physical reads 0, read-
ahead reads 0...

 SQL Server Execution Times:
   CPU time = 406 ms,   elapsed time = 1458 ms.
```

As you can see, CPU time is reduced by more than 50%, and the query executed 33% faster. The improvement is not spectacular, but this is a simple query. In complex queries, interleaved execution can bring significant performance improvements.

Interleaved execution will help with workload performance issues that are due to these fixed cardinality estimates associated with multi-statement table-valued functions.

Batch mode adaptive memory grant feedback

When SQL Server compiles the execution plan for a query, it has to choose appropriate operators and eventually memory that is required for the query execution. This memory grant size is based on the Estimated Number of Rows for the operator and the associated average row size. If the cardinality estimates are significantly inaccurate, this can lead to poor performance. Underestimations can degrade the performance of the execution query since intermediate rows cannot fit in memory and must be spilled to the disk. On the other hand, overestimations lead to large memory grants and the wasting of memory, which can affect other queries and overall performance.

In one of the previous sections, you saw that you can address memory grant issues (without significant refactoring of your queries) by using the `MIN_GRANT_PERCENT` and `MAX_GRANT_PERCENT` hints. SQL Server 2017 introduces another mechanism that deals with this issue—`batch mode adaptive memory grant feedback`. It is a part of the *adaptive query processing* family of features.

`Batch mode adaptive memory grant feedback` is the feature that can update a (correct) memory grant given for a query after the execution plan is created. Interleaved execution allows Query Optimizer to execute a part of the code during the execution plan; here, the action comes after the plan is created. After query execution, the required memory is recalculated and compared with the memory granted during the plan creation. If the difference between them is significant, the memory grant information in the cached plan is updated. Thus, the execution plan remains the same and in the cache, only memory grant is corrected.

To demonstrate this feature, you will use the same sample table used in the *New query hints* section. Before you execute the query, ensure that the compatibility mode is `130` and that there are no cached execution plans in the `WideWorldImportes` database:

```
ALTER DATABASE SCOPED CONFIGURATION CLEAR PROCEDURE_CACHE;
ALTER DATABASE WideWorldImporters SET COMPATIBILITY_LEVEL = 130;
```

The next step is to create a sample stored procedure:

```
CREATE OR ALTER PROCEDURE dbo.GetOrders
@OrderDate DATETIME
AS
BEGIN
```

```
      DECLARE @now DATETIME = @OrderDate;
      SELECT * FROM dbo.Orders
      WHERE orderdate >= @now
      ORDER BY amount DESC;
END
GO
```

Now, call the stored procedure with a parameter representing a date in the future and with the activated **Include Actual Execution Plan** option:

```
EXEC dbo.GetOrders '20180101';
```

The execution plan for this query is shown as follows:

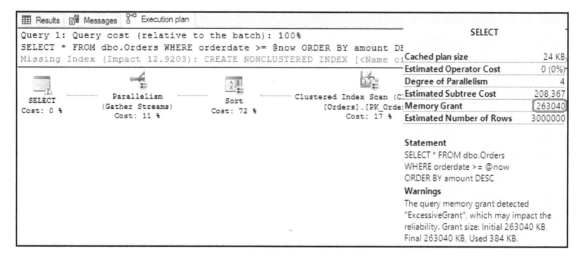

Execution plan for a query with overestimated memory grant in SQL Server 2016

You can see that this query has a **Memory Grant** of **263** MB, although no rows are returned. Prior to SQL Server 2017, this value was fixed, regardless of the number of query executions and required memory for it. You could not change the cached plan without recompiling it. As mentioned earlier, in SQL Server 2017, this is possible. To check how SQL Server 2017 deals with memory grants, clear the cache and enable the compatibility mode 140:

```
ALTER DATABASE SCOPED CONFIGURATION CLEAR PROCEDURE_CACHE;
ALTER DATABASE WideWorldImporters SET COMPATIBILITY_LEVEL = 140;
```

When you execute the query again, you will see the same execution plan and the same amount of memory grant (263 MB). Now, turn off the **Include Actual Execution Plan** option (to allow SSMS to display results faster) and execute the same query 20 times, as in the following code:

```
EXEC dbo.GetOrders '20180101';
GO 20
```

Now, execute the initial code again, with the **Include Actual Execution Plan** option:

```
EXEC dbo.GetOrders '20180101';
```

Observe the execution plan shown in the following screenshot:

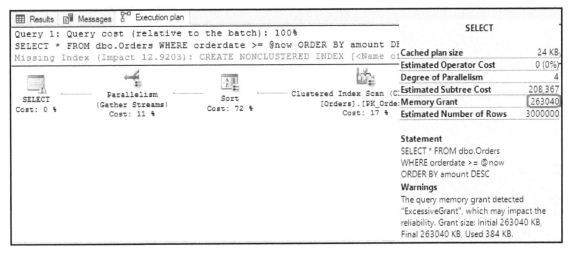

Execution plan for a query with overestimated memory grant in SQL Server 2017

No, this is not a mistake! The execution plan looks the same, as well as the memory grants. But where is the batch mode adaptive memory grant feedback feature? This feature is available only if the affected table has a columnstore index; without an index, it won't work. So, you need to create a columnstore index:

```
CREATE NONCLUSTERED COLUMNSTORE INDEX ixc ON dbo.Orders(id,
orderdate,custid, amount) WHERE id = -4;
```

In this example, you have created a trivial, logically useless index, but you just wanted to fill the requirement about the presence of a columnstore index. Now repeat the previous steps. First, execute the initial query with the **Include Actual Execution Plan** option:

```
ALTER DATABASE SCOPED CONFIGURATION CLEAR PROCEDURE_CACHE;
EXEC dbo.GetOrders '20180101';
```

Observe the **Execution plan** and **Memory Grant** shown as follows:

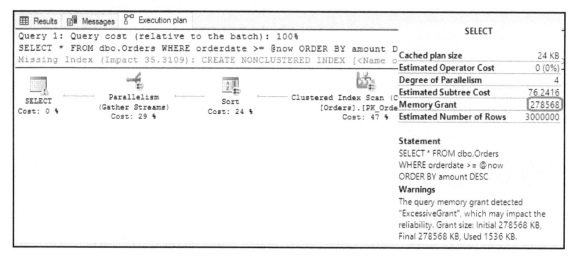

Execution plan for a query with overestimated memory grant in SQL Server 2017

You can see the same execution plan (with different percentages near the plan operators) and slightly higher memory grant, 278 MB.

Now, turn off the **Include Actual Execution Plan** option (to allow SSMS to display results faster) and execute the same query 20 times, as in the following code:

```
EXEC dbo.GetOrders '20180101';
GO 20
```

Finally, execute the initial query again, with the **Include Actual Execution Plan** option:

```
EXEC dbo.GetOrders '20180101';
```

Observe the **Execution plan** and **Memory Grant** shown as follows:

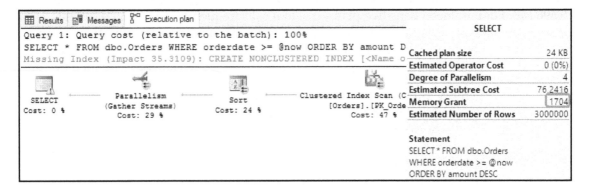

Execution plan for a query with memory grant in SQL Server 2017 corrected by memory grant feedback

You can see that after 20 executions of the stored procedure, the **Memory Grant** has been reduced to 1.7 MB only!

What would happen if you would call the same stored procedure, but with a non-selective parameter? To check this, you can execute the following code:

```
EXEC dbo.GetOrders '20000101';
GO 2
```

The execution plan, including memory grant information, is shown as follows:

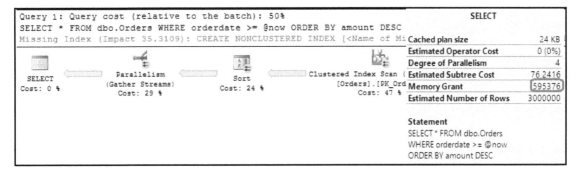

Execution plan for a query with memory grant in SQL Server 2017 corrected by memory grant feedback

You can see that after an additional two executions of the stored procedure, with non-selective parameters, the **Memory Grant** has been corrected again; this time it has increased to 596 MB. For parameter-sensitive plans, if actual calls frequently use (very) different parameters, memory grant feedback will disable itself on a query if it has unstable memory requirements. The plan is disabled after several repeated runs of the query and this can be observed by monitoring the `memory_grant_feedback_loop_disabled` extended event.

Memory grant feedback will only change the cached plan. It is not persisted if the plan is evicted from the cache. Changes are not captured in the Query Store for this version. A statement using OPTION(RECOMPILE) will create a new plan and not cache it. Since it is not cached, no memory grant feedback is produced and it is not stored for that compilation and execution.

Batch mode adaptive memory grant feedback corrects the initial memory grant as follows:

- **Overestimated memory grants**: If the granted memory is more than two times the size of the actual used memory, memory grant feedback will recalculate the memory grant and update the cached plan.
- **Underestimated memory grants**: If the granted memory is too small and the operation is spilled to disk, memory grant feedback will calculate a new memory grant.

Execution plans with memory grants under 1 MB will not be recalculated.

You can track memory grant feedback events using the `memory_grant_updated_by_feedback` extended event.

Batch mode adaptive joins

Logical joins are implemented through three physical join operators in SQL Server: Nested Loop, Hash Match, and Merge Join. For Merge Join, inputs must be sorted in the same manner, thus in most cases, you can see either a Nested Loop or Hash Match Join operator. The decision of which one to use is made during compilation. A significant part of the decision is estimating how many records will be processed in both join inputs. If the estimation is wrong, you can expect the wrong operator. Inappropriate join operators in the execution plan can lead to serious performance issues. Another case where the choice between these two operators could be a problem is stored procedures with parameter sniffing. In this case, the plan is created and optimized for the first execution and this operator will be used later as a cached plan, even for parameters where another join operator would be better.

Prior to SQL Server 2017, the execution plan was created based on the estimation at compile time and the parameters used by the first call in case of stored procedures. Thus, all physical operators used in execution plans are chosen at compile time. In SQL Server 2017, the decision which operators the query and is used in the query plan *is a bit postponed*. Before the decision is made, SQL Server looks a bit into data and then decides dynamically which join operator to use. To support dynamically switching between Nested Loop Join and Hash Match Join operators, SQL Server 2017 introduces a new operator called **Adaptive Join**.

Adaptive Join contains both operators and can switch between them after the first input has been scanned and the number of items is known. It starts as a Hash Match Join operator; it performs the first step in a Hash Match algorithm, scanning the first input. It also defines a threshold; if the number of input rows is less than the threshold, it changes to a Nested Loop Join operator.

To demonstrate the usage of the new operator, create a sample stored procedure:

```
USE WideWorldImporters;
GO
CREATE OR ALTER PROCEDURE dbo.GetSomeOrderDeatils
@UnitPrice DECIMAL(18,2)
AS
SELECT o.OrderID, o.OrderDate, ol.OrderLineID, ol.Quantity, ol.UnitPrice
FROM Sales.OrderLines ol
INNER JOIN Sales.Orders o ON ol.OrderID = o.OrderID
WHERE ol.UnitPrice = @UnitPrice;
GO
```

Now, invoke the stored procedure with the parameter `112`:

```
EXEC dbo.GetSomeOrderDeatils 112;
```

The execution plan for this invocation is shown as follows:

Adaptive Join operator

You can see the new `Adaptive Join` operator in the execution plan. The branch **1** represents a columnstore index scan and it is used to provide rows for the hash join build phase (the `Adaptive Join` operator starts as a Hash Match Join). In the Property Window of the `Adaptive Join` operator, you can see the property **Adaptive Threshold Rows**. This property defines the number of rows in the hash build phase that are required for switching to the Nested Loop Join. In the figure *Adaptive Join operator*, this value is 97.3. That means if the actual number of rows is less than 97, Nested Loop Join will be used, otherwise it will continue with Hash Match Join. Therefore, you can see two additional branches—each implementing one of the two mentioned operators. How do you know which one is used? You can see it in the previously mentioned property window in the value for the property **Actual Join Type**. In this case, the number of rows is 1,004 and it exceeds the threshold, therefore the Hash Match Join operator is implemented. You can also see this in the branches **2** and **3**. Branch **3**, which corresponds to the Nested Loop Join operator for the **Actual Number of Rows**, has a value of 0. So, it is clear that branches **1** and **2** are executed.

Now call the same procedure with a different parameter to see how `Adaptive Join` switches to the Nested Loop Join operator:

```
EXEC dbo.GetSomeOrderDeatils 1;
```

The execution plan is shown in the following screenshot:

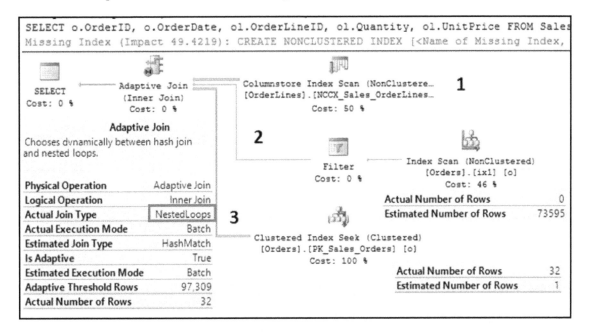

Adaptive Join operator

This time, the actual number of rows is 32 and, since this is under the threshold, branch **3** is executed and the property **Actual Join Type** has a **NestedLoops** value.

> The Adaptive Threshold has been calculated based on the parameter used for the first call (112). Its value is 97.309. If you were to call it with a different parameter, the value would be different. So, this is not solution for parameter sniffing. It is still possible to have an inappropriate plan, but at least you can have two different operators in the same plan.

To see what's going on under the hood, when Adaptive Join is used, you need to enable the trace flag `9415`, as in the following code example:

```
DBCC TRACEON (9415);
EXEC dbo.GetSomeOrderDeatils 112;
```

The following screenshot shows both operators, Hash Match Join and Nested Loops Join, and how they are actually implemented:

Adaptive Join operator under the hood

As you can see, the `Adaptive Join` operator uses the extended `Concatenation` and `Table Spool` operators.

Disabling adaptive batch mode joins

You can disable adaptive batch mode joins by using the `DISABLE_BATCH_MODE_ADAPTIVE_JOINS` database scoped configuration option, as shown in the following code:

```
ALTER DATABASE SCOPED CONFIGURATION SET DISABLE_BATCH_MODE_ADAPTIVE_JOINS =
ON;
```

You can also use the query hint `DISABLE_BATCH_MODE_ADAPTIVE_JOINS` to disable this feature. To demonstrate this, recreate the stored procedure from the beginning of this section:

```
CREATE OR ALTER PROCEDURE dbo.GetSomeOrderDeatils
@UnitPrice DECIMAL(18,2)
AS
SELECT o.OrderID, o.OrderDate, ol.OrderLineID, ol.Quantity, ol.UnitPrice
FROM Sales.OrderLines ol
INNER JOIN Sales.Orders o ON ol.OrderID = o.OrderID
WHERE ol.UnitPrice = @UnitPrice
OPTION (USE HINT ('DISABLE_BATCH_MODE_ADAPTIVE_JOINS'));
```

Now, invoke the procedure, as you already did at the beginning of this section:

```
EXEC dbo.GetSomeOrderDeatils 112;
```

Finally, observe the execution plan, shown as follows:

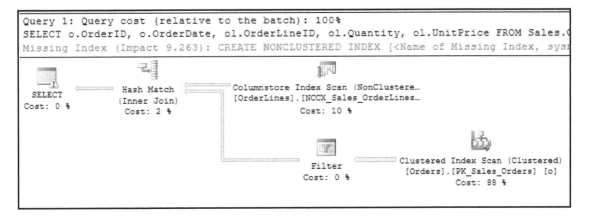

Disabled batch mode Adaptive Join

As expected, no Adaptive Join operator is shown. The fact that you have two options to disable the feature means that the feature is not applicable for many queries. If your queries perform well, or you know that you want to use the Nested Loop Join operator in the execution plan for your query, you might want to avoid overhead introduced by the hash join building phase of the Adaptive Join operator.

`Batch Mode Adaptive Join` allows SQL Server to handle one query with two different execution plans without plan recompiling. The `Adaptive Join` operator's threshold depends on the estimation and parameters used in the first invocation. If the estimation is wrong and initial parameters are not representative, you can still expect performance issues due to parameter sniffing. Adaptive Join in an execution plan does not guarantee usage of an appropriate join operator; you can still see *Hash Match Join* where you expected Nested Loop Join and vice versa. However, `Adaptive Join` will almost always use the expected Nested Loop Join operator for a small number of rows, which was not the case prior to SQL Server 2017.

Summary

This chapter explored new Transact-SQL elements, extensions, and hints. Some of them are small enhancements that make a developer's life easier and increase their productivity. There are also significant operational extensions that increase the availability and deployment of solutions. In addition to this, two newly added query hints address some rare but serious performance problems caused by incorrect query optimizer estimations and assumptions, where it is hard to find a workaround in previous SQL Server versions. Finally, with adaptive query processing, SQL Server additionally optimizes the creation of an execution plan by partially executing part of the code and introducing a new Adaptive Join operator. It also brings opportunities for correction of an execution plan after its creation, depending on runtime parameters and memory usage.

In this chapter, you saw many enhancements to the Transact-SQL language and database engine added in two recent SQL Server versions. Now, it is time to check JSON support in SQL Server 2017.

5

JSON Support in SQL Server

In the last few years, JSON has been established as a standard format for data exchange among applications and services. XML is still the exchange standard (and will remain so), but many applications communicate by exchanging JSON data instead of XML documents. Therefore, the most important relational database management system products need to support JSON.

Two release cycles after the feature was requested by the community, Microsoft has implemented built-in JSON support in SQL Server 2016. The support is not as comprehensive as for XML, but for most databases and workloads, it will be quite fine.

This chapter explores how SQL Server stores and processes JSON data, with a comprehensive comparison between JSON and XML support in SQL Server.

The most important actions related to JSON data in SQL Server are demonstrated in detail:

- Formatting and exporting JSON data from SQL Server
- Converting JSON data to a tabular format
- Importing JSON data to SQL Server
- Validating, querying, and modifying JSON data

Finally, you will be made aware of limitations caused by missing JSON data types and indexes, and given advice on how you can improve the performance of JSON queries despite these limitations.

Why JSON?

The Microsoft Connect site is the place where you can leave your feedback, suggestions, and wishes for Microsoft products. The most popular feature request for SQL Server is the one for JSON support. It was created in June 2011 and at the time of writing (October 2017) it has 1,138 votes. The request is still open, as you can see in the following screenshot, and you will see later in this chapter, why it still makes sense to have it in the active state:

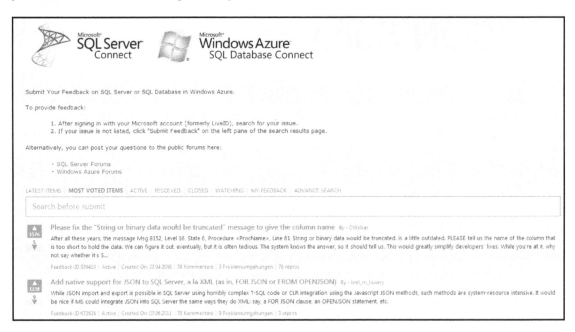

Highly ranked requests for SQL Server on the Microsoft Connect site (October 2017)

What arguments are used by community members to justify the request? They are as follows:

- JSON is already standard, and it should be supported, similar to XML.
- Other vendors support it (Oracle, PostgreSQL, and others)
- Due to the lack of JSON support, my customers want to move from SQL Server to other database systems supporting JSON.

As always with vox populi (the opinions or beliefs of the majority), some of the arguments and given examples represent development and business needs. Some of them, however, are very personal, sometimes guided by passion. But there is one thing upon which they agree and which is common in almost all comments: *a serious relational database management system should have significant support for JSON*. Almost five years after the item was created, Microsoft added JSON support in SQL Server 2016.

Of course, the number of votes on the Microsoft Connect site is not the only reason for this feature. The other competitors (PostgreSQL, Oracle, DB2, MySQL) have already introduced support for JSON; some of them, such as PostgreSQL, are very serious and robust. And if you want to still be a respectable vendor, you need to come up with JSON support.

What is JSON?

JavaScript Object Notation (**JSON**) is an open standard format for data exchange between applications and services. JSON objects are human-readable lists of key-value pairs. Although its name suggests otherwise, JSON is language-independent. It is specified in the ECMA-404 standard (`http://www.ecma-international.org/publications/files/ECMA-ST/ECMA-404.pdf`).

 ECMA International is an industry association founded in 1961 and dedicated to the standardization of **Information and Communication Technology** (**ICT**) and **Consumer Electronics** (**CE**). You can find more information about it at `https://www.ecma-international.org`.

JSON is very simple and very popular. It is commonly used in AJAX applications, configurations, RESTful web services, apps from social media, and NoSQL database management systems such as MongoDB and CouchDB. Many developers prefer JSON to XML because they see JSON as less verbose and easier to read.

JSON support in SQL is defined in the latest SQL standard—SQL:2016. The standard describes how to store, publish, and query JSON data, and defines the SQL/JSON data model and path language. The specification document (*ISO/IEC TR 19075-6:2017*) is available at the following web address: `https://www.iso.org/standard/67367.html`.

Why is it popular?

JSON is a simple data format, but its simplicity is not the only thing that makes it a leading standard for exchanging data among web services and applications. The most important reason for its popularity is the fact that the JSON format is native for many programming languages, such as JavaScript. They can generate and consume JSON data natively, without serialization. One of the biggest problems in software development in recent years is object-relational impedance. The JSON data format is flexible and self-describing and allows you to use it effectively without defining a strict schema for data, which XML might need. This allows for the quick integration of data.

JSON versus XML

Both JSON and XML are simple, open, and interoperable. Since JSON usually contains less data, by using JSON, less data traverses through the network. Both formats are human-readable; JSON is a bit cleaner, since it contains less text. This is because the number of data formats supported by JSON is much smaller than with XML.

JSON is handy for sharing data. Data in JSON is stored in arrays and objects while XML documents form a tree structure. Therefore, data transfer is easier with JSON and native for many programming languages: JavaScript, Python, Perl, Ruby, and so on. On the other hand, XML can store more data types (JSON does not have even a data type for date); it can include photos, videos, and other binary files. XML is more robust and it is better suited for complex documents. XML also offers options for data representation, while JSON just transfers data, without suggesting or defining how to display it.

Generally, JSON is better as a data exchange format, while XML is more convenient as a document exchange format.

JSON objects

According to the ECMA specification, a JSON text is a sequence of tokens formed of Unicode code points that conforms to the JSON value grammar. A JSON value can be:

- **Primitive**: This is a string, number, true/false, or null value
- **Complex**: This is an object or an array

JSON object

A JSON object is a collection of zero or more key-value pairs called **object members**. The collection is wrapped in a pair of curly brackets. The key and value are separated by a single colon, while object members are separated with a comma character. The key is a string. The value can be any primitive or complex JSON data type. The structure of a JSON object is shown in the following figure:

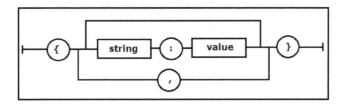

JSON object data type

The member name within a JSON object does not need to be unique. The following strings show a JSON text representing an object:

```
{
"Name":"Mila Radivojevic",
"Age":12,
"Instrument": "Flute"
}
{}
{
"Song":"Echoes",
"Group":"Pink Floyd",
"Album":{
"Name":"Meddle",
"Year":1971
}
}
{
"Name":"Tom Waits",
"Name":"Leonard Cohen"
}
```

Since the value can be any data type, including an object or an array, you can have many nested layers. This makes JSON a good choice for even complex data. Note that white spaces are allowed between the key and the value.

JSON array

A JSON array is an ordered list of zero or more values separated by commas and surrounded by square brackets. The structure is shown in the following figure:

JSON array data type

Unlike JSON objects, here, the order of values is significant. Values can have different data types.

The following strings are JSON conform arrays:

```
["Benfica","Juventus","Rapid Vienna","Seattle Seahawks"]
["NTNK",3,"Käsekrainer","Sejo Kalac","political correctness",true,null]
```

Primitive JSON data types

JSON is designed to be lightweight and supports only four primitive data types:

- **Numbers**: This is a double-precision float
- **String**: Unicode text surrounded by double quotes
- **True/false**: Boolean values; they must be written in lowercase
- **Null**: This represents a null value

As you can see, there is no `date` data type. Dates are represented and processed as strings. A JSON string is a sequence of Unicode code points wrapped with quotation marks. All characters may be placed within the quotation marks, except for the characters that must be escaped. The following table provides the list of characters that must be escaped according to this specification and their JSON conform representation:

JSON escaping rules

Special character	JSON conform character
Double quote	\ "

Solidus	\/
Reverse solidus	\\
Backspace	\b
Form feed	\f
New line	\n
Carriage return	\r
Tabulation	\t

In addition to this, all control characters with character codes in the range 0-31 need to be escaped too. In JSON output, they are represented in the following format: u<code>. Thus, the control character CHAR(0) is escaped as u0000, while CHAR(31) is represented by u001f.

The structure of a JSON string is shown in the following figure:

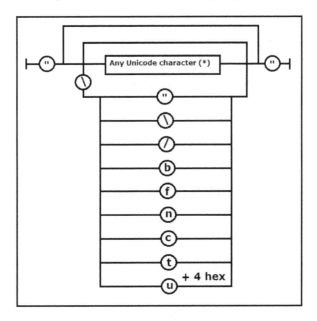

JSON string data type

JSON in SQL Server prior to SQL Server 2016

JSON has become established as a respectable and important data exchange format in the last 6-7 years. You read earlier in this chapter that JSON support in SQL Server was requested six years ago. Since this support was not provided prior to SQL Server 2016, developers had to implement their own solutions. They had to use either CLR or Transact-SQL to process and manipulate JSON data in SQL Server. This section will briefly discuss a few solutions.

JSON4SQL

JSON4SQL is a commercial CLR-based solution (with a trial version). It provides a fast, feature-rich binary JSON type for SQL Server. JSON4SQL stores JSON in a binary format ported from the JSONB format used in the PostgreSQL database. It is available at the following web address: `http://www.json4sql.com`.

JSON.SQL

JSON.SQL is a CLR-based JSON serializer/deserializer for SQL Server written by Bret Lowery, available at this address:
`http://www.sqlservercentral.com/articles/SQLCLR/74160/`. It uses a popular JSON framework—Json.NET.

Transact-SQL-based solution

There is also a Transact-SQL-only solution that does not use `.NET` functionality at all. It is written by Phil Factor and described in two articles:

- *Consuming JSON Strings in SQL Server:* You can find this article at `https://www.simple-talk.com/sql/t-sql-programming/consuming-json-strings-in-sql-server/`.
- *Producing JSON Documents from SQL Server queries via TSQL:* The article is available at
`https://www.simple-talk.com/sql/t-sql-programming/producing-json-documents-from-sql-server-queries-via-tsql/`.

Since it processes text with Transact-SQL only, the solution is not performant, but it can be used to process small or moderate JSON documents.

Retrieving SQL Server data in JSON format

This section explores JSON support in SQL Server with a very common action: formatting tabular data as JSON. In SQL Server 2017, the clause FOR JSON can be used with the SELECT statement to accomplish this. It is analogous to formatting relational data as XML by using the FOR XML extension.

When you use the FOR JSON clause, you can choose between two modes:

- FOR JSON AUTO: The JSON output will be formatted by the structure of the SELECT statement automatically.
- FOR JSON PATH: The JSON output will be formatted by the structure explicitly defined by you. With JSON PATH, you can create a more complex output (nested objects and properties).

In both modes, SQL Server extracts relational data defined by the SELECT statement, converts SQL Server data types to appropriate JSON types, implements escaping rules, and finally formats the output according to explicitly or implicitly defined formatting rules.

FOR JSON AUTO

Use FOR JSON AUTO when you want to let SQL Server format query results for you. When you specify this mode, the JSON format is controlled by how the SELECT statement is written.

FOR JSON AUTO requires a table; you cannot use it without a database table or view. For instance, the following query will fail:

```
SELECT GETDATE() AS today FOR JSON AUTO;
```

Here is the error message:

```
Msg 13600, Level 16, State 1, Line 13
FOR JSON AUTO requires at least one table for generating JSON objects. Use
FOR JSON PATH or add a FROM clause with a table name.
```

To demonstrate how SQL Server automatically generates JSON data, use the `WideWorldImporters` SQL Server 2017 sample database. Consider the following query, which returns the first three rows from the `Application.People` table:

```
USE WideWorldImporters;
SELECT TOP (3) PersonID, FullName, EmailAddress, PhoneNumber
FROM Application.People ORDER BY PersonID ASC;
```

Here is the result in tabular format:

PersonID	FullName	EmailAddress	PhoneNumber
1	Data Conversion Only	NULL	NULL
2	Kayla Woodcock	kaylaw@wideworldimporters.com	(415) 555-0102
3	Hudson Onslow	hudsono@wideworldimporters.com	(415) 555-0102

First, you will recall how SQL Server converts this data automatically to XML. To generate an XML, you can use the FOR JSON AUTO extension:

```
SELECT TOP (3) PersonID, FullName, EmailAddress, PhoneNumber
FROM Application.People ORDER BY PersonID ASC FOR XML AUTO;
```

Here is the portion of XML generated by the previous query:

```
<Application.People PersonID="1" FullName="Data Conversion Only" />
<Application.People PersonID="2" FullName="Kayla Woodcock"
EmailAddress="kaylaw@wideworldimporters.com" PhoneNumber="(415) 555-0102"
/>
<Application.People PersonID="3" FullName="Hudson Onslow"
EmailAddress="hudsono@wideworldimporters.com" PhoneNumber="(415) 555-0102"
/>
```

Analogous to this, the simplest way to convert the result in JSON format is to put the FOR JSON AUTO extension at the end of the query:

```
SELECT TOP (3) PersonID, FullName, EmailAddress, PhoneNumber
FROM Application.People ORDER BY PersonID ASC FOR JSON AUTO;
```

The result is an automatically formatted JSON text. By default, it is a JSON array with objects:

```
[{"PersonID":1,"FullName":"Data Conversion
Only"},{"PersonID":2,"FullName":"Kayla
Woodcock","EmailAddress":"kaylaw@wideworldimporters.com","PhoneNumber":"(41
5) 555-0102"},{"PersonID":3,"FullName":"Hudson
Onslow","EmailAddress":"hudsono@wideworldimporters.com","PhoneNumber":"(415
) 555-0102"}]
```

As you can see, in **SQL Server Management Studio** (**SSMS**), the JSON result is prepared in a single line. This is hard to follow and observe from a human-readable point of view. Therefore, you will need a JSON formatter. In this book, JSON output generated in SSMS is formatted by using the JSON formatter and validator that are available at `https://jsonformatter.curiousconcept.com`. The previous result looks better after additional formatting:

```
[
    {
        "PersonID":1,
        "FullName":"Data Conversion Only"
    },
    {
        "PersonID":2,
        "FullName":"Kayla Woodcock",
        "EmailAddress":"kaylaw@wideworldimporters.com",
        "PhoneNumber":"(415) 555-0102"
    },
    {
        "PersonID":3,
        "FullName":"Hudson Onslow",
        "EmailAddress":"hudsono@wideworldimporters.com",
        "PhoneNumber":"(415) 555-0102"
    }
]
```

As you can see, for each row from the original result set, one JSON object with a flat property structure is generated. Compared to XML, you see less text since the table name does not appear in the JSON output.

The difference in size is significant when you compare JSON with XML generated by using the ELEMENTS option instead of default RAW. To illustrate this, you can use the following code; it compares the data length (in bytes) of XML-and JSON-generated output for all rows in the Sales.Orders table:

```
USE WideWorldImporters;
SELECT
  DATALENGTH(CAST((SELECT * FROM Sales.Orders FOR XML AUTO) AS
NVARCHAR(MAX))) AS xml_raw_size,  DATALENGTH(CAST((SELECT * FROM
Sales.Orders FOR XML AUTO,   ELEMENTS) AS NVARCHAR(MAX))) AS
xml_elements_size,  DATALENGTH(CAST((SELECT * FROM Sales.Orders FOR JSON
AUTO) AS   NVARCHAR(MAX))) AS json_size;
```

The preceding query generates the following results:

xml_raw_size	xml_elements_size	json_size
49161702	81161852	49149364

You can see that the XML representation of data when columns are expressed as XML elements is about 65% larger than the JSON representation. When they are expressed as XML attributes, JSON and XML output have approximately the same size.

The FOR JSON AUTO extension creates a flat structure with single-level properties. If you are not satisfied with the automatically created output and want to create a more complex structure, you should use the FOR JSON PATH extension.

FOR JSON PATH

To maintain full control over the format of the JSON output, you need to specify the PATH option with the FOR JSON clause. The PATH mode lets you create wrapper objects and nest complex properties. The results are formatted as an array of JSON objects.

The FOR JSON PATH clause will use the column alias or column name to determine the key name in the JSON output. If an alias contains dots, the FOR JSON PATH clause will create a nested object.

Assume you want to have more control over the output generated by `FOR JSON AUTO` in the previous subsection, and instead of a flat list of properties you want to represent `EmailAddress` and `PhoneNumbers` as nested properties of a new property named `Contact`. Here is the required output for the `PersonID` property with a value of 2:

```
{
        "PersonID":2,
        "FullName":"Kayla Woodcock",
        "Contact":
    {
        "EmailAddress":"kaylaw@wideworldimporters.com",
        "PhoneNumber":"(415) 555-0102"
    }
}
```

To achieve this, you simply add an alias to columns that need to be nested. In the alias, you have to use a dot syntax, which defines a JSON path to the property. Here is the code that implements the previous request:

```
SELECT TOP (3) PersonID, FullName,
EmailAddress AS 'Contact.Email', PhoneNumber AS 'Contact.Phone'
FROM Application.People ORDER BY PersonID ASC FOR JSON PATH;
```

Here is the expected result:

```
[
    {
        "PersonID":1,
        "FullName":"Data Conversion Only"
    },
    {
        "PersonID":2,
        "FullName":"Kayla Woodcock",
        "Contact":{
            "Email":"kaylaw@wideworldimporters.com",
            "Phone":"(415) 555-0102"
        }
    },
    {
        "PersonID":3,
        "FullName":"Hudson Onslow",
        "Contact":{
            "Email":"hudsono@wideworldimporters.com",
            "Phone":"(415) 555-0102"
        }
    }
]
```

By default, null values are not included in the output as you can see in the first array element; it does not contain the `Contact` property.

`FOR JSON PATH` does not require a database table. The following statement, which was not allowed in the `AUTO` mode, works in the `PATH` mode:

```
SELECT GETDATE() AS today FOR JSON PATH;
```

It returns:

```
[{"today":"2017-08-26T09:13:32.007"}]
```

If you reference more than one table in the query, the results are represented as a flat list, and then `FOR JSON PATH` nests each column using its alias. `JSON PATH` allows you to control generated JSON data and to create nested documents.

FOR JSON additional options

In both modes of the `FOR JSON` clause, you can specify additional options to control the output. The following options are available:

- **Add a root node**: This option allows you to add a top-level element to the JSON output.
- **Include null values**: This option allows you to include null values in the JSON output (by default they are not shown).
- **Remove array wrapper**: By using this option, you can format JSON output as a single object.

Add a root node to JSON output

By specifying the `ROOT` option in the `FOR JSON` query, you can add a single, top-level element to the JSON output. The following code shows this:

```
SELECT TOP (3) PersonID, FullName, EmailAddress, PhoneNumber
FROM Application.People ORDER BY PersonID ASC FOR JSON AUTO,
ROOT('Persons');
```

Here is the result:

```
{
    "Persons":[
        {
            "PersonID":1,
```

```
            "FullName":"Data Conversion Only"
        },
        {
            "PersonID":2,
            "FullName":"Kayla Woodcock",
            "EmailAddress":"kaylaw@wideworldimporters.com",
            "PhoneNumber":"(415) 555-0102"
        },
        {
            "PersonID":3,
            "FullName":"Hudson Onslow",
            "EmailAddress":"hudsono@wideworldimporters.com",
            "PhoneNumber":"(415) 555-0102"
        }
    ]
}
```

By specifying the root element, you have converted the outer array to a single complex property named `Persons`.

Include NULL values in the JSON output

As you can see in the preceding example, the JSON output does not map a column to a JSON property if the column value is NULL. To include null values in the JSON output, you can specify the INCLUDE_NULL_VALUES option. Let's apply it to our initial example:

```
SELECT TOP (3) PersonID, FullName, EmailAddress, PhoneNumber
FROM Application.People ORDER BY PersonID ASC FOR JSON AUTO,
INCLUDE_NULL_VALUES;
```

Let's observe the result:

```
[
  {
    "PersonID":1,
    "FullName":"Data Conversion Only",
    "EmailAddress":null,
    "PhoneNumber":null
  },
  {
    "PersonID":2,
    "FullName":"Kayla Woodcock",
    "EmailAddress":"kaylaw@wideworldimporters.com",
    "PhoneNumber":"(415) 555-0102"
  },
  {
    "PersonID":3,
```

```
      "FullName":"Hudson Onslow",
      "EmailAddress":"hudsono@wideworldimporters.com",
      "PhoneNumber":"(415) 555-0102"
   }
]
```

Now each element has all properties listed even if they don't have a value. This option is similar to the XSINIL option used with the ELEMENTS directive in the case of FOR XML AUTO.

Formatting a JSON output as a single object

The default JSON output is enclosed within square brackets, which means the output is an array. If you want to format it as a single object instead of an array, use the WITHOUT_ARRAY_WRAPPER option.

Even if a query returns only one row, SQL Server will format it by default as a JSON array, as in the following example:

```
SELECT PersonID, FullName, EmailAddress, PhoneNumber
FROM Application.People WHERE PersonID = 2 FOR JSON AUTO;
```

Although only one row is returned, the output is still an array (with a single element):

```
[
  {
    "PersonID":2,
    "FullName":"Kayla Woodcock",
    "EmailAddress":"kaylaw@wideworldimporters.com",
    "PhoneNumber":"(415) 555-0102"
  }
]
```

To return a single object instead of an array, you can specify the WITHOUT_ARRAY_WRAPPER option:

```
SELECT PersonID, FullName, EmailAddress, PhoneNumber
FROM Application.People WHERE PersonID = 2 FOR JSON AUTO,
WITHOUT_ARRAY_WRAPPER;
```

The output looks more convenient now:

```
{
  "PersonID":2,
  "FullName":"Kayla Woodcock",
  "EmailAddress":"kaylaw@wideworldimporters.com",
```

```
    "PhoneNumber":"(415) 555-0102"
}
```

Removing square brackets from the output allows us to choose between an object and an array in the output JSON. However, only square brackets guarantee that the output is JSON conforming. Without the brackets, JSON text will be valid only if the underlined query returns a single row or no rows at all.

To demonstrate this, include `PersonID` with a value of 3 in your initial query:

```
SELECT PersonID, FullName, EmailAddress, PhoneNumber
FROM Application.People WHERE PersonID IN (2, 3) FOR JSON AUTO,
WITHOUT_ARRAY_WRAPPER;
```

The output is expected, but invalid; there is no parent object or array:

```
{
  "PersonID":2,
  "FullName":"Kayla Woodcock",
  "EmailAddress":"kaylaw@wideworldimporters.com",
  "PhoneNumber":"(415) 555-0102"
},
{
  "PersonID":3,
  "FullName":"Hudson Onslow",
  "EmailAddress":"hudsono@wideworldimporters.com",
  "PhoneNumber":"(415) 555-0102"
}
```

But, wait! By specifying the ROOT option, you can wrap the output in an object, can't you? You saw this demonstrated earlier in this chapter. You can add a no-name root element to the preceding output:

```
SELECT PersonID, FullName, EmailAddress, PhoneNumber
FROM Application.People WHERE PersonID IN (2, 3) FOR JSON AUTO,
WITHOUT_ARRAY_WRAPPER, ROOT('');
```

This should add a top-level element, and with that change, the JSON output should be valid. Check this out in the output:

```
Msg 13620, Level 16, State 1, Line 113
ROOT option and WITHOUT_ARRAY_WRAPPER option cannot be used together in FOR
JSON. Remove one of these options.
```

A bitter disappointment! You cannot combine these two options! Therefore, use this option with caution; be aware that the JSON could be invalid.

Converting data types

As mentioned earlier, JSON does not have the same data types as SQL Server. Therefore, when JSON text is generated from relational data, a data type conversion is performed. The `FOR JSON` clause uses the following mapping to convert SQL Server data types to JSON types in the JSON output:

Conversion between SQL Server and JSON data types

SQL Server data type	JSON data type
`Char`, `Varchar`, `Nchar`, `NVarchar`, `Text`, `Ntext`, `Date`, `DateTime`, `DateTime2`, `DateTimeOffset`, `Time`, `UniqueIdentifier`, `Smallmoney`, `Money`, `XML`, `HierarchyId`, `Sql_Variant`	string
`Tinyint`, `Smallint`, `Int`, `Bigint`, `Decimal`, `Float`, `Numeric`	number
`Bit`	`true` or `false`
`Binary`, `Varbinary`, `Image`, `Rowversion`, `Timestamp`	encoded string (BASE 64)

The following data types are not supported: geography, geometry, and CLR-based user-defined data types. Thus, you cannot generate JSON output from tabular data if it includes columns of the aforementioned data types. For instance, the following query will fail:

```
SELECT * FROM Application.Cities FOR JSON AUTO;
```

Instead of returning a JSON output, it will generate an error with the following error message:

```
Msg 13604, Level 16, State 1, Line 282
FOR JSON cannot serialize CLR objects. Cast CLR types explicitly into one
of the supported types in FOR JSON queries.
```

The reason for the error is the `Location` column in the `Cities` table. Its data type is geography.

User-defined data types (UDT) are supported and will be converted following the same rules as underlined data types.

Escaping characters

Another action that is automatically performed when JSON is generated by using the FOR JSON clause is escaping special characters from text columns according to JSON's escaping rules. The rules are explained in detail in the *Primitive JSON data types* section earlier in this chapter.

Converting JSON data in a tabular format

Nowadays, JSON is a recognized format for data representation and exchange. However, most of the existing data still resides in relational databases and you need to combine them to process and manipulate them together. In order to combine JSON with relational data or to import it in relational tables, you need to map JSON data to tabular data, that is, convert it into a tabular format. In SQL Server 2016, you can use the OPENJSON function to accomplish this:

- OPENJSON is a newly added rowset function. A rowset function is a table-valued function and returns an object that can be used as if it were a table or a view. Just as OPENXML provides a rowset view over an XML document, OPENJSON gives a rowset view over JSON data. The OPENJSON function converts JSON objects and properties to table rows and columns respectively.
- It accepts two input arguments:
  - **Expression**: JSON text in the Unicode format.
  - **Path**: This is an optional argument. It is a JSON path expression and you can use it to specify a fragment of the input expression.

The function returns a table with a default or user-defined schema.

To use the OPENJSON function, the database must be in compatibility level 130. If it is not, you will get the following error:

```
Msg 208, Level 16, State 1, Line 78
Invalid object name 'OPENJSON'.
```

As mentioned, the returned table can have an implicit (default) schema or an explicit one, defined by the user. In the next two sections, both schemas will be explored in more detail.

OPENJSON with the default schema

When you don't specify a schema for returned results, the OPENJSON function returns a table with three columns:

- **Key**: This is the name of a JSON property or the index of a JSON element. The data type of the column is nvarchar, the length is 4,000, collation is Latin1_General_BIN2, and the column does not allow null values.
- **Value**: This is the value of the property or index defined by the key column. The data type of the column is nvarchar(max), it inherits collation from the input JSON text, and nulls are allowed.
- **Type**: The JSON data type of the value. The data type of the column is tinyint. Following table lists the possible values for this column and appropriate descriptions:

OPENJSON mapping of JSON data types

Type column value	JSON data type
0	null
1	string
2	number
3	true/false
4	array
5	object

OPENJSON returns only one table; therefore only first-level properties are returned as rows. It returns one row for each JSON property or array element. To demonstrate the different results provided by the OPENJSON function, use the following JSON data with the information about the album *Wish You Were Here* by the British band Pink Floyd. You will provide JSON data as an input string and call the function without specifying an optional path argument:

```
DECLARE @json NVARCHAR(MAX) = N'{
"Album":"Wish You Were Here",
"Year":1975,
"IsVinyl":true,
"Songs":[{"Title":"Shine On You Crazy Diamond","Authors":"Gilmour, Waters,
Wright"},
```

```
{"Title":"Have a Cigar","Authors":"Waters"},
{"Title":"Welcome to the Machine","Authors":"Waters"},
{"Title":"Wish You Were Here","Authors":"Gilmour, Waters"}],
"Members":{"Guitar":"David Gilmour","Bass Guitar":"Roger
Waters","Keyboard":"Richard Wright","Drums":"Nick Mason"}
}';
SELECT * FROM OPENJSON(@json);
```

The function has been invoked without the path expression; simply to convert the whole JSON document into a tabular format. Here is the output of this action:

key	value	type
Album	Wish you Were Here	1
Year	1975	2
IsVinyl	true	3
Songs	[{"Title":"Shine On You Crazy Diamond","Writers":"Gilmour, Waters, Wright" ...]	4
Members	{"Guitar":"David Gilmour","Bass Guitar":"Roger Waters","Keyboard":"Richard Wright","Drums":"Nick Mason"}	5

As you can see, five rows were generated (one row for each JSON property), property names are shown in the `key` column, and their values in the `value` column.

The input JSON expression must be well formatted; otherwise, an error occurs. In the following code, a leading double quote for the `Year` property is intentionally omitted:

```
DECLARE @json NVARCHAR(500) = '{
"Album":"Wish You Were Here",
Year":1975,
"IsVinyl":true
}';
SELECT * FROM OPENJSON(@json);
```

Of course, the optimizer does not forgive this small mistake and its reaction is very conservative:

```
Msg 13609, Level 16, State 4, Line 23
JSON text is not properly formatted. Unexpected character 'Y' is found at
position 34.
```

As already mentioned and demonstrated, only first-level properties are returned with the OPENJSON function. To return properties within complex values of a JSON document (arrays and objects), you need to specify the path argument. In this example, assume you want to return the Songs fragment from the initial Wish You Were Here JSON string:

```
DECLARE @json NVARCHAR(MAX) = N'{
"Album":"Wish You Were Here",
"Year":1975,
"IsVinyl":true,
"Songs":[{"Title":"Shine On You Crazy Diamond","Authors":"Gilmour, Waters,
Wright"},
{"Title":"Have a Cigar","Authors":"Waters"},
{"Title":"Welcome to the Machine","Authors":"Waters"},
{"Title":"Wish You Were Here","Authors":"Gilmour, Waters"}],
"Members":{"Guitar":"David Gilmour","Bass Guitar":"Roger
Waters","Keyboard":"Richard Wright","Drums":"Nick Mason"}
}';
SELECT * FROM OPENJSON(@json,'$.Songs');
```

The $ path expression represents the context item and $.Songs refers to the Songs property and actually extracts this fragment from the JSON document. The rest of the document must be valid; otherwise, the path expression cannot be evaluated.

Here is the result:

key	value	type
0	{"Title":"Shine On You Crazy Diamond","Writers":"Gilmour, Waters, Wright"}	5
1	{"Title":"Have a Cigar","Writers":"Waters"}	5
2	{"Title":"Welcome to the Machine","Writers":"Waters"}	5
3	{"Title":"Wish You Were Here","Writers":"Gilmour, Waters"}	5

You can see four entries for four elements in the JSON array representing songs from this album. Since they contain objects, their values are still in the JSON format in the column value.

When you do the same for the Members property, you get a nice list of properties with their names and values:

```
DECLARE @json NVARCHAR(MAX) = N'{
"Album":"Wish You Were Here",
"Year":1975,
"IsVinyl":true,
"Songs":[{"Title":"Shine On You Crazy Diamond","Authors":"Gilmour, Waters,
Wright"},
{"Title":"Have a Cigar","Authors":"Waters"},
```

```
{"Title":"Welcome to the Machine","Authors":"Waters"},
{"Title":"Wish You Were Here","Authors":"Gilmour, Waters"}],
"Members":{"Guitar":"David Gilmour","Bass Guitar":"Roger
Waters","Keyboard":"Richard Wright","Drums":"Nick Mason"}
}';
SELECT * FROM OPENJSON(@json,'$.Members');
```

Here is the result:

key	value	type
Guitar	David Gilmour	1
Bass Guitar	Roger Waters	1
Keyboard	Richard Wright	1
Drums	Nick Mason	1

Note that the returned type this time is **1** (*string*), while in the previous example it was **5** (*object*).

The function returns an error if the JSON text is not properly formatted. To demonstrate this, the initial string has been slightly changed: a leading double quote has been omitted for the element Drums (value Nick Mason). Therefore, the string is not JSON valid. Invoke the OPENJSON function for such a string:

```
DECLARE @json NVARCHAR(MAX) = N'{
"Album":"Wish you Were Here",
"Members":{"Guitar":"David Gilmour","Bass Guitar":"Roger
Waters","Keyboard":"Richard Wright","Drums":Nick Mason", "Vocal":"Syd
Barrett"}
}';
SELECT * FROM OPENJSON (@json,'$.Members');
```

Here is the result:

Msg 13609, Level 16, State 4, Line 15
JSON text is not properly formatted. Unexpected character 'N' is found at
position 417

key	value	type
Guitar	David Gilmour	1
Bass Guitar	Roger Waters	1
Keyboard	Richard Wright	1

You can see an error message, but also the returned table. The table contains three rows, since the first three properties of the complex Member property are JSON conforming. Instead of a fourth row, an error message has been generated and the fifth row is not shown either, although it is well formatted.

What would happen if the JSON path expression points to a scalar value or to a non-existing property? In the default JSON path mode (lax), the query would return an empty table; and when you specify strict mode, in addition to an empty table, an error message is shown (a batch-level exception is raised), as shown in the following examples:

```
DECLARE @json NVARCHAR(MAX) = N'{
"Album":"Wish you Were Here",
"Year":1975,
"IsVinyl":true,
"Songs" :[{"Title":"Shine On You Crazy Diamond","Writers":"Gilmour, Waters,
Wright"},
{"Title":"Have a Cigar","Writers":"Waters"},
{"Title":"Welcome to the Machine","Writers":"Waters"},
{"Title":"Wish You Were Here","Writers":"Gilmour, Waters"}],
"Members":{"Guitar":"David Gilmour","Bass Guitar":"Roger
Waters","Keyboard":"Richard Wright","Drums":"Nick Mason"}
}';
SELECT * FROM OPENJSON(@json, N'$.Members.Guitar');
SELECT * FROM OPENJSON(@json, N'$.Movies');
```

Both queries return an empty table:

key	value	type

The same calls with the strict option end up with error messages:

```
SELECT * FROM OPENJSON(@json, N'strict $.Members.Guitar');
```

The result for the preceding query is the first error message:

Msg 13611, Level 16, State 1, Line 12
Value referenced by JSON path is not an array or object and cannot be
opened with OPENJSON

The second query from the preceding example:

```
SELECT * FROM OPENJSON(@json, N'strict $.Movies');
```

The result for the preceding query is the second error message:

```
Msg 13608, Level 16, State 3, Line 13
Property cannot be found on the specified JSON path.
```

You can use OPENJSON, not only to convert JSON data into a tabular format, but also to implement some non-JSON related tasks.

Processing data from a comma-separated list of values

The following code example demonstrates how to use the OPENJSON rowset function to return the details of orders for IDs provided in a comma-separated list:

```
USE WideWorldImporters;
DECLARE @orderIds AS VARCHAR(100) = '1,3,7,8,9,11';
SELECT o.OrderID, o.CustomerID, o.OrderDate
FROM Sales.Orders o
INNER JOIN (SELECT value FROM OPENJSON('[' + @orderIds + ']' )) x ON
x.value= o.OrderID;
```

Here is the list of orders produced by the preceding query:

```
OrderID      CustomerID   OrderDate
-----------  -----------  ----------
1            832          2013-01-01
3            105          2013-01-01
7            575          2013-01-01
8            964          2013-01-01
9            77           2013-01-01
11           586          2013-01-01
```

In this example, the input argument is wrapped with square brackets to create a proper JSON text and the OPENJSON function is invoked without the path argument. OPENJSON created one row for each element from the JSON array and that is exactly what you needed.

Returning the difference between two table rows

Another example where you can use OPENJSON is to return the difference between two rows in a table. For instance, when you put application settings for different environments in a database table, you might need to know what is different in the settings between the two environments. You can accomplish this task by comparing values in each column, but this can be annoying and error prone if the table has many columns.

The following example returns the difference for database settings in the **master** and **model** database in an instance of SQL Server 2017:

```
SELECT
  mst.[key],
  mst.[value] AS mst_val,
  mdl.[value] AS mdl_val
FROM OPENJSON ((SELECT * FROM sys.databases WHERE database_id = 1 FOR JSON
AUTO, WITHOUT_ARRAY_WRAPPER)) mst
INNER JOIN OPENJSON((SELECT * FROM sys.databases WHERE database_id = 3 FOR
JSON AUTO, WITHOUT_ARRAY_WRAPPER)) mdl
ON mst.[key] = mdl.[key] AND mst.[value] <> mdl.[value]
```

Here is the list showing columns that have different values for these two databases.

key	mst_val	mdl_val
name	master	model
database_id	1	3
snapshot_isolation_state	1	0
snapshot_isolation_state_desc	ON	OFF
recovery_model	3	1
recovery_model_desc	SIMPLE	FULL
is_db_chaining_on	true	false
target_recovery_time_in_seconds	0	60

This is very handy and efficient; you don't need to know or write a lot of OR statements with column names. For instance, in the system view used in this example (sys.databases), there are 78 columns and you would need to include them all in the WHERE clause in a relational Transact-SQL statement.

OPENJSON with an explicit schema

If you need more control over formatting when it is offered by default, you can explicitly specify your own schema. The function will still return a table but with the columns defined by you. To specify the resultant table schema, use the WITH clause of the OPENJSON function. Here is the syntax for the OPENJSON function with an explicit schema:

```
OPENJSON( jsonExpression [ , path ] )
[
    WITH (
        column_name data_type [ column_path ] [ AS JSON ]
    [ , column_name data_type [ column_path ] [ AS JSON ] ]
    [ , . . . n ]
        )
]
```

When you use the WITH clause, you need to specify at least one column. For each column, you can specify the following attributes:

- column_name: This is the name of the output column.
- data_type: This is the data type for the output column.
- column_path: This is the value for the output column specified with the JSON path expression (it can be a JSON property or value of an array element); this argument is optional.
- AS JSON: Use this to specify that the property referenced in the column path represents an object or array; this argument is optional.

The best way to understand how the function works is to look at examples. The following code shows how to extract JSON properties as columns and their values as rows for JSON primitive data types:

```
DECLARE @json NVARCHAR(MAX) = N'{
"Album":"Wish You Were Here",
"Year":1975,
"IsVinyl":true,
"Songs" :[{"Title":"Shine On You Crazy Diamond","Writers":"Gilmour, Waters,
Wright"},
{"Title":"Have a Cigar","Writers":"Waters"},
{"Title":"Welcome to the Machine","Writers":"Waters"},
{"Title":"Wish You Were Here","Writers":"Gilmour, Waters"}],
"Members":{"Guitar":"David Gilmour","Bass Guitar":"Roger
Waters","Keyboard":"Richard Wright","Drums":"Nick Mason"}
}';
SELECT * FROM OPENJSON(@json)
```

```
WITH
(
  AlbumName NVARCHAR(50) '$.Album',
  AlbumYear SMALLINT '$.Year',
  IsVinyl     BIT '$.IsVinyl'
);
```

The result of the previous action is a table defined with the WITH statement:

AlbumName	AlbumYear	IsVinyl
Wish You Were Here	1975	1

You can add a fourth column to show band members. Here is the code:

```
SELECT * FROM OPENJSON(@json)
WITH
(
  AlbumName NVARCHAR(50) '$.Album',
  AlbumYear SMALLINT '$.Year',
  IsVinyl  BIT '$.IsVinyl',
  Members  VARCHAR(200) '$.Members'
);
```

Here is the resultant table:

AlbumName	AlbumYear	IsVinyl	Members
Wish You Were Here	1975	1	NULL

The result might be unexpected, but the value for the Members property is an object, and therefore the function returns NULL since the JSON path is in default lax mode. If you specified the strict mode, the returned table would be empty and an error would be raised. To solve the problem and show the value of the Members property you need to use the AS JSON option to inform SQL Server that the expected data is properly JSON-formatted, as shown in the following code:

```
SELECT * FROM OPENJSON(@json)
WITH
(
  AlbumName NVARCHAR(50) '$.Album',
  AlbumYear SMALLINT '$.Year',
  IsVinyl  BIT '$.IsVinyl',
  Members  VARCHAR(MAX) '$.Members' AS JSON

);
```

Now it should return the expected result, but it returns an error:

```
Msg 13618, Level 16, State 1, Line 70
AS JSON option can be specified only for column of nvarchar(max) type in
WITH clause.
```

As the error message clearly says, the AS JSON option requires a column with the nvarchar(max) data type. Finally, here is the code that works and returns the expected result:

```
SELECT * FROM OPENJSON(@json)
WITH
(
  AlbumName NVARCHAR(50) '$.Album',
  AlbumYear SMALLINT '$.Year',
  IsVinyl  BIT '$.IsVinyl',
  Members  NVARCHAR(MAX) '$.Members' AS JSON
);
```

AlbumName	AlbumYear	IsVinyl	Members
Wish You Were Here	1975	1	{"Guitar":"David Gilmour","Bass Guitar":"Roger Waters","Keyboard":"Richard Wright","Drums":"Nick Mason"}

To combine property values from different levels and convert them to a tabular format, you would need to have multiple calls of the OPENJSON function. The following example lists all songs and authors and shows the appropriate album name:

```
DECLARE @json NVARCHAR(MAX) = N'{
"Album":"Wish You Were Here",
"Year":1975,
"IsVinyl":true,
"Songs" :[{"Title":"Shine On You Crazy Diamond","Writers":"Gilmour, Waters,
Wright"},
{"Title":"Have a Cigar","Writers":"Waters"},
{"Title":"Welcome to the Machine","Writers":"Waters"},
{"Title":"Wish You Were Here","Writers":"Gilmour, Waters"}],
"Members":{"Guitar":"David Gilmour","Bass Guitar":"Roger
Waters","Keyboard":"Richard Wright","Drums":"Nick Mason"}
}';
SELECT s.SongTitle, s.SongAuthors, a.AlbumName FROM OPENJSON(@json)
WITH
(
  AlbumName NVARCHAR(50) '$.Album',
```

```
    AlbumYear SMALLINT '$.Year',
    IsVinyl BIT '$.IsVinyl',
    Songs  NVARCHAR(MAX) '$.Songs' AS JSON,
    Members NVARCHAR(MAX) '$.Members' AS JSON

) a
CROSS APPLY OPENJSON(Songs)
WITH
(
    SongTitle NVARCHAR(200) '$.Title',
    SongAuthors NVARCHAR(200) '$.Writers'
) s;
```

This time the result meets expectations. No hidden catch! Here is the result:

SongTitle	SongAuthors	AlbumName
Shine On You Crazy Diamond	Gilmour, Waters, Wright	Wish You Were Here
Have a Cigar	Waters	Wish You Were Here
Welcome to the Machine	Waters	Wish You Were Here
Wish You Were Here	Gilmour, Waters	Wish You Were Here

Import the JSON data from a file

Importing JSON data from a file and converting it into a tabular format is straightforward in SQL Server 2016. To import data from a filesystem (local disk or network location) into SQL Server, you can use the OPENROWSET (BULK) function. It simply imports the entire file contents in a single-text value.

To demonstrate this, use your knowledge from the previous section and generate content for a JSON file. Use the following query to create JSON data from the Application.People table:

```
USE WideWorldImporters;
SELECT PersonID, FullName, PhoneNumber, FaxNumber, EmailAddress, LogonName,
IsEmployee, IsSalesperson FROM Application.People FOR JSON AUTO;
```

You then save the resulting JSON text in a file named app.people.json in the C:Temp directory. Now import this JSON file into SQL Server.

By using the OPENROWSET function, the file is imported in a single-text column. Here is the code:

```
SELECT BulkColumn
FROM OPENROWSET (BULK 'C:\Temp\app.people.json', SINGLE_CLOB) AS x;
```

The following screenshot shows the result of this import action. The entire file content is available in the single-text column named BulkColumn:

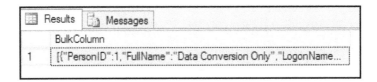

Import JSON file into SQL Server by using OPENROWSET function

To represent a JSON file's contents in a tabular format, you can combine the OPENROWSET function with the OPENJSON function. The following code imports JSON data and displays it with the default schema (columns key, value, and type):

```
SELECT [key], [value], [type]
FROM OPENROWSET (BULK 'C:\Temp\app.people.json', SINGLE_CLOB) AS x
CROSS APPLY OPENJSON(BulkColumn);
```

The result is shown in the following screenshot. You can see one row for each element of a JSON array in the file:

	key	value	type
1	0	{"PersonID":1,"FullName":"Data Conversion Only","Lo...	5
2	1	{"PersonID":2,"FullName":"Kayla Woodcock","Logon...	5
3	2	{"PersonID":3,"FullName":"Hudson Onslow","LogonNa...	5
4	3	{"PersonID":4,"FullName":"Isabella Rupp","LogonNam...	5
5	4	{"PersonID":5,"FullName":"Eva Muirden","LogonName...	5
6	5	{"PersonID":6,"FullName":"Sophia Hinton","LogonNam...	5
7	6	{"PersonID":7,"FullName":"Amy Trefl","LogonName":"...	5
8	7	{"PersonID":8,"FullName":"Anthony Grosse","LogonNa...	5
9	8	{"PersonID":9,"FullName":"Alica Fatnowna","LogonNa...	5
10	9	{"PersonID":10,"FullName":"Stella Rosenhain","Logon...	5

Importing a JSON file into SQL Server and combining with OPENJSON with the default schema

Finally, this code example shows the code that can be used to import a JSON file and represent its content in tabular format, with a user-defined schema:

```
SELECT PersonID, FullName,PhoneNumber, FaxNumber, EmailAddress,LogonName,
IsEmployee, IsSalesperson
FROM OPENROWSET (BULK 'C:\Temp\app.people.json', SINGLE_CLOB) as j
CROSS APPLY OPENJSON(BulkColumn)
WITH
(
  PersonID INT '$.PersonID',
  FullName NVARCHAR(50) '$.FullName',
  PhoneNumber NVARCHAR(20) '$.PhoneNumber',
  FaxNumber NVARCHAR(20) '$.FaxNumber',
  EmailAddress NVARCHAR(256) '$.EmailAddress',
  LogonName NVARCHAR(50) '$.LogonName',
  IsEmployee  BIT '$.IsEmployee',
  IsSalesperson BIT '$.IsSalesperson'
);
```

The following screenshot shows the result of this import procedure:

	PersonID	FullName	PhoneNumber	FaxNumber	EmailAddress	LogonName	IsEmployee	IsSalesperson
1	1	Data Conversion Only	NULL	NULL	NULL	NO LOGON	0	0
2	2	Kayla Woodcock	(415) 555-0102	(415) 555-0103	kaylaw@wideworldimporters.com	kaylaw@wideworldimporters.com	1	1
3	3	Hudson Onslow	(415) 555-0102	(415) 555-0103	hudsono@wideworldimporters.com	hudsono@wideworldimporters.com	1	1
4	4	Isabella Rupp	(415) 555-0102	(415) 555-0103	isabellar@wideworldimporters.com	isabellar@wideworldimporters.com	1	0
5	5	Eva Muirden	(415) 555-0102	(415) 555-0103	evam@wideworldimporters.com	evam@wideworldimporters.com	1	0
6	6	Sophia Hinton	(415) 555-0102	(415) 555-0103	sophiah@wideworldimporters.com	sophiah@wideworldimporters.com	1	1
7	7	Amy Trefl	(415) 555-0102	(415) 555-0103	amyt@wideworldimporters.com	amyt@wideworldimporters.com	1	1
8	8	Anthony Grosse	(415) 555-0102	(415) 555-0103	anthonyg@wideworldimporters.com	anthonyg@wideworldimporters.com	1	1
9	9	Alica Fatnowna	(415) 555-0102	(415) 555-0103	alicaf@wideworldimporters.com	alicaf@wideworldimporters.com	1	0
10	10	Stella Rosenhain	(415) 555-0102	(415) 555-0103	stellar@wideworldimporters.com	stellar@wideworldimporters.com	1	0

Importing a JSON file into SQL Server and combining with OPENJSON with an explicit schema

As expected, the structure is identical to the one generated by the simple SELECT statement against the Application.People table.

JSON storage in SQL Server 2017

Since XML support was introduced in SQL Server 2005, the native XML data type has been implemented as well. SQL Server 2016 introduces built-in support for JSON but unlike XML, there is no native JSON data type. Here are the reasons that the Microsoft team gave for not introducing a new data type:

- **Migration**: Prior to SQL Server 2016, developers already had to deal with JSON data.
- **Cross-feature compatibility**: The data type `nvarchar` is supported in all SQL Server components, so JSON will also be supported everywhere (memory-optimized tables, temporal tables, and Row-Level Security).
- **Client-side support**: Even if a new data type were introduced, most of the client tools would still represent it outside SQL Server as a string.

They also noted that if you believe that the JSON binary format from PostgreSQL, or a compressed format, such as zipped JSON text, is a better option, you can parse JSON text in UDT, store it as JSONB in a binary property of CLR UTD, and create member methods that can use properties from that format. You can find more details about their decision at `https://blogs.msdn.microsoft.com/jocapc/2015/05/16/json-support-in-sql-server-2016`.

A part of the SQL Server community has expected a native data type in the SQL Server 2017 version, but the native JSON data type is still not provided.

Although the arguments mentioned make sense, a native JSON data type would be better, especially from a performance point of view. However, this requires more effort and time frames for development, and release of new features are shorter which should be also taken in account when you judge the feature. JSON support in SQL Server would be complete with a native data type, but built-in support is a respectable implementation and this is a very useful feature.

Since there is no JSON data type, JSON data is stored as text in `NVARCHAR` columns. You can use the newly added `COMPRESS` function to compress JSON data and convert it to a binary format.

Validating JSON data

To validate JSON, you can use the ISJSON function. This is a scalar function and checks whether the input string is valid JSON data. The function has one input argument:

- string: This is an expression of any string data type, except text and ntext.

The return type of the function is int, but only three values are possible:

- 1 , if the input string is JSON conforming
- 0 , if the input string is not valid JSON data
- NULL , if the input expression is NULL

The following statement checks whether the input variable is JSON valid:

```
SELECT
  ISJSON ('test'),
  ISJSON (''),
  ISJSON ('{}'),
  ISJSON ('{"a"}'),
  ISJSON ('{"a":1}'),
  ISJSON ('{"a":1"}');
```

Here is the output:

```
------ ------ ------ ------ ------ ------
0      0      1      0      1      0
```

ISJSON does not check the uniqueness of keys at the same level. Therefore, this JSON data is valid:

```
SELECT ISJSON ('{"id":1, "id":"a"}') AS is_json;
```

It returns:

```
is_json
-----------
1
```

Since there is no JSON data type and data must be stored as text, the ISJSON function is important for data validation before the text is saved into a database table. To ensure that a text column stores only JSON- conforming data, you can use the ISJSON function in the check constraint. The following code creates a sample table with a JSON column and an appropriate check constraint:

```
USE WideWorldImporters;
DROP TABLE IF EXISTS dbo.Users;
CREATE TABLE dbo.Users(
id INT IDENTITY(1,1) NOT NULL,
username NVARCHAR(50) NOT NULL,
user_settings NVARCHAR(MAX) NULL CONSTRAINT CK_user_settings CHECK
(ISJSON(user_settings) = 1),
CONSTRAINT PK_Users PRIMARY KEY CLUSTERED (id ASC)
);
```

To test the constraint, you will have to insert two rows in the table. The first INSERT statement contains a well-formatted JSON text, while in the second the value for the last property is omitted; thus the JSON text is invalid. Now, execute the statements:

```
INSERT INTO dbo.Users(username, user_settings) VALUES(N'vasilije', '{"team"
: ["Rapid", "Bayern"], "hobby" : ["soccer", "gaming"], "color" : "green"
}');

INSERT INTO dbo.Users(username, user_settings) VALUES(N'mila', '{"team" :
"Liverpool", "hobby" }');
```

The first statement has been executed successfully, but the second, as expected, generated the following error message:

```
Msg 547, Level 16, State 0, Line 12
The INSERT statement conflicted with the CHECK constraint
"CK_user_settings". The conflict occurred in database "WideWorldImporters",
table "dbo.Users", column 'user_settings'.
The statement has been terminated.
```

Ensure that you have dropped the table used in this exercise:

```
USE WideWorldImporters;
DROP TABLE IF EXISTS dbo.Users;
```

Extracting values from a JSON text

As mentioned earlier in this chapter, JSON has four primitive types (string, number, Boolean, and null) and two complex (structure) types: object and array. SQL Server 2016 offers two functions to extract values from a JSON text:

- JSON_VALUE: This is used to extract values of primitive data types.
- JSON_QUERY: This is used to extract a JSON fragment or to get a complex value (object or array).

JSON_VALUE

The JSON_VALUE function extracts a scalar value from a JSON string. It accepts two input arguments:

- **Expression**: This is JSON text in the Unicode format.
- **Path**: This is an optional argument; it is a JSON path expression and you can use it to specify a fragment of the input expression.

The return type of the function is nvarchar(4000), with the same collation as in the input expression. If the extracted value is longer than 4,000 characters, the function returns NULL provided the path is in lax mode, or an error message in the case of strict mode.

If either the expression or the path is not valid, the JSON_VALUE function returns an error explaining that the JSON text is not properly formatted.

The following example shows the JSON_VALUE function in action. It is used to return values for properties and an array element:

```
DECLARE @json NVARCHAR(MAX) = N'{
"Album":"Wish You Were Here",
"Year":1975,
"IsVinyl":true,
"Members":["Gilmour","Waters","Wright","Mason"]
}';
SELECT
  JSON_VALUE(@json, '$.Album') AS album,
  JSON_VALUE(@json, '$.Year') AS yr,
  JSON_VALUE(@json, '$.IsVinyl') AS isVinyl,
  JSON_VALUE(@json, '$.Members[0]') AS member1;
```

Here is the result of the previous query:

```
album                  yr   isVinyl   member1
------------------    ----  ------    --------
Wish You Were Here    1975  true      Gilmour
```

Note that all returned values are strings; as already mentioned, the data type of the returned value is `nvarchar`.

The aim of the function is to extract scalar values. Therefore, it won't work if the JSON path specifies an array or an object. The following call with the JSON string in the previous example will return a `NULL` value:

```
DECLARE @json NVARCHAR(MAX) = N'{
"Album":"Wish You Were Here",
"Year":1975,
"IsVinyl":true,
"Members":["Gilmour","Waters","Wright","Mason"]
}';
SELECT
  JSON_VALUE(@json, '$.Members') AS member;
```

The JSON path `$.members` specifies an array and the function expects a scalar value. A `NULL` value will be returned even if the property specified with the path expression does not exist. As mentioned earlier, the JSON path expression has two modes: lax and strict. In the default lax mode, errors are suppressed and functions return `NULL` values or empty tables, while every unexpected or non-existing path raises a batch-level exception. The same call with the JSON path in strict mode would end up with an error:

```
SELECT
  JSON_VALUE(@json, 'strict $.Members') AS member;
```

Here is the error message:

```
Msg 13623, Level 16, State 1, Line 75
Scalar value cannot be found in the specified JSON path.
```

If the length of a JSON property value or string element is longer than 4,000, the function returns NULL. The next example demonstrates this by using two very long strings as values for two properties. The first one has 4,000 characters and the second is one character longer:

```
DECLARE @json NVARCHAR(MAX) = CONCAT('{"name":"', REPLICATE('A',4000),
'",}'),
@json4001 NVARCHAR(MAX) = CONCAT('{"name":"', REPLICATE('A',4001), '",}')
SELECT
  JSON_VALUE(@json, '$.name') AS name4000,
  JSON_VALUE(@json4001, '$.name') AS name4001;
```

The abbreviated result is here:

```
Name4000              name4001
-------------------   ---------
AAAAAAAAAAAAAAAA...   NULL
```

You can see that 4001 is too much for JSON_VALUE, and the function returns NULL. If you specify strict in the previous example, the function returns an error:

```
DECLARE @json4001 NVARCHAR(MAX) = CONCAT('{"name":"', REPLICATE('A',4001),
'",}')
SELECT
  JSON_VALUE(@json4001, ' strict $.name') AS name4001;
```

Here is the error message:

```
Msg 13625, Level 16, State 1, Line 65
String value in the specified JSON path would be truncated.
```

This is a typical change in function behavior regarding the JSON path mode. Lax mode usually returns NULL and does not break the code, while strict mode raises a batch-level exception.

JSON_VALUE can be used in SELECT, WHERE, and ORDER clauses. In the following example, it is used in all three clauses:

```
SELECT
  PersonID,
  JSON_VALUE(UserPreferences, '$.timeZone') AS TimeZone,
  JSON_VALUE(UserPreferences, '$.table.pageLength') AS PageLength
FROM Application.People
WHERE JSON_VALUE(UserPreferences, '$.dateFormat') = 'yy-mm-dd'
  AND JSON_VALUE(UserPreferences, '$.theme') = 'blitzer'
ORDER BY JSON_VALUE(UserPreferences, '$.theme'), PersonID;
```

One important limitation of the `JSON_VALUE` function in SQL Server 2016 is that a variable as a second argument (JSON path) is not allowed. For instance, the following code won't work in SQL Server 2016:

```
DECLARE @jsonPath NVARCHAR(10) = N'$.Album';
DECLARE @json NVARCHAR(200) = N'{
"Album":"Wish You Were Here",
"Year":1975
}';
SELECT
  JSON_VALUE(@json, @jsonPath) AS album;
```

The query fails with the following error message:

```
Msg 13610, Level 16, State 1, Line 137
The argument 2 of the "JSON_VALUE or JSON_QUERY" must be a string literal
```

This was a significant limitation; you had to provide JSON path as a static value in advance and you cannot add or change it dynamically. Fortunately, this limitation has been removed in SQL Server 2017, and the preceding code in SQL Server 2017 provides the following result:

```
album
------------------
Wish You Were Here
```

 You can use variables for both arguments of the `JSON_VALUE` function in SQL Server 2017 even if the database is still in compatibility mode 130 (which corresponds to SQL Server 2016).

There are not many differences between JSON implementations in SQL Server 2016 and 2017; this is the most important one.

JSON_QUERY

The `JSON_QUERY` function extracts a JSON fragment from the input JSON string for the specified JSON path. It returns a JSON object or an array; therefore, its output is JSON conforming. This function is complementary to the `JSON_VALUE` function.

JSON_QUERY always returns JSON conforming text. Thus, if you want to suggest to SQL Server that the string is JSON formatted, you should wrap it with this function.

The function has two input arguments:

- **Expression**: This is a variable or column containing JSON text.
- **Path**: This is a JSON path that specifies the object or the array to extract. This parameter is optional. If it's not specified, the whole input string will be returned.

The return type of the function is nvarchar(max) if the input string is defined as (n)varchar(max); otherwise, it is nvarchar(4000). As already mentioned, the function always returns a JSON conforming string.

If either the expression or the path is not valid, JSON_QUERY returns an error message saying that the JSON text or JSON path is not properly formatted.

In the following self-explanatory examples, how to use this function with different JSON path expressions is demonstrated:

```
DECLARE @json NVARCHAR(MAX) = N'{
"Album":"Wish You Were Here",
"Year":1975,
"IsVinyl":true,
"Songs" :[{"Title":"Shine On You Crazy Diamond","Writers":"Gilmour, Waters,
Wright"},
{"Title":"Have a Cigar","Writers":"Waters"},
{"Title":"Welcome to the Machine","Writers":"Waters"},
{"Title":"Wish You Were Here","Writers":"Gilmour, Waters"}],
"Members":{"Guitar":"David Gilmour","Bass Guitar":"Roger
Waters","Keyboard":"Richard Wright","Drums":"Nick Mason"}
}';
--get Songs JSON fragment (array)
SELECT JSON_QUERY(@json,'$.Songs');
--get Members SON fragment (object)
SELECT JSON_QUERY(@json,'$.Members');
--get fourth Song JSON fragment (object)
SELECT JSON_QUERY(@json,'$.Songs[3]');
```

Here is the result of these invocations:

```
[{"Title":"Shine On You Crazy Diamond","Writers":"Gilmour, Waters,
   Wright"},
{"Title":"Have a Cigar","Writers":"Waters"},
{"Title":"Welcome to the Machine","Writers":"Waters"},
{"Title":"Wish You Were Here","Writers":"Gilmour, Waters"}]
{"Guitar":"David Gilmour","Bass Guitar":"Roger
```

```
Waters","Keyboard":"Richard Wright","Drums":"Nick Mason"}
{"Title":"Wish You Were Here","Writers":"Gilmour, Waters"}
```

You can see that the returned values are JSON objects and arrays. However, if you specify a value that is not an array or object, the function returns NULL in lax mode and an error in strict mode:

```
--get property value (number)
SELECT JSON_QUERY(@json,'$.Year');
--get property value (string)
SELECT JSON_QUERY(@json,'$.Songs[1].Title');
--get value for non-existing property
SELECT JSON_QUERY(@json,'$.Studios');
```

All three calls return NULL, whereas strict mode raises a batch-level exception:

```
SELECT JSON_QUERY(@json,'strict $.Year');
/*Result:
Msg 13624, Level 16, State 1, Line 54
Object or array cannot be found in the specified JSON path.
*/
--get value for non-existing property
SELECT JSON_QUERY(@json,'strict $.Studios');
/*Result:
Msg 13608, Level 16, State 5, Line 60
Property cannot be found on the specified JSON path
*/
```

You can also use JSON_QUERY to ensure data integrity of JSON data in a table column. For instance, the following check constraint ensures that all persons in the People table have the OtherLanguages property within the CustomFields column if this column has a value:

```
USE WideWorldImporters;
ALTER TABLE Application.People
ADD CONSTRAINT CHK_OtherLanguagesRequired
CHECK (JSON_QUERY(CustomFields, '$.OtherLanguages') IS NOT NULL OR
CustomFields IS NULL);
```

The JSON_QUERY function has the same restrictions in SQL Server 2016 for the path argument as JSON_VALUE; only literals are allowed. In SQL Server 2017 you can use variables too.

Modifying JSON data

You might sometimes need to update only a part of JSON data. In SQL Server 2016, you can modify JSON data using the JSON_MODIFY function. It allows you to:

- Update the value of an existing property
- Add a new element to an existing array
- Insert a new property and its value
- Delete a property based on a combination of modes and provided values

The function accepts three mandatory input arguments:

- **Expression**: This is a variable or column name containing JSON text.
- **Path**: This is the JSON path expression with an optional modifier append.
- **new_value**: This is the new value for the property specified in the path expression.

The JSON_MODIFY function returns the updated JSON string. In the next subsections, you will see this function in action.

Adding a new JSON property

In the following code example, you add a new property named IsVinyl with the value true:

```
DECLARE @json NVARCHAR(MAX) = N'{
"Album":"Wish You Were Here",
"Year":1975
}';
PRINT JSON_MODIFY(@json, '$.IsVinyl', CAST(1 AS BIT));
```

You need to cast the value explicitly to the BIT data type; otherwise it will be surrounded by double quotes and interpreted as a string. Here is the result of the modification:

```
{
"Album":"Wish You Were Here",
"Year":1975,
"IsVinyl":true
}
```

Note that the JSON path expression is in default lax mode. By specifying strict mode, the function will return an error:

```
DECLARE @json NVARCHAR(MAX) = N'{
"Album":"Wish You Were Here",
"Year":1975
}';
PRINT JSON_MODIFY(@json, 'strict $.IsVinyl', CAST(1 AS BIT));
```

Strict mode always expects the property specified with the JSON path expression to exist. If it does not exist, it returns the following error message:

```
Msg 13608, Level 16, State 2, Line 34
Property cannot be found on the specified JSON path.
```

Be aware when you add a value that it is already JSON formatted. In the next example, assume you want to add a new property named Members and you have already prepared the whole JSON array:

```
DECLARE @json NVARCHAR(MAX) = N'{
"Album":"Wish You Were Here",
"Year":1975,
"IsVinyl":true
}';
DECLARE @members NVARCHAR(500) = N'["Gilmour","Waters","Wright","Mason"]';
PRINT JSON_MODIFY(@json, '$.Members', @members);
```

A new Members property has been added to the input JSON data, but our JSON conform value has been interpreted as text and therefore all special characters are escaped. Here is the modified input string:

```
{
"Album":"Wish You Were Here",
"Year":1975,
"IsVinyl":true,
"Members":"["Gilmour","Waters","Wright","Mason"]"
}
```

To avoid the escaping of JSON conforming text, you need to tell the function that the text is already JSON and escaping should not be performed. You can achieve this by wrapping the new value with the JSON_QUERY function:

```
DECLARE @json NVARCHAR(MAX) = N'{
"Album":"Wish You Were Here",
"Year":1975,
"IsVinyl":true
}';
```

```
DECLARE @members NVARCHAR(500) = N'["Gilmour","Waters","Wright","Mason"]';
PRINT JSON_MODIFY(@json, '$.Members', JSON_QUERY(@members));
```

As mentioned in the previous section, the JSON_QUERY function returns JSON conforming text and now SQL Server knows that escaping is not required. Here is the expected result:

```
{
"Album":"Wish You Were Here",
"Year":1975,
"IsVinyl":true,
"Members":["Gilmour","Waters","Wright","Mason"]
}
```

This is a drawback of the missing JSON data type. If you had it, it wouldn't be necessary to use JSON_QUERY and SQL Server would distinguish between JSON and string.

Updating the value for a JSON property

In the next examples, you will update the value of an existing property. You will start by updating the Year property from 1973 to 1975. Here is the code:

```
DECLARE @json NVARCHAR(MAX) = N'{
"Album":"Wish You Were Here",
"Year":1973
}';
PRINT JSON_MODIFY(@json, '$.Year', 1975);
PRINT JSON_MODIFY(@json, 'strict $.Year', 1975);
```

You invoked the function twice to demonstrate using both JSON path modes: lax and strict. Here are the output strings:

```
{
"Album":"Wish You Were Here",
"Year":1975
}
{
"Album":"Wish You Were Here",
"Year":1975
}
```

You can see that there is no difference between lax and strict mode if the property specified with the path exists.

The following example demonstrates how to update a value of an array element within a JSON text. Assume you want to replace the first element of the Members array (Gilmour) with the value (Barrett):

```
DECLARE @json NVARCHAR(MAX) = N'{
"Album":"Wish You Were Here",
"Year":1975,
"Members":["Gilmour","Waters","Wright","Mason"]
}';
PRINT JSON_MODIFY(@json, '$.Members[0]', 'Barrett');
```

Here is the expected result:

```
{
"Album":"Wish You Were Here",
"Year":1975,
"Members":["Barrett","Waters","Wright","Mason"]
}
```

If you want to add a new element to an array, you have to use append. In the following example, you simply add another element in the Members array:

```
DECLARE @json NVARCHAR(MAX) = N'{
"Album":"Wish You Were Here",
"Year":1975,
"Members":["Gilmour","Waters","Wright","Mason"]
}';
PRINT JSON_MODIFY(@json, 'append $.Members', 'Barrett');
```

Here is the result:

```
{
"Album":"Wish You Were Here",
"Year":1975,
"Members":["Gilmour","Waters","Wright","Mason","Barrett"]
}
```

If you specify an index that is out of range or if the array does not exist, you will get:

- **Strict mode**: This shows an error message and no return value (batch-level exception).
- **Lax mode**: This shows no error; the original input string is returned.

To update a value of a JSON property to NULL, you have to use a JSON path in strict mode. Use the following code to update the Year property from the input JSON string to a NULL value:

```
DECLARE @json NVARCHAR(MAX) = N'{
"Album":"Wish You Were Here",
"Year":1975,
"Members":["Gilmour","Waters","Wright","Mason"]
}';
PRINT JSON_MODIFY(@json, 'strict $.Year', NULL);
```

Here is the output.

```
{
"Album":"Wish You Were Here",
"Year":null,
"Members":["Gilmour","Waters","Wright","Mason"]
}
```

Removing a JSON property

To remove a property from the input JSON string, you have to use a JSON path expression in lax mode. You will repeat the preceding code, but this time in lax mode:

```
DECLARE @json NVARCHAR(MAX) = N'{
"Album":"Wish You Were Here",
"Year":1975,
"Members":["Gilmour","Waters","Wright","Mason"]
}';
PRINT JSON_MODIFY(@json, '$.Year', NULL);
```

When you observe the result of this action, you can see that the Year property does not exist anymore:

```
{
"Album":"Wish You Were Here",
"Members":["Gilmour","Waters","Wright","Mason"]
}
```

By taking this approach, you can remove only properties and their values. You cannot remove an array element. The following code will not remove the Waters element from the JSON array property Members; it will actually update it to NULL:

```
DECLARE @json NVARCHAR(MAX) = N'{
"Album":"Wish You Were Here",
```

```
"Year":1975,
"Members":["Gilmour","Waters","Wright","Mason"]
}';
PRINT JSON_MODIFY(@json, '$.Members[1]', NULL);
```

The result is as follows:

```
{
"Album":"Wish You Were Here",
"Year":1975,
"Members":["Gilmour",null,"Wright","Mason"]
}
```

If you want to remove the Waters element, you can use the following code:

```
DECLARE @json NVARCHAR(MAX) = N'{
"Album":"Wish You Were Here",
"Year":1975,
"Members":["Gilmour","Waters","Wright","Mason"]
}';
PRINT JSON_MODIFY(@json, '$.Members',
JSON_QUERY('["Gilmour","Wright","Mason"]'));
```

And finally, the expected result:

```
{
"Album":"Wish You Were Here",
"Year":1975,
"Members":["Gilmour","Wright","Mason"]
}
```

Multiple changes

You can change only one property at a time; for multiple changes you need multiple calls. In this example, you want to update the IsVinyl property to false, add a new property Recorded, and add another element called Barrett to the Members property:

```
DECLARE @json NVARCHAR(MAX) = N'{
"Album":"Wish You Were Here",
"Year":1975,
"IsVinyl":true,
"Members":["Gilmour","Waters","Wright","Mason"]
}';
PRINT JSON_MODIFY(JSON_MODIFY(JSON_MODIFY(@json, '$.IsVinyl', CAST(0 AS
BIT)), '$.Recorded', 'Abbey Road Studios'), 'append $.Members', 'Barrett');
```

Here is the output:

```
{
"Album":"Wish You Were Here",
"Year":1975,
"IsVinyl":false,
"Members":["Gilmour","Waters","Wright","Mason","Barrett"],
"Recorded":"Abbey Road Studios"
}
```

Performance considerations

One of the main concerns about JSON in SQL Server 2016 is performance. As mentioned, unlike XML, JSON is not fully supported; there is no JSON data type. Data in XML columns is stored as **binary large objects** (**BLOBs**). SQL Server supports two types of XML indexes that avoid parsing all the data at runtime to evaluate a query and allow efficient query processing. Without an index, these BLOBs are shredded at runtime to evaluate a query. As mentioned several times, there is no JSON data type; JSON is stored as simple Unicode text and the text has to be interpreted at runtime to evaluate a JSON query. This can lead to slow reading and writing performance for large JSON documents. The primary XML index indexes all tags, values, and paths within the XML instances in an XML column. The primary XML index is a shredded and persisted representation of the XML BLOBs in the XML data type column. For each XML **BLOB** in the column, the index creates several rows of data. The number of rows in the index is approximately equal to the number of nodes in the XML BLOB.

Since JSON is stored as text, it will always be interpreted. On JSON columns that are not larger than 1,700 bytes, you could create a non-clustered index, or use them as an included column without the limit.

Without a dedicated data type and storage, performance and options for JSON query improvements in SQL Server 2016 are limited: you can use computed columns and create indexes on them, or use the benefits of full-text indexes. However, you can expect performance problems during the processing of large amounts of JSON data in SQL Server 2016.

Indexes on computed columns

The following code example creates a sample table with a JSON column and populates it with values from the `Application.People` table:

```
USE WideWorldImporters;
DROP TABLE IF EXISTS dbo.T1;
CREATE TABLE dbo.T1(
id INT NOT NULL,
info NVARCHAR(2000) NOT NULL,
CONSTRAINT PK_T1 PRIMARY KEY CLUSTERED(id)
);

INSERT INTO dbo.T1(id, info)
SELECT PersonID, info FROM Application.People t1
CROSS APPLY(
  SELECT (
    SELECT t2.FullName, t2.EmailAddress, t2.PhoneNumber,       t2.FaxNumber
FROM Application.People t2 WHERE t2.PersonID = t1.PersonID FOR      JSON
AUTO, WITHOUT_ARRAY_WRAPPER
  ) info
  ) x
```

Assume you want to return rows that have the `Vilma Niva` value for the `FullName` property. Since this is a scalar value, you can use the `JSON_VALUE` function. Before you execute the code, ensure that the actual execution plan will be displayed as well (on the **Query** menu, click on **Include Actual Execution Plan**, or click on the **Include Actual Execution Plan** toolbar button). Now execute the following code:

```
SELECT id, info
FROM dbo.T1
WHERE JSON_VALUE(info,'$.FullName') = 'Vilma Niva';
```

The execution plan for the query is shown in the following screenshot:

```
Query 1: Query cost (relative to the batch): 100%
SELECT id, info FROM dbo.T1 WHERE JSON_VALUE(info,'$.FullName')='Vilma Niva'
```

SELECT
Cost: 0 %

Clustered Index Scan (Clustered)
[T1].[PK_T1]
Cost: 100 %

Execution plan without computed columns

The plan shows that a `Clustered Index Scan` was performed; SQL Server was not able to search for full names within the JSON column in an efficient manner.

To improve the performance of the query, you can create a computed column by using the same expression as in its `WHERE` clause and then using a non-clustered index on it:

```
ALTER TABLE dbo.T1 ADD FullName AS  JSON_VALUE(info, '$.FullName');
CREATE INDEX IX1 ON dbo.T1(FullName);
```

When you execute the same query again, the execution plan is changed:

```
SELECT id, info
FROM dbo.T1
WHERE JSON_VALUE(info,'$.FullName') = 'Vilma Niva';
```

A newly created index is used and the plan is more efficient, as shown in the following screenshot:

Execution plan using the index on the computed column

Of course, this will work only for a particular JSON path, in this case for the `FullName` property only. For the other properties, you would need to create additional computed columns and indexes on them. In the case of XML indexes, all nodes and values are covered; they are not related to particular values.

An important feature of JSON indexes is that they are collation-aware. The result of the `JSON_VALUE` function is a text value that inherits its collation from the input expression. Therefore, values in the index are ordered using the collation rules defined in the source columns.

By using indexes on computed columns, you can improve performance for frequently used queries.

Full-text indexes

One of the advantages of the fact that JSON data is stored as text in SQL Server is that you can use full-text search features. With computed columns, as demonstrated in the previous section, you can index only one property. To index all JSON properties (actually, to simulate this) you can use full-text indexes.

To demonstrate how full-text searching can improve JSON query performance, you first create a full-text catalog and index it in the sample table that you created earlier in this section:

```
USE WideWorldImporters;
CREATE FULLTEXT CATALOG ftc AS DEFAULT;
CREATE FULLTEXT INDEX ON dbo.T1(info) KEY INDEX PK_T1 ON ftc;
```

Now, after you have created a full-text index, you can execute JSON queries to check whether they can use full-text index benefits. You need to use the CONTAINS predicate; it can identify rows where a word is near another word. Here is the query:

```
SELECT id, info
FROM dbo.T1
WHERE CONTAINS(info, 'NEAR(FullName, "Vilma")');
```

The execution plan for the query shown in the following screenshot clearly demonstrates that a full-text index was helpful for this query:

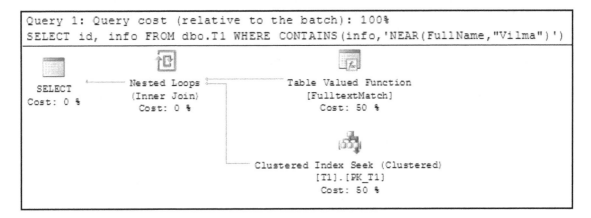

Execution plan with full-text index on the FullName property

To ensure that the same index can improve performance for JSON queries searching the other JSON properties and not only `FullName` (as in the case of the index on the computed column), let's execute another query that searches the `PhoneNumber` property:

```
SELECT id, info
FROM dbo.T1
WHERE CONTAINS(info,'NEAR(PhoneNumber,"(209) 555-0103")');
```

The execution plan is the same as for the previous query, as you can see in the following screenshot:

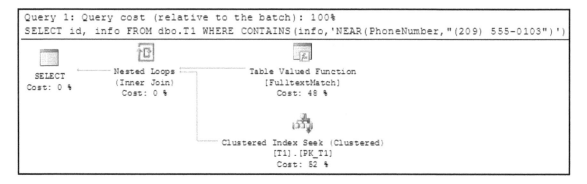

Query 1: Query cost (relative to the batch): 100%
SELECT id, info FROM dbo.T1 WHERE CONTAINS(info,'NEAR(PhoneNumber,"(209) 555-0103")')

Execution plan with full-text index on the PhoneNumber property

The same index covers both queries. Unfortunately, JSON path expressions are not supported in the `CONTAINS` predicate; you can only search for property values, but it is better than scanning the whole table.

You can store and process small and moderate amounts of JSON data within SQL Server with good support of JSON functions and acceptable performance. However, if your JSON documents are large and you need to search them extensively, you should use a NoSQL solution, such as DocumentDB.

Ensure that you have dropped the table used in this exercise:

```
USE WideWorldImporters;
DROP TABLE IF EXISTS dbo.T1;
```

Summary

This chapter explored JSON support in SQL Server 2017. It is not as robust and deep as XML—there is no native data type, and no optimized storage, and therefore you cannot create JSON indexes to improve performance. Thus, we are talking about built-in and not native JSON support.

However, even with built-in support, it is easy and handy to integrate JSON data in SQL Server. For most of JSON data processing, it would be acceptable. For large JSON documents stored in large database tables, it would be more appropriate to use DocumentDB or other NoSQL based solutions.

In this chapter, you learned that SQL Server 2017 brings built-in support for JSON data; unlike XML, there is no native data type. You used the FOR JSON extension to generate JSON from data in a tabular format and converted JSON data into a tabular format by using the OPENJSON rowset function. You learned how to parse, query, and modify JSON data with a function and how to improve the performance of JSON data processing by using indexes on computed columns and full-text indexes. You also discovered the limitations of JSON implementation in SQL Server 2017.

In the next chapter, you will meet another promising SQL Server feature—*Stretch Databases*.

6
Stretch Database

Stretch Database (**Stretch DB**) is a feature introduced in SQL Server 2016 that allows you to move data or a portion of data transparently and securely from your local database to the cloud (Microsoft Azure). All you need to do is mark the tables that you want to migrate, and the data movement is done transparently and securely. The intention of this feature is to let companies store their old or infrequently used data on the cloud. Companies need to store data locally and operate with active data only, thus reducing the cost and using their resources more effectively. This feature is great and very promising, but there are many limitations that reduce its usability.

In this chapter, we will cover the following points:

- Stretch DB architecture
- How to enable Stretch DB
- How to select tables or part of tables for migration
- Managing and troubleshooting Stretch DB
- Under what circumstances should you use Stretch DB

Stretch DB architecture

When you enable `Stretch Database` for an on-premise SQL Server 2017 database, SQL Server automatically creates a new stretch database in MS Azure SQL Database as an external source and a remote endpoint for the database.

When you query the database, the SQL Server's database engine runs the query against the local or remote database, depending on the data location. Queries against stretch-enabled tables return both local and remote data by default. This is completely transparent to the database user. This means that you can use `Stretch Database` without changing Transact-SQL code in your queries, procedures, or applications. You can stretch an entire table or a portion of table data. The data migration is done asynchronously and transparently. In addition, Stretch Database ensures that no data is lost if a failure occurs during migration. It also has retry logic to handle connection issues that may occur during migration. The following figure illustrates the `Stretch Database` architecture:

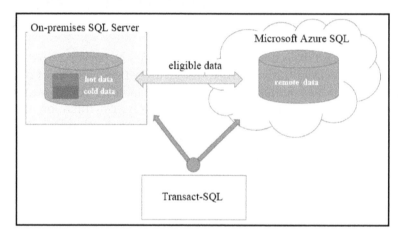

Stretch DB architecture

Data can be located in three stages:

- **Local data**: Local data is data in the table that remains in the on-premise instance. This is usually frequently used or hot data.
- **Staging (eligible data)**: Eligible data is data marked for migration but not migrated yet.
- **Remote data**: Remote data is data that has already been migrated. This data resides in Microsoft Azure SQL Database and is rarely used.

`Stretch Database` does not support stretching to another SQL Server instance. You can stretch a SQL Server database only to Azure SQL Database.

Is this for you?

When SQL Server 2016 RTM was released, there was the tool *Stretch Database Advisor*. This tool could be used to identify databases and tables that were candidates for the `Stretch DB` feature. It was a component of the *SQL Server 2016 Upgrade Advisor*, and by using it, you were also able to identify constraints and blocking issues that prevented the use of the feature.

However, this tool has been removed and replaced by the *Microsoft Data Migration Assistant*. But why I am mentioning this deprecated tool? The *Stretch Database Advisor* checked all tables in the database and creates a report showing the stretching capabilities of each table. I have used it to check which tables in the Microsoft sample SQL Server database `AdventureWorks` are ready for stretching. The results was very disappointing: there was no single table from the Microsoft official SQL Server sample database that this tool marked as recommended and ready for stretching! However, as you will see later in this chapter, this feature is not designed for all tables; it is for special ones.

Data Migration Assistant does not have a separate functionality for `Stretch DB` advises. It analyzes your database and helps you to upgrade it to a new SQL Server version or to Azure SQL Database by detecting compatibility issues that can impact database functionality on your new database version. It also recommends performance and reliability improvements for your target environment. In the Data Migration Assistant, `Stretch DB` is only one of the storage improvements. You can download Data Migration Assistant v3.4 from `https://www.microsoft.com/en-us/download/details.aspx?id=53595`.

Using Data Migration Assistant

In this section, you will use the *Data Migration Assistant* to see what you should expect for your databases when you migrate them to SQL Server 2017 or Azure SQL Database. This is a standalone program and you can run it by executing the `Dma.exe` file in the default install directory `C:\Program FilesMicrosoft Data Migration Assistant`. When you start the tool, you should see an intro screen, as shown in the following screenshot:

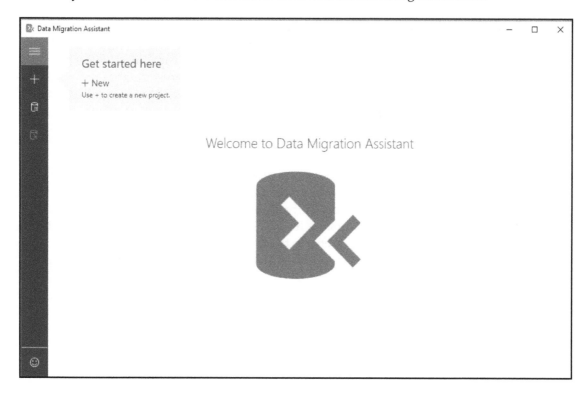

Data Migration Assistant introduction screen

To start a project, you need to click on the + symbol and the new project form appears. On the new project screen, choose **Assessment** as **Project type**, type AdvWorksStretchDB in the **Project name** field, and choose **SQL Server** as **Target server type** (**Source server type** is preselected to **SQL Server**), as displayed here:

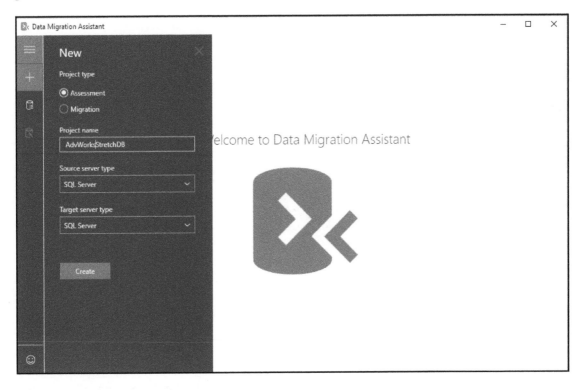

Data Migration Assistant—New Project

After you are done, click on the **Create** button and you will see the next screen, similar to the one shown in the following screenshot:

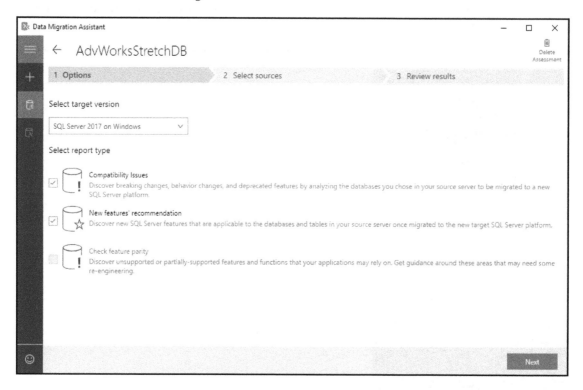

Data Migration Assistant—Select target version

On this screen, you can choose the target SQL Server version. In the dropdown, all versions from 2012 are available; you should, of course, choose **SQL Server 2017 on Windows**. In addition to this, you can select the report type. This time you will choose **New features' recommendation** since you want to see which new features *Data Migration Assistant* recommends to you and not potential compatibility issues.

You then need to click on the **Next** button, connect to a SQL Server 2014 instance, and select the desired databases. In this example, I have selected the Microsoft former standard sample databases AdventureWorks and AdventureWorksDW that I have restored. If you don't have these two databases, you can choose any other database, but you will most probably end up with different results.

After you have established the connection with the SQL Server 2014 instance, you need to choose the databases that should be analyzed by *Data Migration Assistant*. As mentioned, choose the `AdventureWorks2014` and `AdventureWorksDW2014`databases. You should see a screen like the following one:

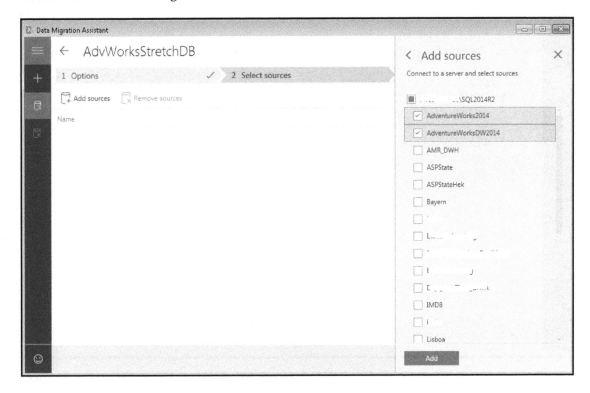

Data Migration Assistant - choose databases for analyzing

When you click the **Add** button, the selected databases are added to the sources collection. You'll get another screen, where you can start the assessment by clicking on the **Start Assessment** button:

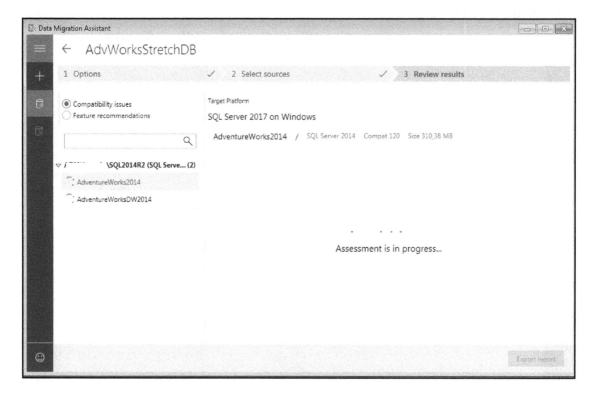

Data Migration Assistant—Start Assessment

The analysis takes less than a minute, and the next figure shows its results for the `AdventureWorks2014` database:

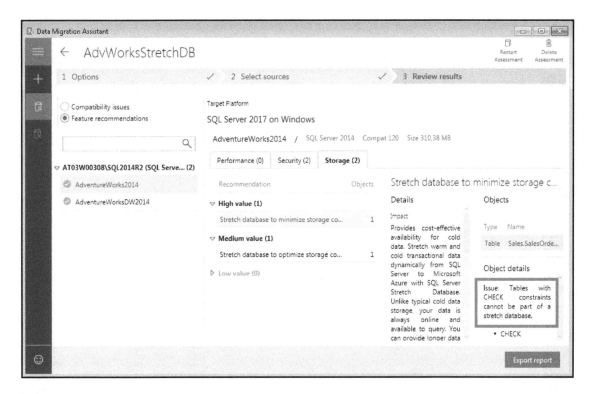

Data Migration Assistant—Review results for the AdventureWorks2014 database

On the left radio-buttons, you need to choose the *Feature recommendations* option. `Stretch DB`-related recommendations are located under the **Storage** tab. In the case of the `AdventureWorks2014` database, two tables are listed as tables that would benefit from using the `Stretch DB` feature: `Sales.SalesOrderDetail` and `Production.TransactionHistory`.

However, both of them have properties that prevent the use of the `Stretch DB`, so you can conclude that this feature is irrelevant for the `AdventureWorks2014` database. The result of the analysis for the `AdventureWorksDW2014` looks a bit better, as shown in the following screenshot:

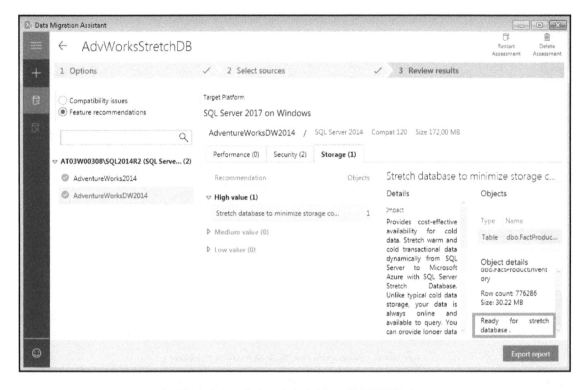

Data Migration Assistant—Review results for the AdventureWorksDW2014 database

Data Migration Assistant has found one table (`dbo.FactProductInventory`) that is ready to use the `Stretch DB` feature. It does not mention the other tables in the report—just three tables from two selected databases. At this point, I need to mention again that although this sample databases have a few very simple tables, with just a few rows, even for them you cannot use the `Stretch DB` feature. In data warehouse databases, tables seem to be more stretch-friendly, but according the tool, it is very hard to find a table that qualifies for stretching.

`Stretch Database` will give you benefits with your data warehouse databases, especially with historical data that is taking up space and is rarely used. On the other hand, this feature might not be eligible for your OLTP system due to the table limitations that your OLTP system has. Now, it is finally time to see in detail what these limitations are.

Limitations of using Stretch Database

As you saw in the previous section, there are many limitations when you work with Stretch Database. You can distinguish between limitations that the prevent usage of Stretch Database and limitations in database tables that are enabled for stretching.

Limitations that prevent you from enabling the Stretch DB features for a table

In this section, you will see the limitations that prevent you from using Stretch DB. They can be divided into table, column, and index limitations.

Table limitations

You cannot enable the `Stretch DB` feature for any SQL Server table. A table should have stretch-friendly properties. The following list shows the table properties that prevent the use of the `Stretch DB` feature:

- It is a memory-optimized table
- It is a file table
- It contains `FILESTREAM` data
- It uses `Change Data Capture` or `Change Tracking` features
- It has more than 1,023 columns or more than 998 indexes
- Tables referenced with a foreign key
- It is referenced by indexed views
- It contains full-text indexes

The list is not so short, but let's see how huge these limitations are in practice. Despite their power and a completely new technology stack behind them, memory-optimized tables are still not in use intensively. From my experience, I can say that most companies still don't use memory-optimized tables in production environments due to the lack of use cases for them, hardware resources, or even the knowledge required for their implementation and configuration. In addition to this, memory-optimized tables usually store hot data, data that is frequently needed and whose content is not intended to be sent to the cloud. Therefore, you cannot say that the first limitation is a huge one. You will spend more time on memory-optimized tables later in this book (in `Chapter 11`, *Introducing SQL Server In-Memory OLTP* and `Chapter 12`, *In-Memory OLTP Improvements in SQL Server 2016*).

`File Table` and `FILESTREAM` tables appear frequently in the list of limitations for new SQL Server features. The same is true for tables using `Change Data Capture` or `Change Tracking` features. They are simply not compatible with many other features since they address specific use cases. Therefore, I am not surprised to see them in this list. Full-text indexes and indexed views also prevent Stretch DB usage. From my experience, in companies that I have worked with or where I was involved as a consultant, less than 10% of tables belong to these categories. According to all of these limitations, I would say that the potential of Stretch DB is slightly reduced, but not significantly. However, the most important limitation is that a table cannot be referenced with a foreign key. This is an implementation of database integrity and many tables are and should be referenced with foreign keys. Therefore, this is a serious limitation for Stretch DB usage and significantly reduces the number of potential tables that can be stretched.

 You should not disable foreign key relationships in order to use the Stretch DB feature! I would never suggest removing any database object or attribute that implements data integrity to gain performance or storage benefits.

However, this is just the beginning; more limitations will come in the next subsection.

Column limitations

Even if your table does not violate constraints from the preceding table of limitations, it is still far away from fulfilling the conditions for stretching. The following properties and characteristics of table columns don't support the Stretch DB feature:

- Unsupported data types: Deprecated large data types (`text`, `ntext`, and `image`), XML, `timestamp`, `sql_variant`, spatial data types (geometry and geography), `hierarchyId`, user-defined CLR data types
- Computed columns
- Default constraints
- Check constraints

Let's repeat a similar analysis of the reduced potential of `Stretch DB` for the items from this list. I think that Microsoft has a balanced approach with deprecated data types; they are not removed in order to prevent the breaking of changes in legacy code, but all new features don't support them. This is completely correct and it should not be considered a limitation.

The other unsupported data types are used rarely and do not represent a huge limitation.

 You can find user-defined CLR data types in a list of limitations for almost all SQL Server features in recent releases. This is also one of the reasons they are not so popular or frequently used.

However, the most important limitation in this list is that a table column in a Stretch Database cannot have a default or check constraint. This is a huge limitation and significantly reduces the usage and importance of the Stretch DB feature!

Also, as mentioned before, you should not remove database objects created to implement database integrity just to enable Stretch DB. Default constraints and foreign keys are the reasons why there is not a single table in the `AdventureWorks2014` database that is ready for stretching.

Limitations for Stretch-enabled tables

If your table survives these limitations and you have enabled it for stretching, you should be aware of these additional constraints:

- Uniqueness is not enforced for UNIQUE constraints and PRIMARY KEY constraints in the Azure table that contains the migrated data.
- You cannot UPDATE or DELETE rows that have been migrated or rows that are eligible for migration in a Stretch-enabled table or in a view that includes Stretch-enabled tables.
- You cannot INSERT rows into a Stretch-enabled table on a linked server.
- You cannot create an index for a view that includes Stretch-enabled tables.
- Filters on SQL Server indexes are not propagated to the remote table.

These limitations are not unexpected; the Azure portion of data is automatically managed and it should be protected from direct access and changes. Therefore, these limitations are acceptable, especially compared to all those listed in the previous sections.

Use cases for Stretch Database

With so many limitations, finding use cases for `Stretch DB` does not seem to be an easy task. You would need tables without constraints and rare data types that are not involved in relations with other tables and that don't use some special SQL Server features. Where to find them? As potential candidates for stretching, you should consider historical or auditing and logging tables.

Archiving of historical data

Historical or auditing data is commonly produced automatically by database systems and does not require constraints to guarantee data integrity. In addition to this, it is usually in large data sets. Therefore, historical and auditing data can be a candidate for using the `Stretch DB` feature. SQL Server 2016 introduced support for system-versioned temporal tables. They are implemented as a pair of tables: a current and a historical table. One of the requirements for historical tables is that they cannot have any constraints. Therefore, historical tables used in system-versioned temporal tables are ideal candidates for stretching. Temporal tables are covered in `Chapter 7`, *Temporal Tables*.

Archiving of logging tables

Sometimes, developers decide to store application and service logging information in database tables. Such tables usually have no constraints, since writing to log must be as fast as possible. They are also possible candidates for using the `Stretch DB` feature.

Testing Azure SQL database

Small or medium companies that are considering whether to use the cloud or to move data completely to it can use `Stretch DB` to start using Azure SQL database. They can learn about data management in Azure and collect experience and then decide whether they need to delegate more or their entire data to the cloud.

Enabling Stretch Database

Before you select tables for stretching, you need to enable the feature at the instance level. Like many other new features, it is disabled by default. To enable it, you need to execute the following statements:

```
EXEC sys.sp_configure N'remote data archive', '1';
RECONFIGURE;
GO
```

Actually, you have to allow remote data archiving; there is no enabling Stretch Database option. Anyway, after enabling it at an instance level, you can choose a database and enable the feature at the database level.

Enabling Stretch Database at the database level

If the feature is enabled at the instance level and you have enough database permissions (db_owner or CONTROL DATABASE), the next step is to enable Stretch DB at the database level. Of course, before you enable it, you need to have a valid Azure account and subscription. You also need to create and configure firewall rules to allow your Azure database to communicate with your local server. In this section, you will enable the Stretch DB feature for a new database. Use this code to create a database named Mila:

```
DROP DATABASE IF EXISTS Mila; --Ensure that you create a new, empty
database
GO
CREATE DATABASE Mila;
GO
```

Since the database is new and has no tables, it does not violate the limitations listed in the previous section. You can enable the Stretch Database feature at the database level by using wizard or with Transact-SQL.

Enabling Stretch Database by using wizard

You can use the **Enable Database for Stretch** wizard to configure a database for Stretch Database. To launch it, you need to right-click on the newly created Mila database in **SQL Server Management Studio** (**SSMS**), and from the right-click context menu, select **Tasks** | **Stretch** | **Enable** respectively. When you launch the wizard, you should get the following screen:

Enable Database for Search Wizard—Introduction page

You can see an intro screen that describes what you can achieve with the Stretch Database feature and what you need to use them. Since your database has no tables, the second section of the wizard is **Configure Azure**. You are asked to enter your Azure credentials and to connect to Azure:

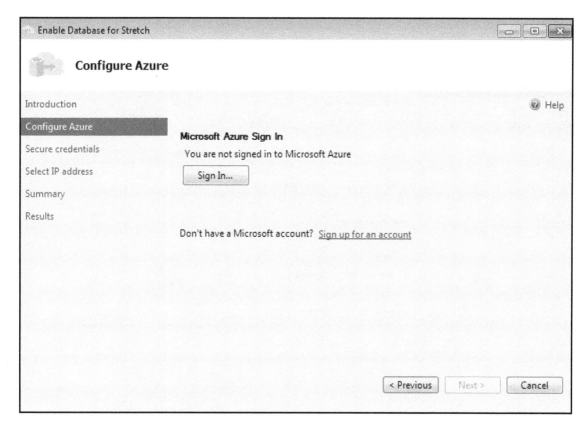

Enable Database for Search Wizard—Configure Azure page

After signing in to Azure, you should select one of your Azure subscriptions and an appropriate Azure region. Create a new or choose an existing Azure server, as follows:

Enable Database for Search Wizard—Sign in to Azure and select subscription and server

The next part of the wizard is **Secure credentials**. The wizard lets you create a database master key (if your database does not have one) in order to protect the database credentials and connection information stored in your SQL Server database. Database security is covered in detail in Chapter 8, *Tightening the Security*. Here is the screen where you can create a database master key:

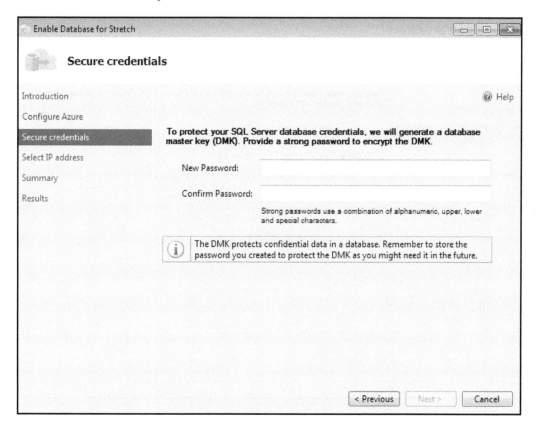

Enable Database for Search Wizard—Secure credentials

As already mentioned, you need to create Azure firewall rules to let your Azure SQL database communicate with your local SQL Server database. You can define a range of IP addresses with the **Enable Database for Stretch** wizard's page **Select IP address**:

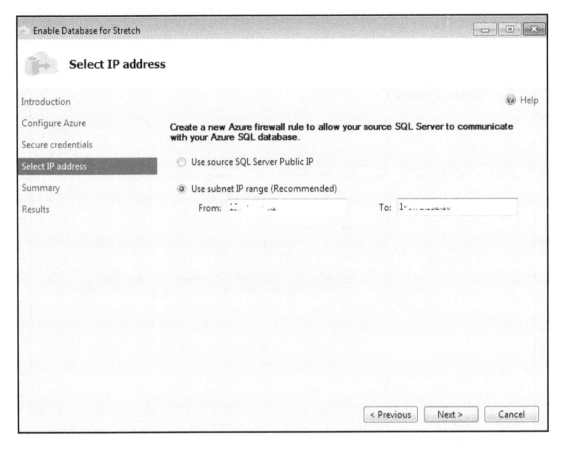

Enable Database for Search Wizard—Select IP address

And the tour is almost done. The next screen is **Summary** and it displays what you have already selected and entered, but it also provides an estimated price for the Stretch DB setup. The following screenshot shows the **Summary** screen:

Enable Database for Search Wizard—Summary

As you can see, the **Summary** screen brings one very important piece of information to you: the estimated price for enabling the Stretch DB feature. The **Estimated Pricing** section in the summary report is a bit strange: it shows two prices: $61 per TB per month and $1,825 per month. If you enable Stretch DB for your database with no tables, you would need to pay at least $1,825 per month! It does not seem to be cheap at all for an empty database. However, there is also a third piece of information in that section—a link to the pricing page at Microsoft Azure—and you can find more details about pricing there. The pricing is covered later in this chapter, in the *SQL Server Stretch Database pricing* section. For now, it is enough to know that you don't need to pay a full month's cost if you remove your database from the cloud before that. The minimum period for payment is 1 hour.

However, this is not immediately clear, and even if you want to just try or play with the feature to find out how it works or to explore it, you need to pay for this or apply for a trial subscription (which involves giving credit card details). I expected a non-complicated trial version with limited functionalities but without required registration and payment data, where I can check and learn about the feature. Stretch DB as a new and promising feature should be easy to try. Now it is time to click on the **Finish** button to instruct the wizard to perform the final step in the process of enabling the Stretch DB feature. After the last wizard action is done, the stretch database is created in Azure. You can use SSMS to see that the action was successful. When you choose the database `Mila`, you will see a different icon near to the database name:

Database in SSMS with enabled Stretch DB feature

After the feature is enabled for your sample database, you should not expect anything, since there are no tables in it. You will create a table and continue to play with stretching later in this chapter.

Enabling Stretch Database by using Transact-SQL

You can enable the `Stretch DB` feature by using Transact-SQL only. As you saw in the previous section, to enable `Stretch DB`, you need to create and secure communication infrastructure between our local database and the Azure server. Therefore, you need to accomplish the following three tasks:

1. Create a database master key to protect server credentials
2. Create a database credential
3. Define the Azure server

The following code creates a database master key for the sample database `Mila`:

```
USE Mila;
CREATE MASTER KEY ENCRYPTION BY PASSWORD='<very secure password>'; --you
need to put your password here
```

Next, we create a credential. This is saved authentication information that is required to connect to external resources. You need a credential for only one database; therefore you should create a database-scoped credential:

```
CREATE DATABASE SCOPED CREDENTIAL MilaStretchCredential
WITH
IDENTITY = 'Vasilije',
SECRET = '<very secure password>'; --you need to put your password here
```

Now you can finally enable the Stretch DB feature by using the `ALTER DATABASE` statement. You need to set `REMOTE_DATA_ARCHIVE` and define two parameters: Azure server and just-created database scoped credential. Here is the code that can be used to enable the Stretch DB feature for the database `Mila`:

```
ALTER DATABASE Mila
    SET REMOTE_DATA_ARCHIVE = ON
        (
            SERVER = '<address of your Azure server>,
            CREDENTIAL = [MilaStretchCredential]
        );
```

With this action, you have created an infrastructure, necessary for communication between your local database and the Azure server that will hold the stretched data. Note that this action can take a few minutes. When I executed the command, it took more than three minutes:

Enabling Stretch Database by using Transact-SQL

The next and final step is to select and enable tables for stretching.

Enabling Stretch Database for a table

To enable Stretch DB for a table, you can also choose between the wizard and Transact-SQL. You can migrate an entire table or just part of a table. If your cold data is stored in a separated table, you can migrate the entire table; otherwise you must specify a filter function to define which rows should be migrated. To enable the Stretch DB feature for a table, you must be a member of the db_owner role. In this section, you will create a new table in the Mila database, populate it with a few rows, and enable it for stretching. Use this code to create and populate the table:

```
USE Mila;
CREATE TABLE dbo.T1(
id INT NOT NULL,
c1 VARCHAR(20) NOT NULL,
c2 DATETIME NOT NULL,
CONSTRAINT PK_T1 PRIMARY KEY CLUSTERED (id)
);
```

```
GO
INSERT INTO dbo.T1 (id, c1, c2) VALUES
    (1, 'Benfica Lisbon','20180115'),
    (2, 'Manchester United','20180202'),
    (3, 'Rapid Vienna','20180128'),
    (4, 'Juventus Torino','20180225'),
    (5, 'Red Star Belgrade','20180225');
```

In the next sections, you will enable and use the `Stretch DB` feature for the T1 table. Assume that you want to move all rows from this table with a value in the c2 column that is older than *1st February 2018* to the cloud.

Enabling Stretch DB for a table by using wizard

You can create a new table with the `Stretch DB` feature enabled or enable it for an existing table using the **Enable Table for Stretch** wizard. To launch it, you need to navigate to the T1 table under the database `Mila` in SSMS. Then, after right-clicking, you need to select the option **Tasks/Stretch/Enable** respectively. You should get a following screenshot:

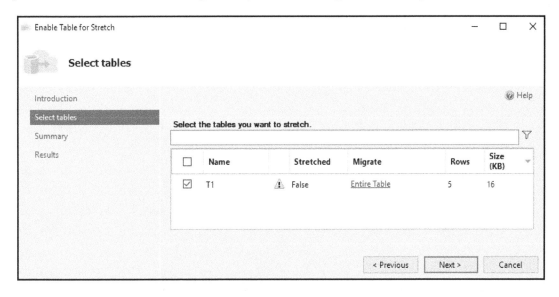

Enable Table for Stretch Wizard—Select tables

As you can see, T1 can be selected for stretching, since it meets the `Stretch DB` requirements discussed in the previous sections. You can choose to migrate the entire table or (by clicking on the link **Entire Table)** only a part of it. When you click on the link, you'll get this screen:

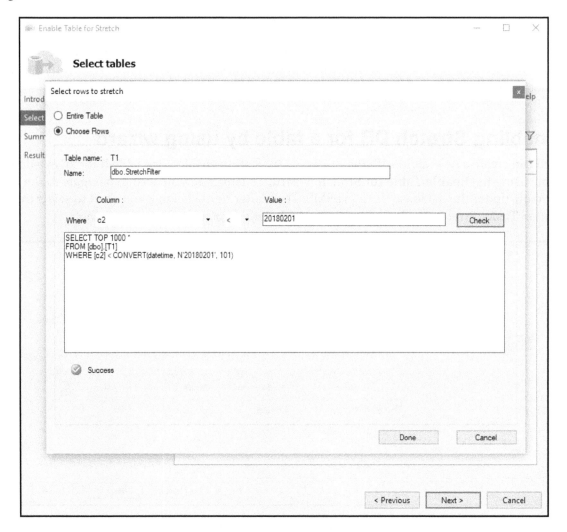

Enable Table for Stretch Wizard—Select rows to stretch

You see a query builder that can help you to write the correct filter function. Filter function is used to define which rows have to be migrated to the cloud. In this example, you are going to return all rows from the T1 table, where the value in the c2 column is less than *2018/02/01*.

However, developers find query builders a bit clumsy, and most of them prefer to work with Transact-SQL. In the next section, you will see how to use Transact-SQL to configure Stretch DB.

Enabling Stretch Database for a table by using Transact-SQL

In order to support table stretching, the CREATE and ALTER TABLE statements have been extended in SQL Server 2016. Here is the syntax extension for the ALTER TABLE statement that supports the Stretch DB feature:

```
<stretch_configuration> ::=
    {
      SET (
        REMOTE_DATA_ARCHIVE
        {
            = ON ( <table_stretch_options>  )
          | = OFF_WITHOUT_DATA_RECOVERY ( MIGRATION_STATE = PAUSED )
          | ( <table_stretch_options> [, ...n] )
        }
          )
    }
<table_stretch_options> ::=
    {
     [ FILTER_PREDICATE = { null | table_predicate_function } , ]
       MIGRATION_STATE = { OUTBOUND | INBOUND | PAUSED }
    }
```

You can specify the following options to enable Stretch DB:

- REMOTE_DATA_ARCHIVE is required and can have these values: ON, OFF_WITHOUT_DATA_RECOVERY or no value.

- MIGRATION_STATE is also mandatory and can have one of the following values: OUTBOUND, INBOUND, or PAUSED.

- FILTER_PREDICATE is optional and is used to define the part of the data that needs to be migrated. If it's not specified, the entire table will be moved.

If your table contains both hot and cold data, you can specify a filter predicate to select the rows that should be migrated. The filter predicate is an inline table-valued function. Its parameters are identifiers for stretch table columns. At least one parameter is required. Here is the function syntax:

```
CREATE FUNCTION dbo.fn_stretchpredicate(@column1 datatype1, @column2
datatype2 [, ...n])
RETURNS TABLE
WITH SCHEMABINDING
AS
RETURN  SELECT 1 AS is_eligible
        WHERE <predicate>
```

The function returns either a non-empty result or no result set. In the first case, the row is eligible to be migrated, otherwise it remains in the local system.

 Note that the function is defined with the SCHEMABINDING option to prevent columns that are used by the filter function from being dropped or altered.

The <predicate> can consist of one condition, or of multiple conditions joined with the AND logical operator:

```
<predicate> ::= <condition> [ AND <condition> ] [ ...n ]
```

Each condition in turn can consist of one primitive condition, or of multiple primitive conditions joined with the OR logical operator. You cannot use subqueries or non-deterministic functions. For a detailed list of limitations, please visit this page in the SQL Server Books Online: https://msdn.microsoft.com/en-us/library/mt613432.aspx.

The following code example shows how to enable the Stretch DB feature for the T1 table in the database Mila:

```
CREATE FUNCTION dbo.StretchFilter(@col DATETIME)
RETURNS TABLE
WITH SCHEMABINDING
AS
        RETURN SELECT 1 AS is_eligible WHERE @col < CONVERT(DATETIME,
'01.02.2018', 104);
GO
ALTER TABLE dbo.T1
  SET (
          REMOTE_DATA_ARCHIVE = ON (
                                        FILTER_PREDICATE =
dbo.StretchFilter(c2),
```

```
                              MIGRATION_STATE = OUTBOUND
                      )
          ) ;
```

After executing the preceding commands, Stretch DB is enabled for `T1` table. The following screenshot shows the SSMS screen immediately after the execution:

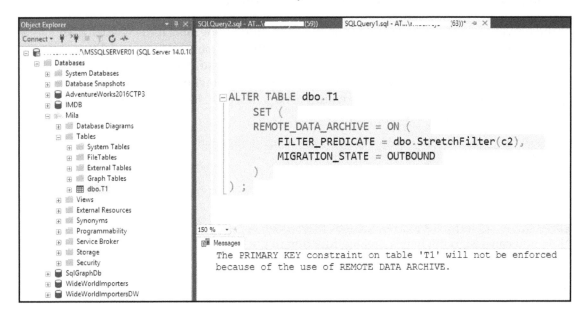

Enabling table for stretch by using Transact-SQL

The `Stretch DB` feature is enabled, but you can also see a warning message that informs you that although your `T1` table has a primary key constraint, it will not be enforced! Thus, you can have multiple rows in your table with the same ID, just because you have enabled the Stretch DB. This schema and integrity change silently implemented as part of Stretch DB enabling can be dangerous; some developers will not be aware of it, since the information is delivered through a message warning.

When you ignore this issue, the rest of the action looks correct. After the table is enabled for stretching, you can expect three rows to remain in the local database (they have a value in the `c2` column later than *1st February 2018*). Two rows should be moved to the Azure SQL database. You will confirm this by querying stretch tables, but before that you will learn a tip about the creation of a filter predicate with sliding window.

Filter predicate with sliding window

As mentioned earlier, you cannot call a non-deterministic function in a filter predicate. If you, for instance, want to migrate all rows older than 1 month (where a date column has a value older than 1 month), you cannot simply use the DATEADD function in the filter function because DATEADD is a non-deterministic function.

In the previous example, you created the filter function to migrate all rows older than 1 June 2016. Assume that you want to send all rows older than 1 month to the cloud. Since the function must be deterministic and you cannot alter the existing one because it is defined with SCHEMABINDING attribute, you need to create a new function with the literal date again. For instance, on 1 August, you would need a function that instructs the system to migrate rows older than 1 July:

```
CREATE FUNCTION dbo.StretchFilter20180301(@col DATETIME)
RETURNS TABLE
WITH SCHEMABINDING
AS
        RETURN SELECT 1 AS is_eligible
WHERE @col < CONVERT(DATETIME, '01.03.2018', 104);
```

Now you can assign the newly created function to the T1 table:

```
ALTER TABLE dbo.T1
SET (REMOTE_DATA_ARCHIVE = ON
    (FILTER_PREDICATE = dbo.StretchFilter20180301(c2), MIGRATION_STATE =
OUTBOUND ) );
```

Finally, you should remove the old filter function:

```
DROP FUNCTION IF EXISTS dbo.StretchFilter;
```

Querying stretch databases

When you query a stretch database, the SQL Server Database Engine runs the query against the local or remote database depending on data location. This is completely transparent to the database user. When you run a query that returns both local and remote data, you can see the Remote Query operator in the execution plan. The following query returns all rows from the stretch T1 table:

```
USE Mila;
SELECT * FROM dbo.T1;
```

As expected, it returns five rows:

id	c1	c2
2	Manchester United	2018-02-02 00:00:00.000
4	Juventus Torino	2018-02-25 00:00:00.000
5	Red Star Belgrade	2018-02-25 00:00:00.000
1	Benfica Lisbon	2018-01-15 00:00:00.000
3	Rapid Vienna	2018-01-28 00:00:00.000

You are surely much more interested in how the execution plan looks:

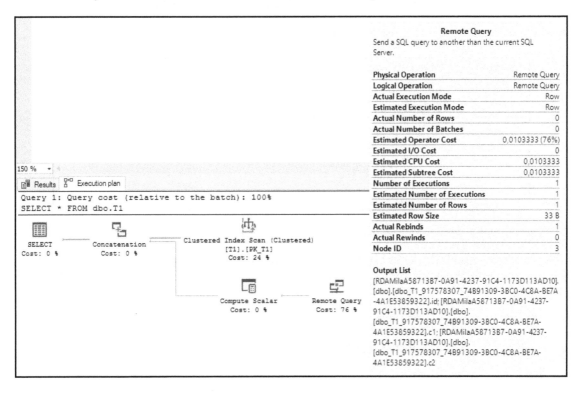

Execution plan for query with stretch tables

You can see that the Remote Query operator operates with an Azure database and that its output is concatenated with the output of the Clustered Index Scan that collected data from the local SQL Server instance. Note that the property window for the Remote Query operator has been shortened to show only context-relevant information.

What does SQL Server do when only local rows are returned? To check this, run the following code:

```
SELECT * FROM dbo.T1 WHERE c2 >= '20180201';
```

The query returns three rows, as expected:

```
id              c1                      c2
-----------     --------------------    ------------------------
2               Manchester United       2018-02-02 00:00:00.000
4               Juventus Torino         2018-02-25 00:00:00.000
5               Red Star Belgrade       2018-02-25 00:00:00.000
```

And the execution plan is shown as follows:

Execution plan for query with stretch tables returning local data only

The plan looks good; it checks only the local database and there is no connection to Azure. Finally, you will check the plan for a query that logically returns remote data only. Here is the query:

```
SELECT * FROM dbo.T1 WHERE c2 < '20180201';
```

You will again get the expected result:

```
id              c1                      c2
-----------     --------------------    ------------------------
1               Benfica Lisbon          2018-01-15 00:00:00.000
3               Rapid Vienna            2018-01-28 00:00:00.000
```

Here is the execution plan:

Execution plan for query with stretch tables returning remote data only

You probably did not expect both operators here only `Remote Query` should be shown. However, even if the returned data resides in the Azure SQL database only, both operators should be used since data can be in an eligible state, which means that it has not yet been moved to Azure!

Querying stretch tables is straightforward; you don't need to change anything in your queries. One of the most important things about stretch databases is that the entire execution is transparent to the user and you don't need to change your code when working with stretch tables.

However, you should not forget that enabling `Stretch DB` can suspend primary key constraints in your stretched tables; uniqueness is not enforced for UNIQUE constraints and PRIMARY KEY constraints in the Azure table that contains the migrated data.

Querying and updating remote data

As mentioned earlier, queries with stretch-enabled tables return both local and remote data by default. You can manage the scope of queries by using the system stored procedure `sys.sp_rda_set_query_mode` to specify whether queries against the current Stretch-enabled database and its tables return both local and remote data, or local data only. The following modes are available:

- LOCAL_AND_REMOTE (queries against Stretch-enabled tables return both local and remote data). This is the default mode.

- LOCAL_ONLY (queries against Stretch-enabled tables return only local data).
- DISABLED (queries against Stretch-enabled tables are not allowed).

When you specify the scope of queries against the Stretch Database, this is applied to all queries for all users. However, there are additional options at the single query level for an administrator (member of the db_owner group). As administrator, you can add the query hint WITH (REMOTE_DATA_ARCHIVE_OVERRIDE = value) to the SELECT statement to specify data location. The option REMOTE_DATA_ARCHIVE_OVERRIDE can have one of the following values:

- LOCAL_ONLY (query returns only local data)
- REMOTE_ONLY (query returns only remote data)
- STAGE_ONLY (query returns eligible data)

The following code returns eligible data for the T1 table:

```
USE Mila;
SELECT * FROM dbo.T1 WITH (REMOTE_DATA_ARCHIVE_OVERRIDE = STAGE_ONLY);
```

Here is the output:

id	c1	c2	batchID--917578307
1	Benfica Lisbon	2018-01-15 00:00:00.000	1
3	Rapid Vienna	2018-01-28 00:00:00.000	1

Run this code to return data from the T1 table already moved to Azure:

```
SELECT * FROM dbo.T1 WITH (REMOTE_DATA_ARCHIVE_OVERRIDE = REMOTE_ONLY);
```

Here is the output:

id	c1	c2	batchID--917578307
1	Benfica Lisbon	2018-01-15 00:00:00.000	1
3	Rapid Vienna	2018-01-28 00:00:00.000	1

Finally, this code returns data in the T1 table from the local database server:

```
SELECT * FROM dbo.T1 WITH (REMOTE_DATA_ARCHIVE_OVERRIDE = LOCAL_ONLY);
```

As you expected, three rows are returned:

```
id              c1                    c2
-----------     --------------------  -----------------------
2               Manchester United     2018-02-02 00:00:00.000
4               Juventus Torino       2018-02-25 00:00:00.000
5               Red Star Belgrade     2018-02-25 00:00:00.000
```

By default, you can't update or delete rows that are eligible for migration or rows that have already been migrated in a Stretch-enabled table. When you have to fix a problem, a member of the db_owner role can run an UPDATE or DELETE operation by adding the preceding hint and will be able to update data in all locations.

SQL Server Stretch Database pricing

You can see price details on the https://azure.microsoft.com/en-us/pricing/details/sql-server-stretch-database/ page. Stretch Database bills compute and storage separately. Compute usage is represented by **Database Stretch Unit** (**DSU**) and customers can scale up and down the level of performance/DSUs they need at any time. The prices given here were valid at 28th February 2018:

Performance level (DSU)	Price in $ per month
100	1,825
200	3,650
300	5,475
400	7,300
500	9,125
600	10,950
1,000	18,250
1,200	21,900
1,500	27,375
2,000	36,500

Stretch DB price list

Database sizes are limited to 240 TB. Monthly price estimates are based on 730 hours per month at constant DSU levels. `Stretch DB` is generally available in all regions except southern India, Northern China, southern Brazil, north-central America, western India, Australia, Japan, and US Gov.

Data storage is charged based on $0.16/GB/month. Data storage includes the size of your `Stretch DB` and backup snapshots. All Stretch databases have 7 *days* of incremental backup snapshots.

You can also use the Azure Pricing calculator to estimate expenses for your planned Azure activities. It is available at `https://azure.microsoft.com/en-us/pricing/calculator/?service=sql-server-stretch-database`. You can choose the Azure region and specify the time period, data storage, and DSU, as shown in the following screenshot:

Azure Pricing calculator—Calculating price for Stretch DB

This screen shows the price you would pay when you play with the Stretch DB feature for two hours in a database with less than **1 GB** of data and with **100 DSU(s)** using Azure database in **Western Europe**.

It is also possible to try the feature for free. You can apply for it at `https://azure.`
`microsoft.com/en-us/free/`. When you do this, you'll see this screen:

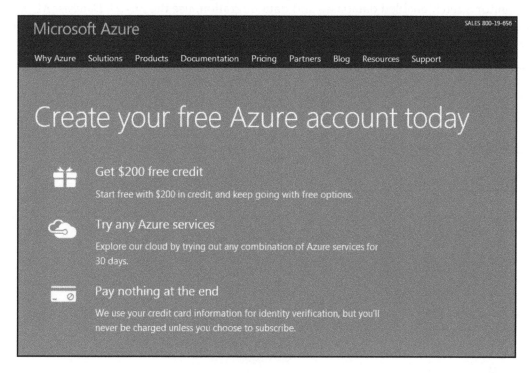

Creating a free Azure account

It is good that you can try the new feature for free, but in this case you must also give your
payment details, which could reduce the number of developers who will try the feature.

Stretch DB management and troubleshooting

To monitor stretch-enabled databases and data migration, you can use the *Stretch Database
Monitor* feature, the `sys.remote_data_archive_databases` and
`sys.remote_data_archive_tables` catalog views, and the
`sys.dm_db_rda_migration_status` dynamic management view.

Monitoring Stretch Databases

To monitor Stretch-enabled databases and data migration, use the *Stretch Database Monitor* feature. It is part of SQL Server Management Studio and you open it when you select your database and then choose **Tasks/Stretch/Monitor**:

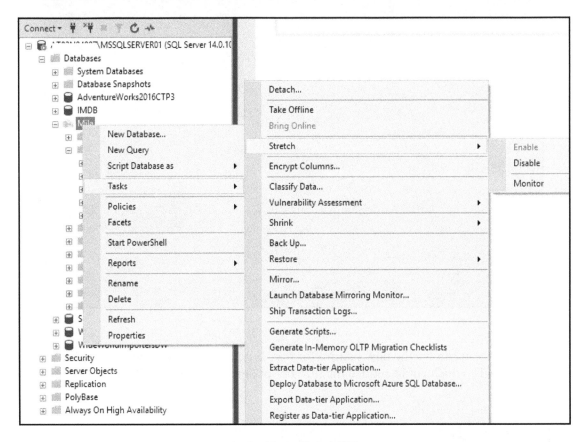

Open Stretch Database Monitor in SSMS

The top portion of the monitor displays general information about both the stretch-enabled SQL Server database and the remote Azure database, while the status of data migration for each stretch-enabled table in the database is shown in the bottom part of the screen:

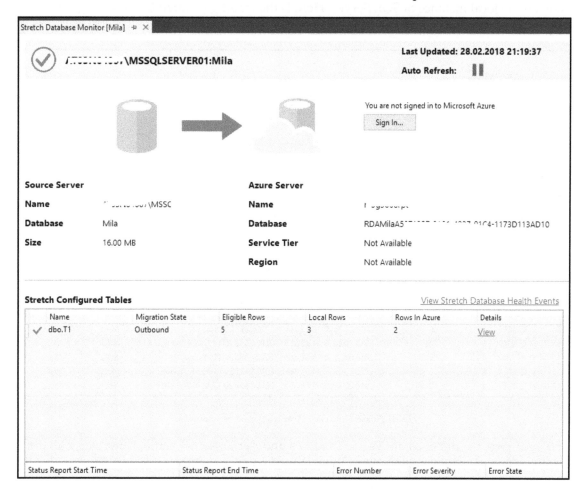

Stretch Database Monitoring

You can also use the dynamic management view `sys.dm_db_rda_migration_status` to check the status of migrated data (how many batches and rows of data have been migrated). It contains one row for each batch of migrated data from each stretch-enabled table on the local instance of SQL Server. Here is the result generated by executing this view:

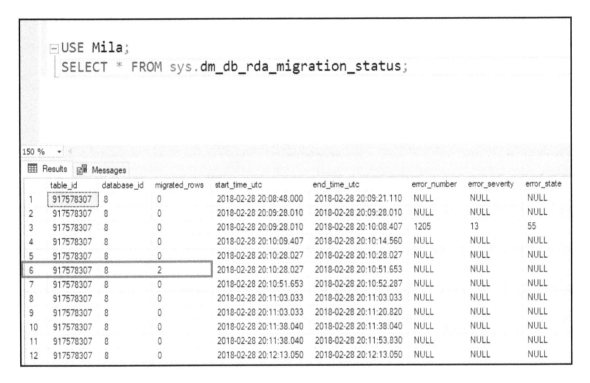

Checking migration status by using DMV sys.dm_db_rda_migration_status

The `sys.remote_data_archive_databases` and `sys.remote_data_archive_tables` catalog views give information about the status of migration at the table and database level.

This query provides archive database information:

```
USE Mila;
SELECT * FROM sys.remote_data_archive_databases;
```

Here is the output:

remote_database_id	remote_database_name	data_source_id	federated_service_account
65536	RDAMilaA58713B7-0A91-4237-91C4-1173D113AD10	65536	0

By using the following command, you can get information about archive tables on the Azure side :

```
USE Mila;
SELECT * FROM sys.remote_data_archive_tables;
```

And here is the output:

object_id	remote_database_id	remote_table_name	filter_predicate
917578307	65536	dbo_T1_917578307_74B91309-3B...	([dbo].[StretchFilter]([c2]))

migration_direction	migration_direction_desc	is_migration_paused	is_reconciled
0	OUTBOUND	0	1

Finally, to see how much space a stretch-enabled table is using in Azure, run the following statement:

```
USE Mila;
EXEC sp_spaceused 'dbo.T1', 'true', 'REMOTE_ONLY';
```

Here is the result of this command:

name	rows	reserved	data	index_size	unused
dbo.T1	2	288 KB	16 KB	48 KB	224 KB

In the next sections, you will see how to pause or disable the Stretch DB feature.

Pause and resume data migration

To pause data migration for a table, choose the table in SSMS and then select the option **Stretch | Pause**. You can achieve the same with the following Transact-SQL command; it temporarily breaks the data migration for the T1 table:

```
USE Mila;
ALTER TABLE dbo.T1 SET (REMOTE_DATA_ARCHIVE (MIGRATION_STATE = PAUSED));
```

To resume data migration for a table, choose the table in SSMS and then select the **Stretch/Resume** option or write the Transact-SQL code, similar to the following one:

```
USE Mila;
ALTER TABLE dbo.T1 SET (REMOTE_DATA_ARCHIVE (MIGRATION_STATE = OUTBOUND));
```

To check whether migration is active or paused, you can open Stretch Database Monitor in SQL Server Management Studio and check the value of the `Migration State` or column check the value of the flag `is_migration_paused` in the system catalog view `sys.remote_data_archive_tables`.

Disabling Stretch Database

Disabling the Stretch DB features for a database and the tables stops data migration immediately and queries don't include remote data anymore. You can copy the already-migrated data back to the local system, or you can leave it in Azure. As with Stretch Database enabling, you can disable it for tables and databases using SSMS and Transact-SQL. In order to disable Stretch DB for a database, you have to disable it for tables involved in stretching. Otherwise, you will get an error that instructs you to disable stretch tables before that action.

Disable Stretch Database for tables by using SSMS

To disable `Stretch DB` for a table, you need to select it in SQL Server Management Studio (SSMS); right-click on it, and select the option **Stretch**. Then, go to one of the following options:

- **Disable | Bring data back from Azure** to copy remote data for the table to the local system and then disable the Stretch DB feature
- **Disable | Leave data in Azure** to disable the Stretch DB feature immediately, without transferring it back to the local system (data remains in Azure)

Be aware that the first option includes data transfer costs! When you choose the second option, you don't have transfer costs, but the data remains in Azure and you still need to pay for storage. You can remove it through the Azure Management portal:

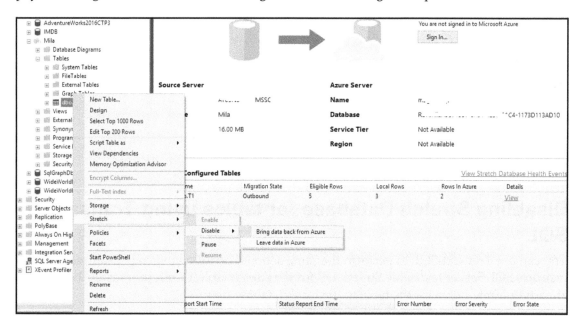

Disable stretching for a table in SSMS

After the `Stretch DB` feature has been disabled for the `T1` table, you can see the following screenshot:

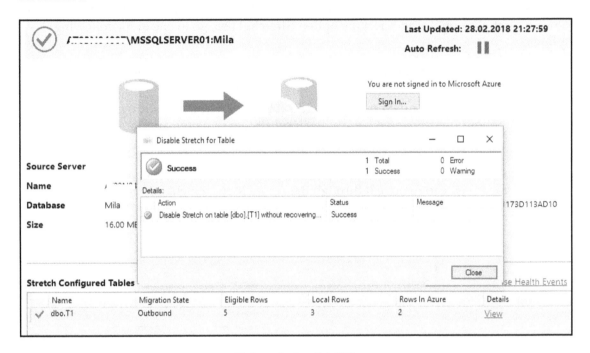

Disable stretching for a table in SSMS

Disabling Stretch Database for tables using Transact-SQL

You can use Transact-SQL to perform the same action. The following code example instructs SQL Server to disable Stretch DB for the stretch table `T1` but to transfer the already-migrated data for the table to the local database first:

```
USE Mila;
ALTER TABLE dbo.T1 SET (REMOTE_DATA_ARCHIVE (MIGRATION_STATE = INBOUND));
```

If you don't need the already-migrated data (or you want to avoid data transfer costs), use the following code:

```
USE Mila;
ALTER TABLE dbo.T1 SET (REMOTE_DATA_ARCHIVE = OFF_WITHOUT_DATA_RECOVERY
(MIGRATION_STATE = PAUSED));
```

Disabling Stretch Database for a database

After you have disabled Stretch DB for all stretch tables in a database, you can disable it for the database. You can do this by selecting the database in SSMS and choosing the **Task/Stretch/Disable** option in the database context menu.

Alternatively, you can use Transact-SQL to achieve the same:

```
ALTER DATABASE Mila SET (REMOTE_DATA_ARCHIVE = OFF_WITHOUT_DATA_RECOVERY
(MIGRATION_STATE = PAUSED));
```

You can check if the action was successful by using this query:

```
SELECT * FROM sys.remote_data_archive_tables;
```

You should get an empty set as the result of this query. As already mentioned for stretch tables, disabling Stretch DB does not drop a database remotely. You need to drop it by using the Azure management portal.

Backing up and restoring Stretch-enabled databases

Since you have delegated a part of your database to the remote Azure instance, when you perform a database backup, only local and eligible data will be backed up; remote data is the responsibility of the Azure service. By default, Azure automatically creates storage snapshots at least every 8 hours and retains them for seven days so that you can restore data to a point in time (by default, 21 points). You can change this behavior and increase the number of hours or backup frequency by using the system stored procedure `sys.sp_rda_set_rpo_duration`. Since the Azure service is not free, this can have additional costs.

As expected, to remotely restore a database you have to log in to the Azure portal. How to restore a live Azure database to an earlier point in time using the Azure portal is shown in the following screenshot:

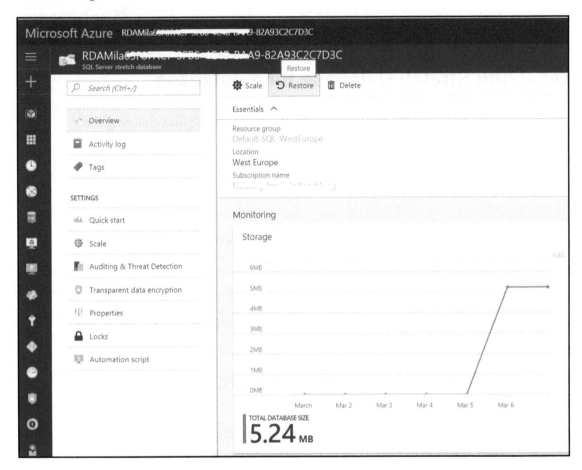

Restore Azure database to an earlier point in time

To restore your Azure database to an earlier point in time, you need to perform the following steps:

1. Log in to the Azure portal.
2. On the left-hand side of the screen, select **BROWSE** and then select **SQL Databases**.
3. Navigate to your database and select it.

4. At the top of the database blade, click on **Restore**.

5. Specify a new **Database name**, select a `Restore Point`, and then click on **Create**.

6. The database restore process will begin and can be monitored using **NOTIFICATIONS**.

After you restore the local SQL Server database, you have to run the `sys.sp_rda_reauthorize_db` stored procedure to re-establish the connection between the stretch-enabled SQL Server database and the remote Azure database. The same action is required if you restore the Azure database with a different name or in a different region. You can also restore a deleted database up to 7 days after dropping it. The *SQL Server Stretch Database service* on Azure takes a database snapshot before a database is dropped and retains it for seven days.

Summary

`Stretch DB` allows the moving of historical or less frequently needed data dynamically and transparently to Microsoft Azure. Data is always available and online, and you don't need to change queries in your solutions; SQL Server takes care of the location of data and combines retrieving data from the local server and remote Azure location. Therefore, you can completely delegate your cold data to Azure and reduce storage, maintenance, and implementation costs of an on-premises solution for cold data storage and availability. However, there are many limitations to using Stretch DB and most OLTP tables cannot be stretched to the cloud—at least not without schema and constraint changes. Stretch Database brings maximum benefits to tables with historical data that is rarely used. You can calculate the price for data storage and querying against the Azure database and decide whether you would benefit from using the `Stretch DB` feature.

In the next chapter, you will learn about temporal data support in SQL Server 2017.

7

Temporal Tables

Databases that serve business applications often need to support temporal data. For example, suppose a contract with a supplier is valid for a limited time only. It could be valid from a specific point in time onward, or it could be valid for a specific time interval—from a starting time point to an ending time point. In addition, often you'll need to audit all changes in one or more tables. You might also need to be able to show the state at a specific point in time, or all changes made to a table in a specific period of time. From a data integrity perspective, you might need to implement many additional temporal-specific constraints.

This chapter introduces temporal problems, deals with manual solutions, and shows you out-of-the-box features in SQL Server 2016 and 2017, including the following:

- Defining temporal data
- Using temporal data in SQL Server before version 2016
- History of temporal data implementation
- System versioned tables in SQL Server 2016 and 2017
- What kind of temporal support is still missing in SQL Server 2017?

What is temporal data?

In a table with temporal support, the header represents a predicate with at least one time parameter that represents when the rest of the predicate is valid; the complete predicate is therefore a **timestamped predicate**. Rows represent timestamped propositions, and the row's valid time period is expressed with one of two attributes: since (for **semi temporal** data) or during (for **fully temporal** data); the latter attribute is usually represented with two values, from and to. The following table shows the original and two additional timestamped versions of an exemplary Suppliers table:

Suppliers		Suppliers_Since		Suppliers_FromTo	
PK	**supplierid**	**PK**	**supplierid**	**PK**	**supplierid**
	companyname		companyname		companyname
	contactname		contactname		contactname
	contacttitle		contacttitle		contacttitle
	address		address		address
	city		city		city
	region		region		region
	postalcode		postalcode		postalcode
	country		country		country
	phone		phone		phone
	fax		fax		fax
			since		from
					to

Original Suppliers table and two tables with temporal support

From the original table header, you can read a predicate saying that a supplier with identification supplierid, named companyname, with a contact contactname, and so on is currently our supplier, or is currently under contract. You pretend that this supplier is the supplier forever. The Suppliers_Since table header has this predicate modified with a time parameter; a supplier with the identification supplierid, named companyname, with a contact contactname, and so on has been under contract since some specific point in time. In the Suppliers_FromTo table, the header has this predicate modified with an even more specific time attribute; a supplier with the ID supplierid, named companyname, with a contact contactname, and so on is (or was, or will be, depending on the current time) under contract *from* some specific point in time *to* another point in time.

There is no need to implement semi-temporal tables. You can simply use the maximum possible date and time for the *to* time point. Therefore, the rest of the chapter focuses on fully temporal data only.

In this section, you will learn about:

- Types of temporal tables
- Temporal data algebra
- Temporal constrains
- Temporal data implementation in SQL Server before version 2016
- Optimization of temporal queries

Types of temporal tables

You might have noticed during the introduction part at the beginning of this chapter that there are two kinds of temporal issues. The first one is the **validity time** of the proposition—a time period in which the proposition that a timestamped row in a table represents was actually true. For example, a contract with a supplier was valid only from time point 1 to time point 2. This kind of validity time is meaningful to people and meaningful for the business. The validity time is also called **application time** or **human time**. We can have multiple valid periods for the same entity. For example, the aforementioned contract that was valid from time point 1 to time point 2 might also be valid from time point 7 to time point 9.

The second temporal issue is the **transaction time**. A row for the contract mentioned previously was inserted in time point 1 and was the only version of the truth known to the database until somebody changed it, or even to the end of time. When the row is updated in time point 2, the original row is known as being true to the database from time point 1 to time point 2. A new row for the same proposition is inserted with a time valid for the database from time point 2 to the end of time. The transaction time is also known as **system time** or **database time**.

The **database management systems** (**DBMSs**) can, and should, maintain the transaction times automatically. The system has to take care to insert a new row for every update and change the transaction validity period in the original row. The system also needs to allow for querying the current and the historical data, and show the state at any specific point in time. There are not many additional issues with the transaction time. The system has to take care that the start time of the database time period is lower than the end time, and that the two periods in two rows for the same entity don't overlap. The database system has to know a single truth at a single point in time. Finally, the database does not care about the future. The end of the database time of the current row is actually the end of time. Database time is about the present and past states only.

Implementing application time might be much more complex. Of course, you might have validity time periods that end or even begin in the future. DBMSs can't take care of future times automatically, and for example check whether they are correct. Therefore, you need to take care of all the constraints you need. The DBMS can only help you by implementing time-aware objects, such as declarative constraints. For example, a foreign key from the products to the suppliers table, which ensures that each product has a supplier, could be extended to check not only whether the supplier for the product exists, but also if the supplier is a valid supplier at the time point when the foreign key is checked.

So far, I've talked about time as though it consists of discrete time points; I used the term *time point* as if it represented a single, indivisible, infinitely small point in time. Of course, time is continuous. Nevertheless, in common language, we talk about time as though it consists of discrete points. We talk in days, hours, and other time units; the granularity we use depends on what we are talking about. The time points we are talking about are actually intervals of time; a day is an interval of 24 hours, an hour is an interval of 60 minutes, and so on.

So what is the granularity level of the time points for the system and application intervals? For the system times, the decision is simple: use the lowest granularity level that a system supports. In SQL Server, with the `datetime2` data type, you can support 100-nanosecond granularity. For application time, the granularity depends on the business problem. For example, for a contract with a supplier, the day level could work well. For measuring the intervals when somebody is using services, such as mobile phone services, the granularity of seconds could be more appropriate. This looks very complex. However, you can make a generalized solution for the application times. You can translate time points to integers, and then use a lookup table that gives you the context—gives the meaning to the integer time points.

Of course, you can also implement both application and system versioned tables. Such tables are called **bitemporal** tables.

Allen's interval algebra

The theory for temporal data in a relational model started to evolve more than thirty years ago. I will define quite a few useful Boolean operators and a couple of operators that work on intervals and return an interval. These operators are known as **Allen's operators**, named after J. F. Allen, who defined a number of them in a 1983 research paper on temporal intervals. All of them are still accepted as valid and needed. A DBMS could help you deal with application times by implementing these operators out of the box.

Let me first introduce the notation I will use. I will work on two intervals, denoted as i_1 and i_2. The beginning time point of the first interval is b_1, and the end is e_1; the beginning time point of the second interval is b_2 and the end is e_2. Allen's **Boolean operators** are defined in the following table:

Name	Notation	Definition
Equals	$(i_1 = i_2)$	$(b_1 = b_2)$ AND $(e_1 = e_2)$
Before	$(i_1 \, before \, i_2)$	$(e_1 < b_2)$
After	$(i_1 \, after \, i_2)$	$(i_2 \, before \, i_1)$
Includes	$(i_1 \supseteq i_2)$	$(b_1 \leq b_2)$ AND $(e_1 \geq e_2)$
Properly includes	$(i_1 \supset i_2)$	$(i_1 \supseteq i_2)$ AND $(i_1 \neq i_2)$
Meets	$(i_1 \, meets \, i_2)$	$(b2 = e1 + 1)$ OR $(b1 = e2 + 1)$
Overlaps	$(i_1 \, overlaps \, i_2)$	$(b_1 \leq e_2)$ AND $(b_2 \leq e_1)$
Merges	$(i_1 \, merges \, i_2)$	$(i_1 \, overlaps \, i_2)$ OR $(i_1 \, meets \, i_2)$
Begins	$(i_1 \, begins \, i_2)$	$(b_1 = b_2)$ AND $(e_1 \leq e_2)$
Ends	$(i_1 \, ends \, i_2)$	$(e_1 = e_2)$ AND $(b_1 \geq b_2)$

In addition to Boolean operators, three of Allen's operators accept intervals as input parameters and return an interval. These operators constitute simple **interval algebra**. Note that these operators have the same name as relational operators you are probably already familiar with: Union, Intersect, and Minus. However, they don't behave exactly like their relational counterparts.

In general, using any of the three interval operators, if the operation will result in an empty set of time points or in a set that cannot be described by one interval, then the operator should return NULL. A union of two intervals makes sense only if the intervals meet or overlap. An intersection makes sense only if the intervals overlap. The Minus interval operator makes sense only in some cases. For example, (3:10) Minus (5:7) returns NULL because the result cannot be described by one interval. The following table summarizes the definitions of the operators in interval algebra:

Name	Notation	Definition
Union	$(i_1 \ union \ i_2)$	$(Min(b_1, b_2) : Max(e_1, e_2))$, when $(i_1 \ merges \ i_2)$; NULL otherwise
Intersect	$(i_1 \ intersect \ i_2)$	$(Max(b_1, b_2) : Min(e_1, e_2))$, when $(i_1 \ overlaps \ i_2)$; NULL otherwise
Minus	$(i_1 \ minus \ i_2)$	$(b_1: Min(b_2 - 1, e_1))$, when $(b_1 < b_2)$ AND $(e_1 \le e_2)$; $(Max(e_2 + 1, b_1) : e_1)$, when $(b_1 \ge b_2)$ AND $(e_1 > e_2)$; NULL otherwise

The following figure shows the interval algebra operators graphically:

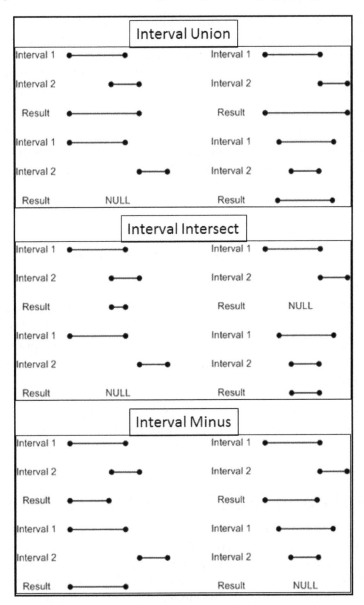

Interval algebra operators

Temporal constraints

Depending on the business problem you are solving, you might need to implement many temporal constraints. Remember that for application time, SQL Server does not help you much. You need to implement the constraints in your code, using SQL Server declarative constraints where possible. However, most of the constraints you need to implement through custom code, either in triggers or in stored procedures, or even in the application code.

Imagine the `Suppliers` table example. One supplier can appear multiple times in the table because the same supplier could be under contract for separate periods of time. For example, you could have two tuples like this in the relation with the shortened header `Suppliers (supplierid, companyname, from, to)`:

```
{2, Supplier VHQZD, d05, d07}
{2, Supplier VHQZD, d12, d27}
```

Here are some possible constraints you might need to implement:

- *To* should never be less than *from*
- Two contracts for the same supplier should not have overlapping time intervals
- Two contracts for the same supplier should not have abutting time intervals
- No supplier can be under two distinct contracts at the same point in time
- There should be no supplies from a supplier at a point in time when the supplier is not under contract

You might find even more constraints. Anyway, SQL Server 2016 brings support for system versioned tables only. To maintain application validity times, you need to develop the code by yourself.

Temporal data in SQL Server before 2016

As mentioned, in SQL Server versions before 2016, you need to take care of temporal data by yourself. Even in SQL Server 2016, you still need to take care of the human, or application, times. The following code shows an example of how to create a table with validity intervals expressed with the b and e columns, where the beginning and the end of an interval are represented as integers. The table is populated with demo data from the `WideWorldImporters.Sales.OrderLines` table:

```
USE tempdb;
GO
```

```
SELECT OrderLineID AS id,
  StockItemID * (OrderLineID % 5 + 1) AS b,
  LastEditedBy + StockItemID * (OrderLineID % 5 + 1) AS e
INTO dbo.Intervals
FROM WideWorldImporters.Sales.OrderLines;
-- 231412 rows
GO
ALTER TABLE dbo.Intervals ADD CONSTRAINT PK_Intervals PRIMARY KEY(id);
CREATE INDEX idx_b ON dbo.Intervals(b) INCLUDE(e);
CREATE INDEX idx_e ON dbo.Intervals(e) INCLUDE(b);
GO
```

Please note also the indexes created. The two indexes are optimal for searches at the beginning of an interval or on the end of an interval. You can check the minimum beginning and maximum end of all intervals with the following code:

```
SELECT MIN(b), MAX(e)
FROM dbo.Intervals;
```

You can see in the results that the minimum beginning time point is 1 and the maximum end time point is 1155. Now you need to give the intervals some time context. In this case, a single time point represents a day. The following code creates a date lookup table and populates it. Note that the starting date is July 1, 2014:

```
CREATE TABLE dbo.DateNums
  (n INT NOT NULL PRIMARY KEY,
   d DATE NOT NULL);
GO
DECLARE @i AS INT = 1,
  @d AS DATE = '20140701';
WHILE @i <= 1200
BEGIN
INSERT INTO dbo.DateNums
  (n, d)
SELECT @i, @d;
SET @i += 1;
SET @d = DATEADD(day,1,@d);
END;
GO
```

Now you can join the `dbo.Intervals` table to the `dbo.DateNums` table twice, to give context to the integers that represent the beginning and the end of the intervals:

```
SELECT i.id,
  i.b, d1.d AS dateB,
  i.e, d2.d AS dateE
FROM dbo.Intervals AS i
  INNER JOIN dbo.DateNums AS d1
  ON i.b = d1.n
  INNER JOIN dbo.DateNums AS d2
  ON i.e = d2.n
ORDER BY i.id;
```

The abbreviated result from the previous query is:

```
id    b      dateB          e      date
--    ---    ----------     ---    ----------
1     328    2015-05-24     332    2015-05-28
2     201    2015-01-17     204    2015-01-20
3     200    2015-01-16     203    2015-01-19
```

Now you can see which day is represented by which integer.

Optimizing temporal queries

The problem with temporal queries is that when reading from a table, SQL Server can use only one index, successfully eliminate rows that are not candidates for the result from one side only, and then scan the rest of the data. For example, you need to find all intervals in the table that overlap with a given interval. Remember, two intervals overlap when the beginning of the first one is lower than or equal to the end of the second one, and the beginning of the second one is lower than or equal to the end of the first one, or mathematically when $(b_1 \le e_2)$ *AND* $(b_2 \le e_1)$.

The following query searches for all of the intervals that overlap with the interval (`10`, `30`). Note that the second condition $(b_2 \le e_1)$ is turned around to $(e_1 \ge b_2)$ for simpler reading (the beginning and the end of intervals from the table are always on the left side of the condition). The given or searched interval is at the beginning of the timeline for all intervals in the table:

```
SET STATISTICS IO ON;
DECLARE @b AS INT = 10,
  @e AS INT = 30;
SELECT id, b, e
FROM dbo.Intervals
```

```
WHERE b <= @e
  AND e >= @b
OPTION (RECOMPILE);
GO
```

The query used 36 logical reads. If you check the execution plan, you can see that the query used the index seek in the `idx_b` index with the seek predicate `[tempdb].[dbo].[Intervals].b <= Scalar Operator((30))` and then scanned the rows and selected the resulting rows using the residual predicate `[tempdb].[dbo].[Intervals].[e]>=(10)`. Because the searched interval is at the beginning of the timeline, the seek predicate successfully eliminated a majority of the rows; only a few intervals in the table have a beginning point lower than or equal to 30.

You would get a similarly efficient query if the searched interval was at the end of the timeline; it's just that SQL Server would use the `idx_e` index for the seek. However, what happens if the searched interval is in the middle of the timeline, like the following query shows:

```
DECLARE @b AS INT = 570,
  @e AS INT = 590;
SELECT id, b, e
FROM dbo.Intervals
WHERE b <= @e
  AND e >= @b
OPTION (RECOMPILE);
GO
```

This time, the query used 111 logical reads. With a bigger table, the difference with the first query would be even bigger. If you check the execution plan, you can find out that SQL Server used the `idx_e` index with the `[tempdb].[dbo].[Intervals].e >= Scalar Operator((570))` seek predicate and the `[tempdb].[dbo].[Intervals].[b]<=(590)` residual predicate. The seek predicate excludes approximately half of the rows from one side, while half of the rows from the other side are scanned and the resulting rows extracted with the residual predicate.

There is a solution that uses that index to eliminate rows from both sides of the searched interval by using a single index. The following figure shows this logic:

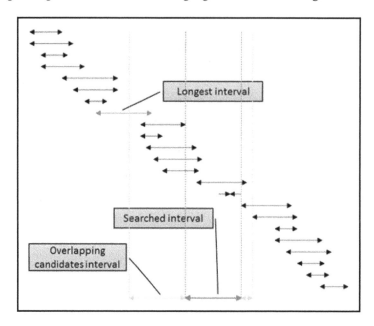

Optimizing a temporal query

The intervals in the figure are sorted by the lower boundary, representing SQL Server's usage of the idx_b index. Eliminating intervals from the right side of the given (searched) interval is simple: just eliminate all intervals where the beginning is at least one unit bigger (more to the right) of the end of the given interval. You can see this boundary in the figure denoted with the rightmost dotted line. However, eliminating from the left is more complex. In order to use the same index, the idx_b index for eliminating from the left, I need to use the beginning of the intervals in the table in the WHERE clause of the query. I have to go to the left side, away from the beginning of the given (searched) interval at least for the length of the longest interval in the table, which is marked with a callout in the figure. The intervals that begin before the left-hand yellow line cannot overlap with the given (blue/dark gray) interval.

Since I already know that the length of the longest interval is 20, I can write an enhanced query in a quite simple way:

```
DECLARE @b AS INT = 570,
  @e AS INT = 590;
DECLARE @max AS INT = 20;
```

```
SELECT id, b, e
FROM dbo.Intervals
WHERE b <= @e AND b >= @b - @max
  AND e >= @b AND e <= @e + @max
OPTION (RECOMPILE);
```

This query retrieves the same rows as the previous one with 20 logical reads only. If you check the execution plan, you can see that the `idx_b` was used, with the seek predicate `Seek Keys[1]: Start: [tempdb].[dbo].[Intervals].b >= Scalar Operator((550)), End: [tempdb].[dbo].[Intervals].b <= Scalar Operator((590))`, which successfully eliminated rows from both sides of the timeline, and then the residual predicate `[tempdb].[dbo].[Intervals].[e]>=(570) AND [tempdb].[dbo].[Intervals].[e]<=(610)` was used to select rows from a very limited partial scan.

Of course, the figure could be turned around to cover cases where the `idx_e` index would be more useful. With this index, elimination from the left is simple—eliminate all of the intervals that end at least one unit before the beginning of the given interval. This time, elimination from the right is more complex—the end of the intervals in the table cannot be more to the right than the end of the given interval plus the maximum length of all intervals in the table.

 Please note that this performance is the consequence of the specific data in the table.

The maximum length of an interval is 20. This way, SQL Server can very efficiently eliminate intervals from both sides. However, if there were to be only one long interval in the table, the code would become much less efficient, because SQL Server would not be able to eliminate a lot of rows from one side, either left or right, depending on which index it would use. Anyway, in real life, interval length often does not vary a lot, so this optimization technique might be very useful, especially because it is simple.

After you finish with the temporal queries in this section, you can clean up your `tempdb` database with the following code:

```
DROP TABLE dbo.DateNums;
DROP TABLE dbo.Intervals;
```

Temporal features in SQL:2011

Temporal data support was introduced in the SQL:2011—ANSI standard. There were also attempts to define support in the previous standard versions, but without success (TSQL2 extensions in 1995). They were not widely accepted and vendors did not implement them.

The SQL:2011 standard proposed that temporal data should be supported in relational database management systems. A very important thing is that SQL:2011 did not introduce a new data type to support temporal data; rather, it introduced the period.

A period is a table attribute and it's defined by two table columns of date type, representing start time and end time, respectively. It is defined as follows:

- A period must have a name.
- The end time must be greater than the start time.
- It is a closed-open period model. The start time is included in the period and the end time is excluded.

The SQL:2011 standard recognizes two dimensions of temporal data support:

- Application time or valid time tables
- System time or transaction time tables

Application time period tables are intended to meet the requirements of applications that capture time periods during which the data is believed to be valid in the real world. A typical example of such an application is an insurance application, where it is necessary to keep track of the specific policy details of a given customer that are in effect at any given point in time.

System-versioned tables are intended to meet the requirements of applications that must maintain an accurate history of data changes either for business reasons, legal reasons, or both. A typical example of such an application is a banking application, where it is necessary to keep previous states of customer account information so that customers can be provided with a detailed history of their accounts. There are also plenty of examples where certain institutions are required by law to preserve historical data for a specified length of time to meet regulatory and compliance requirements.

Bitemporal tables are tables that implement both application time and system-versioned time support.

After the standard was published, many vendors came up with the temporal table implementation:

- **IDM DB2 10** added full support for temporal tables (for both application time and system-versioned).
- **Oracle** implemented a feature called the **Flashback Data Archive** (**FDA**). It automatically tracks all changes made to data in a database and maintains an archive of historical data. Oracle 12c introduced valid time temporal support.
- **PostgreSQL** does not support temporal tables natively, but temporal tables approximate them.
- **Teradata** implements both valid time and transaction time table types based on the TSQL2 specification.

All these implementations most probably affected Microsoft's decision to implement temporal tables in SQL Server 2016.

System-versioned temporal tables in SQL Server 2017

SQL Server 2016 introduces support for system-versioned temporal tables. Unfortunately, application-time tables are not implemented neither in this version, nor in SQL Server 2017. System-versioned temporal tables bring built-in support for providing information about data stored in the table at any point in time rather than only the data that is correct at the current moment in time. They are implemented according to the specifications in the ANSI SQL:2011 standard with a few extensions.

How temporal tables work in SQL Server 2017

A system-versioned temporal table is implemented in SQL Server 2017 as a pair of tables: the current table containing the actual data, and the history table where only historical entries are stored. There are many limitations for both current and history tables. Here are limitations and considerations that you must take into account for the current table of a system-versioned temporal table:

- It must have a primary key defined
- It must have one PERIOD FOR SYSTEM_TIME defined with two DATETIME2 columns

- Cannot be `FILETABLE` and cannot contain `FILESTREAM` data type
- `INSERT`, `UPDATE`, and `MERGE` statements cannot reference and modify period columns; the start column is always set to system time, the end column to max date value
- `INSTEAD OF` triggers are not allowed
- `TRUNCATE TABLE` is not supported

The list of limitations for a history table is significantly longer and brings many additional restrictions. The following applies to the history table of a system-versioned temporal table:

- Cannot have constraints defined (primary or foreign keys, check, table, or column constraints). Only default column constraints are allowed.
- You cannot modify data in the history table.
- You can neither `ALTER` nor `DROP` a history table.
- It must have the same schema as the current table (column names, data types, ordinal position.
- Cannot be defined as the current table.
- Cannot be `FILETABLE` and cannot contain `FILESTREAM` data type.
- No triggers are allowed (neither `INSTEAD OF` nor `AFTER`).
- `Change Data Capture` and `Change Data Tracking` are not supported.

You can read more about considerations and limitations when working with temporal tables at `https://msdn.microsoft.com/en-us/library/mt604468.aspx`.

The list might look long and discouraging, but all these limitations are there to protect data consistency and accuracy in history tables. However, although you cannot change logical attributes, you can still perform actions related to the physical implementations of the history table: you can switch between rowstore and columnstore table storage, you can choose columns for clustered indexes, and you can create additional non-clustered indexes.

Creating temporal tables

To support the creation of temporal tables, the `CREATE TABLE` and `ALTER TABLE` Transact-SQL statements have been extended. To create a temporal table, you need to perform the following steps:

1. Define a column of `DATETIME2` data type for holding the info since when the row has been valid from a system point of view

2. Define a column of DATETIME2 data type for holding the info until the row is valid from the same point of view

3. Define a period for system time by using previously defined and described columns

4. Set the newly added SYSTEM_VERSIONING table attribute to ON

The following code creates a new temporal table named Product in the dbo schema in the WideWorldImporters database:

```
USE WideWorldImporters;
CREATE TABLE dbo.Product
(
    ProductId INT NOT NULL CONSTRAINT PK_Product PRIMARY KEY,
    ProductName NVARCHAR(50) NOT NULL,
    Price MONEY NOT NULL,
    ValidFrom DATETIME2 GENERATED ALWAYS AS ROW START NOT NULL,
    ValidTo DATETIME2 GENERATED ALWAYS AS ROW END NOT NULL,
    PERIOD FOR SYSTEM_TIME (ValidFrom, ValidTo)
)
WITH (SYSTEM_VERSIONING = ON);
```

You can identify all four elements related to temporal table creation from the previous list: *two period columns*, the *period*, and the SYSTEM_VERSIONING attribute. Note that all elements marked bold are predefined and you must write them exactly like this; data type, nullability, and default values for both period columns are also predefined and you can only choose their names and define data type precision. The data type must be DATETIME2; you can only specify its precision. Furthermore, the period definition itself is predefined too; you must use the period column names you have chosen in the previous step.

By defining period columns and the period, you have created the infrastructure required for implementing temporal tables. However, if you create a table with them but without the SYSTEM_VERSIONING attribute, the table will not be temporal. It will contain an additional two columns with values that are maintained by the system, but the table will not be a system-versioned temporal table.

The final, fourth part is to set the SYSTEM_VERSIONING attribute to ON. When you execute the previous code, you implicitly instruct SQL Server to automatically create a history table for the dbo.Product temporal table. The table will be created in the same schema (dbo), with a name according to the following naming convention:

MSSQL_TemporalHistoryFor_<current_temporal_table_object_id>_[suffix].
The suffix is optional and it will be added only if the first part of the table name is not unique. The following screenshot shows what you will see when you open **SQL Server Management Studio** (**SSMS**) and find the dbo.Product table:

Temporal table in SQL Server Management Studio

You can see that all temporal tables have a small clock icon indicating temporality. Under the table name, you can see its history table. Note that columns in both tables are identical (column names, data types, precision, nullability), but also that the history table does not have constraints (primary key).

 Period columns must be of the DATETIME2 data type. If you try to define them with the DATETIME data type, you will get an error. The SQL:2011 standard does not specify data type precision, thus system-versioned temporal tables in SQL Server 2017 are not implemented strictly according to standard. This is very important when you migrate your existing temporal solution to one that uses new temporal tables in SQL Server 2017. Usually, columns that you were using are of the DATETIME data type and you have to extend their data type to DATETIME2.

You can also specify the name of the history table and let SQL Server create it with the same attributes as described earlier. Use the following code to create a temporal table with a user-defined history table name:

```
USE WideWorldImporters;
CREATE TABLE dbo.Product2
(
    ProductId INT NOT NULL CONSTRAINT PK_Product2 PRIMARY KEY,
    ProductName NVARCHAR(50) NOT NULL,
    Price MONEY NOT NULL,
    ValidFrom DATETIME2 GENERATED ALWAYS AS ROW START NOT NULL,
    ValidTo DATETIME2 GENERATED ALWAYS AS ROW END NOT NULL,
    PERIOD FOR SYSTEM_TIME (ValidFrom, ValidTo)
)
WITH (SYSTEM_VERSIONING = ON (HISTORY_TABLE = dbo.ProductHistory2));
```

What storage type is used for the automatically created history table? By default, it is a rowstore table with a clustered index on the period columns. The table is compressed with PAGE compression, if it can be enabled for compression (has no SPARSE or (B)LOB columns). To find out the storage type of the history table, use the following code:

```
SELECT temporal_type_desc, p.data_compression_desc
FROM sys.tables t
INNER JOIN sys.partitions p ON t.object_id = p.object_id
WHERE name = 'ProductHistory2';
```

The result of the preceding query shows that PAGE compression has been applied:

temporal_type_desc	data_compression_desc
HISTORY_TABLE	PAGE

You can also see that the history table has a clustered index. The following code extracts the index name and the columns used in the index:

```
SELECT i.name, i.type_desc, c.name, ic.index_column_id
FROM sys.indexes i
INNER JOIN sys.index_columns ic on ic.object_id = i.object_id
INNER JOIN sys.columns c on c.object_id = i.object_id AND ic.column_id =
c.column_id
WHERE OBJECT_NAME(i.object_id) = 'ProductHistory2';
```

The output of this query shows that the automatically created history table has a clustered index on the period columns and the name in the following ix_<history_tablename> format:

name	type_desc	name	index_column_id
ix_ProductHistory2	CLUSTERED	ValidFrom	1
ix_ProductHistory2	CLUSTERED	ValidTo	2

This index is a good choice, when you want to query the history table only by using dates as criteria. However, when you want to browse through the history of one item, that would be an inappropriate index.

If the predefined implementation of the history table (rowstore and period columns in a clustered index) does not meet your criteria for historical data, you can create your own history table. Of course, you need to respect all constraints and limitations listed at the beginning of the chapter. The following code first creates a history table, then a temporal table, and finally assigns the history table to it. Note that, in order to proceed with the code execution, you need to remove the temporal table created in the first example in this chapter:

```
USE WideWorldImporters;
ALTER TABLE dbo.Product SET (SYSTEM_VERSIONING = OFF);
ALTER TABLE dbo.Product DROP PERIOD FOR SYSTEM_TIME;
DROP TABLE IF EXISTS dbo.Product;
DROP TABLE IF EXISTS dbo.ProductHistory;
GO
CREATE TABLE dbo.ProductHistory
(
    ProductId INT NOT NULL,
    ProductName NVARCHAR(50) NOT NULL,
    Price MONEY NOT NULL,
    ValidFrom DATETIME2 NOT NULL,
    ValidTo DATETIME2 NOT NULL
);
CREATE CLUSTERED COLUMNSTORE INDEX IX_ProductHistory ON dbo.ProductHistory;
CREATE NONCLUSTERED INDEX IX_ProductHistory_NC ON
dbo.ProductHistory(ProductId, ValidFrom, ValidTo);
GO
CREATE TABLE dbo.Product
(
    ProductId INT NOT NULL CONSTRAINT PK_Product PRIMARY KEY,
    ProductName NVARCHAR(50) NOT NULL,
    Price MONEY NOT NULL,
    ValidFrom DATETIME2 GENERATED ALWAYS AS ROW START NOT NULL,
    ValidTo DATETIME2 GENERATED ALWAYS AS ROW END NOT NULL,
    PERIOD FOR SYSTEM_TIME (ValidFrom, ValidTo)
)
WITH (SYSTEM_VERSIONING = ON (HISTORY_TABLE = dbo.ProductHistory));
```

You will learn how to alter and drop system-versioned tables in more detail later in this chapter. Here, you should focus on the fact that you can create your own history table with a clustered columnstore index on it. The following screenshot shows what you will see when you look at SSMS and find the created temporal table:

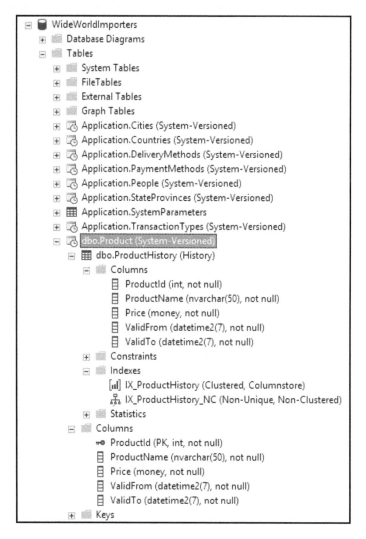

Temporal table in SQL Server Management Studio with user-defined history table

You can see that the table created by you acts as a history table and has a clustered columnstore index.

Period columns as hidden attributes

Period columns are used to support the temporality of data and have no business logic value. By using the HIDDEN clause, you can hide the new PERIOD columns to avoid impacting on existing applications that are not designed to handle new columns. The following code will create two temporal tables, one with default values (visible period column) and the other with hidden period columns:

```
CREATE TABLE dbo.T1(
    Id INT NOT NULL CONSTRAINT PK_T1 PRIMARY KEY,
    Col1 INT NOT NULL,
    ValidFrom DATETIME2 GENERATED ALWAYS AS ROW START NOT NULL,
    ValidTo DATETIME2 GENERATED ALWAYS AS ROW END NOT NULL,
    PERIOD FOR SYSTEM_TIME (ValidFrom, ValidTo)
)
WITH (SYSTEM_VERSIONING = ON (HISTORY_TABLE = dbo.T1_Hist));
GO
INSERT INTO dbo.T1(Id, Col1) VALUES(1, 1);
GO
CREATE TABLE dbo.T2(
    Id INT NOT NULL CONSTRAINT PK_T2 PRIMARY KEY,
    Col1 INT NOT NULL,
    ValidFrom DATETIME2 GENERATED ALWAYS AS ROW START HIDDEN NOT NULL,
    ValidTo DATETIME2 GENERATED ALWAYS AS ROW END HIDDEN NOT NULL,
    PERIOD FOR SYSTEM_TIME (ValidFrom, ValidTo)
)
WITH (SYSTEM_VERSIONING = ON (HISTORY_TABLE = dbo.T2_Hist));
GO
INSERT INTO dbo.T2(Id, Col1) VALUES(1, 1);
GO
```

When you query both tables, you can see that period columns are not listed for the second table:

```
SELECT * FROM dbo.T1;
SELECT * FROM dbo.T2;
```

Here is the result:

```
Id   Col1      ValidFrom                   ValidTo
---  ------    --------------------------  --------------------------
1    1         2017-12-14 23:05:44.2068702 9999-12-31 23:59:59.9999999


Id        Col1
--------  -----------
1         1
```

As you can see, period columns are not shown, even when you use * in your queries. So, you can implement temporal functionality for a table transparently and you can be sure that your existing code will still work. Of course, if you explicitly specify period columns with their names, they will be shown in the result set.

 I need here to express my concerns about another implementation that takes care of solutions where SELECT * is implemented. I can understand that the vendor does not want to introduce a feature that can break customers' existing applications, but on the other hand, you cannot expect a developer to stop using SELECT * when new features and solutions don't sanction bad development habits.

Hidden attributes let you convert normal tables to temporal tables without worrying about breaking changes in your applications.

Converting non-temporal tables to temporal tables

In SQL Server 2017, you can create temporal tables from scratch, but you can also alter an existing table and add attributes to it to convert it to a system-versioned temporal table. All you need to do is to add period columns, define the SYSTEM_TIME period on them, and set the temporal attribute. In this section, for example, you will convert the Department table from the AdventureWorks2017 database into a temporal table. The following screenshot shows the table's content:

DepartmentID	Name	GroupName	ModifiedDate
1	Engineering	Research and Development	2008-04-30 00:00:00.000
2	Tool Design	Research and Development	2008-04-30 00:00:00.000
3	Sales	Sales and Marketing	2008-04-30 00:00:00.000
4	Marketing	Sales and Marketing	2008-04-30 00:00:00.000
5	Purchasing	Inventory Management	2008-04-30 00:00:00.000
6	Research and Development	Research and Development	2008-04-30 00:00:00.000
7	Production	Manufacturing	2008-04-30 00:00:00.000
8	Production Control	Manufacturing	2008-04-30 00:00:00.000
9	Human Resources	Executive General and Administration	2008-04-30 00:00:00.000
10	Finance	Executive General and Administration	2008-04-30 00:00:00.000
11	Information Services	Executive General and Administration	2008-04-30 00:00:00.000
12	Document Control	Quality Assurance	2008-04-30 00:00:00.000
13	Quality Assurance	Quality Assurance	2008-04-30 00:00:00.000
14	Facilities and Maintenance	Executive General and Administration	2008-04-30 00:00:00.000
15	Shipping and Receiving	Inventory Management	2008-04-30 00:00:00.000
16	Executive	Executive General and Administration	2008-04-30 00:00:00.000

Data in the HumanResources.Department table

You can see that the table has one column representing temporality. The `ModifiedDate` column shows the time a table row became valid, that is, when it was recently updated. However, since there is no history table, you don't know previous row versions. By converting the table to a temporal table, you can retain the existing functionality, and add the temporal one. The following code example demonstrates how to convert the `Department` table in the `AdventureWorks2017` database to a temporal table:

```
USE AdventureWorks2017;
--the ModifiedDate column will be replaced by temporal table functionality
ALTER TABLE HumanResources.Department DROP CONSTRAINT
DF_Department_ModifiedDate;
ALTER TABLE HumanResources.Department DROP COLUMN ModifiedDate;
GO
ALTER TABLE HumanResources.Department
ADD ValidFrom DATETIME2 GENERATED ALWAYS AS ROW START HIDDEN NOT NULL
CONSTRAINT DF_Validfrom DEFAULT '20080430 00:00:00.0000000',
    ValidTo DATETIME2 GENERATED ALWAYS AS ROW END HIDDEN NOT NULL CONSTRAINT
DF_ValidTo DEFAULT '99991231 23:59:59.9999999',
    PERIOD FOR SYSTEM_TIME (ValidFrom, ValidTo);
GO
ALTER TABLE HumanResources.Department SET (SYSTEM_VERSIONING = ON
(HISTORY_TABLE = HumanResources.DepartmentHistory));
```

Since the existing temporal data implementation will be replaced by an SQL Server 2017 temporal table, the `ModifiedDate` column is not necessary anymore and can be removed. Furthermore, you have to use two `ALTER` statements; with the first statement, you define the period columns and the period, while the second statement sets the `SYSTEM_VERSIONING` attribute to `ON` and defines the name of the history table that will be created by the system.

You should be aware that you need to provide default constraints for both columns, since they must be non-nullable. You can even use a date value from the past for the default constraint of the first period column (as shown in the preceding code example, where the value is set to the one from the removed column); however, you cannot set values in the future. Finally, period date columns are defined with the `HIDDEN` attribute to ensure that there will be no breaking changes in the existing code.

Adding a non-nullable column with a default constraint is a metadata operation in Enterprise Edition only; in all other editions that means a physical operation with the allocation space to update all table rows with newly added columns. For large tables, this can take a long time, and be aware that, during this action, the table is locked.

Any further change in the table will be automatically handled by the system and written in the `HumanResources.DepartmentHistory` history table. For instance, you can update the `Name` attribute for the department with the ID of 2 and then check the values in both tables:

```
UPDATE HumanResources.Department SET Name='Political Correctness' WHERE
DepartmentID = 2;
SELECT * FROM HumanResources.Department WHERE DepartmentID = 2;
SELECT * FROM HumanResources.DepartmentHistory;
```

The first table simply shows the new value, while the second shows the previous one, with appropriate validity dates from a system point of view (the time part of the date is shortened for brevity):

DepartmentID	Name	GroupName
2	Political Correctness	Research and Development

DepartmentID	Name	GroupName	ValidFrom	ValidTo
2	Tool Design	Research and Development	2008-04-30	2017-12-15

As you can see, it is very easy and straightforward to add temporal functionality to an existing non-temporal table. It works transparently; all your queries and commands will work without changes.

Migrating an existing temporal solution to system-versioned tables

Most probably, you have had to deal with historical data in the past. Since there was no out-of-the-box feature in previous SQL Server versions, you had to create a custom temporal data solution. Now that the feature is available, you might think to use it for your existing temporal solutions. You saw earlier in this chapter that you can define your own history table. Therefore, you can also use an existing and populated historical table. If you want to convert your existing solution to use system-versioned temporal tables in SQL Server 2017, you have to prepare both tables so that they fill all requirements for temporal tables. To achieve this, you will again use the AdventureWorks2017 database and create both current and history tables by using tables that exist in this database. Use the following code to create and populate the tables:

```
USE WideWorldImporters;
CREATE TABLE dbo.ProductListPrice
(
    ProductID INT NOT NULL CONSTRAINT PK_ProductListPrice PRIMARY KEY,
    ListPrice MONEY NOT NULL,
);
INSERT INTO dbo.ProductListPrice(ProductID,ListPrice)
SELECT ProductID,ListPrice FROM AdventureWorks2017.Production.Product;
GO
CREATE TABLE dbo.ProductListPriceHistory
(
    ProductID INT NOT NULL,
    ListPrice MONEY NOT NULL,
    StartDate DATETIME NOT NULL,
    EndDate DATETIME    NULL,
    CONSTRAINT PK_ProductListPriceHistory PRIMARY KEY CLUSTERED
    (
        ProductID ASC,
        StartDate ASC
    )
);
INSERT INTO
dbo.ProductListPriceHistory(ProductID,ListPrice,StartDate,EndDate)
SELECT ProductID, ListPrice, StartDate, EndDate FROM
AdventureWorks2017.Production.ProductListPriceHistory;
```

Consider the rows for the product with an ID of 707 in both tables:

```
SELECT * FROM dbo.ProductListPrice WHERE ProductID = 707;
SELECT * FROM dbo.ProductListPriceHistory WHERE ProductID = 707;
```

Here are the rows in the current and history tables respectively:

```
ProductID   ListPrice
----------  ----------
707         34.99
ProductID   ListPrice   StartDate               EndDate
----------  ----------  ----------------------  ----------------------
707         33.6442     2011-05-31 00:00:00.000 2012-05-29 00:00:00.000
707         33.6442     2012-05-30 00:00:00.000 2013-05-29 00:00:00.000
707         34.99       2013-05-30 00:00:00.000 NULL
```

Assume that this data has been produced by your temporal data solution and that you want to use system-versioned temporal tables in SQL Server 2017 instead of it, but also use the same tables. The first thing you have to do is align the columns in both tables. Since the current table has no date columns, you need to add two period columns and define the period. The columns should have the same name as the counterpart columns from the history table. Here is the code that creates the temporal infrastructure in the current table:

```
ALTER TABLE dbo.ProductListPrice
ADD StartDate DATETIME2 GENERATED ALWAYS AS ROW START HIDDEN NOT NULL
CONSTRAINT DF_StartDate1 DEFAULT '20170101 00:00:00.0000000',
    EndDate DATETIME2 GENERATED ALWAYS AS ROW END HIDDEN NOT NULL CONSTRAINT
DF_EndDate1 DEFAULT '99991231 23:59:59.9999999',
    PERIOD FOR SYSTEM_TIME (StartDate, EndDate);
GO
```

The next steps are related to the history table. As you can see from the sample data, your current solution allows gaps in the history table and also contains the current value with the undefined end date. As mentioned earlier in this chapter, the history table only contains historical data and there are no gaps between historical entries (the new start date is equal to the previous end date). Here are the steps you have to implement in order to prepare the dbo.ProductLisPriceHistory table to act as a history table in a system-versioned temporal table in SQL Server 2017:

- Update the non-nullable EndDate column to remove the gap between historical values described earlier and to support the open-closed interval
- Update all rows where the EndDate column is null to the StartDate of the rows in the current table

- Remove the primary key constraint
- Change the data type for both date columns `StartDate` and `EndDate` to `DATETIME2`

Here is the code that implements all these requests:

```
--remove gaps
UPDATE dbo.ProductListPriceHistory SET EndDate = DATEADD(day,1,EndDate);
--update EndDate to StartDate of the actual record
UPDATE dbo.ProductListPriceHistory SET EndDate = (SELECT MAX(StartDate)
FROM dbo.ProductListPrice) WHERE EndDate IS NULL;
--remove constraints
ALTER TABLE dbo.ProductListPriceHistory DROP CONSTRAINT
PK_ProductListPriceHistory;
--change data type to DATETIME2
ALTER TABLE dbo.ProductListPriceHistory ALTER COLUMN StartDate DATETIME2
NOT NULL;
ALTER TABLE dbo.ProductListPriceHistory ALTER COLUMN EndDate DATETIME2 NOT
NULL;
```

Now, both tables are ready to act as a system-versioned temporal table in SQL Server 2017:

```
ALTER TABLE dbo.ProductListPrice SET (SYSTEM_VERSIONING = ON (HISTORY_TABLE
= dbo.ProductListPriceHistory,  DATA_CONSISTENCY_CHECK = ON));
```

The command has been executed successfully and the `dbo.ProductListPriceHistory` table is now a system-versioned temporal table. Note that the `DATA_CONSISTENCY_CHECK = ON` option is used to check that all rows in the history table are valid from a temporal data point of view (no gaps and the end date is not before the start date). Now, you can check the new functionality by using the `UPDATE` statement. You will update the price for the product by changing the ID of `707` to `50` and then check the rows in both tables:

```
UPDATE dbo.ProductListPrice SET ListPrice = 50 WHERE ProductID = 707;
SELECT * FROM dbo.ProductListPrice WHERE ProductID = 707;
SELECT * FROM dbo.ProductListPriceHistory WHERE ProductID = 707;
```

Here are the rows for this product in both tables:

```
ProductID   ListPrice
---------   ---------
707         50.00
ProductID ListPrice  StartDate                   EndDate
--------- ---------  -------------------------   -------------------------
707       33.6442 2011-05-31 00:00:00.0000000 2012-05-30 00:00:00.0000000
707       33.6442 2012-05-30 00:00:00.0000000 2013-05-30 00:00:00.0000000
707       34.99   2013-05-30 00:00:00.0000000 2017-12-12 21:21:08.4382496
```

707   34.99   2017-12-12 21:21:08.4382496 2017-12-12 21:21:08.4382496

You can see another row in the history table (compare with the previous result). Of course, when you try these examples, you will get different values for the columns `StartDate` and `EndDate`, since they are managed by the system.

 AdventureWorks has long been one of the most used SQL Server sample databases. After introducing the `WideWorldImporter` database, it was not supported in the SQL Server 2016 RTM, but `AdventureWorks` is back in SQL Server 2017. You can download it at `https://github.com/Microsoft/sql-server-samples/releases/tag/adventureworks`.

As you can see, it is not so complicated to migrate an existing solution to a system-versioned table in SQL Server 2017, but it is not a single step. You should take into account that most probably it will take time to update the data type to `DATETIME2`. However, by using the system-versioned temporal tables feature, your history tables are completely and automatically protected from changes by anyone except the system. This is a great out-of-the-box data consistency improvement.

Altering temporal tables

You can use the `ALTER TABLE` statement to perform schema changes on system-versioned temporal tables. When you use it to add a new data type, change a data type, or remove an existing column, the system will automatically perform the action against both the current and the history table. However, some of these actions will not be metadata operations only; there are changes that will update the entire table. To check this, run the following code to create (and populate with sample data) the temporal table from the previous section:

```
USE tempdb;
CREATE TABLE dbo.Product
(
    ProductId INT NOT NULL CONSTRAINT PK_Product PRIMARY KEY,
    ProductName NVARCHAR(50) NOT NULL,
    Price MONEY NOT NULL,
    ValidFrom DATETIME2 GENERATED ALWAYS AS ROW START NOT NULL,
    ValidTo DATETIME2 GENERATED ALWAYS AS ROW END NOT NULL,
    PERIOD FOR SYSTEM_TIME (ValidFrom, ValidTo)
)
WITH (SYSTEM_VERSIONING = ON (HISTORY_TABLE = dbo.ProductHistory));
GO
INSERT INTO dbo.Product (ProductId,ProductName,Price)
SELECT message_id,'PROD' + CAST(message_id AS NVARCHAR), severity FROM
sys.messages WHERE language_id = 1033;
```

Now, you will add three new columns into the temporal table:

- A column named `Color`, which allows NULL values
- A column named `Category`, where a non-nullable value is mandatory
- A **Large Object** (**LOB**) column named `Description`

But before you add them, you will create an **Extended Events** (**XE**) session to trace what happens under the hood when you add a new column to a temporal table. Use the following code to create and start the XE session:

```
CREATE EVENT SESSION AlteringTemporalTable ON SERVER
ADD EVENT sqlserver.sp_statement_starting(
    WHERE (sqlserver.database_id = 2)),
ADD EVENT sqlserver.sp_statement_completed(
    WHERE (sqlserver.database_id = 2)),
ADD EVENT sqlserver.sql_statement_starting(
    WHERE (sqlserver.database_id = 2)),
ADD EVENT sqlserver.sql_statement_completed(
    WHERE (sqlserver.database_id = 2))
ADD TARGET package0.event_file (SET filename = N'AlteringTemporalTable')
WITH (MAX_DISPATCH_LATENCY = 1 SECONDS)
GO
ALTER EVENT SESSION AlteringTemporalTable ON SERVER STATE = start;
GO
```

Now you can issue the following three `ALTER` statements that correspond to the previously described new columns:

```
ALTER TABLE dbo.Product ADD Color NVARCHAR(15);
ALTER TABLE dbo.Product ADD Category SMALLINT NOT NULL CONSTRAINT
DF_Category DEFAULT 1;
ALTER TABLE dbo.Product ADD Description NVARCHAR(MAX) NOT NULL CONSTRAINT
DF_Description DEFAULT N'N/A';
```

The content collected by the XE session is shown as follows:

Displaying 10 Events		
name	timestamp	statement
sql_statement_starting	2017-12-17 23:28:28.5382499	SELECT @@SPID
sql_statement_completed	2017-12-17 23:28:28.5382623	SELECT @@SPID
sql_statement_starting	2017-12-17 23:28:28.5418307	ALTER TABLE dbo.Product ADD Color NVARCHAR(15)
sql_statement_completed	2017-12-17 23:28:28.5429845	ALTER TABLE dbo.Product ADD Color NVARCHAR(15)
sql_statement_starting	2017-12-17 23:28:28.5433065	ALTER TABLE dbo.Product ADD Category SMALLINT NOT NULL CONSTRAINT DF_Category DEFAULT 1
sql_statement_completed	2017-12-17 23:28:28.5447483	ALTER TABLE dbo.Product ADD Category SMALLINT NOT NULL CONSTRAINT DF_Category DEFAULT 1
sql_statement_starting	2017-12-17 23:28:28.5447855	ALTER TABLE dbo.Product ADD Description NVARCHAR(MAX) NOT NULL CONSTRAINT DF_Description DEFAULT N'N/A'
sp_statement_starting	2017-12-17 23:28:28.5472037	UPDATE [dbo].[Product] SET [Description] = DEFAULT
sp_statement_completed	2017-12-17 23:28:28.6044360	UPDATE [dbo].[Product] SET [Description] = DEFAULT
sql_statement_completed	2017-12-17 23:28:28.6047962	ALTER TABLE dbo.Product ADD Description NVARCHAR(MAX) NOT NULL CONSTRAINT DF_Description DEFAULT N'N/A'

Data collected by Extended Event session

It clearly shows that the first two ALTER statements have been executed without additional actions. However, adding a LOB column triggers the updating of all rows with the default value as an offline operation.

The first statement adds a column that accepts null values, so the action is done instantly.

When you add a non-nullable column, the situation is different, as illustrated in the second statement. First, you need to provide a default constraint to ensure that all rows will have a value in this column. This action will be online (metadata operation) in the Enterprise and Developer editions only. In all the other editions, all rows in both the current and the history table will be updated to add additional columns with their values.

However, adding LOB or BLOB columns will cause a mass update in both the current and the history table in all SQL Server editions! This action will internally update all rows in both tables. For large tables, this can take a long time and during this time, both tables are locked.

You can also use the ALTER TABLE statement to add the HIDDEN attribute to period columns or to remove it. This code line adds the HIDDEN attribute to the columns ValidFrom and ValidTo:

```
ALTER TABLE dbo.Product ALTER COLUMN ValidFrom ADD HIDDEN;
ALTER TABLE dbo.Product ALTER COLUMN ValidTo ADD HIDDEN;
```

Clearly, you can also remove the HIDDEN attribute:

```
ALTER TABLE dbo.Product ALTER COLUMN ValidFrom DROP HIDDEN;
ALTER TABLE dbo.Product ALTER COLUMN ValidTo DROP HIDDEN;
```

However, there are some changes that are not allowed for temporal tables:

- Adding an IDENDITY or computed column
- Adding a ROWGUIDCOL column or changing an existing column to it
- Adding a SPARSE column or changing an existing column to it, when the history table is compressed

When you try to add a SPARSE column, you will get an error, as in the following example:

```
ALTER TABLE dbo.Product ADD Size NVARCHAR(5) SPARSE;
```

The command ends up with the following error message:

Msg 11418, Level 16, State 2, Line 20
Cannot alter table 'ProductHistory' because the table either contains
sparse columns or a column set column which are incompatible with
compression.

The same happens when you try to add an IDENTITY column, as follows:

```
ALTER TABLE dbo.Product ADD ProductNumber INT IDENTITY (1,1);
```

And here is the error message:

Msg 13704, Level 16, State 1, Line 26
System-versioned table schema modification failed because history table
'WideWorldImporters.dbo.ProductHistory' has IDENTITY column specification.
Consider dropping all IDENTITY column specifications and trying again.

If you need to perform schema changes to a temporal table not supported in the ALTER statement, you have to set its SYSTEM_VERSIONING attribute to false to convert the tables to non-temporal tables, perform the changes, and then convert back to a temporal table. The following code demonstrates how to add the identity column ProductNumber and the sparse column Size into the temporal table dbo.Product:

```
ALTER TABLE dbo.ProductHistory REBUILD PARTITION = ALL WITH
(DATA_COMPRESSION=NONE);
GO
BEGIN TRAN
ALTER TABLE dbo.Product SET (SYSTEM_VERSIONING = OFF);
ALTER TABLE dbo.Product ADD Size NVARCHAR(5) SPARSE;
```

```
ALTER TABLE dbo.ProductHistory ADD Size NVARCHAR(5) SPARSE;
ALTER TABLE dbo.Product ADD ProductNumber INT IDENTITY (1,1);
ALTER TABLE dbo.ProductHistory ADD ProductNumber INT NOT NULL DEFAULT 0;
ALTER TABLE dbo.Product SET(SYSTEM_VERSIONING = ON (HISTORY_TABLE = dbo.
ProductHistory));
COMMIT;
```

To perform ALTER TABLE operations, you need to have CONTROL permission on the current and history tables. During the changes, both tables are locked with schema locks.

Dropping temporal tables

You cannot drop a system-versioned temporal table. Both current and history tables are protected until the SYSTEM_VERSIONING attribute of the current table is set to ON. When you set it to OFF, both tables automatically become non-temporal tables and are fully independent of each other. Therefore, you can perform all operations against them that are allowed according to your permissions. You can also drop the period if you definitely want to convert a temporal table to a non-temporal one. The following code converts the Product table into a non-temporal table and removes the defined SYSTEM_TIME period:

```
ALTER TABLE dbo.Product SET (SYSTEM_VERSIONING = OFF);
ALTER TABLE dbo.Product DROP PERIOD FOR SYSTEM_TIME);
```

Note that the period columns ValidFrom and ValidTo remain in the table and will be further updated by the system. However, the history table will not be updated when data in the current table is changed.

Data manipulation in temporal tables

In this section, you will see what happens when data is inserted, updated, or deleted into/in/from a temporal table. Note that all manipulations will be done against the current table. The history table is protected; only the system can write to it.

 Even members of the sysadmin server role cannot insert, update, or delete rows from a history table of a system-versioned temporal table in SQL Server 2017.

As an example, you will use the `dbo.Product` temporal table created in the previous section. Use this code to recreate the table:

```
USE WideWorldImporters;
--remove existing temporal table if exists
ALTER TABLE dbo.Product SET (SYSTEM_VERSIONING = OFF);
ALTER TABLE dbo.Product DROP PERIOD FOR SYSTEM_TIME;
DROP TABLE IF EXISTS dbo.Product;
DROP TABLE IF EXISTS dbo.ProductHistory;
GO
CREATE TABLE dbo.Product
(
    ProductId INT NOT NULL CONSTRAINT PK_Product PRIMARY KEY,
    ProductName NVARCHAR(50) NOT NULL,
    Price MONEY NOT NULL,
    ValidFrom DATETIME2 GENERATED ALWAYS AS ROW START NOT NULL,
    ValidTo DATETIME2 GENERATED ALWAYS AS ROW END NOT NULL,
    PERIOD FOR SYSTEM_TIME (ValidFrom, ValidTo)
)
WITH (SYSTEM_VERSIONING = ON (HISTORY_TABLE = dbo.ProductHistory));
GO
```

Now, you can insert, update, and delete rows in this table to demonstrate how these actions affect the current and history table.

Inserting data in temporal tables

Assume that the table is empty and you have added the `Fog` product with a `150` price on 12th November 2017. Here is the code for this action:

```
INSERT INTO dbo.Product(ProductId, ProductName, Price) VALUES(1, N'Fog',
150.00) ;-- on 12th November
```

The state of the current table is as follows:

ProductId	ProductName	Price	ValidFrom	ValidTo
1	Fog	150	12.11.2017	31.12.9999

The state of the history table is as follows:

ProductId	ProductName	Price	ValidFrom	ValidTo

Note that the dates in the `ValidFrom` and `ValidTo` columns are displayed in short format for clarity; their actual value is of `DATETIME2` data type.

As you can see, after an `INSERT` into a temporal table, the following transitions occur:

- **Current table**: A new row has been added with attributes from the `INSERT` statement, the period start date column is set to the system date and the period end date column is set to the maximum value for the `DATETIME2` data type
- **History table**: Not affected at all

Updating data in temporal tables

Now, assume that the price for the product has been changed to `200` and that this change was entered into the database on 28th November 2017. Here is the code for this action:

```
UPDATE dbo.Product SET Price = 200.00 WHERE ProductId = 1;-- on 28th
November
```

The state of the current table is as follows after the preceding statement's execution:

ProductId	ProductName	Price	ValidFrom	ValidTo
1	Fog	200	28.11.2017	31.12.9999

The state of the history table is as follows after the preceding statement's execution:

ProductId	ProductName	Price	ValidFrom	ValidTo
1	Fog	150	12.11.2017	28.11.2017

Note again that values in the `ValidFrom` and `ValidTo` columns are displayed in short format for clarity. The value in the `ValidTo` column in the history table is identical to the `ValidFrom` value in the current table; there are no gaps.

The start and end time period columns store time in the UTC time zone!

Now, assume that you reduced the price the next day to `180`. Here is the code for this action:

```
UPDATE dbo.Product SET Price = 180.00 WHERE ProductId = 1;-- on 29th
November
```

The state of the current table is as follows after the preceding statement's execution:

ProductId	ProductName	Price	ValidFrom	ValidTo
1	Fog	180	29.11.2017	31.12.9999

The state of the history table is as follows after the preceding statement's execution:

ProductId	ProductName	Price	ValidFrom	ValidTo
1	Fog	150	12.11.2017	28.11.2017
1	Fog	200	28.11.2017	29.11.2017

You can see another entry in the history table indicating that the price `200` was valid for one day. What would happen if you execute the same statement again, say on 30th November? There is no real change; no business logic attributes are changed, but what does it mean for temporal tables? Here is the code for this action:

```
UPDATE dbo.Product SET Price = 180.00 WHERE ProductId = 1;-- on 30th
November
```

The state of the current table is as follows after the preceding statement's execution:

ProductId	ProductName	Price	ValidFrom	ValidTo
1	Fog	180	30.11.2017	31.12.9999

The state of the history table is as follows after the preceding statement's execution:

ProductId	ProductName	Price	ValidFrom	ValidTo
1	Fog	150	12.11.2017	28.11.2017
1	Fog	200	28.11.2017	29.11.2017
1	Fog	180	29.11.2017	30.11.2017

As you can see in the history table, even if there is no real change to the attributes in the current table, an entry in the history table is created and period date columns are updated.

 You can think about this as a bug, but although no attributes have been changed, if you use temporal tables for auditing you probably want to see all attempts at data manipulation in the main table.

Here is how an UPDATE of a single row in a temporal table affects the current and history tables:

- **Current table**: Values in the current table are updated to those provided by the UPDATE statement, the period start date column is set to the system date, and the period end date column is set to the maximum value for the DATETIME2 data type
- **History table**: The row from the current table before updating is copied to the history table, and only the period end date column is set to the system date

You can also see that there are no gaps in the dates in the same row of the history table. Even duplicates are possible; the history table does not have constraints to prevent them! Therefore, it is possible to have multiple records for the same row with the same values in period columns. Moreover, even values in period columns can be identical! The only constraint that is enforced is that the date representing the period end date column cannot be before the date representing the period start date (therefore, it is guaranteed that ValidFrom <= ValidTo).

Deleting data in temporal tables

You will finally remove the row from the current table in order to demonstrate how the DELETE statement affects temporal tables. Here is the code for this action:

```
DELETE FROM dbo.Product WHERE ProductId = 1;-- on 15th December
```

The state of the current table is as follows after the preceding statement's execution:

ProductId	ProductName	Price	ValidFrom	ValidTo

The state of the history table is as follows after the preceding statement's execution:

ProductId	ProductName	Price	ValidFrom	ValidTo
1	Fog	150	12.11.2017	28.11.2017
1	Fog	200	28.11.2017	29.11.2017
1	Fog	180	29.11.2017	30.11.2017
1	Fog	180	30.11.2017	15.12.2017

As you expected, there are no rows the current table, but another row has been added to the history table. After executing the DELETE statement against a single row in a temporal table:

- **Current table**: The row has been removed
- **History table**: The row from the current table before deleting is copied to the history table, and only the period end date column is set to the system date

Use this opportunity to clean up the temporal table created in this section:

```
ALTER TABLE dbo.Product SET (SYSTEM_VERSIONING = OFF);
ALTER TABLE dbo.Product DROP PERIOD FOR SYSTEM_TIME;
DROP TABLE IF EXISTS dbo.Product;
DROP TABLE IF EXISTS dbo.ProductHistory;
```

Querying temporal data in SQL Server 2017

System-versioned tables are primarily intended for tracking historical data changes. Queries on system-versioned tables often tend to be concerned with retrieving table content as of a given point in time, or between any two given points in time. As you saw, Microsoft has implemented them according to the SQL:2011 standard, which means that two physical tables exist: a table with actual data and a history table. In order to simplify queries against temporal tables, the SQL:2011 standard introduced a new SQL clause, FOR SYSTEM_TIME. In addition to it, some new temporal-specific sub-clauses have been added too. SQL Server 2017 has not only implemented these extensions, but added two more extensions. Here is the complete list of clauses and extensions you can use to query temporal data in SQL Server 2017:

- FOR SYSTEM_TIME AS OF
- FOR SYSTEM_TIME FROM TO

- FOR SYSTEM_TIME BETWEEN AND
- FOR SYSTEM TIME CONTAINED_IN
- FOR SYSTEM_TIME ALL

Retrieving temporal data at a specific point in time

When you want to retrieve temporal data that was valid at a given point in time, the resulting set could contain both actual and historical data. For instance, the following query would return all rows from the People temporal table in the WideWorldImporters sample database that were valid at 20th May 2013 at 8 A.M.:

```
SELECT PersonID, FullName, OtherLanguages, ValidFrom, ValidTo
FROM Application.People WHERE ValidFrom <= '20130520 08:00:00' AND ValidTo
> '20130520 08:00:00'
UNION ALL
SELECT PersonID, FullName, OtherLanguages, ValidFrom, ValidTo
FROM Application.People_Archive WHERE ValidFrom <= '20130520 08:00:00' AND
ValidTo > '20130520 08:00:00';
```

The query returns 1,060 rows. For a single person, only one row is returned: either the actual or a historical row. A row is valid if its start date was before or exactly on the given date and its end date is greater than the given date.

The new FOR SYSTEM_TIME clause with the AS OF sub-clause can be used to simplify the preceding query. Here is the same query with temporal Transact-SQL extensions:

```
SELECT PersonID, FullName, OtherLanguages, ValidFrom, ValidTo
FROM Application.People FOR SYSTEM_TIME AS OF '20130520 08:00:00';
```

Of course, it returns the same result set and the execution plans are identical, as shown in the following screenshot:

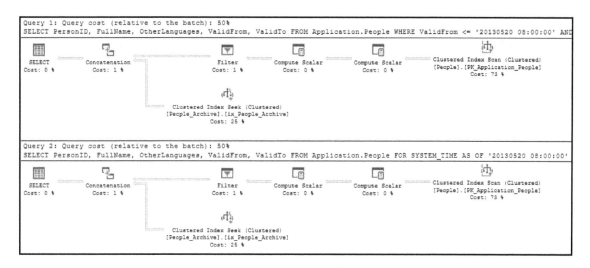

```
Query 1: Query cost (relative to the batch): 50%
SELECT PersonID, FullName, OtherLanguages, ValidFrom, ValidTo FROM Application.People WHERE ValidFrom <= '20130520 08:00:00' AND
```

```
Query 2: Query cost (relative to the batch): 50%
SELECT PersonID, FullName, OtherLanguages, ValidFrom, ValidTo FROM Application.People FOR SYSTEM_TIME AS OF '20130520 08:00:00'
```

Execution plans for point-in-time queries against temporal tables

Under the hood, the query processor touches both tables and retrieves data, but the query with temporal extensions looks simpler.

The special case of a point-in-time query against a temporal table is a query where you specify the actual date as the point in time. The following query returns actual data from the same temporal table:

```
DECLARE @Now AS DATETIME = SYSUTCDATETIME();
SELECT PersonID, FullName, OtherLanguages, ValidFrom, ValidTo
FROM Application.People FOR SYSTEM_TIME AS OF @Now;
```

The previous query is logically equivalent to this one:

```
SELECT PersonID, FullName, OtherLanguages, ValidFrom, ValidTo FROM
Application.People;
```

However, when you look at the execution plans (see the following screenshot) for the execution of the first query, both tables have been processed, while the non-temporal query had to retrieve data from the current table only:

Comparing execution plans for temporal and non-temporal queries that retrieve actual data only

So, you should not use temporal queries with the FOR SYSTEM_TIME AS clause to return data from the current table.

Retrieving temporal data from a specific period

You can use the new FOR SYSTEM_TIME clause to retrieve temporal data that was or is valid between two points in time. These queries are typically used for getting changes to specific rows over time. To achieve this, you could use one of two SQL:2011 standard-specified sub-clauses:

- FROM...TO returns all data that started before or at the beginning of a given period and ended after the end of the period (closed-open interval)
- BETWEEN...AND returns all data that started before or at the beginning of a given period and ended after or at the end of the period (closed-closed interval)

As you can see, the only difference between these two sub-clauses is how data with a starting date to the right side of the given period is interpreted: BETWEEN includes this data, FROM...TO does not.

The following queries demonstrate the usage of these two sub-clauses and the difference between them:

```
--example using FROM/TO
SELECT PersonID, FullName, OtherLanguages, ValidFrom, ValidTo
FROM Application.People FOR SYSTEM_TIME FROM '2016-03-20 08:00:00' TO
'2016-05-31 23:14:00' WHERE PersonID = 7;

--example using BETWEEN
SELECT PersonID, FullName, OtherLanguages, ValidFrom, ValidTo
FROM Application.People FOR SYSTEM_TIME BETWEEN '2016-03-20 08:00:01' AND
'2016-05-31 23:14:00' WHERE PersonID = 7;
```

Here are the result sets generated by the preceding queries:

PersonID	FullName	OtherLanguages	ValidFrom	ValidTo
7	Amy Trefl	NULL	2016-03-20 08:00	2016-05-31 23:13
7	Amy Trefl	["Slovak","Spanish","Polish"]	2016-05-31 23:13	2016-05-31 23:14

PersonID	FullName	OtherLanguages	ValidFrom	ValidTo
7	Amy Trefl	["Slovak","Spanish","Polish"]	2016-05-31 23:14	9999-12-31 23:59
7	Amy Trefl	NULL	2016-03-20 08:00	2016-05-31 23:13
7	Amy Trefl	["Slovak","Spanish","Polish"]	2016-05-31 23:13	2016-05-31 23:14

As you can see, the second query returns three rows, as it includes the row where the start date is equal to the value of the right boundary of the given period.

These two sub-clauses return row versions that overlap with a specified period. If you need to return rows that existed within specified period boundaries, you need to use another extension, CONTAINED IN. This extension (an implementation of one of Allen's operators) is not defined in the SQL:2011 standard; it is implemented in SQL Server 2017. Rows that either start or end outside a given interval will not be part of a result set when the CONTAINED IN sub-clause is used. When you replace the sub-clause BETWEEN with it in the previous example, only rows whose whole life belongs to the given interval will survive:

```
SELECT PersonID, FullName, OtherLanguages, ValidFrom, ValidTo
FROM Application.People FOR SYSTEM_TIME CONTAINED IN ('2016-03-20
08:00:01','2016-05-31 23:14:00') WHERE PersonID = 7;
```

Instead of three rows using BETWEEN, or two with FROM...TO sub-clauses, this time only one row is returned:

```
PersonID   FullName   OtherLanguages                  ValidFrom          ValidTo
---------  ---------- ------------------------------- ----------------  ----------------
7          Amy Trefl  ["Slovak","Spanish","Polish"]  2016-05-31 23:13  2016-05-31 23:14
```

Although this extension is not standard, its implementation in SQL Server 2017 is welcomed; it covers a reasonable and not-so-rare use case, and simplifies the development of database solutions based on temporal tables.

Retrieving all temporal data

Since temporal data is separated into two tables, to get all temporal data you need to combine data from both tables, but there is no sub-clause defined in the SQL:2011 standard for that purpose. However, the SQL Server team has introduced the extension (sub-clause) ALL to simplify such queries.

Here is a temporal query that returns both actual and historical data for the person with the ID of 7:

```
SELECT PersonID, FullName, OtherLanguages, ValidFrom, ValidTo FROM
Application.People FOR SYSTEM_TIME ALL WHERE PersonID = 7;
```

The query returns *14* rows, since there are 13 historical rows and one entry in the actual table. Here is the logically equivalent, standard, but a bit more complex query:

```
SELECT PersonID, FullName, OtherLanguages, ValidFrom, ValidTo FROM
Application.People WHERE PersonID = 7
UNION ALL
SELECT PersonID, FullName, OtherLanguages, ValidFrom, ValidTo FROM
Application.People_Archive WHERE PersonID = 7;
```

The only purpose of this sub-clause is to simplify queries against temporal tables.

Performance and storage considerations with temporal tables

Introducing temporal tables and adding this functionality to existing tables can significantly increase storage used for data in your system. Since there is no out-of-the-box solution for managing the retention of history tables, if you don't do something, data will remain there forever. This can be painful for storage costs, maintenance, and performance of queries on temporal tables, especially if rows in your current tables are heavily updated.

History retention policy in SQL Server 2017

A temporal history retention policy lets you define which rows should stay and which should be cleaned up from the history tables. It can be configured at the individual table level, which allows users to create flexible aging polices. Applying temporal retention is simple; it requires only one parameter to be set during table creation or schema change.

Configuring the retention policy at the database level

The temporal historical retention feature must be enabled at the database level. For new databases, this flag is enabled by default. For databases restored from previous database versions (as with the WideWorldImporters database used in this book), you need to set it manually. The following code enables the temporal historical retention feature for this database:

```
ALTER DATABASE WideWorldImporters SET TEMPORAL_HISTORY_RETENTION ON;
```

Now, you can define the retention policy at the (temporal) table level.

Configuring the retention policy at the table level

To configure the retention policy, you need to specify a value for the HISTORY_RETENTION_PERIOD parameter during table creation or after the table is created. Use the following code to create and populate a sample temporal table:

```
USE WideWorldImporters;
GO
CREATE TABLE dbo.T1(
    Id INT NOT NULL PRIMARY KEY CLUSTERED,
    C1 INT,
    Vf DATETIME2 NOT NULL,
    Vt DATETIME2 NOT NULL
)
GO
CREATE TABLE dbo.T1_Hist(
    Id INT NOT NULL,
    C1 INT,
    Vf DATETIME2 NOT NULL,
    Vt DATETIME2 NOT NULL
)
GO
--populate tables
INSERT INTO dbo.T1_Hist(Id, C1, Vf, Vt) VALUES
(1,1,'20171201','20171210'),
(1,2,'20171210','20171215');
GO
INSERT INTO dbo.T1(Id, C1, Vf, Vt) VALUES
(1,3,'20171215','99991231 23:59:59.9999999');
GO
```

Here is the content of both tables after the script execution:

Id	C1	Vf	Vt
1	3	2017-12-15 00:00:00.0000000	9999-12-3 23:59:59.9999999

Id	C1	Vf	Vt
1	1	2017-12-01 00:00:00.0000000	2017-12-10 00:00:00.0000000
1	2	2017-12-10 00:00:00.0000000	2017-12-15 00:00:00.0000000

The actual value in the C1 column for the row with the ID of 1 is 3, and there are two historical values. You will now convert the T1 table into a temporal table and so define a retention policy that states historical entries should be retained for one day only. Here is the appropriate code:

```
ALTER TABLE dbo.T1 ADD PERIOD FOR SYSTEM_TIME (Vf, Vt);
GO
ALTER TABLE dbo.T1 SET
  (
      SYSTEM_VERSIONING = ON
      (
          HISTORY_TABLE = dbo.T1_Hist,
          HISTORY_RETENTION_PERIOD = 3 DAYS
      )
  );
```

You had to use two statements to achieve this task: the first one is used for adding a period to the table, and the second converts the table to a temporal table with a retention policy of 3 days. However, when you execute the query, you will see the following message:

```
Msg 13765, Level 16, State 1, Line 31
Setting finite retention period failed on system-versioned temporal table
'WideWorldImporters.dbo.T1' because the history table
'WideWorldImporters.dbo.T1_Hist' does not contain required clustered index.
Consider creating a clustered columnstore or B-tree index starting with the
column that matches end of SYSTEM_TIME period, on the history table.
```

The history table must have a row clustered index on the column representing the end of period; it won't work without it. Use this code to create the index and run the previous code again:

```
CREATE CLUSTERED INDEX IX_CL_T1_Hist ON dbo.T1_Hist(Vt, Vf);
GO
ALTER TABLE dbo.T1 SET
  (
      SYSTEM_VERSIONING = ON
      (
          HISTORY_TABLE = dbo.T1_Hist,
          HISTORY_RETENTION_PERIOD = 3 DAYS
      )
  );
```

The execution was successful. This section is written on 17th December, so the results of the further actions will be shown according to this date. In this example, there are two historical records with the end period dates 10.12. and 15.12. According to the retention policy, only one row should be shown as a history row. To check this, use the following query:

```
SELECT * FROM dbo.T1 FOR SYSTEM_TIME ALL;
```

The query returns the following result:

Id	C1	Vf	Vt
1	3	2017-12-15 00:00:00.0000000	9999-12-31 23:59:59.9999999
1	2	2017-12-10 00:00:00.0000000	2017-12-15 00:00:00.0000000

Rows that do not meet the retention policy have been removed from the result set. The execution plan for the query is shown in the following screenshot:

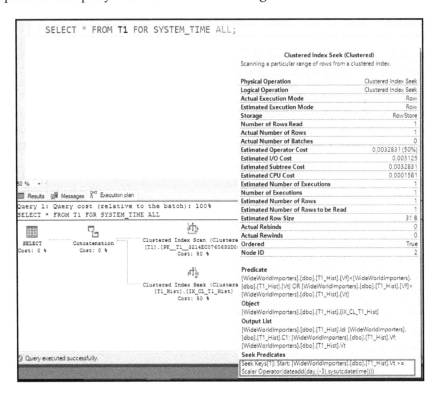

Execution plan for a query with a temporal table with a finite retention period defined

When you look at the execution plan, you can see that the retention policy filter is automatically applied. Therefore, historical rows older than three days are removed from the result set and it contains one actual and one historical row. Rows that meet the following criteria are not shown:

```
Vt < DATEADD (Day, -3, SYSUTCDATETIME ());
```

However, when you query the history table directly, you can still see all rows:

```
SELECT * FROM dbo.T1
UNION ALL
SELECT * FROM dbo.T1_Hist;
```

The query returns the following result:

```
Id   C1      Vf                            Vt
---  ------  ----------------------------  ----------------------------
1    3       2017-12-15 00:00:00.0000000   9999-12-31 23:59:59.9999999
1    1       2017-12-01 00:00:00.0000000   2017-12-10 00:00:00.0000000
1    2       2017-12-10 00:00:00.0000000   2017-12-15 00:00:00.0000000
```

This is not what you expected! How does SQL Server remove the aged rows? Identification of matching rows and their removal from the history table occur transparently, alongside the background tasks that are scheduled and run by the system. Since aged rows can be removed at any point in time and in arbitrary order, you should use Transact-SQL extensions for querying temporal data, as shown in the previous section.

In this example, you have used three days in the retention policy. This information is stored in the `sys.tables` catalog. Run the following query to check retention policy settings for the `T1` table:

```
SELECT temporal_type_desc, history_retention_period,
history_retention_period_unit
FROM sys.tables WHERE name = 'T1';
```

The previous query returns this result set:

temporal_type_desc	history_retention_period	history_retention_period_unit
SYSTEM_VERSIONED_TEMPORAL_TABLE	3	3

The second 3 in the results represents days. If you include the other tables, you can see that all temporal tables in the `WideWorldImporters` database have a value of −1 in this column, which means that the retention period is not defined for a temporal table, thus the historical rows will be kept forever. Here is the list of possible retention period units you can define in an SQL Server 2017 retention policy:

- **-1**: INFINITE
- **3**: DAY
- **4**: WEEK
- **5**: MONTH
- **6**: YEAR

A history retention policy is good and lets you manage and control data size. However, currently you can use only one criteria to define aged rows: the end of period. If you have a lot of historical entries for some rows and a few for most of the others, this will not help you. It would be nice if you could choose additional criteria such as the number of rows or table size. You also cannot define where aged data will be moved; currently it is simply cleaned up.

Custom history data retention

Unfortunately, you cannot configure a history table to automatically move data to some other table or repository according to a user-defined retention policy. That means that you have to implement this kind of data retention manually. This is not very complicated, but it is not a trivial action. I expected it as a part of the implementation and would be disappointed if this was not delivered in the next SQL Server version. As mentioned, you can use some other SQL Server features to implement data retention for history tables:

- **Stretch databases** allow you to move entire parts of historical data transparently to Azure.
- **Partitioning** history tables allows you to easily truncate the oldest historical data by implementing the sliding window approach.
- **Custom Cleanup** doesn't require any other features. You use Transact-SQL scripts to convert a temporal table to non-temporal, delete old data, and convert the table back to a temporal table.

 You can find more details about data retention at Books Online at the following address: https://docs.microsoft.com/en-us/sql/relational-databases/tables/manage-retention-of-historical-data-in-system-versioned-temporal-tables.

History table implementation

As mentioned in the *Creating temporal tables* section, you can create the history table in advance, or let SQL Server create it for you. In the former case, the created table is a row stored table with a clustered index on period columns. If the current table does not contain data types that prevent the usage of data compression, the table is created with PAGE compression. This physical implementation is acceptable if you query the history table by using period columns as filter criteria. However, if your temporal queries usually look for historical records for individual rows, this is not a good implementation. To check potential performance issues of an automatic created history table, use the following code to create and populate a sample temporal table:

```
CREATE TABLE dbo.Mila
(
    Id INT NOT NULL IDENTITY (1,1) PRIMARY KEY CLUSTERED,
    C1 INT NOT NULL,
    C2 NVARCHAR(4000) NULL
)
GO
INSERT INTO dbo.Mila(C1, C2)  SELECT message_id, text FROM sys.messages
WHERE language_id = 1033;
GO 50

ALTER TABLE dbo.Mila
ADD ValidFrom DATETIME2 GENERATED ALWAYS AS ROW START NOT NULL CONSTRAINT
DF_Mila_ValidFrom DEFAULT '20170101',
    ValidTo DATETIME2 GENERATED ALWAYS AS ROW END NOT NULL CONSTRAINT
DF_Mila_ValidTo DEFAULT '99991231 23:59:59.9999999',
    PERIOD FOR SYSTEM_TIME (ValidFrom, ValidTo);
GO
ALTER TABLE dbo.Mila SET (SYSTEM_VERSIONING = ON (HISTORY_TABLE =
dbo.Mila_History));
GO
```

As you can see, the INSERT statement is repeated 50 times, so that the sample table has a lot of rows (661,150 rows). At this point, the history table is empty; all rows are in the current table only. To create a history row for each row in the current table, and one additional history row for the row with the ID of 1, use the following command:

```
UPDATE dbo.Mila SET C1 = C1 + 1;
UPDATE dbo.Mila SET C1 = 44 WHERE Id = 1;
```

Now, assume that you want to check the state of the row with the ID of 1 at some time in the past. Ensure also that query statistics parameters are set to on:

```
SET STATISTICS IO ON;
SET STATISTICS TIME ON;
SELECT * FROM dbo.Mila FOR SYSTEM_TIME AS OF '20170505 08:00:00' WHERE Id = 1;
```

This query returns one row:

```
Id  C1    C2                    ValidFrom          ValidTo
---  -----  --------------------  -----------------  --------------------
1   21    Warning:Fatal error   2017-01-01 00:00   2017-12-13 16:57
              %d occurred
```

However, it is most interesting to check the execution parameters. The execution plan for the query is shown as follows:

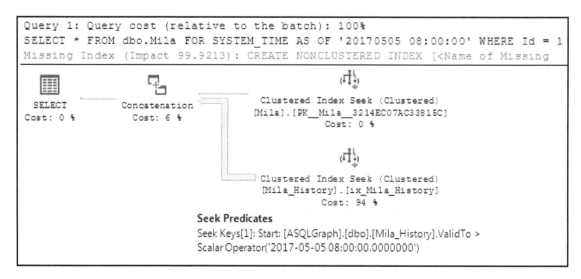

Execution plan with a default index on the history table

You can see the **Index Seek** operator in the plan, but the plan is not efficient since it uses the ValidTo column as filter criteria. Observe the execution parameters:

```
SQL Server Execution Times:
   CPU time = 0 ms,  elapsed time = 0 ms.
SQL Server parse and compile time:
   CPU time = 0 ms, elapsed time = 0 ms.

Table 'Mila_History'. Scan count 1, logical reads 10583, physical reads 0,
```

```
read-ahead reads 0, lob logical reads 0, lob physical reads 0, lob read-
ahead reads 0.
Table 'Mila'. Scan count 0, logical reads 3, physical reads 0, read-ahead
reads 0, lob logical reads 0, lob physical reads 0, lob read-ahead reads 0.

 SQL Server Execution Times:
   CPU time = 188 ms,  elapsed time = 193 ms.
SQL Server parse and compile time:
   CPU time = 0 ms, elapsed time = 0 ms.

 SQL Server Execution Times:
   CPU time = 0 ms,  elapsed time = 0 ms.
```

The query that returns a single row takes almost 200 milliseconds and SQL Server had to read more than 10,000 pages to generate this row! Since you have the Id column in the filter, it is clear that you need an index with this column as the leading column:

```
CREATE CLUSTERED INDEX ix_Mila_History ON dbo.Mila_History(Id, ValidTo,
ValidFrom) WITH DROP_EXISTING;
```

When you execute the same query again, you can see the execution plan shown as follows:

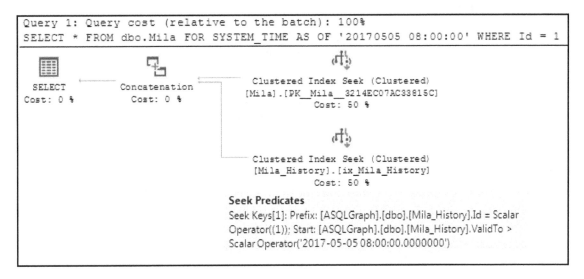

Execution plan with a custom index on the history table

Actually, the plan looks the same, but the `Id` as the leading column in the clustered index on the history table allows SQL Server to search efficiently, as shown in the execution parameters' output:

```
SQL Server Execution Times:
   CPU time = 0 ms,  elapsed time = 0 ms.
SQL Server parse and compile time:
   CPU time = 0 ms, elapsed time = 0 ms.

Table 'Mila_History'. Scan count 1, logical reads 4, physical reads 0,
read-ahead reads 0, lob logical reads 0, lob physical reads 0, lob read-
ahead reads 0.
Table 'Mila'. Scan count 0, logical reads 3, physical reads 0, read-ahead
reads 0, lob logical reads 0, lob physical reads 0, lob read-ahead reads 0.

 SQL Server Execution Times:
   CPU time = 0 ms,  elapsed time = 0 ms.
SQL Server parse and compile time:
   CPU time = 0 ms, elapsed time = 0 ms.

 SQL Server Execution Times:
   CPU time = 0 ms,  elapsed time = 0 ms.
```

It is good when SQL Server can create and configure some objects for you, but you should not forget to check what it means for the performance of your queries.

Finally, if you plan to process a lot of data in temporal queries or to aggregate them, the best approach is to create your own history table with a clustered columnstore index and eventual, additional, non-clustered, normal B-tree indexes.

History table overhead

Converting a non-temporal table into a temporal table is very easy. With two ALTER TABLE statements you get the full temporal table functionality. However, this cannot be completely free. Adding temporal features to a table brings performance overhead in all data modification operations. According to Microsoft, a single update operation against a row in a temporal table is about 30% slower than it would be when the table is non-temporal.

I have performed a simple test where I have updated a different number of rows in a table before it is converted to a temporal table and afterwards. The following graph displays results of this test. For a small amount of rows (<1000), locking, calculating, and inserting data into a history table slows the update down by 50%. Updating 50,000 rows in a temporal table takes about eight times longer than the same operation against the same table when it is implemented as a non-temporal table:

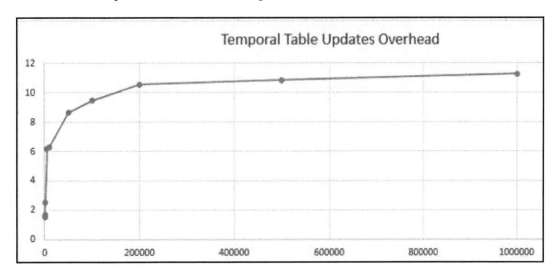

Temporal table updates overhead

Finally, massive updates (>100K rows) are 10 times slower for temporal tables compared to those against their non-temporal counterparts.

Temporal tables with memory-optimized tables

System-versioned temporal tables are also supported for memory-optimized tables. You can assign or let SQL Server create a history table for your memory-optimized table. The history table must be a disk table, but this is exactly what you want; frequently used (hot) data remains in memory, while cold data can reside in disk tables. By taking this approach, you can use all the benefits provided by memory-optimized tables (high transactional throughput, lock-free concurrency), save their historical data on disk-based tables, and leave memory for active datasets only. The following figure shows the architecture of system-versioned memory-optimized tables. It is taken from the Books Online page at `https://msdn.microsoft.com/en-us/library/mt590207.aspx`:

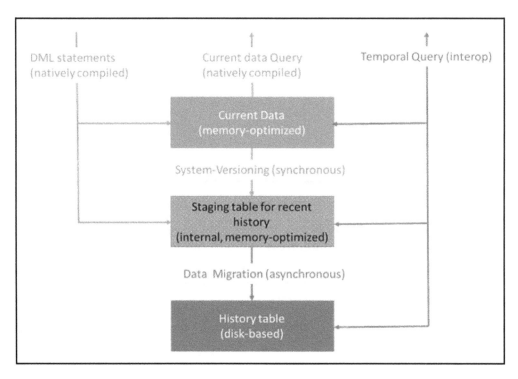

System-versioned temporal tables with memory-optimized table architecture (Source: SQL Server Books Online)

As you can see, system-versioned temporal tables are implemented with three tables:

- **Current table** is a memory-optimized table and all native compiled operations are supported
- **Recent history table** is an internal memory-optimized table that handles changes in the current table synchronously and enables DMLs to be executed from natively compiled code
- **History table** is a disk table that contains changes in the current table and manages them asynchronously

Historical data is a union of data in the recent history and history tables. A history row is either in the staging memory table or in the disk table; it cannot be in both tables. The following code example creates a new memory-optimized temporal table:

```
USE WideWorldImporters;
CREATE TABLE dbo.Product
(
    ProductId INT NOT NULL PRIMARY KEY NONCLUSTERED,
    ProductName NVARCHAR(50) NOT NULL,
    Price MONEY NOT NULL,
    ValidFrom DATETIME2 GENERATED ALWAYS AS ROW START HIDDEN NOT NULL,
    ValidTo DATETIME2 GENERATED ALWAYS AS ROW END HIDDEN NOT NULL,
    PERIOD FOR SYSTEM_TIME (ValidFrom, ValidTo)
)
WITH (MEMORY_OPTIMIZED = ON, DURABILITY = SCHEMA_AND_DATA,
SYSTEM_VERSIONING = ON (HISTORY_TABLE = dbo.ProductHistory));
```

After the execution of this query, you will see that the history table is a memory-optimized table.

```
SELECT CONCAT(SCHEMA_NAME(schema_id),'.', name) AS table_name,
is_memory_optimized, temporal_type_desc FROM sys.tables WHERE name IN
('Product', 'ProductHistory');
```

The result of the preceding query is as follows:

table_name	is_memory_optimized	temporal_type_desc
dbo.Product	1	SYSTEM_VERSIONED_TEMPORAL_TABLE
dbo.ProductHistory	0	HISTORY_TABLE

As mentioned earlier, SQL Server creates a third table automatically: an internal memory-optimized table. Here is the code that you can use to find its name and properties:

```
SELECT CONCAT(SCHEMA_NAME(schema_id),'.', name) AS table_name,
internal_type_desc FROM  sys.internal_tables WHERE name =
CONCAT('memory_optimized_history_table_', OBJECT_ID('dbo.Product'));
```

And here is its output:

table_name	internal_type_desc
sys.memory_optimized_history_table_1575676661	INTERNAL_TEMPORAL_HISTORY_TABLE

Only durable, memory-optimized tables can be system-versioned temporal tables, and history tables must be disk based. Since all current rows are in memory, you can use natively compiled modules to access this data. Use the following code to create a natively compiled stored procedure that handles the inserting and updating of products:

```
CREATE OR ALTER PROCEDURE dbo.SaveProduct
(
@ProductId INT,
@ProductName NVARCHAR(50),
@Price MONEY
)
WITH NATIVE_COMPILATION, SCHEMABINDING, EXECUTE AS OWNER
AS
    BEGIN ATOMIC WITH
    (TRANSACTION ISOLATION LEVEL = SNAPSHOT, LANGUAGE = N'English')
    UPDATE dbo.Product SET ProductName = @ProductName, Price = @Price WHERE
ProductId = @ProductId
    IF @@ROWCOUNT = 0
        INSERT INTO dbo.Product(ProductId,ProductName,Price) VALUES
(@ProductId, @ProductName, @Price);
END
GO
```

Now you can, for instance, add two rows and update one of them by using the previous procedure:

```
EXEC dbo.SaveProduct 1, N'Home Jersey Benfica', 89.95;
EXEC dbo.SaveProduct 2, N'Away Jersey Juventus', 89.95;
EXEC dbo.SaveProduct 1, N'Home Jersey Benfica', 79.95;
```

Under the hood, everything works perfectly; both the current and history tables are updated. Here are the resulting datasets in the current and historical table:

ProductId	ProductName	Price
2	Away Jersey Juventus	89.95
1	Home Jersey Benfica	79.95

ProductId	ProductName	Price	ValidFrom	ValidTo
1	Home Jersey Benfica	89.95	2017-12-17 20:25:50	2017-12-17 20:25:51

The querying of historical data is effectively under the SNAPSHOT isolation level and always returns a union between the in-memory staging buffer and the disk-based table without duplicates. Since temporal queries (queries that use the FOR SYSTEM_TIME clause) touch memory-optimized and disk tables, they can be used only in interop mode; it is not possible to use them in natively compiled procedures.

Data from the internal memory-optimized staging table is regularly moved to the disk-based history table by the asynchronous data flush task. This data flush mechanism has the goal of keeping the internal memory buffers at less than 10% of the memory consumption of their parent objects.

When you add system-versioning to an existing non-temporal table, expect a performance impact on update and delete operations because the history table is updated automatically. Every update and delete is recorded in the internal memory-optimized history table, so you may experience unexpected memory consumption if your workload uses those two operations.

What is missing in SQL Server 2017?

SQL Server 2016 is the first SQL Server version that has some built-in support for temporal data. However, even in SQL Server version 2017, the support is still quite basic. SQL Server 2016 and 2017 support system-versioned tables only. You have seen at the beginning of this chapter that application versioned tables, and of course bitemporal tables, add much more complexity to temporal problems. Unfortunately, in order to deal with application validity times, you need to develop your own solution, including your own implementation of all constraints, on which you need to enforce data integrity. In addition, you need to deal with the optimization of temporal queries by yourself as well.

In SQL Server 2017, you can define the retention period for historical rows. Therefore, you do not have to do the history data cleanup by yourself, like you needed to do in SQL Server 2016. Nevertheless, it would be very useful to also have the ability to define the absolute maximum number of historical rows you want to keep, and the maximum number of versions per row. This way, you could prevent a scenario where frequent updates of some rows occupy the most space in the historical table, overwhelming the history of the rows that are not updated that frequently.

If you are familiar with analytical applications and data warehouses, you might think that system-versioned temporal tables can help you in analytical scenarios. However, as you will learn in the next section, which briefly introduces data warehouses and the slowly changing dimensions problem, analytical applications have typically different granularity requests and system-versioned temporal tables don't help there.

SQL Server 2016 and 2017 temporal tables and data warehouses

For analytical purposes, **data warehouses** have evolved. Data warehouses support historical data. You should not confuse a data warehouse's historical data with temporal data, the subject of this chapter. In a data warehouse, historical data means just archived non-temporal data from the past; a typical data warehouse holds from 5 to 10 years of data for analytical purposes. Data warehouses are not suitable for business applications because a data warehouse typically has no constraints.

Data warehouses have a simplified data model that consists of multiple **star schemas**. You can see a typical star schema in the following figure:

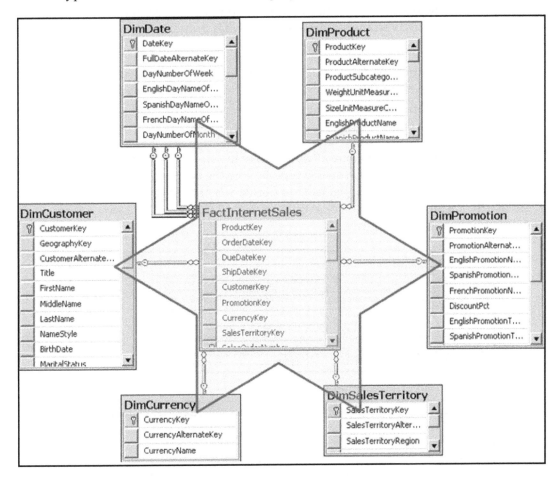

Star schema

One schema covers one business area. It consists of a single central table, called the **fact table**, and multiple surrounding tables, called **dimensions**. The fact table is always on the many side every single relationship, with every single dimension table. Star schema is deliberately denormalized. The fact table includes measures, while dimensions give context to those measures. Shared dimensions connect star schemas in a data warehouse.

Dimensions can change over time. The pace of the changes is usually slow compared to the pace of the changes in fact tables. Transactional systems often show the current state only, and don't preserve the history. In a data warehouse, you might need to preserve the history. This is known as the **slowly changing dimensions (SCD)** problem, which has two common solutions:

- A type 1 solution means not preserving the history in the data warehouse by simply overwriting the values when the values in the sources change
- A type 2 solution means adding a new row for a change, and marking which row is the current one

You can also mix both types; for some attributes, like the city in the example, you use type 2, while for some, like occupation, you use type 1. Note the additional problem: when you update the OCCUPATION attribute, you need to decide whether to update the current row only or also the historical rows that come from the type 2 changes. You can see these possibilities in the following figure:

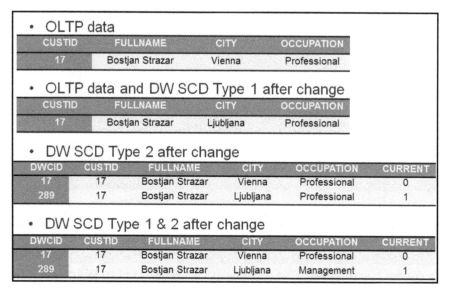

- OLTP data

CUSTID	FULLNAME	CITY	OCCUPATION
17	Bostjan Strazar	Vienna	Professional

- OLTP data and DW SCD Type 1 after change

CUSTID	FULLNAME	CITY	OCCUPATION
17	Bostjan Strazar	Ljubljana	Professional

- DW SCD Type 2 after change

DWCID	CUSTID	FULLNAME	CITY	OCCUPATION	CURRENT
17	17	Bostjan Strazar	Vienna	Professional	0
289	17	Bostjan Strazar	Ljubljana	Professional	1

- DW SCD Type 1 & 2 after change

DWCID	CUSTID	FULLNAME	CITY	OCCUPATION	CURRENT
17	17	Bostjan Strazar	Vienna	Professional	0
289	17	Bostjan Strazar	Ljubljana	Management	1

Slowly changing dimensions

On first glance, SQL Server system-versioned tables might be the solution to the SCD problem when using the type 2 implementation. However, this is typically not true. In a data warehouse, most of the time you need to implement a mixed solution: type 1 for some attributes and type 2 for others. The granularity of the time points in system-versioned tables is 100 nanoseconds; in a data warehouse, typical granularity is 1 day. In the source system, the same entity, like customer, can be updated multiple times per day. You can have multiple historical rows for the same entity in a single day. Therefore, when transferring the data from a transactional database to a data warehouse, you need to take care to transfer the last state for each day. The following query illustrates the problem:

```
USE WideWorldImporters;
SELECT PersonID, FullName,
 ValidFrom, ValidTo
FROM Application.People
 FOR SYSTEM_TIME ALL
WHERE IsEmployee = 1
  AND PersonID = 14;
```

In the `WideWorldImporters` database, `Application.People` is a system-versioned table. The previous query returns all rows for an employee called `Lily Code`. Here is the abbreviated result:

PersonID	FullName	ValidFrom	ValidTo
14	Lily Code	2016-05-31 23:14:00.0000000	9999-12-31 23:59:59.9999999
14	Lily Code	2013-01-01 00:00:00.0000000	2013-01-01 08:00:00.0000000
14	Lily Code	2013-01-01 08:00:00.0000000	2013-01-19 08:00:00.0000000
14	Lily Code	2013-01-19 08:00:00.0000000	2013-02-14 08:00:00.0000000

You can see that this person has multiple rows for a single date. For example, there are two rows for `Lily` where the `ValidTo` date (just the date part) equals `2013-01-01`. You need to select only the last row per employee per day. This is done with the following query. You can run it and check the results:

```
WITH PersonCTE AS
(
SELECT PersonID, FullName,
 CAST(ValidFrom AS DATE) AS ValidFrom,
 CAST(ValidTo AS DATE) AS ValidTo,
 ROW_NUMBER() OVER(PARTITION BY PersonID, CAST(ValidFrom AS Date)
                ORDER BY ValidFrom DESC) AS rn
FROM Application.People
 FOR SYSTEM_TIME ALL
WHERE IsEmployee = 1
)
```

```
SELECT PersonID, FullName,
 ValidFrom, ValidTo
FROM PersonCTE
WHERE rn = 1;
```

Summary

SQL Server 2016 and 2017 system-versioned temporal tables are a very nice feature you can start using immediately, without changes to your applications. You can use them for auditing all changes in specific tables. You can retrieve the state of those tables at any point in time in history. You can find all states and changes in a specific period. SQL Server automatically updates the period in the current row and inserts the old version of the row into the history table as soon as you update the current row.

Nevertheless, there is still a lot to do in future versions of SQL Server. We still need better support for application validity times, including support for constraints and optimization of temporal queries, and more flexibility in the history retention policy.

In the next chapter, you will learn the basics of SQL Server security, together with new security features in SQL Server 2016 and 2017.

8

Tightening Security

Developers like to forget about security and simply leave security issues to **database administrators** (**DBAs**). However, it is much harder for a DBA to tighten security for a database where developers did not plan and design for security. To secure your data, you must understand the potential threats as well as the security mechanisms provided by SQL Server and the other components your application is using, including the operating system and programming language.

When talking about securing SQL Server, we are actually talking about defending data access to the database platform and guaranteeing the integrity of that access. In addition, you have to protect all SQL Server components included in your solution. Remember that your system is only as secure as the least secure component. As a defender, you have to close all holes, while an attacker only has to find a single hole. However, dealing with all aspects of security would be beyond the scope of this chapter. Therefore, this chapter will cover only the most important security features of the SQL Server Database Engine, and introduces three new SQL Server 2016 and 2017 security features.

With **Always Encrypted**, SQL Server 2016 and 2017 finally enable full data encryption, so that no tools or people, regardless of their database and server permissions, can read encrypted data except the client application with an appropriate key. **Row-Level Security** (**RLS**), on the other hand, restricts which data in a table can be seen by a specific user. This is very useful in multi-tenant environments where you usually want to avoid a data-reading intersection between different customers. **Dynamic data masking** is a soft feature that limits sensitive data exposure by masking it to non-privileged users.

This chapter will cover the following points:

- SQL Server security basics
- Data encryption
- Row-Level Security
- Dynamic data masking

SQL Server security basics

The structure of secure systems generally consists of three parts: authentication, authorization, and enforcement of rules. **Authentication** is the process of checking the identity of a principal by examining the credentials and validating those credentials against some authority. **Authorization** is the process of determining whether a principal is allowed to perform a requested action. Authorization occurs after authentication, and uses information about the principal's identity and roles to determine what resources the principal can access. The enforcement of rules provides the mechanism to block direct access to resources. Blocking access is essential to securing any system. The following figure shows the structure of a secure system:

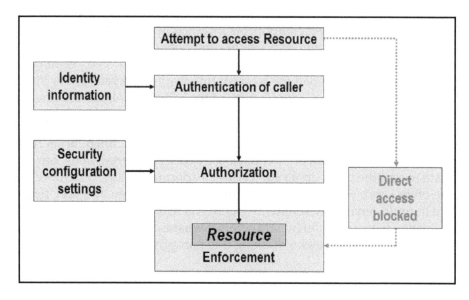

Structure of secure systems

You will learn how SQL Server implements the logic of a secure system, including:

- Principals
- Securables
- Schemas
- Object permissions
- Statement permissions

Defining principals and securables

SQL Server supports two authentication modes: Windows mode and mixed mode. In Windows mode, when a user connects through a Windows user account, SQL Server validates the account name and password by using information from the operating system. In mixed mode, in addition to Windows authentication, a user can provide a SQL login and password to connect to SQL Server. SQL Server can use and enforce Windows password policy mechanisms.

SQL Server defines two fundamental terms for security: principals and securables. **Principals** are entities that can request SQL Server resources. They are arranged in a hierarchy in the principal's scope: you can have Windows, server, and database-level principals. A principal can be a Windows domain login, a Windows local login, a Windows group, a SQL Server login, a server role, a database user, a database role, or an application role in a database. In addition to having regular users, you can create a SQL Server login or a database user from a certificate or an asymmetric key.

Securables are the resources you are protecting. Some securables can be contained within others in nested hierarchies (scopes). You can secure a complete scope, and the objects in the scope inherit permissions from the upper level of the hierarchy. The securable scopes are server, database, and schema.

After authentication, in the authorization phase, SQL Server checks whether a principal has appropriate permissions to use the securables. The following figure shows the most important principals, securables, and permissions in SQL Server, including the level where they are defined:

Principals	Permissions	Securables
Windows level		
• Groups • Domain user accounts • Local user accounts		
SQL Server level		

• Fixed server roles
• SQL Server logins
	• Grant – Deny – Revoke
	   – Control
	   – Create
	   – Alter
	   – Drop
		• SQL Server logins and roles
		• Endpoints
		• Databases

Database level	– Select – Insert	

• Fixed database roles
• Database users
• Application roles
	– Update
	   – Delete
	   – Execute
	   – Connect
	   – Reference
	   – Take ownership
	   – View definition
		• Users and roles
		• Assemblies
		• Keys and certificates
		• Full-text catalogs and stoplists
		• Service Broker services, bindings, contracts, routes, and message types
		• Schemas
		   – Tables
		   – Views
		   – Functions
		   – Procedures
		   – Types
		   – XML schema collections
		   – Service Broker queues
		   – Synonyms

Principals, securables, and permissions

You manage principals with **Data Definition Language** (**DDL**) statements. You maintain permissions with **Data Control Language** (**DCL**) statements. You create a principal as you do any other objects, by using the CREATE statement. You modify them by using the ALTER statement and delete them by using the DROP statement.

You can create SQL Server logins, which are security principals, or you can create logins from different sources, such as from Windows, certificates, or asymmetric keys. When you create SQL Server logins, you can specify that you want to bypass password expiration and account policies. However, these policies help to secure your system, for example, preventing brute-force password attacks, and therefore this option is not recommended.

Database users are still part of the authentication. SQL Server supports two models: the traditional login and user model and the contained database user model, described as follows:

- In the traditional model, a login is created in the master database and then mapped to a user in some other database. The end user connects to SQL Server with a login, and, through the mapping to one or more databases, the user gets access to the database(s).
- In the contained model, a database user is either mapped to a Windows user directly or one is created with a password. The end user connects to a single database directly, without having to log in to the master database.

The following code shows how to create a SQL Server login with a weak password. If you execute this code, you get an error because the password does not meet Window's password policy requirements:

```
USE master;
CREATE LOGIN LoginA WITH password='LoginA';
GO
```

However, the following code succeeds. It creates a SQL Server login with a weak password, this time bypassing the Windows password policy, and creates a login from a built-in Windows group:

```
CREATE LOGIN LoginA WITH password='LoginA',
CHECK_POLICY=OFF;
CREATE LOGIN [BuiltinPower Users] FROM WINDOWS;
```

Bypassing password expiration and complexity policies is definitely not recommended. The SQL Server login just created is now very prone to brute-force attacks. You can check the `sys.sql_logins` catalog view to see which SQL logins do not enforce the policies mentioned, as the following code shows:

```
SELECT name,
type_desc,
is_disabled,
is_policy_checked,
is_expiration_checked
```

```
FROM sys.sql_logins
WHERE name LIKE 'L%';
```

The result shows the login that was just created:

name	type_desc	is_disabled	is_policy_checked	is_expiration_checked
LoginA	SQL_LOGIN	0	0	0

In SQL Server, you have some special principals. On the server level, you have the sa SQL Server login, which is created when you install SQL Server. The default database for this login is master. This login has all permissions on the server and you cannot revoke any permissions from this login. You should protect the sa login with a strong password. If you use Windows authentication only, this login cannot be used to connect to SQL Server.

In every database, you get the public fixed role and the guest user account. You cannot drop them. You can only disable the guest user account. Any login without a directly mapped user in a database can access the database through the guest account. Application roles can also use this account to access the data in databases other than the database in the context for which they were invoked. Before you give any permission to the guest user account, make sure you consider all the ramifications. Every database user and every database role is a member of the public role. Therefore, any user or role—including an application role—inherits all permissions given to the public role. You should be careful when giving any permission to the public role; the best practice is to never give any permission to it.

The privileged database user dbo still exists in SQL Server. This user is a member of the db_owner role and, therefore, has all permissions on the database. You cannot drop dbo from the db_owner role.

Every database includes two additional principals: INFORMATION_SCHEMA and sys. You cannot drop these principals because SQL Server needs them. They serve as schemas (namespaces) for ANSI-standard information schema views and for SQL Server catalog views. Finally, SQL Server provides some special logins based on certificates, where their name starts and ends with two hash characters, such as ##MS_dqs_db_owner_login##. These logins are for SQL Server internal use only.

The principals are securables by themselves. You can control who can modify logins using membership in the sysadmin and securityadmin server-level roles, and the ALTER ANY LOGIN server-level permission. You can control who can modify database users and roles by memberships in the db_owner and db_securityadmin roles, and the ALTER ANY USER and ALTER ANY ROLE permissions.

In SQL Server, object metadata is not visible to the public role (that is, everyone) by default. You can control metadata visibility by using two permissions: VIEW ANY DATABASE and VIEW DEFINITION.

The VIEW ANY DATABASE permission is granted to the public role by default, so all logins can still see the list of all databases on a SQL Server instance unless you revoke this permission from the public role. You can check this server-level permission by querying the sys.server_permissions catalog view:

```
SELECT pr.name,
pe.state_desc,
pe.permission_name
FROM sys.server_principals AS pr
INNER JOIN sys.server_permissions AS pe
ON pr.principal_id = pe.grantee_principal_id
WHERE permission_name = 'VIEW ANY DATABASE';
```

The result of this query is as follows:

```
name          state_desc  permission_name
------        ----------  ------------------
public        GRANT       VIEW ANY DATABASE
```

The VIEW DEFINITION permission lets a user see the definition of the securable for which this permission is granted. However, this permission does not give the user access to the securable; you have to give other permissions to the user if the user must work with database objects. If the user has any other permission on an object, the user can see the metadata of the object as well.

Managing schemas

The complete name of a **relational database management system** (RDBMS) object consists of four parts. In SQL Server, the complete name form is server.database.schema.object. Objects also have owners, and owners are database users and roles. However, the owners are hidden; you typically never refer to an object owner in the code that deals with data, whereas you intensively use schemas. **Schemas** are more than just namespaces for database objects; they are securables as well. Instead of giving permissions to specific database objects, a DBA can give users permissions to schemas. For example, granting the Execute permission to the Sales schema gives the grantees the Execute permission on all objects in this schema for which this permission makes sense, such as stored procedures and functions. Therefore, you should plan your schemas carefully.

When you refer to database objects in your code, you should always use a two-part name, in the form `schema.object`. You don't want to use more than two parts because you don't want to make your application dependent on a specific server or database name. However, because of the way SQL Server handles name resolution, you should not use a single-part name either.

In SQL Server, every user has a default schema. You can specify the default schema for a user when you create the user. You can change the default schema of a user at any later time. If you do not specify an explicit default schema for a user, the default schema is `dbo`. This schema exists in all SQL Server databases and is owned by the `dbo` user. Thus, SQL Server first checks for a partially specified object name if the object exists in the user's default schema and then checks the `dbo` schema. To fully understand this behavior, let's work through the following code; note that this code assumes you are working in the `dbo` database user context because it uses the `EXECUTE AS` command to impersonate a database user and you must have the correct permission to use this command.

The first part of the code creates a demo database and another login called `LoginB`. Note that a login called `LoginA` should already exist at this point:

```
USE master;
IF DB_ID(N'SQLDevGuideDemoDb') IS NULL
CREATE DATABASE SQLDevGuideDemoDb;
CREATE LOGIN LoginB WITH password='LB_ComplexPassword';
GO
```

The next part of the code creates a new schema called `Sales` in the `SQLDevGuideDemoDb` demo database, and then two tables with the same name and structure, one in the `dbo` schema and one in the new `Sales` schema:

```
USE SQLDevGuideDemoDb;
GO
CREATE SCHEMA Sales;
GO
CREATE TABLE dbo.Table1
(id INT, tableContainer CHAR(5));
CREATE TABLE Sales.Table1
(id INT, tableContainer CHAR(5));
GO
```

The following two insert statements insert one row into each table. The value of the character column shows the name of the table schema:

```
INSERT INTO dbo.Table1(id, tableContainer)
VALUES(1,'dbo');
INSERT INTO Sales.Table1(id, tableContainer)
```

```
VALUES(1,'Sales');
GO
```

The next part of the code creates two database users, one for LoginA and one for LoginB, with the same name as their respective login name. Note that the default schema for user LoginA is dbo, while for LoginB it is Sales. Both users are also granted the permission to select data from both demo tables:

```
CREATE USER LoginA FOR LOGIN LoginA;
GO
CREATE USER LoginB FOR LOGIN LoginB
 WITH DEFAULT_SCHEMA = Sales;
GO
GRANT SELECT ON dbo.Table1 TO LoginA;
GRANT SELECT ON Sales.Table1 TO LoginA;
GRANT SELECT ON dbo.Table1 TO LoginB;
GRANT SELECT ON Sales.Table1 TO LoginB;
GO
```

Next, you impersonate LoginA. In a query, you refer to the table you are reading with a single-part name only (that is, with the table name only):

```
EXECUTE AS USER='LoginA';
SELECT USER_NAME() AS WhoAmI,
id,
tableContainer
FROM Table1;
REVERT;
GO
```

Here are the results:

WhoAmI	id	tableContainer
LoginA	1	dbo

You can see that you read from the dbo.Table1 table. Repeat the same thing for the database user LoginB:

```
EXECUTE AS USER='LoginB';
SELECT USER_NAME() AS WhoAmI,
id,
tableContainer
FROM Table1;
REVERT;
GO
```

This time the results show that you read the data from the `Sale.Table1` table:

```
WhoAmI   id   tableContainer
------   --   --------------
LoginB    1   Sales
```

Now you drop the `Sales.Table1` table. Then you impersonate user `LoginB` again, and read from the table using the table name only:

```
DROP TABLE Sales.table1;
GO
EXECUTE AS USER='LoginB';
SELECT USER_NAME() AS WhoAmI,
id,
tableContainer
FROM Table1;
REVERT;
GO
```

Here are the results:

```
WhoAmI   id   tableContainer
------   --   --------------
LoginA    1   dbo
```

Now that you know how schemas work, you should be able to understand the following guidelines for managing schemas:

- You should group objects in schemas based on application-access requirements. Classify applications by access requirements and then create appropriate schemas. For example, if an application module deals with sales data, create a `Sales` schema to serve as a container for all database objects that pertain to sales.
- Typically, you can map end users to application modules. You should specify the appropriate default schemas for database users and roles. For example, you should specify `Sales` as the default schema for users in the Sales department.
- Because SQL Server uses a permissions hierarchy, you can manage permissions efficiently if you set up appropriate schemas. For example, you can give permissions on data to sales-department users quickly by giving them appropriate permissions on the `Sales` schema. Later, you can define exceptions by denying permissions to some users on the objects contained in the `Sales` schema.

- You should use either the `dbo` user or database roles as the owners of schemas and objects. This way, you can drop a database user without worrying about orphaned objects.
- Although you set appropriate default schemas for users, you should still always refer to database objects by using two-part names. With this strategy, you can avoid confusion in your application if the default schema for a user changes, or if an object from the user's default schema is dropped and an object with the same name exists in the `dbo` schema (as you saw in the code example).
- You can use schemas to control development environments as well. You can identify different developer groups based on application requirements and then map those groups to schemas.
- In SQL Server, you can control permissions on schemas and objects with a lot of precision. For example, giving developers permission to create objects does not imply that they can create objects in all schemas. On the contrary, developers must have an `ALTER` or `CONTROL` schema permission on every schema they want to modify by creating, altering, or dropping objects contained in that schema.
- You can move objects between schemas by using the `ALTER SCHEMA` command.
- Your documentation should include schema information.

Object and statement permissions

All the demo code so far has supposed that you are authorized inside a database as the `dbo` user. This user has all possible permissions inside a database. However, in real life it might be necessary for other users to create and modify objects. These users could be developers or other database administrators. To modify objects, they need statement permissions. Statement permissions are on the server, database, schema, or at the object level, depending on which level you work at. In addition, end users must use objects, and thus need object permissions. Object permissions depend on the type of the object you are working with.

Statement permissions include permissions to use any DDL statements (that is, to create, alter, and drop objects). Object permissions include permissions to use objects (that is, to use the **Data Modification Language** (**DML**) statements). However, the two permissions classes slightly overlap, and you can treat a couple of permissions as both statement and object permissions.

You control permissions by using these DCL elements: the GRANT, REVOKE, and DENY statements. You already know that without explicitly granted permission, a user cannot use an object. You give the permissions by using the GRANT statement. You explicitly prohibit the usage of an object by using the DENY statement. You clear an explicit GRANT or an explicit DENY permission by using the REVOKE statement. You might wonder why you need an explicitly DENY statement when, without an explicit GRANT, a user cannot use an object. The DENY statement exists because all grants are cumulative. For example, if a user gets a GRANT permission to select from table1 and the role that the user is a member of is granted permission to select from table2, the user can select from both tables. If you want to be sure that the user can never select from table2, you should deny the select permission from table2 to this user. A DENY for an ordinary user always supersedes every GRANT.

You cannot grant, deny, or revoke permissions to or from special roles at the server or database level. For example, you cannot deny anything inside a database to the db_owner role. You cannot grant, deny, or revoke permissions to special logins and database users (that is, to sa, dbo, INFORMATION_SCHEMA, and sys). Finally, you cannot grant, deny, or revoke permissions to yourself.

Statement permissions let users create and alter objects, or back up a database and transaction log. Permissions granted on a higher level include implicit permissions on a lower level. For example, permissions granted at the schema level are implicitly granted on all objects in the schema. In addition, there is a hierarchy between permissions on the same level; some are stronger and implicitly include weaker permissions. The CONTROL permission is the strongest. For example, the CONTROL permission on the database level implies all other permissions on the same database. Therefore, you have two different kinds of hierarchy: a hierarchy between securables and a hierarchy between permissions. You can treat high-level permissions as covering the more detailed, low-level permissions that they imply. For example, if a user needs to alter an object, the user needs either the ALTER OBJECT permission or any other higher permission, such as the ALTER ANY SCHEMA permission.

The types of permission depend on the types of database object. You can get a list of permissions applicable for an object or objects by using the sys.fn_builtin_permissions system function. For example, you can check which permissions are applicable for user-defined types, or check the objects for which the SELECT permission is applicable, like the following two queries do:

```
SELECT * FROM sys.fn_builtin_permissions(N'TYPE');
SELECT * FROM sys.fn_builtin_permissions(DEFAULT)
WHERE permission_name = N'SELECT';
GO
```

In SQL Server, you can specify very detailed permissions. For example, you can specify that a user can select or update only some columns of a table. Specifying permissions on such a granular level means a lot of administrative work, and is nearly impossible to do in a limited time with graphical tools such as SSMS. You should rarely go that far.

 You should specify permissions on the higher levels of the object hierarchy, namely on the schema level, and then handle exceptions. If you need column-level permissions, you should use programmable objects such as views and stored procedures. You should keep permissions as simple as possible.

The GRANT statement includes the WITH GRANT OPTION. This option indicates that the principal to whom you grant permission on an object can grant this permission on the same object to other principals.

The DENY statement comes with the CASCADE option. When you use this option with the DENY statement, you indicate that the permission you are denying is also denied to other principals to which it has been granted by this principal.

The REVOKE statement has the GRANT OPTION FOR and the CACSCADE options. GRANT OPTION FOR means you are revoking the permission to grant the same permission to other principals (that is, you are revoking the WITH GRANT OPTION permission you gave to this principal by using the GRANT statement). The CASCADE option means you are revoking a permission not just from the principal you mention in the statement but also from other principals to which permission has been granted by this principal. Note that such a cascading revocation revokes both the GRANT and DENY of that permission.

The following code shows how to use object permissions. First, the code grants the CONTROL permission on dbo.Table1 to LoginB. LoginB can read the table:

```
GRANT CONTROL ON dbo.Table1 TO LoginB;
GO
EXECUTE AS USER = 'LoginB';
SELECT *
FROM dbo.Table1;
REVERT;
GO
```

Next, you deny the SELECT permission on dbo.Table1 to LoginB. Note that LoginB still has the CONTROL permission on this table, so this user can insert into the table:

```
DENY SELECT ON dbo.Table1 TO LoginB;
GO
EXECUTE AS USER = 'LoginB';
```

```
INSERT INTO dbo.Table1(id, tableContainer)
VALUES (2, 'dbo');
REVERT;
GO
```

However, you denied the SELECT permission to LoginB. An explicit DENY for an ordinary user always supersedes every explicit GRANT. Therefore, the following code produces an error, stating that the SELECT permission is denied:

```
EXECUTE AS USER = 'LoginB';
SELECT *
FROM dbo.Table1;
REVERT;
GO
```

Finally, security would not be worth much if a user could change their own settings. The following code impersonates LoginB and tries to change the permissions to the same database user:

```
EXECUTE AS USER = 'LoginB';
REVOKE SELECT ON dbo.Table1 FROM LoginB;
REVERT;
GO
```

Of course, the previous code produced an error. However, you, as the dbo database user, can change the permissions for the user LoginB, and therefore the following code succeeds:

```
REVOKE SELECT ON dbo.Table1 FROM LoginB;
GO
```

Encrypting the data

If you need to store confidential data in your database, you can use **data encryption**. SQL Server supports encryption with symmetric keys, asymmetric keys, certificates, and password phrases. Let's first have a theoretical look at each of these encryption techniques.

When you use **symmetric key** encryption, the party that encrypts the data shares the same key with the party that decrypts the data. Because the same key is used for encryption and decryption, this is called **symmetric key encryption**. This encryption is very fast. However, if an unauthorized party somehow acquires the key, that party can decrypt the data. Protecting symmetric keys is a challenge. The symmetric key must remain secret. Symmetric encryption is also called **secret key** encryption.

In **asymmetric key** encryption, you use two different keys that are mathematically linked. You must keep one key secret and prevent unauthorized access to it; this is the **private key**. You make the other key public to anyone; this is the **public key**. If you encrypt the data with the public key, you can decrypt the data with the private key; if you encrypt the data with the private key, you can decrypt it with the public key. Asymmetric encryption is very strong; however, it is much slower than symmetric encryption. Asymmetric encryption is useful for digital signatures. A developer applies a **hash algorithm** to the code to create a **message digest**, which is a compact and unique representation of data. Then the developer encrypts the digest with the private key. Anybody with a public key from the same pair can decrypt the digest and use the same hash algorithm to calculate the digest from the code again. If the re-calculated and decrypted digests match, you can identify who created the code.

A **certificate** is a digitally signed statement that binds the value of a public key to the identity of the person, device, or service that holds the corresponding private key. It identifies the owner of the public/private keys. You can use certificates for authentication. A certificate can be issued by a trusted authority or by SQL Server. You can create a certificate from a file (if the certificate was issued by a trusted authority) or a digitally signed executable file (assembly), or you can create a self-signed certificate in SQL Server directly. You can use certificates to encrypt data; of course, this way you are actually using asymmetric encryption.

You should use symmetric keys to encrypt data because secret key encryption is much faster than public-key encryption. You can then use asymmetric encryption to protect symmetric keys and use certificates for authentication. You combine certificates and keys to encrypt data in the following manner:

1. The server sends a certificate and public key to a client. The certificate identifies the server to the client.
2. The client creates two symmetric keys. The client encrypts one symmetric key with the public key and sends it to the server.
3. The server's private key can decrypt the symmetric key. The server and client encrypt and decrypt data with symmetric keys.

When encrypting data, you should consider all possible surface areas for an attack. For example, if you encrypt data in SQL Server, but send clear text over the network, an attacker could use a network monitor to intercept the clear text. You should use on-the-wire encryption, such as **Internet Protocol Security** (**IPSec**), a framework of open source standards for network security, or **Secure Sockets Layer** (**SSL**)/**Transport Layer Security** (**TLS**), which are protocols based on public key cryptography. An attacker can even sniff client computer memory to retrieve clear text. Therefore, you should use .NET encryption in client applications in addition to or instead of server encryption.

Consider the following trade-offs when you design a solution that uses data encryption:

- Encrypted data is typically stored in a binary data type column; space is not allocated according to the original data type as it is with unencrypted data. This means you need to change your database schema to support data encryption.
- Sorting encrypted data is different from sorting unencrypted data and, of course, makes no sense from a business point of view.
- Similarly, indexing and filtering operations on encrypted data are useless from a business point of view.
- You might need to change applications to support data encryption.
- Encryption is a processor-intensive process.
- Longer keys mean stronger encryption. However, the stronger the encryption, the higher the consumption of CPU resources.
- When the length of the keys is the same, then asymmetric encryption is weaker than symmetric encryption. Asymmetric key encryption is also slower than symmetric encription.
- Although you probably already know this, it is still worth mentioning that long and complex passwords are stronger than short and simple ones.

Instead of storing all keys in SQL Server, you can also use an external cryptographic provider to store asymmetric keys used to encrypt and decrypt symmetric keys stored in SQL Server, or to store both asymmetric and symmetric keys outside SQL Server. This is called **Extensible Key Management** (**EKM**). For example, you can use the Azure Key Vault service as the external cryptographic provider.

As already mentioned, you can protect symmetric keys with asymmetric keys or certificates. In addition, you can protect them with passwords or even other symmetric keys. You can protect certificates and asymmetric keys stored in SQL Server with the **Database Master Key** (**DMK**) and passwords. You protect the DMK when you create it with the **Service Master Key** (**SMK**) and password. The SMK is created by SQL Server Setup, and is protected by the Windows system **Data Protection Application Programming Interface** (**DPAPI**). This whole encryption hierarchy looks quite complex. The following figure shows the encryption hierarchy in a condensed way. It shows all components and a couple of possible paths to the encrypted data:

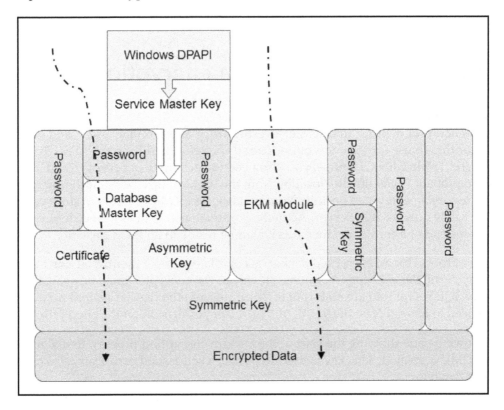

Encryption hierarchy

SQL Server supports many encryption algorithms. You can choose from DES, Triple DES, TRIPLE_DES_3KEY, RC2, RC4, 128-bit RC4, DESX, 128-bit AES, 192-bit AES, and 256-bit AES. However, from SQL Server 2016 onwards, you should use only the AES-128, AES-192, and AES-256 algorithms; all other algorithms have been deprecated.

You don't need to encrypt all of the data all of the time. SQL Server provides many encryption options, and you should choose the one that suits you the best. In addition, you should also consider encrypting and decrypting the data in the client application. In this section, you will learn about the different encryption options in SQL Server, including the strengths and weaknesses of each option. These options include:

- Backup encryption
- Column-level encryption
- Transparent data encryption
- Always encrypted

Leveraging SQL Server data encryption options

SQL Server encryption options start with **backup encryption**. This encryption was introduced in version 2014. You can encrypt data while creating a backup. You need to specify an **encryptor**, which can be either a certificate or an asymmetric key, and define which algorithm to use for the encryption. The supported algorithms are AES-128, AES-192, AES-256, and Triple DES. Of course, you also need to back up the encryptor, and store it in a different, probably even off-site, location from the backup files. Without the encryptor, you can't restore an encrypted backup. You can also use EKM providers to store your encryptor safely outside SQL Server. Actually, if you are using an asymmetric key as an encryptor instead of a certificate, then this key must reside in an EKM provider.

The restore process for an encrypted backup is completely transparent. You don't need to specify any particular encryption options. However, the encryptor must be available on the instance of SQL Server you are restoring to. In addition to the regular restore permissions, you also need to have at least the VIEW DEFINITION permission on the encryptor.

In the following code showing the start of the backup encryption process, first a master database DMK is created. This key is used to protect a self-issued certificate, also created in the master database:

```
USE master;
CREATE MASTER KEY ENCRYPTION BY PASSWORD = 'Pa$$w0rd';
CREATE CERTIFICATE DemoBackupEncryptCert
WITH SUBJECT = 'SQLDevGuideDemoDb Backup Certificate';
GO
```

The master DMK is encrypted using the SMK created during the setup. You can check both keys with the following query:

```
SELECT name, key_length, algorithm_desc
FROM sys.symmetric_keys;
```

The query returns the following result set:

```
Name                      key_length   algorithm_desc
-----------------------   ----------   --------------
##MS_DatabaseMasterKey##  256          AES_256
##MS_ServiceMasterKey##   256          AES_256
```

For a test, the following code creates an unencrypted backup in the `C:SQL2017DevGuide` folder, which should be created in advance:

```
BACKUP DATABASE SQLDevGuideDemoDb
TO DISK = N'C:SQL2017DevGuideSQLDevGuideDemoDb_Backup.bak'
WITH INIT;
```

Next, you can create an encrypted backup, as shown in the following code:

```
BACKUP DATABASE SQLDevGuideDemoDb
TO DISK = N'C:SQL2017DevGuideSQLDevGuideDemoDb_BackupEncrypted.bak'
WITH INIT,
ENCRYPTION
  (
   ALGORITHM = AES_256,
   SERVER CERTIFICATE = DemoBackupEncryptCert
  );
```

Note that this time you get a warning telling you that the certificate used for encrypting the database encryption key has not been backed up. Therefore, you should back up the certificate used for the backup encryption and, in addition, the master DMK used to protect the certificate and the SQL Server SMK used to protect the master DMK, as the following code shows:

```
-- Backup SMK
BACKUP SERVICE MASTER KEY
 TO FILE = N'C:SQL2017DevGuideSMK.key'
 ENCRYPTION BY PASSWORD = 'Pa$$w0rd';
-- Backup master DMK
BACKUP MASTER KEY
 TO FILE = N'C:SQL2017DevGuidemasterDMK.key'
 ENCRYPTION BY PASSWORD = 'Pa$$w0rd';
-- Backup certificate
BACKUP CERTIFICATE DemoBackupEncryptCert
```

```
TO FILE = N'C:SQL2017DevGuideDemoBackupEncryptCert.cer'
WITH PRIVATE KEY
  (
   FILE = N'C:SQL2017DevGuideDemoBackupEncryptCert.key',
   ENCRYPTION BY PASSWORD = 'Pa$$w0rd'
  );
GO
```

Now you are ready to simulate a failure. Drop the demo database, the certificate used for the encryption, and the master DMK:

```
DROP DATABASE SQLDevGuideDemoDb;
DROP CERTIFICATE DemoBackupEncryptCert;
DROP MASTER KEY;
```

Try to restore the encrypted backup. You should get `error 33111`, telling you that SQL Server cannot find the server certificate. The following code is used to restore the encrypted backup:

```
RESTORE DATABASE SQLDevGuideDemoDb
FROM  DISK = N'C:SQL2017DevGuideSQLDevGuideDemoDb_BackupEncrypted.bak'
WITH  FILE = 1;
```

You have to start the restore process by restoring the master DMK, as shown in the following code:

```
RESTORE MASTER KEY
FROM FILE = N'C:SQL2017DevGuidemasterDMK.key'
DECRYPTION BY PASSWORD = 'Pa$$w0rd'
ENCRYPTION BY PASSWORD = 'Pa$$w0rd';
```

Next, you open the master DMK and restore the certificate, as shown in the following code:

```
OPEN MASTER KEY DECRYPTION BY PASSWORD = 'Pa$$w0rd';
CREATE CERTIFICATE DemoBackupEncryptCert
 FROM FILE = N'C:SQL2017DevGuideDemoBackupEncryptCert.cer'
 WITH PRIVATE KEY (FILE = N'C:SQL2017DevGuideDemoBackupEncryptCert.key',
  DECRYPTION BY PASSWORD = 'Pa$$w0rd');
```

Now you are ready to restore the encrypted backup. The following code should restore the demo database successfully:

```
RESTORE DATABASE SQLDevGuideDemoDb
FROM  DISK = N'C:SQL2017DevGuideSQLDevGuideDemoDb_BackupEncrypted.bak'
WITH  FILE = 1, RECOVERY;
```

Finally, you can check which backups are encrypted by querying the
`msdb.dbo.backupset` table as shown in the following code:

```
SELECT b.database_name,
 c.name,
 b.encryptor_type,
 b.encryptor_thumbprint
FROM sys.certificates AS c
 INNER JOIN msdb.dbo.backupset AS b
  ON c.thumbprint = b.encryptor_thumbprint;
```

Backup encryption encrypts backups only. It does not encrypt data in data files. You can
encrypt data in tables with T-SQL using **column-level encryption**. Column-level encryption
is present in SQL Server from version 2008 onwards. You encrypt the data in a specific
column by using a symmetric key. You protect the symmetric key with an asymmetric key
or a certificate. The keys and the certificate are stored inside your database where the tables
with the encrypted columns are. You protect the asymmetric key or the certificate with the
database master key. The following code, which created the DMK in the demo database,
issues a SQL Server certificate and then creates the symmetric key used for column
encryption:

```
USE SQLDevGuideDemoDb;
-- Create the SQLDevGuideDemoDb database DMK
CREATE MASTER KEY ENCRYPTION BY PASSWORD = 'Pa$$w0rd';
-- Create the column certificate in SQLDevGuideDemoDb
CREATE CERTIFICATE DemoColumnEncryptCert
 WITH SUBJECT = 'SQLDevGuideDemoDb Column Certificate';
-- Create the symmetric key
CREATE SYMMETRIC KEY DemoColumnEncryptSimKey
 WITH ALGORITHM = AES_256
 ENCRYPTION BY CERTIFICATE DemoColumnEncryptCert;
GO
```

Next, you can prepare an additional column to store the encrypted data. The `dbo.Table1`
should already exist from the demo code earlier in this chapter. The following code adds an
additional column to store the encrypted data:

```
ALTER TABLE dbo.Table1
ADD tableContainer_Encrypted VARBINARY(128);
GO
```

Now you are ready to encrypt data in the new column. You need to open the symmetric key and decrypt it with the certificate used for the encryption. The following code opens the symmetric key and then updates the new column in the table with the values from an unencrypted column. The code uses the ENCRYPTBYKEY() T-SQL function to encrypt the data with a symmetric key:

```
OPEN SYMMETRIC KEY DemoColumnEncryptSimKey
 DECRYPTION BY CERTIFICATE DemoColumnEncryptCert;
UPDATE dbo.Table1
SET tableContainer_Encrypted =
    ENCRYPTBYKEY(Key_GUID('DemoColumnEncryptSimKey'), tableContainer);
GO
```

You can check the data with the following query, which uses the DECRYPTBYKEY() T-SQL function for decryption:

```
OPEN SYMMETRIC KEY DemoColumnEncryptSimKey
 DECRYPTION BY CERTIFICATE DemoColumnEncryptCert;
-- All columns
SELECT id, tableContainer,
 tableContainer_Encrypted,
 CAST(DECRYPTBYKEY(tableContainer_Encrypted) AS CHAR(5))
  AS tableContainer_Decrypted
FROM dbo.Table1;
GO
```

Here are the results, with the encrypted value abbreviated for simpler reading:

Id	tableContainer	tableContainer_Encrypted	tableContainer_Decrypted
1	dbo	0x003D10428AE86248A44F70	dbo
2	dbo	0x003D10428AE86248A44F70	dbo

You can use the following code to clean up your SQL Server instance. The code also deletes backups in the demo folder. You need to run SSMS as administrator and turn on the SQLCMD mode in SSMS to successfully execute the clean-up code (go to the **Query** menu and select the SQLCMD mode option):

```
USE master;
!!del C:SQL2017DevGuideDemoBackupEncryptCert.cer
!!del C:SQL2017DevGuideDemoBackupEncryptCert.key
!!del C:SQL2017DevGuidemasterDMK.key
!!del C:SQL2017DevGuideSMK.key
!!del C:SQL2017DevGuideSQLDevGuideDemoDb_Backup.bak
!!del C:SQL2017DevGuideSQLDevGuideDemoDb_BackupEncrypted.bak
GO
```

```
IF DB_ID(N'SQLDevGuideDemoDb') IS NOT NULL
    DROP DATABASE SQLDevGuideDemoDb;
DROP LOGIN LoginA;
DROP LOGIN [BuiltinPower Users];
DROP LOGIN LoginB;
DROP CERTIFICATE DemoBackupEncryptCert;
DROP MASTER KEY;
GO
```

Column-level encryption protects the data in the database, not just backups. However, it protects data at rest only. When data is used by an application, the data is decrypted. If you don't use network encryption, the data travels over the network in an unencrypted way. All the keys are in a SQL Server database, and therefore a DBA can always decrypt the data. End users who don't have access to the certificates and keys can't decrypt the encrypted data. In addition, the implementation of column-level encryption might be quite complex because you might need to modify a lot of T-SQL code. Column-level encryption is available in all editions of SQL Server.

Another option to protect data at rest is **Transparent Data Encryption** (TDE). You can use the TDE for real-time encryption and decryption of data and log files. You encrypt data with the **database encryption key** (DEK), which is a symmetric key. It is stored in the database boot record and is therefore already available during the database recovery process. You protect the DEK with a certificate in the master database. You can also use an asymmetric key instead of the certificate; however, the asymmetric key must be stored in an EKM module. TDE uses the AES and Triple DES encryptions only. TDE was first implemented in SQL Server with version 2012.

You can use TDE on user databases only. You cannot export the database encryption key. This key is used by the SQL Server Database Engine only. End users never use it. Even if you change the database owner, you don't need to regenerate the DEK.

TDE encrypts data on a page level. In addition, it also encrypts the transaction log. You should back up the certificate used to protect the DEK and the private key used to protect the certificate immediately after you enable TDE. If you need to restore or attach the encrypted database to another SQL Server instance, you need to restore both the certificate and the private key, or you are not able to open the database. Note again that you don't export the DEK as it is a part of the database itself. You need to keep and maintain the certificate used to protect the DEK even after you disable the TDE on the database. This is because parts of the transaction log might still be encrypted. The certificate is needed until you perform a full database backup.

The following code starts the process of enabling the TDE by creating a DMK in the master database:

```
USE master;
CREATE MASTER KEY ENCRYPTION BY PASSWORD = 'Pa$$w0rd';
GO
```

You can check whether the master DMK was created successfully with the following code:

```
SELECT name, key_length, algorithm_desc
FROM sys.symmetric_keys;
```

Let's back up the SMK and the master DMK immediately, as the next part of the code shows:

```
BACKUP SERVICE MASTER KEY
  TO FILE = N'C:SQL2017DevGuideSMK.key'
  ENCRYPTION BY PASSWORD = 'Pa$$w0rd';
-- Backup master DMK
BACKUP MASTER KEY
  TO FILE = N'C:SQL2017DevGuidemasterDMK.key'
  ENCRYPTION BY PASSWORD = 'Pa$$w0rd';
GO
```

The next portion of the code creates a demo database:

```
IF DB_ID(N'TDEDemo') IS NULL
CREATE DATABASE TDEDemo;
GO
```

While still in the context of the master database, use the following code to create the certificate you will use to protect the DEK:

```
CREATE CERTIFICATE DemoTDEEncryptCert
WITH SUBJECT = 'TDEDemo TDE Certificate';
GO
```

Of course, you need to back up this certificate immediately, as shown in the following code:

```
BACKUP CERTIFICATE DemoTDEEncryptCert
  TO FILE = N'C:SQL2017DevGuideDemoTDEEncryptCert.cer'
  WITH PRIVATE KEY
    (
    FILE = N'C:SQL2017DevGuideDemoTDEEncryptCert.key',
    ENCRYPTION BY PASSWORD = 'Pa$$w0rd'
    );
GO
```

You create the database encryption key in the demo user database, as shown in the following code:

```
USE TDEDemo;
CREATE DATABASE ENCRYPTION KEY
 WITH ALGORITHM = AES_128
 ENCRYPTION BY SERVER CERTIFICATE DemoTDEEncryptCert;
GO
```

The final step of this process is to actually turn the TDE on, as shown in the following code:

```
ALTER DATABASE TDEDemo
SET ENCRYPTION ON;
GO
```

You can check which databases are encrypted by querying the sys.dm_database_encryption_keys dynamic management view. This view exposes the information about the encryption keys and the state of encryption of a database, as shown in the following code:

```
SELECT DB_NAME(database_id) AS DatabaseName,
    key_algorithm AS [Algorithm],
    key_length AS KeyLength,
   encryption_state AS EncryptionState,
   CASE encryption_state
        WHEN 0 THEN 'No database encryption key present, no encryption'
        WHEN 1 THEN 'Unencrypted'
        WHEN 2 THEN 'Encryption in progress'
        WHEN 3 THEN 'Encrypted'
        WHEN 4 THEN 'Key change in progress'
        WHEN 5 THEN 'Decryption in progress'
    END AS EncryptionStateDesc,
    percent_complete AS PercentComplete
FROM sys.dm_database_encryption_keys;
```

The results of this query are as follows:

DatabaseName	Algorithm	KeyLength	EncryptionState	EncryptionStateDesc	PercentComplete
Tempdb	AES	256	3	Encrypted	0
TDEDemo	AES	128	3	Encrypted	0

Note that the `Tempdb` system database also inherited the encryption. The demo database is empty and thus very small. The encryption process on such a small database is very fast. However, in a production database, you would be able to monitor the percentage complete rising from 0 to 100, while the encryption state would be *Encryption in progress*. SQL Server needs to scan all of the data files and log files to finish the encryption.

Now let's turn encryption off for the demo database:

```
ALTER DATABASE TDEDemo
SET ENCRYPTION OFF;
GO
```

Using the same query, you can check the encryption status again:

```
SELECT DB_NAME(database_id) AS DatabaseName,
    key_algorithm AS [Algorithm],
    key_length AS KeyLength,
  encryption_state AS EncryptionState,
   CASE encryption_state
        WHEN 0 THEN 'No database encryption key present, no encryption'
        WHEN 1 THEN 'Unencrypted'
        WHEN 2 THEN 'Encryption in progress'
        WHEN 3 THEN 'Encrypted'
        WHEN 4 THEN 'Key change in progress'
        WHEN 5 THEN 'Decryption in progress'
    END AS EncryptionStateDesc,
    percent_complete AS PercentComplete
FROM sys.dm_database_encryption_keys;
```

Please note the result. The `tempdb` system database is still encrypted:

DatabaseName	Algorithm	KeyLength	EncryptionState	EncryptionStateDesc	PercentComplete
Tempdb	AES	256	3	Encrypted	0
TDEDemo	AES	128	1	Unencrypted	0

Restart your SQL Server instance and execute the previous query again. This time, the `tempdb` system database is unencrypted.

You can use the following code to clean up your SQL Server instance. Again, use SQLCMD mode to execute it:

```
USE master;
!!del C:SQL2017DevGuideDemoTDEEncryptCert.cer
!!del C:SQL2017DevGuideDemoTDEEncryptCert.key
!!del C:SQL2017DevGuidemasterDMK.key
!!del C:SQL2017DevGuideSMK.key
IF DB_ID(N'TDEDemo') IS NOT NULL
    DROP DATABASE TDEDemo;
DROP CERTIFICATE DemoTDEEncryptCert;
DROP MASTER KEY;
GO
```

Always Encrypted

SQL Server 2016 and 2017 introduce a new level of encryption, the **Always Encrypted** (**AE**) feature. This feature enables the same level of data protection as encrypting the data in the client application. Actually, although this is a SQL Server feature, the data is encrypted and decrypted on the client side. The encryption keys are never revealed to the SQL Server Database Engine. This way, a DBA can't also see sensitive data without the encryption keys, just by having sysadmin permissions on the SQL Server instance with the encrypted data. This way, AE makes a separation between the administrators who manage the data and the users who own the data.

You need two keys for AE. First you create the **column master key** (**CMK**). Then you create the **column encryption key** (**CEK**) and protect it with the CMK. An application uses the CEK to encrypt the data. SQL Server stores only encrypted data, and can't decrypt it. This is possible because the column master keys aren't really stored in a SQL Server database. In the database, SQL Server stores only the link to those keys. The column master keys are stored outside SQL Server, in one of the following possible places:

- Windows Certificate Store for the current user
- Windows Certificate Store for the local machine
- Azure Key Vault service
- A **hardware security module** (**HSM**) that supports Microsoft CryptoAPI or Cryptography API: Next Generation

The column encryption keys are stored in the database. Inside a SQL Server Database, only the encrypted part of the values of the column encryption keys are stored, together with the information about the location of the column master keys. CEKs are never stored as plain text in a database. CMKs are, as mentioned, actually stored in external trusted key stores.

An application can use AE keys and encryption by using an AE-enabled driver, such as .NET Framework Data Provider for SQL Server version 4.6 or higher, Microsoft JDBC Driver for SQL Server 6.0 or higher, or Windows ODBC driver for SQL Server version 13.1 or higher. The application must send parameterized queries to SQL Server. The AE-enabled driver works together with the SQL Server Database Engine to determine which parameters should be encrypted or decrypted. For each parameter that needs to be encrypted or decrypted, the driver obtains the metadata needed for the encryption from the Database Engine, including the encryption algorithm, the location of the corresponding CMK, and the encrypted value for the corresponding CEK. Then the driver contacts the CMK store, retrieves the CMK, decrypts the CEK, and uses the CEK to encrypt or decrypt the parameter. Next the driver caches the CEK in order to speed up the next usage of the same CEK. The following figure shows the process graphically:

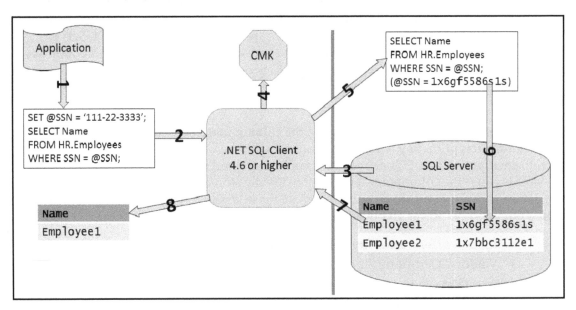

Always Encrypted process

The preceding figure represents the whole process in these steps:

1. The client application creates a parameterized query.
2. The client application sends the parameterized query to the AE-enabled driver.
3. The AE-enabled driver contacts SQL Server to determine which parameters need encryption or decryption, the location of the CMK, and the encrypted value of the CEK.
4. The AE-enabled driver retrieves the CMK and decrypts the CEK.
5. The AE-enabled driver encrypts the parameter(s).
6. The driver sends the query to the Database Engine.
7. The Database Engine retrieves the data and sends the result set to the driver.
8. The driver performs decryption, if needed, and sends the result set to the client application.

The Database Engine never operates on the plain text data stored in the encrypted columns. However, some queries on the encrypted data are possible, depending on the encryption type. There are two types of encryption:

- **Deterministic encryption**, which always generates the same encrypted value for the same input value. With this encryption, you can index the encrypted column and use point lookups, equality joins, and grouping expressions on the encrypted column. However, a malicious user could try to guess the values by analyzing the patterns of the encrypted values. This is especially dangerous when the set of possible values for a column is discrete, with a small number of distinct values.
- **Randomized encryption**, which encrypts data in an unpredictable manner.

It is time to show how AE works through some demo code. First, let's create and use a demo database:

```
USE master;
IF DB_ID(N'AEDemo') IS NULL
    CREATE DATABASE AEDemo;
GO
USE AEDemo;
GO
```

Next, create the CMK in the SSMS GUI. In Object Explorer, refresh the database folder to see the `AEDemo` database. Expand this database folder, expand the `Security` subfolder and the `Always Encrypted Keys` subfolder, right-click on the `Column Master Key` subfolder, and select the **New Column Master Key** option from the pop-up menu. In the **Name** text box, write `AE_ColumnMasterKey`, and make sure you select the **Windows Certificate Store-Local Machine** option in the **Key store** drop-down list, as shown in the following screenshot. Then click **OK**:

Creating a CMK

You can check if the CMK was created successfully with the following query:

```
SELECT *
FROM sys.column_master_keys;
```

Next, you create the CEK. In SSMS, in Object Explorer, right-click on the `Column Encryption Keys` subfolder, right under the `Column Master Key` subfolder, and select the **New Column Encryption Key** option from the pop-up menu. Name the CEK `AE_ColumnEncryptionKey` and use the `AE_ColumnMasterKey` CMK to encrypt it. You can check whether the CEK creation was successful with the following query:

```
SELECT *
FROM sys.column_encryption_keys;
GO
```

Now try to create a table with one deterministic encryption column and one randomized encryption column. My database used the default `SQL_Latin1_General_CP1_CI_AS` collation:

```
CREATE TABLE dbo.Table1
(id INT,
 SecretDeterministic NVARCHAR(10)
  ENCRYPTED WITH (COLUMN_ENCRYPTION_KEY = AE_ColumnEncryptionKey,
   ENCRYPTION_TYPE = DETERMINISTIC,
   ALGORITHM = 'AEAD_AES_256_CBC_HMAC_SHA_256') NULL,
 SecretRandomized NVARCHAR(10)
  ENCRYPTED WITH (COLUMN_ENCRYPTION_KEY = AE_ColumnEncryptionKey,
   ENCRYPTION_TYPE = RANDOMIZED,
   ALGORITHM = 'AEAD_AES_256_CBC_HMAC_SHA_256') NULL
);
GO
```

The previous statement produced an error number `33289`, which tells me that I cannot create an encrypted column for character strings that use a non-BIN2 collation. Currently, only new binary collations (that is, collations with the `BIN2` suffix) are supported by AE.

So let's try to create the table again, this time with correct collations for character columns:

```
CREATE TABLE dbo.Table1
(id INT,
 SecretDeterministic NVARCHAR(10) COLLATE Latin1_General_BIN2
  ENCRYPTED WITH (COLUMN_ENCRYPTION_KEY = AE_ColumnEncryptionKey,
   ENCRYPTION_TYPE = DETERMINISTIC,
   ALGORITHM = 'AEAD_AES_256_CBC_HMAC_SHA_256') NULL,
 SecretRandomized NVARCHAR(10) COLLATE Latin1_General_BIN2
  ENCRYPTED WITH (COLUMN_ENCRYPTION_KEY = AE_ColumnEncryptionKey,
```

```
    ENCRYPTION_TYPE = RANDOMIZED,
    ALGORITHM = 'AEAD_AES_256_CBC_HMAC_SHA_256') NULL
);
GO
```

This time, table creation succeeds. Now you can try to insert a row of data with the following statement:

```
INSERT INTO dbo.Table1
(id, SecretDeterministic, SecretRandomized)
VALUES (1, N'DeterSec01', N'RandomSec1');
```

You get error `206` with the following error text Operand type clash: nvarchar is incompatible with nvarchar(4000) encrypted with (`encryption_type = 'DETERMINISTIC'`, `encryption_algorithm_name = 'AEAD_AES_256_CBC_HMAC_SHA_256'`, `column_encryption_key_name = 'AE_ColumnEncryptionKey'`, `column_encryption_key_database_name = 'AEDemo'`). SQL Server cannot encrypt or decrypt the data. You need to modify it from a client application. You can perform a limited set of operations on the table from SQL Server. For example, you can use the `TRUNCATE TABLE` statement on a table with `AE` columns.

I created a very simple client Windows Console application in Visual C#. The application actually just retrieves the keys and inserts a single row into the table that was created with the previous code. Here is the C# code. The first part of the code just defines the namespaces used in the application or added by default in a new project in Visual Studio 2015:

```
using System;
using System.Collections.Generic;
using System.Data;
using System.Data.SqlClient;
using System.Linq;
using System.Text;
using System.Threading.Tasks;
```

The next part of the code defines the connection string to my local SQL Server. Please note the new connection string property in .NET 4.6 and exceeding ones, the `Column Encryption Setting=enabled` property. Then the application opens the connection:

```
namespace AEDemo
{
    class Program
    {
        static void Main(string[] args)
        {
```

```
string connectionString = "Data Source=localhost; " +
    "Initial Catalog=AEDemo; Integrated Security=true; " +
    "Column Encryption Setting=enabled";
SqlConnection connection = new SqlConnection(connectionString);
connection.Open();
```

The next part is just a simple check to see whether the three arguments were passed. Please note that in a real application you should use a try-catch block when parsing the first argument to an integral number. The following code is used to check whether the three arguments were passed correctly:

```
if (args.Length != 3)
    {
        Console.WriteLine("Please enter a numeric " +
            "and two string arguments.");
        return;
    }
int id = Int32.Parse(args[0]);
```

The next part of the code defines the parameterized INSERT statement and executes it, as shown in the following code:

```
{
    using (SqlCommand cmd = onnection.CreateCommand())
    {
     cmd.CommandText = @"INSERT INTO dbo.Table1 " +
      "(id, SecretDeterministic, SecretRandomized)" +
         " VALUES (@id, @SecretDeterministic,
             @SecretRandomized);";

     SqlParameter paramid= cmd.CreateParameter();
     paramid.ParameterName = @"@id";
     paramid.DbType = DbType.Int32;
     paramid.Direction = ParameterDirection.Input;
     paramid.Value = id;
     cmd.Parameters.Add(paramid);

     SqlParameter paramSecretDeterministic =
        cmd.CreateParameter();
                    paramSecretDeterministic.ParameterName =
    @"@SecretDeterministic";
    paramSecretDeterministic.DbType = DbType.String;
    paramSecretDeterministic.Direction =
       ParameterDirection.Input;
   paramSecretDeterministic.Value = "DeterSec01";
   paramSecretDeterministic.Size = 10;
 cmd.Parameters.Add(paramSecretDeterministic);
```

```
    SqlParameter paramSecretRandomized = cmd.CreateParameter();
    paramSecretRandomized.ParameterName =
@"@SecretRandomized";
paramSecretRandomized.DbType = DbType.String;
paramSecretRandomized.Direction = ParameterDirection.Input;
paramSecretRandomized.Value = "RandomSec1";
paramSecretRandomized.Size = 10;
                    cmd.Parameters.Add(paramSecretRandomized);

cmd.ExecuteNonQuery();
    }
    }
```

Finally, the code closes the connection and informs you that a row was inserted successfully:

```
    connection.Close();
    Console.WriteLine("Row inserted successfully");
        }
    }
}
```

If you don't have Visual Studio installed, you can just run the AEDemo.exe application provided with the code examples associated with this book. As mentioned, the application inserts a single row into a previously created table with two AE-enabled columns. Please run the application from SSMS in SQLCMD mode, as the following example shows; there is no prompting for values in the application:

```
!!C:SQL2017DevGuideAEDemo 1 DeterSec01 RandomSec1
!!C:SQL2017DevGuideAEDemo 2 DeterSec02 RandomSec2
```

Now try to read the data from the same session in SSMS that you used to create the table, using the following code:

```
SELECT *
FROM dbo.Table1;
```

You can see only encrypted data. Now open a second query window in SSMS. Right-click in this window and choose **Connection**, then **Change Connection**. In the connection dialog, click the **Options** button at the bottom. Type in AEDemo for the database name and then click the **Additional Connection Parameters** tab. In the text box, enter Column Encryption Setting=enabled (without the double quotes). Then click on **Connect**.

Try again to insert a row from SSMS. Use the following query:

```
INSERT INTO dbo.Table1
  (id, SecretDeterministic, SecretRandomized)
VALUES (3, N'DeterSec03', N'RandomSec3');
```

You get error message 206 again. You need to use a parameterized query. SSMS from version 17.0 adds support for inserting, updating, and filtering by values stored in columns that use **Always Encrypted** from a **Query Editor** window. However, parameterization is disabled by default. You need to enable it for your current session:

- From the **Query** menu, select **Query Options...**
- Navigate to **Execution** | **Advanced**
- Select the **Enable Parameterization for Always Encrypted** check box and click **OK**.

In addition, you need to declare and initialize the variables in the same statement (with inline initialization). The initialization value must be a single literal. The following code shows an example:

```
DECLARE @p1 NVARCHAR(10) = N'DeterSec03';
DECLARE @p2 NVARCHAR(10) = N'RandomSec3';
INSERT INTO dbo.Table1
  (id, SecretDeterministic, SecretRandomized)
VALUES (3, @p1, @p2);
```

Let's try to read the data with the following query:

```
SELECT *
FROM dbo.Table1;
```

This time, the query works and you get the following result:

```
Id   SecretDeterministic   SecretRandomized
---  --------------------  ----------------
1    DeterSec01            RandomSec1
2    DeterSec02            RandomSec2
3    DeterSec03            RandomSec3
```

You can now close this query window and continue in the first one. Try to index the column with deterministic encryption. The following code creates a nonclustered index on the dbo.Table1 with the SecretDeterministic column used as the key:

```
CREATE NONCLUSTERED INDEX NCI_Table1_SecretDeterministic
ON dbo.Table1(SecretDeterministic);
GO
```

The creation succeeds. Now try to also create an index on the column with randomized encryption, as shown in the following code:

```
CREATE NONCLUSTERED INDEX NCI_Table1_SecretRandomized
ON dbo.Table1(SecretRandomized);
GO
```

This time you get an error message telling you that you cannot index a column with randomized encryption. Finally, execute the following code to clean up your SQL Server instance:

```
USE master;
IF DB_ID(N'AEDemo') IS NOT NULL
DROP DATABASE AEDemo;
GO
```

You have already seen some of the limitations of AE, including:

- Only BIN2 collations are supported for strings
- You can only index columns with deterministic encryption, and use a limited set of T-SQL operations on those columns
- You cannot index columns with randomized encryption
- AE is limited to the Enterprise and Developer editions only
- Working with AE in SSMS can be painful

Refer to Books Online for a more detailed list of AE's limitations. However, please also note the strengths of AE. It is simple to implement because it does not need modifications in an application, except the modification for connection strings. Data is encrypted end-to-end, from client memory, through network-to-database storage. Even DBAs can't view the data within SQL Server only; they need access to the key storage outside SQL Server to read the CMK. AE and other encryption options in SQL Server provide a complete set of possibilities, and it is up to you to select the appropriate method for the business problem you are solving.

Row-Level Security

In the first part of this chapter, you learned about permissions on database objects, including objects with data, namely tables, views, and table-valued, user-defined functions. Sometimes you need to give permissions to end users in a more granular way. For example, you might need to give permissions to a specific user to read and update only a subset of columns in the table, and to see only a subset of rows in a table.

You can use programmable objects, such as stored procedures, to achieve these granular permission needs. You can use declarative permissions with DCL statements (GRANT, REVOKE, and DENY) on the column level already available in previous versions of SQL Server. However, SQL Server 2016 and 2017 also offer **declarative Row-Level Security**, abbreviated to RLS. In this section, you will learn how to:

- Use programmable objects to maintain security
- Use SQL Server 2016 and 2017 RLS

Using programmable objects to maintain security

In Transact-SQL, you can write views, stored procedures, scalar and table-valued user-defined functions, and triggers. Views serve best as a layer for selecting data, although you can modify data through views as well. Views are especially useful for columns and RLS. You can grant column permissions directly; however, doing this means a lot of administrative work. You can create a view as a projection on the base table with selected columns only, and then maintain permissions on a higher granularity level (that is, on the view instead of on the columns). In addition, you cannot give row-level permissions through a predicate in the GRANT statement. Of course, you can use the same predicate in the WHERE clause of the SELECT statement of the view you are using as a security layer. You can use table-valued functions as parameterized views.

Stored procedures are appropriate for all update activity, and also for querying data. Maintaining security through stored procedures is the easiest method of administration; with stored procedures, you typically need to grant the EXECUTE permission only. You can use triggers and scalar functions for advanced security checking; for example, for validating users input.

Programmable objects refer to base tables and to each other in a kind of chain. For example, a stored procedure can use a view that selects from a base table. All the objects in SQL Server have owners. As long as there is a single owner for all the objects in the chain, you can manage permissions on the highest level only. Using the previous example, if the stored procedure, view, and base table have the same owner, you can manage permissions for the stored procedure only. SQL Server trusts that the owner of the procedure knows what the procedure is doing. This works for any DML statement (SELECT, INSERT, UPDATE, DELETE, and MERGE).

If the chain of owners between dependent objects is broken, SQL Server must check the permissions for any objects where the chain is broken. For example, if the owner of the procedure from the previous example is different from the owner of the view, SQL Server will check the permissions on the view as well. If the owner of the table is different from the owner of the view, SQL Server will also check permissions on the base table. In addition, if you use dynamic T-SQL code, concatenate a T-SQL statement as a string, and then use the EXECUTE command to execute them, SQL Server checks the permissions on all the objects the dynamic code is using. This is logical because SQL Server cannot know which objects the dynamic code is going to use until it actually executes the code, especially if you concatenate a part of the dynamic code from user input. Besides the threat of code injection, this extra checking is another reason why you should not use dynamic string concatenation in T-SQL code in production.

To start testing programmable-object-based RLS, let's create a new demo database and change the context to this database:

```
USE master;
IF DB_ID(N'RLSDemo') IS NULL
CREATE DATABASE RLSDemo;
GO
USE RLSDemo;
```

The next step is to create four database users without logins. Three of them represent regular users from the sales department, and the fourth one represents the sales department manager. We will use the following program to create the databases:

```
CREATE USER SalesUser1 WITHOUT LOGIN;
CREATE USER SalesUser2 WITHOUT LOGIN;
CREATE USER SalesUser3 WITHOUT LOGIN;
CREATE USER SalesManager WITHOUT LOGIN;
GO
```

The next piece of code creates a table for the employee data. This table needs RLS:

```
CREATE TABLE dbo.Employees
(
 EmployeeId   INT          NOT NULL PRIMARY KEY,
 EmployeeName NVARCHAR(10) NOT NULL,
 SalesRegion  NVARCHAR(3)  NOT NULL,
 SalaryRank   INT          NOT NULL
);
GO
```

Now let's insert some data into the dbo.Employees table. The three rows inserted represent the three regular users from the sales department. You can check the inserted rows immediately with a query. Note that the sales region for the first two users is USA, and for the third one it is EU:

```
INSERT INTO dbo.Employees
(EmployeeId, EmployeeName, SalesRegion, SalaryRank)
VALUES
  (1, N'SalesUser1', N'USA', 5),
  (2, N'SalesUser2', N'USA', 4),
  (3, N'SalesUser3', N'EU', 6);
-- Check the data
SELECT *
FROM dbo.Employees;
GO
```

The dbo.Customers table, created with the following code, will also need RLS:

```
CREATE TABLE dbo.Customers
(
 CustomerId   INT          NOT NULL PRIMARY KEY,
 CustomerName NVARCHAR(10) NOT NULL,
 SalesRegion  NVARCHAR(3)  NOT NULL
);
GO
```

Again, let's insert some rows into this table and check them. There are two customers from the USA and two from the EU:

```
INSERT INTO dbo.Customers
(CustomerId, CustomerName, SalesRegion)
VALUES
  (1, N'Customer01', N'USA'),
  (2, N'Customer02', N'USA'),
  (3, N'Customer03', N'EU'),
  (4, N'Customer04', N'EU');
-- Check the data
SELECT *
FROM dbo.Customers;
GO
```

None of the users have been given any permissions yet. Therefore, you can read the data only as the dbo user. If you execute the following five lines of code, only the first SELECT succeeds. For the four EXECUTE commands, you get an error:

```
SELECT * FROM dbo.Employees;
EXECUTE (N'SELECT * FROM dbo.Employees') AS USER = N'SalesUser1';
EXECUTE (N'SELECT * FROM dbo.Employees') AS USER = N'SalesUser2';
EXECUTE (N'SELECT * FROM dbo.Employees') AS USER = N'SalesUser3';
EXECUTE (N'SELECT * FROM dbo.Employees') AS USER = N'SalesManager';
```

In the next step, the code creates a stored procedure that reads the data from the dbo.Employees table. It filters the rows for regular users and returns all rows for the sales department manager:

```
CREATE PROCEDURE dbo.SelectEmployees
AS
SELECT *
FROM dbo.Employees
WHERE EmployeeName = USER_NAME()
OR USER_NAME() = N'SalesManager';
GO
```

You must give the permission to execute this procedure to the database users:

```
GRANT EXECUTE ON dbo.SelectEmployees
TO SalesUser1, SalesUser2, SalesUser3, SalesManager;
GO
```

Users still cannot see the data by querying the tables directly. You can test this fact by executing the following code again. You can read the data as the dbo user, but will get errors when you impersonate other database users:

```
SELECT * FROM dbo.Employees;
EXECUTE (N'SELECT * FROM dbo.Employees') AS USER = N'SalesUser1';
EXECUTE (N'SELECT * FROM dbo.Employees') AS USER = N'SalesUser2';
EXECUTE (N'SELECT * FROM dbo.Employees') AS USER = N'SalesUser3';
EXECUTE (N'SELECT * FROM dbo.Employees') AS USER = N'SalesManager';
GO
```

Try to execute the stored procedure, once as dbo and once by impersonating each database user:

```
EXEC dbo.SelectEmployees;
EXECUTE AS USER = N'SalesUser1' EXEC dbo.SelectEmployees;
REVERT;
EXECUTE AS USER = N'SalesUser2' EXEC dbo.SelectEmployees;
REVERT;
```

```
EXECUTE AS USER = N'SalesUser3' EXEC dbo.SelectEmployees;
REVERT;
EXECUTE AS USER = N'SalesManager' EXEC dbo.SelectEmployees;
REVERT;
GO
```

As the dbo user, you can execute the procedure; however, you don't see any rows because the filter in the query in the procedure did not take the dbo user into consideration. Of course, the dbo user can still query the table directly. The regular users see their rows only. The sales department manager sees all of the rows in the table.

The next procedure uses dynamic SQL to read the data from the table for a single user. By using dynamic SQL, the procedure creates a broken ownership chain. The following code illustrates this process:

```
CREATE PROCEDURE dbo.SelectEmployeesDynamic
AS
DECLARE @sqlStatement AS NVARCHAR(4000);
SET @sqlStatement = N'
SELECT *
FROM dbo.Employees
WHERE EmployeeName = USER_NAME();'
EXEC(@sqlStatement);
GO
```

The following code is used to give the users permission to execute this procedure:

```
GRANT EXECUTE ON dbo.SelectEmployeesDynamic
TO SalesUser1, SalesUser2, SalesUser3, SalesManager;
GO
```

Now, try to execute the procedure by impersonating different users, with the help of the following code:

```
EXEC dbo.SelectEmployeesDynamic;
EXECUTE AS USER = N'SalesUser1' EXEC dbo.SelectEmployeesDynamic;
REVERT;
EXECUTE AS USER = N'SalesUser2' EXEC dbo.SelectEmployeesDynamic;
REVERT;
EXECUTE AS USER = N'SalesUser3' EXEC dbo.SelectEmployeesDynamic;
REVERT;
EXECUTE AS USER = N'SalesManager' EXEC dbo.SelectEmployeesDynamic;
REVERT;
```

When you execute this as the `dbo` user, the execution succeeds, but you don't get any data returned. However, when you execute the procedure while impersonating other users, you get an error because other users don't have permission to read the underlying table.

Predicate-based Row-Level Security

Using programmable objects for RLS protects sensitive data very well because users don't have direct access to the tables. However, the implementation of such a security might be very complex for existing applications that don't use stored procedures, and other programmable objects. This is why SQL Server 2016 and 2017 include predicate-based RLS. A DBA creates the security filters and policies. The new security policies are transparent to the application. RLS is available in the Standard, Enterprise, and Developer editions. There are two types of RLS security predicates:

- **Filter predicates** that silently filter the rows the application reads. For these predicates, no application change is needed. Note that, besides reading, filter predicates also filter the rows when an application updates or deletes the rows; this is because the application again simply does not see the filtered rows.

- **Block predicates** that explicitly block write operations. You can define them for after-insert and after-update operations, when the predicates block inserts or updates that would move a row beyond the scope of the block predicate. After-insert block predicates also apply to minimally logged or bulk inserts. You can also define block predicates for before-update and before-delete operations, when they serve as filter predicates for the updates and deletes. Note that if you already use filter predicates, before-update and before-delete predicates are not needed. You might want to change the affected applications to catch additional errors produced by block predicates.

You define predicates through a `predicate` function. In the body of this function, you can use other tables with the `JOIN` or `APPLY` operators. If the function is schema-bound, no additional permission checks are needed. If the function is not schema-bound, users need permissions to read the data from the joined tables. When a `predicate` function is schema-bound, you cannot modify the objects it refers to.

A security policy adds an RLS predicate to a table using a `predicate` function. The policy can be disabled. If it is disabled, users see all of the rows. A security policy also filters and/or blocks the rows for the database owners (the `dbo user`, `db_owner` database, and `sysadmin` server roles).

Before testing SQL Server 2016 and 2017 RLS, users need permissions to read the data. The following code gives users permissions to read data from both tables in the demo database:

```
GRANT SELECT ON dbo.Employees
TO SalesUser1, SalesUser2, SalesUser3, SalesManager;
GRANT SELECT ON dbo.Customers
TO SalesUser1, SalesUser2, SalesUser3, SalesManager;
GO
```

To check the permissions, you can try to read from the dbo.Employees table by impersonating each of the users again. All of the users see all of the rows. The following code illustrates this process:

```
SELECT * FROM dbo.Employees;
EXECUTE (N'SELECT * FROM dbo.Employees') AS USER = N'SalesUser1';
EXECUTE (N'SELECT * FROM dbo.Employees') AS USER = N'SalesUser2';
EXECUTE (N'SELECT * FROM dbo.Employees') AS USER = N'SalesUser3';
EXECUTE (N'SELECT * FROM dbo.Employees') AS USER = N'SalesManager';
GO
```

The following command creates a separate schema for security objects. It is good practice to move security objects into a separate schema. If they are in a regular schema, a DBA might inadvertently give permission to modify the security objects when giving the ALTER SCHEMA permission to users for some other reason, such as allowing them to alter the procedures in that schema. The following code illustrates this process:

```
CREATE SCHEMA Security;
GO
```

The following predicate function limits the users to seeing only their own rows in a table. The Sales department manager role can see all rows. In addition, the predicate also takes care of the dbo users, enabling these users to see all of the rows as well:

```
CREATE FUNCTION Security.EmployeesRLS(@UserName AS NVARCHAR(10))
RETURNS TABLE
WITH SCHEMABINDING
AS
RETURN SELECT 1 AS SecurityPredicateResult
  WHERE @UserName = USER_NAME()
     OR USER_NAME() IN (N'SalesManager', N'dbo');
GO
```

The next step is to create the security policy. The security policy created with the following code adds a filter predicate for the `dbo.Employees` table. Note that the `EmployeeName` column is used as the argument for the `predicate` function:

```
CREATE SECURITY POLICY EmployeesFilter
ADD FILTER PREDICATE Security.EmployeesRLS(EmployeeName)
ON dbo.Employees
WITH (STATE = ON);
GO
```

You can test the filter predicate by querying the `dbo.Employees` table again. This time, each regular user gets their own row only, while the `Sales` department manager and the `dbo` users see all of the rows. The following code illustrates this process:

```
SELECT * FROM dbo.Employees;
EXECUTE (N'SELECT * FROM dbo.Employees') AS USER = N'SalesUser1';
EXECUTE (N'SELECT * FROM dbo.Employees') AS USER = N'SalesUser2';
EXECUTE (N'SELECT * FROM dbo.Employees') AS USER = N'SalesUser3';
EXECUTE (N'SELECT * FROM dbo.Employees') AS USER = N'SalesManager';
GO
```

Note that users can still gain access to sensitive data if they can write queries. With carefully crafted queries, they can conclude that a specific row exists, for example. The salary rank for the `SalesUser1` user is 5. This user might be interested if another user with salary rank 6 exists. The user can execute the following query:

```
EXECUTE (N'SELECT * FROM dbo.Employees
WHERE SalaryRank = 6')
AS USER = N'SalesUser1';
```

The query returns zero rows. The `SalesUser1` did not get any information yet. However, when a query is executed, the `WHERE` predicate is evaluated before the security policy filter predicate. Imagine that the `SalesUser1` tries to execute the following query:

```
EXECUTE (N'SELECT * FROM dbo.Employees
WHERE SalaryRank / (SalaryRank - 6) = 0')
AS USER = N'SalesUser1';
```

When you execute this code, you get error 8134, divide by zero error encountered. Now `SalesUser1` knows that an employee with salary rank equal to 6 exists.

Now let's create another predicate function that will be used to filter the rows in the dbo. Customers table. It applies a tabular expression to each row in the dbo.Customers table to include rows with the same sales region as the sales region value for the user who is querying the tables. It does not filter the data for the sales department manager and the dbo database user. The following code illustrates this process:

```
CREATE FUNCTION Security.CustomersRLS(@CustomerId AS INT)
RETURNS TABLE
WITH SCHEMABINDING
AS
RETURN
SELECT 1 AS SecurityPredicateResult
FROM dbo.Customers AS c
 CROSS APPLY(
  SELECT TOP 1 1
  FROM dbo.Employees AS e
  WHERE c.SalesRegion = e.SalesRegion
    AND (e.EmployeeName = USER_NAME()
         OR USER_NAME() IN (N'SalesManager', N'dbo')))
 AS E(EmployeesResult)
WHERE c.CustomerId = @CustomerId;
GO
```

The next step is, of course, to add a security policy. Note that you need to use a column from the dbo.Customers table for the argument of the predicate function. This argument is a dummy one, and does not filter the rows; the actual filter is implemented in the body of the function. The following code illustrates this process:

```
CREATE SECURITY POLICY CustomersFilter
ADD FILTER PREDICATE Security.CustomersRLS(CustomerId)
ON dbo.Customers
WITH (STATE = ON);
GO
```

The following queries test the filter predicate:

```
SELECT * FROM dbo.Customers;
EXECUTE (N'SELECT * FROM dbo.Customers') AS USER = N'SalesUser1';
EXECUTE (N'SELECT * FROM dbo.Customers') AS USER = N'SalesUser2';
EXECUTE (N'SELECT * FROM dbo.Customers') AS USER = N'SalesUser3';
EXECUTE (N'SELECT * FROM dbo.Customers') AS USER = N'SalesManager';
GO
```

The rows from the dbo.Customers table are filtered for regular users. However, note that SalesUser1 and SalesUser2 see the same rows—the rows for the customers from the USA—because the sales territory for both of them is USA. Now let's give users permissions to modify the data in the dbo.Customers table, using the following code:

```
GRANT INSERT, UPDATE, DELETE ON dbo.Customers
TO SalesUser1, SalesUser2, SalesUser3, SalesManager;
```

Try to impersonate the SalesUser1 user, and delete or update a row that SalesUser1 does not see because of the filter predicate. In both cases, zero rows are affected. The code for this is given here:

```
EXECUTE (N'DELETE FROM dbo.Customers WHERE CustomerId = 3')
 AS USER = N'SalesUser1';
EXECUTE (N'UPDATE dbo.Customers
 SET CustomerName =' + '''' + 'Updated' + '''' +
  'WHERE CustomerId = 3')
 AS USER = N'SalesUser1';
```

However, SalesUser1 can insert a row that is filtered out when the same user queries the data. In addition, the user can also update a row in such a way that it disappears from the users scope. The following code illustrates this process:

```
EXECUTE (N'INSERT INTO dbo.Customers
(CustomerId, CustomerName, SalesRegion)
 VALUES(5, ' + '''' + 'Customer05' + '''' + ',' +
  '''' + 'EU' + '''' + ');'
) AS USER = N'SalesUser1';
EXECUTE (N'UPDATE dbo.Customers
 SET SalesRegion =' + '''' + 'EU' + '''' +
 'WHERE CustomerId = 2')
 AS USER = N'SalesUser1';
```

Now try to read the data, using the following code. The dbo user sees all of the rows, while SalesUser1 sees neither the row(s) he just inserted nor the row(s) he just updated:

```
SELECT * FROM dbo.Customers;
EXECUTE (N'SELECT * FROM dbo.Customers') AS USER = N'SalesUser1';
```

You need to add a block predicate to block the inserts and updates that would move a row outside the scope of the user performing the write operation:

```
ALTER SECURITY POLICY CustomersFilter
ADD BLOCK PREDICATE Security.CustomersRLS(CustomerId)
ON dbo.Customers AFTER INSERT,
ADD BLOCK PREDICATE Security.CustomersRLS(CustomerId)
```

```
ON dbo.Customers AFTER UPDATE;
GO
```

Try to do similar data modifications while impersonating the `SalesUser1` user again:

```
EXECUTE (N'INSERT INTO dbo.Customers
(CustomerId, CustomerName, SalesRegion)
 VALUES(6, ' + '''' + 'Customer06' + '''' + ',' +
 '''' + 'EU' + '''' + ');'
) AS USER = N'SalesUser1';
EXECUTE (N'UPDATE dbo.Customers
SET SalesRegion =' + '''' + 'EU' + '''' +
'WHERE CustomerId = 1')
 AS USER = N'SalesUser1';
```

This time, you get an error for both commands. You can see that the block predicate works. Finally, you can clean up your SQL Server instance:

```
USE master;
IF DB_ID(N'RLSDemo') IS NOT NULL
    ALTER DATABASE RLSDemo SET SINGLE_USER WITH ROLLBACK IMMEDIATE;
    DROP DATABASE RLSDemo;
GO
```

Exploring dynamic data masking

With the new SQL Server 2016 and **Dynamic Data Masking** (DDM), you have an additional tool that helps you limit the exposure of sensitive data by masking it to non-privileged users. The masking is done on the SQL Server side, and thus you don't need to implement any changes to applications so they can start using it. DDM is available in the Standard, Enterprise, and Developer Editions; you can read the official documentation about it at:

https://docs.microsoft.com/en-us/sql/relational-databases/security/dynamic-data-masking.

This section introduces DDM, including:

- Defining masked columns
- DDM limitations

Defining masked columns

You define DDM at the column level. You can obfuscate values from a column in a table by using four different masking functions:

- The `default` function implements full masking. The mask depends on the data type of the column. A string is masked by changing each character of a string to X. Numeric values are masked to zero. Date and time data type values are masked to `01.01.2000 00:00:00.0000000` (without double quotes). Binary data is masked to a single byte of ASCII value 0.
- The `email` function masks strings that represent e-mail addresses in the form: `aXXX@XXXX.com`.
- The `random` function masks numeric values to a random value in a specified range.
- The `partial` function uses a custom string to mask character data. You can skip masking some characters at the beginning of the string (prefix) or at the end of the string (suffix).

You must give the users the `UNMASK` database level permission if you want them to see unmasked data.

Let's start testing the DDM feature by creating a new demo database and changing the context to the newly created database:

```
USE master;
IF DB_ID(N'DDMDemo') IS NULL
CREATE DATABASE DDMDemo;
GO
USE DDMDemo;
```

Next, you need a couple of database users for the test:

```
CREATE USER SalesUser1 WITHOUT LOGIN;
CREATE USER SalesUser2 WITHOUT LOGIN;
```

The following code creates and populates a demo table using the `SELECT INTO` statement. It uses the employees from the `WideWorldImporters` demo database, and adds a randomized salary:

```
SELECT PersonID, FullName, EmailAddress,
 CAST(JSON_VALUE(CustomFields, '$.HireDate') AS DATE)
  AS HireDate,
 CAST(RAND(CHECKSUM(NEWID()) % 100000 + PersonID) * 50000 AS INT) + 20000
```

```
  AS Salary
INTO dbo.Employees
FROM WideWorldImporters.Application.People
WHERE IsEmployee = 1;
```

You must grant the SELECT permission on this table to the two database users, with the help of the following code:

```
GRANT SELECT ON dbo.Employees
TO SalesUser1, SalesUser2;
```

If you execute the following queries, you can see that you, as the dbo user, and both database users you created, can see all of the data:

```
SELECT * FROM dbo.Employees;
EXECUTE (N'SELECT * FROM dbo.Employees') AS USER = N'SalesUser1';
EXECUTE (N'SELECT * FROM dbo.Employees') AS USER = N'SalesUser2';
```

Here is the partial result of one of the three previous queries:

PersonID	FullName	EmailAddress	HireDate	Salary
2	Kayla Woodcock	kaylaw@wideworldimporters.com	2008-04-19	45823
3	Hudson Onslow	hudsono@wideworldimporters.com	2012-03-05	39344

The following code adds masking to the previous queries:

```
ALTER TABLE dbo.Employees ALTER COLUMN EmailAddress
  ADD MASKED WITH (FUNCTION = 'email()');
ALTER TABLE dbo.Employees ALTER COLUMN HireDate
  ADD MASKED WITH (FUNCTION = 'default()');
ALTER TABLE dbo.Employees ALTER COLUMN FullName
  ADD MASKED WITH (FUNCTION = 'partial(1, "&&&&&", 3)');
ALTER TABLE dbo.Employees ALTER COLUMN Salary
  ADD MASKED WITH (FUNCTION = 'random(1, 100000)');
GO
```

Now we will try to read the data as one of the regular users, using the following code:

```
EXECUTE (N'SELECT * FROM dbo.Employees') AS USER = N'SalesUser1';
```

The result for this user is masked, as shown here:

PersonID	FullName	EmailAddress	HireDate	Salary
2	K&&&&&ock	kXXX@XXXX.com	1900-01-01	57709
3	H&&&&&low	hXXX@XXXX.com	1900-01-01	44627

Note that you might get different values for the salary because this column uses the random masking function. Now you can grant the UNMASK permission to the SalesUser1 user, and try to read the data again. This time, the result is unmasked:

```
GRANT UNMASK TO SalesUser1;
EXECUTE (N'SELECT * FROM dbo.Employees') AS USER = N'SalesUser1';
```

Dynamic data masking limitations

You might have already noticed the first DDM limitation. The UNMASK permission currently works at the database level only. You also cannot mask columns encrypted with the AE feature. FILESTREAM and COLUMN_SET (sparse) columns don't support masking either. A masked column cannot be used in a full-text index. You cannot define a mask on a computed column. If a user who does not have permission to unmask the columns creates a copy of the data with the SELECT INTO statements, then the data in the destination is converted to masked values and the original data is lost. For example, the following code gives the CREATE TABLE and ALTER SCHEMA permissions to both test users, while only the first user has the UNMASK permission. Both users execute the SELECT INTO statement:

```
GRANT CREATE TABLE TO SalesUser1, SalesUser2;
GRANT ALTER ON SCHEMA::dbo TO SalesUser1, SalesUser2;
EXECUTE (N'SELECT * INTO dbo.SU1 FROM dbo.Employees') AS USER =
N'SalesUser1';
EXECUTE (N'SELECT * INTO dbo.SU2 FROM dbo.Employees') AS USER =
N'SalesUser2';
GO
```

You can query the two new tables as the dbo user. The values in the table created by the SalesUser2 user are converted into masked values.

Carefully crafted queries can also bypass DDM. Some numeric system functions automatically unmask data in order to perform the calculation. The following query is executed in the context of the SalesUser2 user, who does not have permission to unmask data:

```
EXECUTE AS USER = 'SalesUser2';
SELECT Salary AS SalaryMaskedRandom,
 EXP(LOG(Salary)) AS SalaryExpLog,
 SQRT(SQUARE(salary)) AS SalarySqrtSquare
FROM dbo.Employees
WHERE PersonID = 2;
REVERT;
```

If you execute the preceding code in SQL Server 2016, you get the following results:

```
SalaryMaskedRandom   SalaryExpLog    SalarySqrtSquare
------------------   ------------    ----------------
70618                45822.96875     45823
```

This problem is mitigated in SQL Server 2017. If you execute the same code in SQL Server 2017, you get the following results:

```
SalaryMaskedRandom   SalaryExpLog    SalarySqrtSquare
------------------   ------------    ----------------
70618                0               0
```

Filtering in a query also works on the unmasked value. This issue is present in both, SQL Server 2016 and 2017. For example, the `SalesUser2` user can check which employees have a salary greater than `50000` with the following query:

```
EXECUTE AS USER = 'SalesUser2';
SELECT *
FROM dbo.Employees
WHERE Salary > 50000;
REVERT;
```

Here are the abbreviated results:

```
PersonID  FullName    EmailAddress    HireDate     Salary
--------  ----------  --------------  -----------  ------
4         I&&&&&upp   iXXX@XXXX.com   1900-01-01   8347
8         A&&&&&sse   aXXX@XXXX.com   1900-01-01   60993
```

Please note that you might get different results because the `Salary` column is masked with the random masking function. Finally, you can clean up your SQL Server instance:

```
USE master;
DROP DATABASE DDMDemo;
GO
```

Summary

In this chapter, you have learned about SQL Server security. You have learned about principals and securables. When designing a database, you should carefully implement schemas. You give object and statement permissions to database users. To enhance data protection, SQL Server implements encryption in many different ways. The new SQL Server 2016 and 2017 Always Encrypted feature might be extremely useful because you don't need to change existing applications (except for the connection string) to use it. You can filter the rows the users can see and modify these with the help of programmable objects or SQL Server 2016 predicate-based Row-Level Security. Finally, in SQL Server 2016 and 2017, you can also mask data with dynamic data masking for non-privileged users.

In the next chapter, you will learn how to use Query Store to keep your execution plans optimal.

9
Query Store

Query Store is a new performance troubleshooting tool, fully integrated into the database engine. In my opinion, it is one of the best database engine features since 2005 and the introduction of `OPTION(RECOMPILE)`. Query Store helps you to troubleshoot query performance by collecting information about queries, resource utilization, execution plans, and the other execution parameters. This information is stored in a database and therefore it survives server crashes, restarts, and failovers.

Query Store not only helps you to identify issues with query executions, but also lets you easily and quickly fix or work-around problems caused by poorly chosen execution plans. This fix can even be done automatically.

In this chapter, you will learn about the following points:

- Why Query Store has been introduced
- What Query Store is intended for and what it is not
- Query Store architecture
- How Query Store can help you to quickly identify and solve performance issues
- Automatic tuning in SQL Server 2017

Why Query Store?

I am sure that everyone who reads this book has to deal with a situation where a stored procedure or query suddenly started to perform poorly. In other words, performance was good in the past and it was working regularly up to some point in time, but the same procedure or query does not perform well anymore: either you got a timeout when you executed it, or the execution time has been significantly increased. Usually you need to fix this as soon as possible, especially when it happens in an important application module and/or during non-working or peak hours.

How do you proceed with this? What is the first step you take when you start such troubleshooting? By gathering information such as system information, query stats and plans, execution parameters, and so on, right? When a query or stored procedure is slow, you want to see its execution plan. Therefore, the first thing is to check the execution plan in the server cache. You can use this query to return the execution plan for a given stored procedure:

```
SELECT c.usecounts, c.cacheobjtype, c.objtype, q.text AS query_text,
p.query_plan
FROM
sys.dm_exec_cached_plans c
CROSS APPLY sys.dm_exec_sql_text(c.plan_handle) q
CROSS APPLY sys.dm_exec_query_plan(c.plan_handle) p
WHERE
c.objtype = 'Proc' AND q.text LIKE '%<SlowProcedureName>%';
```

By observing the execution plan of a poorly performed query you can find the reason why the execution is slow: you can see Scan, Hash Join, and Sort operators, and at least make some assumptions about the slow execution. You can also find out when the plan was generated. In addition to the plan info, you can also use execution statistics. The following query returns info about the execution time and logical reads for the execution of a given stored procedure:

```
SELECT p.name, s.execution_count,
ISNULL(s.execution_count*60/(DATEDIFF(second, s.cached_time, GETDATE())),
0) AS calls_per_minute,
(s.total_elapsed_time/(1000*s.execution_count)) AS avg_elapsed_time_ms,
s.total_logical_reads/s.execution_count AS avg_logical_reads,
s.last_execution_time,
s.last_elapsed_time/1000 AS last_elapsed_time_ms,
s.last_logical_reads
FROM sys.procedures p
INNER JOIN sys.dm_exec_procedure_stats AS s ON p.object_id = s.object_id
AND s.database_id = DB_ID()
WHERE p.name LIKE '%<SlowProcedureName>%';
```

By using the results of this query, you can compare current and average execution parameters, and also discover if only occasional executions are slow or if each execution under the current circumstances runs longer. These two queries can help you to find out how the execution looks now and to see how it differs from the execution in the past (from the response time and used resources point of view). You can also include a third query that returns current waiting tasks on the server within your database, to see if bad performance is caused by blocking issues.

However, there are some limitations to the set of information in the server cache. First, dynamic management views reflect particular or aggregated information from the last server restart only. When a server crashes, is restarted, or fails over, all cache information disappears. This could be a huge limitation in the query troubleshooting process. In the server cache, only the actual execution plan for a query is available and even this is not guaranteed. Sometimes, the plan is not in the cache due to memory pressure or infrequent usage. For queries with OPTION (RECOMPILE), for instance, only the latest version of the execution plan is in the cache, although the plan is generated by every execution. Since only the latest execution plan for a query is available, you don't know if and how the execution plan changed over time.

Every upgrade to a new SQL Server version, and every failover, patch, and installation of a new version of an application or service could lead to new execution plans. In most cases, these plans look the same after the aforementioned action; sometimes they are even better (new versions and installing cumulative updates and service packs usually improve overall performance), but in some cases newly-generated plans could be significantly slower than before the change. However, in the server cache, the old, good plan cannot be found.

What do we do in such cases? For the most critical stored procedures, I collect execution plans and statistics from dynamic management views mentioned at the beginning of this chapter and save them regularly into a database table by using a SQL job. The job runs every five minutes; data is persistent, belongs to the database, and is not lost when the server is restarted. On the top of the tables, I create a few PowerPivot reports and notifications. I check them immediately after a failover, patch, or the installation of a new application version and use them to confirm that the action was successful or to quickly identify performance degradations. A typical report is shown in the following screenshot:

Report using previously collected execution data

It clearly shows one regressed stored procedure after an application release.

This approach works very well and I had a good experience with it. It helped me many times not only to identify performance issues, but also to confirm that an update action was successful and learn more about my workload and how it behaves over time. However, I had to write, maintain, and deploy this custom solution to every database, and ensure that the aforementioned SQL job will run on all servers for all databases, regardless of failover or restart. It also requires consideration for, and even negotiations with, database administrators to ensure that server performance will not be significantly affected by the SQL job that collects my statistics. I would prefer an out-of-box solution for this, but such a solution did not exist, until **SQL Server 2016**.

What is Query Store?

Query Store is the answer to the challenges described previously. It was introduced in SQL Server 2016 and extended in SQL Server 2017. It collects the most relevant information about executed queries: query text, parameters, query optimization and compilation details, execution plans, execution statistics (execution time, CPU and memory usage, I/O execution details), and wait statistics; Query Store stores them in a database so that they are available after server restarts, failovers, or crashes.

You can use Query Store not only to identify performance issues, but also to fix some of them. Query Store offers a solution for issues caused by changed execution plans. By using Query Store, you can easily enforce an old plan; it is not required to rewrite the query or to write any code. You don't affect the business logic, therefore there is no need for testing; there is neither code deployment nor an application restart. By taking this approach, you can quickly implement a solution, or at least a work-around, and save time and money.

 In addition to this, stored information can be used (exposed through catalog views) outside of SQL Server, usually in reports and notifications, to let you get a better or more complete picture about your workload and help you to be more familiar with it.

Query Store also captures some information that is not available in the server cache, such as unfinished queries or queries with broken execution, either using the caller or by an exception. You can easily find out how many executions of a single query were successful and how many executions ended with exceptions. This was not possible prior to SQL Server 2016 by querying the server cache.

Query Store architecture

Query Store is integrated with the query processor in the database engine. A simplified Query Store architecture in SQL Server 2017 is shown in the following figure:

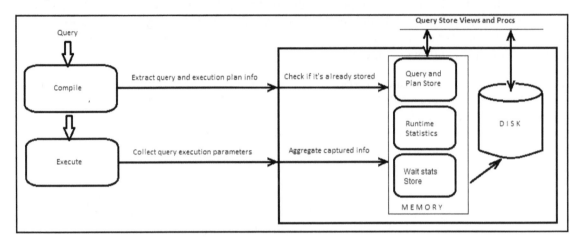

Query Store architecture

Query Store actually has three stores:

- **Query and Plan Store**: This stores information about executed queries and execution plans used for their execution
- **Runtime Statistics store**: This store holds aggregated execution parameters (execution time, logical reads, and so on) for executed queries within a specified time
- **Wait Stats Store**: This store persists wait statistics information

All three stores have instances in memory and persisted representation through disk tables. Due to performance reasons, captured info is not immediately written to disk; rather it is written asynchronously. Query Store physically stores this info into the database primary file group.

When a query is submitted to the database engine and Query Store is enabled for the database, during query compilation, Query Store captures information about the query and execution plan. This is then sent into the **Query and Plan Store**, if the information is not already there. Information about a single query is stored only once in Query Store; the same for execution plans. For every execution plan we have only one row (up to 200 different execution plans are supported by default).

When the query is executed, Query Store captures the most relevant execution parameters (duration, logical reads, CPU time, used memory, and so on), uses them in aggregated calculations, and sends them into the **Runtime Statistics** store only at configured time intervals. Therefore, Query Store does not store info about every single execution. If the time interval is 10 minutes, for instance, it stores runtime stats for a single execution plan every 10 minutes.

Captured data is persistently stored in internal database tables. It is not directly available for reading and manipulation. Instead of that, Query Store functionalities are exposed through Query Store catalog views and stored procedures. There are eight Query Store catalog views:

- `sys.database_query_store_options`
- `sys.query_context_settings`
- `sys.query_store_plan`
- `sys.query_store_query`
- `sys.query_store_query_text`
- `sys.query_store_runtime_stats`
- `sys.query_store_runtime_stats_interval`
- `sys.query_store_wait_stats`

The `sys.database_query_store_options` system catalog view holds information about Query Store configuration such as actual state, current storage size, maximal storage size, maximum number of plans per query, and so on. You can use this view to check the status and available space and create appropriate alerts when Query Store has switched to *Read-Only* mode or there isn't enough free space.

The `sys.database_query_store_query` view contains information about queries and associated overall aggregated runtime execution statistics. There is exactly one row for each query in the system. Queries within a stored procedure, function, or trigger have the same `object_id` property. There are 30 columns in this view: they cover details about parameterization, the aforementioned `object_id`, statistics about duration, CPU and memory usage during compilation, binding, and optimization. There are also two columns that are used for connection to other catalog views: `query_text_id` and `context_settings_id`. This view does not contain the text of the query. To get the query text, you need to join it with the `sys.query_store_query_text` catalog view.

The `sys.database_query_store_query_text` view contains query text (including whitespaces and comments) and SQL handle and a few flags about encryption or restricted words.

The `sys.query_context_settings` view contains information about the semantics affecting context settings associated with a query. It contains information about date settings, language, and *SET* options (`ARITHABORT`, `ANSI_NULLS`, `QUOTED_IDENTIFIER`).

The `sys.query_store_plan` view stores information about the execution plans for captured queries. It contains an XML representation of the execution plan, flags related to it, and information about the compilation and execution time.

To get execution statistics for execution plans captured by Query Store, you need to query the `sys.query_store_runtime_stats` catalog view. It has exactly one row for a combination of the `plan_id`, `execution_type` and `runtime_stats_interval_id` attributes. Query Store collects, calculates, and aggregates execution parameters for each execution plan and store them for all successfully executed queries in a single row at the specified interval. If there were aborted executions or executions that ended with an exception, the collected information for them is stored in separated rows. It stores dozens of aggregated statistical values (min, max, avg, stdev, count) for execution parameters such as duration, CPU time, logical and physical IO, memory usage, degree of parallelism, and different time stamp information. This is a very detailed catalog view; it has 68 columns!

The `sys.query_store_runtime_stats_interval` view contains information about the start and end time of each interval over which runtime execution statistics information for a query has been collected.

The `sys.query_store_wait_stats` catalog view was added in SQL Server 2017 and stores wait information about queries captured in Query Store. Like the `query_store_runtime_stats` view, it contains exactly one row per `plan_id`, `runtime_stats_interval_id`, `execution_type`, and `wait_category` attribute combination. To simplify troubleshooting and reduce stored information, wait types are grouped in 24 wait categories.

 Detailed info about *Query Store Catalog Views* can be found in SQL Server Books Online at `https://msdn.microsoft.com/en-us/library/dn818149.aspx`.

You can also interact, and perform some actions, with Query Store by using six Query Store stored procedures:

- `sp_query_store_flush_db`
- `sp_query_store_force_plan`
- `sp_query_store_remove_plan`
- `sp_query_store_remove_query`
- `sp_query_store_reset_exec_stats`
- `sp_query_store_unforce_plan`

Of course, SQL Server Books Online describes Query Store stored procedures in detail at `https://msdn.microsoft.com/en-us/library/dn818153.aspx`.

Enabling and configuring Query Store

As with all new features, Query Store is not active for a database by default. You can enable and configure it in **SQL Server Management Studio** (**SSMS**) by using the database properties (**Query Store** page) or by using Transact-SQL. To enable Query Store, your account must be the `db_owner` of the database or a member of the sysadmin fixed server role.

Enabling Query Store with SSMS

To enable Query Store for a database, you need to select it and click on **Properties**. You can find a new **Query Store** property page at the bottom of the list. As mentioned at the beginning of the section, it is disabled by default, which is indicated by the values **Off** for both **Operation Mode (Actual)** and **Operation Mode (Requested)**. To enable it, you need to change the value for the parameter **Operation Mode (Requested)** to **Read Write**, as shown in the following screenshot:

Enabling Query Store in SQL Server Management Studio

Enabling Query Store with Transact-SQL

The same action can be performed by using **Transact-SQL**. Use the following statement to enable Query Store in the `WideWorldImporters` database:

```
ALTER DATABASE WideWorldImporters SET QUERY_STORE = ON;
```

Configuring Query Store

As shown in the previous section, to enable Query Store you need to set only one parameter or click once. When you do this, you have enabled it with default values for all of its parameters. There is a collection of Query Store options that can be configured. Again, you can set them through SSMS or Transact-SQL. However, some of them have different names and even metrics in both tools. Here is a list of configurable Query Store parameters:

- **Operation Mode** defines the operation mode of the Query Store. Only two modes are supported: `READ_WRITE` and `READ_ONLY`. The default value is `READ_WRITE`, which means that Query Store collects query plans and runtime statistics and writes them to the disk. `READ_ONLY` mode makes sense only when the collected info in the Query Store exceeds the maximum allocated space for it. In this case, the mode is set to `READ_ONLY` automatically. The name of the parameter in the `ALTER DATABASE` Transact-SQL statement is `OPERATION_MODE`.

- **Max Size (MB)** determines the space in megabytes allocated to the Query Store. The parameter data type is `bigint`; the default value is `100`. The name of the parameter in the `ALTER DATABASE` Transact-SQL statement is `STORAGE_SIZE_MB`.

- **Statistics Collection Interval** defines a fixed time window at which runtime execution statistics data is aggregated into the Query Store. The parameter data type is `bigint`; the default value is `60`.The name of the parameter in the `ALTER DATABASE` Transact-SQL statement is `INTERVAL_LENGTH_MINUTES`.

- **Data Flush Interval (Minutes)** determines the frequency at which data written to the Query Store is persisted to disk. The parameter data type is `bigint`; the default value is `15`. The minimum value is 1 minute. If you want to use it in the `ALTER DATABASE` Transact-SQL statement its name is `DATA_FLUSH_INTERVAL_SECONDS`. As you can see, in Transact-SQL you need to use seconds, and in SSMS minutes as the parameter metric. It seems that consistency is lost somewhere between these two configuration modes.

- **Query Store Capture Mode** defines the scope of queries that will be captured. The parameter data type is `nvarchar`, and it has the following values: `AUTO` (only relevant queries based on execution count and resource consumption are captured), `ALL` (all queries are captured), and `NONE` (new queries are not captured, only info about already captured queries). The default value is `ALL`. The name of the parameter in the `ALTER DATABASE` Transact-SQL statement is `QUERY_CAPTURE_MODE`.

- **Stale Query Threshold (Days)** controls the retention period of persisted runtime statistics and inactive queries. The parameter data type is `bigint`; the default value is `30` days. When you use Transact-SQL you need to know that this parameter is a part of another parameter called `CLEANUP_POLICY`. The following Transact-SQL code configures the Stale Query Threshold parameter for Query Store in the `WideWorldImporters` database to `60` days:

```
ALTER DATABASE WideWorldImporters
SET QUERY_STORE (CLEANUP_POLICY = (STALE_QUERY_THRESHOLD_DAYS =
60));
```

- **Size Based Cleanup Mode** controls whether cleanup will be automatically activated when the total amount of data gets close to the maximum size. The parameter data type is `nvarchar`, and it has the following values: `AUTO` (size-based cleanup will be automatically activated when its size on the disk reaches 90% of `max_storage_size_mb`)). Size-based cleanup removes the least expensive and oldest queries first. It stops at approximately 80% of `max_storage_size_mb`, `ALL` (all queries are captured) and `OFF` (size based cleanup won't be automatically activated). The default value is `OFF`. The name of the parameter in the `ALTER DATABASE` Transact-SQL statement is `SIZE_BASED_CLEANUP_MODE`.

- `MAX_PLANS_PER_QUERY` determines the maximum number of plans maintained for a single query. The parameter data type is `int`; the default value is `200`. This parameter is inconsistently implemented, too. It is not even shown on the Query Store property page and can be set only using Transact-SQL.

Query Store default configuration

Enabling Query Store with default values is equivalent to this Transact-SQL statement:

```
ALTER DATABASE WideWorldImporters
SET QUERY_STORE = ON
  (
```

```
    OPERATION_MODE = READ_WRITE,
    MAX_STORAGE_SIZE_MB = 100,
    DATA_FLUSH_INTERVAL_SECONDS = 900,
    INTERVAL_LENGTH_MINUTES = 60,
    CLEANUP_POLICY = (STALE_QUERY_THRESHOLD_DAYS = 367),
    QUERY_CAPTURE_MODE = ALL,
    SIZE_BASED_CLEANUP_MODE = OFF,
    MAX_PLANS_PER_QUERY = 200
);
```

The default configuration is good for small databases or when you want to enable the feature and learn about it with a real query workload. However, for large databases and volatile database workloads you might need to change values for some Query Store options.

Query Store recommended configuration

What are the most important settings, and are default values a good starting point for using Query Store in your database? The most important values are Max Size, Size Based Cleanup Mode, Statistics Collection Interval, and Query Capture Mode, which are explained as follows:

- Max Size: When the maximum storage size allocated for Query Store is reached, then Query Store switches to Read-Only operation mode and no info is captured anymore: you can only read already captured data. In most of the cases, this is not what you want—you are usually interested in recent data. To leave the most recent data in Query Store the you would need to set Size Based Cleanup Mode to Auto, which instructs a background process to remove the oldest data from the Query Store, when the data size approaches the max size, keeping the most recent data in Query Store, similar to flight recorders in aircraft. However, even for a moderate workload, *100 MB* for Query Store storage is not enough. I've seen moderate databases where Query Store contains queries from the last 24 hours only, therefore, I would suggest you increase this value to *1 GB* at least and set Size Based Cleanup Mode to Auto to ensure that the most recent data is available and to avoid switching to Read-Only operation mode.

- Statistics Collection Interval: You can leave this on its default value (1 hour) if you don't need to track queries over time less granular intervals. If your database workload is volatile and depends on time patterns, you can consider using a smaller value. However, bear in mind that this will increase the amount of runtime statistics data.

- `Query Store Capture Mode`: Should be set to auto to instruct Query Store to capture info about only relevant queries based on execution count and resource consumption. This will exclude some queries and the captured info will not reflect the whole workload, but the most relevant and important information will be there.

Disabling and cleaning Query Store

You might need to remove collected data from Query Store sometimes, for instance, when you use it for demo purposes or when you fixed queries that were a long time in regression and will be shown in Query Store reports in the next period too, because of their significant regression. You can remove captured information by clicking on the **Purge Query Data** button in the Query Store properties page inside SSMS.

In addition to this, you can use the following Transact-SQL command:

```
ALTER DATABASE WideWorldImporters SET QUERY_STORE CLEAR;
```

To disable Query Store, you would need to set the operation mode property to OFF either through SQL Server Management Studio (The **Query Store** page within database properties) or the Transact-SQL command:

```
ALTER DATABASE WideWorldImporters SET QUERY_STORE = OFF;
```

Query Store in action

In this section, you will see how Query Store collects information about queries and query plans and how it can identify and fix regressed queries. We will demonstrate how Query Store supports and facilitates an upgrade to SQL Server 2017.

In this exercise, you will use the `WideWorldImporters` sample database. To simulate having created that database with SQL Server 2012, set the compatibility level to `110`:

```
ALTER DATABASE WideWorldImporters SET COMPATIBILITY_LEVEL = 110;
```

Now, you will enable and configure Query Store for the database. It will accompany you in your migration adventures. The following statement enables and configures Query Store for the sample database:

```
ALTER DATABASE WideWorldImporters
SET QUERY_STORE = ON
```

```
(
  OPERATION_MODE = READ_WRITE,
  INTERVAL_LENGTH_MINUTES = 1
);
```

You can check the status and configured parameters of your Query Store by using the following view:

```
SELECT * FROM sys.database_query_store_options;
```

The following screenshots show the Query Store configuration, created by the previous command:

desired_state	desired_state_desc	actual_state	actual_state_desc	readonly_reason	current_storage_size_mb	flush_interval_seconds	interval_length_minutes	max_storage_size_mb
2	READ_WRITE	2	READ_WRITE	0	0	900	60	100

Checking Query Store configuration

As you noticed, in this example you have used a minimal value (one minute) for the parameter INTERVAL_LENGTH_MINUTES. This is done for demonstration purposes; you want to see collected data immediately. On the production system, this action can generate a lot of runtime statistics rows and could mean, for instance, that data is available for the last few hours only.

After you have enabled and configured Query Store, it immediately starts to collect information about executed queries.

Capturing the Query info

To simulate a database workload, you will execute one simple query. Ensure that the database is in compatibility mode 110, and that Query Store is empty, in order to track your queries easily:

```
ALTER DATABASE WideWorldImporters SET COMPATIBILITY_LEVEL = 110;
ALTER DATABASE WideWorldImporters SET QUERY_STORE CLEAR;
```

Run this code to execute one statement 100 times, as shown in the following command:

```
SET NOCOUNT ON;
SELECT * FROM Sales.Orders o
INNER JOIN Sales.OrderLines ol ON o.OrderID = ol.OrderID
WHERE SalespersonPersonID IN (0, 897);
GO 100
```

The previous query returns no rows; there are no orders in the `Sales.Orders` table handled by sales persons with given IDs. After executing this single query 100 times, you can check what has been captured by Query Store by using the following query:

```
SELECT * FROM sys.query_store_query;
```

The query repository contains a single row for each compiled query. You can see in the following screenshot one row representing the query you have executed in the previous step.

query_id	query_text_id	context_settings_id	object_id	batch_sql_handle	query_hash	is_internal_query	query_parameterization_type
1	1	2	0	NULL	0x855B1D2AFF9FD4A6	0	0

Checking captured queries in Query Store

You have cleared Query Store before executing the previous query, and since you have executed only a single query, Query Store captured only one query. However, you could still get more rows from this catalog view if you run this code when you try code examples from this chapter, because some system queries such as updated statistics could also run at this time. Use the following query to return `query_text`, besides the `query_id` for all captured queries in Query Store, so that you can identify your query:

```
SELECT q.query_id, qt.query_sql_text FROM sys.query_store_query q
INNER JOIN sys.query_store_query_text AS qt ON q.query_text_id =
qt.query_text_id;
```

The preceding query produces the following output:

```
query_id         query_sql_text
--------         -----------------------------------------------------
1                SELECT id, custid, details, status FROM dbo.Orders
                 WHERE status IN (0, 2)
2                SELECT * FROM sys.query_store_query
```

You can find the text of your initial query and the `query_id` associated to it (1 in our case).

As you can see, the `query_id` of your initial query has a value of 1, and you will use it for further queries. If you get some other value when you run these examples, use it later instead of 1. In this section, the initial query will be tracked by using `query_id =1`.

The `sys.query_store_query` catalog view contains information about query hashes, query compilation details, binding and optimizing, and also parameterization. A full list and descriptions of all attributes of the catalog view can be found in Books Online at `https://msdn.microsoft.com/en-us/library/dn818156.aspx`.

The `sys.query_store_query_text` catalog view contains query text and statement SQL handles for all queries captured in Query Store. It has only five attributes and is linked to the `sys.query_store_query` catalog view via the attribute `query_id`. A full list and descriptions of all attributes of the catalog view can be found in Books Online at `https://msdn.microsoft.com/en-us/library/dn818159.aspx`.

Capturing plan info

For each query, you can have at least one execution plan. Therefore, in the plan repository, at least one entry exists for each query from the query repository. The following query returns rows from the plan repository:

```
SELECT * FROM sys.query_store_plan;
```

You can see four plans for four executed queries in the `WideWorldImporters` database. The first query is your initial query; the rest are queries against catalog views as shown in the following screenshot. As mentioned earlier in this section, you can see more entries if you execute the code examples from this chapter.

plan_id	query_id	plan_group_id	engine_version	compatibility_level	query_plan_hash	query_plan
1	1	0	14.0.1000.169	110	0xE743243FB9189904	<ShowPlanXML xmlns="http
2	4	0	14.0.1000.169	110	0x3C42727B6F21D1CA	<ShowPlanXML xmlns="http
3	3	0	14.0.1000.169	110	0xE2E1199F3FE566C6	<ShowPlanXML xmlns="http
4	2	0	14.0.1000.169	110	0x6FA179640875F159	<ShowPlanXML xmlns="http

Check captured query plans in Query Store

The `sys.query_store_plan` catalog view contains information about query plan generation, including the plan in XML format. A full list and descriptions of all attributes of the catalog view can be found in Books Online at `https://msdn.microsoft.com/en-us/library/dn818155.aspx`.

Retuning query text beside IDs is always a good idea. Run the following code to show query text info, too:

```
SELECT qs.query_id, q.query_sql_text, CAST(p.query_plan AS XML) AS qplan
FROM sys.query_store_query AS qs
```

```
INNER JOIN sys.query_store_plan AS p ON p.query_id = qs.query_id
INNER JOIN sys.query_store_query_text AS q ON qs.query_text_id =
q.query_text_id
ORDER BY qs.query_id;
```

The output is more user-friendly as the following screenshot clearly shows:

query_id	query_sql_text	qplan
1	SELECT * FROM Sales.Orders o INNER JOIN Sales.OrderLines ol ON o.OrderID = ol.OrderID WHERE SalespersonPersonID IN (0, 897)	<ShowPlanXML
2	SELECT * FROM sys.query_store_query	<ShowPlanXML
3	SELECT q.query_id, qt.query_sql_text FROM sys.query_store_query q INNER JOIN sys.query_store_query_text AS qt ON q.query_tex...	<ShowPlanXML
4	SELECT * FROM sys.query_store_plan	<ShowPlanXML

Checking captured queries and query plans in Query Store

As you can see, queries against catalog views are also there, but you are interested in user queries only. For the initial query, you can see that all its executions were done with the same execution plan.

Here, you can already see the first great thing about Query Store. You can identify all queries that are executed with more than one execution plan. Use the following query to identify `query_id` for queries that have at least two different plans:

```
SELECT query_id, COUNT(*) AS cnt
FROM sys.query_store_plan p
GROUP BY query_id
HAVING COUNT(*) > 1 ORDER BY cnt DESC;
```

The query returns no rows in this case. You have simply executed only one query, but this is very useful information: you can instantly identify unstable queries in your system.

Collecting runtime statistics

In the previous two subsections, you saw two kinds of information: query details and execution plan. Now it is time for execution statistics parameters. You will query a new catalog view:

```
SELECT * FROM sys.query_store_runtime_stats;
```

The output is shown in the following screenshot:

runtime_stats_id	plan_id	runtime_stats_interval_id	execution_type	execution_type_desc	count_executions	avg_duration	last_duration	min_duration	max_
1	1	1	0	Regular	98	79,2755102040816	66	65	221
2	2	8	0	Regular	1	4450	4450	4450	4450
3	2	9	0	Regular	1	24473	24473	24473	2447
4	2	10	0	Regular	1	8090	8090	8090	8090
5	2	11	0	Regular	1	4934	4934	4934	4934
6	3	12	0	Regular	1	14081	14081	14081	1408

Check collected runtime statistics in Query Store

Again, the output generated when you execute the previous query can differ from the one shown in the preceding screenshot. The `sys.query_store_runtime_stats` catalog view contains runtime execution statistics information for the query. A full list and descriptions of all attributes of the catalog view can be found in Books Online at `https://msdn.microsoft.com/en-us/library/dn818158.aspx`. Every minute (you have configured Query Store in this way), one entry per query plan will be entered in this store.

Actually, for each execution plan, you can have more than one entry in the runtime statistics store per unit defined with the **Statistics Collection Interval** option. If all queries were successfully executed, one row will be added to the store. However, if some executions with the same plan were aborted by the client or ended with an exception, you can have more rows representing each execution type. Three execution types are supported: Regular, Aborted, and Exception, which means that for each execution plan you can have up to three rows in the runtime statistics store per unit defined with the Statistics Collection Interval option.

Query Store and migration

In previous sections, you saw how Query Store captures and stores data about queries and their execution plans. It is now time to see how Query Store can help you with migration. You will execute the same queries under different compatibility levels; firstly under `110` (which corresponds to SQL Server 2012) and `140`, the compatibility level of SQL Server 2017. This action will simulate what can happen when you migrate a database to SQL Server 2017.

To simulate migration to SQL Server 2017, you will now change the compatibility level of the sample database to `110`:

```
ALTER DATABASE WideWorldImporters SET COMPATIBILITY_LEVEL = 140;
```

Now, execute the same query from the previous section:

```
SET NOCOUNT ON;
SELECT * FROM Sales.Orders o
INNER JOIN Sales.OrderLines ol ON o.OrderID= ol.OrderID
WHERE SalespersonPersonID IN (0, 897);
GO 100
```

This time, the execution will take much longer thane under the old compatibility mode; you will see why later. It is clear that a new plan has been created for the query and it is also clear that the old one was better. After the execution is done, you can check query and plan repositories. Since you already know the `query_id` for the query, you can check the plan repository to confirm that the plan has been changed under the new compatibility mode, with the help of the following code:

```
SELECT * FROM sys.query_store_plan WHERE query_id = 1;
```

The following screenshot shows two entries in the plan repository. You can also see that two plans have been generated with different compatibility levels: `110` and `140` respectively:

plan_id	query_id	plan_group_id	engine_version	compatibility_level	query_plan_hash	query_plan
1	1	0	14.0.1000.169	110	0xE743243FB9189904	<ShowPlanXML xmlns="http://schemas.microsoft.com…
2	1	0	14.0.1000.169	140	0x1D5497927C129D03	<ShowPlanXML xmlns="http://schemas.microsoft.com…

Multiple plans for a single query in Query Store

Setting the compatibility level for the sample database to `140` triggers the generation of new execution plans for queries in this database. Most of them will probably be the same as they were before, but some of them will change. You can expect small or big improvements for most of them, but the upgrade to the latest compatibility mode will introduce significant regression for some queries, as in the sample query in this section. In the next section, you will see how Query Store can help you to solve these issues.

Query Store – identifying regressed queries

To see how Query Store represents regression, you will use a new Query Store node within SSMS. From four integrated reports, you will choose **Tracked Queries** as shown in the following screenshot:

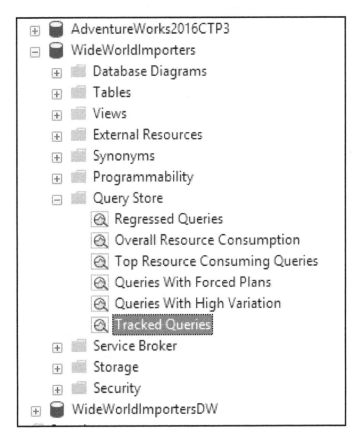

Tracked Queries report in the Query Store section of SQL Server Management Studio

When you click **Tracked Queries**, a new window will be opened in SSMS. In the text field, `Tracking query`, enter 1 and click on the button with the small play icon. As mentioned earlier, assume that the ID of your initial query is 1. You will see a screen similar to the one displayed in the following screenshot:

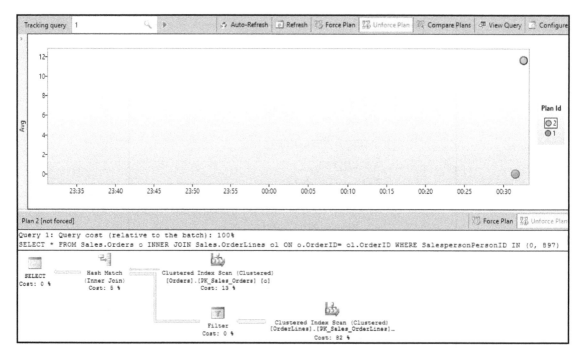

Tracked Queries report showing the new execution plan (compatibility level 140)

You can see two different colors for bullets, representing two execution plans used for the execution of the query with ID set to 1. The vertical axis shows the average execution time for the plans in milliseconds. It is clear that the yellow plan performs better and that the average execution time for the blue plan is significantly increased. In the bottom pane, you can see the execution plan for the selected circle (in this case this is a plan with the id set to 2 which represents the execution plan under compatibility level 140). The plan uses the Clustered Index Scan and Hash Match operators, which is not efficient for a query that returns no rows.

When you click on the green circle on the screen, you get the window shown in the following screenshot:

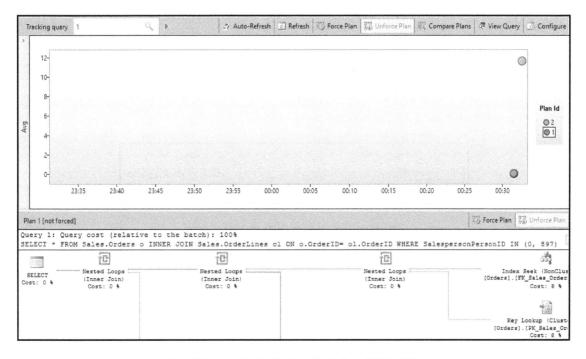

Tracked Queries report showing the old execution plan (compatibility level 110)

You can see that, for this case, the old execution plan uses the appropriate and efficient `Nested Loops` join operator, which explains why the old execution plan is better for this highly selective query (no rows are returned).

 Changes in the cardinality estimator introduced in SQL Server 2014 are responsible for new execution plans in this example. The old CE estimates 10 rows, while the new CE expects 3,129 rows to be returned, which leads to an execution plan with the Scan and Hash Match Join operators. Since the query returns no rows, the estimation done by the old CE is more suitable in this case. The same plan (Clustered Index Scan and Hash Match) would be generated under compatibility level 120.

Of course, you can get this info by querying catalog views, too. The following query returns rows from the collected runtime statistics for two plans in the Query Store:

```
SELECT plan_id, CAST(avg_duration AS INT) AS avg_duration,
avg_logical_io_reads FROM sys.query_store_runtime_stats WHERE plan_id = 1
UNION ALL
SELECT plan_id, CAST(avg_duration AS INT) AS avg_duration,
avg_logical_io_reads FROM sys.query_store_runtime_stats WHERE plan_id = 2;
```

The output is shown in the following screenshot. You can see that all execution parameters are significantly increased for the second plan:

plan_id	avg_duration	avg_logical_io_reads	avg_cpu_time
1	80	4	80,3775510204082
2	52329	692	11690,06

Comparing multiple runtime statistics for two different execution plans

Query Store – fixing regressed queries

Of course, after migration, you need to fix regression as soon as possible. It is obvious in this case that the old plan is better: both the average execution time and the number of logical reads are significantly increased. What can you do with this information? All you want is to have the same (or similar) execution parameters as you had before the migration. How can you get them back? Here are the steps you usually need to perform prior to SQL Server 2016 when an important query suddenly starts to run slow:

- You need to understand why SQL Server decided to change the plan
- You can try to rewrite the query and hope that the optimizer will choose a better plan or the old plan
- You can apply a query hint to enforce a better plan or the old execution plan
- If you have saved the old plan, you can try to enforce it by using plan guides

All these tasks require time and knowledge to implement, and since they include code changes there is a risk that the change will break the application's functionality. Therefore, it introduces testing, which means additional time, resources, and money. You usually don't have a lot of time, and company management is not happy when an action requires more money.

As you can guess, Query Store will save you time and money. It allows you to instruct the optimizer to use the old plan. All you have to do is to choose the plan you want to be applied, click the **Force Plan** button, and then confirm the decision by clicking on **Yes** in the **Confirmation** dialog box as shown in the following screenshot:

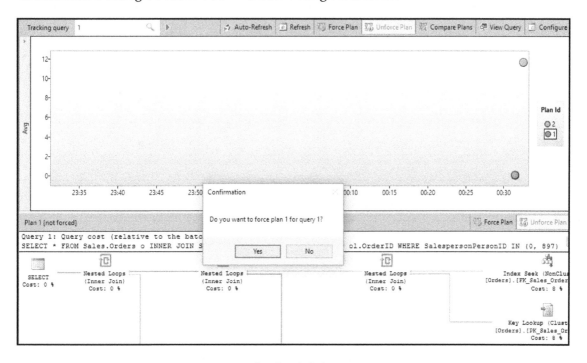

Query Store plan forcing

Now, we will execute the query again, as shown in the following code:

```
SET NOCOUNT ON;
SELECT * FROM Sales.Orders o
INNER JOIN Sales.OrderLines ol ON o.OrderID= ol.OrderID
WHERE o.SalespersonPersonID IN (0, 897);
```

Now, you will see a third color (with the circle representing the third execution plan) as shown in the following screenshot:

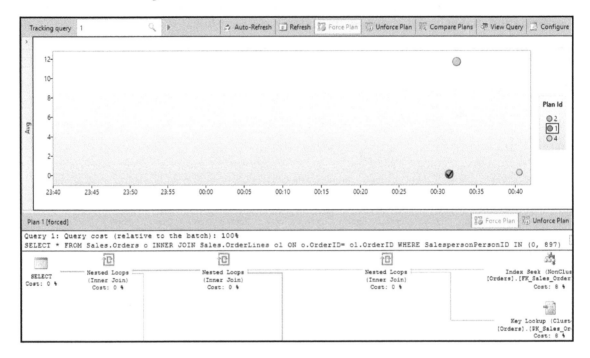

Plan forcing in action

The execution is faster, you get the old plan again and there is no risk of a breaking change. And also, you did not spend much time fixing the issue!

You can also force and unforce a plan by using Query Store stored procedures. The following command unforces the execution plan that you forced in the previous step:

```
EXEC sp_query_store_unforce_plan @query_id = 1, @plan_id = 1;
```

Now we will execute the query again, as shown in the following code:

```
SET NOCOUNT ON;
SELECT * FROM Sales.Orders o
INNER JOIN Sales.OrderLines ol ON o.OrderID= ol.OrderID
WHERE o.SalespersonPersonID IN (0, 897);
```

Now, you will see that the plan is not forced anymore and that the execution is slow again, as shown in the following screenshot:

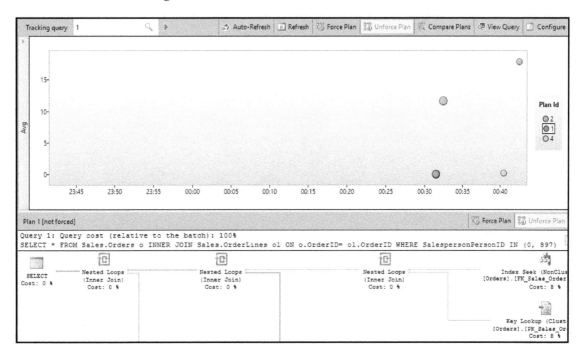

Query Store plan unforcing

Now you can use Transact-SQL to force the old plan again:

```
EXEC sp_query_store_force_plan @query_id = 1, @plan_id = 1;
```

When you re-execute the query, you will see that the plan is forced again and another circle has appeared in the main pane as you can see in the following screenshot:

```
SET NOCOUNT ON;
SELECT * FROM Sales.Orders o
INNER JOIN Sales.OrderLines ol ON o.OrderID= ol.OrderID
WHERE o.SalespersonPersonID IN (0, 897);
```

When you re-execute the query, you will see that the plan is forced again and another circle has appeared to the main pane as you can see in the following screenshot:

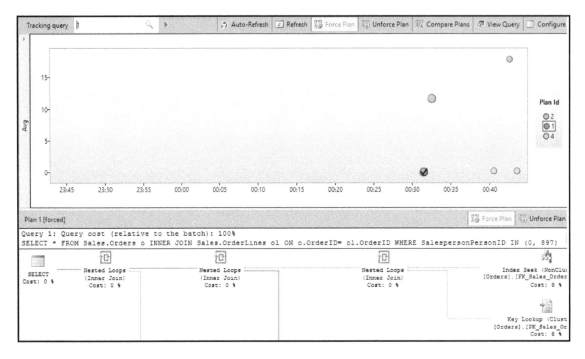

Query Store plan forcing

In this section, you saw that Query Store can help you not only to identify performance regressions, but also to solve them quickly, elegantly, and with almost no effort. However, bear in mind that forcing an old plan is a *forever decision*; the plan will always be applied whenever the query is executed. You have to be absolutely sure that you want this when you force the plan.

 Forcing a plan will instruct SQL Server to use one plan whenever the query is executed regardless of its costs or improvement in the database engine. However, if the execution plan requires database objects that don't exist anymore (for instance, an index used in the plan is dropped), the query execution will not fail, but a new plan will be generated. The forced plan will be saved and set in the "hold on" mode and will be applied again when the missing object is available.

You should also notice that forcing an old, good-looking execution plan in a Query Store report does not guarantee that the execution with it will be better. A typical example would be issues with parameter sniffing, where different parameter combinations require different plans. Forcing an old plan in that case might be good for some parameter combinations only; but for others, it could be even worse than the actual, bad execution plan. Generally, Query Store helps you to solve problems with queries whose execution plans have changed over time but that have stable input parameters. You should not force the old plan for all queries when you see that the old execution parameters look better!

I am using Query Store intensively, and it is an excellent tool and a great help for me during query troubleshooting. I have forced an old execution plan several times in a production system to solve or mitigate a significant performance degradation. In my company, massive workload and peaks happen on a weekend, and if you have an issue on a weekend, you usually want to solve it or find a workaround as quickly as possible. Query Store allows me to force a well-known and good plan and solve the issue temporarily. I review and evaluate the situation later, during regular working time, without pressure and the risk of breaking some applications. Sometimes, I rewrite the code and unforce the plan; sometimes, when I am completely sure that I want exactly the plan that I have forced, I leave it in the production database. When you know what you are doing, you can use all Query Store features. Query Store can save time and money.

Query Store reports in SQL Server Management Studio

In the previous section, you saw that migration to SQL Server 2017 can lead to performance regressions for some database queries. In this example, you had only one query and since the regression was significant, you could immediately detect it; you did not need help from Query Store. However, in a production system, you could have hundreds or thousands of queries, and you will not be able to check them to see if they perform well after migration. To find regressed queries or queries that are consuming the most server resources, you can use Query Store reports.

When Query Store is enabled for a database, in the **Object Explorer** of the SSMS you can find a new node called Query Store for this database. When you expand the node, you find six reports under it:

- Regressed queries
- Overall resource consumption
- Top resource consuming queries
- Queries with forced plans
- Queries with high variation
- Tracked queries

However, when you right-click the node, you can see another report, so there are six Query Store reports.

 SQL Server Management Studio in versions prior to version 17.4 displays only five reports. However, the Regressed Queries report is available when you right-click the node. This is a bug in SQL Server Management Studio version 17.3 and it was fixed in version 17.4.

You have already seen the Tracked Queries report in action; here we will describe the other five reports.

Regressed queries

The `Regressed queries` report page shows queries with regressed performance over time. Query Store analyzes database workload and extracts the 25 most regressed queries according to the chosen metrics. You can choose between the following metrics: *CPU time, Duration, Logical reads, Logical writes, Physical reads, Memory consumption, CLR time, DOP,* and *Row Count*. You can also decide whether you want to see total numbers or maybe average, max, min, or standard deviation of the value chosen in the first step. The following screenshot shows regressed queries in a moderate database in a chart format:

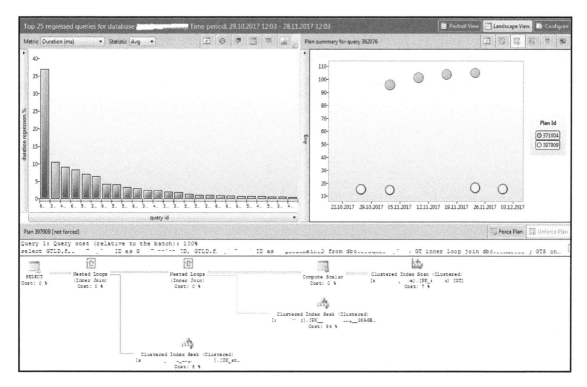

View regressed queries in a chart format

The chart format allows you to focus on the most regressed queries. As you can see, there are three panes on the page. In the first pane, you can see up to 25 of the most regressed queries. The pane on the right side shows execution plans over time for the query chosen in the left pane. Finally, the bottom pane shows a graphical representation of the plan chosen in the second pane.

In the top-right corner in the left pane, you can find an option which allows you to choose between the chart and grid format of regressed queries. The same regressed queries but in a grid format are shown in the following screenshot:

View regressed queries in a grid format

Compared to the other display mode, only the left pane is different. It contains textual information such as query text, the procedure name, and numerical values for many metrics with significantly more information than chart view.

In the top-right corner in the right pane, you can configure time intervals for query executions. In the previous figure, the time interval is set to a custom one (*22.10.–03.12.*).

Top resource – consuming queries

The `Top resource consuming queries` report shows you the most expensive queries (25), based on your chosen metric, analogous to the previous report type. The displayed panes are the same as in the regressed queries report. The only difference between them is extracted queries: top resource consumers can also see queries that did not regress, but just use a lot of server resources. A sample report is shown in the following screenshot:

Top resource-consuming queries report

This Query Store report will not find plan regressions, but can help you to quickly identify the most expensive queries in a database in a given time interval.

Overall Resource Consumption report

The Overall Resource Consumption report can be used to determine the impact of particular queries on all database resources. The report has predefined panes where you can see the impact of queries for overall duration, execution count, CPU time, and logical reads. You can define an additional three parameters (logical writes, memory consumption, and physical reads) and you can also show this info in a grid format. A common report with default windows is shown in the following screenshot:

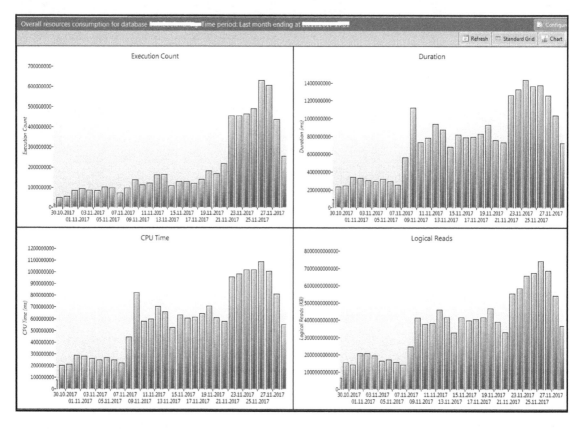

Overall Resource Consumption report

This Query Store report will not find plan regressions, but can help you to quickly identify the most expensive queries in a database in a given time interval.

Queries With Forced Plans

This report is new in SSMS 17 and, as its name suggests, it shows queries that are executed under an execution plan forced in Query Store. The following shows this report for a database that has one query with a forced execution plan:

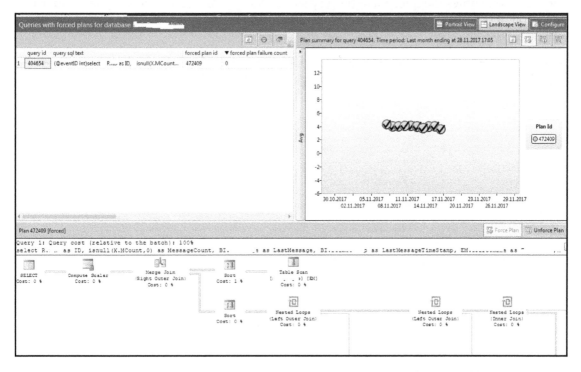

Queries With Forced Plans report

The report contains panes similar to the top resource consuming queries report; in the right pane, you can see the execution statistics, while the bottom pane shows the execution plan.

Queries With High Variation

In SSMS 17, the newly added Queries With High Variation report allows you to easily identify queries with parameterization problems. When a query has parameterization problems, there is a high variation in query execution. Sometimes the query runs well and very fast, sometimes the query will be very slow. Query Store keeps track of the standard deviation of query execution; due to the parameterization problem, the standard deviation will be high:

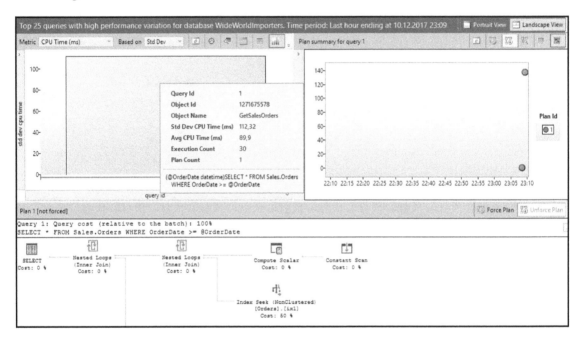

Queries With High Variation report

In productions systems, there are usually hundreds or thousands of stored procedures and parameterized queries. Use this view to identify quickly those with widely variant performance.

Automatic tuning in SQL Server 2017

As mentioned, Query Store was introduced in SQL Server 2016 and it is a great tool for identifying regressed queries, especially after the version upgrade. You can use different reports to search for regressed queries or query the appropriate catalog views. However, in production databases, you could have thousands of queries, and if regressed queries are top-consuming queries, you will need time and patience to identify significantly regressed but less frequently executed queries. It would be nice if Query Store did this and created notifications for you, so that you can easily and quickly see all regressed queries in a database. This feature was not available in SQL Server 2016, but SQL Server 2017 brings it in as part of the new `Automatic Tuning` feature.

 In the SQL Server 2016 production environment, I have created notifications on top of Query Store catalog views, in order to quickly identify queries that recently got new execution plan(s) with an increased execution or CPU time that exceeds the defined threshold. This is not necessary in SQL Server 2017; it monitors regressed queries and writes info about them in internal tables and you can get them by querying a new dynamic management view.

`Automatic tuning` lets SQL Server automatically detect plan choice regression including the plan that should be used instead of the regressed plan. When it detects it, it can apply the last known good plan. It continues to monitor automatically the performance of the forced plan. If the forced plan is not better than the regressed plan, the new plan will be unforced and the database engine will compile a new plan. If the forced plan is better than the regressed one, the forced plan will be retained until a recompile (for example, on the next statistics or schema change). You can use the `Automatic tuning` feature by choosing between two modes:

- **Offline recommendations**: SQL Server detects and stores info about regressed queries that includes instructions on which execution plan to force in order to solve regression problems, but without forcing plans
- **Automatic tuning**: SQL Server detects regression and forces last good plans automatically

In the next sections, you will see both modes in action.

Regressed queries in the sys.dm_db_tuning_recommendations view

The new SQL Server 2017 `sys.dm_db_tuning_recommendations` system dynamic management view returns detailed information about tuning recommendations for queries which execution details are captured by Query Store. To see this feature in action, you will repeat the scenario from the previous section, executing a query in two different compatibility levels, but this time you'll let SQL Server automatically identify the regression and suggest the fix.

Open your SSMS and turn on the `Discard results after execution` option. You need to choose the **Query Options** menu item, click on the **Results node** in the left pane tree view, and check the **Discard results after execution** checkbox. This option will prevent SSMS from writing output in the results pane and speed up the overall execution in this exercise. After you have set this option, run the following code in the `WideWorldImporters` database:

```
USE WideWorldImporters;
GO
ALTER DATABASE WideWorldImporters SET QUERY_STORE CLEAR;
ALTER DATABASE WideWorldImporters SET QUERY_STORE = OFF;
GO
ALTER DATABASE WideWorldImporters
SET QUERY_STORE = ON
(
    OPERATION_MODE = READ_WRITE,
    INTERVAL_LENGTH_MINUTES = 1
);
GO
ALTER DATABASE WideWorldImporters SET COMPATIBILITY_LEVEL = 110;
GO
SET NOCOUNT ON;
SELECT *
FROM Sales.Orders o
INNER JOIN Sales.OrderLines ol ON o.OrderID = ol.OrderID
WHERE o.SalespersonPersonID IN (0,897);
GO 1000
ALTER DATABASE WideWorldImporters SET COMPATIBILITY_LEVEL = 140;
GO
SET NOCOUNT ON;
SELECT *
FROM Sales.Orders o
INNER JOIN Sales.OrderLines ol ON o.OrderID = ol.OrderID
WHERE o.SalespersonPersonID IN (0,897);
```

```
GO 1000
```

The first few statements ensure that Query Store is enabled and empty for the sample database. After that, the code looks the same as at the beginning of the chapter, and the same thing happened. The second execution is slower because the old execution plan for that query is better than the new one. Instead of searching for regression in Query Store reports, this time you will query the new `sys.dm_db_tuning_recommendations` dynamic management view:

```
SELECT * FROM sys.dm_db_tuning_recommendations;
```

The output produced by this query is shown as follows:

name	type	reason	valid_since	last_refresh	state
PR_1	FORCE_LAST_GOOD_PLAN	Average query CPU time changed from 0.03ms to 10...	2017-10-29 13:08:09.7466667	2017-10-29 13:08:09.7466667	{"currentValue":"Active","reason":"AutomaticTuni...

Output produced by querying the sys.dm_db_tuning_recommendations view

Maybe the most interesting detail here is the value in the **reason** column. You can see the sentence **Average query CPU time changed from 0.03 ms to 10.2 ms**, which describes the reason why this entry is shown. Since you know the nature of the queries that you ran, you know that the first time is related to the average CPU time for the query where the compatibility level was 110, while the second refers to the execution under the latest compatibility mode. From the CPU usage point of view, the regression is significant; the second query uses 340 times more CPU time!

The figure does not show the other attributes in detail, but you can check them in SSMS. In addition to the `reason` column, there are two more interesting columns: `state` and `details`. Both of them contain JSON data. Here is the content of the `state` column:

```
{"currentValue":"Active","reason":"AutomaticTuningOptionNotEnabled"}
```

You can see two JSON keys: `currentValue` and `reason`, which say more about the current recommendation. The value `Active` means that the recommendation is active, but not applied. You can find a full list and a description of all keys and values at `https://docs.microsoft.com/en-us/sql/relational-databases/system-dynamic-management-views/sys-dm-db-tuning-recommendations-transact-sql`.

The **details** column is also JSON, but has more data. Here is the content, but formatted with the JSON formatter used in `Chapter 5`, *JSON Support in SQL Server*:

```
{
"planForceDetails":{
   "queryId":1,
   "regressedPlanId":2,
```

```
        "regressedPlanExecutionCount":18,
        "regressedPlanErrorCount":0,
        "regressedPlanCpuTimeAverage":1.019883333333333e+004,
        "regressedPlanCpuTimeStddev":2.017456808018999e+003,
        "recommendedPlanId":1,
        "recommendedPlanExecutionCount":998,
        "recommendedPlanErrorCount":0,
        "recommendedPlanCpuTimeAverage":2.860120240480962e+001,
        "recommendedPlanCpuTimeStddev":2.651439807288578e+001
    },
    "implementationDetails":{
        "method":"TSql",
        "script":"exec sp_query_store_force_plan @query_id = 1, @plan_id = 1"
    }
}
```

Here are more details showing the `query_id` and `plan_id` of the regressed query, average CPU time for both plans, and so on. You can also see the recommended command that can solve the regression by forcing the old plan. Since the data in these two columns is JSON data, to get the most important information from the view you need to parse JSON data. Here is a query that returns the most important details from the `sys.dm_db_tuning_recommendations` view:

```
SELECT
    reason,
    score,
    details.[query_id],
    details.[regressed_plan_id],
    details.[recommended_plan_id],
    JSON_VALUE(details, '$.implementationDetails.script') AS command
FROM sys.dm_db_tuning_recommendations
    CROSS APPLY OPENJSON (details, '$.planForceDetails')
        WITH (
                query_id INT '$.queryId',
                regressed_plan_id INT '$.regressedPlanId',
                recommended_plan_id INT '$.recommendedPlanId'
            ) AS details;
```

This query produces the output shown in the following screenshot:

reason	score	query_id	regressed_plan_id	recommended_plan_id	command
Average query CPU time changed from 0.03ms to 10.2ms	100	1	2	1	exec sp_query_store_force_plan @query_id = 1, @plan_id = 1

Output produced by querying the sys.dm_db_tuning_recommendations view

You can see `query_id`, `reason`, and `command`, which you need to execute to fix the query. Execute the following command to fix the plan:

```
EXEC sp_query_store_force_plan @query_id = 1, @plan_id = 1;
GO
SET NOCOUNT ON;
SELECT *
FROM Sales.Orders o
INNER JOIN Sales.OrderLines ol ON o.OrderID = ol.OrderID
WHERE o.SalespersonPersonID IN (0,897);
```

To confirm that the old plan is enforced for that query, you can check the Queries With Forced Plan report as shown in the following screenshot:

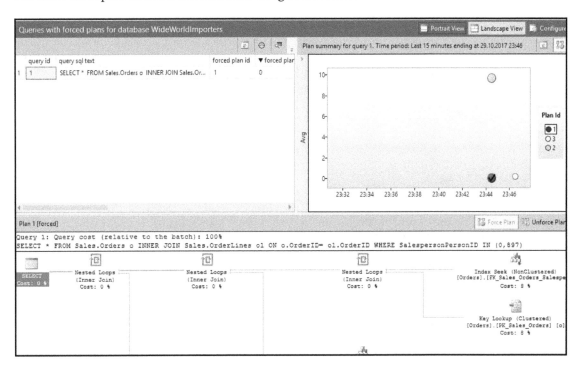

Queries with forced plans report

You can see that the old plan is forced, and also used when you executed the query under the latest compatibility level.

Automatic tuning

As you might guess, automatic tuning is the process where by the last step from the preceding example (in that case performed by you) is automatically done by SQL Server. To see automatic tuning in action, you will again execute the code from the previous subsection, but with an additional database setting. Ensure that the `Discard results after execution` option is turned on in your SSMS and execute the following code:

```
USE WideWorldImporters;
GO
ALTER DATABASE WideWorldImporters SET QUERY_STORE CLEAR;
ALTER DATABASE WideWorldImporters SET QUERY_STORE = OFF;
GO
ALTER DATABASE WideWorldImporters
SET QUERY_STORE = ON
(
OPERATION_MODE = READ_WRITE,
INTERVAL_LENGTH_MINUTES = 1
);
GO
ALTER DATABASE current SET AUTOMATIC_TUNING (FORCE_LAST_GOOD_PLAN = ON);
GO
ALTER DATABASE WideWorldImporters SET COMPATIBILITY_LEVEL = 110;
GO
SET NOCOUNT ON;
SELECT *
FROM Sales.Orders o
INNER JOIN Sales.OrderLines ol ON o.OrderID = ol.OrderID
WHERE o.SalespersonPersonID IN (0,897);
GO 1000
ALTER DATABASE WideWorldImporters SET COMPATIBILITY_LEVEL = 140;
GO
SET NOCOUNT ON;
SELECT *
FROM Sales.Orders o
INNER JOIN Sales.OrderLines ol ON o.OrderID = ol.OrderID
WHERE o.SalespersonPersonID IN (0,897);
GO 1000
```

In the preceding code, you ensure that Query Store is turned on and empty and then execute the same query under the same circumstances as in the previous subsection. The only difference compared to the previous case is the `FORCE_LAST_GOOD_PLAN` option. It is turned on to instruct SQL Server to automatically enforce an old plan, whenever a regression plan is detected.

After executing the code, you can re-check the queries with forced plans report. The following screenshot shows that plan forcing is done automatically:

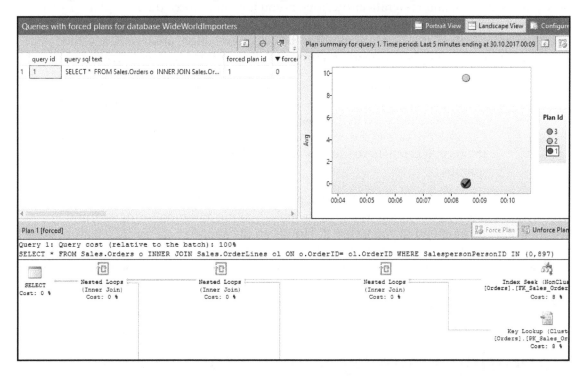

Queries with forced plans report for an automatically tuned query

As you can see, this time you did not need to perform any action: SQL Server silently identified and fixed the problem with the plan regression. That sounds perfect and very promising for SQL Server performance troubleshooting. However, before you turn this feature on, you have to be sure that you want to enforce the old plan whenever SQL Server detects a plan regression. I have to confess that this code example did not always work when I tried it. As you can see in the code, I had to execute the query at least 1,000 times to get desired results. And even this did not work every time. Thus, you should not expect that every regression will be automatically fixed. On the other hand, in the offline mode, each execution was successful and ended with appropriate recommendations.

As a rule of thumb—if the old execution plan was stable (CPU time was relatively constant for different calls and different parameters) and suddenly (or after an upgrade or a patch) a new plan is created, and is significantly slower, you'll want to force the new plan. If you had several plans in the past, or the execution or CPU time varies with the same plan from execution to execution, it is better to monitor the query execution, analyze it, and then eventually force the old plan, instead of letting SQL Server force it automatically.

 Automatic tuning and Query Store in general allow you to fix plan regressions. That means that you can fix a problem for a query that had a good execution plan in the past, but whose new plan does not work well. Query Store cannot fix performance issues for queries that were slow in the past. It can help to identify them, if they are under the most consuming queries.

In my experience, collected during the book preparation and usage in our test and production systems, Query Store is a great troubleshooting and monitoring tool and I would highly recommend to you to use it. However, the `Automatic tuning` feature does not seem to be stable and does not work always as expected. Therefore, for dealing with regressed queries, I would not recommend this option automatically, I would rather refer to the results of the `sys.dm_db_tuning_recommendations` dynamic management view and decide about potential tuning actions manually.

Capturing waits by Query Store in SQL Server 2017

As mentioned earlier, Query Store uses CPU time as the main criterion for execution plan comparison. Execution time often differs from CPU time, sometimes very significantly. In production environments, thousands or even hundreds of thousands of queries are running simultaneously and since most of them refer to the same database objects and SQL Server resources are limited, a query is usually not executed at once; during the execution, there are phases where instructions in the query are executed, and phases where the query waits for resources to be available to proceed with the execution. What a query is waiting for is very important information in performance troubleshooting. Unfortunately, waits were not captured by Query Store in SQL Server 2016, but SQL Server 2017 removes this limitation and increased captured data with this important information.

Since there are more than 900 wait types, in order to reduce Query Store's impact on customer workload and to simplify recommended tuning actions, Query Store groups wait types into wait categories. Different wait types similar by nature are combined in the same category. The following table shows how common wait types are mapped into wait categories:

Wait category	Wait types
CPU	`SOS_SCHEDULER_YIELD`
Memory	`RESOURCE_SEMAPHORE, CMEMTHREAD, CMEMPARTITIONED, EE_PMOLOCK, MEMORY_ALLOCATION_EXT, RESERVED_MEMORY_ALLOCATION_EXT, MEMORY_GRANT_UPDATE`
Network IO	`ASYNC_NETWORK_IO, NET_WAITFOR_PACKET, PROXY_NETWORK_IO, EXTERNAL_SCRIPT_NETWORK_IOF`
Parallelism	`CXPACKET, EXCHANGE`
Lock	`LCK_M_%`
Latch	`LATCH_%`

Mapping between wait types and wait categories

You can find the complete mapping table at: `https://docs.microsoft.com/en-us/sql/relational-databases/system-catalog-views/sys-query-Query Store-wait-stats-transact-sql`.

Catalog view sys.query_store_wait_stats

Captured information about waits is stored in the `sys.query_store_wait_stats` system catalog view. To check the output of this view, you will create two connections and execute two queries simultaneously. Before that, ensure that Query Store is enabled and empty by running these statements from previous sections:

```
USE WideWorldImporters;
GO
ALTER DATABASE WideWorldImporters SET QUERY_STORE CLEAR;
ALTER DATABASE WideWorldImporters SET QUER_STORE = OFF;
GO
ALTER DATABASE WideWorldImporters
SET QUERY_STORE = ON
(
```

```
OPERATION_MODE = READ_WRITE,
INTERVAL_LENGTH_MINUTES = 1
);
GO
```

To see how Query Store captures waits, you need to open two connections to a SQL Server 2017 instance. In the first connection, you need to type these statements:

```
USE WideWorldImporters;
SET NOCOUNT ON;
SELECT *
FROM Sales.Orders o
GO 5
```

In the second connection, type the following code:

```
USE WideWorldImporters;
BEGIN TRAN
UPDATE Sales.Orders SET ContactPersonID = 3003 WHERE OrderID = 1;
--ROLLBACK
```

As you may have guessed, in the second connection you will simulate the LOCK wait type since the transaction is neither committed nor rolled back. Now execute the query from the first connection and, a few seconds later, execute the command in the second connection. At this point, the first query cannot proceed with the execution until you finish the transaction in the second connection. After 20 seconds, for instance, finish the transaction by removing the comment near to the ROLLBACK and executing it. In this way, the commands from the second connection are finished and the query from the first connection continue with the execution. To check what Query Store has collected during these actions, execute the following query:

```
SELECT * FROM sys.query_store_wait_stats;
```

This exercise is performed to explore the output of this view, so let's have a look at the following screenshot:

wait_stats_id	plan_id	runtime_stats_interval_id	wait_category	wait_category_desc	execution_type	execution_type_desc	total_query_wait_time_ms
28	2	1	3	Lock	0	Regular	7648
40	2	1	15	Network IO	0	Regular	1671

Output of the sys.query_store_wait_stats view

You can see two rows for two category waits for the plan for the first query: `Lock` and `Network IO`. They correspond to the `LCK_M_S` and `ASYNC_NETWORK_IO` wait types respectively.

You can see the following, if you repeat the preceding scenario by opening a third connection, where you will execute this query (use the `session_id` of the query in the first connection):

```
SELECT * FROM sys.dm_os_waiting_tasks WHERE session_id = <Your_Session_Id>;
```

During the query execution following the preceding scenario, this query will (most probably) return one row at a time: either a `ASYNC_NETWORK_IO` wait type or `LCK_M_S`, depending on the status of the transaction in the second connection, as shown in the following screenshot:

waiting_task_address	session_id	exec_context_id	wait_duration_ms	wait_type	resource_address	blocking_task_address	blocking_session_id	blocking_exec_context_id	resource_description
0x00000026B8011D848	52	0	1	ASYNC_NETWORK_IO	NULL	NULL	NULL	NULL	NULL

waiting_task_address	session_id	exec_context_id	wait_duration_ms	wait_type	resource_address	blocking_task_address	blocking_session_id	blocking_exec_context_id	resource_description
0x00000026B8011D848	52	0	579	LCK_M_S	0x0000002B6F39F180	NULL	53	NULL	pagelock fileid=3 pageid=1544 dbid=5 subresource...

Output of the sys.dm_os_waiting_tasks dynamic management view

You cannot see both entries at the same time, since this DMV returns only active waits; if a resource is free, previous waits for it are not shown. Query Store waits on the other hand are cumulative and all waits during the query execution are included in the wait category statistics.

> For a full list of columns returned by the `sys.query_store_wait_stats` catalog view and their description, see the following page in SQL Server Books Online: `https://docs.microsoft.com/en-us/sql/relational-databases/system-catalog-views/sys-query-Query Store-wait-stats-transact-sql`.

Capturing wait statistics is a great Query Store improvement in SQL Server 2017 and makes Query Store an excellent tool for fast performance troubleshooting.

Query Store use cases

Query Store is a very useful feature and can help you identify and solve some performance problems, and also learn about your workload and to be more familiar with it.

The main use cases are related to issues caused by changed execution plans. Complex queries can have many potential execution plans and some of them can be performant, while others lead to serious performance problems. The *Query Optimizer* does a great job when it generates execution plans but sometimes it comes up with a suboptimal plan. It is possible that two totally different execution plans have similar costs. When a complex query has a good plan, it can happen that the next plan for the same query performs badly. And the next plan will be generated when the old plan is not in the cache anymore. This happens when SQL Server is upgrading to a new version, when a cumulative update or a Service Pack is installed, when patching is performed, when a failover happens, and also when a new application or service version is deployed. In all these cases, when a new plan performs badly, Query Store can help, not only for identifying, but also finding a solution or a workaround for, the problem.

SQL Server version upgrades and patching

The main use case, and most probably the one that triggered the introduction of this feature, is upgrading to a new SQL Server version. An upgrade is never a trivial action; it brings improvements (that's the reason why you upgrade, right?) but sometimes also regressions. These regressions are not always predictable and it happens often that companies do not perform a full upgrade to the latest SQL Server version, but instead leave the most important or most volatile databases in the old compatibility mode. This means execution plans will use the logic, rules, and algorithms from the previous database version. By taking this approach, you can reduce the risk of performance regression, but you will not be able to use some of the new features because they are available only in the latest compatibility mode. In my experience, after changes in the Cardinality Estimator in SQL Server 2014, more than 50% of companies did not upgrade all large and volatile databases to compatibility mode 120 because of significant regressions. Most queries perform well, but some of them got different, suboptimal execution plan and fixing them on a production system would be too expensive and risky.

Query Store can help you to perform upgrades without many worries about issues with different plans in the new version. It can easily and quickly identify issues with execution plans and offers you an option to force the old plan in cases of regression, without a big impact on the production workload.

In measurements and tests that I have performed, I could not detect a significant impact from Query Store activities on database workload. I would estimate that the Query Store impact is roughly 3–5% of server resources.

A typical scenario for a SQL Server version upgrade is as follows:

- Upgrade SQL Server to the latest version (SQL Server 2017), but leave all user databases in the old compatibility mode
- Enable and configure Query Store
- Let Query Store work and collect information about your representative workload
- Change queries with forced plan compatibility level to the latest one (140)
- Check recommendations in the `sys.dm_db_tuning_recommendations` dynamic management view
- Force old plans for regressed queries

Query Store will let you fix problems by choosing the old plan. However, as mentioned earlier, this might not be a final solution and it is good idea to analyze why regression happened and to try to fine-tune the query. Of course, this could be time-and resource-consuming and it is better to do this later, when you have enough time, than when under pressure, at a time when problems occur on the production system.

Application and service releases, patching, failovers, and cumulative updates

In all these cases, Query Store can help you to identify issues after the actions and to fix problems caused by changed execution plans very quickly, efficiently, and without risking business applications. A typical scenario include:

- Ensuring that Query Store is enabled and configured
- Letting Query Store work and capture information about your representative workload

- Performing the install action; this can be one of the following actions:
  - Server failover
  - Installing a SQL Server Service Pack
  - Installing a SQL Server Cumulative Update
  - Upgrading hardware configuration
  - Operating system and network patching
  - Application and service deployment
  - Letting Query Store collect information about queries and plans
  - Checking recommendations in the `sys.dm_db_tuning_recommendations` dynamic management view or run the *Top Resources Consuming Queries* report

Query Store will let you fix problems by choosing the old plan. It is a good idea to analyze why regression happened, but it is better to do this later, when you have enough time, than when problems occur on the production system.

Identifying ad hoc queries

You can use Query Store to identify ad hoc workloads, which are typically characterized by a relatively large number of different queries executed very rarely, and usually only once. Use the following query to identify all queries that are executed exactly once:

```
SELECT p.query_id
FROM sys.query_store_plan p
INNER JOIN sys.query_store_runtime_stats s ON p.plan_id = s.plan_id
GROUP BY p.query_id
HAVING SUM(s.count_executions) = 1;
```

Identifying unfinished queries

In the *Query Store in action* section, you saw that Query Store does not capture runtime statistics only for successfully executed queries. When query execution is aborted by the caller or ends with an exception, this info is not stored in the server cache, but Query Store collects that info too. This can help you easily identify queries with an incomplete execution process.

To see an example, you first need to clean-up info that was captured in the previous sections of this chapter:

```
ALTER DATABASE WideWorldImporters SET QUERY_STORE CLEAR ALL;
ALTER DATABASE WideWorldImporters SET QUERY_STORE = OFF;
ALTER DATABASE WideWorldImporters
SET QUERY_STORE = ON
    (
      OPERATION_MODE = READ_WRITE
    , DATA_FLUSH_INTERVAL_SECONDS = 2000
    , INTERVAL_LENGTH_MINUTES = 1
    );
```

You should also ensure that the latest compatibility mode is applied:

```
ALTER DATABASE WideWorldImporters SET COMPATIBILITY_LEVEL = 140;
```

Now, you can execute the same query as you did in the *Query Store in action* section:

```
SELECT *
FROM Sales.Orders o
INNER JOIN Sales.OrderLines ol ON o.OrderID = ol.OrderID;
GO 10
```

You should execute the query, then click the **Cancel Executing Query** button in the SSMS, then click again to execute it in order to simulate the execution and query abortion.

In addition to this you should execute the following query, too:

```
SELECT TOP (1) OrderID/ (SELECT COUNT(*)
FROM Sales.Orders o
INNER JOIN Sales.OrderLines ol ON o.OrderID = ol.OrderID
WHERE o.SalespersonPersonID IN (0,897))
FROM Sales.Orders;
```

This query will not be successfully executed; it will raise a `Divide by zero` exception. Now, you can check what Query Store has captured. To do this run the following code:

```
SELECT * FROM sys.query_store_runtime_stats;
```

In the following screenshot, you can see two entries for your initial query (regular executed and aborted) and also an entry for the query with the `Divide by zero` exception:

runtime_stats_id	plan_id	runtime_stats_interval_id	execution_type	execution_type_desc	count_executions	avg_duration
1	1	1	3	Aborted	1	2171616
2	1	1	0	Regular	9	4895207.22222222
3	1	2	0	Regular	1	5002603
4	2	2	4	Exception	8	7754

Identifying unfinished queries by using Query Store

As you can see, by using Query Store you can easy identify started but not executed queries in your database.

Summary

In this chapter, you have learned that Query Store is a great troubleshooting tool and captures all execution-relevant parameters for database queries: query details, execution plans, and runtime statistics and stores them in the same database so that they can survive after server failures. All that is done out-of-the-box, with minimal impact on the database workload.

By using Query Store, you can not only quickly identify performance regressions, but also mitigate them by forcing a well-known and previously used execution plan. Query Store will save you time and money. It also helps you to learn how your database workload changes over time and to identify queries that did not execute successfully.

With the automatic tuning feature, you can get a list of regressed queries with tuning actions recommended by Query Store, which significantly reduces troubleshooting time and even offers you fully automated tuning for queries with a regressed executed plan.

In the next chapter, you will discover the power of columnstore indexes and memory-optimized objects.

10
Columnstore Indexes

Analytical queries that scan huge amounts of data are always problematic in relational databases. Nonclustered balanced tree indexes are efficient for transactional query seeks; however, they rarely help with analytical queries. A great idea occurred nearly 30 years ago: why do we need to store data physically in the same way we work with it logically, row by row? Why don't we store it column by column and transform columns back into rows when we interact with the data? Microsoft played with this idea for a long time and finally implemented it in SQL Server.

Columnar storage was first added to SQL Server in the 2012 version. It included **nonclustered columnstore indexes (NCCI)** only. **Clustered columnstore indexes (CCIs)** were added in the 2014 version. In this chapter, readers can revise columnar storage and then explore huge improvements for columnstore indexes in SQL Server 2016 and 2017—updatable nonclustered columnstore indexes, columnstore indexes on in-memory tables, and many other new features for operational analytics.

In the first section, you will learn about SQL Server support for analytical queries without using columnar storage. The next section of this chapter jumps directly to columnar storage and explains the internals, with the main focus on columnar storage compression. In addition, batch execution mode is introduced.

Then it is time to show you columnar storage in action. The chapter starts with a section that introduces nonclustered columnstore indexes. The demo code shows the compression you can get with this storage and also how to create a filtered nonclustered columnstore index.

Clustered columnstore indexes can have even better compression. You will learn how these clustered and nonclustered columnstore indexes compress data and improve the performance of your queries. You can also combine columnar indexes with regular B-tree indexes. In addition, you will learn how to update data in a clustered columnstore index, especially how to insert new data efficiently. Finally, the chapter introduces method to use columnar indexes, together with regular B-tree indexes, to implement a solution for operational analytics.

This chapter will cover the following points:

- Data compression in SQL Server
- Indexing for analytical queries
- T-SQL support for analytical queries
- Columnar storage basics
- Nonclustered columnstore indexes
- Using clustered columnstore indexes
- Creating regular B-tree indexes for tables with CCI
- Discovering support for primary and foreign keys for tables with CCI
- Discovering additional performance improvements with batch mode
- Columnstore index query performance
- Columnstore for real-time operational analytics
- Data loading for columnstore indexes

Analytical queries in SQL Server

Supporting analytical applications in SQL Server differs quite a lot from supporting transactional applications. The typical schema for reporting queries is the star schema. In a star schema, there is one central table called a **fact table** and multiple surrounding tables called **dimensions**. The fact table is always on the many side of every relationship with every dimension. A database that supports analytical queries and uses the star schema design is called **Data Warehouse** (**DW**). Dealing with data warehousing design in detail is beyond the scope of this book. Nevertheless, there is a lot of literature available. For a quick start, you can read the data warehouse concepts MSDN blog at
`https://blogs.msdn.microsoft.com/syedab/2010/06/01/data-warehouse-concepts/`. The `WideWorldImportersDW` demo database implements multiple star schemas. The following screenshot shows a subset of tables from this database that supports analytical queries for sales:

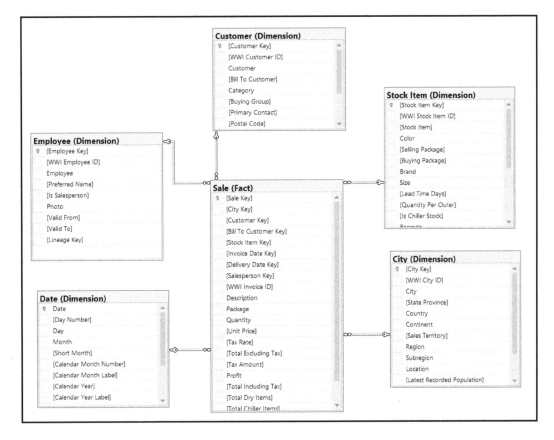

Sales star schema

Typical analytical queries require huge amounts of data, for example, sales data for two years, which is then aggregated. Therefore, index seeks are quite rare. Most of the time, you need to optimize the number of IO reads using different techniques from those you would use in a transactional environment, where you have mostly selective queries that benefit a lot from index seeks. Columnstore indexes are the latest and probably the most important optimization for analytical queries in SQL Server. However, before going into columnar storage, you should be familiar with other techniques and possibilities for optimizing data warehousing scenarios. Everything you will learn about in this and the upcoming section will help you understand the need for, and the implementation of, columnstore indexes. You will learn about the following:

- Join types
- Bitmap filtered hash joins
- B-tree indexes for analytical queries

- Filtered nonclustered indexes
- Table partitioning
- Indexed views
- Row compression
- Page compression
- Appropriate query techniques

Joins and indexes

SQL Server executes a query by a set of physical **operators**. Because these operators iterate through rowsets, they are also called **iterators**. There are different join operators, because when performing joins, SQL Server uses different algorithms. SQL Server supports three basic algorithms: nested loops joins, merge joins, and hash joins.

The nested loops algorithm is a very simple and, in many cases, efficient algorithm. SQL Server uses one table for the outer loop, typically the table with the fewest rows. For each row in this outer input, SQL Server seeks matching rows in the second table, which is the inner table. SQL Server uses the join condition to find the matching rows. The join can be a **non-equijoin**, meaning that the equality operator does not need to be part of the join predicate. If the inner table has no supporting index to perform seeks, then SQL Server scans the inner input for each row of the outer input. This is not an efficient scenario. A nested loop join is efficient when SQL Server can perform an index seek in the inner input.

Merge join is a very efficient join algorithm. However, it has its own limitations. It needs at least one **equijoin** predicate and sorted inputs from both sides. This means that the merge join should be supported by indexes on both tables involved in the join. In addition, if one input is much smaller than another, then the nested loop join could be more efficient than a merge join.

In a one-to-one or one-to-many scenario, a merge join scans both inputs only once. It starts by finding the first rows on both sides. If the end of the input is not reached, the merge join checks the join predicate to determine whether the rows match. If the rows match, they are added to the output. Then the algorithm checks the next rows from the other side and adds them to the output until they match the predicate. If the rows from the inputs do not match, then the algorithm reads the next row from the side with the lower value from the other side. It reads from this side and compares the row to the row from the other side until the value is bigger than the value from the other side. Then it continues reading from the other side, and so on. In a many-to-many scenario, the merge join algorithm uses a worktable to put the rows from one input side aside for reuse when duplicate matching rows are received from the other input.

If none of the input is supported by an index and an equijoin predicate is used, then the hash join algorithm might be the most efficient one. It uses a searching structure named a hash table. This is not a searching structure you can build, like a balanced tree used for indexes. SQL Server builds the hash table internally. It uses a **hash function** to split the rows from the smaller input into **buckets**. This is the build phase. SQL Server uses the smaller input for building the hash table because SQL Server wants to keep the hash table in memory. If it needs to get spilled out to `tempdb` on disk, then the algorithm might become much slower. The hash function creates buckets of approximately equal size.

After the hash table is built, SQL Server applies the hash function on each of the rows from the other input. It checks to see which bucket the row fits. Then it scans through all rows from the bucket. This phase is called the **probe phase**.

A hash join is a kind of compromise between creating a fully balanced tree index and then using a different join algorithm and performing a full scan of one side of the input for each row of the other input. At least in the first phase, a seek of the appropriate bucket is used. You might think that the hash join algorithm is not efficient. It is true that in single-thread mode, it is usually slower than the merge and nested loop join algorithms, which are supported by existing indexes.

However, SQL Server can split rows from the probe input in advance. It can push the filtering of rows that are candidates for a match with a specific hash bucket down to the storage engine. This kind of optimization of a hash join is called a **bitmap filtered hash join**. It is typically used in a data warehousing scenario, in which you can have large inputs for a query that might not be supported by indexes. In addition, SQL Server can parallelize query execution and perform partial joins in multiple threads. In data warehousing scenarios, it is not uncommon to have only a few concurrent users, so SQL Server can execute a query in parallel. Although a regular hash join can be executed in parallel as well, a bitmap filtered hash join is even more efficient because SQL Server can use bitmaps for early elimination of rows not used in the join from the bigger table involved in the join.

In the bitmap filtered hash join, SQL Server first creates a bitmap representation of a set of values from a dimension table to prefilter rows to join from a fact table. A bitmap filter is a bit array of *m* bits. Initially, all bits are set to 0. Then SQL Server defines *k* different hash functions. Each one maps some set elements to one of the *m* positions with a uniform random distribution. The number of hash functions *k* must be smaller than the number of bits in array *m*. SQL Server feeds each of the *k* hash functions to get *k* array positions with values from dimension keys. It set the bits at all these positions to 1. Then SQL Server tests the foreign keys from the fact table. To test whether any element is in the set, SQL Server feeds it to each of the *k* hash functions to get *k* array positions. If any of the bits at these positions are 0, the element is not in the set. If all are 1, then either the element is in the set, or the bits have been set to 1 during the insertion of other elements. The following figure shows the bitmap filtering process:

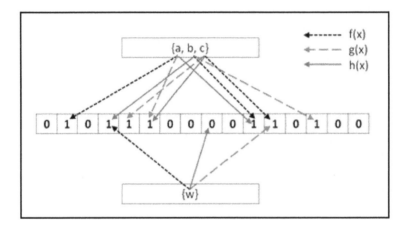

Bitmap filtering

In the preceding figure, the length *m* of the bit array is 16. The number *k* of hash functions is 3. When feeding the hash functions with the values from the set *{a, b, c}*, which represents dimension keys, SQL Server sets bits at positions 2, 4, 5, 6, 11, 12, and 14 to 1 (starting numbering positions at 1). Then SQL Server feeds the same hash functions with the value *w* from the smaller set at the bottom **{w}**, which represents a key from a fact table. The functions set bits at positions 4, 9, and 12 to 1. However, the bit at position 9 is set to 0. Therefore, the value *w* is not in the set *{a, b, c}*.

 If all of the bits for the value *w* were set to 1, this could mean either that the value *w* is in the set *{a, b, v}* or that this is a coincidence.

Bitmap filters return so-called false positives. They never return false negatives. This means that when you declare that a probe value might be in the set, you still need to scan the set and compare it to each value from the set. The more false positive values a bitmap filter returns, the less efficient it is. Note that if the values in the probe side in the fact table are sorted, it will be quite easy to avoid the majority of false positives.

The following query reads the data from the tables introduced earlier in this section and implements star schema-optimized bitmap filtered hash joins:

```
USE WideWorldImportersDW;
SELECT cu.[Customer Key] AS CustomerKey, cu.Customer,
  ci.[City Key] AS CityKey, ci.City,
  ci.[State Province] AS StateProvince, ci.[Sales Territory] AS
SalesTeritory,
  d.Date, d.[Calendar Month Label] AS CalendarMonth,
  d.[Calendar Year] AS CalendarYear,
  s.[Stock Item Key] AS StockItemKey, s.[Stock Item] AS Product, s.Color,
  e.[Employee Key] AS EmployeeKey, e.Employee,
  f.Quantity, f.[Total Excluding Tax] AS TotalAmount, f.Profit
FROM Fact.Sale AS f
  INNER JOIN Dimension.Customer AS cu
    ON f.[Customer Key] = cu.[Customer Key]
  INNER JOIN Dimension.City AS ci
    ON f.[City Key] = ci.[City Key]
  INNER JOIN Dimension.[Stock Item] AS s
    ON f.[Stock Item Key] = s.[Stock Item Key]
  INNER JOIN Dimension.Employee AS e
    ON f.[Salesperson Key] = e.[Employee Key]
  INNER JOIN Dimension.Date AS d
    ON f.[Delivery Date Key] = d.Date;
```

The following figure shows a part of the execution plan. Please note that you can get a different execution plan based on differences in resources available to SQL Server to execute this query. You can see the **Bitmap Create** operator, which is fed with values from the dimension date table. The filtering of the fact table is done in the **Hash Match** operator:

Bitmap Create operator in the execution plan

Benefits of clustered indexes

SQL Server stores a table as a **heap** or as a **balanced tree** (**B-tree**). If you create a clustered index, a table is stored as a B-tree. As a general best practice, you should store every table with a clustered index because storing a table as a B-tree has many advantages, as listed here:

- You can control table fragmentation with the ALTER INDEX command using the REBUILD or REORGANIZE option.
- A clustered index is useful for range queries because the data is logically sorted on the key.
- You can move a table to another filegroup by recreating the clustered index on a different filegroup. You do not have to drop the table as you would to move a heap.
- A clustering key is a part of all nonclustered indexes. If a table is stored as a heap, then the row identifier is stored in nonclustered indexes instead. A short integer-clustering key is shorter than a row identifier, thus making nonclustered indexes more efficient.
- You cannot refer to a row identifier in queries, but clustering keys are often part of queries. This raises the probability for covered queries. Covered queries are queries that read all data from one or more nonclustered indexes without going to the base table. This means that there are fewer reads and less disk IO.

Clustered indexes are particularly efficient when the clustering key is short. Creating a clustering index with a long key makes all nonclustered indexes less efficient. In addition, the clustering key should be unique. If it is not unique, SQL Server makes it unique by adding a 4-byte sequential number called a **uniquifier** to duplicate keys. The uniquifier becomes a part of the clustering key, which is duplicated in every nonclustered index. This makes keys longer and all indexes less efficient. Clustering keys can be useful if they are ever-increasing. With ever-increasing keys, minimally logged bulk inserts are possible even if a table already contains data, as long as the table does not have additional nonclustered indexes.

Data warehouse surrogate keys are often ideal for clustered indexes. Because you are the one who defines them, you can define them as efficiently as possible. Use integers with auto-numbering options. The primary key constraint creates a clustered index by default. In addition, clustered indexes can be very useful for **partial scans**. Remember that analytical queries typically involve a lot of data and, therefore, don't use seeks a lot. However, instead of scanning the whole table, you can find the first value with a seek and then perform a partial scan until you reach the last value needed for the query result. Many times, analytical queries use date filters; therefore, a clustering key over a date column might be ideal for such queries.

You need to decide whether to optimize your tables for data load or for querying. However, with partitioning, you can get both—efficient data load without a clustered key on an ever-increasing column, and more efficient queries with partial scans. In order to show the efficiency of partial scans, let's first create a new table organized as a heap with the following query:

```
SELECT 1 * 1000000 + f.[Sale Key] AS SaleKey,
  cu.[Customer Key] AS CustomerKey, cu.Customer,
  ci.[City Key] AS CityKey, ci.City,
  f.[Delivery Date Key] AS DateKey,
  s.[Stock Item Key] AS StockItemKey, s.[Stock Item] AS Product,
  f.Quantity, f.[Total Excluding Tax] AS TotalAmount, f.Profit
INTO dbo.FactTest
FROM Fact.Sale AS f
  INNER JOIN Dimension.Customer AS cu
    ON f.[Customer Key] = cu.[Customer Key]
  INNER JOIN Dimension.City AS ci
    ON f.[City Key] = ci.[City Key]
  INNER JOIN Dimension.[Stock Item] AS s
    ON f.[Stock Item Key] = s.[Stock Item Key]
  INNER JOIN Dimension.Date AS d
    ON f.[Delivery Date Key] = d.Date;
```

Now you can turn STATISTICS IO on to show the number of logical reads in the following two queries:

```
SET STATISTICS IO ON;
-- All rows
SELECT *
FROM dbo.FactTest;
-- Date range
SELECT *
FROM dbo.FactTest
WHERE DateKey BETWEEN '20130201' AND '20130331';
SET STATISTICS IO OFF;
```

SQL Server used a `Table Scan` operator to execute both queries. For both of them, even though the second one used a filter on the delivery date column, SQL Server performed 5,893 logical IOs.

 Note that your results for the logical IOs might vary slightly for every query in this chapter. However, you should be able to notice which query is more efficient and which is less.

Now let's create a clustered index in the delivery date column:

```
CREATE CLUSTERED INDEX CL_FactTest_DateKey
ON dbo.FactTest(DateKey);
GO
```

If you execute the same two queries, you get around 6,091 reads with the `Clustered Index Scan` operator for the first query, and 253 logical reads for the second query, with the `Clustered Index Seek` operator, which finds the first value needed for the query and performs a partial scan afterwards.

Leveraging table partitioning

Loading even very large fact tables is not a problem if you can perform incremental loads. However, this means that data in the source should never be updated or deleted; data should only be inserted. This is rarely the case with LOB applications. In addition, even if you have the possibility of performing an incremental load, you should have a parameterized **Extract- Transform-Load** (**ETL**) procedure in place so you can reload portions of data loaded already in earlier loads. There is always the possibility that something might go wrong in the source system, which means that you will have to reload historical data. This reloading will require you to delete part of the data from your DW.

Deleting large portions of fact tables might consume too much time unless you perform a minimally logged deletion. A minimally logged deletion operation can be done using the `TRUNCATE TABLE` command; however, in previous versions of SQL Server, this command deleted all the data from a table, and deleting all the data is usually not acceptable. More commonly, you need to delete only portions of the data. With SQL Server 2016 and 2017, truncation is somewhat easier, because you can truncate one or more partitions.

Inserting huge amounts of data can consume too much time as well. You can do a minimally logged insert, but as you already know, minimally logged inserts have some limitations. Among other limitations, a table must either be empty, have no indexes, or use a clustered index only on an ever-increasing (or ever-decreasing) key so that all inserts occur on one end of the index.

You can resolve all of these problems by *partitioning a table*. You can achieve even better query performance using a partitioned table because you can create partitions in different filegroups on different drives, thus parallelizing reads. In addition, the SQL Server query optimizer can do early partition elimination, so SQL Server does not even touch a partition with data excluded from the results set of a query. You can also perform maintenance procedures on a subset of filegroups, and thus on a subset of partitions. That way, you can also speed up regular maintenance tasks. Partitions have many benefits.

Although you can partition a table on any attribute, partitioning over dates is most common in data warehousing scenarios. You can use any time interval for a partition. Depending on your needs, the interval could be a day, a month, a year, or any other interval.

In addition to partitioning tables, you can also partition indexes. If indexes are partitioned in the same way as the base tables, they are called **aligned indexes**. Partitioned table and index concepts include the following:

- **Partition function**: This is an object that maps rows to partitions by using values from specific columns. The columns used for the function are called **partitioning columns**. A partition function performs logical mapping.
- **Partition scheme**: A partition scheme maps partitions to filegroups. A partition scheme performs physical mapping.
- **Aligned index**: This is an index built on the same partition scheme as its base table. If all indexes are aligned with their base table, switching a partition is a metadata operation only, so it is very fast. Columnstore indexes have to be aligned with their base tables. Nonaligned indexes are, of course, indexes that are partitioned differently from their base tables.
- **Partition switching**: This is a process that switches a block of data from one table or partition to another table or partition. You switch the data by using the ALTER TABLE T-SQL command. You can perform the following types of switching:
    - Reassign all data from a nonpartitioned table to an empty existing partition of a partitioned table
    - Switch a partition of a one-partitioned table to a partition of another partitioned table
    - Reassign all data from a partition of a partitioned table to an existing empty nonpartitioned table

- **Partition elimination**: This is a query optimizer process in which SQL Server accesses only those partitions needed to satisfy query filters.

For more information about table and index partitioning, refer to the MSDN *Partitioned Tables and Indexes* article at `https://msdn.microsoft.com/en-us/library/ms190787.aspx`.

Nonclustered indexes in analytical scenarios

As mentioned, DW queries typically involve large scans of data and aggregation. Very selective seeks are not common for reports from a DW. Therefore, nonclustered indexes generally don't help DW queries much. However, this does not mean that you shouldn't create any nonclustered indexes in your DW.

An attribute of a dimension is not a good candidate for a nonclustered index key. Attributes are used for pivoting and typically contain only a few distinct values. Therefore, queries that filter based on attribute values are usually not very selective. Nonclustered indexes on dimension attributes are not good practice.

DW reports can be parameterized. For example, a DW report could show sales for all customers or for only a single customer, based perhaps on parameter selection by an end user. For a single-customer report, the user would choose the customer by selecting that customer's name. Customer names are selective, meaning that you retrieve only a small number of rows when you filter by customer name. Company names, for example, are typically unique, so by filtering by a company name, you typically retrieve a single row. For reports like these, having a nonclustered index on a name column or columns could lead to better performance.

You can create a filtered nonclustered index. A filtered index spans a subset of column values only and thus applies to a subset of table rows. Filtered nonclustered indexes are useful when some values in a column occur rarely, whereas other values occur frequently. In such cases, you would create a filtered index over the rare values only. SQL Server uses this index for seeks of rare values but performs scans for frequent values. Filtered nonclustered indexes can be useful not only for name columns and member properties but also for attributes of a dimension, and even foreign keys of a fact table. For example, in our demo fact table, the customer with an ID equal to 378 has only 242 rows. You can execute the following code to show that even if you select data for this customer only, SQL Server performs a full scan:

```
SET STATISTICS IO ON;
-- All rows
SELECT *
FROM dbo.FactTest;
```

```
-- Customer 378 only
SELECT *
FROM dbo.FactTest
WHERE CustomerKey = 378;
SET STATISTICS IO OFF;
```

Both queries needed 6,091 logical reads. Now you can add a filtered nonclustered index to the table:

```
CREATE INDEX NCLF_FactTest_C378
 ON dbo.FactTest(CustomerKey)
 WHERE CustomerKey = 378;
GO
```

If you execute the same two queries again, you get much less IO for the second query. It needed 752 logical reads in my case and uses the Index Seek and Key Lookup operators.

You can drop the filtered index when you don't need it anymore with the following code:

```
DROP INDEX NCLF_FactTest_C378
 ON dbo.FactTest;
GO
```

Using indexed views

You can optimize queries that aggregate data and perform multiple joins by permanently storing the aggregated and joined data. For example, you could create a new table with joined and aggregated data and then maintain that table during your ETL process.

However, creating additional tables for joined and aggregated data is not best practice because using these tables means you have to change queries used in your reports. Fortunately, there is another option for storing joined and aggregated tables. You can create a view with a query that joins and aggregates data. Then you can create a clustered index on the view to get an **indexed view**. With indexing, you are materializing a view; you are storing, physically, the data the view is returning when you query it. In the Enterprise or Developer Edition of SQL Server, SQL Server Query Optimizer uses an indexed view automatically, without changing the query. SQL Server also maintains indexed views automatically. However, to speed up data loads, you can drop or disable the index before the load and then recreate or rebuild it after the load.

For example, note the following query, which aggregates the data from the test fact table:

```
SET STATISTICS IO ON;
SELECT StockItemKey,
 SUM(TotalAmount) AS Sales,
 COUNT_BIG(*) AS NumberOfRows
FROM dbo.FactTest
GROUP BY StockItemKey;
SET STATISTICS IO OFF;
```

In my case, this query used 6,685 logical IOs. It used the Clustered Index Scan operator on the fact table to retrieve the whole dataset. Now let's create a view with the same query used for the definition:

```
CREATE VIEW dbo.SalesByProduct
WITH SCHEMABINDING AS
SELECT StockItemKey,
 SUM(TotalAmount) AS Sales,
 COUNT_BIG(*) AS NumberOfRows
FROM dbo.FactTest
GROUP BY StockItemKey;
GO
```

Indexed views have many limitations. One of them is that they have to be created with the SCHEMABINDING option if you want to index them, as you can see in the previous code. Now let's index the view:

```
CREATE UNIQUE CLUSTERED INDEX CLU_SalesByProduct
 ON dbo.SalesByProduct (StockItemKey);
GO
```

Try to execute the last query before creating the VIEW again. Make sure you notice that the query refers to the base table and not the view. This time, the query needed only four logical reads. If you check the execution plan, you should see that SQL Server used the Clustered Index Scan operator on the indexed view. If your indexed view was not used automatically, please check which edition of SQL Server you are using. When you finish testing, you can drop the view with the following code:

```
DROP VIEW dbo.SalesByProduct;
GO
```

Data compression and query techniques

SQL Server supports data compression. Data compression reduces the size of the database, which helps improve query performance because queries on compressed data read fewer pages from the disk and thus use less IO. However, data compression requires extra CPU resources for updates, because data must be decompressed before and compressed after the update. Data compression is therefore suitable for data warehousing scenarios in which data is mostly read and only occasionally updated.

SQL Server supports three compression implementations:

- **Row compression**: Row compression reduces metadata overhead by storing fixed data type columns in a variable-length format. This includes strings and numeric data. Row compression has only a small impact on CPU resources and is often appropriate for OLTP applications as well.
- **Page compression**: Page compression includes row compression, but also adds prefix and dictionary compressions. **Prefix compression** stores repeated prefixes of values from a single column in a special compression information structure that immediately follows the page header, replacing the repeated prefix values with a reference to the corresponding prefix. **Dictionary compression** stores repeated values anywhere in a page in the compression information area. Dictionary compression is not restricted to a single column.
- **Unicode compression**: In SQL Server, Unicode characters occupy an average of two bytes. Unicode compression substitutes single-byte storage for Unicode characters that don't truly require two bytes. Depending on collation, Unicode compression can save up to 50 % of the space otherwise required for Unicode strings. Unicode compression is very cheap and is applied automatically when you apply either row or page compression.

You can gain quite a lot from data compression in a data warehouse. Foreign keys are often repeated many times in a fact table. Large dimensions that have Unicode strings in name columns, member properties, and attributes can benefit from Unicode compression.

The following figure explains dictionary compression:

Dictionary compression

As you can see from the figure, dictionary compression (corresponding to the first arrow) starts with prefix compression. In the compression information space on the page right after the page header, you can find stored prefixes for each column. If you look at the top left cell, the value in the first row, and first column, is **aaabb**. The next value in this column is **aaabcc**. A prefix value **aaabcc** is stored for this column in the first column of the row for the prefix compression information. Instead of the original value in the top left cell, the **4b value** is stored. This means use four characters from the prefix for this column and add the letter *b* to get the original value back. The value in the second row for the first column is empty because the prefix for this column is equal to the whole original value in that position. The value in the last row for the first column after the prefix compression is **3ccc**, meaning that in order to get the original value, you need to take the first three characters from the column prefix and add a string **ccc**, thus getting the value **aaaccc**, which is, of course, equal to the original value. Check prefix compression for the other two columns also.

After prefix compression, dictionary compression is applied (corresponding to the second arrow in the *Dictionary compression* figure). It checks all strings across all columns to find common substrings. For example, the value in the first two columns of the first row after the prefix compression was applied is **4b**. SQL Server stores this value in the dictionary compression information area as the first value in this area, with index 0. In the cells, it stores just the index value 0 instead of the value **4b**. The same happens for the **0bbbb** value, which you can find in the second row, second column, and third row, third column, after prefix compression is applied. This value is stored in the dictionary compression information area in the second position with index 1; in the cells, the value 1 is left.

You might wonder why prefix compression is needed. For strings, a prefix is just another substring, so dictionary compression could cover prefixes as well. However, prefix compression can work on nonstring data types as well. For example, instead of storing integers 900, 901, 902, 903, and 904 in the original data, you can store a 900 prefix and leave values 0, 1, 2, 3, and 4 in the original cells.

Now it's time to test SQL Server compression. First of all, let's check the space occupied by the test fact table:

```
EXEC sys.sp_spaceused N'dbo.FactTest', @updateusage = N'TRUE';
GO
```

The result is as follows:

Name	rows	reserved	data	index_size	unused
dbo.FactTest	227981	49672 KB	48528 KB	200 KB	944 KB

The following code enables row compression on the table and checks the space used again:

```
ALTER TABLE dbo.FactTest
  REBUILD WITH (DATA_COMPRESSION = ROW);
EXEC sys.sp_spaceused N'dbo.FactTest', @updateusage = N'TRUE';
```

This time, the result is as follows:

Name	rows	reserved	data	index_size	unused
dbo.FactTest	227981	25864 KB	24944 KB	80 KB	840 KB

You can see that a lot of space was saved. Let's also check the page compression:

```
ALTER TABLE dbo.FactTest
  REBUILD WITH (DATA_COMPRESSION = PAGE);
EXEC sys.sp_spaceused N'dbo.FactTest', @updateusage = N'TRUE';
```

Now the table occupies even less space, as the following result shows:

Name	rows	reserved	data	index_size	unused
dbo.FactTest	227981	18888 KB	18048 KB	80 KB	760 KB

If these space savings are impressive to you, wait for columnstore compression! Anyway, before continuing, you can remove the compression from the test fact table with the following code:

```
ALTER TABLE dbo.FactTest
  REBUILD WITH (DATA_COMPRESSION = NONE);
```

Before continuing with other SQL Server features that support analytics, I want to explain another compression algorithm because this algorithm is also used in columnstore compression. The algorithm is called **LZ77 compression**. It was published by Abraham Lempel and Jacob Ziv in 1977; the name of the algorithm comes from the first letters of the author's last names plus the publishing year. The algorithm uses sliding window dictionary encoding, meaning it encodes chunks of an input stream with dictionary encoding. The following are the steps of the process:

1. Set the coding position to the beginning of the input stream
2. Find the longest match in the window for the look-ahead buffer
3. If a match is found, output the pointer P and move the coding position (and the window) L bytes forward
4. If a match is not found, output a null pointer and the first byte in the look-ahead buffer and move the coding position (and the window) one byte forward
5. If the look-ahead buffer is not empty, return to step 2

The following figure explains this process via an example:

Input stream	Position	1	2	3	4	5	6	7	8	9
	Byte	A	A	B	C	B	B	A	B	C

Step	Position	Match	Byte	Output
1.	1	~	A	(0, 0) A
2.	2	A	~	(1, 1)
3.	3	~	B	(0, 0) B
4.	4	A	C	(0, 0) C
5.	5	B	~	(2, 1)
6.	6	B	~	(1, 1)
7.	7	A B C	~	(5, 3)

LZ77 compression

The input stream chunk that is compressed in the figure is **AABCBBABC**:

- The algorithm starts encoding from the beginning of the window of the input stream. It stores the first byte (the **A** value) in the result, together with the pointer **(0,0)**, meaning this is a new value in this chunk.
- The second byte is equal to the first one. The algorithm stores just the pointer **(1,1)** to the output. This means that in order to recreate this value, you need to move one byte back and read one byte.
- The next two values, **B** and **C**, are new and are stored to the output together with the pointer **(0,0)**.
- Then the **B** value repeats. Therefore, the pointer **(2,1)** is stored, meaning that in order to find this value, you need to move two bytes back and read one byte.
- Then the **B** value repeats again. This time, you need to move one byte back and read one byte to get the value, so the value is replaced with the pointer **(1,1)**. You can see that when you move back and read the value, you get another pointer. You can have a chain of pointers.
- Finally, the substring **ABC** is found in the stream. This substring can be also found in positions 2 to 4. Therefore, in order to recreate the substring, you need to move five bytes back and read 3 bytes, and the pointer **(5,3)** is stored in the compressed output.

Writing efficient queries

Before finishing this section, I also need to mention that no join, compression algorithm, or any other feature that SQL Server offers can help you if you write inefficient queries. A good example of a typical DW query is one that involves running totals. You can use non-equi self joins for such queries, which is a very good example of an inefficient query. The following code calculates the running total for the profit ordered over the sale key with a self join. The code also measures the IO and time needed to execute the query. Note that the query uses a CTE first to select 12,000 rows from the fact table. A non-equi self join is a quadratic algorithm; with double the number of the rows, the time needed increases by a factor of four. You can play with different number of rows to prove that:

```
SET STATISTICS IO ON;
SET STATISTICS TIME ON;
WITH SalesCTE AS
(
SELECT [Sale Key] AS SaleKey, Profit
FROM Fact.Sale
WHERE [Sale Key] <= 12000
)
SELECT S1.SaleKey,
 MIN(S1.Profit) AS CurrentProfit,
 SUM(S2.Profit) AS RunningTotal
FROM SalesCTE AS S1
 INNER JOIN SalesCTE AS S2
  ON S1.SaleKey >= S2.SaleKey
GROUP BY S1.SaleKey
ORDER BY S1.SaleKey;
SET STATISTICS IO OFF;
SET STATISTICS TIME OFF;
```

With 12,000 rows, the query needed 817,584 logical reads in a worktable, which is a temporary representation of the test fact table on the right side of the self join, and on the top of this, more than 3,000 logical reads for the left representation of the fact table. On my computer, it took more than 12 seconds (elapsed time) to execute this query, with more than 72 seconds of CPU time, as the query was executed with a parallel execution plan. With 6,000 rows, the query would need approximately four times less IO and time.

You can calculate running totals very efficiently with window aggregate functions. The following example shows the query rewritten. The new query uses the window aggregate functions:

```
SET STATISTICS IO ON;
SET STATISTICS TIME ON;
WITH SalesCTE AS
```

```
(
SELECT [Sale Key] AS SaleKey, Profit
FROM Fact.Sale
WHERE [Sale Key] <= 12000
)
SELECT SaleKey,
 Profit AS CurrentProfit,
 SUM(Profit)
   OVER(ORDER BY SaleKey
       ROWS BETWEEN UNBOUNDED PRECEDING
                  AND CURRENT ROW) AS RunningTotal
FROM SalesCTE
ORDER BY SaleKey;
SET STATISTICS IO OFF;
SET STATISTICS TIME OFF;
```

This time, the query used 331 reads in the fact table, 0 (zero) reads in the worktable, 0.15 second elapsed time, and 0.02 second CPU time. SQL Server didn't even bother to find a parallel plan.

Columnar storage and batch processing

Various researchers started to think about **columnar storage** in the 80s. The main idea is that a **relational database management system** (RDBMS) does not need to store the data in exactly the same way we understand it and work with it. In a relational model, a tuple represents an entity and is stored as a row of a table, which is an entity set. Traditionally, database management systems store entities row by row. However, as long as we get rows back to the client application, we do not care how an RDBMS stores the data.

This is actually one of the main premises of the relational model—we work with data on the logical level, which is independent of the physical level of the physical storage. However, it was not until approximately 2000 when the first attempts to create columnar storage came to life. SQL Server added columnar storage first in version 2012.

Columnar storage is highly compressed. Higher compression means more CPU usage because the data must be decompressed when you want to work with it and recompressed when you store it. In addition, SQL Server has to transform columns back to rows when you work with data and vice versa when you store the data. Add to this picture parallelized query execution, and suddenly CPU becomes a bottleneck. CPU is rarely a bottleneck in a transactional application. However, analytical applications have different requests. SQL Server solves the CPU problem by introducing **batch processing**.

In this section, you will learn about SQL Server columnar storage and batch processing, including the following:

- How SQL Server creates columnar storage
- Columnstore compression
- Nonclustered columnstore indexes
- Clustered columnstore indexes
- The limitations of columnar storage in different versions of SQL Server
- Batch processing
- The limitations of batch processing in different versions of SQL Server

Columnar storage and compression

Storing the data column by column instead of row by row gives you the opportunity to store each column in a sorted way. Imagine that you have every column totally sorted. Then for every equijoin, the merge join algorithm could be used, which is, as you already know, a very efficient algorithm. In addition, with sorted data, you get one more type of compression for free—**run-length encoding** (RLE) compression.

The following figure explains the idea graphically:

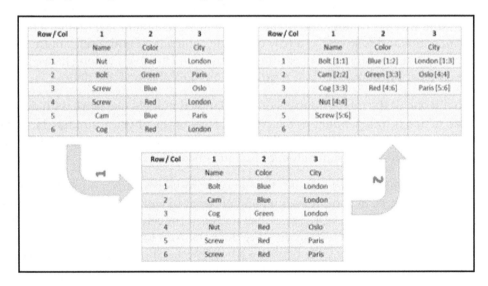

Sorted columnar storage and RLE

An RDBMS in the first step reorders every single column. Then RLE compression is implemented. For example, if you look at the **Color** column, you don't need to repeat the value **Red** three times; you can store it only once and store either the frequency of the value or the index in the form from position to position, as shown in the figure.

Note that SQL Server does not implement total sorting. Total sorting of every single column would simply be too expensive. Creating such storage would take too much time and too many resources. SQL Server uses its own patented **row-rearranging algorithm**, which rearranges the rows in the most optimal way to order all columns as best as possible, with a single pass through the data. This means that SQL Server does not totally sort any column; however, all columns are at least partially sorted. Therefore, SQL Server does not target the merge join algorithm; the hash join algorithm is preferred. Partial sorts still optimizes the use of bitmap filters because fewer false positives are returned from a bitmap filter when compared to randomly organized values. RLE compression can still reduce the size of the data substantially.

Recreating rows from columnar storage

Of course, there is still the question of how to recreate rows from columnar storage. In 1999, Stephen Tarin patented the Tarin Transform Method, which uses a **row reconstruction table** to regenerate the rows. Mr. Tarin called columnar storage the Trans-Relational Model. This does not mean the model is beyond relational; this was more a marketing term, short for Transform Relational Model.

SQL Server documentation does not publish the row recreation algorithm it uses. I am presenting the Tarin's method here. It should still be good enough to give you a better understanding of the amount of work SQL Server has to do when it recreates rows from columns.

The following figure explains the Tarin Transform Method:

Row / Col	1	2	3
	Name	Color	City
1	3	6	4
2	1	4	6
3	6	5	3
4	4	1	5
5	2	2	1
6	5	3	2

Row / Col	1	2	3
	Name	Color	City
1	Bolt [1:1]	Blue [1:2]	London [1:3]
2	Cam [2:2]	Green [3:3]	Oslo [4:4]
3	Cog [3:3]	Red [4:6]	Paris [5:6]
4	Nut [4:4]		
5	Screw [5:6]		
6			

Tarin Transform Method

In the figure, the top table is the row reconstruction table. You start reconstructing the rows in the top left corner. For the first column of the first row value, take the top left value in the columnar storage table at the bottom, in this case the value **Bolt**. In the first cell of the row reconstruction table, there is a pointer to the row number of the second column in this table. In addition, it is an index for the value of the second column in the columnar storage table. In the figure, this value is **3**. This means that you need to find the value in the second column of the columnar storage table with index 3, which is **Green**. In the row reconstruction table, you read the value **5** in the second column, third row. You use this value as an index for the value of the third column in the columnar storage table, which, in the example, is **Paris**. In the row reconstruction table, you read the value **1**. Because this is the last column in the table, this value is used for a cyclic redundancy check, checking whether you can correctly get to the starting point of the row reconstruction process. The row **Bolt**, **Green**, and **Paris**, the second row from the original table from the previous figure, was successfully reconstructed.

As mentioned, how SQL Server reconstructs the rows has not been published. Nevertheless, you can appreciate that this is quite an intensive process. You can also imagine changes in the original data. Just a small update to the original values might cause the complete recreation of the row reconstruction table. This would simply be too expensive. This is why columnar storage, once it is created, is actually read-only. In SQL Server 2014 and 2016, columnstore indexes are updateable; however, SQL Server does not update the columnar storage online. SQL Server uses additional row storage for the updates. You will learn further details later in this chapter.

Columnar storage creation process

SQL Server starts creating the columnar storage by first splitting the data into **rowgroups**. The maximum number of rows per rowgroup is 1,048,576. The idea here is that the time-consuming row rearranging is done on smaller datasets, just like how the hash join algorithm splits the data into buckets and then performs smaller joins on portions of the data. SQL Server performs row rearranging in each of the groups separately. Then SQL Server encodes and compresses each column. Each column's data in each rowgroup is called a **segment**. SQL Server stores segments in blobs in database files. Therefore, SQL Server leverages the existing storage for columnar storage. The following figure shows the process:

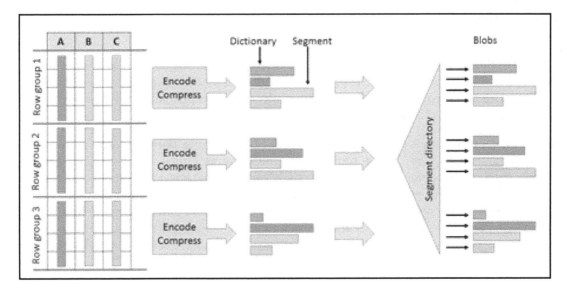

How SQL Server creates columnar storage

SQL Server implements different compressing algorithms:

- SQL Server does bit-packing. Bit-packing is similar to row compression, just pushed one level further. Instead of storing the minimal number of bytes, SQL Server stores the minimal number of bits that can represent the value. For example, with row compression, you would get one byte instead of four bytes for value 5, if this value is an integer. With bit-packing, SQL Server would store this value using three bits only *(101)*.
- Then SQL Server encodes the values to integers with **value encoding** and **dictionary encoding**. Value encoding is similar to prefix encoding in page compression, and dictionary encoding is the same. Therefore, this part of compression uses the ideas of page compression. However, dictionaries for columnar storage are much more efficient because they are built on more values than dictionaries in page compression. With page compression, you get a separate dictionary for each 8 KB page. With columnar storage, you get one dictionary per rowgroup plus one global dictionary over all rowgroups.
- Because of the partial ordering, the run-length encoding algorithm is also used.
- Finally, SQL Server can also use the LZ77 algorithm to compress columnar data.

All of these compression algorithms except the LZ77 one are implemented automatically when you create a columnstore index. This is called COLUMNSTORE compression. You must turn LZ77 compression on manually to get so-called the COLUMNSTORE_ARCHIVE compression.

With all of these compression algorithms implemented, you can count on at least 10 times more compression compared to the original, non-compressed row storage. In reality, you can get much better compression levels, especially when you also implement archive compression with the LZ77 algorithm.

However, compression is not the only advantage of large scans. Because each column is stored separately, SQL Server can retrieve only the columns a query is referring to. This is like having a covering nonclustered index. Each segment also has additional metadata associated with it. This metadata includes the minimal and the maximal value in the segment. SQL Server query optimizer can use this metadata for early segment elimination, just as SQL Server can do early partition elimination if a table is partitioned. Finally, you can combine partitioning with columnstore indexes to maintain even very large tables.

Development of columnar storage in SQL Server

SQL Server introduced columnar storage in version 2012. Only NCCIs were supported. This means that you still need to have the original row storage, either organized as a heap or as a **clustered index** (**CI**). There are many other limitations, including the following:

- Nonclustered columnstore index only
- One per table
- Must be partition-aligned
- Table becomes read-only (partition switching allowed)
- Unsupported types
    - Decimals greater than 18 digits
    - Binary, Image, CLR (including Spatial, HierarchyId)
    - (N)varchar(max), XML, Text, Ntext
    - Uniqueidentifier, Rowversion, SQL_Variant
    - Date/time types greater than 8 bytes

SQL Server 2014 introduced **clustered columnstore indexes** (**CCI**). This means that the original row storage does not exist anymore; CCI is the only storage you need. Just like in a regular clustered index, SQL Server needs to identify each row in a clustered columnstore index as well. Note that SQL Server 2014 does not support constraints on the columnar storage. Therefore, SQL Server 2014 adds a **bookmark**, which is a unique tuple ID inside a rowgroup, stored as a simple sequence number. SQL Server 2014 has many data types unsupported for columnar storage, including the following:

- Varbinary(MAX), Image, CLR (including Spatial, HierarchyId)
- (N)Varchar(max), XML, Text, Ntext
- Rowversion, SQL_Variant

SQL Server 2014 also optimizes the columnstore index build. For example, SQL Server 2012 used a fixed number of threads to build the index. This number was estimated in advance. If, for some reason, the operating system took some threads away from SQL Server while SQL Server was building a columnstore index, the build might have failed. In SQL Server 2014, the degree of parallelism or the number of threads can be adjusted dynamically while SQL Server builds the columnstore index.

The CCI in SQL 2014 is updateable. However, its columnar storage is immutable. The following figure explains the update process:

How SQL Server updates columnar storage

Data modification is implemented as follows:

- **Insert**: The new rows are inserted into a delta store
- **Delete**: If the row to be deleted is in a column store row group, a record containing its row ID is inserted into the B-tree storing the delete bitmap; if it is in a delta store, the row is simply deleted
- **Update**: Split into a delete and an insert
- **Merge**: Split into a delete, an insert, and an update

A delta store can be either open or closed. When a new delta store is created, it is open. After you insert the maximum number of rows for a rowgroup in an open delta store, SQL Server changes the status of this delta store to closed. If you remember, this means a bit more than one million rows. Then a background process called tuple-mover converts the closed delta stores to column segments. This process starts by default every five minutes. You can run it manually with the ALTER INDEX ... REORGANIZE or ALTER INDEX ... REBUILD commands.

Non-bulk (trickle) inserts go to an open delta store. Bulk inserts up to 102,400 rows; smaller ones go to an open delta store, and larger ones go directly to column segments. More delta stores mean less compression. Therefore, when using bulk insert, you should try to optimize the batches to contain close to 1,000,000 rows. You can also rebuild the index occasionally.

SQL Server 2016 brings many additional features to the columnstore indexes. The most important features in version 2016 include the following:

- CCI supports additional NCI (B-tree) indexes
- CCI supports through NCI primary and foreign key constraints
- CCI supports snapshot and read-committed snapshot isolation levels
- NCCI on a heap or B-tree updateable and filtered
- Columnstore indices on in-memory tables
- Defined when you create the table in the CREATE TABLE statement
- Must include all columns and all rows (not filtered)
- NCI indexes can be filtered

SQL Server 2017 adds only small improvements to columnar storage, compared to version 2016:

- You can build and rebuild NCCIs online
- CCIs now support LOB columns: VARCHAR(MAX), NVARCHAR(MAX), and VARBINARY(MAX)

Batch processing

With columnar storage, the CPU can become a bottleneck. SQL Server solves these problems with **batch mode processing**. In batch mode processing, SQL Server processes data in batches rather than processing one row at a time. A batch represents roughly 900 rows of data. Each column within a batch is stored as a vector in a separate memory area, meaning that batch mode processing is vector-based. Batch mode processing interrupts a processor with metadata only once per batch rather than once per row, as in row mode processing, which lowers the CPU burden substantially. This means that batch mode spreads the metadata access costs over all of the 900 rows in a batch.

Batch mode processing is orthogonal to columnar storage. This means SQL Server can use it with many different operators, no matter whether the data is stored in row or column storage. However, batch mode processing gives the best results when combined with columnar storage. DML operations, such as insert, update, or delete, work in row mode. Of course, SQL Server can mix batch and row mode operators in a single query.

SQL Server introduced batch mode also in version 2012. The batch mode operators in this version include the following:

- Filter
- Project
- Scan
- Local hash (partial) aggregation
- Hash inner join
- Batch hash table build, but only in-memory, no spilling
- Bitmap filters limited to a single column, data types represented with a 64-bit integer

In SQL Server 2014, the following batch mode operators were added:

- All join types
- Union all
- Scalar aggregation
- Spilling support
- Complex bitmap filters, all data types supported

SQL Server 2016 added the following improvements to batch mode processing:

- Single-threaded queries
- Sort operator
- Multiple distinct count operations
- Left anti-semi join operators
- Window aggregate functions
- Window analytical functions
- String predicate and aggregate pushdown to the storage engine
- Row-level locking on index seeks against a nonclustered index and rowgroup-level locking on full table scans against the columnstore

Finally, SQL Server 2017 added two more improvements to batch mode processing:

- Batch mode adaptive joins
- Batch mode memory grant feedback

The following table summarizes the most important features and limitations of columnar storage and batch mode processing in SQL Server versions 2012 to 2106:

Columnstore Index/Batch Mode Feature	SQL 2012	SQL 2014	SQL 2016	SQL 2017
Batch execution for multi-threaded queries	yes	yes	yes	yes
Batch execution for single-threaded queries			yes	yes
Batch mode adaptive joins				yes
Batch mode memory grant feedback				yes
Archival compression		yes	yes	yes
Snapshot isolation and read-committed snapshot isolation			yes	yes
Specify CI when creating a table			yes	yes
AlwaysOn supports CIs	yes	yes	yes	yes
AlwaysOn readable secondary supports read-only NCCI	yes	yes	yes	yes
AlwaysOn readable secondary supports updateable CIs			yes	yes
Read-only NCCI on heap or B-tree	yes	yes	yes	yes
Updateable NCCI on heap or B-tree			yes	yes
NCCI online build and rebuild				yes
B-tree indexes allowed on a table that has a NCCI	yes	yes	yes	yes
Updateable CCI		yes	yes	yes
CCI LOB columns support				yes
B-tree index on a CCI			yes	yes
CCI on a memory-optimized table			yes	yes

Filtered NCCI			yes	yes

You can check whether SQL Server uses row or batch mode for an operator by analyzing the properties of the operator in the execution plan. Before checking the batch mode, the following code adds nine time as many rows to the test fact table:

```
DECLARE @i AS INT = 1;
WHILE @i < 10
BEGIN
SET @i += 1;
INSERT INTO dbo.FactTest
(SaleKey, CustomerKey,
 Customer, CityKey, City,
 DateKey, StockItemKey,
 Product, Quantity,
 TotalAmount, Profit)
SELECT @i * 1000000 + f.[Sale Key] AS SaleKey,
  cu.[Customer Key] AS CustomerKey, cu.Customer,
  ci.[City Key] AS CityKey, ci.City,
  f.[Delivery Date Key] AS DateKey,
  s.[Stock Item Key] AS StockItemKey, s.[Stock Item] AS Product,
  f.Quantity, f.[Total Excluding Tax] AS TotalAmount, f.Profit
FROM Fact.Sale AS f
  INNER JOIN Dimension.Customer AS cu
    ON f.[Customer Key] = cu.[Customer Key]
  INNER JOIN Dimension.City AS ci
    ON f.[City Key] = ci.[City Key]
  INNER JOIN Dimension.[Stock Item] AS s
    ON f.[Stock Item Key] = s.[Stock Item Key]
  INNER JOIN Dimension.Date AS d
    ON f.[Delivery Date Key] = d.Date;
END;
```

Let's check how much space this table uses now:

```
EXEC sys.sp_spaceused N'dbo.FactTest', @updateusage = N'TRUE';
GO
```

The result is as follows:

```
Name            rows      reserved     data         index_size   unused
-------------   -------   ----------   ----------   -----------   --------
dbo.FactTest    2279810   502152 KB    498528 KB    2072 KB       1552 KB
```

Now let's start querying this table. Before executing the following query, make sure you turn the actual execution plan on:

```
SELECT f.StockItemKey,
  SUM(f.TotalAmount) AS Sales
FROM dbo.FactTest AS f
WHERE f.StockItemKey < 30
GROUP BY f.StockItemKey
ORDER BY f.StockItemKey;
```

You can hover the mouse over any of the operators. For example, the following screenshot shows the details of the Hash Match (Partial Aggregate) operator:

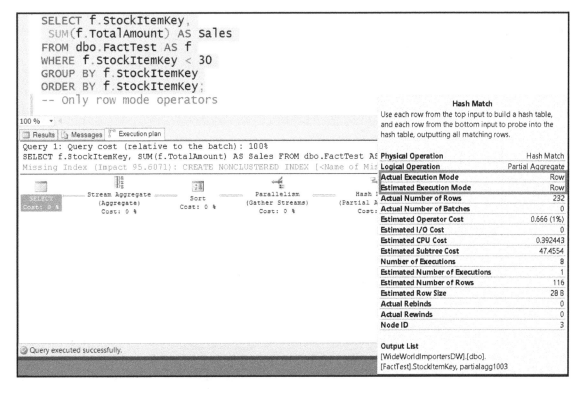

Row mode operators

You can see that SQL Server used row mode processing. As mentioned, batch mode is not strictly bound to columnar storage; however, it is much more likely that SQL Server would use it as you use the columnar storage. The following code creates a filtered nonclustered columnstore index. It is actually empty:

```
CREATE NONCLUSTERED COLUMNSTORE INDEX NCCI_FactTest
ON dbo.FactTest
(SaleKey, CustomerKey,
 Customer, CityKey, City,
 DateKey, StockItemKey,
 Product, Quantity,
 TotalAmount, Profit)
WHERE SaleKey = 0;
GO
```

Now, execute the same query again. As you can see from the following screenshot, this time batch mode is used for the `Hash Match` (Partial Aggregate) operator:

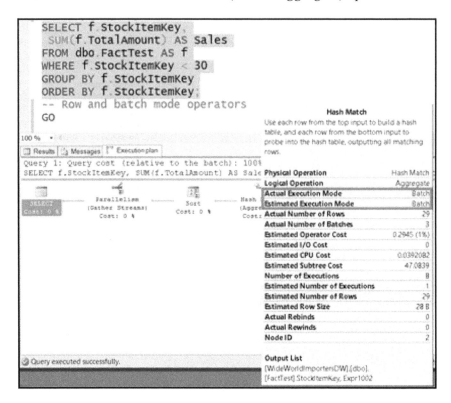

Batch mode operators

Nonclustered columnstore indexes

After a theoretical introduction, it is time to start using columnar storage. You will start by learning how to create and use NCCI. You already know from the previous section that an NCCI can be filtered. Now you will learn how to create, use, and ignore an NCCI. In addition, you will measure the compression rate of the columnar storage.

Because of the different burdens on SQL Server when a transactional application uses it compared to analytical applications usage, traditionally, companies split these applications and created data warehouses. Analytical queries are diverted to the data warehouse database. This means that you have a copy of data in your data warehouse, of course with a different schema. You also need to implement the ETL process for scheduled loading of the data warehouse. This means that the data you analyze is somehow stalled. Frequently, the data is loaded overnight and is thus one day old when you analyze it. For many analytical purposes, this is good enough. However, in some cases, users would like to analyze current data together with archived data. This is called **operational analytics**. SQL Server 2016 with columnar storage and in-memory tables makes operational analytics realistically possible.

In this section, you will learn how to do the following:

- Create nonclustered columnstore indexes
- Ignore an NCCI in a query
- Use NCCI in a query
- Architect an operational analytics solution

Compression and query performance

Without any further hesitation, let's start with the code. The first thing is to drop the filtered (empty) NCCI created in the previous section:

```
DROP INDEX NCCI_FactTest
ON dbo.FactTest;
GO
```

The test fact table is organized as a B-tree with no additional nonclustered index, neither a rowstore nor columnstore one. The clustering key is the date. In order to make a comparison to NCCIs, let's set a baseline. First, recheck the space used by the test fact table:

```
EXEC sys.sp_spaceused N'dbo.FactTest', @updateusage = N'TRUE';
GO
```

The result is as follows:

Name	rows	reserved	data	index_size	unused
dbo.FactTest	2279810	502152 KB	498528 KB	2072 KB	1552 KB

You can measure IO with the `SET STATISTICS IO ON` command. In addition, you can turn on the actual execution plan. Here is the first sample query; let's call it the *simple* query:

```
SET STATISTICS IO ON;
SELECT f.StockItemKey,
 SUM(f.TotalAmount) AS Sales
FROM dbo.FactTest AS f
WHERE f.StockItemKey < 30
GROUP BY f.StockItemKey
ORDER BY f.StockItemKey;
```

The query did a full clustered index scan, and there were 63,601 logical reads. You may also notice in the execution plan that only row mode operators were used.

 You can get slightly different results for the IO. The exact number of pages used by the table might vary slightly based on your dataset file organization, parallel operations when you load the data or change the table from a heap to a B-tree, and other possibilities. Nevertheless, your numbers should be very similar, and the point is to show how much less space will be used by columnar storage because of the compression.

The next query involves multiple joins; let's call it the *complex* query:

```
SELECT f.SaleKey,
  f.CustomerKey, f.Customer, cu.[Buying Group],
  f.CityKey, f.City, ci.Country,
  f.DateKey, d.[Calendar Year],
  f.StockItemKey, f.Product,
  f.Quantity, f.TotalAmount, f.Profit
FROM dbo.FactTest AS f
  INNER JOIN Dimension.Customer AS cu
    ON f.CustomerKey = cu.[Customer Key]
  INNER JOIN Dimension.City AS ci
    ON f.CityKey = ci.[City Key]
  INNER JOIN Dimension.[Stock Item] AS s
    ON f.StockItemKey = s.[Stock Item Key]
  INNER JOIN Dimension.Date AS d
    ON f.DateKey = d.Date;
```

This time, SQL Server created a much more complex execution plan, yet SQL Server used a full clustered index scan to read the data from the test fact table. SQL Server used 62,575 logical reads in this table.

The third test query is very selective—it selects only the rows for customer 378. If you remember, this customer has only 242 rows in the fact table. Let's call the third query the *point* query:

```
SELECT CustomerKey, Profit
FROM dbo.FactTest
WHERE CustomerKey = 378;
SET STATISTICS IO OFF;
```

The query again did a full clustered index scan, and there were 63,601 logical reads.

Testing the nonclustered columnstore index

The following code creates an NCCI on the fact table, this time without a filter, so all data is included in the NCCI:

```
CREATE NONCLUSTERED COLUMNSTORE INDEX NCCI_FactTest
ON dbo.FactTest
(SaleKey, CustomerKey,
 Customer, CityKey, City,
 DateKey, StockItemKey,
 Product, Quantity,
 TotalAmount, Profit);
GO
```

So how much space is used by the test fact table now? Let's check it again with the following code:

```
EXEC sys.sp_spaceused N'dbo.FactTest', @updateusage = N'TRUE';
GO
```

The result is as follows:

Name	rows	reserved	data	index_size	unused
dbo.FactTest	2279810	529680 KB	498528 KB	29432 KB	1720 KB

Note the numbers. The index size is about 17 times less than the data size! And remember, in this preceding reported size are also the non-leaf levels of the clustered index, so the actual compression rate was even more than 17 times. This is impressive. So what does this mean for queries? Before measuring the improvements in queries, I want to show how you can ignore the NCCI you just created with a specific option in the `OPTION` clause of the `SELECT` statement. So here is a *simple* query that ignores the NCCI:

```
SET STATISTICS IO ON;
SELECT f.StockItemKey,
 SUM(f.TotalAmount) AS Sales
FROM dbo.FactTest AS f
WHERE f.StockItemKey < 30
GROUP BY f.StockItemKey
ORDER BY f.StockItemKey
OPTION (ignore_nonclustered_columnstore_index);
```

Because the NCCI was ignored, the query still did the full-clustered index scan with 63,301 logical reads. However, you can see from the execution plan that this time row mode operators were used, as shown in the following screenshot:

Row mode processing operators

This is different compared to the execution plan SQL Server used for the same query when the NCCI was empty, when SQL Server used batch mode operators. The ignore option really means that SQL Server completely ignores the NCCI. You can check that this is also true for the other two queries, the *complex* and the *point* one. You can also check the execution plans when ignoring the NCCI with the *complex* and *point* queries:

```
-- Complex query
SELECT f.SaleKey,
   f.CustomerKey, f.Customer, cu.[Buying Group],
   f.CityKey, f.City, ci.Country,
   f.DateKey, d.[Calendar Year],
   f.StockItemKey, f.Product,
   f.Quantity, f.TotalAmount, f.Profit
FROM dbo.FactTest AS f
   INNER JOIN Dimension.Customer AS cu
     ON f.CustomerKey = cu.[Customer Key]
   INNER JOIN Dimension.City AS ci
     ON f.CityKey = ci.[City Key]
   INNER JOIN Dimension.[Stock Item] AS s
     ON f.StockItemKey = s.[Stock Item Key]
   INNER JOIN Dimension.Date AS d
     ON f.DateKey = d.Date
OPTION (ignore_nonclustered_columnstore_index);
-- Point query
SELECT CustomerKey, Profit
FROM dbo.FactTest
WHERE CustomerKey = 378
OPTION (ignore_nonclustered_columnstore_index);
SET STATISTICS IO OFF;
```

For both queries, SQL Server did a full table scan on the fact table, with around 63,000 logical reads in this table. Now let's finally see how the queries can benefit from the NCCI. The first query is the *simple* query again:

```
SET STATISTICS IO ON;
SELECT f.StockItemKey,
 SUM(f.TotalAmount) AS Sales
FROM dbo.FactTest AS f
WHERE f.StockItemKey < 30
GROUP BY f.StockItemKey
ORDER BY f.StockItemKey;
```

As you can see from the following screenshot, the columnstore index scan was used, and only four segments were read, with 2,001 LOB reads. Remember that the columnstore indexes are stored in blobs in SQL Server. Compare this to the number of logical reads when the NCCI was ignored. You can also check by yourself that batch mode operators were used:

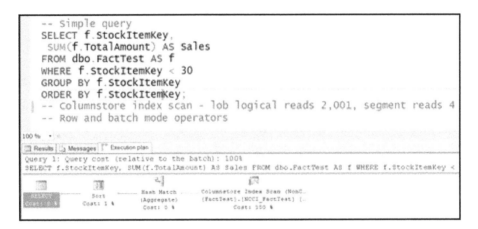

Row mode processing operators

You can check how many segments in total are occupied by the NCCI with the following query using the `sys.column_store_segments` catalog view:

```
SELECT ROW_NUMBER()
        OVER (ORDER BY s.column_id, s.segment_id) AS rn,
 COL_NAME(p.object_id, s.column_id) AS column_name,
 S.segment_id, s.row_count,
 s.min_data_id, s.max_data_id,
 s.on_disk_size AS disk_size
FROM sys.column_store_segments AS s
INNER JOIN sys.partitions AS p
    ON s.hobt_id = p.hobt_id
INNER JOIN sys.indexes AS i
    ON p.object_id = i.object_id
WHERE i.name = N'NCCI_FactTest'
ORDER BY s.column_id, s.segment_id;
```

Here is the abbreviated result of this query:

rn	column_name	segment_id	row_count	min_data_id	max_data_id	disk_size
1	SaleKey	0	1048576	1000001	10106307	4194888
2	SaleKey	1	336457	1001951	10185925	1346560

3	SaleKey	2	441851	1106610	10227981	1768336
4	SaleKey	3	452926	1001228	10213964	1812656
5	CustomerKey	0	1048576	0	402	773392
...	...					
44	Profit	3	452926	−64500	920000	25624
45	NULL	0	1048576	0	3539	1678312
...	...					
48	NULL	3	452926	0	3879	725640

The total number of segments used is 48. SQL Server created four rowgroups and then one segment per column inside each rowgroup, plus one segment per rowgroup for the rowgroup dictionary. You can also see the number of rows and disk space used per segment. In addition, the min_data_id and max_data_id columns point to the minimal and the maximal value in each segment. The SQL Server query optimizer uses this information for early segment elimination.

You can also execute the other two queries:

```
-- Complex query
SELECT f.SaleKey,
    f.CustomerKey, f.Customer, cu.[Buying Group],
    f.CityKey, f.City, ci.Country,
    f.DateKey, d.[Calendar Year],
    f.StockItemKey, f.Product,
    f.Quantity, f.TotalAmount, f.Profit
FROM dbo.FactTest AS f
    INNER JOIN Dimension.Customer AS cu
        ON f.CustomerKey = cu.[Customer Key]
    INNER JOIN Dimension.City AS ci
        ON f.CityKey = ci.[City Key]
    INNER JOIN Dimension.[Stock Item] AS s
        ON f.StockItemKey = s.[Stock Item Key]
    INNER JOIN Dimension.Date AS d
        ON f.DateKey = d.Date;
-- Point query
SELECT CustomerKey, Profit
FROM dbo.FactTest
WHERE CustomerKey = 378;
SET STATISTICS IO OFF;
```

For the `Complex query`, the number of LOB reads is 7,128. For the `Point query`, the number of LOB reads is 2,351. In both cases, a columnstore index scan was used to read the data from the fact table. The *point* query used fewer LOB reads than the *complex* query because the query refers to fewer columns, and SQL Server retrieves only the columns needed to satisfy the query. Still, the results for the *point* query are not overly exciting. You should be able to get much less IO with a B-tree nonclustered index, especially with a covering one.

In my case, the *complex* query used a serial plan. Note that, depending on the hardware resources and concurrent work, you might get a different execution plan. SQL Server sees eight logical processors in my virtual machine, so you might have expected a parallel plan. SQL Server 2016 is much more conservative about using a parallel plan compared to previous versions. This is better for the majority of queries. If you really need to get a parallel execution plan, you could change the compatibility level to the version 2014, as the following code shows:

```
USE master;
GO
ALTER DATABASE WideWorldImportersDW SET COMPATIBILITY_LEVEL = 120;
GO
```

Now you can try to execute the *complex* query again:

```
USE WideWorldImportersDW;
SET STATISTICS IO ON;
SELECT f.SaleKey,
    f.CustomerKey, f.Customer, cu.[Buying Group],
    f.CityKey, f.City, ci.Country,
    f.DateKey, d.[Calendar Year],
    f.StockItemKey, f.Product,
    f.Quantity, f.TotalAmount, f.Profit
FROM dbo.FactTest AS f
    INNER JOIN Dimension.Customer AS cu
      ON f.CustomerKey = cu.[Customer Key]
    INNER JOIN Dimension.City AS ci
      ON f.CityKey = ci.[City Key]
    INNER JOIN Dimension.[Stock Item] AS s
      ON f.StockItemKey = s.[Stock Item Key]
    INNER JOIN Dimension.Date AS d
      ON f.DateKey = d.Date;
SET STATISTICS IO OFF;
```

This time, SQL Server used a parallel plan on my computer. Before continuing, reset the compatibility level to 2017:

```
USE master;
GO
ALTER DATABASE WideWorldImportersDW SET COMPATIBILITY_LEVEL = 140;
GO
```

Operational analytics

Real-time operational analytics has become a viable option in SQL Server 2016 and 2017, especially if you combine columnar storage together with in-memory tables. Here is just a brief overview of two possible solutions for operational analytics—one with on-disk and another with in-memory storage. You will learn more about in-memory tables in Chapter 11, *Introducing SQL Server In-Memory OLTP* and Chapter 12, *In-Memory OLTP Improvements in SQL Server 2017*.

The following figure shows the architecture of an operational analytics solution with on-disk tables:

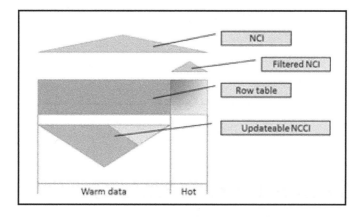

On-disk operational analytics

The majority of the data does not change much (so-called **warm data**), or may even be historical, immutable data (so-called **cold data**). You use a filtered nonclustered columnstore index over this warm or cold data. For **hot data**—data that is changed frequently—you can use a regular filtered nonclustered index. You can also use additional nonclustered indexes over the whole table. The table can be organized as a heap or as B-tree.

For in-memory tables, you can implement a slightly different architecture. You have to take into account that nonclustered columnstore indexes on an in-memory table cannot be filtered. Therefore, they must cover both warm and hot data areas. However, they are updateable, and in-memory updates are much faster than on-disk updates.

You can combine a columnstore index with other in-memory index types, namely with hash indexes and nonclustered indexes.

The in-memory operational analytics solution is shown in the following figure:

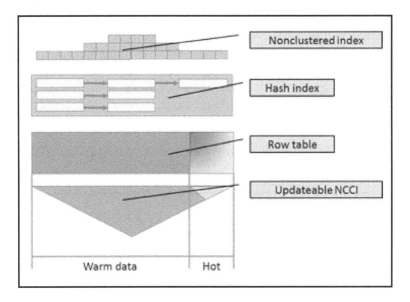

In-memory operational analytics

Clustered columnstore indexes

In the last sections of this chapter, you will learn how to manage a CCI. Besides optimizing query performance, you will also learn how to add a regular B-tree **nonclustered index** (**NCI**) to a CCI and use it instead of the primary key or unique constraints. When creating the NCCI in the previous sections, we didn't use LZ77 or archive compression. You will use it with a CCI in this section. Altogether, you will learn how to do the following:

- Create clustered columnstore indexes
- Use archive compression
- Add B-tree NCI to a CCI

- Use B-tree NCI for a constraint
- Update data in a CCI

Compression and query performance

Let's start by dropping both indexes from the demo fact table, the NCCI and the CI, to make a heap again:

```
USE WideWorldImportersDW;
-- Drop the NCCI
DROP INDEX NCCI_FactTest
  ON dbo.FactTest;
-- Drop the CI
DROP INDEX CL_FactTest_DateKey
  ON dbo.FactTest;
GO
```

Now let's create the CCI:

```
CREATE CLUSTERED COLUMNSTORE INDEX CCI_FactTest
  ON dbo.FactTest;
GO
```

And, of course, the next step is to recheck the space used by the test fact table:

```
EXEC sys.sp_spaceused N'dbo.FactTest', @updateusage = N'TRUE';
GO
```

The result is as follows:

Name	rows	reserved	data	index_size	unused
dbo.FactTest	2279810	23560 KB	23392 KB	0 KB	168 KB

The CCI even uses slightly less space than the NCCI. You can check the number of segments with the following query:

```
SELECT ROW_NUMBER() OVER (ORDER BY s.column_id, s.segment_id) AS rn,
 COL_NAME(p.object_id, s.column_id) AS column_name,
 S.segment_id, s.row_count,
 s.min_data_id, s.max_data_id,
 s.on_disk_size
FROM sys.column_store_segments AS s
INNER JOIN sys.partitions AS p
    ON s.hobt_id = p.hobt_id
INNER JOIN sys.indexes AS i
```

```
        ON p.object_id = i.object_id
WHERE i.name = N'CCI_FactTest'
ORDER BY s.column_id, s.segment_id;
```

This time, the number of segments is 44. The CCI does not show a dictionary segment per row group; it has a global dictionary that apparently covers the whole table. How does that influence the queries?

Testing the clustered columnstore index

Again, the first test is with the *simple* query:

```
SET STATISTICS IO ON;
SELECT f.StockItemKey,
 SUM(f.TotalAmount) AS Sales
FROM dbo.FactTest AS f
WHERE f.StockItemKey < 30
GROUP BY f.StockItemKey
ORDER BY f.StockItemKey;
```

From the IO output, you can see that SQL Server used only 82 logical reads. This time, this is really impressive. Note that the execution plan again used the `Columnstore Index Scan` operator, this time scanning the CCI and selecting only the rowgroups and segments needed to satisfy the query. You can see the execution plan in the following screenshot:

CCI scan execution plan

The next query to test is the *complex* query:

```
SELECT f.SaleKey,
  f.CustomerKey, f.Customer, cu.[Buying Group],
  f.CityKey, f.City, ci.Country,
  f.DateKey, d.[Calendar Year],
  f.StockItemKey, f.Product,
  f.Quantity, f.TotalAmount, f.Profit
FROM dbo.FactTest AS f
  INNER JOIN Dimension.Customer AS cu
    ON f.CustomerKey = cu.[Customer Key]
  INNER JOIN Dimension.City AS ci
    ON f.CityKey = ci.[City Key]
  INNER JOIN Dimension.[Stock Item] AS s
    ON f.StockItemKey = s.[Stock Item Key]
  INNER JOIN Dimension.Date AS d
    ON f.DateKey = d.Date;
```

This time, SQL Server needed 6,101 LOB logical reads. SQL Server used a serial plan on my virtual machine, a mixed batch (for CCI scan and for hash joins), and row mode operators (for other index scans). This is only slightly better than when using an NCCI. How about the *point* query?:

```
SELECT CustomerKey, Profit
FROM dbo.FactTest
WHERE CustomerKey = 378;
SET STATISTICS IO OFF;
```

The *point* query this time used 484 LOB logical reads. Better, but still not the best possible.

Using archive compression

You might remember that there is still one option left for columnar storage compression—archive compression. Let's turn it on with the following code:

```
ALTER INDEX CCI_FactTest
 ON dbo.FactTest
 REBUILD WITH (DATA_COMPRESSION = COLUMNSTORE_ARCHIVE);
GO
```

You can imagine what comes next; recheck the space used by the test fact table:

```
EXEC sys.sp_spaceused N'dbo.FactTest', @updateusage = N'TRUE';
GO
```

The result is as follows:

```
Name              rows      reserved    data       index_size  unused
------------      -------   ----------  ---------- ----------  -------
dbo.FactTest      2279810   19528 KB    19336 KB       0 KB    192 KB
```

The LZ77 algorithm added some additional compression. Compare the data size now with the initial data size when the data size was 498,528 KB; now it is only 19,336 KB. The compression rate is more than 25 times! This is really impressive. Of course, you'd expect test queries to be even more efficient now. For example, here is the *simple* query:

```
SET STATISTICS IO ON;
SELECT f.StockItemKey,
 SUM(f.TotalAmount) AS Sales
FROM dbo.FactTest AS f
WHERE f.StockItemKey < 30
GROUP BY f.StockItemKey
ORDER BY f.StockItemKey;
```

This time, SQL Server needed only 23 LOB logical reads. The next query to test is the *complex* query:

```
SELECT f.SaleKey,
  f.CustomerKey, f.Customer, cu.[Buying Group],
  f.CityKey, f.City, ci.Country,
  f.DateKey, d.[Calendar Year],
  f.StockItemKey, f.Product,
  f.Quantity, f.TotalAmount, f.Profit
FROM dbo.FactTest AS f
  INNER JOIN Dimension.Customer AS cu
    ON f.CustomerKey = cu.[Customer Key]
  INNER JOIN Dimension.City AS ci
    ON f.CityKey = ci.[City Key]
  INNER JOIN Dimension.[Stock Item] AS s
    ON f.StockItemKey = s.[Stock Item Key]
  INNER JOIN Dimension.Date AS d
    ON f.DateKey = d.Date;
```

This time, SQL Server needed 4,820 LOB logical reads in the test fact table. It can't get much better than this for scanning all of the data. And what about the *point* query?:

```
SELECT CustomerKey, Profit
FROM dbo.FactTest
WHERE CustomerKey = 378;
```

This time, it used 410 LOB logical reads. This number can still be improved.

Adding B-tree indexes and constraints

There is still one query, the *point* query, which needs additional optimization. In SQL Server 2016 and 2017, you can create regular, rowstore B-tree nonclustered indexes on a clustered columnstore index, on a table that is organized as columnar storage. The following code adds a nonclustered index with an included column, an index that is going to cover the *point* query:

```
CREATE NONCLUSTERED INDEX NCI_FactTest_CustomerKey
 ON dbo.FactTest(CustomerKey)
 INCLUDE(Profit);
GO
```

Before executing the queries, let's check the space used by the demo fact table:

```
EXEC sys.sp_spaceused N'dbo.FactTest', @updateusage = N'TRUE';
GO
```

The result is as follows:

Name	rows	reserved	data	index_size	unused
dbo.FactTest	2279810	90256 KB	19344 KB	70192 KB	720 KB

You can see that row storage uses much more space than columnar storage. However, a regular NCI is very efficient for seeks. Let's test the queries, starting with the *simple* query:

```
SET STATISTICS IO ON;
SELECT f.StockItemKey,
 SUM(f.TotalAmount) AS Sales
FROM dbo.FactTest AS f
WHERE f.StockItemKey < 30
GROUP BY f.StockItemKey
ORDER BY f.StockItemKey;
```

This query still needed 23 LOB logical reads. If you check the execution plan, you can see that SQL Server is still using the columnstore index scan. Of course, the NCI is not very useful for this query. How about the *complex* query?:

```
SELECT f.SaleKey,
   f.CustomerKey, f.Customer, cu.[Buying Group],
   f.CityKey, f.City, ci.Country,
   f.DateKey, d.[Calendar Year],
   f.StockItemKey, f.Product,
   f.Quantity, f.TotalAmount, f.Profit
FROM dbo.FactTest AS f
   INNER JOIN Dimension.Customer AS cu
```

```
    ON f.CustomerKey = cu.[Customer Key]
INNER JOIN Dimension.City AS ci
    ON f.CityKey = ci.[City Key]
INNER JOIN Dimension.[Stock Item] AS s
    ON f.StockItemKey = s.[Stock Item Key]
INNER JOIN Dimension.Date AS d
    ON f.DateKey = d.Date;
```

Again, SQL Server needed 4,820 LOB logical reads in the test fact table. The NCI didn't improve this query; it is already optimized. Finally, let's check the *point* query:

```
SELECT CustomerKey, Profit
FROM dbo.FactTest
WHERE CustomerKey = 378;
SET STATISTICS IO OFF;
```

This time, the query needed only 13 logical reads. The SQL Server query optimizer decided to use the covering NCI index, as you can see in the following screenshot, showing the execution plan for the *point* query for this execution:

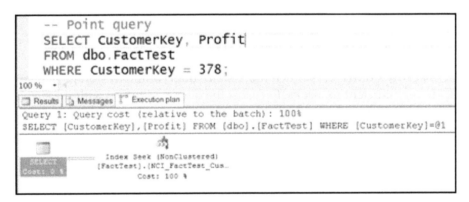

Execution plan for the point query that uses the nonclustered covering index

We don't need the nonclustered index anymore, so let's drop it:

```
DROP INDEX NCI_FactTest_CustomerKey
 ON dbo.FactTest;
GO
```

You can check the physical status of the rowgroups of the CCI using the `sys.dm_db_column_store_row_group_physical_stats` **Dynamic Management View (DMV)**, as the following query shows:

```
SELECT OBJECT_NAME(object_id) AS table_name,
 row_group_id, state, state_desc,
 total_rows, deleted_rows
FROM sys.dm_db_column_store_row_group_physical_stats
WHERE object_id = OBJECT_ID(N'dbo.FactTest')
ORDER BY row_group_id;
```

Here is the result:

table_name	row_group_id	state	state_desc	total_rows	deleted_rows
FactTest	0	3	COMPRESSED	1048576	0
FactTest	1	3	COMPRESSED	343592	0
FactTest	2	3	COMPRESSED	444768	0
FactTest	3	3	COMPRESSED	442874	0

You can see that all rowgroups are closed and compressed.

In SQL 2016 and 2017, you can also add a primary key and unique constraints to a CCI table. The following code adds a unique constraint to the test fact table. Note that you cannot add a primary key constraint because the `SaleKey` column is nullable:

```
ALTER TABLE dbo.FactTest
 ADD CONSTRAINT U_SaleKey UNIQUE (SaleKey);
GO
```

You can check in the **Object Explorer** that the Unique constraint is enforced with help from the unique rowstore nonclustered index. The following screenshot of the **Object Explorer** window shows that the SaleKey column is nullable as well:

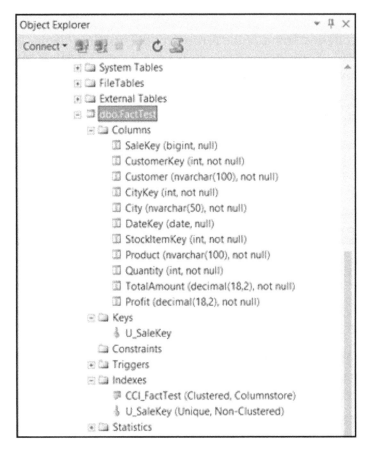

Unique constraint on a CCI table

Let's test the constraint. The following command tries to insert 75,993 rows into the test fact table that already exist in the table:

```
INSERT INTO dbo.FactTest
(SaleKey, CustomerKey,
 Customer, CityKey, City,
 DateKey, StockItemKey,
 Product, Quantity,
 TotalAmount, Profit)
SELECT 10 * 1000000 + f.[Sale Key] AS SaleKey,
```

```
    cu.[Customer Key] AS CustomerKey, cu.Customer,
    ci.[City Key] AS CityKey, ci.City,
    f.[Delivery Date Key] AS DateKey,
    s.[Stock Item Key] AS StockItemKey, s.[Stock Item] AS Product,
    f.Quantity, f.[Total Excluding Tax] AS TotalAmount, f.Profit
FROM Fact.Sale AS f
    INNER JOIN Dimension.Customer AS cu
        ON f.[Customer Key] = cu.[Customer Key]
    INNER JOIN Dimension.City AS ci
        ON f.[City Key] = ci.[City Key]
    INNER JOIN Dimension.[Stock Item] AS s
        ON f.[Stock Item Key] = s.[Stock Item Key]
    INNER JOIN Dimension.Date AS d
        ON f.[Delivery Date Key] = d.Date
WHERE f.[Sale Key] % 3 = 0;
```

If you execute the code, you get error 2627, violating Unique constraint. Let's recheck the status of the rowgroups:

```
SELECT OBJECT_NAME(object_id) AS table_name,
 row_group_id, state, state_desc,
 total_rows, deleted_rows
FROM sys.dm_db_column_store_row_group_physical_stats
WHERE object_id = OBJECT_ID(N'dbo.FactTest')
ORDER BY row_group_id;
```

This time, the result differs slightly:

table_name	row_group_id	state	state_desc	total_rows	deleted_rows
FactTest	0	3	COMPRESSED	1048576	0
FactTest	1	3	COMPRESSED	343592	0
FactTest	2	3	COMPRESSED	444768	0
FactTest	3	3	COMPRESSED	442874	0
FactTest	4	1	OPEN	0	0

Although the insert was rejected, SQL Server did not close or delete the delta storage. Of course, this makes sense since this storage might become useful pretty soon for data updates. You can rebuild the index to get rid of this delta storage. The following command rebuilds the CCI, this time without archive compression:

```
ALTER INDEX CCI_FactTest
 ON dbo.FactTest
 REBUILD WITH (DATA_COMPRESSION = COLUMNSTORE);
GO
```

You can check the rowgroup's status again:

```
SELECT OBJECT_NAME(object_id) AS table_name,
 row_group_id, state, state_desc,
 total_rows, deleted_rows
FROM sys.dm_db_column_store_row_group_physical_stats
WHERE object_id = OBJECT_ID(N'dbo.FactTest')
ORDER BY row_group_id;
```

Here is the result:

table_name	row_group_id	state	state_desc	total_rows	deleted_rows
FactTest	0	3	COMPRESSED	1048576	0
FactTest	1	3	COMPRESSED	343592	0
FactTest	2	3	COMPRESSED	444768	0
FactTest	3	3	COMPRESSED	442874	0

Note that your results for the number of rows in each row group may vary slightly.

Updating a clustered columnstore index

So far, only an unsuccessful insert was tested. Of course, you can also try to insert some valid data. Before that, let's drop the constraint since it is not needed for further explanation:

```
ALTER TABLE dbo.FactTest
 DROP CONSTRAINT U_SaleKey;
GO
```

Next, you can insert some valid rows. The following statement inserts 113,990 rows into the test fact table. Note that this is more than the 102,400 row limit for trickle inserts; therefore, you should expect this to be treated as a bulk insert:

```
INSERT INTO dbo.FactTest
(SaleKey, CustomerKey,
 Customer, CityKey, City,
 DateKey, StockItemKey,
 Product, Quantity,
 TotalAmount, Profit)
SELECT 11 * 1000000 + f.[Sale Key] AS SaleKey,
  cu.[Customer Key] AS CustomerKey, cu.Customer,
```

```
    ci.[City Key] AS CityKey, ci.City,
    f.[Delivery Date Key] AS DateKey,
    s.[Stock Item Key] AS StockItemKey, s.[Stock Item] AS Product,
    f.Quantity, f.[Total Excluding Tax] AS TotalAmount, f.Profit
FROM Fact.Sale AS f
    INNER JOIN Dimension.Customer AS cu
        ON f.[Customer Key] = cu.[Customer Key]
    INNER JOIN Dimension.City AS ci
        ON f.[City Key] = ci.[City Key]
    INNER JOIN Dimension.[Stock Item] AS s
        ON f.[Stock Item Key] = s.[Stock Item Key]
    INNER JOIN Dimension.Date AS d
        ON f.[Delivery Date Key] = d.Date
WHERE f.[Sale Key] % 2 = 0;
```

You can check whether this was a bulk insert by checking the rowgroups again:

```
SELECT OBJECT_NAME(object_id) AS table_name,
 row_group_id, state, state_desc,
 total_rows, deleted_rows
FROM sys.dm_db_column_store_row_group_physical_stats
WHERE object_id = OBJECT_ID(N'dbo.FactTest')
ORDER BY row_group_id;
```

The result shows you that you have only compressed rowgroups:

table_name	row_group_id	state	state_desc	total_rows	deleted_rows
FactTest	0	3	COMPRESSED	1048576	0
FactTest	1	3	COMPRESSED	343592	0
FactTest	2	3	COMPRESSED	444768	0
FactTest	3	3	COMPRESSED	442874	0
FactTest	4	3	COMPRESSED	113990	0

Although all rowgroups are compressed, you will notice that the last rowgroups have fewer rows than the other rowgroups. It would be more efficient if you could use bulk inserts with more rows, closer to 1,000,000 rows. Now let's try to insert a smaller number of rows. This time, you can also turn on the graphical execution plan:

```
INSERT INTO dbo.FactTest
(SaleKey, CustomerKey,
 Customer, CityKey, City,
 DateKey, StockItemKey,
 Product, Quantity,
 TotalAmount, Profit)
SELECT 12 * 1000000 + f.[Sale Key] AS SaleKey,
    cu.[Customer Key] AS CustomerKey, cu.Customer,
    ci.[City Key] AS CityKey, ci.City,
```

```
   f.[Delivery Date Key] AS DateKey,
   s.[Stock Item Key] AS StockItemKey, s.[Stock Item] AS Product,
   f.Quantity, f.[Total Excluding Tax] AS TotalAmount, f.Profit
FROM Fact.Sale AS f
   INNER JOIN Dimension.Customer AS cu
     ON f.[Customer Key] = cu.[Customer Key]
   INNER JOIN Dimension.City AS ci
     ON f.[City Key] = ci.[City Key]
   INNER JOIN Dimension.[Stock Item] AS s
     ON f.[Stock Item Key] = s.[Stock Item Key]
   INNER JOIN Dimension.Date AS d
     ON f.[Delivery Date Key] = d.Date
WHERE f.[Sale Key] % 3 = 0;
```

In the execution, you can see that the insert was a row mode operation. SQL Server does not use batch mode operators for DDL operations. The following screenshot shows a portion of the execution plan, with the `Columnstore Index Insert` operator highlighted to show that row mode processing was used:

Messages	Execution plan		
Query 1: Query cost (rela		**Columnstore Index Insert**	
INSERT INTO dbo.FactTest		Insert rows in a columnstore index.	
T-SQL		**Physical Operation**	Columnstore Index Insert
INSERT	Columnstore I	**Logical Operation**	Insert
Cost: 0 %	[FactTest].[CC	**Actual Execution Mode**	Row
	Cost:	**Estimated Execution Mode**	Row
		Actual Number of Rows	75993
		Actual Number of Batches	0
		Estimated Operator Cost	19.57413 (86%)
		Estimated I/O Cost	19.4973
		Estimated CPU Cost	0.0759963
		Estimated Subtree Cost	22.7992
		Number of Executions	1
		Estimated Number of Executions	1
		Estimated Number of Rows	75996.3
		Estimated Row Size	9 B
		Actual Rebinds	0
		Actual Rewinds	0
		Node ID	0
Query executed successfully.		**Object**	
		[WideWorldImportersDW].[dbo].[FactTest].[CCI_FactTest]	

DDL operations are processed in row mode in SQL Server 2016

Note that SSMS in version 17.0 and higher also changed the icons in execution plans. That's why the icons in the previous screenshot are different from those in previous screenshots of execution plans, where I used SSMS version 16.

Anyway, let's recheck the status of the rowgroups:

```
SELECT OBJECT_NAME(object_id) AS table_name,
 row_group_id, state, state_desc,
 total_rows, deleted_rows
FROM sys.dm_db_column_store_row_group_physical_stats
WHERE object_id = OBJECT_ID(N'dbo.FactTest')
ORDER BY row_group_id;
```

This time, another open rowgroup is in the result:

table_name	row_group_id	state	state_desc	total_rows	deleted_rows
FactTest	0	3	COMPRESSED	1048576	0
FactTest	1	3	COMPRESSED	343592	0
FactTest	2	3	COMPRESSED	444768	0
FactTest	3	3	COMPRESSED	442874	0
FactTest	4	3	COMPRESSED	113990	0
FactTest	5	1	OPEN	75993	0

Let's rebuild the index to get only compressed rowgroups again:

```
ALTER INDEX CCI_FactTest
 ON dbo.FactTest REBUILD;
GO
```

After the rebuild, let's see what happened to the rowgroups:

```
SELECT OBJECT_NAME(object_id) AS table_name,
 row_group_id, state, state_desc,
 total_rows, deleted_rows
FROM sys.dm_db_column_store_row_group_physical_stats
WHERE object_id = OBJECT_ID(N'dbo.FactTest')
ORDER BY row_group_id;
```

The result shows you that you have only compressed rowgroups:

table_name	row_group_id	state	state_desc	total_rows	deleted_rows
FactTest	0	3	COMPRESSED	1048576	0
FactTest	1	3	COMPRESSED	428566	0
FactTest	2	3	COMPRESSED	495276	0
FactTest	3	3	COMPRESSED	497375	0

SQL Server has added the rows from the trickle insert to other rowgroups. Let's now select the rows from the last trickle insert:

```
SELECT *
FROM dbo.FactTest
WHERE SaleKey >= 12000000
ORDER BY SaleKey;
```

Deleting from a clustered columnstore index

Let's test what happens when you delete rows from a CCI with the following DELETE command. Before executing the command, you can check the estimated execution plan. Therefore, don't execute the following command yet:

```
DELETE
FROM dbo.FactTest
WHERE SaleKey >= 12000000;
```

The following screenshot shows the actual execution plan. You can see that, for the Columnstore Index Delete operator, row mode was used again:

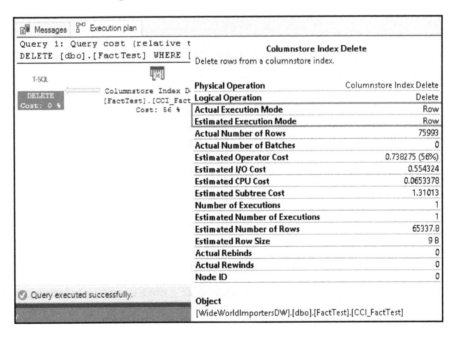

Estimated execution plan for a DELETE

And here is a final check of the state of the rowgroups:

```
SELECT OBJECT_NAME(object_id) AS table_name,
  row_group_id, state, state_desc,
  total_rows, deleted_rows
FROM sys.dm_db_column_store_row_group_physical_stats
WHERE object_id = OBJECT_ID(N'dbo.FactTest')
ORDER BY row_group_id;
```

The result shows you that you have only compressed rowgroups:

table_name	row_group_id	state	state_desc	total_rows	deleted_rows
FactTest	0	3	COMPRESSED	1048576	0
FactTest	1	3	COMPRESSED	428566	0
FactTest	2	3	COMPRESSED	495276	0
FactTest	3	3	COMPRESSED	497375	75993

You can see that one of the rowgroups has deleted rows. Although the total number of rows in this rowgroup did not change, you cannot access the deleted rows; the deleted bitmap B-tree structure for this rowgroup defines which rows are deleted. You can try to retrieve the deleted rows:

```
SELECT *
FROM dbo.FactTest
WHERE SaleKey >= 12000000
ORDER BY SaleKey;
```

This time, no rows are returned.

Finally, let's clean the WideWorldImporters database with the following code:

```
USE WideWorldImportersDW;
GO
DROP TABLE dbo.FactTest;
GO
```

Before finishing this chapter, look at the following table summarizing the space needed for different versions of row and columnar storage:

Storage	Rows	Reserved	Data	Index
CI	227,981	49,672 KB	48,528 KB	200 KB
CI row compression	227,981	25,864 KB	24,944 KB	80 KB
CI page compression	227,981	18,888 KB	18,048 KB	80 KB

CI (10 times more rows)	2,279,810	502,152 KB	498,528 KB	2,072 KB
CI with NCCI	2,279,810	529,680 KB	498,528 KB	29,432 KB
CCI	2,279,810	23,560 KB	23,392 KB	0 KB
CCI archive compression	2,279,810	19,528 KB	19,336 KB	0 KB
CCI archive compression and NCI	2,279,810	90,256 KB	19,344 KB	70,192 KB

Summary

Columnar storage brings a completely new set of possibilities to SQL Server. You can get lightning performance in analytical queries right from your data warehouse, without a special analytical database management system. This chapter started by describing features that support analytical queries in SQL Server other than columnar storage. You can use row or page data compression levels, bitmap filtered hash joins, filtered indexes, indexed views, window analytical and aggregate functions, table partitioning, and more. However, columnar storage adds an additional level of compression and performance boost. You learned about the algorithms behind the fantastic compression delivered by columnar storage. This chapter also included a lot of code, showing you how to create and use the nonclustered and the clustered columnstore indexes, including updating the data, creating constraints, and adding additional B-tree nonclustered indexes.

In the next two chapters, you are going to learn about a completely different way of improving the performance of your databases: memory-optimized tables. In addition, this chapter only started you off with analytics in SQL Server; Chapters 13 and 14 introduce R, a whole analytical language supported by SQL Server 2016. Chapter 15 introduces Python, another language useful for advanced analytics, for which support was added in SQL Server 2017.

11

Introducing SQL Server In-Memory OLTP

IT systems today are required to deliver the maximum performance with zero downtime and with maximum flexibility for developers and administrators. As developers, we all know that if performance of our applications is somehow lacking, then the cause of the slowdown *must* be in the database!

A major cause for performance problems inside database projects can be followed back to database design mistakes or to the limitations built in to the database engine to ensure data consistency for concurrent connections, or a mixture of both of these aspects.

Microsoft SQL Server adheres to the ACID theory. A simplified explanation of the **ACID** theory is that it describes how changes made to a database are required to fulfill four properties: **A**tomicity, **C**onsistency, **I**solation and **D**urability:

- **Atomicity** states that the contents of each transaction are either processed successfully and completely or fail in their entirety; *half-transactions* are not possible.
- **Consistency** states that a transaction brings a database from one valid state to another. This includes the adherence to the logical model inside the database (constraints, rules, triggers, and more). A transaction may not change a database from a logically valid state to a logically invalid state, for example, perform a data change that violates a unique constraint.
- **Isolation** states that the changes made inside a transaction are isolated from and are unaffected by other concurrent operations/transactions.
- **Durability** states that the changes made inside a transaction remain inside the database permanently, regardless of whether a system should go offline immediately after the transaction has completed.

To adhere to the ACID theory, Microsoft SQL Server employs the pessimistic concurrency model. Pessimistic concurrency assumes there will be conflicting concurrent transactions attempting to change the same data simultaneously. Therefore, transactions must (temporarily) lock the data they are changing to prevent other transactions from interfering with the isolation of those changes.

However, a system with enough concurrent users will eventually reach a logical limitation for transactional throughput through the design of the pessimistic concurrency model. Assuming unlimited hardware resources, the locking of data through pessimistic concurrency will become the bottleneck for transaction processing inside SQL Server.

Microsoft has developed a solution to this logical limitation, by implementing a method for employing the optimistic concurrency model. This model uses row versioning to avoid the need to lock and block data changes between concurrent users. Their implementation was made available in SQL Server 2014 under the codename **Hekaton** (Greek for a 100-fold), hinting at the possible performance increases) and the official feature name, **In-Memory OLTP**.

 This chapter will introduce the In-Memory OLTP feature as it was initially made available in SQL Server 2014. We will discuss the feature implementation and limitations before the specific additions and improvements in SQL Server 2016/2017 are expanded upon in `Chapter 12`, *In-Memory OLTP Improvements in SQL Server 2017*.

In-Memory OLTP architecture

In-Memory OLTP is the name of the optimistic concurrency model implementation offered from SQL Server 2014 onwards. The challenge that **In-Memory OLTP** is designed to solve is the ability to process massively concurrent transaction workloads, while removing the logical limitations of the pessimistic concurrency model present in the traditional transaction processing engine in SQL Server. Microsoft also wanted to introduce In-Memory OLTP as an *additional* transaction processing engine and *not* as a replacement for the standard transaction processing engine. This decision was made to ensure that existing applications running on SQL Server would be compatible with newer SQL Server versions, but offer the ability to allow newer applications to take advantage of the new engine without separating the two systems.

In this section, we will take a look at the architecture of the In-Memory OLTP engine and see how data is stored and processed.

Row and index storage

The first major difference in In-Memory OLTP is the storage structure of both tables and indexes. The traditional storage engine in SQL Server was optimized for disk storage, especially for the block storage of hard disk subsystems. However, In-Memory OLTP was designed from the ground up to be memory resident, or memory optimized. This small, but important difference allowed a design with byte storage in mind. This means that memory-optimized tables avoid the needs of data pages and extents that we know from the normal, disk-optimized tables in SQL Server. Through this change, a significant overhead in page and extent management is removed. This reduction in overhead provides a major performance increase in itself.

Row structure

Rows in memory-optimized tables are stored as heaps. These heaps are not to be confused with heaps in the traditional storage engine, but are memory structures storing the row data itself. These rows have no specific physical ordering and no requirement or expectation of being located *near* to other rows in memory. They also have no *knowledge* of connected rows themselves, they are solely created to store row data. The connection of these rows is controlled via the indexes created on memory-optimized tables. Knowing that the index stores and controls the connection of the memory-optimized row data heaps, we can infer that a table must have at least one index. This index (or indexes) must be defined during table creation.

In the introduction to the chapter, we mentioned that the In-Memory OLTP system is an implementation of the optimistic concurrency model. This model uses row versioning to allow concurrent connections to change data and still provide the necessary isolation. Row versioning is an important part of how memory-optimized tables are structured. Let's look at how a row is structured for a memory-optimized table.

In the following figure, we can see a depiction of a memory-optimized table, which is split into a row header (information about the row) and payload (the actual row data). The **Row Header** structure is expanded in the lower part of the image:

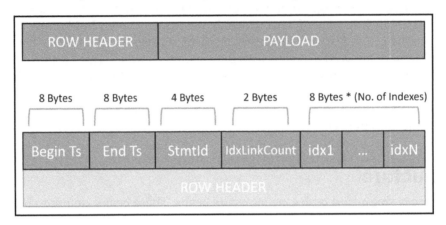

Memory-optimized table row structure—Header and Payload

Row header

The row header is split into five sections:

- **Begin Ts**: This is the timestamp of the transaction that inserted the row into the database.
- **End Ts**: This is the timestamp of the transaction that deleted the row from the database. For rows that have not yet been deleted, this field contains a value infinity.
- **StmtId**: This field stores a unique statement ID corresponding to the statement inside the transaction that created this row.
- **IdxLinkCount**: This field is a counter for the number of indexes that reference this row. An In-Memory table stores data only and has no reference to other rows in the table. The indexes that are linked to the table control which rows belong together.
- Finally, we have a set of pointers that reference the indexes connected to this row. The number of pointers stored here corresponds directly to the number of indexes that reference this row.

Row payload

The row payload is where the actual row data is stored. The key columns and all other columns are stored here. The structure of the payload depends upon the columns and data types that make up the table from the CREATE TABLE command.

Index structure

All memory-optimized tables must have at least one index. The indexes on a memory-optimized table store the connections between the rows. It is also important to remember that, as the name suggests, In-Memory OLTP indexes reside inside non-permanent memory (RAM) and are not written to disk. The only portions written to disk are the data rows of the base memory-optimized table and data changes, which are written to the transaction log (which is a requirement to fulfill the *Durability* part of the ACID concept).

There are two types of index available for memory-optimized tables:

- Non-clustered index
- Hash index

Non-clustered index

To be able to discuss the structure of a non-clustered index itself, we first need to understand how the storage engine creates, references, and processes these indexes.

The name of this type of index should be well known to all SQL Server developers. A non-clustered index for a memory-optimized table is widely similar to a non-clustered index in the traditional storage engine. This type of index uses a variation of the B-tree structure called a **Bw-tree** and is very useful for searching on ranges of data in a memory-optimized table. A Bw-tree is essentially a B-tree structure, without the locking and latching used to maintain a traditional B-tree. The index contains ordered key values which themselves store pointers to the data rows. With the Bw-tree, these pointers do not point to a physical page number (these data page structures don't exist for memory-optimized tables); the pointers direct to a logical **Page ID** (**PID**), which directs to an entry in a Page Mapping Table. This Page Mapping Table stores the physical memory address of the row data. This behavior mimics a covering index from the traditional disk-based non-clustered indexes, containing the columns of the key columns of the index.

As mentioned, memory-optimized tables run in optimistic concurrency and use versioning to avoid the need for locks and latches. The memory-optimized non-clustered index never updates a page when a change occurs, updated pages are simply replaced by adding a new page to the index and adding the physical memory address to the Page Mapping Table.

In the following figure, we see an example of a memory-optimized non-clustered index:

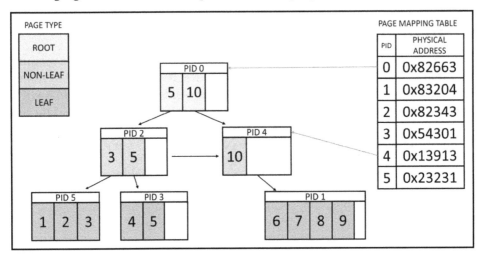

Memory-optimized non-clustered index Bw-tree structure

We can see in the preceding figure, the Bw-tree looks a lot like a B-tree, except we have a connection into the Page Mapping Table (instead of an Index Allocation Map for disk-based tables), which translates the index to the physical memory location of the row data. The root page and the non-leaf pages store key value information and a PID of the page beneath themselves in the tree. Particularly noteworthy here is that the key value stored is the highest value in the page in the next level down and not, like with a traditional B-tree, the lowest value. The leaf level also stores the PID to the memory address of the row that the index references. If multiple data rows have the same key, they will be stored as a *chain of rows* where the rows reference the same physical address for the value. Data changes in a memory-optimized non-clustered index are processed through a delta record process. The value that was originally referenced is then no longer referenced by the index and can be physically removed using the **Garbage Collector (GC)**.

A memory-optimized non-clustered index page follows a familiar pattern, with each page having a header which carries uniform control information:

- **PID**: The Page ID pointer which references the Page Mapping Table
- **Page Type**: Indicates the type of the page: leaf, internal or delta
- **Right PID**: The PID of the page to the right of the current page in the Bw-tree
- **Height**: The distance of the current page to the leaf
- **Page statistics**: The count of records on the page including the delta records
- **Max Key**: The maximum key value on the page

For pages lower down the Bw-tree structure, that is, internal and leaf, there are additional fields containing more detailed information required for deeper traversal than the root page:

- **Values**: This is an array of pointers that directs to either (for internal pages) the PID of the page in the next level down, or (for leaf pages) the memory location for the first row in a chain of rows with the same key values.
- **Keys**: This represents the first value on the page (for internal pages) or the value in a chain of rows (for leaf pages).
- **Offsets**: Stores the key value start offset for indexes with variable length keys.

Hash indexes

The second type of index for memory-optimized tables is the hash index. An array of pointers is created, with each element in the array representing a single value—this element is known as a **hash bucket**. The index key column of a table which should have a hash index created on it has a hashing function applied to it, and the resulting hash value is used to **bucketize** rows. Values that generate the same hash value are stored in the same hash bucket as a linked chain of values. To access this data, we pass in the key value we wish to search for, this value is also hashed to determine which hash bucket should be accessed, and the hash index translates the hash value to the pointer and allows us to retrieve all the duplicate values in a chain.

In the following diagram, we can see a very simplified representation of the hashing and retrieval of data. The row header has been removed for clarity's sake:

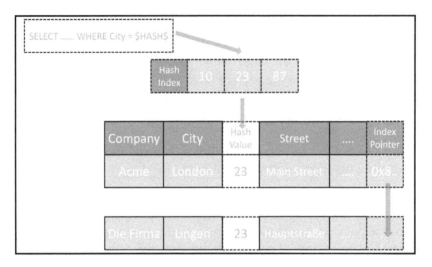

Simplified representation of hashing and retrieval of data

In the preceding figure, we can see a table storing company address information. We are interested in the City column, which is the key for a hash index. If we were to insert a value of London into this hash index, we would get a value, 23 (the hash function is simplified here for illustration purposes). This stores the key value London and the memory address of the table row of the memory-optimized table. If we then insert the second row with a city value of Lingen and our hash function hashes Lingen to 23 too, then this will be added to the hash index in the hash bucket for the value 23 and added to the chain started with London. Each hash index on a memory-optimized table adds an index pointer column (shown here with a dashed outline). This is an internal column that is used to store the pointer information for the next row in the chain. Every row of a chain has a pointer to the next row, bar the last row, which can have no following chain row. When no pointer is in this column, the retrieval routine knows it has reached the end of the chain and can stop loading rows.

The creation of a hash index requires some thought. We have seen that we can have multiple values that hash to the same hash value, which creates chains of records. However, the idea of a hashing function is to try and keep these chains as short as possible. An optimal hash index will have enough hash buckets to store as many unique values as possible, but has as few buckets as possible to reduce the overhead of maintaining these buckets (more buckets = more memory consumption for the index). Having more buckets than is necessary will also not improve performance, but rather hinder it, as each additional bucket makes a scan of the buckets slower. We must decide how many buckets to create when we initially create the index, which we will see with a sample script shortly. It is also important to realize that the hash index and hashing function considers *all* key columns of an index we create, so a multi-column index raises the chances that hash values will be unique and can require more hash buckets to assist with keeping these buckets emptier.

Creating memory-optimized tables and indexes

Now that we have looked at the theory behind the storage of memory-optimized tables, we want to get to the real fun and create some of these objects.

Laying the foundation

Before we can start creating our memory-optimized objects, we need to create a database with a FILEGROUP designed for memory-optimized objects. This can be achieved as follows:

```
CREATE DATABASE InMemoryTest
    ON
    PRIMARY(NAME = [InMemoryTest_disk],
                FILENAME = 'C:tempInMemoryTest_disk.mdf', size=100MB),
    FILEGROUP [InMemoryTest_inmem] CONTAINS MEMORY_OPTIMIZED_DATA
                (NAME = [InMemoryTest_inmem],
                FILENAME = 'C:tempInMemoryTest_inmem')
    LOG ON (name = [InMemoryTest_log],
 Filename='c:tempInMemoryTest_log.ldf', size=100MB)
    COLLATE Latin1_General_100_BIN2;
```

The first main thing to note is that we have a separate FILEGROUP dedicated to the memory-optimized objects, with the keyword CONTAINS MEMORY_OPTIMIZED_DATA. This FILEGROUP is used to persist the memory-optimized objects between server restarts (if required). The filestream APIs are used for this, you can observe what objects are created by navigating to the folder location and accessing the folder (with administrator permissions).

Also of note is that the database has been created with the windows BIN2 collation. This is an initial implementation limitation of In-Memory OLTP with SQL Server 2014 and limited the support for comparisons, grouping and sorting with memory-optimized objects.

It is equally possible to add a FILEGROUP to an existing database using the ALTER DATABASE command, specifying the FILEGROUP and then the location for the filestream folder:

```
ALTER DATABASE AdventureWorks2014
        ADD FILEGROUP InMemTest CONTAINS MEMORY_OPTIMIZED_DATA;
GO
ALTER DATABASE AdventureWorks2014
        ADD FILE (NAME='InMemTest', FILENAME='c:tempInMemTest')
    TO FILEGROUP InMemTest;
GO
```

As we can see, Microsoft has tried to keep the integration of the In-Memory OLTP engine as seamless as possible. A simple filegroup addition is all it takes to be able to start creating memory-optimized objects. We are one step closer to a faster database, let's keep going.

Creating a table

Now that we have a filegroup/database that is ready for high-performance workloads, we need to take a moment and consider what limitations there are with the In-Memory OLTP engine.

The following data types are supported:

- All integer types—tinyint, smallint, int, and bigint
- All float types—float and real
- All money types—smallmoney and money
- Numeric and decimal
- All non-LOB string types—char(n), varchar(n), nchar(n), nvarchar(n), and sysname
- Non-LOB binary types—binary(n) and varbinary(n)

- Date/time types—`smalldatetime`, `datetime`, `date`, `time`, and `datetime2`
- Unique identifier

This leaves out the LOB data types, that is, XML, max types (for example, `varchar(max)`) and CLR types (remembering that this is valid for the initial implementation in SQL Server 2014). This also includes row lengths exceeding 8,060 bytes. This limit is generally not recommended, as it will cause issues even in regular tables. However, with memory-optimized tables we cannot even create a table whose row length exceeds 8,060 bytes.

Other than the data type limitations, the following restrictions also apply:

- No `FOREIGN KEY` or `CHECK` constraints
- No `UNIQUE` constraints (except for `PRIMARY KEY`)
- No DML Triggers
- A maximum of eight indexes (including the `PRIMARY KEY` index)
- No schema changes after table creation

More specifically to the last restriction, absolutely no DDL commands can be issued on a memory-optimized table: no `ALTER TABLE`, `CREATE INDEX`, or `ALTER INDEX`, `DROP INDEX`. Effectively, once you create a memory-optimized table, it is unchangeable.

So, with the bad news out of the way, let's create our first memory-optimized table. But before we do, we must note that memory-optimized tables cannot be created in system databases (including `tempdb`). If we attempt to do so, we will receive an error message:

```
Msg 41326, Level 16, State 1, Line 43
Memory optimized tables cannot be created in system databases.
```

The following code will therefore change the connection into the previously created `InMemoryTest` database and then create a test memory-optimized table:

```
 USE InMemoryTest
GO
CREATE TABLE InMemoryTable
(
   UserId INT NOT NULL PRIMARY KEY NONCLUSTERED,
   UserName VARCHAR(255) NOT NULL,
   LoginTime DATETIME2 NOT NULL,
   LoginCount INT NOT NULL,
CONSTRAINT PK_UserId PRIMARY KEY NONCLUSTERED (UserId),  INDEX NCL_IDX HASH
(UserName) WITH (BUCKET_COUNT=10000)
) WITH (MEMORY_OPTIMIZED = ON, DURABILITY=SCHEMA_AND_DATA)
GO
```

Let's consider a few of the previous lines of code. Firstly, the table creation command resembles that of many other tables that can be created in SQL Server. We are not confronted with anything unfamiliar. Only in the last two lines of code do we notice anything peculiar. We have the previously mentioned hash index, with a bucket count of 10,000 on the `UserName` column. The last line of code has two new keywords: `MEMORY_OPTIMIZED=ON`, is simple enough— we are informing SQL Server that this table should be created as a memory-optimized table. However, the `DURABILITY` keyword is something that we have only tangentially mentioned so far.

The durability options available to us are either `SCHEMA_AND_DATA` or `SCHEMA_ONLY`. These keyword options are clear enough to understand. Either the schema *and* the data will be recovered after a server restart, or only the schema. With `SCHEMA_ONLY` we have the ability to completely bypass writing data changes to the transaction log, because our memory-optimized table has no requirements in terms of data recovery. This has a major positive performance impact if the data in a `SCHEMA_ONLY` table meets the requirement of not needing recovery.

After making our decisions about columns, indexes, and the durability of our table, we issue the `CREATE TABLE` command. At this point, SQL Server receives the command and generates the table as a memory-optimized object. This results in a compiled DLL being created for the memory-optimized table, including the compiled access methods for the memory-resident object. This compilation process is the main factor in the limitations listed previously, especially the reason for alterations of the table and indexes *after* creation.

Querying and data manipulation

Now that we have a memory-optimized table, the next logical step is to start querying the table and manipulating the data stored inside it.

We have two methods of interacting with these memory-optimized objects. Firstly, we can issue standard T-SQL queries and allow the SQL Server Query Optimizer to deal with accessing this new type of table. The second method is to use natively compiled stored procedures:

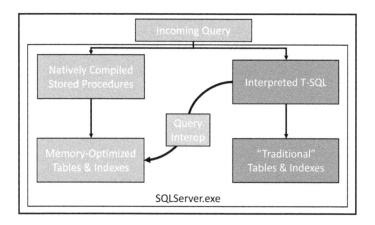

Overview of SQL Server engine illustrating Query Interop between In-Memory OLTP and normal OLTP

In the preceding figure, we can see a simplified diagram of a query that is either querying *normal* tables or memory-optimized tables. In the center of the diagram is a node titled **Query Interop**. This is a mechanism that is responsible for enabling *normal* interpreted T-SQL statements to access memory optimized tables. Please note that this is a one-way mechanism and that the natively compiled stored procedures are *not* able to access traditional objects, only memory-optimized objects.

Back to querying memory-optimized tables! Let's take a look at the following code:

```
SELECT *
FROM dbo.InMemoryTable;
```

This SELECT statement is standard T-SQL and has no special syntax to query the memory-optimized table we created earlier. At this point, we are unaware that this table is a memory-optimized table and that is a good thing. This is further proof of Microsoft's commitment to integrating this high-performance feature as a seamless extension of the storage engine. Essentially, it should not be of major interest whether we are using In-Memory OLTP or the traditional storage engine for our table—it should just be fast. We could even extrapolate that, in future, it may be possible that the entire SQL Server storage engine becomes purely memory-optimized.

If we can select data without any syntax changes, then we can expect that inserting data is equally simple, as you can see from the following code:

```
INSERT INTO dbo.InMemoryTable
        ( UserId ,
          UserName ,
          LoginTime ,
          LoginCount
```

```
            )
VALUES   ( 1 ,
            'John Smith' ,
            SYSDATETIME() ,
            1
          )
;
SELECT *
FROM dbo.InMemoryTable
;
```

Of course, this insert works flawlessly and the final select returns a single row:

```
UserId        UserName       LoginTime            LoginCount
-----------   -------------  --------------------  ----------------------
1             John Smith     2016-12-09           20:27:04.3424133 1
```

The important thing to realize here is that we are using **normal** T-SQL. This may sound rather uninteresting; however, this means that if we want to start migrating some of our tables to be memory-optimized, then we are free to do so without needing to refactor our code (provided we adhere to the limitations of the engine). This makes the possibilities of using this feature much more attractive, especially in legacy projects where logical design limitations are leading to locking and latching issues.

Due to the way that this interoperability works and the lock-free nature of memory-optimized tables, there are some further limitations with the T-SQL language and querying itself that we need to consider. Luckily, the large majority of T-SQL language features are available to us, so the list of unsupported commands is mercifully short:

- The MERGE statement when a memory-optimized table is the target of the MERGE
- Dynamic cursors (to adhere to memory-optimized rules; these are automatically changed to static cursors)
- TRUNCATE TABLE
- Cross database transactions
- Cross database queries
- Linked servers
- Locking hints—XLOCK, TABLOCK, PAGLOCK, and others
- READUNCOMMITTED, READCOMMITTED, and READCOMMITTEDLOCK isolation level hints

If we consider how each of these unsupported features work, it becomes clear that these limitations exist. Many, if not all, of these limitations are linked to how locking and latching is controlled in one way or another with those features. The only way to continue our high-performance adventure is to accept these limitations and adjust our system design accordingly.

There is a similar list of limitations for natively compiled stored procedures. This list is unfortunately quite a bit longer, and if we look back at figure *Overview of SQL Server engine illustrating Query Interop between In-Memory OLTP and normal OLTP* with the diagram of the SQL Server engine, we see that natively compiled stored procedures are only able to access memory-optimized tables and *not* the traditional storage engine objects. This main limitation causes the list of unsupported features to be quite a lot longer. You can find an exhaustive list of which features are supported and which aren't by visiting Microsoft's Books Online site and reading the list. You will be able to also change the documentation website to a different version of SQL Server to see that newer versions support an increasing number of features inside the In-Memory OLTP engine.

The official Microsoft website for In-Memory OLTP
is: `https://msdn.microsoft.com/en-us/library/dn246937(v=sql.120).aspx#Anchor_4`.

Performance comparisons

We have seen the lists of limitations at both the table structure level and at the T-SQL language level, it is not all doom and gloom, but these restrictions may be causing some readers to re-think their enthusiasm for memory-optimized objects.

In this section, we will take a look at how traditional disk-based tables compare to their younger brothers, the memory-optimized tables. According to the codename of the In-Memory OLTP feature, Hekaton (Greek for a 100-fold), the new feature should be in the order of 100x faster.

We begin our test by creating a comparable disk-based table and inserting one row into it:

```
USE InMemoryTest
GO
CREATE TABLE DiskBasedTable
(
    UserId INT NOT NULL PRIMARY KEY NONCLUSTERED,
    UserName VARCHAR(255) NOT NULL,
    LoginTime DATETIME2 NOT NULL,
```

```
    LoginCount INT NOT NULL,

    INDEX NCL_IDX NONCLUSTERED (UserName)
)
GO
INSERT INTO dbo.DiskBasedTable
        ( UserId ,
          UserName ,
          LoginTime ,
          LoginCount
        )
VALUES  ( 1 ,
          'John Smith' ,
          SYSDATETIME() ,
          1
        )
;
```

We have an identical table structure, with the only difference being that the disk-based table doesn't have a hash index, but rather a normal non-clustered index.

We will now run a test, inserting 500,000 rows of data into each table, measuring solely the execution time of each run. We begin by creating a stored procedure that will insert one row into the disk-based table:

```
CREATE PROCEDURE dbo.DiskBasedInsert
    @UserId INT,
    @UserName VARCHAR(255),
    @LoginTime DATETIME2,
    @LoginCount INT
AS
BEGIN

    INSERT dbo.DiskBasedTable
    (UserId, UserName, LoginTime, LoginCount)
    VALUES
    (@UserId, @UserName, @LoginTime, @LoginCount);

END;
```

This stored procedure is then called 500,000 times in a simple loop and the time difference between start and finish is recorded:

```
USE InMemoryTest
GO
TRUNCATE TABLE dbo.DiskBasedTable
GO

DECLARE @start DATETIME2;
SET @start = SYSDATETIME();

DECLARE @Counter int = 0,
        @_LoginTime DATETIME2 = SYSDATETIME(),
        @_UserName VARCHAR(255);
   WHILE @Counter < 50000
   BEGIN
        SET @_UserName = 'UserName ' + CAST(@Counter AS varchar(6))

        EXECUTE dbo.DiskBasedInsert
             @UserId = @Counter,
             @UserName = @_UserName,
             @LoginTime = @_LoginTime,
             @LoginCount = @Counter
        SET @Counter += 1;
   END;

SELECT DATEDIFF(ms, @start, SYSDATETIME()) AS 'insert into disk-based table
(in ms)';
GO

insert into disk-based table (in ms)
------------ -------------- ---------------------------- -----------
6230
```

The execution on my machine was repeatable with an average execution time between 6 and 7 seconds for 50,000 rows with a disk-based table.

The first step of optimizing this insert is to move from a disk-based table to a memory-optimized table:

```
USE InMemoryTest
GO
SET NOCOUNT ON
GO
CREATE PROCEDURE dbo.InMemoryInsert
    @UserId INT,
    @UserName VARCHAR(255),
```

```
        @LoginTime DATETIME2,
        @LoginCount INT
AS
BEGIN

        INSERT dbo.InMemoryTable
        (UserId, UserName, LoginTime, LoginCount)
        VALUES
        (@UserId, @UserName, @LoginTime, @LoginCount);

END;
GO


USE InMemoryTest
GO
DELETE FROM dbo.InMemoryTable
GO


DECLARE @start DATETIME2;
SET @start = SYSDATETIME();

DECLARE @Counter int = 0,
        @_LoginTime DATETIME2 = SYSDATETIME(),
        @_UserName VARCHAR(255);
    WHILE @Counter < 50000
    BEGIN
        SET @_UserName = 'UserName ' + CAST(@Counter AS varchar(6))

        EXECUTE dbo.InMemoryInsert
            @UserId = @Counter,
            @UserName = @_UserName,
            @LoginTime = @_LoginTime,
            @LoginCount = @Counter
        SET @Counter += 1;
    END;

SELECT DATEDIFF(ms, @start, SYSDATETIME()) AS 'insert into memory-optimized
table (in ms)';
GO

insert into memory-optimized table (in ms)
----------- ------------- ---------------------------- ------------
1399
```

OK, we have made a massive leap in terms of execution time. We are down from ~6 seconds to a quite respectable ~1.4 seconds. That improvement is purely down to the difference in locking and latching of our two tables. We swapped the disk-based table for a memory-optimized table.

Natively compiled stored procedures

When we issue T-SQL commands to SQL Server, the commands are parsed and compiled into machine code, which is then executed. This parsing and compiling becomes a major bottleneck when the locking and latching caused by pessimistic concurrency is removed. This is where natively compiled stored procedures come into play. They are effectively T-SQL code that is compiled into machine code once, and then instead of the parse and compile of a standard T-SQL command, the compiled DLL for the stored procedure is called. The improvements in execution time can be phenomenal.

Our next possibility of improvement is to reduce our parse and compile time of the insert command (the *Query Interop* mentioned earlier in this chapter). This can be achieved by natively compiling the insert stored procedure. Let's do just that, and run the same test with our memory-optimized table also using a natively compiled stored procedure:

```
USE InMemoryTest
GO
CREATE PROCEDURE dbo.InMemoryInsertOptimized
    @UserId INT,
    @UserName VARCHAR(255),
    @LoginTime DATETIME2,
    @LoginCount INT
WITH NATIVE_COMPILATION, SCHEMABINDING
AS
BEGIN ATOMIC WITH
(
    TRANSACTION ISOLATION LEVEL = SNAPSHOT,
    LANGUAGE = N'English'
)

    INSERT dbo.InMemoryTable
    (UserId, UserName, LoginTime, LoginCount)
     VALUES
     (@UserId, @UserName, @LoginTime, @LoginCount);
    RETURN 0;
END;
GO
```

```
USE InMemoryTest
GO
DELETE FROM dbo.InMemoryTable
GO

DECLARE @start DATETIME2;
SET @start = SYSDATETIME();

DECLARE @Counter int = 0,
        @_LoginTime DATETIME2 = SYSDATETIME(),
        @_UserName VARCHAR(255);
   WHILE @Counter < 50000
   BEGIN
        SET @_UserName = 'UserName ' + CAST(@Counter AS varchar(6))

        EXECUTE dbo.InMemoryInsertOptimized
             @UserId = @Counter,
             @UserName = @_UserName,
             @LoginTime = @_LoginTime,
             @LoginCount = @Counter
        SET @Counter += 1;
   END;

SELECT DATEDIFF(ms, @start, SYSDATETIME()) AS 'insert into memory-optimized
table & native stored procedure (in ms)';
GO
```

insert into memory-optimized table & native stored procedure (in ms)
----------- ------------- ---------------------------- -----------
631

We can see from the results that the execution time has been reduced from ~1.4 seconds down to ~600 milliseconds. This is an impressive improvement, considering we have again only made minimal changes.

However, there is *still* room for improvement here. At present, we have created a native compiled stored procedure, which allows us to save on compile time for the insert statement itself. With this solution, we are still using non-compiled T-SQL for the loop. This optimization is easily achieved and we can run the final test to see how fast we can get:

```
USE InMemoryTest
GOCREATE PROCEDURE dbo.FullyNativeInMemoryInsertOptimized
WITH NATIVE_COMPILATION, SCHEMABINDING
AS
BEGIN ATOMIC WITH
(
    TRANSACTION ISOLATION LEVEL = SNAPSHOT,
```

```
        LANGUAGE = N'English'
    )

    DECLARE @Counter int = 0,
    @_LoginTime DATETIME2 = SYSDATETIME(),
    @_UserName VARCHAR(255)
    ;
    WHILE @Counter < 50000
    BEGIN
                SET  @_UserName = 'UserName ' + CAST(@Counter AS varchar(6))

                INSERT dbo.InMemoryTable
                (UserId, UserName, LoginTime, LoginCount)
                VALUES
                (@Counter, @_UserName, @_LoginTime, @Counter);

        SET @Counter += 1;
    END;
    RETURN 0;
END;
GO

USE InMemoryTest
GO
DELETE FROM dbo.InMemoryTable
GO

DECLARE @start DATETIME2;
SET @start = SYSDATETIME();

EXEC dbo.FullyNativeInMemoryInsertOptimized

SELECT DATEDIFF(ms, @start, SYSDATETIME()) AS 'insert into fully native
memory-optimized table (in ms)';
GO
```

insert into fully native memory-optimized table (in ms)
------------ -------------- --------------------------- -----------
155

With a fully optimized workflow, taking advantage of both memory-optimized tables as well as natively compiled stored procedures, the execution time has dropped from 6.2 seconds to 155 milliseconds. With just a few simple steps, the execution time of the example insert has been reduced by 40 times. While not quite the 100-fold improvement that the codename suggests, this is a serious improvement by any measure.

Looking behind the curtain of concurrency

So far, we have seen that we can easily create a table with indexes, query, and insert data into that table with our traditional T-SQL knowledge. It is now also clear that we are able to change an existing implementation of disk-based tables into memory-optimized tables with some simple changes. If we want to push the performance to the max, we can also consider natively compiled stored procedures to further improve upon some quite large performance gains. We have also seen how the two types of index; hash index and non-clustered index, are implemented in the storage engine. However, to better understand how the magic happens, we need to have a closer look at what is happening to our sample table and indexes while we are manipulating them.

We already mentioned at the beginning of this chapter that SQL Server uses a pessimistic concurrency model in the disk-based storage engine and an optimistic concurrency model for the memory-optimized objects. The implementation of this optimistic concurrency model is achieved using a **Multi-Version Concurrency Control** (**MVCC**), or to describe it another way, snapshotting the data. MVCC is not a new technology; it has been around in one form or another since the early 1980s and has been an optional isolation level in SQL Server since SQL Server 2005 (READ COMMITTED SNAPSHOT). This technology has been repurposed in the In-Memory OLTP engine to allow for lock and latch-free optimistic concurrency. READ COMMITTED snapshot isolation level provides row versioning for disk-based tables by redirecting write operations into the row version store inside `tempdb`; however, In-Memory OLTP works entirely inside memory and cannot push row versions into `tempdb`.

If we take a look at our row header from the beginning of the chapter again, we can investigate the, **Begin Ts** and **End Ts** fields:

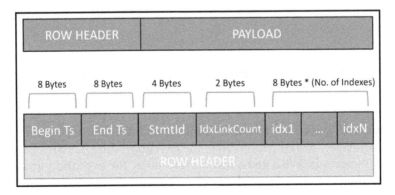

Memory-optimized table row structure—Header and Payload

When a row is inserted, the **Begin Ts** timestamp is filled. This timestamp is constructed from two pieces of information. The first is the transaction ID, which is a globally unique value on the instance. This value increments whenever a transaction starts on the instance and is reset when the server restarts. The second portion of this generated timestamp is created from the **Global Transaction Timestamp**. This is equally unique across the instance, but is *not* reset at server restart and increments whenever a transaction completes.

In order to avoid the requirement of locking records to update them, memory-optimized tables only ever add new records to a table. Whenever an insert occurs (the simplest change operation), a new row is added to a table, with a **Begin Ts** at the transaction start time. The **End Ts** is left empty, allowing SQL Server to know that this row exists inside the database from the **Begin Ts** and is valid until **End Ts** (or in the case of the row not being deleted, it is valid until *infinite*).

The interesting changes occur when we wish to update or delete an existing row. To avoid having to lock the row and perform a delete (for a pure delete) or a delete and insert (for an update), a memory-optimized table will simply insert the updated version of the row with a **Begin Ts** of the transaction timestamp and insert the same timestamp in the **End Ts** of the newly *deleted* row:

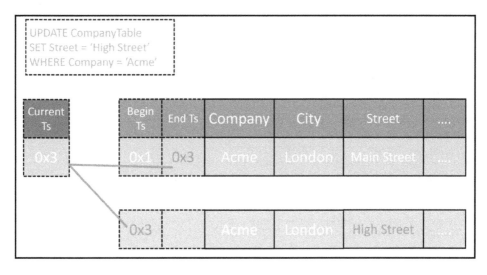

Update of a memory-optimized table—row versioning

In the preceding figure, we can see this behavior illustrated. The update statement in the top-left corner shows that an existing row (blue row) needs to be updated. The concurrency model then creates a new copy of the row (green) while noting the current transaction timestamp (orange). At this point, we have a new row which is valid from timestamp **0x3** and an old row that was valid from timestamp **0x1** until **0x3**. Any transaction that started at timestamp **0x2** would see the original row (blue), while any transaction from **0x3** onwards would see the new row (green).

As you may realize, the action of continually appending new versions of a row will cause this linked list of row versions to grow over time. This is where the GC comes into play. The GC is a background process which periodically traverses the tables and indexes in the In-Memory storage engine and removes the old and invalidated rows. In order to further accelerate this cleanup process, user processes also assist with identifying entries that can be cleaned up. When a user process scans across a table or index that has stale row version data, it will remove their links from the row chains as it passes them.

As with many features inside SQL Server, we can gain insight into the inner workings of this row version mechanism using **Dynamic Management Objects** (**DMOs**).

To take a look at the table we created previously and see the row version information, we query `sys.dm_db_xtp_index_stats` joining to `sys.indexes` to retrieve the corresponding object information:

```
SELECT i.name AS 'index_name',
    s.rows_returned,
    s.rows_expired,
    s.rows_expired_removed
FROM sys.dm_db_xtp_index_stats s
    JOIN sys.indexes i
        ON s.object_id = i.object_id
            AND s.index_id = i.index_id
WHERE OBJECT_ID('InMemoryTable') = s.object_id;
GO

index_name   rows_returned    rows_expired    rows_expired_removed
-----------  ---------------  --------------  ----------------
NULL         594115           0               0
NCL_IDX      0                0               0
PK_UserId    0                649901          399368
```

Here, we can see that after our data wrangling using the different methods, the table has rows added and also *expired* (detected as stale) or *expired removed* (how many rows have been unlinked from the index).

Data durability concerns

Now that we have a better understanding of how data moves inside a memory-optimized table, we need to also dive a little deeper into the durability of memory-optimized tables. Earlier in the chapter, we saw that we can choose between SCHEMA_AND_DATA or SCHEMA_ONLY for durability of these objects. The succinct description for SCHEMA_ONLY durability is that any data (or changes) inside a memory-optimized table that has SCHEMA_ONLY durability, will be lost when the server restarts. The reason for the server restart is irrelevant; when the server is brought back online, the table (and any associated indexes) is recreated and will be empty.

The SCHEMA_AND_DATA option informs SQL Server that you wish the data inside the memory-optimized table to be permanently stored on non-volatile storage. This will ensure that the data is available even after a server restart. This initially sounds like it would be a problem for a high-performance data processing system, especially when we consider the speed differences between mass storage (HDDs/SSDs) versus main system memory (DIMMs). However, the type and amount of data required to be stored on durable storage is kept to a minimum, so that the chances of a bottleneck in making the data durable are greatly reduced.

The data that gets written to disk contains only the data that has changed, and only the row data of the memory-optimized table and not the index data. Only the index definitions are stored durably, the index content is recreated every time the server is restarted. This recreation is rapid, because SQL Server can create the index based on the data that is already in main memory, which is extremely low latency and high throughput.

There are two streams of data processed and written to disk: *checkpoint streams* and *log streams*.

A checkpoint stream is itself split into two files, together known as **checkpoint file pairs** (**CFPs**). These CFPs utilize the filestream API which we addressed when creating our test In-Memory OLTP database. The two file types in this file pair are *data streams* (containing all row versions inserted in a timestamp interval) and *delta streams* (containing a list of deleted row versions matching the data stream file pair).

The *log streams* contain the changes made by committed transactions, and like *normal* transactions, are stored in the SQL Server transaction log. This allows SQL Server to use the entries in the transaction log to reconstruct information during the redo phase of crash recovery.

We can investigate the behavior of Durability, by running our insert stored procedures for the disk-based table and then our SCHEMA_ONLY memory-optimized table. After running each stored procedure we can then investigate the contents of the transaction log using the undocumented and unsupported (but on a test machine, perfectly usable) fn_dblog() to view how these two processes affect the transaction log:

	Current LSN	Operation	Context	Transaction ID	Log Record Fixed Length	Log Record Length	Previous LSN	Flag Bits	Log Reserve	AllocUnitId	AllocUnitName
1	00000058:00001a35:0005	LOP_COMMIT_XACT	LCX_NULL	0000:002700d3	80	84	00000058:00001a35:0001	0x0002	90	NULL	NULL
2	00000058:00001a35:0004	LOP_INSERT_ROWS	LCX_INDEX_LEAF	0000:002700d3	62	116	00000058:00001a35:0003	0x0002	74	72057594048544768	dbo.DiskBasedTable.PK_
3	00000058:00001a35:0003	LOP_INSERT_ROWS	LCX_INDEX_LEAF	0000:002700d3	62	128	00000058:00001a35:0002	0x0002	74	72057594048479232	dbo.DiskBasedTable.NCL
4	00000058:00001a35:0002	LOP_INSERT_ROWS	LCX_HEAP	0000:002700d3	62	132	00000058:00001a35:0001	0x0002	178	72057594048413696	dbo.DiskBasedTable
5	00000058:00001a35:0001	LOP_BEGIN_XACT	LCX_NULL	0000:002700d3	76	124	00000000:00000000:0000	0x0002	9436	NULL	NULL
6	00000058:00001a33:0005	LOP_COMMIT_XACT	LCX_NULL	0000:002700d2	80	84	00000058:00001a33:0001	0x0002	90	NULL	NULL
7	00000058:00001a33:0004	LOP_INSERT_ROWS	LCX_INDEX_LEAF	0000:002700d2	62	116	00000058:00001a33:0003	0x0002	74	72057594048544768	dbo.DiskBasedTable.PK
8	00000058:00001a33:0003	LOP_INSERT_ROWS	LCX_INDEX_LEAF	0000:002700d2	62	128	00000058:00001a33:0002	0x0002	74	72057594048479232	dbo.DiskBasedTable.NCL
9	00000058:00001a33:0002	LOP_INSERT_ROWS	LCX_HEAP	0000:002700d2	62	132	00000058:00001a33:0001	0x0002	178	72057594048413696	dbo.DiskBasedTable
10	00000058:00001a33:0001	LOP_BEGIN_XACT	LCX_NULL	0000:002700d2	76	124	00000000:00000000:0000	0x0002	9436	NULL	NULL
11	00000058:00001a31:0005	LOP_COMMIT_XACT	LCX_NULL	0000:002700d1	80	84	00000058:00001a31:0001	0x0002	90	NULL	NULL
12	00000058:00001a31:0004	LOP_INSERT_ROWS	LCX_INDEX_LEAF	0000:002700d1	62	116	00000058:00001a31:0003	0x0002	74	72057594048544768	dbo.DiskBasedTable.PK
13	00000058:00001a31:0003	LOP_INSERT_ROWS	LCX_INDEX_LEAF	0000:002700d1	62	128	00000058:00001a31:0002	0x0002	74	72057594048479232	dbo.DiskBasedTable.NCL
14	00000058:00001a31:0002	LOP_INSERT_ROWS	LCX_HEAP	0000:002700d1	62	132	00000058:00001a31:0001	0x0002	178	72057594048413696	dbo.DiskBasedTable
15	00000058:00001a31:0001	LOP_BEGIN_XACT	LCX_NULL	0000:002700d1	76	124	00000000:00000000:0000	0x0002	9436	NULL	NULL
16	00000058:00001a2f:0005	LOP_COMMIT_XACT	LCX_NULL	0000:002700d0	80	84	00000058:00001a2f:0001	0x0002	90	NULL	NULL
17	00000058:00001a2f:0004	LOP_INSERT_ROWS	LCX_INDEX_LEAF	0000:002700d0	62	116	00000058:00001a2f:0003	0x0002	74	72057594048544768	dbo.DiskBasedTable.PK

fn_dblog() output after disk-based insert run

The output after the memory-optimized insert is as follows:

	Current LSN	Operation	Context	Transaction ID	Log Record Fixed Length	Log Record Length	Previous LSN	Flag Bits	Log Reserve	AllocUnitId	AllocUnitName
1	00000058:00001a4f:0002	LOP_HK	LCX_NULL	0000:00000000	28	152	00000000:00000000:0000	0x0000	0	NULL	NULL
2	00000058:00001a4f:0001	LOP_HK	LCX_NULL	0000:00000000	28	88	00000000:00000000:0000	0x0000	0	NULL	NULL
3	00000058:00001a4e:0001	LOP_END_CKPT	LCX_NULL	0000:00000000	136	136	00000058:00001a4c:0001	0x0000	0	NULL	NULL
4	00000058:00001a4d:0001	LOP_XACT_CKPT	LCX_BOOT_PAGE_CKPT	0000:00000000	24	28	00000000:00000000:0000	0x0000	0	NULL	NULL
5	00000058:00001a4c:0001	LOP_BEGIN_CKPT	LCX_NULL	0000:00000000	96	96	00000058:00001a37:002c	0x0000	0	NULL	NULL
6	00000058:00001a4b:0002	LOP_HK	LCX_NULL	0000:00000000	28	152	00000000:00000000:0000	0x0000	0	NULL	NULL

fn_dblog() output after memory-optimized insert run

In the preceding screenshots, we see a snapshot of the data retrieved immediately after running first the disk-based insert (figure *fn_dblog() output after disk-based insert run*) and the memory-optimized insert (figure *fn_dblog() output after disk-based insert run*). The disk-based insert created thousands of log record entries for each iteration of the loop. This takes time to process and inflates the transaction log unnecessarily. The memory-optimized insert causes zero entries in the transaction log, because the table was defined as SCHEMA_ONLY, and as such has no requirement for log redo or crash recovery. The schema will be loaded at server startup and will be immediately ready for normal operations.

We can now take a look at our `filestream` folder, where the checkpoint stream is directed. We will find multiple checkpoint files in this folder. Each checkpoint file will contain either data or delta streams, as described earlier in this section of the chapter. The checkpoint files are created and filled with an append-only mechanism, adding data to the end of the file. A single checkpoint file pair will continue to be used until either a manual CHECKPOINT command is used, or 512 MB of transaction information has accumulated since the last automatic checkpoint. When this occurs, the checkpoint process generates a checkpoint file inventory of multiple data and delta files, this inventory file catalogues the data and delta files and writes this information to the transaction log. These files are used in a recovery scenario to be able to reconstruct data for SCHEMA_AND_DATA defined memory-optimized tables:

Name	Type	Size
> This PC > OS (C:) > Temp > InMemoryTest_inmem > $HKv2		
{659C3B5A-93DD-4036-B9CB-198916371D65}.hkckp	HKCKP File	65,536 KB
{45078208-9E87-46E1-844C-ABE566F1B42E}.hkckp	HKCKP File	65,536 KB
{BB5D2943-DED2-474A-9B27-8F891BDA9B56}.hkckp	HKCKP File	65,536 KB
{BCBB7428-00DE-4E07-921C-64EC96557BDB}.hkckp	HKCKP File	16,384 KB
{23EB0035-BF08-43D8-8A64-853A385045A9}.hkckp	HKCKP File	16,384 KB
{025CFA00-4A01-43E1-8E8F-B84228B081C5}.hkckp	HKCKP File	131,072 KB
{EE7C6290-8A4D-4E1E-96E1-28E3A0FE8E1F}.hkckp	HKCKP File	16,384 KB
{4B3A1792-7CDB-4CBD-AC02-EC31E23DC8BF}.hkckp	HKCKP File	131,072 KB
{717E9794-AECB-48C8-B8E1-137C5370F0F8}.hkckp	HKCKP File	131,072 KB
{B7BBE7E7-3D17-4C6F-8CEE-F5502FAE2171}.hkckp	HKCKP File	8,192 KB

Filestream folder used for storing memory-optimized checkpoint file pairs

Database startup and recovery

Recovery of memory-optimized tables is performed in an optimized manner compared to disk-based tables.

The In-Memory OLTP engine gathers information on which checkpoints are currently valid and their locations. Each checkpoint file pair (delta and data) is identified, and the delta file is used to filter out rows from the data file (delete data doesn't need to be recovered). The In-Memory OLTP engine creates one recovery thread per CPU core, allowing for parallel recovery of memory-optimized tables. These recovery threads load the data from the data and delta files, creating the schema and all indexes. Once the checkpoint files have been processed, the tail of the transaction log is replayed from the timestamp of the latest valid checkpoint.

The ability to process recovery in parallel is a huge performance gain and allows objects that are memory-optimized to be recovered in a much shorter time than if only serial recovery was available.

Management of In-Memory objects

Managing memory-optimized tables is similar to disk-based tables. SQL Server Management Studio provides a full syntax and GUI support for memory-optimized tables. There is a long list of DMOs that provide detailed insights into each aspect of the feature, but also the legacy management objects such as `sys.tables` or `sys.indexes` have also received some updates to include pertinent memory-optimized information.

Dynamic management objects

The DMOs concerned with the In-Memory OLTP engine all have **eXtreme Transaction Processing (XTP)** in their name:

- `sys.dm_db_xtp_checkpoint_stats`
- `sys.dm_db_xtp_checkpoint_files`
- `sys.dm_db_xtp_gc_cycles_stats`
- `sys.dm_xtp_gc_stats`
- `sys.dm_xtp_system_memory_consumers`
- `sys.dm_xtp_threads`
- `sys.dm_xtp_transaction_stats`
- `sys.dm_db_xtp_index_stats`
- `sys.dm_db_xtp_memory_consumers`

- `sys.dm_db_xtp_object_stats`
- `sys.dm_db_xtp_transactions`
- `sys.dm_db_xtp_table_memory_stats`

Full details to the columns and meanings for each DMO can be found in Microsoft Books Online (`https://msdn.microsoft.com/library/dn133203(SQL.130).aspx`).

Extended events

As with all new features inside SQL Server, In-Memory OLTP also provides Extended Events session details. There is an extensive set of events that can be captured by Extended Events. Using the Extended Events Wizard will allow you to easily choose which events you wish to collect. Extended Events is the preferred method for collecting internal system information on any feature of SQL Server (where possible). Extended Events is a lightweight collection framework that allows you to collect system runtime statistics while keeping resource usage to a minimum.

A T-SQL query to return a list of the Extended Events that are available for the In-Memory OLTP engine would be:

```
SELECT p.name,
    o.name,
    o.description
FROM sys.dm_xe_objects o
    JOIN sys.dm_xe_packages p
        ON o.package_guid = p.guid
WHERE p.name = 'XtpEngine';
```

PerfMon counters

SQL Server also provides perfmon counters for the In-Memory OLTP engine; however, PerfMon is a much older technology than Extended Events and has certain limitations that prevent it from exposing all the details that Extended Events can. Be that as it may, it is still possible to collect certain information on the In-Memory OLTP engine.

A T-SQL query to return a list of the PerfMon counters that are available for the In-Memory OLTP engine would be:

```
SELECT object_name,
    counter_name
FROM sys.dm_os_performance_counters
WHERE object_name LIKE '%XTP%';
```

Assistance in migrating to In-Memory OLTP

Now that we have explored the possibilities that memory-optimized tables offer, it would be fantastic to be able to somehow evaluate our existing databases. Ideally this evaluation would show how many tables or stored procedures could potentially be converted from traditional disk-based objects into ultra-fast memory-optimized objects.

Luckily for us, Microsoft has also provided us with some help here too. Inside SQL Server Management Studio are two interesting standard reports that help us to analyze our databases and see how we can benefit from the memory-optimized objects.

The first report is the **Transaction Performance Analysis Overview**. This report allows us to quickly identify possible candidates for a move from disk-based to memory-optimized. We can reach this report by navigating through SQL Server Management Studio, shown as follows:

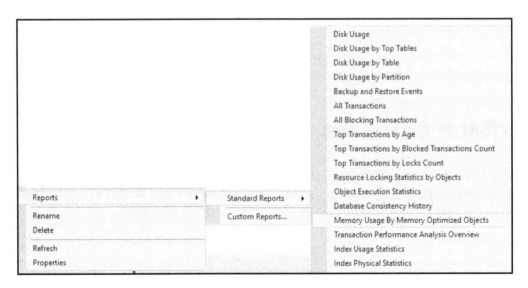

Transaction Performance Analysis Overview Report in SQL Server Management Studio

Once we select the standard **Transaction Performance Analysis Overview** report, we are greeted with a start page asking whether we want to evaluate tables or stored procedures. Our example queries are focused on tables, so choosing **Tables Analysis** will give us a little sample data for illustration purposes:

Transaction Performance Analysis Overview

[InMemoryTest]   SQL Server

This report helps you identify bottlenecks in your database and provide assistance to migrate them to In-Memory OLTP. The estimated migration effort is based on the SQL Server 2014 feature set. To begin, choose an option from below to see the report.

This server has been continuously operating since 18/12/2016 15:47:13

Tables Analysis

Stored Procedure Analysis

Transaction Performance Analysis Overview Report

Clicking on **Tables Analysis** brings up a detailed report of all tables in the database that are eligible candidates for a migration to memory-optimized tables.

As the report states, eligible candidate tables are shown on this report. The higher up and the further to the right of the table, the higher the recommendation for a conversion to a memory-optimized table. Based on our sample queries, it should be no surprise that the table called `DiskBasedTable` is an ideal candidate for memory-optimized storage. The data types are perfect, the behavior of the data movement is ideal. There is pretty much no reason at this point to not migrate this table to the In-Memory OLTP engine:

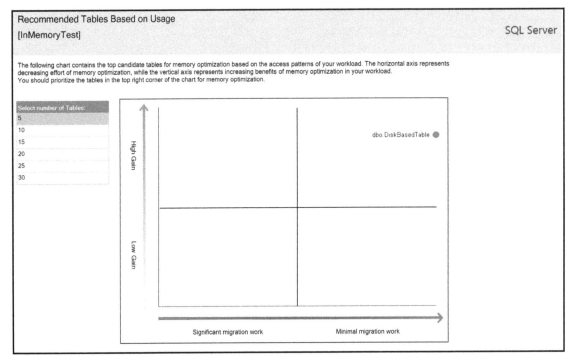

In-Memory OLTP Table analysis report

A further click on the table name pulls up a report based on the table itself, providing details on lock and latch statistics for the table, along with recommendations on what indexes are currently available and what index these should be migrated into (either hash or non-clustered):

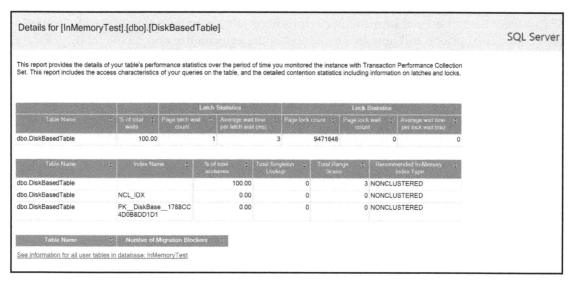

Table-level report for the Transaction Performance Analysis Overview

Summary

In this chapter, we have taken a look at the In-Memory OLTP engine, which was introduced in SQL Server 2014. Along the way, we have investigated how the In-Memory OLTP differs from the traditional SQL Server storage engine with respect to the concurrency model. The main difference is the ability to allow multiple concurrent users to access the data structure without relying on the pessimistic concurrency model of using locking and latching to uphold data isolation within transactions.

We continued our journey by exploring what T-SQL constructs and data types the In-Memory OLTP engine can support in the first version of the feature inside SQL Server 2014. At the same time, we were able to find out that although there are limitations, there is still a wide range of available data types and programming approaches that can be used immediately. Especially exciting is the fact that the T-SQL language receives (almost) transparent support for the powerful new capabilities. Memory-optimized tables appear at first glance to be just normal tables that somehow process data at a much higher rate than normal.

The chapter then discussed how memory-optimized tables can take advantage of different data durability options and how this can affect both performance and recoverability of data. The new storage engine provides solutions that were previously impossible in the traditional storage engine.

We rounded off the first encounter with the In-Memory OLTP engine with a discussion around how the internals of the storage engine work. We also saw how to interrogate the system using different methods to explore how data flows through the In-Memory OLTP engine.

Finally, we also had a glimpse at a useful migration assistant that can help in the preparation or identification of objects in existing databases that are possible candidates for a migration into the In-Memory OLTP engine.

12
In-Memory OLTP Improvements in SQL Server 2017

When In-Memory OLTP was introduced in SQL Server 2014, many developers were initially excited. The hope of a new, ultra-high-performance data processing engine, coupled with a leading relational database engine, offered the potential of significant improvement for many SQL Server developers. However, this excitement quickly turned into mild disappointment due to the number of restrictions assigned to In-Memory OLTP. Many of these restrictions prevented a widespread adoption of the technology and forced it into a niche set of very tight implementation scenarios. Some of these restrictions, such as minimal support for **large data object types** (**LOBs**) and missing support for ALTER commands, dampened many people's enthusiasm for the technology.

As with previous features inside SQL Server, In-Memory OLTP has followed a similar pattern. SQL Server 2014 saw the introduction of the In-Memory OLTP Engine. With SQL Server 2016 and again in 2017, the feature has experienced an evolution: many of the restrictions that were present in SQL Server 2014 have been removed and existing functionality has been extended. In this chapter, we will take a look at the improvements that should now make In-Memory OLTP attractive to almost every developer out there.

This chapter will demonstrate these improvements and additions (many of which were made available in SQL Server 2016), including altering existing memory-optimized objects, expanded data type support, expanded functionality/reduced limitations, and the integration of In-Memory OLTP into other areas of the database engine.

We will cover the following topics in this chapter:

- Ch-Ch-Changes
- Feature improvements
- Improvements in the In-Memory OLTP Engine

Ch-Ch-Changes

It's not only the legend that is Mr. David Bowie who sings about changes. In SQL Server 2014, we were destined to create In-Memory OLTP objects that were unchangeable after creation. If we needed to change the structure of a memory-optimized table, we had to resort to dropping and re-creating the object with the new, updated structure.

For many developers and customers, this was a deal breaker. Being able to add and remove columns or indexes is something that every SQL Server developer is used to being able to do without any restriction. With the advent of agile software development and similar development strategies such as continuous integration, being able to make changes to a software application is something many developers look for.

Now it is possible to do just that. We will be continuing this chapter with the same database as in Chapter 11, *Introducing SQL Server In-Memory OLTP*. We will use the following code to create a simple memory-optimized table, shown as follows:

```
USE master
GO
CREATE DATABASE InMemoryTest
    ON
    PRIMARY(NAME = [InMemoryTest_disk],
                FILENAME = 'C:tempInMemoryTest_disk.mdf', size=100MB),
    FILEGROUP [InMemoryTest_inmem] CONTAINS MEMORY_OPTIMIZED_DATA
                (NAME = [InMemoryTest_inmem],
                FILENAME = 'C:tempInMemoryTest_inmem')
   LOG ON (name = [InMemoryTest_log],
Filename='c:tempInMemoryTest_log.ldf', size=100MB)
   COLLATE Latin1_General_100_BIN2;
GO
USE InMemoryTest
GO
CREATE TABLE InMemoryTable
(
   UserId INT NOT NULL,
   UserName VARCHAR(20) COLLATE Latin1_General_CI_AI NOT NULL,
   LoginTime DATETIME2 NOT NULL,
```

```
      LoginCount INT NOT NULL,
      CONSTRAINT PK_UserId  PRIMARY KEY NONCLUSTERED (UserId),
      INDEX HSH_UserName HASH (UserName) WITH (BUCKET_COUNT=10000)
) WITH (MEMORY_OPTIMIZED = ON, DURABILITY=SCHEMA_AND_DATA);
GO
INSERT INTO dbo.InMemoryTable
        ( UserId, UserName , LoginTime, LoginCount )
VALUES ( 1, 'Mickey Mouse', '2016-01-01', 1 );
GO
```

The list of supported ALTER statements for a table in SQL Server 2017 are as follows:

- Changing, adding, and removing columns
- Adding and removing indexes
- Adding and removing constraints
- Changing the bucket count
- sp_rename is fully supported to memory-optimized tables

First up, we will add a column to the demo table, as shown in the following code. Note how the DDL statement is no different to adding a column to a disk-based table:

```
USE InMemoryTest;
GO
ALTER TABLE dbo.InMemoryTable ADD NewColumn INT NULL;
GO
```

We can also remove columns too, using the following code. Here the DDL has also not changed:

```
USE InMemoryTest;
GO
ALTER TABLE dbo.InMemoryTable DROP COLUMN NewColumn;
GO
```

We are also able to add indexes after a table has already been created, using the following code:

```
 USE InMemoryTest;
GO
ALTER TABLE dbo.InMemoryTable ADD INDEX HSH_LoginTime NONCLUSTERED HASH
(LoginTime) WITH (BUCKET_COUNT = 250);
GO
```

Until now, the DDL statements looked normal. However, adding an index to a memory-optimized table is performed using ALTER TABLE, rather than CREATE INDEX. The same can be said for dropping an index or altering an index:

```
USE InMemoryTest;
GO
ALTER TABLE dbo.InMemoryTable ALTER INDEX HSH_LoginTime REBUILD WITH
(BUCKET_COUNT=10000);
GO
ALTER TABLE dbo.InMemoryTable DROP INDEX HSH_LoginTime;
GO
```

In the last chapter, we discovered that the indexes on a memory-optimized table are the Bw-tree linked lists that provide us with an access path to the memory pages of the *actual* data in a memory-optimized table. As such, they are more an extension of the table definition (similar to constraints), rather than an index on a disk-based table. This is reflected in the requirement of issuing an ALTER TABLE command to add, remove, or alter an index on a memory-optimized table.

Altering the bucket count of an index (as shown in the preceding listing) is quite interesting. We always strive to implement new code with the plan of ensuring it is fit for purpose *before* we deploy to production. We also know that the first implementation of code rarely survives the first encounter with production usage. Predicting the correct bucket count is like predicting the future: the more information we have, the better our predictions can be, but who has full knowledge of how a new feature will be used? It is nearly impossible to get a 1:1 comparison of production to a development environment. As such, changing the bucket count is something that we will more than likely need to do. Later in this chapter we will be looking at the internal aspect of indexing memory-optimized tables, and will cover bucket counts in more detail.

To rename a memory-optimized table, we issue a simple sp_rename command, as shown in the following code:

```
USE InMemoryTest
GO

sp_rename 'dbo.InMemoryTable','InMemoryTable2'
GO
sp_rename 'dbo.InMemoryTable2','InMemoryTable'
```

A further interesting addition is the ability to bundle multiple changes (specifically, multiple change types: columns and indexes) together in one ALTER statement, using the following code:

```
USE InMemoryTest
GO
ALTER TABLE dbo.InMemoryTable
ADD ANewColumn INT NULL,
    AnotherColumn TINYINT NULL,
INDEX HSH_ANewColumn NONCLUSTERED HASH (ANewColumn) WITH (BUCKET_COUNT =
250);
```

Adding multiple columns was possible in previous versions of SQL Server, but the ability to add an index in the same statement is new. This has to do with how the In-Memory OLTP engine creates and manages memory-optimized objects in general. In Chapter 11, *Introducing SQL Server In-Memory OLTP*, we discovered that memory-optimized objects are memory resident objects with matching access methods (in fact, compiled C code). Indexes for memory-optimized tables are part of the memory-optimized table insomuch as they require the C constructs and access methods to ensure that the SQL Server can work with them. Because these objects require compilation into machine code, they are somewhat static—even with the new ability to issue ALTER commands to them.

To overcome this logical limitation of unchangeable compiled code, SQL Server receives the desired changes inside the ALTER statement and proceeds to create a new version of the existing object. Upon creation of this copy, the desired changes are incorporated into the new version. If the object being changed is a table, the rows from the old version are then copied to the new version. The background process then compiles the access methods (including the changed columns) and the new version is ready for use. At this point, SQL Server dereferences the old version and redirects future calls to the new version.

As the ALTER command of a table requires that the entire contents of a table be copied from the old version to the new version, we must be mindful of the fact that we are doubling the memory requirements for the table for the duration of the ALTER transaction (and until the background garbage collection has cleaned up the old structure). Equally, ALTER commands for memory-optimized tables are *offline* operations. This means that the memory-optimized table is blocked for the duration of the ALTER transaction.

As such, if we are manipulating a large table, we must ensure that we have enough memory available for the operation to succeed and understand that the table will be blocked for the duration of the transaction. It may, therefore, be prudent to consider emptying extremely large tables *before* issuing the ALTER command, in order to allow the change to complete quicker.

Many `ALTER` statements require meta-data changes only. These types of changes are able to be processed in parallel and have a reduced impact on the transaction log. When only meta-data changes need to be processed, only those changes are processed through the transaction log. Coupled with parallel processing, we can expect the execution of those meta-data changes to be extremely fast.

However, parallel processing is *excluded* for a few operations that require more than simple meta-data changes; these are as follows:

- Altering or adding a column to use a LOB type such as `nvarchar(max)`, `varchar(max)`, or `varbinary(max)`
- Adding or dropping a `COLUMNSTORE` index
- Almost anything that affects an off-row column:
    - Causing an on-row column to move off-row
    - Causing an off-row column to move on-row
    - Creating a new off-row column
    - Exception—Lengthening an already off-row column that has been logged in the optimized way

As well as serial processing being forced for the operations listed, making changes to these data types causes a complete copy of the table to be processed and copied into the transaction log; this can cause the transaction log to fill up and may produce extra load on the storage sub-system.

The removal of restrictions on altering tables extends to altering natively compiled stored procedures. The well-known `ALTER PROCEDURE` command can now be used to make changes to the previously created natively compiled stored procedures (this demo code creates the stored procedure with no content to allow the `ALTER` statement to then be run):

```
USE InMemoryTest
GO
CREATE PROCEDURE dbo.InMemoryInsertOptimized
    @UserId INT,
    @UserName VARCHAR(255),
    @LoginTime DATETIME2,
    @LoginCount INT
WITH NATIVE_COMPILATION, SCHEMABINDING
AS
BEGIN ATOMIC WITH
(
    TRANSACTION ISOLATION LEVEL = SNAPSHOT,
    LANGUAGE = N'English'
```

```
)
    RETURN 0;
END;
GO

ALTER PROCEDURE dbo.InMemoryInsertOptimized
    @UserId INT,
    @UserName VARCHAR(255),
    @LoginTime DATETIME2,
    @LoginCount INT
WITH NATIVE_COMPILATION, SCHEMABINDING, EXECUTE AS OWNER
AS
BEGIN ATOMIC WITH
(
    TRANSACTION ISOLATION LEVEL = SNAPSHOT,
    LANGUAGE = N'English'
)
    -- Add an Insert
    INSERT dbo.InMemoryTable
    (UserId, UserName, LoginTime, LoginCount)
     VALUES
     (@UserId, @UserName, @LoginTime, @LoginCount);
    RETURN 0;
END;
GO
```

The following aspects of an existing natively compiled stored procedure can be changed using the ALTER PROCEDURE syntax:

- Parameters
- EXECUTE AS
- TRANSACTION ISOLATION LEVEL
- LANGUAGE
- DATEFIRST
- DATEFORMAT
- DELAYED_DURABILITY

However, it is important to note that using the ALTER command to turn a natively compiled stored procedure into one that is non-natively compiled, and vice versa, is *not supported*.

If we wish to make such a change, we are required to perform a DROP PROCEDURE and a CREATE PROCEDURE. This should make sense, as we are moving from In-Memory into the normal Relational Engine. As such, we are recreating these objects in their entirety to achieve the desired change. This also means that we have to consider that any permissions assigned to such an object need to be re-assigned at (re)creation time.

During the recompile process, when an ALTER command is issued, the old version of the natively compiled stored procedure can still be executed. Upon compilation of the altered stored procedure, the old version will be destroyed, and all subsequent calls of the stored procedure will use the new definition. This allows an ALTER command to be issued without causing long waiting periods, but may allow transactions to execute using potentially old code.

Feature improvements

While being able to alter existing objects without having to drop them first is a welcome improvement, many developers are more interested in being able to use data types and T-SQL syntax in the In-Memory OLTP engine that go beyond the basics. In SQL Server 2016 and 2017, we were presented with a great deal of extra support, as is typical with a feature that has matured beyond initial introduction. In this section of the chapter, we will take a look at what areas of the database engine are now supported in the In-Memory OLTP engine.

Collations

The first major addition is the fact that both memory-optimized tables and natively compiled stored procedures support all code pages and collations that SQL Server supports. The previous limitation of only a supporting a subset of collations otherwise available in SQL Server has been completely removed from the product (a newly supported collation has been used in the test table in the demo scripts in this chapter)

This improvement allows us to incorporate tables and stored procedures using the collations that we are used to, or have already used in our database designs.

Computed columns for greater performance

SQL Server 2017 brought further support for table design with the introduction of full support for computed columns, including the indexing of computed columns. All the rules of disk-based table computed columns apply to memory-optimized tables.

Types of data

SQL Server now supports the vast majority of data types in the In-Memory OLTP engine. In fact, the list of supported data types is now so long that it is easier to list the *unsupported* types instead. The data types that are currently *unsupported* are:

- Datetimeoffset
- Geography
- Geometry
- Hierarchyid
- Rowversion
- Xml
- Sql_variant

This means that (except for XML), **Large Binary Objects** (**LOBs**) are supported, and this covers the max data types varchar(max), nvarchar(max), and varbinary(max). This is great news, as there are many cases where disk-based tables that had only one LOB column, but multiple supported columns, were barred from the In-Memory OLTP engine.

LOB data type support is not limited to tables and indexes—it is now also possible to use LOB data types in memory-optimized stored procedures too. This will allow parameters to be passed into and out of natively compiled stored procedures.

Interestingly, as of SQL Server 2017, the JSON data type is supported. This is possible because JSON is not a native data type like XML, but is stored as nvarchar data, which is listed as a supported data type. This is yet another reason to accept JSON as a possible unstructured data storage type over XML in future SQL Server programming.

An exhaustive list of current In-Memory OLTP limitations can be found on Microsoft Books Online: https://msdn.microsoft.com/en-us/library/dn246937.aspx

What's new with indexes?

Indexing memory-optimized tables was quite restrictive in the initial version of the In-Memory OLTP engine. However, thus far in this chapter, we have seen that there have been a number of improvements (including adding, removing, and rebuilding indexes), but there are more to come!

It is now possible to define non-unique indexes with NULLable key columns for memory-optimized tables. The NULLability is something that is widely used, and the move towards parity between memory-optimized and disk-based indexes is continued here.

Similarly, it is possible to declare UNIQUE indexes (other than the primary key) for memory-optimized tables.

We will take a deeper look at indexing later on in this chapter in the section titled, *Down the index rabbit-hole*.

Unconstrained integrity

Referential integrity and data integrity are important foundational rules within relational databases. The In-Memory OLTP engine introduced an extremely limited set of constraints that could be used in SQL Server 2014. This meant that solutions had to widely forgo many expectations of assigning referential and data integrity to memory-optimized tables.

Starting with SQL Server 2016, it is now possible to implement the following referential and data integrity rules for memory-optimized tables:

- FOREIGN KEY constraints (between memory-optimized tables)
- CHECK constraints
- DEFAULT constraints
- UNIQUE constraints
- AFTER triggers for INSERT, UPDATE, and DELETE operations; triggers for memory-optimized tables must be created using WITH NATIVE_COMPILATION so that the trigger is natively compiled at creation time

These changes will now allow developers to create tables with some semblance of sane referential and data integrity rules (such as they are used to with disk-based tables).

Not all operators are created equal

While the number of commands that are supported for natively compiled T-SQL in SQL Server 2017 has expanded, unfortunately, a significant number of the most powerful T-SQL commands are still not available for In-Memory OLTP solutions.

The following notable operators are *unsupported* in SQL Server 2017:

- `LIKE`
- `CASE`
- `INTERSECT`
- `EXCEPT`

Attempting to use these operators inside a natively compiled stored procedure or scalar function will result in an error message explaining that the syntax is not supported, shown as follows:

```
The operator 'LIKE' is not supported with natively compiled modules.
```

 The list of unsupported operators and commands is getting smaller with each subsequent release of SQL Server. One major addition in the 2017 release is the `APPLY` operator, which is now fully supported in natively compiled T-SQL.
A full list of unsupported operators can be found on the Microsoft Books Online page: `https://msdn.microsoft.com/en-us/library/dn246937.aspx#Anchor_4`.

It is important to understand that these T-SQL limitations are for *natively compiled T-SQL* (stored procedures and scalar functions). You are still able to write interpreted T-SQL (non-natively compiled T-SQL) using these commands. For example, it is perfectly fine to query a memory-optimized table and issue a `LIKE` operator to search in a character column.

Size is everything!

When the In-Memory OLTP engine was introduced in SQL Server 2014, Microsoft announced that the maximum size of any memory-optimized table was 256 GB. This limit was reached using internal testing at Microsoft and was introduced to ensure the stability and reliability of the feature in production environments. The main decision here involved the design of the storage subsystem, particularly around the checkpoint file pairs. There was a hard limit of 8,192 checkpoint file pairs, each capable of storing 128 MB of data, however the limit of 256 GB was not a hard limit, and was rather a suggested maximum.

The memory requirements for a memory-optimized table are dynamic. This dynamism is grounded in the memory requirements for merging data changes into memory-optimized tables (inserts, deletes, and updates) and the follow-on redundancies of versioned rows and rows waiting for garbage collection.

When SQL Server 2016 was released, Microsoft quoted a maximum size of 2 TB for a memory-optimized table. Again, this was due to testing and reliability measurements inside the development team at Microsoft. The development team has re-architected the storage subsystem for the checkpoint file pairs, removing the 8,192-pair limit, effectively allowing a memory-optimized table to have no upper size limit. In other words, as long as you have memory available, the table can grow. This *does not* mean that any and all tables should be memory-optimized, but it *does* mean that we are now able to consider using the In-Memory OLTP engine to store any size of table that we can design.

Improvements in the In-Memory OLTP engine

Further to the previously mentioned size limitation removal, there have been a number of improvements of the In-Memory OLTP engine that may not be immediately apparent, but can still drastically improve performance and scalability.

First up is a range of improvements to the storage subsystem; not only was the checkpoint file pair limit removed, but there was also the introduction of multi-threaded checkpointing. In SQL Server 2014, the offline checkpoint process was a single-threaded system. This thread would scan the transaction log for changes to memory-optimized tables and write those changes to the checkpoint file pairs. This meant that a potentially multi-core system would have a *busy* core for the checkpointing process. With SQL Server 2016, this checkpointing system was redesigned to run on multiple threads, therefore increasing throughput to the checkpoint file pairs and thus increasing overall performance and the scalability of the In-Memory OLTP engine.

Similar improvements have been made to the recovery process. When the server is performing crash recovery, or bringing a database online after a server was taken offline, the log apply operations are now also processed using multiple threads.

The theme of multi-threading, or parallel processing, has also been continued in the query processing portion of the In-Memory OLTP engine. Here, we can expect performance improvements for a range of queries, both interpreted and natively compiled.

The query processing engine is now able to process the MERGE statement using multiple threads (as long as your server and database MAXDOP settings allow for this). This allows the query optimizer to use parallelism where it deems parallel processing to be more efficient than serial processing.

Equally, in SQL Server 2014, hash indexes could only be scanned using a single thread or serial scan rather than a parallel scan. SQL Server 2016 implemented a parallel scan method to provide a significant performance gain when scanning a hash index. This helps to mitigate the inherent performance pain that is experienced when performing an index scan over a hash index.

Down the index rabbit-hole

So far in this chapter we have looked at the introduction of features and functionalities that were available in disk-based objects to the In-Memory OLTP engine. The improvements in indexing and the ability to alter your indexing strategy with memory-optimized tables without dropping it are particularly attractive. With that in mind, we will now spend some time investigating how the indexes are treated inside the storage engine. This will include a journey through the system catalogs and **Dynamic Management Views** (**DMVs**) to allow us to see how index information can be queried.

We will now take this opportunity to explore what the alteration of a bucket count can have on the data in our demonstration table.

Let's begin by rolling back two of our changes from earlier in the chapter by dropping the HSH_ANewColumn hash index, dropping the two columns ANewColumn and AnotherColumn, and finally re-creating a HSH_LoginTime hash index, using an extremely irregular and sub-optimal value of 2, as shown in the following code:

```
USE InMemoryTest
GO
ALTER TABLE dbo.InMemoryTable DROP INDEX HSH_ANewColumn
GO
ALTER TABLE dbo.InMemoryTable DROP COLUMN ANewColumn
GO
ALTER TABLE dbo.InMemoryTable DROP COLUMN AnotherColumn
GO
ALTER TABLE dbo.InMemoryTable ADD INDEX HSH_LoginTime NONCLUSTERED HASH
(LoginTime) WITH (BUCKET_COUNT=2);
GO
```

We will begin by taking a look at the system catalog views we've used in past versions of SQL Server to inspect the table and indexes we have created so far, using the following code:

```
USE InMemoryTest
GO
SELECT OBJECT_NAME(i.object_id) AS [table_name],
    COALESCE(i.name,'--HEAP--') AS [index_name],
    i.index_id,
    i.type,
    i.type_desc
FROM sys.indexes AS i
WHERE i.object_id = OBJECT_ID('InMemoryTable');
```

table_name	index_name	index_id	type	type_desc
InMemoryTable	--HEAP--	0	0	HEAP
InMemoryTable	HSH_UserName	2	7	NONCLUSTERED HASH
InMemoryTable	PK_InMemory	3	2	NONCLUSTERED
InMemoryTable	HSH_LoginTime	4	7	NONCLUSTERED HASH

The results of this first query against `sys.indexes` shows us that we have a HEAP hash index(the data pages of the memory-optimized table), as well as the three additional indexes we have already created. Particularly noteworthy here are the two non-clustered hash indexes that we created: `HSH_UserName` and `HSH_LoginTime`. Both appear as index type 7 and with the index description NONCLUSTERED HASH. This should come as no great surprise, but it shows us that the old system views have been extended to include information regarding memory-optimized tables and indexes. The previous listing may be executed without the WHERE clause to see that the details for both memory-optimized and disk-based tables and indexes can be queried simultaneously.

We already know that hash indexes are exclusive to memory-optimized tables. However, if we go through the demo code so far, we also know that the primary key of this table is also memory-optimized. The query referencing `sys.indexes`, however, only shows us that the primary key is a non-clustered index. So, we have no way of knowing if this non-clustered index is a memory-optimized or disk-based index.

The information about whether a table is memory-optimized or disk-based is stored in the newly extended `sys.tables` catalog view, as shown in the following code:

```
SELECT COALESCE(i.name,'--HEAP--') AS [index_name],
    i.index_id,
    i.type,
    t.is_memory_optimized,
    t.durability,
```

```
        t.durability_desc
FROM sys.tables t
    INNER JOIN sys.indexes AS i
        ON i.object_id = t.object_id
WHERE t.name = 'InMemoryTable'
```

```
index_name   index_id type is_memory_optimized durability durability_desc
----------   -------- ---- ------------------- ---------- --------------
--HEAP--         0      0         1                0       SCHEMA_AND_DATA
HSH_UserName     2      7         1                0       SCHEMA_AND_DATA
PK_InMemory      3      2         1                0       SCHEMA_AND_DATA
HSH_LoginTime    4      7         1                0       SCHEMA_AND_DATA
```

As the results of the query show, the table and all indexes are memory-optimized (is_memory_optimized = 1). We are also able to determine which durability option has been chosen for the table.

With these two queries, we are able to take our first look at the index information for memory-optimized tables. However, we are not able to see any particular information regarding our hash index (bucket counts or chain lengths). To access that information, we leave the general system catalog views sys.indexes and sys.tables behind and venture forwards into more feature specific catalog views.

Our first port of call is the obviously named sys.hash_indexes , which displays information on any hash index in a database. The sys.hash_indexes catalog view has the same columns as the sys.indexes catalog view with the exception of the bucket_count column. This column displays the bucket count for the index from creation time, or the last rebuild, with the BUCKET_COUNT option supplied:

```
USE InMemoryTest
GO
SELECT hi.name AS [index_name],
    hi.index_id,
    hi.type,
    hi.bucket_count
FROM sys.hash_indexes AS hi;
```

```
index_name       index_id    type bucket_count
--------------   ----------- ---- ------------
HSH_UserName         2        7      16384
HSH_LoginTime        4        7         2
```

This catalog view only provides us with information about the index structure from the time of creation, it does *not* provide us with any details on chain length inside each bucket (the number of rows that are assigned to each bucket via the hashing algorithm).

To access this more important and relevant information, we must access another catalog view specifically created for the memory-optimized indexes, `sys.dm_db_xtp_hash_index_stats`

By joining the system `sys.dm_db_xtp_hash_index_stats` catalog view to `sys.indexes` (or even directly to `sys.hash_indexes`), we are able to finally see our bucket count and our usage statistics. We are now able to see how many buckets are empty, the average chain length, and the maximum chain length for each hash index. The following code illustrates this technique:

```
SELECT COALESCE(i.name, '--HEAP--') AS [index_name],
    i.index_id,
    i.type,
    ddxhis.total_bucket_count AS [total_buckets],
    ddxhis.empty_bucket_count AS [empty_buckets],
    ddxhis.avg_chain_length,
    ddxhis.max_chain_length
FROM sys.indexes AS i
    LEFT JOIN sys.dm_db_xtp_hash_index_stats AS ddxhis
        ON ddxhis.index_id = i.index_id
            AND ddxhis.object_id = i.object_id
    WHERE i.object_id = OBJECT_ID('InMemoryTable');
```

index_name	index_id	type	total_buckets	empty_buckets	avg_chain_length	max_chain_length
--HEAP--	0	0	NULL	NULL	NULL	NULL
HSH_UserName	2	7	16384	16383	1	1
PK_UserId	3	2	NULL	NULL	NULL	NULL
HSH_LoginTime	4	7	2	1	1	1

We will want to monitor the statistics of our hash indexes to see whether the bucket count is optimal or not. As each bucket takes up 8 bytes of memory, the higher the bucket count, the more memory we will use for the index. A higher bucket count also results in a slower traversal of the index when performing index scans. So, if we note a high number of empty buckets, we may consider reducing the bucket count to improve potential scan speeds. In general, it is best to avoid performing index scans on a hash index, as the scan must first scan the hash buckets and then the chains of rows for each bucket. This has considerable overhead versus scanning a non-clustered index, which doesn't have the added complexity of the bucket structure to traverse.

Equally, if we see a high average or maximum chain length, this could indicate that there are not enough buckets available for the data coming into the index. Higher chain lengths can also impact performance when performing seeks or inserts.

The general idea of a hash index is to have just enough buckets to cover all possible unique values going into the index (or as near to this as possible), so that when a query seeks a single hash value, the storage engine can retrieve the one (or very few) row(s) that belong to that hash value.

The recommendation from Microsoft is to aim for an empty bucket percentage of 33% or higher. If the bucket count matches the number of unique values for the index, the hashing algorithm's distribution will cause around 33% of buckets to remain empty.

The recommendation from Microsoft is to aim for a chain length of less than *10*, with the ideal value being 1—one row per hash value and therefore bucket.

If you have wildly non-unique values with many duplicates, a non-clustered index would, more than likely, be a better choice versus a hash index.

We can see from the following code how the empty buckets and chain lengths are affected by inserting a handful of rows into the test table and re-running the previous query:

```
USE InMemoryTest
GO
INSERT INTO dbo.InMemoryTable
        ( UserId, UserName , LoginTime, LoginCount )
VALUES
            (2,  'Donald Duck'     , '2016-01-02', 1),
            (3,  'Steve Jobs'      , '2016-01-03', 1),
            (4,  'Steve Ballmer'   , '2016-01-04', 1),
            (5,  'Bill Gates'      , '2016-01-05', 1),
            (6,  'Ted Codd'        , '2016-01-06', 1),
            (7,  'Brian Kernighan', '2016-01-07', 1),
            (8,  'Dennis Ritchie' , '2016-01-08', 1);
GO
SELECT COALESCE(i.name, '--HEAP--') AS [index_name],
    i.index_id,
    i.type,
    ddxhis.total_bucket_count AS [total_buckets],
    ddxhis.empty_bucket_count AS [empty_buckets],
    ddxhis.avg_chain_length,
    ddxhis.max_chain_length
FROM sys.indexes AS i
    LEFT JOIN sys.dm_db_xtp_hash_index_stats AS ddxhis
        ON ddxhis.index_id = i.index_id
            AND ddxhis.object_id = i.object_id
WHERE i.object_id = OBJECT_ID('InMemoryTable');
```

index_name	index_id	type	total_buckets	empty_buckets	avg_chain_length	max_chain_length
--HEAP--	0	0	NULL	NULL	NULL	NULL
HSH_UserName	2	7	16384	16376	1	1
PK_UserId	3	2	NULL	NULL	NULL	NULL
HSH_LoginTime	4	7	2	0	4	5

Here, we can see that the two hash indexes now have slightly different information in them. We now have a total of eight rows in the table (and the indexes). HSH_UserName has 16384 buckets with a hash function applied to the UserName column. As we inserted seven new rows, each with a unique value for UserName, they will all be stored in an empty bucket. This leaves the average and maximum chain lengths at 1. The data inserted into LoginTime was also unique for each of the seven rows. However, there are only two buckets assigned to HSH_LoginTime. This results in the seven rows hashing to one of two possible values and being placed in one of the two available buckets. The average and maximum chain lengths are then no longer 1.

This example is simplified, but allows us to recognize that the implementation of the hash index on LoginTime requires attention. Either the bucket count needs raising, or the choice of a hash index may be incorrect. Equally, the hash index on UserName provides ideal chain lengths, but has an excessive empty bucket count. The index therefore uses more memory than is necessary and may need the bucket count reducing to release memory for other memory-optimized objects. Now that we know that bucket counts and chain lengths can affect the amount of memory required to store memory-optimized tables and indexes, we should also take a quick look at how the two hash indexes in the example can differ by using the following code:

```
USE InMemoryTest
GO
SELECT COALESCE(i.name, '--HEAP--') AS [index_name],
    i.index_id,
    i.type,
    c.allocated_bytes,
    c.used_bytes
FROM sys.dm_db_xtp_memory_consumers c
    JOIN sys.memory_optimized_tables_internal_attributes a
        ON a.object_id = c.object_id
            AND a.xtp_object_id = c.xtp_object_id
    LEFT JOIN sys.indexes i
        ON c.object_id = i.object_id
            AND c.index_id = i.index_id
WHERE c.object_id = OBJECT_ID('InMemoryTable')
    AND a.type = 1
ORDER BY i.index_id;
```

index_name	index_id	type	allocated_bytes	used_bytes
--HEAP--	NULL	NULL	131072	696
HSH_UserName	2	7	131072	131072
PK_UserId	3	2	196608	1368
HSH_LoginTime	4	7	16	16

The results show an interesting fact. The index HSH_LoginTime was created with two buckets and has 16 bytes allocated and used. This makes sense when we think about how each bucket takes up 8 bytes of memory. However, HSH_UserName takes up 128 MB of memory even though the index has 10,000 buckets. We would expect ~78 MB (10,000 * 8 bytes = 80,000 bytes), however the memory allocation follows base—2 size allocations. As the size is larger than 64 MB, the next largest size in base—2 is 128, and therefore 128 MB are allocated. We can test this theory by altering the number of buckets to a value low enough for the size to be below 64 (the next step down the base—2 scale), as shown in the following code:

```
USE InMemoryTest
GO
ALTER TABLE dbo.InMemoryTable ALTER INDEX HSH_UserName REBUILD WITH
(BUCKET_COUNT=8000);
GO
SELECT COALESCE(i.name, '--HEAP--') AS [index_name],
    i.index_id,
    i.type,
    c.allocated_bytes,
    c.used_bytes
FROM sys.dm_db_xtp_memory_consumers c
    JOIN sys.memory_optimized_tables_internal_attributes a
        ON a.object_id = c.object_id
            AND a.xtp_object_id = c.xtp_object_id
    LEFT JOIN sys.indexes i
        ON c.object_id = i.object_id
            AND c.index_id = i.index_id
WHERE c.object_id = OBJECT_ID('InMemoryTable')
    AND a.type = 1
ORDER BY i.index_id;
```

index_name	index_id	type	allocated_bytes	used_bytes
--HEAP--	NULL	NULL	131072	760
HSH_UserName	2	7	65536	65536
PK_InMemory	3	2	196608	1368
HSH_LoginTime	4	7	16	16

We now see that the index `HSH_UserName` has 64 MB allocated, although 8000 buckets equates to ~62.5 MB. This gives us further information regarding memory use for indexing memory-optimized tables, and tells us that we have a certain amount of overhead for the storage of indexes in relation to the number of buckets we assign to a hash index.

Large object support

We will now take a look at exactly what LOB data types are supported in SQL Server from SQL Server 2016 and higher, and what aspects of these data types need to be considered when using them with memory-optimized objects.

Let's begin by adding a LOB column to our test table using the following code:

```
USE InMemoryTest
GO
ALTER TABLE dbo.InMemoryTable Add NewColumnMax VARCHAR(MAX) NULL
GO
```

This follows the same scheme as the previous code examples: adding a LOB column is no different with a memory-optimized table than a disk-based table. At least on the surface, anyway!

Let's take another look at our index meta-data to see how exactly LOB columns are handled by the storage engine, using the following code:

```
USE InMemoryTest
GO
SELECT COALESCE(i.name, '--HEAP--') AS [index_name],
    c.allocated_bytes AS allocated,
    c.used_bytes AS used,
    c.memory_consumer_desc AS memory_consumer,
    a.type_desc
FROM sys.dm_db_xtp_memory_consumers c
    JOIN sys.memory_optimized_tables_internal_attributes a
        ON a.object_id = c.object_id
            AND a.xtp_object_id = c.xtp_object_id
    LEFT JOIN sys.indexes i
        ON c.object_id = i.object_id
            AND c.index_id = i.index_id
WHERE c.object_id = OBJECT_ID('InMemoryTable')
        AND i.index_id IS NULL;
GO
```

```
index_name  allocated  used  memory_consumer       type_desc
----------  ---------  ----  ------------------     --------------------
--HEAP--     131072     760  Table Heap            USER_TABLE
--HEAP--          0       0  LOB Page Allocator    INTERNAL OFF-ROW DATA TABLE
--HEAP--          0       0  Table heap            INTERNAL OFF-ROW DATA TABLE
```

There are a number of things to note here:

- We are filtering on the table/heap only (`AND i.index_id IS NULL`). This will allow us to concentrate on the base table.
- Two additional columns have been added, showing what type of memory consumer each row represents.
- We now see two additional rows displayed.

The previous listing returns two additional rows: one marked `LOB Page Allocator` and one marked `Table heap`, both with an internal table attribute of `Internal off row data table`. These are references to how LOB data is stored for memory-optimized tables.

LOB data is not stored along with the other data pages for a memory-optimized table. Rather, the LOB data is stored in a separate data structure that is optimized for LOB style data. `LOB Page Allocator` stores the actual LOB data, while `Table heap` stores references to the LOB data, referring back to the original data pages. This arrangement has been designed so that the row-versioning mechanism, which is the foundation of the multi-version concurrency control inside the In-Memory OLTP engine (described in `Chapter 11`, *Introducing SQL Server In-Memory OLTP*), doesn't need to keep multiple versions of the LOB data in the same way as it must for regular columns. By decoupling the two data storage classes, SQL Server can be much more efficient with the storage of these two relatively different data types. In particular, LOB data has been regarded as a data type that is likely to be modified less often compared to non-LOB columns. As such, processing LOB data separately will greatly reduce memory resource usage, which will in turn reduce the overhead of storing LOB data in a memory-optimized table while still affording the ability of processing data types through one interface.

At the moment, the LOB column is empty (allocated = 0 and used = 0). If we now run a simple update to copy the `UserName` column data into the LOB column, we can run the same query, as shown in the following code, to investigate how the data is stored in the LOB data structures:

```
USE InMemoryTest
GO
UPDATE dbo.InMemoryTable
SET NewColumnMax = UserName
```

```
GO
SELECT COALESCE(i.name, '--HEAP--') AS [index_name],
    c.allocated_bytes AS allocated,
    c.used_bytes AS used,
    c.memory_consumer_desc AS memory_consumer,
    a.type_desc
FROM sys.dm_db_xtp_memory_consumers c
    JOIN sys.memory_optimized_tables_internal_attributes a
        ON a.object_id = c.object_id
            AND a.xtp_object_id = c.xtp_object_id
    LEFT JOIN sys.indexes i
        ON c.object_id = i.object_id
            AND c.index_id = i.index_id
WHERE c.object_id = OBJECT_ID('InMemoryTable')
    AND i.index_id IS NULL;
GO
```

index_name	allocated	used	memory_consumer	type_desc
--HEAP--	131072	1520	Table Heap	USER_TABLE
--HEAP--	131072	376	LOB Page Allocator	INTERNAL OFF-ROW DATA TABLE
--HEAP--	65536	512	Table heap	INTERNAL OFF-ROW DATA TABLE

Here, we are observing a similar behavior as seen earlier in the chapter, where allocation is occurring in base—2 steps. The LOB Page Allocator has allocated 128 MB and the supporting table heap has allocated 64 MB—although both are using much less space. This is an efficient step that avoids having to perform unnecessary additional allocations too often. Despite this, we notice a behavior that could cause memory resource contention if large amounts of LOB data were to be processed in this way.

Please note, if you run the index meta-data queries shortly after modifying the table structure you may notice that the memory allocations of the table are larger than shown in the example results here. This has to do with how ALTER statements are processed by the In-Memory OLTP engine. Earlier in the chapter, this mechanism was described, where it was stated that an ALTER makes a copy of the original table and incorporates the desired changes into the new copy. This leads to a doubling of the memory allocation until ghost record cleanup can remove the old copy of the data from memory.

When SQL Server processes LOB data in the In-Memory OLTP engine, the decision whether or not to push the data from in-row to off-row storage is made according to the table schema. This is a different mechanism than the disk-based storage engine uses, which bases the decision on the data being processed at execution time. Disk-based storage only places data off-row when it won't fit on a data page, while memory-optimized tables place data off-row when the table schema describes a column as being either a max data type or that the row could store more than 8060 bytes when completely full. When LOB data is stored off-row for a memory-optimized table, there is a significant overhead associated with that storage. A reference must be stored for the in-row data (the base memory-optimized table), the off-row data (the LOB data itself in `LOB Page Allocator`), and the leaf level of the range index (the intermediary heap referencing between the on-row and off-row data). In addition to this, the actual data must be stored in `LOB Page Allocator`. This overhead can go beyond 50 bytes per row. This additional overhead is created and must be maintained for each and every LOB column that a memory-optimized table has. The more LOB columns there are, the more overhead and bloated referencing is required. As you may see, writing an additional 50+ bytes for each row with a LOB column (or multiples of this) can quickly cause significant resource and performance issues.

Storage differences of on-row and off-row data

Let's now take a look at the difference in storage and processing between two tables with variable length character columns. One table has varchar(5) columns, which will be small enough to fit in the in-row storage. The other table will have a series of varchar(max) columns, which will automatically be stored in the off-row storage. These tables will be created and filled with 100,000 rows each to demonstrate both the storage and also the performance differences between the two storage types. We will create the two tables using the following code:

```
USE InMemoryTest
GO
DROP TABLE IF EXISTS dbo.InMemoryTableMax
DROP TABLE IF EXISTS dbo.InMemoryTableNotMax
GO

CREATE TABLE dbo.InMemoryTableMax
(
    UserId INT NOT NULL IDENTITY (1,1),
    MaxCol1 VARCHAR(max) COLLATE Latin1_General_CI_AI NOT NULL ,
    MaxCol2 VARCHAR(max) COLLATE Latin1_General_CI_AI NOT NULL ,
    MaxCol3 VARCHAR(max) COLLATE Latin1_General_CI_AI NOT NULL ,
    MaxCol4 VARCHAR(max) COLLATE Latin1_General_CI_AI NOT NULL ,
    MaxCol5 VARCHAR(max) COLLATE Latin1_General_CI_AI NOT NULL ,
```

```
        CONSTRAINT PK_InMemoryTableMax  PRIMARY KEY NONCLUSTERED (UserId),

) WITH (MEMORY_OPTIMIZED = ON, DURABILITY=SCHEMA_AND_DATA)
GO

CREATE TABLE dbo.InMemoryTableNotMax
(
    UserId INT NOT NULL IDENTITY (1,1),
    Col1 VARCHAR(5) COLLATE Latin1_General_CI_AI NOT NULL ,
    Col2 VARCHAR(5) COLLATE Latin1_General_CI_AI NOT NULL ,
    Col3 VARCHAR(5) COLLATE Latin1_General_CI_AI NOT NULL ,
    Col4 VARCHAR(5) COLLATE Latin1_General_CI_AI NOT NULL ,
    Col5 VARCHAR(5) COLLATE Latin1_General_CI_AI NOT NULL ,
    CONSTRAINT PK_InMemoryTableNotMax  PRIMARY KEY NONCLUSTERED (UserId),

) WITH (MEMORY_OPTIMIZED = ON, DURABILITY=SCHEMA_AND_DATA)
GO
```

The only difference between these two tables is the column data type: one
uses varchar(max), while the other uses a varchar(5) data type. We are leaving the
tables with a primary key and no other indexes because we only want to investigate the on-
row and off-row storage differences.

If we now run our memory consumers query from earlier on in this section, we can
investigate how LOB Page Allocator and the corresponding Table heap objects are
created for each table, using the following code:

```
SELECT OBJECT_NAME(c.object_id) AS [table_name],
    c.allocated_bytes AS allocated,
    c.used_bytes AS used,
    c.memory_consumer_desc AS memory_consumer,
    a.type_desc
FROM sys.dm_db_xtp_memory_consumers c
    JOIN sys.memory_optimized_tables_internal_attributes a
        ON a.object_id = c.object_id
            AND a.xtp_object_id = c.xtp_object_id
    LEFT JOIN sys.indexes i
        ON c.object_id = i.object_id
            AND c.index_id = i.index_id
WHERE
(
    c.object_id = OBJECT_ID('InMemoryTableNotMax')
    OR c.object_id = OBJECT_ID('InMemoryTableMax')
)
AND i.index_id IS NULL
```

table_name	allocated	used	memory_consumer	type_desc
InMemoryTableNotMax	0	0	Table heap	USER_TABLE
InMemoryTableMax	0	0	Table heap	USER_TABLE
InMemoryTableMax	0	0	LOB Page Allocator	INTERNAL OFF-ROW DATA TABLE
InMemoryTableMax	0	0	Table heap	INTERNAL OFF-ROW DATA TABLE
InMemoryTableMax	0	0	LOB Page Allocator	INTERNAL OFF-ROW DATA TABLE
InMemoryTableMax	0	0	Table heap	INTERNAL OFF-ROW DATA TABLE
InMemoryTableMax	0	0	LOB Page Allocator	INTERNAL OFF-ROW DATA TABLE
InMemoryTableMax	0	0	Table heap	INTERNAL OFF-ROW DATA TABLE
InMemoryTableMax	0	0	LOB Page Allocator	INTERNAL OFF-ROW DATA TABLE
InMemoryTableMax	0	0	Table heap	INTERNAL OFF-ROW DATA TABLE
InMemoryTableMax	0	0	LOB Page Allocator	INTERNAL OFF-ROW DATA TABLE
InMemoryTableMax	0	0	Table heap	INTERNAL OFF-ROW DATA TABLE;

The results of the memory consumer query show that we have a single table heap for the
InMemoryTableNotMax table (the table with the varchar(5) columns) and that we have
several internal off-row data tables for the table InMemoryTableMax. In fact, we have LOB
Page Allocator and a matching Table heap for each varchar(max) column in the table.

We then fill each table with 100,00 rows of data while running a basic timing comparison to
see what performance overhead LOB Page Allocator and Table heap maintenance
causes. We do this using the following code:

```
SET NOCOUNT ON
GO

SET STATISTICS TIME ON
GO

INSERT INTO dbo.InMemoryTableMax
        ( MaxCol1 ,
          MaxCol2 ,
          MaxCol3 ,
          MaxCol4 ,
          MaxCol5
        )
SELECT TOP 100000
    'Col1',
    'Col2',
    'Col3',
    'Col4',
    'Col5'
FROM sys.columns a
    CROSS JOIN sys.columns;
GO

INSERT INTO dbo.InMemoryTableNotMax
        ( Col1 ,
```

```
                   Col2 ,
                   Col3 ,
                   Col4 ,
                   Col5
                )
       SELECT TOP 100000
            'Col1',
            'Col2',
            'Col3',
            'Col4',
            'Col5'
       FROM sys.columns a
            CROSS JOIN sys.columns
       GO

       SET STATISTICS TIME OFF
       GO
       SQL Server Execution Times:
          CPU time = 1797 ms,   elapsed time = 1821 ms.

       SQL Server Execution Times:
          CPU time = 281 ms,   elapsed time = 382 ms.
```

The results at the end of this listing show that the elapsed time for inserting 100,000 rows into the table with varchar(max) columns took roughly five times longer than it did to insert the same rows into the table with varchar(5) columns. This timing difference is down to the overhead of inserting data into off-row storage (LOB Page Allocator and matching Table heap).

If we also take another look at the memory consumption statistics, we will see that there is also a significant difference in memory consumption between the two tables, as shown in the following code:

```
       SELECT OBJECT_NAME(c.object_id) AS [table_name],
            SUM(c.allocated_bytes) / 1024. AS allocated,
            SUM(c.used_bytes) / 1024. AS used
       FROM sys.dm_db_xtp_memory_consumers c
            JOIN sys.memory_optimized_tables_internal_attributes a
               ON a.object_id = c.object_id
                  AND a.xtp_object_id = c.xtp_object_id
            LEFT JOIN sys.indexes i
               ON c.object_id = i.object_id
                  AND c.index_id = i.index_id
       WHERE
       (
            c.object_id = OBJECT_ID('InMemoryTableNotMax')
```

```
        OR c.object_id = OBJECT_ID('InMemoryTableMax')
)
AND i.index_id IS NULL
GROUP BY c.object_id;
```

table_name	allocated	used
InMemoryTableMax	59392.000000	58593.750000
InMemoryTableNotMax	7104.000000	7031.250000

We can see that we should very carefully consider the use of LOB data types for memory-optimized tables. If LOB data types are required, then the performance and resource consumption overhead should be noted, especially where high performance is the driving factor for the adoption of a memory-optimized solution.

Cross-feature support

We have seen that the In-Memory OLTP engine has increasingly added support for features outside the engine itself, allowing interoperability between disk-based and memory-optimized objects with increasing parity with each new release. However, developers need to also be aware of how the feature support of In-Memory OLTP is also expanding into more administrator-focused areas of SQL Server.

Security

The first important feature we will discuss of cross feature support is the ability to use **Transparent Data Encryption** (**TDE**) on memory-optimized objects. TDE, as the name suggests, allows a database administrator to apply an encryption mechanism to an entire database. This encryption will protect all the data stored inside the database. The encryption is designed in such a way that should the database fall into the wrong hands (or the data and log files are copied or a backup is misplaced), then the data inside those files will be completely encrypted. Any encryption key(s) and certificate(s) will be stored separately from the database files themselves. The scope of this book does not allow for a full excursion into the inner-workings of TDE; however, it is enough to know that should you wish to use this simple but effective encryption solution, you are able to use memory-optimized objects in such a database without restriction.

For developers wishing to implement In-Memory OLTP using the newest security features introduced in *SQL Server 2016: Always Encrypted, Row-Level Security, and Dynamic Data Masking* (all explained in detail in `Chapter 8`, *Tightening the Security*), you can also rest assured that memory-optimized tables can also take advantage of these improved security features.

Programmability

We are now also able to take full advantage of the extremely useful Query Store feature, which was also introduced in SQL Server 2016 and has a chapter dedicated to it in this book: `Chapter 9`, *Query Store*. There is no additional configuration required to include memory-optimized tables or natively compiled code. When Query Store is activated, memory-optimized objects will be collected in the Query Store analysis along with disk-based objects and queries.

The focus on feature inclusion continues to also cover Temporal Tables. A chapter explaining what Temporal Tables are and how they can be implemented is available in this book: `Chapter 7`, *Temporal Tables*. Temporal Tables allow for a transparent implementation of memory-optimized tables versus disk-based tables. There are no special requirements to accommodate memory-optimized tables with this feature.

High availability

High availability support is of great importance for systems that are processing large volumes of data.

Starting with SQL Server 2016, SQL Server fully supports the use of memory-optimized objects in conjunction with Always On Availability Groups. Any memory-optimized table will be replicated to the secondary server(s) in the same way that disk-based tables are. For `SCHEMA_ONLY` tables, the table schema will be replicated to the secondary server(s), but not the data (because the data is never logged for schema only tables). As such, if schema only tables are replicated, a mechanism to re-fill these tables must be included for a failover scenario. If the memory-optimized tables are defined as `SCHEMA_AND_DATA`, the data will be replicated to the secondary server(s) and will be available to any readable secondary connections that may be reading from the secondary server(s).

Failover Cluster Instances are also fully supported for high availability with the In-Memory OLTP engine. The memory-optimized tables behave in exactly the same way as a standalone instance, meaning that tables defined with the SCHEMA_AND_DATA property will be instantiated at server startup. In other words, they are created and filled using the checkpoint file pairs at startup. Depending on how large these tables are, this initialization can take some time. This is *not* unique to Failover Cluster Instances, but rather to any SQL Server that uses the In-Memory OLTP engine.

It is now also possible to use replication in conjunction with memory-optimized tables. The initial implementation inside SQL Server 2016 allowed for a transactional or snapshot replication publisher to publish tables to a subscriber, and for the subscriber tables to be created as memory-optimized tables. This means that memory-optimized tables are in fact available on the subscriber-side of replication topology. Using this topology removes the bottleneck of locking and blocking on the subscriber-side and allows the subscriber to keep up with the replication data flow.

Tools and wizards

As with many of the features in SQL Server, In-Memory OLTP also has some useful tools to assist in working with the technology.

The main desire for many developers is to take their existing database solutions and to convert them to memory-optimized solutions (ideally automatically). Microsoft has provided a few options for investigating a database and delivering feedback on a database design with suggestions of memory-optimized solutions where possible.

The simplest of these tools is the In-Memory OLTP Migration Checklist. This is a wizard provided inside SQL Server Management Studio, which performs a variety of checks against an entire database and provides a set of checklists and reports that inform the user exactly what objects inside a database are candidates for conversion into memory-optimized objects. An overview of the work required is also provided (for example, supported and unsupported data types). The Checklist Wizard can be found by right-clicking a database and choosing **Tasks** and then **Generate In-Memory OLTP Migration Checklists**.

The following screenshot illustrates the checklist:

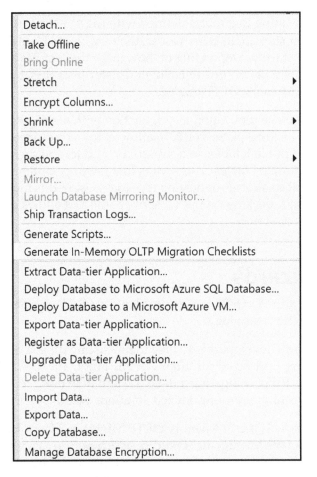

Detach...
Take Offline
Bring Online
Stretch ▶
Encrypt Columns...
Shrink ▶
Back Up...
Restore ▶
Mirror...
Launch Database Mirroring Monitor...
Ship Transaction Logs...
Generate Scripts...
Generate In-Memory OLTP Migration Checklists
Extract Data-tier Application...
Deploy Database to Microsoft Azure SQL Database...
Deploy Database to a Microsoft Azure VM...
Export Data-tier Application...
Register as Data-tier Application...
Upgrade Data-tier Application...
Delete Data-tier Application...
Import Data...
Export Data...
Copy Database...
Manage Database Encryption...

Generate In-Memory OLTP Migration Checklists

This will then launch the wizard for the chosen database, which guides us through the process of evaluating a database for compatibility with the In-Memory OLTP engine. After choosing the objects to be processed by the wizard, and where to store the resulting report, the wizard can be started.

The wizard then runs through all the chosen objects in the database. Depending on the number of objects, this can take some time, as shown in the following screenshot:

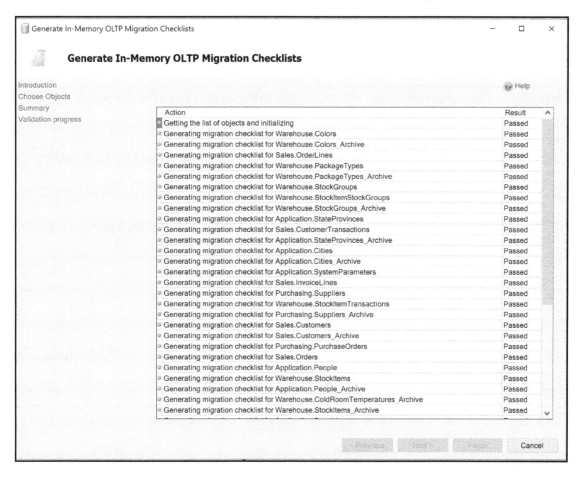

In-Memory OLTP Migration Checklist Progress

Upon completion, the wizard can be closed and the reports found in the location specified before running the analysis. The resulting report files are HTML files, and there will be one per database object that has been analyzed that shows what changes, if any, are required to make the object compatible with the In-Memory OLTP engine. As we can see in the following screenshot, the report files generated by the wizard provide an overview of what properties of an object are or are not supported by the In-Memory OLTP engine:

Memory optimization checklist for [WideWorldImporters].[BuyingGroups]	
Description	**Validation Result**
No unsupported data types are defined on this table.	Succeeded
No sparse columns are defined for this table.	Succeeded
No identity columns with unsupported seed and increment are defined for this table.	Succeeded
Supported foreign key relationships are defined on this table but the table cannot be migrated through the memory-optimization wizard. To migrate this table as well as the other tables involved in the FOREIGN KEY references, first remove the FOREIGN KEYs, then migrate the tables using the memory-optimization wizard, and finally add the FOREIGN KEY references to the migrated memory-optimized tables.	Failed: More information
- FK_Sales_BuyingGroups_Application_People: Foreign Key on this table (referencing Application.People)	
- FK_Sales_Customers_BuyingGroupID_Sales_BuyingGroups: Foreign Key as primary table (referenced by Sales.Customers)	
- FK_Sales_SpecialDeals_BuyingGroupID_Sales_BuyingGroups: Foreign Key as primary table (referenced by Sales.SpecialDeals)	
No unsupported constraints are defined on this table.	Succeeded
No unsupported indexes are defined on this table.	Succeeded
No unsupported triggers are defined on this table.	Succeeded
Post migration row size does not exceed the row size limit of memory-optimized tables.	Succeeded
Table is not partitioned or replicated.	Succeeded

Example Migration Checklist Report for a table

Where appropriate, a link is supplied that loads a Books Online support page describing the issue found and possible solutions.

The next tool to assist in evaluating a database for possible object-migration is a standard report delivered with SSMS, the **Transaction Performance Analysis Overview**. This report does not require the pre-configuration of a database as long as the database being hosted is on a SQL Server 2016 instance or later. The report collects execution statistics for queries in the database that has been chosen and shows which tables or stored procedures are possible candidates for migration. The report will only have meaningful data in it *after* the database has been in use for a few hours, or even days:

Disk Usage
Disk Usage by Top Tables
Disk Usage by Table
Disk Usage by Partition
Backup and Restore Events
All Transactions
All Blocking Transactions
Top Transactions by Age
Top Transactions by Blocked Transactions Count
Top Transactions by Locks Count
Resource Locking Statistics by Objects
Object Execution Statistics
Database Consistency History
Memory Usage By Memory Optimized Objects
Transaction Performance Analysis Overview
Index Usage Statistics
Index Physical Statistics
Schema Changes History
User Statistics

Transaction Performance Analysis Overview Report

The report loads inside SSMS and offers the choice of table or stored procedure analysis. Both options deliver a similar report, displaying the objects that have been recently accessed. These objects are plotted on a graph showing the potential performance impact of a migration to the In-Memory OLTP engine versus the estimated work required to make the change. The best candidates are objects plotted towards the top-right of the graph, indicating a high impact and minimal migration work.

These two analysis options allow us to get an idea of how much impact and how much work would be involved in migrating to the In-Memory OLTP engine. The results should be considered as a basic indication only and offer by no means a guarantee of accuracy:

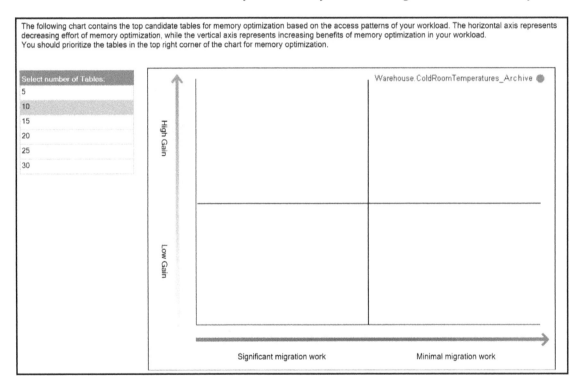

Transaction Performance Analysis Overview result

Summary

In this chapter, we covered how the In-Memory OLTP engine has evolved from the first version released with SQL Server 2014 to the latest version in SQL Server 2017.

Many of the restrictions around data types, constraints, large binary objects, and collations, along with the ability to alter objects without having to drop and recreate them, signal the need for huge improvements for developers. We have also learned that there are still limitations and areas where the use of In-Memory OLTP is not the best choice, or must at least be carefully considered before being chosen.

A vastly more efficient processing engine allows us to consider scenarios where current implementations may benefit from the reduced overhead of the In-Memory OLTP engine. The ability to seamlessly interact between memory-optimized and disk-based objects makes for a very compelling programming experience. The tooling that Microsoft provides allows us to quickly create an overview of how and where time and resources need investing to take a disk-based implementation and convert it to a memory-optimized solution.

The In-Memory OLTP engine has made good progress from its initial incarnation in SQL Server 2014 and it is clear that the feature is here to stay. The evolution from SQL Server 2014 to 2016 and finally to 2017 shows that the engine continues to be improved, adding further integration and support for the remaining data types and programming constructs currently unsupported. I, for one, look forward to seeing this evolution take place and am excited to see developers adopting this fantastic technology in their projects. Now, go forth and see where *you* can accelerate your SQL Server database projects and remove those locks and blocks!

13

Supporting R in SQL Server

SQL Server R Services in version 2017, because of added Python support renamed to *Machine Learning Services*, combines the power and flexibility of the open source R language with enterprise-level tools for data storage and management, workflow development, reporting, and visualization. This chapter introduces R Machine Learning Services globally and the R language. R is developing quite fast, so it is worth mentioning that the R version used in this book is 3.2.2 (2015-08-14).

In the first section, you will learn about the free version of the R language and engine. You will also become familiar with the basic concepts of programming in R.

When developing an advanced analytical solution, you spend the vast majority of time with data. Typically, data is not in a shape useful for statistical and other algorithms. Data preparation is not really glamorous but is an essential part of analytical projects. You will learn how to create a new, or use an existing, dataset and learn about basic data manipulation with R in the second section of this chapter.

The data preparation part of an analytical project is interleaved with the data understanding part. You need to gather in-depth knowledge of your data and data values before you can analyze it. Showing data graphically is a very efficient and popular method of data understanding. Fortunately, R support for data visualization is really comprehensive. However, sometimes numbers tell us more, in a more condensed way, than graphs. Introductory statistics, like descriptive statistics, provide you with the numbers you need to understand your data. Again, R support for introductory statistics is astonishing.

Open source products also have some disadvantages. For example, scalability might be an issue. SQL Server 2016 and 2017 bring R support inside the database engine. With this support, many of your problems are solved. You get many scalable procedures and enhanced security for your R applications.

This chapter will cover the following points:

- R—basics and concepts
- Core elements of the R language
- R data structures
- Basic data management
- Simple visualizations
- Introductory statistics
- SQL Server R (ML) Services architecture
- Creating and using scalable R solutions in SQL Server
- Using the new T-SQL PREDICT function

Introducing R

R is the most widely used language for statistics, data mining, and machine learning. Besides the language, R is also the environment and the engine that executes the R code. You need to learn how to develop R programs, just as you need to learn any other programming language you intend to use.

Before going deeper into the R language, let's explain what the terms **statistics**, **data mining**, and **machine learning** mean. Statistics is the study and analysis of data collections, and the interpretation and presentation of the results of the analysis. Typically, you don't have all the population data, or *census* data, collected. You have to use **samples**—often survey samples. Data mining is again a set of powerful analysis techniques used on your data in order to discover patterns and rules that might improve your business. Machine learning is programming to use data to solve a given problem automatically. You can immediately see that all three definitions overlap. There is no big distinction between them; you can even use them as synonyms. Small differences are visible when you think of the users of each method. Statistics is a science, and the users are scientists. Data mining users are typically business people. Machine learning users are, as the name suggests, often machines. Nevertheless, in many cases, the same algorithms are used, so there is really a lot of overlapping among the three branches of applied mathematics in analytical applications.

Let's not get lost in these formal definitions and instead start with R immediately. You will learn about:

- Parts of open source R
- Basic description of the R language

- Obtaining help
- R core syntax elements
- R variables
- R vectors
- R packages

This chapter assumes that you are already familiar with SQL Server and R tools, including **SQL Server Management Studio** (**SSMS**), RStudio, or R Tools for Visual Studio, so you can start to write the code immediately.

Starting with R

You can download R from the **Comprehensive R Archive Network** (**CRAN**) site at `http://cran.r-project.org`. You can get the R engine for Windows, Linux, or macOS X. Microsoft also maintains its own R portal, the **Microsoft R Application Network** (**MRAN**) site at `https://mran.revolutionanalytics.com/`. You can use this site to download Microsoft R Open, the enhanced distribution of open source R from Microsoft. After installation, you start working in an interactive mode. You can use the R console client tool to write code, line by line. As you already know, there are many additional tools. Let's just repeat here that the most widely used free tool for writing and executing R code is RStudio. It is free and you can download it from `https://www.rstudio.com/`. This section assumes you use RStudio for the code examples.

R is a case-sensitive, functional, and interpreted language. The R engine interprets your commands one by one. You don't type commands but rather call functions to achieve results, even a function called `q()` to quit an R session. As in any programming language, it is good practice to comment the code well. You can start a comment with a hash mark (#) anywhere in the line; any text after the hash mark is not executed and is treated as a comment. You end a command with a semicolon (;) or a new line. Commands finished by a semicolon can be combined in a single line. Similarly, as in T-SQL, explicitly ending a command with a semicolon is a better practice than just entering a new command on a new line. Here is the first example of R code, showing a comment and using the `contributors()` function to list the authors and other contributors to the language:

```
# R Contributors
contributors();
```

The abbreviated results are:

```
R is a project which is attempting to provide a modern piece of
statistical software for the GNU suite of software.
The current R is the result of a collaborative effort with
contributions from all over the world.
Authors of R.
R was initially written by Robert Gentleman and Ross Ihaka-also known as "R
& R"
of the Statistics Department of the University of Auckland.
Since mid-1997 there has been a core group with write access to the R
source, currently consisting of
...
```

In R, help is always at your fingertips. With the help() function, you can get onto help first, and then search for the details you need. Using help.start() gives the links to the free documentation about R. With help("options"), you can examine the global options that are used to affect the way in which R computes and displays the results. You can get help for a specific function. For example, help("exp") displays the help for the exponential function. You can use a shorter version of the help function—just the question mark. For example, ?"exp" also displays help for the exponential function. With example("exp"), you can get examples of usage of the exponential function. You can also search in help using a command—either help.search("topic") or ??"topic". With RSiteSearch("exp"), you can perform an online search for documentation about exponential functions over multiple R sites. The following code summarizes these help options:

```
# Getting help on help
help();
# General help
help.start();
# Help about global options
help("options");
# Help on the function exp()
help("exp");
# Examples for the function exp()
example("exp");
# Search
help.search("constants");
??"constants";
# Online search
RSiteSearch("exp");
```

Finally, there is also the `demo()` function. This function runs some more advanced `demo` scripts, showing you the capabilities of R code. For example, the following call to this function shows you some graphic capabilities:

```
demo("graphics");
```

In RStudio, you get the code to execute in the **Console** window (bottom-left window by default). You need to move the cursor to that window and hit the *Enter* key to execute the first part of the code. You get the first graph in the bottom-right window. Then you hit the *Enter* key a couple of times more to scroll through all demo graphs. One part of the code that creates a nice pie chart is shown here:

```
pie.sales <- c(0.12, 0.3, 0.26, 0.16, 0.04, 0.12);
names(pie.sales) <- c("Blueberry", "Cherry", "Apple",
                "Boston Cream", "Other", "Vanilla Cream");
pie(pie.sales,
    col = c("purple","violetred1","green3","cornsilk","cyan","white"));

title(main = "January Pie Sales", cex.main = 1.8, font.main = 1);
title(xlab = "(Don't try this at home kids)", cex.lab = 0.8, font.lab = 3);
```

The graphical results are shown in the following figure:

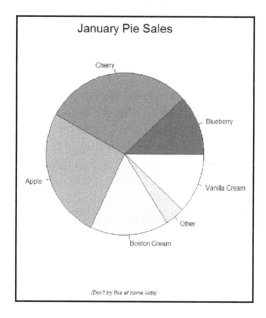

Demo pie chart

All of the objects created exist in memory. Each session has its own **workspace**. When you finish a session, you can save the workspace or the objects from memory to disk in an .RData file and load them in the next session. The workspace is saved in the folder from which R reads the source code files, or in a default folder. You can check the objects in the current workspace with the objects() function or with the ls() function. You can check the working folder, or directory, with the getwd() call. You can change it interactively with the setwd(dir) function, where the dir parameter is a string representing the new working directory. You can remove single objects from the workspace and memory with the rm(objectname) function, or a full list of objects using the same function with the list of objects as a parameter (you will learn about lists and other data structures later in this chapter). There are many more possibilities, including saving images, getting the history of recent commands, saving the history, reloading the history, and even saving a specific object to a specific file. You will learn about some of them later in this chapter.

R language basics

You can start investigating R by writing simple expressions that include literals and operators. Here are some examples:

```
1 + 1;
2 + 3 * 4;
3 ^ 3;
sqrt(81);
pi;
```

This code evaluates three mathematical expressions first using the basic operators. Check the results and note that R, as expected, evaluates the expressions using operator precedence as we know from mathematics. Then it calls the sqrt() function to calculate the square root of 81. Finally, the code checks the value of the base package built-in constant for the number pi (π). R has some built-in constants. Check them by searching help for them with ??"constants".

It is easy to generate **sequences**. The following code shows some examples:

```
rep(1,10);
3:7;
seq(3,7);
seq(5,17,by=3);
```

The first command replicates the number 1 10 times using the `rep()` function. The second line generates the sequence of numbers between 3 and 7. The third line does exactly the same, this time using the `seq()` function. This function gives you additional possibilities, as the fourth line shows. This command generates a sequence of numbers between 5 and 17, but this time with an increment of 3.

Writing ad hoc expressions means you need to rewrite them whenever you need them. To reuse the values, you need to store them in variables. You assign a value to a variable with an assignment operator. R supports multiple assignment operators. You can use the left assignment operator (<–), where the variable name is on the left side, or the right assignment operator (–>), where the variable name is on the right side. You can also use the equals (=) operator. The left assignment operator is the one you will see most commonly in R code. The following code stores the numbers 2, 3, and 4 in variables and then performs a calculation using the variables:

```
x <- 2;
y <- 3;
z <- 4;
x + y * z;
```

The result is 14. Note again that R is case-sensitive. For example, the following line of code produces an error, because variables X, Y, and Z are not defined:

```
X + Y + Z;
```

You can separate part of a variable name with a dot. This way, you can organize your objects into namespaces, just as you can in .NET languages. Here is an example:

```
This.Year <- 2016;
This.Year;
```

You can check whether the equals assignment operator really works:

```
x = 2;
y = 3;
z = 4;
x + y * z;
```

If you executed the last code, you would get the same result as with the code that used the left assignment operator instead of the equals operator.

Besides mathematical operators, R supports logical operators as well. To test exact equality, use the double equals (==) operator. Other logical operators include <, <=, >, >=, and != to test inequality. In addition, you can combine two logical expressions into a third one using the logical AND (&) and logical OR (|) operators. The following code checks a variable for exact equality with a number literal:

```
x <- 2;
x == 2;
```

The result is TRUE.

Every variable in R is actually an object. A simple scalar variable is a **vector** of length one. A vector is a one-dimensional array of scalars of the same **type**, or **mode**: numeric, character, logical, complex (imaginary numbers), and raw (bytes). You use the combine function c() to define the vectors. Here are the ways to assign variable values as vectors. Note that the variables with the same names will be overwritten:

```
x <- c(2,0,0,4);
assign("y", c(1,9,9,9));
c(5,4,3,2) -> z;
q = c(1,2,3,4);
```

The first line uses the left assignment operator. The second assigns the second vector to the variable y using the assign() function. The third line uses the right assignment operator, and the fourth line, the equals operator.

You can perform operations on vectors just like you would perform them on scalars (remember, after all, a scalar is just a vector of length 1). Here are some examples of vector operations:

```
x + y;
x * 4;
sqrt(x);
```

The results of the previous three lines of code are:

```
3   9   9 13
8   0   0 16
1.414214 0.000000 0.000000 2.000000
```

You can see that the operations were performed element by element. You can operate on a selected element only as well. You use numerical index values to select specific elements. Here are some examples:

```
x <- c(2,0,0,4);
x[1];
x[-1];
x[1] <- 3; x;
x[-1] = 5; x;
```

First, the code assigns a vector to a variable. The second line selects the first element of the vector. The third line selects all elements except the first one and returns a vector of three elements. The fourth line of the code assigns a new value to the first element and then shows the vector. The last line assigns new values to all elements but the first one, and then shows the vector. The results are, therefore:

```
2
0 0 4
3 0 0 4
3 5 5 5
```

You can also use logical operators on vectors. Here are some examples:

```
y <- c(1,9,9,9);
y < 8;
y[4] = 1;
y < 8;
y[y<8] = 2; y;
```

The first line assigns a vector to variable y. The second line compares each vector value to a numeric constant 8 and returns TRUE for those elements where the value is lower than the given value. The third line assigns a new value to the fourth element of the vector. The fourth line performs the same comparison of the vector elements to number 8 again and returns TRUE for the first and fourth element. The last line edits the elements of vector y that satisfy the condition in the parentheses—those elements where the value is less than 8. The result is:

```
TRUE FALSE FALSE FALSE
TRUE FALSE FALSE  TRUE
2 9 9 2
```

Vectors and scalars are very basic data structures. You will learn about more advanced data structures in the next section of this chapter. Before that, it is high time to mention a very important concept in R—packages.

 The R code shown in this chapter has used only core capabilities so far; capabilities that you get when you install the R engine. Although these capabilities are already very extensive, the real power of R comes with additional packages.

Packages are optional modules you can download and install. Each package brings additional functions, or demo data, in a well-defined format. The number of available packages is growing year by year. At the time of writing this book, in winter 2017, the number of downloadable packages was already almost 10,000. A small set of standard packages is already included when you install the core engine. You can check out installed packages with the `installed.packages()` command. Packages are stored in the folder called `library`. You can get the path to the library with the `.libPaths()` function (note the dot in the name). You can use the `library()` function to list the packages in your library.

The most important command to learn is `install.packages("packagename")`. This command searches the CRAN sites for the package, downloads it, unzips it, and installs it. Of course, you need a web connection in order to execute it successfully. You can imagine that such a simplistic approach is not very welcome in highly secure environments. Of course, in order to use R Machine Learning Services in SQL Server, the package installation is more secure and more complex, as you will learn later in this chapter.

Once a package is installed, you load it into memory with the `library(packagename)` command. You can get help on the content of the package with the `help(package = "packagename")` command. For example, if you want to read the data from a SQL Server database, you need to install the RODBC library. The following code installs this library, loads it, and gets the help for functions and methods available in it:

```
install.packages("RODBC");
library(RODBC);
help(package = "RODBC");
```

Before reading the data from SQL Server, you need to perform two additional tasks. First, you need to create a login and a database user for the R session and give the user the permission to read the data. Then, you need to create an ODB **data source name** (**DSN**) that points to this database. In SSMS, connect to your SQL Server, and then in **Object Explorer**, expand the `Security` folder. Right-click on the `Logins` subfolder. Create a new login and a database user in the `WideWorldImportersDW` database, and add this user to the `db_datareader` role.

I created a SQL Server login called `RUser` with the password as `Pa$$w0rd`, and a user with the same name, as the following screenshot shows:

Generating the RUser login and database user

After that, I used the ODBC Data Sources tool to create a system DSN called WWIDW. I configured the DSN to connect to my local SQL Server with the RUser SQL Server login and appropriate password, and changed the context to the WideWorldImportersDW database. If you've successfully finished both steps, you can execute this R code to read the data from SQL Server:

```
con <- odbcConnect("WWIDW", uid="RUser", pwd="Pa$$w0rd");
sqlQuery(con,
        "SELECT c.Customer,
           SUM(f.Quantity) AS TotalQuantity,
           SUM(f.[Total Excluding Tax]) AS TotalAmount,
           COUNT(*) AS SalesCount
         FROM Fact.Sale AS f
          INNER JOIN Dimension.Customer AS c
          ON f.[Customer Key] = c.[Customer Key]
         WHERE c.[Customer Key] <> 0
         GROUP BY c.Customer
         HAVING COUNT(*) > 400
         ORDER BY SalesCount DESC;");
close(con);
```

The code returns the following (abbreviated) result:

	Customer	TotalQuantity	TotalAmount	SalesCount
1	Tailspin Toys (Vidrine, LA)	18899	340163.8	455
2	Tailspin Toys (North Crows Nest, IN)	17684	313999.5	443
3	Tailspin Toys (Tolna, ND)	16240	294759.1	443
4	Wingtip Toys (Key Biscayne, FL)	18658	335053.5	441
5	Tailspin Toys (Peeples Valley, AZ)	15874	307461.0	437
6	Wingtip Toys (West Frostproof, FL)	18564	346621.5	436
7	Tailspin Toys (Maypearl, TX)	18219	339721.9	436

Manipulating data

Before you can extract information from your data, you need to understand how the data is stored. First, you need to understand data structures in R.

Scalars and vectors are the most basic data structures. In R terminology, you analyze a dataset. A dataset consists of rows with cases or observations, to analyze and columns representing the variables or attributes of the cases. This definition of a dataset looks like a SQL Server table. However, R does not work with tables in the relational sense. For example, in a relational database, the order of rows and columns is not defined. In order to get a value, you need the column name and the key of the row. However, in R, you can use the position of a cell for most data structures. You have already seen this position reference for vectors.

In this section, you will learn about data structures in R and the basic manipulation of datasets, including:

- Arrays and matrices
- Factors
- Data frames
- Lists
- Creating new variables
- Recoding variables
- Dealing with missing values
- Type conversions
- Merging datasets

Introducing data structures in R

A **matrix** is a two-dimensional array of values of the same type, or mode. You generate matrices from vectors with the `matrix()` function. Columns and rows can have labels. You can generate a matrix from a vector by rows or by columns (default). The following code shows some matrices and the difference of the generation, by rows or by columns:

```
x = c(1,2,3,4,5,6); x;
Y = array(x, dim=c(2,3)); Y;
Z = matrix(x,2,3,byrow=F); Z
U = matrix(x,2,3,byrow=T); U;   # A matrix - fill by rows
rnames = c("Row1", "Row2");
cnames = c("Col1", "Col2", "Col3");
V = matrix(x,2,3,byrow=T, dimnames = list(rnames, cnames)); V;
```

The first line generates and shows a one-dimensional vector. The second line creates a two-dimensional array, which is the same as a matrix, with two rows and three columns. The matrix is filled from a vector, column by column. The third row actually uses the matrix() function to create a matrix, and fill it by columns. The matrix is equivalent to the previous one. The fourth row fills the matrix by rows. The fifth and sixth rows define row and column names. The last row again creates a matrix filled by rows; however, this time it adds row and column names in a list of two vectors. Here are the results:

```
[1] 1 2 3 4 5 6
      [,1] [,2] [,3]
[1,]    1    3    5
[2,]    2    4    6
      [,1] [,2] [,3]
[1,]    1    3    5
[2,]    2    4    6
      [,1] [,2] [,3]
[1,]    1    2    3
[2,]    4    5    6
      Col1 Col2 Col3
Row1    1    2    3
Row2    4    5    6
```

You can see the difference between filling by rows or by columns. The following code shows how you can refer to matrix elements by position, or even by name, if you've named columns and rows:

```
U[1,];
U[1,c(2,3)];
U[,c(2,3)];
V[,c("Col2", "Col3")];
```

The results are:

```
[1] 1 2 3
[1] 2 3
      [,1] [,2]
[1,]    2    3
[2,]    5    6
      Col2 Col3
Row1    2    3
Row2    5    6
```

As you can see from the matrix examples, a matrix is just a two-dimensional array. You generate arrays with the `array()` function. This function again accepts a vector of values as the first input parameter, then a vector specifying the number of elements on dimensions, and then a list of vectors for the names of the dimensions' elements. An array is filled by columns, then by rows, then by the third dimension (let's call it pages), and so on. Here is an example that generates a three-dimensional array:

```
rnames = c("Row1", "Row2");
cnames = c("Col1", "Col2", "Col3");
pnames = c("Page1", "Page2", "Page3");
Y = array(1:18, dim=c(2,3,3), dimnames = list(rnames, cnames, pnames)); Y;
```

The result is as follows:

```
, , Page1
     Col1 Col2 Col3
Row1    1    3    5
Row2    2    4    6
, , Page2
     Col1 Col2 Col3
Row1    7    9   11
Row2    8   10   12
, , Page3
     Col1 Col2 Col3
Row1   13   15   17
Row2   14   16   18
```

Variables can store **discrete** or **continuous** values. Discrete values can be **nominal**, or **categorical**, where they represent labels only, or **ordinal**, where there is an intrinsic order in the values. In R, **factors** represent nominal and ordinal variables. **Levels** of a factor represent distinct values. You create factors from vectors with the `factor()` function. It is important to properly determine the factors because advanced data mining and machine learning algorithms treat discrete and continuous variables differently. Here are some examples of factors:

```
x = c("good", "moderate", "good", "bad", "bad", "good");
y = factor(x); y;
z = factor(x, order=TRUE); z;
w = factor(x, order=TRUE,
          levels=c("bad", "moderate","good")); w;
```

The first line defines a vector of six values denoting whether the observed person was in a good, moderate, or bad mood. The second line generates a factor from the vector and shows it. The third line generates an ordinal variable. Note the results—the order is defined alphabetically. The last commands in the last two lines generate another ordinal variable from the same vector, this time specifying the order explicitly. Here are the results:

```
[1] good      moderate good      bad      bad      good
Levels: bad good moderate
[1] good      moderate good      bad      bad      good
Levels: bad < good < moderate
[1] good      moderate good      bad      bad      good
Levels: bad < moderate < good
```

Lists are the most complex data structures in R. Lists are ordered collections of different data structures. You typically do not work with them a lot. You need to know them because some functions return multiple results, or complex results, packed in a list, and you need to extract specific parts. You create lists with the list() function. You refer to objects of a list by position, using the index number enclosed in double parentheses. If an element is a vector or a matrix, you can additionally use the position of a value in a vector enclosed in single parentheses. Here is an example:

```
L = list(name1="ABC", name2="DEF",
         no.children=2, children.ages=c(3,6));
L;
L[[1]];
L[[4]];
L[[4]][2];
```

The example produces the following result:

```
$name1
[1] "ABC"
$name2
[1] "DEF"
$no.children
[1] 2
$children.ages
[1] 3 6
[1] "ABC"
[1] 3 6
[1] 6
```

Finally, the most important data structure is a **data frame**. Most of the time, you analyze data stored in a data frame. Data frames are matrices where each variable can be of a different type. Remember, a variable is stored in a column, and all values of a single variable must be of the same type. Data frames are very similar to SQL Server tables. However, they are still matrices, meaning that you can refer to the elements by position, and that they are ordered. You create a data frame with the `data.frame()` function from multiple vectors of the same length. Here is an example of generating a data frame:

```
CategoryId = c(1,2,3,4);
CategoryName = c("Bikes", "Components", "Clothing", "Accessories");
ProductCategories = data.frame(CategoryId, CategoryName);
ProductCategories;
```

The result is as follows:

```
     CategoryId     CategoryName
1        1          Bikes
2        2          Components
3        3          Clothing
4        4          Accessories
```

Most of the time, you get a data frame from your data source, for example from a SQL Server database. The results of the earlier example reading from SQL Server can be actually stored in a data frame. You can also enter the data manually, or read it from many other sources, including text files, Excel, and many more. The following code retrieves the data from a **comma-separated values** (**CSV**) file in a data frame, and then displays the first four columns for the first five rows of the data frame. The CSV file is provided in the download for the accompanying code for this book, as described in the preface of the book:

```
TM = read.table("C:\\SQL2017DevGuide\\Chapter13_TM.csv",
                sep=",", header=TRUE, row.names = "CustomerKey",
                stringsAsFactors = TRUE);
TM[1:5,1:4];
```

The code specifies that the first row of the file holds column names (header), and that the `CustomerKey` column represents the row names (or row identifications). If you are interested, the data comes from the `dbo.vTargetMail` view from the `AdventureWorksDW2014` demo SQL Server database you can download from Microsoft CodePlex at `https://msftdbprodsamples.codeplex.com/`. The first five rows are presented here:

	MaritalStatus	Gender	TotalChildren	NumberChildrenAtHome
11000	M	M	2	0
11001	S	M	3	3
11002	M	M	3	3

| 11003 | S | F | 0 | 0 |
| 11004 | S | F | 5 | 5 |

Getting sorted with data management

After you've imported the data to be analyzed in a data frame, you need to prepare it for further analysis. There are quite a few possible ways to retrieve values from a data frame. You can refer to the data by position, or by using the subscript notation. However, if you use a single subscript only, then you retrieve columns defined by the subscript and all rows. The same is true if you use a vector of column names only, without specifying the rows. If you specify two indexes or index ranges, then the first one is used for rows and the second one for columns. The following code shows these options:

```
TM[1:2];                             # Two columns
TM[c("MaritalStatus", "Gender")];    # Two columns
TM[1:3,1:2];                         # Three rows, two columns
TM[1:3,c("MaritalStatus", "Gender")];
```

The first command returns all rows and two columns only. The second command produces the same result. The third command returns three rows, again for the MaritalStatus and Gender columns only. The fourth row produces the same result as the third one.

The most common notation uses the data frame name and column name, separated by the dollar ($) sign, such as TM$Gender. You can also avoid excessive writing of the data frame name by using the attach() or with() functions. With the attach() function, you add the data frame to the search path that R uses to find the objects. You can refer to a variable name directly without the data frame name, if the variable name is unique in the search path. The detach() function removes the data frame from the search path, to avoid possible ambiguity with duplicate variable names later. The with() function allows you to name the data frame only once, and then use the variables in a set of statements enclosed in {} brackets inside the body of the function. The following code shows these approaches:

```
table(TM$MaritalStatus, TM$Gender);
attach(TM);
table(MaritalStatus, Gender);
detach(TM);
with(TM,
     {table(MaritalStatus, Gender)});
```

The first line produces a cross-tabulation of `MaritalStatus` and `Gender`. Please note the `dataframe$variable` notation. The second line adds the data frame to the search path. The third command produces the same cross-tabulation as the first one, however, this time referring to variable names only. The fourth command removes the data frame from the search path. The last command uses the `with()` function to allow you to define the data frame name only once and then use only variable names in the commands inside the function. Note that, because there is only one command in the function, the brackets `{}` can be omitted. All three cross-tabulations return the same result:

```
                    Gender
MaritalStatus    F     M
          M  4745  5266
          S  4388  4085
```

Sometimes, you get numeric categorical variable values and you want to use character labels. The `factor()` function can help you here. For example, in the `TM` data frame, there is the `BikeBuyer` variable. For this variable, `0` means the person never purchased a bike and `1` means this person is a bike buyer. The following code shows you how to add labels to the numerical values:

```
table(TM$BikeBuyer, TM$Gender);
TM$BikeBuyer <- factor(TM$BikeBuyer,
                       levels = c(0,1),
                       labels = c("No","Yes"));
table(TM$BikeBuyer, TM$Gender);
```

The results are shown here. Note that, the second time, the labels for the values of the `BikeBuyer` variable are used:

```
        F     M
0   4536  4816
1   4597  4535
        F     M
No   4536  4816
Yes  4597  4535
```

You can easily get the metadata about your objects. Some useful functions that give you information about your objects include the following:

- `class()`: This function returns the type of object
- `names()`: This function returns the names of the components, such as variable names in a data frame

- length(): This function returns the number of elements, for example, the number of variables in a data frame
- dim(): This function returns the dimensionality of an object, for example, the number of rows and columns in a data frame
- str(): This function gives details about the structure of an object

Here are examples of using these metadata functions:

```
class(TM);
names(TM);
length(TM);
dim(TM);
str(TM);
```

The results are as follows:

```
[1] "data.frame"
[1] "MaritalStatus"         "Gender"          "TotalChildren"
[4] "NumberChildrenAtHome" "Education"        "Occupation"
[7] "HouseOwnerFlag"        "NumberCarsOwned" "CommuteDistance"
[10] "Region"               "BikeBuyer"       "YearlyIncome"
[13] "Age"
[1] 13
[1] 18484    13
'data.frame':      18484 obs. of  13 variables:
$ MaritalStatus : Factor w/ 2 levels "M","S": 1 2 1 2 2 2 2 1 2 2 ...
$ Gender        : Factor w/ 2 levels "F","M": 2 2 2 1 1 2 1 2 1 2 ...
$ TotalChildren : int  2 3 3 0 5 0 0 3 4 0 ...
```

Note that the CustomerKey column is not listed among the 13 columns of the data frame, because when the data was imported, this column was set to row names. In addition, only string variables were converted to factors. In the abbreviated result of the last command, you can see that the TotalChildren is an integer and not a factor, although it can occupy only values from 0 to 5.

Many times, calculated variables are much more meaningful for an analysis than just the base ones you read from your data source. For example, in medicine, the **body mass index (BMI)**, defined as weight divided by the square of the height, is much more meaningful than the base variables of height and weight it is derived from. You can add new variables to a data frame, recode continuous values to a list of discrete values, change the data type of variable values, and more.

The following example uses the `within()` function, which is similar to the `with()` function. It's just that it allows updates of a data frame, to add a new variable `MartitalStatusInt`, derived from the `MaritalStatus` as an integer. This variable tells us the number of additional people in the household of the case observed:

```
TM <- within(TM, {
  MaritalStatusInt <- NA
  MaritalStatusInt[MaritalStatus == "S"] <- 0
  MaritalStatusInt[MaritalStatus == "M"] <- 1
});
str(TM);
```

In the body of the function, firstly the new variable is defined as missing. Then, the `MaritalStatus` values are used to define the number of additional persons in the household. If the person in the case observed is married, then the value is 1; if the person is single, then 0. The last line of the code shows the new structure of the data frame. The abbreviated structure is:

```
'data.frame':    18484 obs. of  14 variables:
$ MaritalStatus    : Factor w/ 2 levels "M","S": 1 2 1 2 2 2 2 1 2 2...
$ MaritalStatusInt : num  1 0 1 0 0 0 0 1 0 0 ...
```

You can see that the new variable values are correct; however, the mode is defined as numeric. You can change the data type with one of the `as.targettype()` functions, where `targettype()` is a placeholder for the actual target type function, as the following example shows:

```
TM$MaritalStatusInt <- as.integer(TM$MaritalStatusInt);
str(TM);
```

Now, the abbreviated structure of the TM data frame shows that the mode of the new column is integer.

In the next example, a new variable is added to the data frame, just as a simple calculation. The new variable, `HouseholdNumber`, is used to define the total number of people in the household of the person in the case observed. The calculation summarizes the number of children at home plus 1 if the person is married, plus 1 for the person herself/himself. Finally, the mode is changed to an integer:

```
TM$HouseholdNumber = as.integer(
  1 + TM$MaritalStatusInt + TM$NumberChildrenAtHome);
str(TM);
```

The structure of the data frame shows that the calculation is correct:

```
'data.frame':     18484 obs. of  15 variables:
$ MaritalStatus    : Factor w/ 2 levels "M","S": 1 2 1 2 2 2 2 1 2 2 ...
$ MaritalStatusInt : int  1 0 1 0 0 0 0 1 0 0 ...
$ HouseholdNumber  : int  2 4 5 1 6 1 1 5 5 1 ...
```

On many occasions, you have to deal with missing values, denoted with a literal NA. R treats missing values as completely unknown. This influences the results of the calculations. For example, adding a missing value to a known integer produces a missing value. You have to decide how to deal with missing data. You can exclude rows with missing data completely, you can recode the missing values to a predefined value, or you can exclude the missing values from a single calculation. The following code defines a vector of six values; however, the last value is missing. You can use the is.na() function to check for each value, whether it is missing or not. Then, the code tries to calculate the mean value for all values of the vector. The last line of code tries to calculate the mean again, this time by disregarding the missing value by using the na.rm = TRUE option. This option is available in most numeric functions and simply removes missing values from the calculation:

```
x <- c(1,2,3,4,5,NA);
is.na(x);
mean(x);
mean(x, na.rm = TRUE);
```

The results of the previous code are here:

```
[1] FALSE FALSE FALSE FALSE FALSE  TRUE
[1] NA
[1] 3
```

You can see that the is.na() function evaluated each element separately, and returned a vector of the same dimensionality as the vector checked for the missing values. The mean() function returned a missing value when, in the calculation, a missing value was present, and the result you might have expected when the missing values were removed.

Frequently, you need to merge two datasets, or to define a new dataset as a projection of an existing one. Merging is similar to joining two tables in SQL Server, and a projection means selecting a subset of variables only. The merge() function joins two data frames based on a common identification of each case. Of course, the identification must be unique. The following code shows how to do the projection:

```
TM = read.table("C:\\SQL2017DevGuide\\Chapter13_TM.csv",
                sep=",", header=TRUE,
                stringsAsFactors = TRUE);
TM[1:3,1:3];
cols1 <- c("CustomerKey", "MaritalStatus");
TM1 <- TM[cols1];
cols2 <- c("CustomerKey", "Gender");
TM2 <- TM[cols2];
TM1[1:3, 1:2];
TM2[1:3, 1:2];
```

The code first re-reads the TM data frame, this time without using the CustomerKey column for the row names. This column must be available in the data frame, because this is the unique identification of each case. Then the code defines the columns for the two projection data frames and shows the first three rows of each new data frame, as you can see in the results of the last two commands:

```
  CustomerKey MaritalStatus
1       11000             M
2       11001             S
3       11002             M
  CustomerKey Gender
1       11000      M
2       11001      M
3       11002      M
```

Now, let's join the two new datasets:

```
TM3 <- merge(TM1, TM2, by = "CustomerKey");
TM3[1:3, 1:3];
```

The results show that the join was done correctly:

```
  CustomerKey MaritalStatus Gender
1       11000             M      M
2       11001             S      M
3       11002             M      M
```

A data frame is a matrix. Sort order is important. Instead of merging two data frames by columns, you can bind them by columns. However, you need to be sure that both data frames are sorted in the same way; otherwise you might bind variables from one case with variables from another case. The following code binds two data frames by columns:

```
TM4 <- cbind(TM1, TM2);
TM4[1:3, 1:4];
```

The results show that, unlike the merge() function, the cbind() function did not use the CustomerKey for a common identification. It has blindly bound columns case by case, and preserved all variables from both source data frames. That's why the CustomerKey column appears twice in the result:

```
  CustomerKey MaritalStatus CustomerKey.1 Gender
1     11000         M            11000       M
2     11001         S            11001       M
3     11002         M            11002       M
```

You can also use the rbind() function to bind two data frames by rows. This is equal to the union of two rowsets in SQL Server. The following code shows how to filter a dataset by creating two new datasets, each one with two rows and two columns only. Then the code uses the rbind() function to unite both data frames:

```
TM1 <- TM[TM$CustomerKey < 11002, cols1];
TM2 <- TM[TM$CustomerKey > 29481, cols1];
TM5 <- rbind(TM1, TM2);
TM5;
```

The results are here:

```
        CustomerKey     MaritalStatus
1          11000             M
2          11001             S
18483      29482             M
18484      29483             M
```

Finally, what happens if you want to bind two data frames by columns but you are not sure about the ordering? Of course, you can sort the data. The following code shows how to create a new data frame from the TM data frame, this time sorted by the Age column in descending order. Note the usage of the minus (−) sign in the order() function to achieve the descending sort:

```
TMSortedByAge <- TM[order(-TM$Age),c("CustomerKey", "Age")];
TMSortedByAge[1:5,1:2];
```

The result is shown here:

```
       CustomerKey Age
1726         12725  99
5456         16455  98
3842         14841  97
3993         14992  97
7035         18034  97
```

Understanding data

As already mentioned, understanding data is interleaved with data preparation. In order to know what to do, which variables need recoding, which variables have missing values, and how to combine variables into a new one, you need to deeply understand the data you are dealing with. You can get this understanding with a simple overview of the data, which might be a method good enough for small datasets, or a method for checking just a small subset of a large dataset.

You can get more information about the distribution of variables by showing the distributions graphically. Basic statistical methods are also useful for data overview. Finally, sometimes these basic statistical results and graphs are already exactly what you need for a report.

R is an extremely powerful language and environment for both visualizations and statistics. You will learn how to:

- Create simple graphs
- Show plots and histograms
- Calculate frequencies distribution
- Use descriptive statistics methods

Basic visualizations

In R, you build a graph step by step. You start with a simple graph, and then add features to it with additional commands. You can even combine multiple plots and other graphs into a single graph. Besides viewing the graph interactively, you can save it to a file. There are many functions for drawing graphs. Let's start with the most basic one, the `plot()` function.

Note that, if you removed the TM dataset from memory or didn't save the workspace when you exited the last session, you need to re-read the dataset. Here is the code that uses it to draw a graph for the Education variable of the TM dataset, which is also added to the search path to simplify further addressing to the variables:

```
TM = read.table("C:\\SQL2017DevGuide\\Chapter13_TM.csv",
                sep=",", header=TRUE,
                stringsAsFactors = TRUE);
attach(TM);

# A simple distribution
plot(Education);
```

The following screenshot shows the graph:

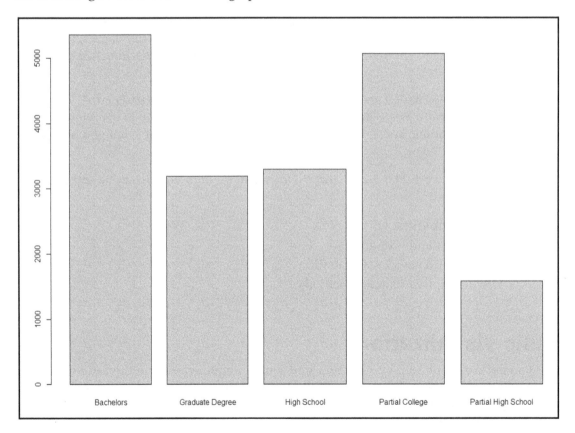

Basic plot for Education

The plot does not look too good. The Education variable is correctly identified as a factor; however, the variable is ordinal, so the levels should be defined. You can see the problem in the graph in the previous figure, where the values are sorted alphabetically. In addition, the graph and axes could also have titles, and a different color might look better. The plot() function accepts many parameters. In the following code, the parameters main for the main title, xlab for the *x* axis label, ylab for the *y* axis label, and col for the fill color are introduced:

```
Education = factor(Education, order=TRUE,
                   levels=c("Partial High School",
                            "High School","Partial College",
                            "Bachelors", "Graduate Degree"));
plot(Education, main = 'Education',
     xlab='Education', ylab ='Number of Cases',
     col="purple");
```

This code produces a nicer graph, as you can see in the following screenshot:

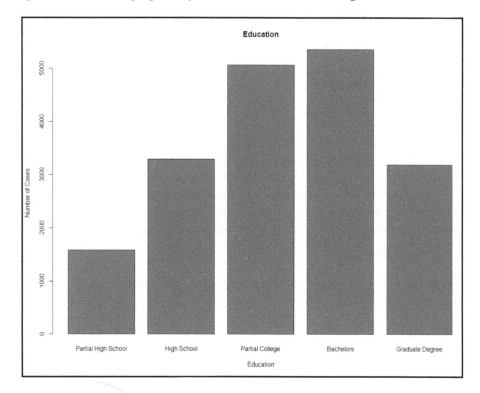

Enhanced plot for Education

Now, let's make some more complex visualizations with multiple lines of code! For a start, the following code generates a new data frame TM1 as a subset of the TM data frame, selecting only 10 rows and 3 columns. This data frame will be used for line plots, where each case is plotted. The code also renames the variables to get unique names and adds the data frame to the search path:

```
cols1 <- c("CustomerKey", "NumberCarsOwned", "TotalChildren");
TM1 <- TM[TM$CustomerKey < 11010, cols1];
names(TM1) <- c("CustomerKey1", "NumberCarsOwned1", "TotalChildren1");
attach(TM1);
```

The next code cross-tabulates the NumberCarsOwned and the BikeBuyer variables and stores the result in an object. This cross-tabulation is used later for a bar plot:

```
nofcases <- table(NumberCarsOwned, BikeBuyer);
nofcases;
```

The cross-tabulation result is shown here:

```
                    BikeBuyer
NumberCarsOwned    0     1
              0  1551 2687
              1  2187 2696
              2  3868 2589
              3   951  694
              4   795  466
```

You can specify graphical parameters directly or through the par() function. When you set parameters with this function, these parameters are valid for all subsequent graphs until you reset them. You can get a list of parameters by simply calling the function without any arguments. The following line of code saves all modifiable parameters to an object by using the no.readonly = TRUE argument when calling the par() function. This way, it is possible to restore the default parameters later, without exiting the session:

```
oldpar <- par(no.readonly = TRUE);
```

The next line defines that the next four graphs will be combined in a single graph in a 2 x 2 invisible grid, filled by rows:

```
par(mfrow=c(2,2));
```

Now let's start filling the grid with smaller graphs. The next command creates a stacked bar showing marital status distribution at different education levels. It also adds a title and *x* and *y* axis labels. It changes the default colors used for different marital statuses to blue and yellow. This graph appears in the top-left corner of the invisible grid:

```
plot(Education, MaritalStatus,
    main='Education and marital status',
    xlab='Education', ylab ='Marital Status',
    col=c("blue", "yellow"));
```

The `hist()` function produces a histogram for numeric variables. Histograms are especially useful if they don't have too many bars. You can define breakpoints for continuous variables with many distinct values. However, the `NumberCarsOwned` variable has only five distinct values, and therefore defining breakpoints is not necessary. This graph fills the top-right cell of the grid:

```
hist(NumberCarsOwned, main = 'Number of cars owned',
    xlab='Number of Cars Owned', ylab ='Number of Cases',
    col="blue");
```

The next part of the code is slightly longer. It produces a line chart with two lines: one for the `TotalChildren1` and one for the `NumberCarsOwned1` variable. Note that the limited dataset is used, in order to get just a small number of plotting points. Firstly, a vector of colors is defined. This vector is used to define the colors for the legend. Then, the `plot()` function generates a line chart for the `TotalChildren1` variable. Here, two new parameters are introduced: the `type="o"` parameter defines the over-plotted points and lines, and the `lwd=2` parameter defines the line width. Then, the `lines()` function is used to add a line for the `NumberCarsOwned1` variable to the current graph, to the current cell of the grid. Then, a legend is added with the `legend()` function to the same graph. The `cex=1.4` parameter defines the character expansion factor relative to the current character size in the graph. The `bty="n"` parameter defines that there is no box drawn around the legend. The `lty` and `lwd` parameters define the line type and the line width for the legend. Finally, a title is added. This graph is positioned in the bottom-left cell of the grid:

```
plot_colors=c("blue", "red");
plot(TotalChildren1,
    type="o",col='blue', lwd=2,
    xlab="Key",ylab="Number");
lines(NumberCarsOwned1,
    type="o",col='red', lwd=2);
legend("topleft",
    c("TotalChildren", "NumberCarsOwned"),
    cex=1.4,col=plot_colors,lty=1:2,lwd=1, bty="n");
title(main="Total children and number of cars owned line chart",
    col.main="DarkGreen", font.main=4);
```

There is one more cell in the grid to fill. The `barplot()` function generates a histogram of the `NumberCarsOwned` variable in groups of the `BikeBuyer` variable and shows the histograms side by side. Note that the input for this function is the cross-tabulation object generated with the `table()` function. The `legend()` function adds a legend in the top-right corner of the chart. This chart fills the bottom-right cell of the grid:

```
barplot(nofcases,
        main='Number of cars owned and bike buyer gruped',
        xlab='BikeBuyer', ylab ='NumberCarsOwned',
        col=c("black", "blue", "red", "orange", "yellow"),
        beside=TRUE);
legend("topright",legend=rownames(nofcases),
        fill = c("black", "blue", "red", "orange", "yellow"),
        ncol = 1, cex = 0.75);
```

The following figure shows the overall results, all four graphs combined into one:

Four graphs in an invisible grid

The last part of the code is the cleanup part. It restores the old graphics parameters and removes both data frames from the search path:

```
par(oldpar);
detach(TM);
detach(TM1);
```

Introductory statistics

Sometimes, numbers tell us more than pictures. After all, the name *descriptive statistics* tells you it is about describing something. Descriptive statistics describe a distribution of a variable. Inferential statistics tell you about the associations between variables. There are a plethora of possibilities for introductory statistics in R. However, before calculating the statistical values, let's quickly define some of the most popular measures of descriptive statistics.

The **mean** is the most common measure for determining the center of a distribution. It is also probably the most abused statistical measure. The mean does not mean anything without the standard deviation or some other measure, and it should never be used alone. Let me give you an example. Imagine there are two pairs of people. In the first pair, both people earn the same—let's say, $80,000 per year. In the second pair, one person earns $30,000 per year, while the other earns $270,000 per year. The mean salary for the first pair is $80,000, while the mean for the second pair is $150,000 per year. By just listing the mean, you could conclude that each person from the second pair earns more than either of the people in the first pair. However, you can clearly see that this would be a seriously incorrect conclusion.

The definition of a mean is simple; it is the sum of all values of a continuous variable divided by the number of cases, as shown in the following formula:

$$\mu = \frac{1}{n} * \sum_{i=1}^{n} v_i$$

The **median** is the value that splits the distribution into two halves. The number of rows with a value lower than the median must be equal to the number of rows with a value greater than the median for a selected variable. If there are an odd number of rows, the median is the middle row. If the number of rows is even, the median can be defined as the average value of the two middle rows (the financial median), the smaller of them (the lower statistical median), or the larger of them (the upper statistical median).

The **range** is the simplest measure of the spread; it is the plain distance between the maximum value and the minimum value that the variable takes.

A quick review: a variable is an attribute of an observation represented as a column in a table.

The first formula for the range is:

$$R = v_{max} - v_{min}$$

You can split the distribution more—for example, you can split each half into two halves. This way, you get quartiles as three values that split the distribution into quarters. Let's generalize this splitting process. You start with sorting rows (cases, observations) on selected columns (attributes, variables). You define the rank as the absolute position of a row in your sequence of sorted rows. The percentile rank of a value is a relative measure that tells you what percentage of all (n) observations have a lower value than the selected value.

By splitting the observations into quarters, you get three percentiles (at 25%, 50%, and 75% of all rows), and you can read the values at those positions that are important enough to have their own names: the quartiles. The second quartile is, of course, the median. The first one is called the **lower quartile** and the third one is known as the **upper quartile**. If you subtract the lower quartile (the first one) from the upper quartile (the third one), you get the formula for the **inter-quartile range (IQR)**:

$$IQR = Q_3 - Q_1$$

Let's suppose for a moment you have only one observation *(n=1)*. This observation is also your sample mean, but there is no spread at all. You can calculate the spread only if *n* exceeds 1. Only *(n-1)* pieces of information help you calculate the spread, considering that the first observation is your mean. These pieces of information are called **degrees of freedom**. You can also think of degrees of freedom as the number of pieces of information that can vary. For example, imagine a variable that can take five different discrete states. You need to calculate the frequencies of four states only to know the distribution of the variable; the frequency of the last state is determined by the frequencies of the first four states you calculated, and they cannot vary because the cumulative percentage of all states must equal 100.

You can measure the distance between each value and the mean value and call it the **deviation**. The sum of all distances gives you a measure of how spread out your population is. But you must consider that some of the distances are positive, while others are negative; actually, they mutually cancel themselves out, so the total gives you exactly zero. So there are only *(n-1)* deviations free; the last one is strictly determined by the requirement just stated. In order to avoid negative deviation, you can square them. So, here is the formula for **variance**:

$$Var = \frac{1}{n-1} * \sum_{i=1}^{n}(v_i - \mu)^2$$

This is the formula for the variance of a sample, used as an estimator for the variance of the population. Now, imagine that your data represents the complete population, and the mean value is unknown. Then, all the observations contribute to the variance calculation equally, and degrees of freedom make no sense. The **variance for a population** is defined in a similar way to the variance for a sample. You just use all n cases instead of *n-1* degrees of freedom:

$$Var = \frac{1}{n} * \sum_{i=1}^{n}(v_i - \mu)^2$$

Of course, with large samples, both formulas return practically the same number. To compensate for having the deviations squared, you can take the square root of the variance. This is the definition of **standard deviation** (σ):

$$\sigma = \sqrt{Var}$$

Of course, you can use the same formula to calculate the **standard deviation for the population**, and the standard deviation of a sample as an estimator of the standard deviation for the population; just use the appropriate variance in the formula.

You probably remember **skewness** and **kurtosis** from Chapter 2, *Review of SQL Server Features for Developers*. These two measures measure the skew and the peakedness of a distribution. The formulas for skewness and kurtosis are:

$$Skewness = \frac{n}{(n-1)*(n-2)} * \sum_{i=1}^{n}(\frac{v_i - \mu}{\sigma})^3$$

$$Kurtosis = \frac{n*(n+1)}{(n-1)*(n-2)*(n-3)} * \sum_{i=1}^{n}(\frac{v_i - \mu}{\sigma})^4 - \frac{3*(n-1)^2}{(n-2)*(n-3)}$$

Where:

- *n*: number of cases
- v_i: ith value
- μ: mean
- σ: standard deviation

These are the descriptive statistics measures for continuous variables. Note that some statisticians calculate kurtosis without the last subtraction, which is approximating 3 for large samples; therefore, a kurtosis around 3 means a normal distribution, neither significantly peaked nor flattened.

For a quick overview of discrete variables, you use frequency tables. In a frequency table, you can show values, the absolute frequency of those values, absolute percentage, cumulative percentage, and a histogram of the absolute percentage.

One very simple way to calculate most of the measures introduced so far is by using the `summary()` function. You can feed it with a single variable or with a whole data frame. For a start, the following code re-reads the CSV file in a data frame and correctly orders the values of the `Education` variable. In addition, the code attaches the data frame to the search path:

```
TM = read.table("C:\\SQL2017DevGuide\\Chapter13_TM.csv",
                sep=",", header=TRUE,
                stringsAsFactors = TRUE);
attach(TM);
Education = factor(Education, order=TRUE,
                   levels=c("Partial High School",
                            "High School","Partial College",
                            "Bachelors", "Graduate Degree"));
```

Note that you might get a warning, `"The following object is masked _by_ .GlobalEnv: Education"`. You get this warning if you didn't start a new session with this section. Remember, the `Education` variable was already ordered earlier in the code, and is already part of the global search path, and therefore hides or masks the newly `read` column, `Education`. You can safely disregard this message and continue with defining the order of the `Education` values again.

The following code shows the simplest way to get a quick overview of descriptive statistics for the whole data frame:

```
summary(TM);
```

The partial results are here:

```
CustomerKey    MaritalStatus Gender TotalChildren   NumberChildrenAtHome
Min.   :11000  M:10011      F:9133  Min.   :0.000   Min.   :0.000
1st Qu.:15621  S: 8473      M:9351  1st Qu.:0.000   1st Qu.:0.000
Median :20242                       Median :2.000   Median :0.000
Mean   :20242                       Mean   :1.844   Mean   :1.004
3rd Qu.:24862                       3rd Qu.:3.000   3rd Qu.:2.000
Max.   :29483                       Max.   :5.000   Max.   :5.000
```

As mentioned, you can get a quick summary for a single variable as well. In addition, there are many functions that calculate a single statistic, for example, sd() to calculate the standard deviation. The following code calculates the summary for the Age variable, and then calls different functions to get the details. Note that the dataset was added to the search path. You should be able to recognize which statistic is calculated by which function from the function names and the results:

```
summary(Age);
mean(Age);
median(Age);
min(Age);
max(Age);
range(Age);
quantile(Age, 1/4);
quantile(Age, 3/4);
IQR(Age);
var(Age);
sd(Age);
```

Here are the results, with added labels for better readability:

```
   Min. 1st Qu.  Median   Mean 3rd Qu.    Max.
  28.00   36.00   43.00  45.41   53.00   99.00
Mean  45.40981
Median       43
Min    28
Max    99
Range  28 99
25%    36
75%    53
IQR    17
Var    132.9251
StDev  11.52931
```

To calculate the skewness and kurtosis, you need to install an additional package. One possibility is the moments package. The following code installs the package, loads it in memory, and then calls the skewness() and kurtosis() functions from the package:

```
install.packages("moments");
library(moments);
skewness(Age);
kurtosis(Age);
```

The kurtosis() function from this package does not perform the last subtraction in the formula and therefore, a kurtosis of three means no peakedness. Here are the results:

```
0.7072522
2.973118
```

Another possibility to calculate the skewness and the kurtosis is to create a custom function. Creating your own function is really simple in R. Here is an example, together with a call:

```
skewkurt <- function(p){
  avg <- mean(p)
  cnt <- length(p)
  stdev <- sd(p)
  skew <- sum((p-avg)^3/stdev^3)/cnt
  kurt <- sum((p-avg)^4/stdev^4)/cnt-3
  return(c(skewness=skew, kurtosis=kurt))
};
skewkurt(Age);
```

Note that this is a simple example, not taking into account all the details of the formulas, and not checking for missing values. Nevertheless, here is the result. Note that in this function, the kurtosis was calculated with the last subtraction in the formula and is therefore different from the kurtosis from the moments package for approximately 3:

```
skewness      kurtosis
0.70719483   -0.02720354
```

Before finishing with these introductory statistics, let's calculate some additional details for discrete variables. The `summary()` function returns absolute frequencies only. The `table()` function can be used for the same task. However, it is more powerful, as it can also do cross tabulation of two variables. You can also store the results in an object and pass this object to the `prop.table()` function, which calculates the proportions. The following code shows how to call the last two functions:

```
edt <- table(Education);
edt;
prop.table(edt);
```

Here are the results:

```
Partial High School      High School   Partial College        Bachelors
               1581             3294              5064             5356
    Graduate Degree
               3189
Partial High School      High School   Partial College        Bachelors
         0.08553343       0.17820818        0.27396667       0.28976412
    Graduate Degree
         0.17252759
```

Of course, there is a package that includes a function that gives you a more condensed analysis of a discrete variable. The following code installs the `descr` package, loads it to memory, and calls the `freq()` function:

```
install.packages("descr");
library(descr);
freq(Education);
```

Here are the results:

```
                     Frequency Percent Cum Percent
Partial High School       1581   8.553       8.553
High School               3294  17.821      26.374
Partial College           5064  27.397      53.771
Bachelors                 5356  28.976      82.747
Graduate Degree           3189  17.253     100.000
Total                    18484 100.000
```

SQL Server R Machine Learning Services

In SQL Server suite, **SQL Server Analysis Services** (**SSAS**) supports data mining from version 2000. SSAS includes some of the most popular algorithms with very explanatory visualizations. SSAS data mining is very simple to use. However, the number of algorithms is limited, and the whole statistical analysis is missing in the SQL Server suite. By introducing R in SQL Server, Microsoft made a quantum leap forward in statistics, data mining, and machine learning.

Of course, the R language and engine have their own issues. For example, installing packages directly from code might not be in accordance with the security policies of an enterprise. In addition, most calculations are not scalable. Scalability might not be an issue for statistical and data mining analyses, because you typically work with samples. However, machine learning algorithms can consume huge amounts of data.

With SQL Server 2016 and 2017, you get a highly scalable R engine. Not every function and algorithm is rewritten as a scalable one. Nevertheless, you will probably find the one you need for your analysis of a big dataset. You can store an R data mining or machine learning model in a SQL Server table and use it for predictions on new data. You can even store graphs in a binary column and use it in **SQL Server Reporting Services** (**SSRS**) reports. Finally, R support is not limited to SQL Server only. You can use R code also in **Power BI** Desktop and Power BI Service, and in **Azure Machine Learning** (**Azure ML**) experiments.

Installing packages is not that simple, and must be done by a DBA. In SQL Server, you call R code through a stored procedure. This way, a DBA can apply all SQL Server security to R code as well. In addition, you need a SQL Server, a Windows login, or Windows to run the code that uses SQL Server R Machine Learning Services. This login must also have enough permissions on SQL Server objects. It needs to access the database where you run the R code, permissions to read SQL Server data, and potentially, if you need to store the results in a SQL Server table, permissions to write data.

This section introduces R support in SQL Server, including:

- Architecture
- Using R code in T-SQL
- Scalable solutions
- Security
- Deploying R models in SQL Server

Discovering SQL Server R Machine Learning Services

Microsoft provides the highly scalable R engine in two flavors:

- **R Machine Learning Services (In-Database)**: This is the installation that integrates R into SQL Server. It includes a database service that runs outside the SQL Server Database Engine and provides a communication channel between the Database Engine and R runtime. You install it with SQL Server setup. The R engine includes open source R components and, in addition, a set of scalable R packages.
- **Microsoft R Server**: This is a standalone R server with the same open and scalable packages that run on multiple platforms.

For development, you prepare a client installation. You can download Microsoft R Client from `http://aka.ms/rclient/download`. This installation includes the open R engine and the scalable packages as well. In addition to the engine, you will probably want to also install a development IDE, either RStudio or R Tools for Visual Studio. Of course, you can also download and install the Developer Edition of SQL Server 2017 instead. This way, you get both the R runtime with the scalable packages and the database engine.

Some scalable packages shipped with SQL Server R Machine Learning Services are:

- **RevoScaleR**: This is a set of parallelized scalable R functions for processing data, data overview and preliminary analysis, and machine-learning models. The procedures in this package can work with chunks of data at a time, so they don't need to load all of the data in memory immediately.
- **RevoPemaR**: This package allows you to write custom parallel external algorithms.
- **MicrosoftML**: This is a new package from December 2016, with many additional scalable machine learning algorithms implemented.

The following figure shows how the communication process between SQL Server and R engine works:

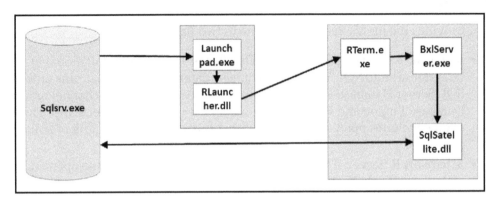

The communication between SQL Server and R runtime

The components involved and their communications are as follows:

- In SQL Server Database Engine, you run an R script with the sys.sp_execute_external_script system stored procedure. SQL Server sends the request to the **Launchpad** service, a new service that supports the execution of external scripts.
- The Launchpad service starts the launcher appropriate for the language of your script. Currently, the only launcher available is the RLauncher, and therefore you can launch an external script from SQL Server using the R language only. However, you can see that the infrastructure is prepared to enable the execution of scripts in additional programming languages.
- The RLauncher starts **RTerm**, the R terminal application for executing R scripts.
- The RTerm sends the script to **BxlServer.** This is a new executable used for communication between SQL Server and the R engine. The scalable R functions are implemented in this executable as well.
- The BxlServer uses **SQL Satellite**, a new extensibility API that provides a fast data transfer between SQL Server and an external runtime. Again, currently only the R runtime is supported.

Time to test the execution of an R script in SQL Server! First, you need to use the sys.sp_configure system stored procedure to enable external scripts. You can do this with the following code:

```
USE master;
EXEC sys.sp_configure 'show advanced options', 1;
RECONFIGURE
EXEC sys.sp_configure 'external scripts enabled', 1;
RECONFIGURE;
```

After that, you can call the sys.sp_execute_external_script system stored procedure. The most important parameters of this procedure include:

- @language: Currently limited to value R
- @script: The actual script in the external language
- @input_data_1_name: The name of the data frame, as seen in the R code in the @script parameter for the first input dataset; the default name is InputDataSet
- @input_data_1: The T-SQL query that specifies the first input dataset
- @output_data_1_name: The name of the R object, most probably a data frame, with the output dataset; the default name is OutputDataSet
- WITH RESULT SETS: The option where you specify the column names and data types of the output of the R script, as seen in SQL Server
- @params: a list of input and output parameters for the script

In the following example, the R script called from SQL Server retrieves a list of installed packages:

```
EXECUTE sys.sp_execute_external_script
 @language=N'R',
 @script =
 N'str(OutputDataSet);
   packagematrix <- installed.packages();
   NameOnly <- packagematrix[,1];
   OutputDataSet <- as.data.frame(NameOnly);'
WITH RESULT SETS ( ( PackageName nvarchar(20) ) );
```

The shortened results are:

```
PackageName
--------------------
base
boot
class
...
```

```
RevoIOQ
revoIpe
RevoMods
RevoPemaR
RevoRpeConnector
RevoRsrConnector
RevoScaleR
RevoTreeView
RevoUtils
RevoUtilsMath
...
spatial
splines
stats
...
```

You can see that besides some base packages, there is a set of packages where the name starts with the string Revo, including the RevoScaleR and RevoPemaR packages. These are two packages with scalable functions and their associated packages.

Creating scalable solutions

You can use the scalable server resources from the client. You start development in RStudio or R Tools for Visual Studio by setting the execution context to the server. Of course, you must do it with a function from the RevoScaleR package, which is loaded in memory at the beginning of the following R code. The code defines the execution context on SQL Server, in the context of the AdventureWorksDW2014 database. Remember, the dbo.vTargetMail view comes from this database. Also note that the RUser used to connect to SQL Server needs permission to use the sys.sp_execute_external_script procedure. For the sake of simplicity, I just added the RUser database user in the AdventureWorksDW2014 database on my local SQL Server instance to the db_owner database role. The following code changes the execution context to SQL Server:

```
library(RevoScaleR);
sqlConnStr <- "Driver=SQL Server;Server=SQL2017EIM;
 Database=AdventureWorksDW2014;Uid=RUser;Pwd=Pa$$w0rd";
sqlShare <- "C:\\SQL2017DevGuide";
chunkSize = 1000;
srvEx <- RxInSqlServer(connectionString = sqlConnStr, shareDir = sqlShare,
                       wait = TRUE, consoleOutput = FALSE);
rxSetComputeContext(srvEx);
```

The parameters define the connection string to my SQL Server instance, the shared folder used to exchange the data between SQL Server and R engine, and the chunk size, which is actually used later when reading the data. Please note that you need to change the name of the SQL Server to your SQL Server instance. The `RxInSqlServer()` object creates the compute context in SQL Server. The `wait` parameter defines whether the execution in SQL Server is blocking and the control does not return to the client until the execution is finished or the execution is not blocking. The `consoleOutput` parameter defines whether the output of the R code started by SQL Server should be returned to the user console. The `rxSetComputeContext()` function actually sets the execution context to SQL Server.

After the execution context has been set to SQL Server, you can try to use other scalable functions. For example, `rxImport()` can be used to import comma-separated value file data to a data frame. The `rowsPerRead` parameter reads in batches, using the chunk size defined earlier in the code. The batch size of 1,000 rows is quite small, just to show how this import in chunks works. For larger datasets, you should use much larger batches. You should test what the best size is for your datasets and the processing power you have:

```
TMCSV = rxImport(inData = "C:\\SQL2017DevGuide\\Chapter13_TM.csv",
                 stringsAsFactors = TRUE, type = "auto",
                 rowsPerRead = chunkSize, reportProgress = 3);
```

The `reportProgress` parameter defines a detailed output. The abbreviated result of the previous code is as follows:

```
ReadNum=1, StartRowNum=1, CurrentNumRows=1000, TotalRowsProcessed=1000,
ReadTime=0.01, ProcessDataTime = 0, LoopTime = 0.01
ReadNum=2, StartRowNum=1001, CurrentNumRows=1000, TotalRowsProcessed=2000,
ReadTime=0.007, ProcessDataTime = 0.002, LoopTime = 0.007
...
Overall compute summaries time: 0.133 secs.
Total loop time: 0.132
Total read time for 19 reads: 0.115
Total process data time: 0.041
Average read time per read: 0.00605263
Average process data time per read: 0.00215789
Number of threads used: 2
```

You can see that the chunk size was really 1,000 rows, how much time was needed for each chunk, the total time, the number of threads used, and more. This confirms that `RevoScaleR` functions use parallelism. Note that you might get a different number of threads, depending on your system configuration and available resources.

The next code reads the same data again, this time from SQL Server. Note that an ODBC connection is not needed; the code is already executed on the server side in the context of the AdventureWorksDW2014 database. The RxSqlServerData() function generates a SQL Server data source object. You can think of it as a proxy object to the SQL Server rowset, which is the result of the query:

```
TMquery <-
"SELECT CustomerKey, MaritalStatus, Gender,
  TotalChildren, NumberChildrenAtHome,
  EnglishEducation AS Education,
  EnglishOccupation AS Occupation,
  HouseOwnerFlag, NumberCarsOwned, CommuteDistance,
  Region, BikeBuyer,
  YearlyIncome, Age
 FROM dbo.vTargetMail";
sqlTM <- RxSqlServerData(sqlQuery = TMquery,
                         connectionString = sqlConnStr,
                         stringsAsFactors = TRUE,
                         rowsPerRead = chunkSize);
TMSQL <- rxImport(inData = sqlTM, reportProgress = 3);
```

The sqlTM object is the pointer to the SQL Server data, and exposes the metadata of the result set of the query to the client R code. Note that the last line creates a new data frame and physically transfers data to the client. Therefore, if you executed the code in this section step by step, you should have two data frames—TMCSV and TMSQL—with data in local client memory, and the sqlTM data source connection, which you can use as a data frame. You can see the difference if you try to get info about all three objects with the rxGetInfo() function:

```
rxGetInfo(TMCSV);
rxGetInfo(sqlTM);
```

The previous code returns the following result:

```
Data frame: TMCSV
Number of observations: 18484
Number of variables: 14
Connection string: Driver=SQL Server;Server=localhost;
 Database=AdventureWorksDW2014;Uid=RUser;Pwd=Pa$$w0rd
Data Source: SQLSERVER
```

You get the details about the metadata of the SQL data source connection object with the rxGetVarInfo() function. You can get summary statistics and different cross tabulations of the SQL Server data with the rxSummary(), rxCrossTabs(), and rxCube() functions. You can create histograms with the rxHistogram() function. All these functions use the SQL Server execution context. The following code shows how to use the functions mentioned:

```
sumOut <- rxSummary(
   formula = ~ NumberCarsOwned + Occupation + F(BikeBuyer),
   data = sqlTM);
sumOut;
cTabs <- rxCrossTabs(formula = BikeBuyer ~
                        Occupation : F(HouseOwnerFlag),
                        data = sqlTM);
print(cTabs, output = "counts");
print(cTabs, output = "sums");
print(cTabs, output = "means");
summary(cTabs, output = "sums");
summary(cTabs, output = "counts");
summary(cTabs, output = "means");
cCube <- rxCube(formula = BikeBuyer ~
                   Occupation : F(HouseOwnerFlag),
                   data = sqlTM);
cCube;
rxHistogram(formula = ~ BikeBuyer | MaritalStatus,
            data = sqlTM);
```

Note that all of these scalable functions accept data from the SQL Server data source connection object. Because they execute on SQL Server, you cannot use the local data frames to feed them. If you used a local data frame, you would get an error. If you want to use the scalable functions with the local datasets, you need to switch the execution context back to local.

The following code shows how to set the execution context back to the client machine:

```
rxSetComputeContext("local");
```

The `RevoScaleR` package includes a function to calculate clusters of similar cases based on the values of the input variables. It uses the **K-means clustering** algorithm. The `rxKmeans()` function in the following code uses a local data frame. It defines two clusters and then assigns each case to one of the clusters. The `summary()` function gives you the details of the clustering model:

```
TwoClust <- rxKmeans(formula = ~ BikeBuyer + TotalChildren +
NumberCarsOwned,
                     data = TMSQL,
                     numClusters = 2);
summary(TwoClust);
```

You can add the cluster membership to the original data frame and rename the variable to a friendlier name:

```
TMClust <- cbind(TMSQL, TwoClust$cluster);
names(TMClust)[15] <- "ClusterID";
```

In order to understand the meaning of the clusters, you need to analyze them. The following code creates a nice graph that consists of three individual small graphs showing the distribution of each input variable in each cluster:

```
attach(TMClust);
oldpar <- par(no.readonly = TRUE);
par(mfrow=c(1,3));

# NumberCarsOwned and clusters
nofcases <- table(NumberCarsOwned, ClusterID);
nofcases;
barplot(nofcases,
        main='Number of cars owned and cluster ID',
        xlab='Cluster Id', ylab ='Number of Cars',
        legend=rownames(nofcases),
        col=c("black", "blue", "red", "orange", "yellow"),
        beside=TRUE);
# BikeBuyer and clusters
nofcases <- table(BikeBuyer, ClusterID);
nofcases;
barplot(nofcases,
        main='Bike buyer and cluster ID',
        xlab='Cluster Id', ylab ='BikeBuyer',
        legend=rownames(nofcases),
        col=c("blue", "yellow"),
        beside=TRUE);
# TotalChildren and clusters
nofcases <- table(TotalChildren, ClusterID);
nofcases;
```

```
barplot(nofcases,
        main='Total children and cluster ID',
        xlab='Cluster Id', ylab ='Total Children',
        legend=rownames(nofcases),
        col=c("black", "blue", "green", "red", "orange", "yellow"),
        beside=TRUE);

# Clean up
par(oldpar);
detach(TMClust);
```

You should already be familiar with this code from the examples earlier in this chapter. The next screenshot shows the results:

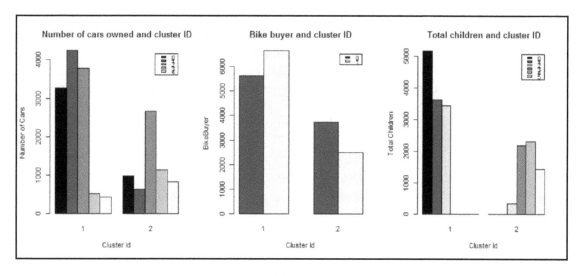

The analysis of the clusters

Deploying R models

Once you have created a model, you can deploy it to a SQL Server table and use it later for predictions. You can also do the predictions in R and store just the results in a SQL Server table.

Let's start by creating another model in R. This time, the model uses the **Logistic Regression** algorithm. The model uses the SQL Server data and the `dbo.vTargetMail` view to learn how the values of the `NumberCarsOwned`, `TotalChildren`, `Age`, and `YearlyIncome` input variables influence the value of the `BikeBuyer` target variable. The following code sets the execution context back to SQL Server, creates the model with the RevoScale `rxLogit()` function, and shows the summary of the model:

```
rxSetComputeContext(srvEx);
bbLogR <- rxLogit(BikeBuyer ~
        NumberCarsOwned + TotalChildren + Age + YearlyIncome,
        data = sqlTM);
summary(bbLogR);
```

You can use the model to perform predictions. In the following example, the model is used to make predictions on the same dataset that was used for training the model. In a real-life situation, you would perform predictions on a new dataset. The code stores the predictions, together with the input values used, in a SQL Server table. The `RxSqlServerData()` function prepares the connection to the SQL Server database and the target table name. The `rxPredict()` function performs the predictions, physically creates the SQL Server table, and inserts the data. Of course, the database user used to connect to SQL Server must have appropriate permissions to create a table:

```
bbLogRPredict <- RxSqlServerData(connectionString = sqlConnStr,
                                 table = "dbo.TargetMailLogR");
rxPredict(modelObject = bbLogR,
        data = sqlTM, outData = bbLogRPredict,
        predVarNames = "BikeBuyerPredict",
        type = "response", writeModelVars = TRUE);
```

If you get a warning message when executing the `rxPredict()` function, just ignore it. Warnings should be gone with the next version of the `RevoScaleR` library. Just check the results. You can use a T-SQL query to check the results, as shown here:

```
USE AdventureWorksDW2014;
SELECT *
FROM dbo.TargetMailLogR;
```

The partial results are shown here. Values exceed 0.5 mean positive predictions:

BikeBuyerPredict	BikeBuyer	NumberCarsOwned	TotalChildren	Age	YearlyIncome
0.733910292274223	1	0	2	44	90000
0.540550204813772	1	1	3	40	60000
0.529196837245225	1	1	3	45	60000

As mentioned, you can store a model in a SQL Server table. The following T-SQL code creates a table where the models are going to be stored and a stored procedure that actually inserts a model:

```
CREATE TABLE dbo.RModels
(Id INT NOT NULL IDENTITY(1,1) PRIMARY KEY,
 ModelName NVARCHAR(50) NOT NULL,
 Model VARBINARY(MAX) NOT NULL);
GO
CREATE PROCEDURE dbo.InsertModel
(@modelname NVARCHAR(50),
 @model NVARCHAR(MAX))
AS
BEGIN
    SET NOCOUNT ON;
    INSERT INTO dbo.RModels (ModelName, Model)
    VALUES (@modelname, CONVERT(VARBINARY(MAX), @model, 2));
END;
```

The infrastructure is created. Now you can store the model in a SQL Server table from R. However, in order to call a stored procedure, you need to use an ODBC connection. Therefore, the following code first loads the RODBC library to memory, and creates a connection to the SQL Server database. Then it serializes the model to a binary variable, and creates a string from the binary variable using the paste() function. The same function is used to prepare a string with the T-SQL code to insert the model in the table. Finally, the sqlQuery() function sends the T-SQL command to SQL Server. Again, the R user used to execute this code must have permission to execute the stored procedure:

```
library(RODBC);
conn <- odbcDriverConnect(sqlConnStr);
modelbin <- serialize(bbLogR, NULL);
modelbinstr=paste(modelbin, collapse="");
sqlQ <- paste("EXEC dbo.InsertModel @modelname='bbLogR', @model='",
              modelbinstr,"'", sep="");
sqlQuery(conn, sqlQ);
close(conn);
```

The final step is to use the model from T-SQL. The following code uses the
`sys.sp_execute_external_script` system procedure to use the model and perform a
prediction on a single case. First, it creates an input dataset that consists of a single row with
four input variables. Then, it retrieves the stored model. Then the R code is executed, which
un-serializes the model and uses the `rxPredict()` function again to generate the output
dataset, which includes the input variables and the prediction:

```
DECLARE @input AS NVARCHAR(MAX)
SET @input = N'
    SELECT *
    FROM (VALUES
          (0, 2, 44, 90000)) AS
          inpQ(NumberCarsOwned, TotalChildren, Age, YearlyIncome);'
DECLARE @mod VARBINARY(max) =
 (SELECT Model
  FROM DBO.RModels
  WHERE ModelName = N'bbLogR');
EXEC sys.sp_execute_external_script
 @language = N'R',
 @script = N'
  mod <- unserialize(as.raw(model));
  OutputDataSet<-rxPredict(modelObject = mod, data = InputDataSet,
  outData =  NULL,
          predVarNames = "BikeBuyerPredict", type = "response",
           checkFactorLevels=FALSE,
           writeModelVars = TRUE, overwrite = TRUE);
 ',
 @input_data_1 = @input,
 @params = N'@model VARBINARY(MAX)',
 @model = @mod
WITH RESULT SETS ((
 BikeBuyerPredict FLOAT,
 NumberCarsOwned INT,
 TotalChildren INT,
 Age INT,
 YearlyIncome FLOAT));
```

The results are as follows:

BikeBuyerPredict	NumberCarsOwned	TotalChildren	Age	YearlyIncome
0.733910292274223	0	2	44	90000

The input values used were the same as the values in the first row of the batch predictions from the dbo.vTargetMail view used in the previous prediction example. You can see that the predicted value is also the same.

You can also deploy a model from T-SQL code directly. The following code creates a **Decision Trees** predictive model using the rxDTree() function using the same data as the logistic regression model did. The data is this time read directly from the SQL Server database. The R code then serializes the model and passes the serialized model as an output parameter. T-SQL code inserts it into the table with the models.

```
DECLARE @model VARBINARY(MAX);
EXECUTE sys.sp_execute_external_script
  @language = N'R'
 ,@script = N'
   bbDTree <- rxDTree(BikeBuyer ~ NumberCarsOwned +
                       TotalChildren + Age + YearlyIncome,
                     data = sqlTM);
   model <- rxSerializeModel(bbDTree, realtimeScoringOnly = TRUE);'
 ,@input_data_1 = N'
     SELECT CustomerKey, BikeBuyer, NumberCarsOwned,
   TotalChildren, Age, YearlyIncome
     FROM dbo.vTargetMail;'
 ,@input_data_1_name = N'sqlTM'
 ,@params = N'@model VARBINARY(MAX) OUTPUT'
 ,@model = @model OUTPUT;
INSERT INTO dbo.RModels (ModelName, Model)
VALUES('bbDTree', @model);
```

You can also deploy a model from T-SQL code directly. The following code creates a Decision Trees predictive model using the rxDTree() function using the same data as the logistic regression model did. The data is this time read directly from the SQL Server database. The R code then serializes the model and passes the serialized model as an output parameter. T-SQL code inserts it into the table with the models.

In SQL Server 2017, there is a new PREDICT() T-SQL function. This function generates predictions based on stored models. In order to use this function, you don't even need to have ML Services with R and Python installed. You just need to serialize your model in a SQL Server table. However, there is an important limitation for using this function. The model you are using for the predictions must have been created with one of the supported algorithms from the RevoScaleR package. You can find the list of supported algorithms at https://docs.microsoft.com/en-us/sql/advanced-analytics/real-time-scoring#bkmk_rt_supported_algos.

The following code uses the PREDICT() T-SQL function to make predictions on the target mail data using the decision trees model just created. You can compare the predictions with the predictions from the logistic regression model to see which model performs better. You will learn more about model evaluation in the next chapter:

```
DECLARE @model VARBINARY(MAX) =
(
  SELECT Model
  FROM dbo.RModels
  WHERE ModelName = 'bbDTree'
);
SELECT d.CustomerKey, d.BikeBuyer,
 d.NumberCarsOwned, d.TotalChildren, d.Age,
 d.YearlyIncome, p.BikeBuyer_Pred
FROM PREDICT(MODEL = @model, DATA = dbo.vTargetMail AS d)
WITH(BikeBuyer_Pred FLOAT) AS p
ORDER BY d.CustomerKey;
```

Summary

In this chapter, you learned the basics of the R language. You learned data structures in R (especially the most important one, the data frame) and how to do simple data manipulation. Then you saw some of the capabilities of R by creating graphical visualizations and calculating descriptive statistics in order to get a deeper understanding of your data. Finally, you got a comprehensive view of R integration in SQL Server.

The next chapter, continues the story and gives you more in-depth knowledge about some of the most important data mining and machine learning algorithms and tasks.

14

Data Exploration and Predictive Modeling with R

Using the R language inside SQL Server gives us the opportunity to get knowledge out of data. We introduced R and R support in SQL Server in the previous chapter, and this chapter demonstrates how you can use R for advanced data exploration, statistical analysis, and predictive modeling, way beyond the possibilities offered by using the T-SQL language only.

You will start with intermediate statistics: exploring associations between two discrete and two continuous variables, and one discrete and one continuous variable. You will also learn about linear regression, where you explain the values of a dependent continuous variable with a linear regression formula using one or more continuous input variables.

The second section of this chapter starts by introducing advanced multivariate data mining and machine learning methods. You will learn about methods that do not use a target variable, or so-called **undirected methods**.

In the third part, you will learn about the most popular directed methods.

Finally, to finish the chapter and the book in a slightly lighter way, you will play with graphs again. The last section introduces `ggplot2`, the most popular package for visualizing data in R.

 The target audience of this book is database developers and solution architects who plan to use the new SQL Server 2016 and 2017 features, or simply want to know what is now available and which limitations from previous versions have been removed.

Most of the readers deal daily with simple statistics only, and less often with data mining and machine learning. Because of that, this chapter does not only show how to write the code for advanced analysis in R, it also gives you an introduction to the mathematics behind the code, and explains when you want to use which method.

This chapter will cover the following points:

- Associations between two or more variables
- Undirected data mining and machine learning methods
- Directed data mining and machine learning methods
- Advanced graphing in R
- The mathematics behind the advanced methods explained
- A mapping between problems and algorithms

Intermediate statistics – associations

In the previous chapter, you learned about discrete statistics methods for getting information about the distribution of discrete and continuous variables. In a data science project, the next typical step is to check for the **associations** between pairs of variables.

When checking for the associations between pairs of variables, you have three possibilities:

- Both variables are discrete
- Both variables are continuous
- There is one discrete and one continuous variable

Besides dealing with two variables only, this section also introduces **linear regression**, one of the most important statistical methods, where you model a single **response** (or **dependent**) variable with a regression formula that includes one or more **predictor** (or **independent**) variables.

Altogether, you will learn about the following in this section:

- Chi-squared test of the independence of two discrete variables
- Phi coefficient, contingency coefficient, and Cramer's V coefficient, which measure the association of two discrete variables
- Covariance and correlations between two continuous variables

- T-Test and one-way ANOVA, which measure associations between one continuous and one discrete variable
- Simple and polynomial linear regression

Exploring discrete variables

Contingency tables are used to examine the relationship between a subject's scores on two qualitative or categorical variables. They show the actual and expected distribution of cases in a **cross-tabulated** (pivoted) format for the two variables. The following table is an example of an **actual** (or **observed**) and **expected** distribution of cases over the Occupation column (on rows) and the MaritalStatus column (on columns):

Occupation/MaritalStatus	Married	Single	Total
Clerical Actual	4,745	4,388	**9,133**
Expected	4,946	4,187	**9,133**
Professional Actual	5,266	4,085	**9,351**
Expected	5,065	4,286	**9,351**
Total Actual	**10,011**	**8,473**	**18,484**
Expected	**10,111**	**8,473**	**18,484**

If the two variables are independent, then the actual distribution in every single cell should be approximately equal to the expected distribution in that cell. The expected distribution is used by calculating the marginal probability. For example, the marginal probability for value Married is 10,111/18,484 = 0.5416: there are more than 54% of married people in the sample. If the two variables are independent, then you would expect to have approximately 54% of married people among clericals and 54% among professionals. You might notice a dependency between two discrete variables by just viewing the contingency table for the two. However, a solid numerical measure is preferred.

If the columns are not contingent on the rows, then the rows and column frequencies are independent. The test of whether the columns are contingent on the rows is called the **chi-squared test of independence**. The **null hypothesis** is that there is no relationship between row and column frequencies. Therefore, there should be no difference between the observed (O) and expected (E) frequencies.

Chi-squared is simply a sum of normalized squared frequency deviations (that is, the sum of squares of differences between observed and expected frequencies divided by expected frequencies). This formula is also called the Pearson chi-squared formula, which is as follows:

$$x^2 = \frac{1}{n} * \sum_{i=1}^{n} \frac{(0 - E)^2}{E}$$

There are already prepared tables with critical points for the chi-squared distribution. If the calculated chi-squared value is greater than a critical value in the table for the defined degrees of freedom and for a specific confidence level, you can reject the null hypothesis with that confidence (which means the variables are interdependent). Degrees of freedom, explained for a single variable in the previous chapter, are the product of the degrees of freedom for columns (C) and rows (R), as the following formula shows:

$$DF = (C - 1) * (R - 1)$$

The following table is the **chi-squared critical points** table for the first 10 degrees of freedom. Greater differences between expected and actual data produce a larger chi-squared value. The larger the chi-squared value, the greater the probability that there really is a significant difference. The Probability row in the table shows you the maximal probability that the null hypothesis holds when the chi-squared value is greater than or equal to the value in the table for specific degrees of freedom:

DF	Chi-squared Value									
1	0.004	0.02	0.15	0.46	1.07	1.64	2.71	3.84	6.64	10.83
2	0.10	0.21	0.71	1.39	2.41	3.22	4.60	5.99	9.21	13.82
3	0.35	0.58	1.42	2.37	3.66	4.64	6.25	7.82	11.34	16.27
4	0.71	1.06	2.20	3.36	4.88	5.99	7.78	9.49	13.28	18.47
5	1.14	1.61	3.00	4.35	6.06	7.29	9.24	11.07	15.09	20.52
6	1.63	2.20	3.83	5.35	7.23	8.56	10.64	12.59	16.81	22.46
7	2.17	2.83	4.67	6.35	8.38	9.80	12.02	14.07	18.48	24.32
8	2.73	3.49	5.53	7.34	9.52	11.03	13.56	15.51	20.09	26.12
9	3.32	4.17	6.39	8.34	10.66	12.24	14.68	16.92	21.67	27.88
10	3.94	4.86	7.27	9.34	11.78	13.44	15.99	18.31	23.21	29.59
Probability	0.95	0.90	0.70	0.50	0.30	0.20	0.10	0.05	0.01	0.001
	Not significant						Significant			

For example, you have calculated chi-squared for two discrete variables. The value is 16, and the degrees of freedom are 7. Search for the first smaller and first bigger value for the chi-squared in the row for degrees of freedom 7 in the table. The values are 14.07 and 18.48. Check the appropriate probability for these two values, which are 0.05 and 0.01. This means that there is less than a 5% probability that the two variables are independent of each other, and more than 1% that they are independent. This is a significant percentage, meaning that you can say the variables are dependent with more than 95% probability.

The following code re-reads the target mail data from a CSV file, adds the new data frame to the search path, and defines the levels for the `Education` factor variable:

```
TM = read.table("C:\\SQL2017DevGuide\\Chapter14_TM.csv",
    sep=",", header=TRUE,
    stringsAsFactors = TRUE);
    attach(TM);
Education = factor(Education, order=TRUE,
    levels=c("Partial High School",
        "High School","Partial College",
        "Bachelors", "Graduate Degree"));
```

You can create pivot tables with the `table()` or the `xtabs()` R functions, as the following code shows:

```
table(Education, Gender, BikeBuyer);
table(NumberCarsOwned, BikeBuyer);
xtabs(~Education + Gender + BikeBuyer);
xtabs(~NumberCarsOwned + BikeBuyer);
```

You can check the results yourself. Nevertheless, in order to test for independence, you need to store the pivot table in a variable. The following code checks for independence between two pairs of variables—`Education` and `Gender` and `NumberCarsOwned` and `BikeBuyer`:

```
tEduGen <- xtabs(~ Education + Gender);
tNcaBik <- xtabs(~ NumberCarsOwned + BikeBuyer);
chisq.test(tEduGen);
chisq.test(tNcaBik);
```

Here are the results:

```
data:   tEduGen
X-squared = 5.8402, df = 4, p-value = 0.2114
data:   tNcaBik
X-squared = 734.38, df = 4, p-value < 2.2e-16
```

From the chi-squared critical points table, you can see that you can confirm the null hypothesis for the first pair of variables, while you need to reject it for the second pair. The p-value tells you the probability that the null hypothesis is correct. Therefore, you can conclude that the variables NumberCarsOwned and BikeBuyer are associated.

You can measure the association by calculating one of the following coefficients: the phi coefficient, contingency coefficient, or Cramer's V coefficient. You can use the phi coefficient for two binary variables only. The formulas for the three coefficients are:

$$\Phi = \sqrt{\frac{X^2}{n}}, C = \sqrt{\frac{X^2}{n + X^2}}, V = \sqrt{\frac{X^2}{n * (k - 1)}}$$

where $k = min(n\ of\ rows, n\ of\ columns)$

The contingency coefficient is not scaled between 0 and 1; for example, the highest possible value for a 2 x 2 table is 0.707. Anyway, the function assocstats() from the vcd package calculates all three of them; since the phi coefficient can be calculated for two binary variables only, it is not useful here. The following code installs the package and calls the function:

```
install.packages("vcd");
library(vcd);
assocstats(tEduGen);
assocstats(tNcaBik);
```

In addition, the vcd package includes the strucplot() function, which visualizes the contingency tables very nicely. The following code calls this function to visualize expected and observed frequencies for the two associated variables:

```
strucplot(tNcaBik, shade = TRUE, type = "expected", main = "Expected");
strucplot(tNcaBik, shade = TRUE, type = "observed", main = "Observed");
```

You can see a graphical representation of the observed frequencies in the following screenshot:

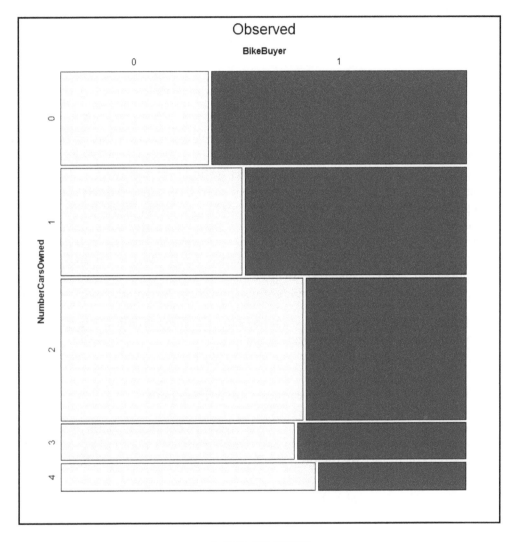

Contingency tables visualization

Finding associations between continuous variables

The first measure for the association of two continuous variables is **covariance**. Here is the formula:

$$cov(X,Y) = \sum_{i-1}^{n}(X_i - \mu(X)) * (Y_i - \mu(Y)) * P(X,Y)$$

Covariance indicates how two variables, X and Y, are related to each other. When large values of both variables occur together, the deviations are both positive (because X_i - Mean(X) > 0 and Y_i - Mean(Y) > 0), and their product is therefore positive. Similarly, when small values occur together, the product is positive as well. When one deviation is negative and one is positive, the product is negative. This can happen when a small value of X occurs with a large value of Y and the other way around. If positive products are absolutely larger than negative products, the covariance is positive; otherwise, it is negative. If negative and positive products cancel each other out, the covariance is zero. And when do they cancel each other out? Well, you can instantly imagine such a situation —when two variables are really independent. So the covariance evidently summarizes the relation between variables:

- If the covariance is positive, when the values of one variable are large, the values of the other one tend to be large as well
- When negative, the values of one variable are large when the values of the other one tend to be small
- If the covariance is zero, the variables are independent

In order to compare the strength of association between two different pairs of variables, a relative measure is better than an absolute one. This is Pearson's correlation coefficient, which divides the covariance by the product of the standard deviations of both variables:

$$\rho(X,Y) = \frac{cov(X,Y)}{\sigma(X) * \sigma(Y)}$$

The reason that the correlation coefficient is a useful measure of the relationship between two variables is that it is always bounded: -1 <= correlation coefficient <= 1. Of course, if the variables are independent, the correlation is zero, because the covariance is zero. The correlation can take the value 1 if the variables have a perfect positive linear relation (if you correlate a variable with itself, for example). Similarly, the correlation would be -1 for a perfect negative linear relation. The larger the absolute value of the coefficient, the more the variables are related. But the significance depends on the size of the sample. The following code creates a data frame that is a subset of the TM data frame used so far. The new data frame includes only continuous variables. Then the code calculates the covariance and the correlation coefficient between all possible pairs of variables:

```
x <- TM[,c("YearlyIncome", "Age", "NumberCarsOwned")];
cov(x);
cor(x);
```

Here are the correlation coefficients shown in a correlation matrix:

	YearlyIncome	Age	NumberCarsOwned
YearlyIncome	1.0000000	0.1446627	0.4666472
Age	0.1446627	1.0000000	0.1836616
NumberCarsOwned	0.4666472	0.1836616	1.0000000

You can see that the income and number of cars owned are correlated better than other pairs of variables.

Pearson's coefficient is not so suitable for ordinal variables so you can calculate Spearman's coefficient instead. The following code shows you how to calculate Spearman's coefficient on ordinal variables:

```
y <- TM[,c("TotalChildren", "NumberChildrenAtHome", "HouseOwnerFlag",
"BikeBuyer")];
cor(y);
cor(y, method = "spearman");
```

Finally, you can also visualize a correlation matrix. A nice visualization is provided by the corrgram() function in the corrgram package, as the following code shows:

```
install.packages("corrgram");
library(corrgram);
corrgram(y, order = TRUE, lower.panel = panel.shade,
         upper.panel = panel.shade, text.panel = panel.txt,
         cor.method = "spearman", main = "Corrgram");
```

In the following figure, you can see Spearman's correlation coefficient between pairs of four ordered variables graphically:

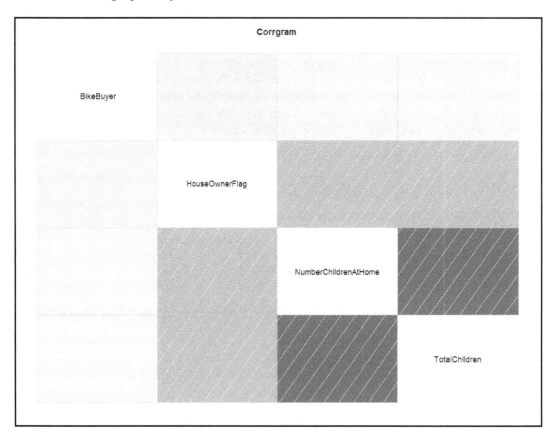

Correlation matrix visualization

The darker the shading in the preceding figure, the stronger the association; a right-oriented texture means a positive association, and a left-oriented texture means a negative association.

Continuous and discrete variables

Finally, it is time to check for linear dependencies between a continuous and a discrete variable. You can do this by measuring the variance between means of the continuous variable in different groups of discrete variable, for example measuring the difference in salary (continuous variable) between different genders (discrete variable). The null hypothesis here is that all variance between means is a result of the variance within each group, for example there is one woman with a very large salary, which raises the mean salary in the female group and makes a difference to the male group. If you reject it, this means that there is some significant variance in the means between groups. This is also known as the residual, or unexplained, variance. You are analyzing the variance of the means, so this analysis is called the **analysis of variance**, or **ANOVA**. A simpler test is the **Student's T-test**, which you can use to test for the differences between means in two groups only.

For a simple **one-way** ANOVA, testing means (averages) of a continuous variable for one independent discrete variable, you calculate the variance between groups, that is, MSA as the sum of squares of deviations of the group mean from the total mean multiplied by the number of cases in each group, with the degrees of freedom equal to the number of groups minus one. The formula is:

$$MS_A = \frac{SS_A}{DF_A}, where \; SS_A = \sum_{i=1}^{a} n_i * (\mu_i - \mu) \; and \; DF_A = (a - 1)$$

The discrete variable has discrete states, μ is the overall mean of the continuous variable, and μ_i is the mean in the continuous variable in the ith group of the discrete variable.

You calculate the variance within groups, that is, MSE as the sum over groups of the sum of squares of deviations of individual values from the group mean, with the degrees of freedom equal to the sum of the number of rows in each group minus 1:

$$MS_E = \frac{SS_E}{DF_E}, where \; SS_E = \sum_{i=1}^{a} \sum_{j=1}^{n_i} (v_{ij} - \mu_i) \; and \; DF_E = \sum_{i=1}^{a} (n_i - 1)$$

The individual value of the continuous variable is denoted as v_{ij}, μ_i is the mean in the continuous variable in the ith group of the discrete variable, and n_i is the number of cases in the ith group of the discrete variable.

Once you have both variances, you calculate the so-called *F* ratio as the ratio between the variance between groups and the variance within groups:

$$F = \frac{MS_A}{MS_E}$$

A large *F* value means you can reject the null hypothesis. Tables for the cumulative distribution under the tails of *F* distributions for different degrees of freedom are already calculated. For a specific *F* value with degrees of freedom between groups and degrees of freedom within groups, you can get critical points where there is, for example, less than a 5% of distribution under the *F* distribution curve up to the *F* point. This means that there is less than a 5% probability that the null hypothesis is correct (that is, there is an association between the means and the groups).

The following code checks for the differences in mean between two groups: it checks the YearlyIncome mean in the groups of Gender and HouseOwnerFlag variables. Note that the last line, after the comment, produces an error, because you can't use t.test for more than two groups:

```
t.test(YearlyIncome ~ Gender);
t.test(YearlyIncome ~ HouseOwnerFlag);
# Error - t-test supports only two groups
t.test(YearlyIncome ~ Education);
```

Instead of using the t.test() function, you can use the aov() function to check for the variance of the YearlyIncome means in the five groups of Education, as the following code shows. Note that the code first correctly orders the Education variable:

```
Education = factor(Education, order=TRUE,
levels=c("Partial High School",
"High School","Partial College",
"Bachelors", "Graduate Degree"));
AssocTest <- aov(YearlyIncome ~ Education);
summary(AssocTest);
```

If you execute the preceding code and check the results, you can conclude that yearly income is associated with the level of the education. You can see that the *F* value (324.7) is quite high and the probability for such a high *F* value being accidental is very low (<2e-16). You can also visualize the differences in the distribution of a continuous variable in groups of a discrete variable with the `boxplot()` function:

```
boxplot(YearlyIncome ~ Education,
        main = "Yearly Income in Groups",
        notch = TRUE,
        varwidth = TRUE,
        col = "orange",
        ylab = "Yearly Income",
        xlab = "Education");
```

The results of the box plot are shown in the following screenshot:

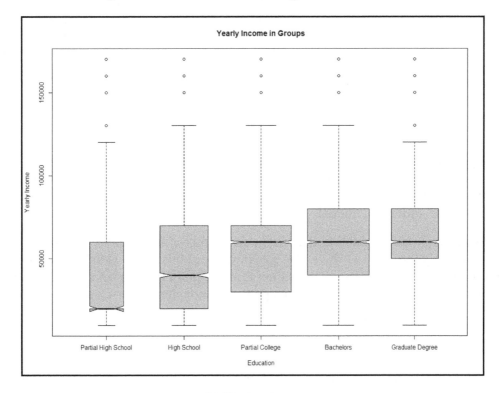

Variability of means in groups

Getting deeper into linear regression

When you get a high correlation between two continuous variables, you might want to express the relation between them in a functional way; that is, one variable as a function of the other one. The **linear function** between two variables is a line determined by its **slope** and its **intercept**. Here is the formula for the linear function:

$$Y' = a + b * X$$

You can imagine that the two variables you are analyzing form a two-dimensional plane. Their values define coordinates of the points in the plane. You are searching for a line that fits all the points best. Actually, it means that you want the points to fall as close to the line as possible. You need the deviations from the line—that is, the difference between the actual value for the Y_i and the line value Y'. If you use simple deviations, some are going to be positive and others negative, so the sum of all deviations is going to be zero for the best-fit line. A simple sum of deviations, therefore, is not a good measure. You can square the deviations, like they are squared to calculate the mean squared deviation. To find the best-fit line, you have to find the minimal possible sum of squared deviations. Here are the formulas for the slope and the intercept:

$$Slope(Y) = \frac{\sum_{i=1}^{n}(X_i - \mu(X)) * (Y_i - \mu(Y))}{\sum_{i=1}^{n}(X_i - \mu(X))^2}$$

$$Intercept\ (Y) = \mu(Y) - Slope(Y) * \mu(X)$$

Linear regression can be more complex. In a **multiple linear regression**, you use multiple independent variables in a formula. You can also try to express the association with a **polynomial regression** model, where the independent variable is introduced in the equation as an nth order polynomial.

The following code creates another data frame as a subset of the original data frame, this time keeping only the first 100 rows. The sole purpose of this action is the visualization at the end of this section, where you will see every single point in the graph. The code also removes the TM data frame from the search path and adds the new TMLM data frame to it:

```
TMLM <- TM[1:100, c("YearlyIncome", "Age")];
detach(TM);
attach(TMLM);
```

The following code uses the lm() function to create a simple linear regression model, where YearlyIncome is modeled as a linear function of Age:

```
LinReg1 <- lm(YearlyIncome ~ Age);
summary(LinReg1);
```

If you check the `summary` results for the model, you can see that there is some association between the two variables; however, the association is not that strong. You can try to express the association with polynomial regression, including squared `Age` in the formula:

```
LinReg2 <- lm(YearlyIncome ~ Age + I(Age ^ 2));
summary(LinReg2);
```

If you plot the values for the two variables in a graph, you can see that there is a non-linear dependency between them. The following code plots the cases as points in the plane, and then adds a linear and a **lowess** line to the graph. A lowess line calculation is more complex; it is used here to represent the polynomial relationship between two variables:

```
plot(Age, YearlyIncome,
     cex = 2, col = "orange", lwd = 2);
abline(LinReg1,
       col = "red", lwd = 2);
lines(lowess(Age, YearlyIncome),
      col = "blue", lwd = 2);
```

The following screenshot shows the results:

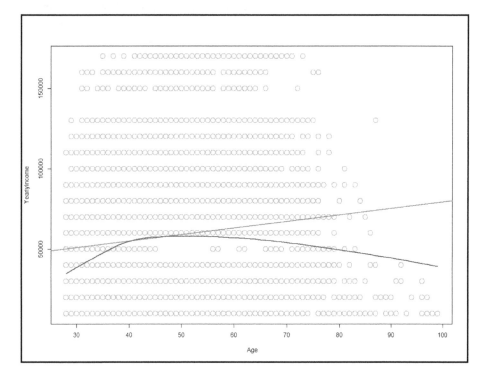

Linear and polynomial regression

You can see that the polynomial line (the curve) fits the data slightly better. The polynomial model is also more logical: you earn less when you are young, then you earn more and more, until at some age your income goes down again, probably after you retire. Finally, you can remove the TMLM data frame from the search path:

```
detach(TMLM);
```

Advanced analysis – undirected methods

Data mining and machine learning techniques are divided into two main classes:

- **The directed, or supervised, approach**: You use known examples and apply information to unknown examples to predict selected target variable(s)
- **The undirected, or unsupervised approach**: You discover new patterns inside the dataset as a whole

The most common undirected techniques are **clustering**, **dimensionality reduction**, and **affinity grouping**, also known as **basket analysis** or **association rules**. An example of clustering is looking through a large number of initially undifferentiated customers and trying to see if they fall into natural groupings based on similarities or dissimilarities in their features. This is a pure example of *undirected data mining* where the user has no preordained agenda and hopes that the data mining tool will reveal some meaningful structure. Affinity grouping is a special kind of clustering that identifies events or transactions that occur simultaneously. A well-known example of affinity grouping is market basket analysis, which attempts to understand what items are sold together at the same time.

In this section, you will learn about four very popular undirected methods:

- Principal Components Analysis
- Exploratory Factor Analysis
- Hierarchical clustering
- K-means clustering

Principal Components and Exploratory Factor Analysis

Principal Component Analysis (**PCA**) is a **data-reduction** technique. You use it as an intermediate step in a more complex analytical session. Imagine that you need to use hundreds of input variables, which can be correlated. With PCA, you convert a collection of possibly correlated variables into a new collection of linearly uncorrelated variables called **principal components**. The transformation is defined in such a way that the first principal component has the largest possible dataset overall variance, and each succeeding component in turn has the highest variance possible under the constraint that it is **orthogonal** to (uncorrelated with) the preceding components. Principal components are orthogonal because they are the **eigenvectors** of the covariance matrix, which is symmetric. The first principal component is the eigenvector with the highest **eigenvalue**, the second with the second highest, and so on. In short, an eigenvector is a direction of an eigenvalue with an explained variance for this point, for this direction. In further analysis, you keep only a few principal components instead of the plethora of original variables. Of course, you lose some variability; nevertheless, the first few principal components should retain the majority of the overall dataset variability.

The following figure explains the process of defining principal components graphically. Initially, variables used in the analysis form a multidimensional space, or matrix, of dimensionality m, if you use m variables. The following screenshot shows a two-dimensional space. Values of the variables **v1** and **v2** define cases in this 2-D space. The variability of the cases is spread across both source variables approximately equally. Finding principal components means finding new m axes, where m is exactly equal to the number of the source variables.

However, these new axes are selected in such a way that most cases variability is spread over a single new variable, or over a principal component, as shown in the following figure:

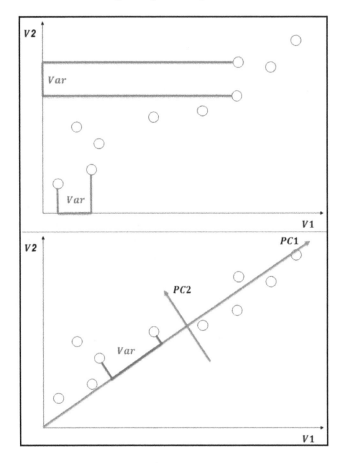

Principal Components Analysis

You use PCA analysis, as mentioned, to reduce the number of variables in further analysis. In addition, you can use PCA for **anomaly detection**, for finding cases that are somehow different from the majority of cases. You use the residual variability not explained by the two first principal components for this task.

Similar to PCA is **Exploratory Factor Analysis** (**EFA**), which is used to uncover the latent structure in the input variables collection. A smaller set of calculated variables called **factors** is used to explain the relations between the input variables.

For a start, the following code creates a subset of the TM data frame by extracting the numerical variables only:

```
TMPCAEFA <- TM[, c("TotalChildren", "NumberChildrenAtHome",
                "HouseOwnerFlag", "NumberCarsOwned",
                "BikeBuyer", "YearlyIncome", "Age")];
```

You can use the `princomp()` function from the base R installation to calculate the principal components. However, the following code uses the `principal()` function from the `psych` package, which returns results that are easier to understand. The following code installs the package, loads it in memory, and calculates two principal components from the seven input variables. Note the comment—the components are not rotated. You will learn about rotation very soon:

```
install.packages("psych");
library(psych);
# PCA not rotated
pcaTM_unrotated <- principal(TMPCAEFA, nfactors = 2, rotate = "none");
pcaTM_unrotated;
```

Here are some partial results:

```
Standardized loadings (pattern matrix) based upon correlation matrix
                        PC1    PC2    h2    u2 com
TotalChildren          0.73   0.43 0.712 0.29 1.6
NumberChildrenAtHome   0.74  -0.30 0.636 0.36 1.3
HouseOwnerFlag         0.20   0.44 0.234 0.77 1.4
NumberCarsOwned        0.70  -0.34 0.615 0.39 1.5
BikeBuyer             -0.23  -0.21 0.097 0.90 2.0
YearlyIncome           0.67  -0.43 0.628 0.37 1.7
Age                    0.46   0.65 0.635 0.36 1.8
                        PC1    PC2
SS loadings            2.32   1.23
Proportion Var         0.33   0.18
Cumulative Var         0.33   0.51
```

In the pattern matrix part, you can see two **principal components** (**PC**) loadings, in the PC1 and PC2 columns. These loadings are correlations of the observed variables with the two PCs. You can use component loading to interpret the meaning of the PCs. The h2 column tells you the amount of the variance explained by the two components. In the SS loadings row, you can see the eigenvalues of the first two PCs, and how much variability is explained by each of them and cumulatively by both of them.

From the pattern matrix, you can see that all of the input variables highly correlate with `PC1`. For most of them, the correlation is higher than with `PC2`. This is logical, because this is how the components were calculated. However, it is hard to interpret the meaning of the two components. Note that for pure machine learning, you might not even be interested in such an interpretation; you might just continue with further analysis using the two principal components only instead of the original variables.

You can improve your understanding of PCs by rotating them. This means you are rotating the axes of the multidimensional hyperspace. The **rotation** is done in such a way that it maximizes associations of PCs with different subsets of input variables each. The rotation can be **orthogonal**, where the rotated components are still uncorrelated, or **oblique**, where correlation between PCs is allowed. In principal component analysis, you typically use orthogonal rotation, because you probably want to use uncorrelated components in further analysis. The following code recalculates the two PCAs using `varimax`, the most popular orthogonal rotation:

```
pcaTM_varimax <- principal(TMPCAEFA, nfactors = 2, rotate = "varimax");
pcaTM_varimax;
```

The abbreviated results are now slightly different, and definitely more interpretable:

```
Standardized loadings (pattern matrix) based upon correlation matrix
                        PC1    PC2    h2    u2  com
TotalChildren           0.38   0.76 0.712 0.29 1.5
NumberChildrenAtHome    0.78   0.15 0.636 0.36 1.1
HouseOwnerFlag         -0.07   0.48 0.234 0.77 1.0
NumberCarsOwned         0.78   0.09 0.615 0.39 1.0
BikeBuyer              -0.08  -0.30 0.097 0.90 1.1
YearlyIncome            0.79   0.01 0.628 0.37 1.0
Age                     0.04   0.80 0.635 0.36 1.0
                        PC1    PC2
SS loadings             2.00  1.56
Proportion Var          0.29  0.22
Cumulative Var          0.29  0.51
```

Now you can easily see that the `PC1` has high loadings, or highly correlates, with the number of children at home, the number of cars owned, yearly income, and also with the total number of children. The second one correlates more with total children and age, quite well with the house ownership flag as well, and negatively with the bike buyer flag.

When you do an EFA, you definitely want to understand the results. The factors are the underlying combined variables that help you understand your data. This is similar to adding computed variables, just in a more complex way, with many input variables. For example, the obesity index could be interpreted as a very simple factor that includes height and weight, and gives you much more information about a person's health than the base two variables do. Therefore, you typically rotate the factors, and also allow correlations between them. The following code extracts two factors from the same dataset as used for the PCA, this time with `promax` rotation, which is an oblique rotation:

```
efaTM_promax <- fa(TMPCAEFA, nfactors = 2, rotate = "promax");
efaTM_promax;
```

Here are the abbreviated results:

```
Standardized loadings (pattern matrix) based upon correlation matrix
                        MR1    MR2    h2    u2  com
    TotalChildren        0.23   0.72 0.684 0.32 1.2
    NumberChildrenAtHome 0.77   0.04 0.618 0.38 1.0
    HouseOwnerFlag       0.03   0.19 0.040 0.96 1.1
    NumberCarsOwned      0.55   0.07 0.332 0.67 1.0
    BikeBuyer           -0.05  -0.14 0.027 0.97 1.2
    YearlyIncome         0.60  -0.02 0.354 0.65 1.0
    Age                 -0.18   0.72 0.459 0.54 1.1
                        MR1    MR2
SS loadings             1.38 1.13
Proportion Var          0.20 0.16
Cumulative Var          0.20 0.36
With factor correlations of
        MR1    MR2
MR1 1.00 0.36
MR2 0.36 1.00
```

Note that this time the results include the correlation between the two factors. In order to interpret the results even more easily, you can use the `fa.diagram()` function, as the following code shows:

```
fa.diagram(efaTM_promax, simple = FALSE,
           main = "EFA Promax");
```

The code produces the following diagram:

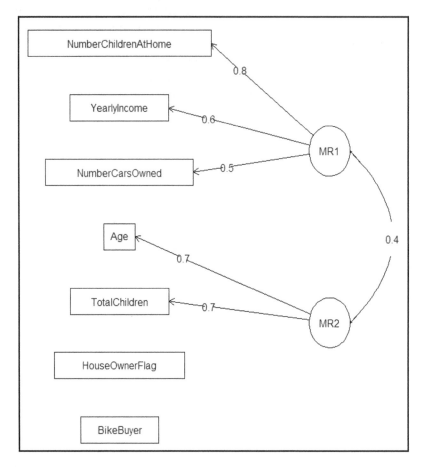

Exploratory Factor Analysis

You can now easily see which variables correlate with which of the two factors, and also the correlation between the two factors.

Finding groups with clustering

Clustering is the process of grouping the data into classes or clusters so that objects within a cluster have high **similarity** in comparison to one another, but are very dissimilar to objects in other clusters. Dissimilarities are assessed based on the attribute values describing the objects.

There are a large number of clustering algorithms. The major methods can be classified into the following categories:

- **Partitioning methods**: A partitioning method constructs K partitions of the data, which satisfy both of the following requirements:
  1. Each group must contain at least one object.
  2. Each object must belong to exactly one group. Given the initial K number of partitions to construct, the method creates initial partitions. It then uses an iterative relocation technique that attempts to improve the partitioning by moving objects from one group to another. There are various kinds of criteria for judging the quality of the partitions. Some of the most popular include the **K-means** algorithm, where each cluster is represented by the mean value of the objects in the cluster, and the **K-medoids** algorithm, where each cluster is represented by one of the objects located near the center of the cluster. You can see an example of K-means clustering in the previous chapter. The example used the scalable `rxKmeans()` function from the `RevoScaleR` package; you can use this function on very large datasets as well.

- **Hierarchical methods**: A hierarchical method creates a hierarchical decomposition of a given set of data objects. These methods are agglomerative or divisive. The agglomerative (bottom-up) approach starts with each object forming a separate group. It successively merges the objects or groups close to one another, until all groups are merged into one. The divisive (top-down) approach starts with all the objects in the same cluster. In each successive iteration, a cluster is split up into smaller clusters, until eventually each object is in one cluster or until a termination condition holds.

- **Density-based methods**: Methods based on the distance between objects can find only spherical-shaped clusters and encounter difficulty in discovering clusters of arbitrary shapes. So other methods have been developed based on the notion of density. The general idea is to continue growing the given cluster as long as the density (number of objects or data points) in the "neighborhood" exceeds some threshold; that is, for each data point within a given cluster, the neighborhood of a given radius has to contain at least a minimum number of points.

- **Model-based methods**: Model-based methods hypothesize a model for each of the clusters and find the best fit of the data to the given model. A model-based technique might locate clusters by constructing a density function that reflects the spatial distribution of the data points. Unlike conventional clustering, which primarily identifies groups of like objects, this conceptual clustering goes one step further by also finding characteristic descriptions for each group, where each group represents a concept or a class.

Hierarchical clustering model training typically starts by calculating a distance matrix—a matrix with distances between data points in a multidimensional hyperspace, where each input variable defines one dimension of that hyperspace. Distance measure can be a geometrical distance or some other, more complex measure. A **dendrogram** is a tree diagram frequently used to illustrate the arrangement of the clusters produced by hierarchical clustering. Dendrograms are also often used in computational biology to illustrate the clustering of genes or samples. The following figure shows the process of building an agglomerative hierarchical clustering dendrogram from six cases in a two-dimensional space (two input variables) in six steps:

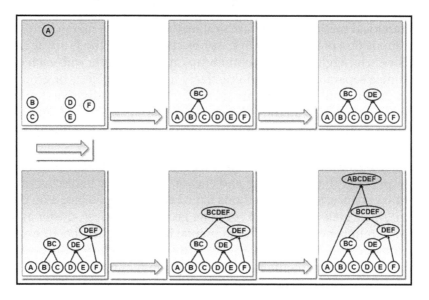

Hierarchical clustering process

The following code creates a subset of the data with 50 randomly selected rows and numerical columns only. You cannot show a dendrogram with thousands of cases. Hierarchical clustering is suitable for small datasets only:

```
TM50 <- TM[sample(1:nrow(TM), 50, replace=FALSE),
           c("TotalChildren", "NumberChildrenAtHome",
             "HouseOwnerFlag", "NumberCarsOwned",
             "BikeBuyer", "YearlyIncome", "Age")];
```

Then you can calculate the distance matrix with the dist() function and create a hierarchical clustering model with the hclust() function:

```
ds <- dist(TM50, method = "euclidean");
TMCL <- hclust(ds, method="ward.D2");
```

In a dendrogram, you can easily see how many clusters you should use. You make a cut where the difference in the distance is the highest. You can plot the model to see the dendrogram. The following code plots the model, and then uses the cutree() function to define two clusters, and the rect.hclust() function to draw two rectangles around the two clusters:

```
plot(TMCL, xlab = NULL, ylab = NULL);
groups <- cutree(TMCL, k = 2);
rect.hclust(TMCL, k = 2, border = "red");
```

You can see the final result in the following screenshot:

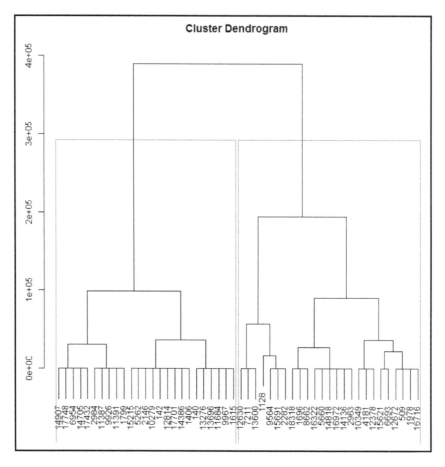

A dendrogram with two clusters

The dendrogram shows the growth of the clusters, and how the cases were associated together. Please note that the decision to cut the population into two clusters is arbitrary: a cut into three or five clusters would work as well. You decide how many clusters to use based on your business perspective because the clusters must be meaningful for you.

Advanced analysis – directed methods

Some of the most important directed techniques include **classification**, **estimation**, and **forecasting**. Classification means to examine a new case and assign it to a predefined discrete class, for example, assigning keywords to articles and assigning customers to known segments. Next is estimation, where you are trying to estimate the value of a continuous variable of a new case. You can, for example, estimate the number of children or the family income. Forecasting is somewhat similar to classification and estimation. The main difference is that you can't check the forecast value at the time of the forecast. Of course, you can evaluate it if you just wait long enough. Examples include forecasting which customers will leave in the future, which customers will order additional services, and the sales amount in a specific region at a specific time in the future.

After you train models, you use them to perform predictions. In most classification and other directed approach projects, you build multiple models, using different algorithms, different parameters of the algorithms, different independent variables, additional calculated independent variables, and more. The question of which model is the best arises. You need to test the accuracy of the predictions of different models. To do so, you simply split the original dataset into training and test sets. You use the training set to train the model. A common practice is to use 70% of the data for the **training set**. The remaining 30% of the data goes into the **test set**, which is used for predictions. When you know the value of the predicted variable, you can measure the quality of the predictions.

In R, there is a plethora of directed algorithms. This section is limited to three only: logistic regression from the base installation, **decision trees** from the base installation, and **conditional inference trees** from the `party` package.

In this section, you will learn how to:

- Prepare training and test datasets
- Use the logistic regression algorithm
- Create decision trees models
- Evaluate predictive models

Predicting with logistic regression

A **logistic regression** model consists of **input units** and an **output unit**, which is the predicted value. Input units are combined into a single transformed output value. This calculation uses the unit's **activation function**. An activation function has two parts: the first part is the **combination function** and merges all of the inputs into a single value (weighted sum, for example); the second part is the **transfer function**, which transfers the value of the combination function to the output value of the unit. The transfer function is called the **sigmoid** or **logistic function** and is S-shaped. Training a logistic regression model is the process of setting the best weights on the inputs of each of the units to maximize the quality of the predicted output. The formula for the logistic function is:

$$S(x) = \frac{1}{1 + e^{-x}}$$

The following figure shows the logistic regression algorithm graphically:

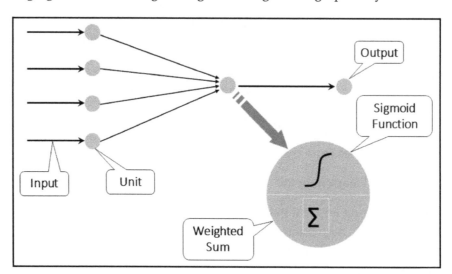

The logistic regression algorithm

In the previous module, you have already seen the `rxLogit()` function from the `RevoScaleR` package in action. Now you are going to learn how to use the `glm()` function from the base installation. In addition, you will see how you can improve the quality of predictions by improving data and selecting different algorithms.

Let's start the advanced analytics session by re-reading the target mail data. In addition, the following code defines the ordered levels of the `Education` factor variables and changes the `BikeBuyer` variable to a labeled factor:

```
TM = read.table("C:\\SQL2017DevGuide\\Chapter14_TM.csv",
                sep=",", header=TRUE,
                stringsAsFactors = TRUE);
TM$Education = factor(TM$Education, order=TRUE,
                levels=c("Partial High School",
                         "High School","Partial College",
                         "Bachelors", "Graduate Degree"));
TM$BikeBuyer <- factor(TM$BikeBuyer,
                levels = c(0,1),
                labels = c("No","Yes"));
```

Next, you need to prepare the training and test sets. The split must be random. However, by defining the `seed`, you can reproduce the same split later, meaning you can get the same cases in the test and in the training set again:

```
set.seed(1234);
train <- sample(nrow(TM), 0.7 * nrow(TM));
TM.train <- TM[train,];
TM.test <- TM[-train,];
```

Now it's time to create the first logistic regression model. For the sake of simplicity, the first model uses three input variables only:

```
TMLogR <- glm(BikeBuyer ~
                YearlyIncome + Age + NumberCarsOwned,
                data=TM.train, family=binomial());
```

You test the model by performing predictions on the `test` dataset. Logistic regression returns the output as a continuous value between zero and 1. The following code recodes the output value to a factor where a value greater than 0.5 is transformed to `Yes`, meaning this is a predicted bike buyer, and otherwise to `No`, meaning this is not a predicted bike buyer. The results are shown in a pivot table together with the actual values:

```
probLR <- predict(TMLogR, TM.test, type = "response");
predLR <- factor(probLR > 0.5,
                levels = c(FALSE, TRUE),
                labels = c("No","Yes"));
perfLR <- table(TM.test$BikeBuyer, predLR,
                dnn = c("Actual", "Predicted"));
perfLR;
```

The pivot table created is called the classification (or confusion) matrix. Here is the result:

```
          Predicted
Actual   No   Yes
    No  1753 1084
   Yes  1105 1604
```

You can compare the predicted and the actual numbers to find the following results to check **true positives** (the values that were predicted correctly as Yes), true negatives (the values that were predicted correctly as No), **false positives** (the values that were predicted incorrectly as Yes), and **false negatives** (the values that were predicted incorrectly as No). The result is not over-exciting. So let's continue the session by creating and testing a new logistic regression model, this time with all possible input variables, to see whether we can get a better result:

```
TMLogR <- glm(BikeBuyer ~
              MaritalStatus + Gender +
              TotalChildren + NumberChildrenAtHome +
              Education + Occupation +
              HouseOwnerFlag + NumberCarsOwned +
              CommuteDistance + Region +
              YearlyIncome + Age,
              data=TM.train, family=binomial());
probLR <- predict(TMLogR, TM.test, type = "response");
predLR <- factor(probLR > 0.5,
                 levels = c(FALSE, TRUE),
                 labels = c("No","Yes"));
perfLR <- table(TM.test$BikeBuyer, predLR,
                dnn = c("Actual", "Predicted"));
perfLR;
```

This time, the results are slightly better, as you can see from the following classification matrix. Still, the results are not very exciting:

```
          Predicted
Actual   No   Yes
    No  1798 1039
   Yes  928  1781
```

In the target mail dataset, there are many variables that are integers, although they actually are factors (nominal or ordinal variables). Let's try to help the algorithm by explicitly defining them as factors. All of them are also ordered. Of course, after changing the original data set, you need to recreate the training and test sets. The following code does all the aforementioned tasks:

```
TM$TotalChildren = factor(TM$TotalChildren, order=TRUE);
TM$NumberChildrenAtHome = factor(TM$NumberChildrenAtHome, order=TRUE);
TM$NumberCarsOwned = factor(TM$NumberCarsOwned, order=TRUE);
TM$HouseOwnerFlag = factor(TM$HouseOwnerFlag, order=TRUE);
set.seed(1234);
train <- sample(nrow(TM), 0.7 * nrow(TM));
TM.train <- TM[train,];
TM.test <- TM[-train,];
```

Now let's rebuild and test the model with all possible independent variables:

```
TMLogR <- glm(BikeBuyer ~
                MaritalStatus + Gender +
                TotalChildren + NumberChildrenAtHome +
                Education + Occupation +
                HouseOwnerFlag + NumberCarsOwned +
                CommuteDistance + Region +
                YearlyIncome + Age,
              data=TM.train, family=binomial());
probLR <- predict(TMLogR, TM.test, type = "response");
predLR <- factor(probLR > 0.5,
                levels = c(FALSE, TRUE),
                labels = c("No","Yes"));
perfLR <- table(TM.test$BikeBuyer, predLR,
                dnn = c("Actual", "Predicted"));
perfLR;
```

The results have improved again:

```
          Predicted
Actual   No   Yes
   No   1850   987
   Yes   841  1868
```

Still, there is room for improving the predictions. However, this time we are going to use a different algorithm.

Classifying and predicting with decision trees

Decision trees are one of the most frequently used data mining algorithms. The algorithm is not very complex, yet it gives very good results in many cases. In addition, you can easily understand the result. You use decision trees for classification and prediction. Typical usage scenarios include:

- Predicting which customers will leave
- Targeting the audience for mailings and promotional campaigns
- Explaining reasons for a decision

Decision trees are a directed technique. Your target variable is the one that holds information about a particular decision, divided into a few discrete and broad categories (yes/no; liked/partially liked/disliked, and so on). You are trying to explain this decision using other gleaned information saved in other variables (demographic data, purchasing habits, and so on). With limited statistical significance, you are going to predict the target variable for a new case using its known values for input variables based on the results of your trained model.

You use **recursive partitioning** to build the tree. The data is split into partitions using a specific value of one of the explaining variables. The partitions are then split again and again. Initially the data is in one big box. The algorithm tries all possible breaks of both input (explaining) variables for the initial split. The goal is to get purer partitions considering the classes of the target variable. The tree continues to grow using the two new partitions as separate starting points and splitting them more. You have to stop the process somewhere. Otherwise, you could get a completely fitted tree that has only one case in each class. The class would be, of course, absolutely pure and this would not make any sense; you could not use the results for any meaningful prediction, because the prediction would be 100% accurate, but for this case only. This phenomenon is called **overfitting**.

The following code uses the `rpart()` function from the base installation to build a decision tree using all possible independent variables, with factors properly defined, as used in the last logistic regression model:

```
TMDTree <- rpart(BikeBuyer ~ MaritalStatus + Gender +
                 TotalChildren + NumberChildrenAtHome +
                 Education + Occupation +
                 HouseOwnerFlag + NumberCarsOwned +
                 CommuteDistance + Region +
                 YearlyIncome + Age,
                 method="class", data=TM.train);
```

You can plot the tree to understand how the splits were made. The following code uses the `prp()` function from the `rpart.plot` package to plot the tree:

```
install.packages("rpart.plot");
library(rpart.plot);
prp(TMDTree, type = 2, extra = 104, fallen.leaves = FALSE);
```

You can see the plot of the decision tree in the following figure. You can easily read the rules from the tree; for example, if the number of cars owned is two, three, or four, and yearly income is not lower than 65,000, then you have approximately 67% of non-buyers (in the following figure, just follow the path to the leftmost node):

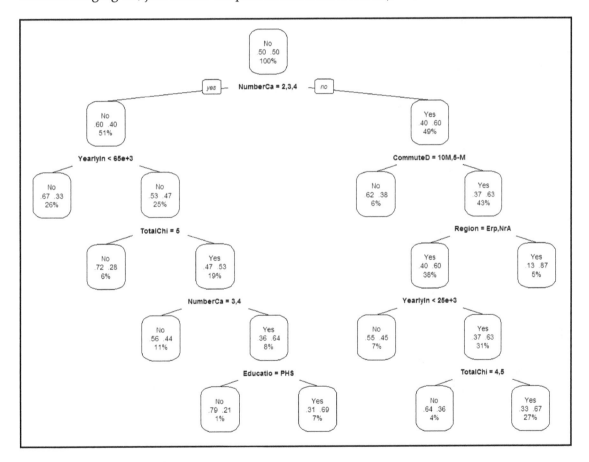

Decision tree plot

So how does this model perform? The following code creates the classification matrix for this model:

```
predDT <- predict(TMDTree, TM.test, type = "class");
perfDT <- table(TM.test$BikeBuyer, predDT,
                dnn = c("Actual", "Predicted"));
perfDT;
```

Here are the results:

```
          Predicted
Actual   No   Yes
   No   2119   718
  Yes   1232  1477
```

The predictions are better in some cells and worse in other cells, compared with the last logistic regression model. The number of false negatives (predicted `No`, actual `Yes`) is especially disappointing. So let's try it with another model. This time, the following code uses the `ctree()` function from the `party` package:

```
install.packages("party", dependencies = TRUE);
library("party");
TMDT <- ctree(BikeBuyer ~ MaritalStatus + Gender +
              TotalChildren + NumberChildrenAtHome +
              Education + Occupation +
              HouseOwnerFlag + NumberCarsOwned +
              CommuteDistance + Region +
              YearlyIncome + Age,
              data=TM.train);
predDT <- predict(TMDT, TM.test, type = "response");
perfDT <- table(TM.test$BikeBuyer, predDT,
                dnn = c("Actual", "Predicted"));
perfDT;
```

The results are:

```
          Predicted
Actual   No   Yes
   No   2190   647
  Yes    685  2024
```

Now you can finally see some big improvements. The version of the decision trees algorithm used by the `ctree()` function is called the **conditional inference trees**. This version uses a different method for deciding how to make the splits. The function accepts many parameters. For example, the following code creates a new model, this time lowering the condition for a split, thus forcing more splits:

```
TMDT <- ctree(BikeBuyer ~ MaritalStatus + Gender +
              TotalChildren + NumberChildrenAtHome +
              Education + Occupation +
              HouseOwnerFlag + NumberCarsOwned +
              CommuteDistance + Region +
              YearlyIncome + Age,
              data=TM.train,
              controls = ctree_control(mincriterion = 0.70));
predDT <- predict(TMDT, TM.test, type = "response");
perfDT <- table(TM.test$BikeBuyer, predDT,
              dnn = c("Actual", "Predicted"));
perfDT;
```

The classification matrix for this model is shown as follows:

```
        Predicted
Actual   No   Yes
   No  2200   637
  Yes   603  2106
```

The predictions have slightly improved again. You could continue with the process until you reach the desired quality of the predictions.

Advanced graphing

Now is the time when we head towards the final section of this chapter. This section is a bit lighter. We will finish the chapter and the book with additional visualizations of data. This section discusses advanced graphing with the help of the `ggplot2` package.

This section introduces the following:

- Basic `ggplot()` function
- Advanced plot types
- Trellis charts

Introducing ggplot2

The `ggplot2` package is a frequently used graphical package among the R community. The package provides a comprehensive and coherent grammar for graphical functions. The grammar is also consistent, and you can create nice graphs with this package. The `ggplot2` package enhances the built-in graphical capabilities and gives a layer-oriented approach to plotting graphs.

The following command installs the package and loads it into memory:

```
install.packages("ggplot2");
library("ggplot2");
```

Here is the code for the first graph that uses the `ggplot()` function. The data used is the TM data frame, as created and modified in the previous section, with all of the factors properly defined:

```
ggplot (TM, aes(Region, fill=Education)) +
  geom_bar(position="stack");
```

The `ggplot()` function defines the dataset used (TM in this case) and initializes the plot. Inside this function, the `aes()` (short for aesthetics) function defines the roles of the variables for the graph. In this case, the graph shows the frequencies of the `Region` variable, where the `Region` bars are filled with the `Education` variable, to show the number of cases with each level of education in each region. The `geom_bar()` function defines the plot type, in this case, a bar plot. There are many other `geom_xxx()` functions for other plot types. The following screenshot shows the results:

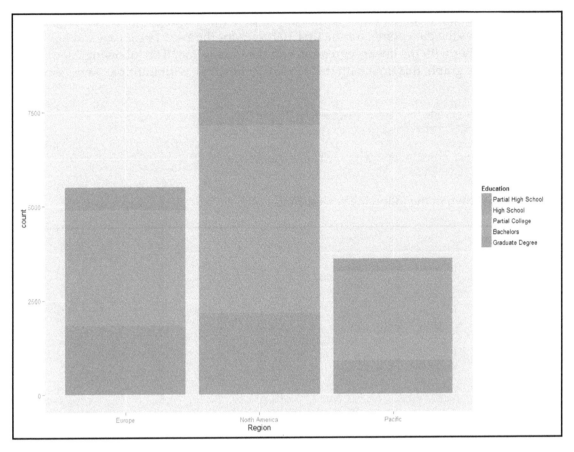

Education in regions

You should also try to create graphs with a different position parameter—you can use `position = "fill"` to create stacked bars, where you can easily see the relative distribution of education inside each region, and `position = "dodge"` to show the distribution of education for each region side by side.

Remember the graph from the linear regression section, the fourth graph in this chapter, the graph that shows the data points for the first 100 cases for the `YearlyIncome` and `Age` variables, together with the linear regression and the lowess line? The following code creates the same graph, this time with the `ggplot()` function, with multiple `geom_xxx()` functions:

```
TMLM <- TM[1:100, c("YearlyIncome", "Age")];
ggplot(data = TMLM, aes(x=Age, y=YearlyIncome)) +
  geom_point() +
  geom_smooth(method = "lm", color = "red") +
  geom_smooth(color = "blue");
```

The result is shown in the following screenshot:

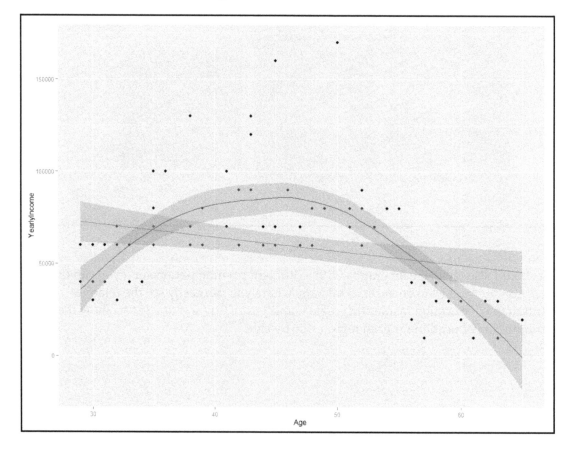

Linear and polynomial regression with ggplot

Advanced graphs with ggplot2

The third figure in this chapter is a box plot showing the YearlyIncome variable distribution in classes of the Education variable. Again, it is possible to make this graph even prettier with ggplot. Besides box plots, ggplot can add violin plots as well. A violin plot shows the kernel density for a continuous variable. This is an effective way to see the distribution of a continuous variable in classes of a discrete variable. The following code produces a combination of a violin and a box plot in order to show the distribution of yearly income in classes of Education:

```
ggplot(TM, aes (x = Education, y = YearlyIncome)) +
  geom_violin(fill = "lightgreen") +
  geom_boxplot(fill = "orange",
               width = 0.2);
```

The graph produced is not just nice, it is really informative, as you can see in the following screenshot:

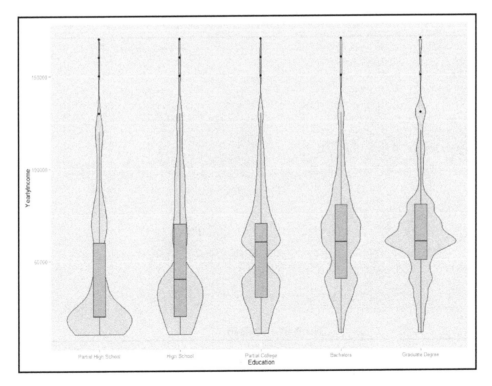

A combination of a violin and a box plot

For the last graph in this book, I selected a **trellis chart**. A trellis chart is a multi-panel chart of small, similar charts, using the same axes and scale. This way you can easily compare them. Trellis graphs are called **faceted graphs** in ggplot semantics. The facet_grid() function defines the discrete variables to be used for splitting the chart in small multiples over rows and columns. The following code creates an example of a trellis chart:

```
ggplot(TM, aes(x = NumberCarsOwned, fill = Region)) +
   geom_bar(stat = "bin") +
   facet_grid(MaritalStatus ~ BikeBuyer) +
   theme(text = element_text(size=30));
```

You can see the results in the next figure. The values of the MaritalStatus variable are used to split the chart into two rows, while the values of the BikeBuyer column are used to split the chart into two columns. The chart has four small multiples, one for each combination of MaritalStatus and BikeBuyer. Inside each of the four small charts, you can see the distribution of the NumberCarsOwned variable, and inside each bar, you can see the distribution of the Region variable for that specific number of cars. The theme() function is used to increase the font size of all of the text in the chart:

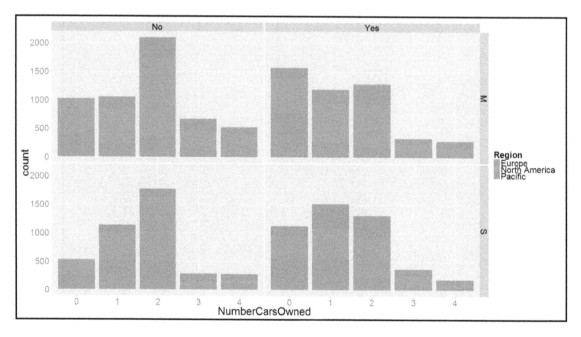

A trellis chart

This is not the end of capabilities of the `ggplot2` package. There are many more additional graphs and visualizations in the package, and the visualization does not stop here. With additional packages, you can plot maps, Google maps, heat maps, areas, circulars, word clouds, networks, tree maps, funnels, and more.

Summary

For SQL Server developers, this must have been quite an exhausting chapter. Of course, the whole chapter is not about the T-SQL language; it's about the R language, and about statistics and advanced analytics. Of course, developers can also profit from the capabilities that the new language has to offer. You learned how to measure associations between discrete, continuous, and combinations of discrete and continuous variables. You learned about directed and undirected data mining and machine learning methods. Finally, you saw how to produce quite advanced graphs in R.

Please be aware that if you want to become a real data scientist, you need to learn more about statistics, data mining and machine learning algorithms, and practice programming in R. Data science is a long learning process, just like programming and development. Therefore, when you start using R, you should have your code double-checked by a senior data scientist for all the tricks and tips that I haven't covered in this chapter. Nevertheless, this and the previous chapter should give you enough knowledge to start your data science learning journey, and even kick off a real-life data science project. However, as of SQL Server 2017, R is not the only language supported by SQL Server that you can use for data science.

You will learn about another option, the Python language, in the next chapter.

15
Introducing Python

Python is one of the most popular programming languages. It is a general purpose high-level language, created by Guido van Rossum, and publicly released in 1991. It is an **interpreted** language. The philosophy of the language is about the code readability. For example, you use **white spaces** to delimit code blocks instead of special characters such as semicolons or curly brackets.

Python supports automatic memory management. It has a dynamic type system. You can use multiple program paradigms in Python, including **procedural**, **object-oriented**, and **functional programming**. You can find Python interpreters for all major operating systems. The reference implementation of Python, namely **CPython**, is open source software, managed by the non-profit Python Software Foundation. Of course, it being open source also means that there is a rich set of libraries available. Even the standard library is impressive and comprehensive.

Like SQL Server 2016 started to support R, SQL Server 2017 supports Python. Now you can select your preferred language for data science and even other tasks. R has even more statistical, data mining, and machine learning libraries, because it is more widely used in the data science community; however, Python has a broader purpose than just data science, and is more readable and therefore might be simpler to learn. This chapter introduces Python for SQL Server developers and **business intelligence** (**BI**) specialists. This means that the chapter is more focused on Python basics and data science, and less on general programming with Python.

This chapter will cover the following points:

- Python basics and concepts
- Python data structures
- Basic data management and visualizations

- Introductory statistics with Python
- Data science with Python
- Creating and using scalable Python solutions in SQL Server

Starting with Python

In order to start working with Python and R, you need to do some installation. General SQL Server setup is not in the scope of this book. However, if you are completely new to Python (and R), it might be helpful to give you a very quick overview of the installation.

Once you prepare the environment, you will start immediately with Python programming. Anyway, time to get our hands dirty. In this section, you will learn about:

- Installing Python
- A quick demo of Python capabilities
- Python core syntax elements
- Python variables
- Basic data structures in Python
- Branching and looping
- Classes and objects

Installing machine learning services and client tools

With SQL Server 2017, you get everything you need from Microsoft. There is no need to download any additional open source interpreter and/or client tool besides **SQL Server**, **SQL Server Management Studio** (**SSMS**), and **Visual Studio** (**VS**), unless you wish so. You just start SQL Server setup, and then from the **Feature Selection** page select **Database Engine Services**, and underneath **Machine Learning Services (In-Database)**, with both languages, **R** and **Python**, selected. This will install both the language engines. After that, all you need is client tools, and you can start writing the code. The following screenshot shows the SQL Server setup's **Feature Selection** page with the appropriate features selected:

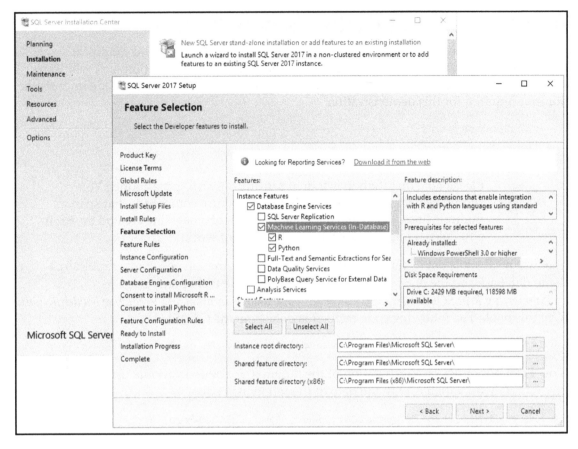

Machine learning feature selection

The next step is installing client tools. Of course, you need SSMS. In addition, you might want to install VS 2017. You can use either a Professional or even a free Community Edition to develop Python (and also R) code.

When installing Visual Studio 2017, be sure to select Python development workload, and then data science and analytical applications, as explained in `Chapter 3`, *SQL Server Tools*. And that's it, you are ready to start Python programming. Just start a new project and select the Python Application template from the `Python` folder. You can also explore the Python Machine Learning templates, which include **Classifier**, **Clustering**, and **Regression** projects. If you selected the **Python Application template**, you should have opened the first empty Python script with the default name the same as the project name and default extension `.py`, waiting for you to write and interactively execute Python code.

A quick demo of Python's capabilities

To start, let me arouse your interest by showing you some analytical and graphical capabilities of Python. I have explained the code just briefly in this section; you will learn more about Python programming in the rest of this chapter. The following code imports the libraries required for this demonstration:

```
import numpy as np
import pandas as pd
import matplotlib.pyplot as plt
```

 Please note that Python is indent sensitive. Every space counts. You should be very careful especially when you use commands that span multiple lines. Just leave the default indent of a new line created by VS; if you delete or add a space, the code does not work.

Then we need some data. I am using the same data from the AdventureWorksDW2014 demo database and the dbo.vTargetMail view as in the R chapters, Chapter 13, *Supporting R in SQL Server*, and Chapter 14, *Data Exploration and Predictive Modeling with R*, of this book. The following code reads this data from the CSV file:

```
TM = pd.read_csv("C:\SQL2017DevGuide\Chapter15_TM.csv")
```

Now I can do a quick cross tabulation of the NumberCarsOwned variable using the TotalChildren variable, with the help of the following code:

```
obb = pd.crosstab(TM.NumberCarsOwned, TM.TotalChildren)
obb
```

And here are the first results, a pivot table of the previously mentioned variables:

TotalChildren NumberCarsOwned	0	1	2	3	4	5
0	990	1668	602	419	449	110
1	1747	1523	967	290	286	70
2	1752	162	1876	1047	1064	556
3	384	130	182	157	339	453
4	292	136	152	281	165	235

Now, let me show you the results of the pivot table in a graph. I need just the following two lines:

```
obb.plot(kind = 'bar')
plt.show()
```

You can see the graph in the following figure:

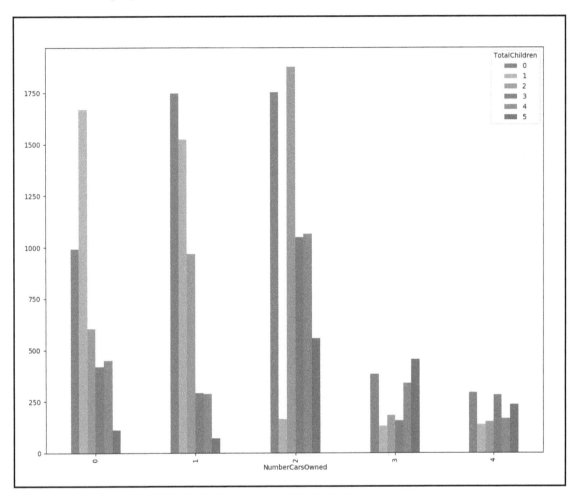

NumberCarsOwned and TotalChildren pivot table

It is quite simple to create even more complex graphs. The following code shows the distribution of the Age variable in histograms and with a kernel density plot:

```
(TM['Age'] - 20).hist(bins = 25, normed = True,
                      color = 'lightblue')
(TM['Age'] - 20).plot(kind='kde', style='r--', xlim = [0, 80])
plt.show()
```

You can see the results in the following figure. Note that in the code, I subtracted 20 from the actual age, to get a slightly younger population than exists in the demo database:

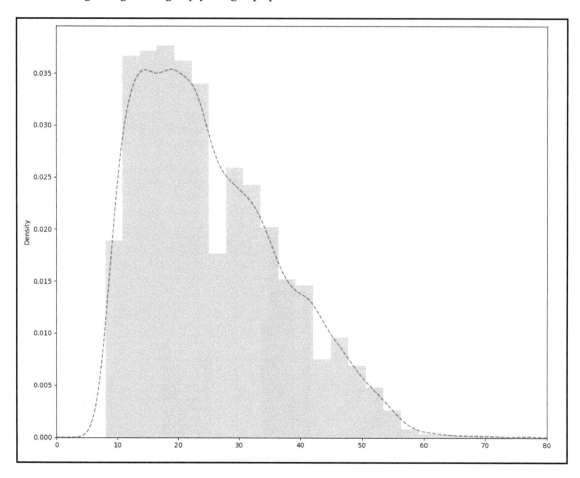

Distribution of age

I hope that you are interested in learning Python after this brief introduction of its capabilities.

Python language basics

Python uses the hash mark for a comment, just like R. You can execute Python code in VS 2017 by highlighting the code and simultaneously pressing the *Ctrl* and *Enter* keys. Again this is completely the same as you need to do either in RStudio IDE or in R Tools for VS. You can use either single or double apostrophes for delimiting strings. The first command you will learn is the print command. Write and execute the following code in the Visual Studio 2017 Python script window:

```
# Introducing Python
# Hash starts a comment
print("Hello World!")
# Next command ignored
# print("Nice typing")
print('Printing again.')
print('O"Hara')    # In-line comment
print("O'Hara")
```

You can observe the code you wrote and the results in the interactive window, which, by default, follows the script window, at the bottom left-side of the screen.

Python supports all the basic mathematical and comparison operators, as you would expect. Note that you can combine strings and expressions in a single print statement. The following code introduces them:

```
1 + 2
print("The result of 3 + 20 / 4 is:", 3 + 20 / 4)
10 * 2 - 7
10 % 4
print("Is 7 less or equal to 5?", 7 <= 5)
print("Is 7 greater than 5?", 7 > 5)
7 is 5
2 == 3
2 != 3
2 ** 3
2 / 3
2 // 3   # integer division
5 // 2
```

Here are the results of the last three lines of the previous code:

```
>>> 2 / 3
0.6666666666666666
>>> 2 // 3
0
>>> 5 // 2
2
```

The next step is to introduce the variables. Note that Python is case sensitive. The following code shows how you can assign values to variables and use them for direct computations and as the arguments of a function. You can also note the case sensitivity error from the following code:

```
# Integer
a = 2
b = 3
a ** b
# Case sensitivity
a + B
# NameError: name 'B' is not defined
# Float
c = 7.0
d = float(5)
print(c, d)
round(4.33777, 3)
```

You can define strings inside double or single quotes. This enables you to use single quotes inside a double-quoted string, and vice versa. You can use the %? operator for formatting strings to include variables, where the question mark stands for a single letter denoting the data type of the variable, for example s for strings and d for numbers. Here are some examples:

```
e = "String 1"
f = "String 2"
print(e + ", " + f)
print("Let's concatenate %s and %s in a single string." % (e, f))
g = 10
print("Let's concatenate string %s and number %d." % (e, g))
```

The resulting strings are:

```
String 1, String 2
Let's concatenate String 1 and String 2 in a single string.
Let's concatenate string String 1 and number 10.
```

Note that because double quotes were used as the string delimiters, it was possible to use a single quote inside a string, in the word `Let's`.

The `str.format()` method of the string data type allows you to do variable substitutions in a string, as the following example shows:

```
four_cb = "String {} {} {} {}"
print(four_cb.format(1, 2, 3, 4))
print(four_cb.format("a", "b", "c", "d"))
```

The result of the previous code is:

```
String 1 2 3 4
String a b c d
```

You can also create multi-line strings. Just enclose the strings in a pair of three double quotes. You can also use special characters, such as tab and line feed. Escape them with a single backslash character plus a letter, for example letter `t` for a tab and letter `n` for a line feed. The following code shows some examples:

```
print("""Note three double quotes.
Allow you to print multiple lines.
As many as you wish.""")
a = "I am 5'11\" tall"
b = 'I am 5\'11" tall'
print("\t" + a + "\n\t" + b)
```

Here are the results:

```
Note three double quotes.
Allow you to print multiple lines.
As many as you wish.
        I am 5'11" tall
        I am 5'11" tall
```

You can always get interactive help with the `help()` command. A Python module is a file with the default extension `.py` containing Python definitions and statements. You can import a module into your current script with the `import` command, and then use the functions and variables defined in that module. Besides modules provided with the installation, you can, of course, develop your own modules, distribute them, and reuse the code. The following example shows how you can import the module `sys`, get help about it, and check the version of the Python engine:

```
import sys
help(sys)
sys.version
```

 Like R, Python also includes many additional libraries. However, for the code shown in this chapter, you don't need to download anything. All necessary libraries for a data science project are already included in SQL Server Python installation.

As in any serious programming language, you can encapsulate your code inside a function. You define a function with the `def name():` command. Functions can use arguments. Functions can also return values. The following code defines three functions, one that has no arguments, one that has two arguments, and one that has two arguments and returns a value. Note that there is no special ending mark of a function body—the correct indentation tells the Python interpreter where the body of the first function ends, and the definition of the second function starts:

```
def p_n():
    print("No args...")
def p_2(arg1, arg2):
    print("arg1: {}, arg2: {}".format(arg1, arg2))
def add(a, b):
    return a + b
```

When you call a function, you can pass parameters as literals, or through variables. You can also do some manipulation with the variables when you pass them as the arguments to a function. The following code shows these possibilities:

```
p_n()
p_2("a", "b")
# Call with variables and math
a = 10
b = 20
p_2(a / 5, b / 4)
add(10,20)
```

You can make branches in the flow of your code with the `if..elif..else:` statement. The following code shows you an example:

```
a = 10
b = 20
c = 30
if a > b:
    print ("a > b")
elif a > c:
    print ("a > c")
elif (b < c):
    print ("b < c")
    if a < c:
        print ("a < c")
    if b in range(10, 30):
        print ("b is between a and c")
else:
    print ("a is less than b and less than c")
```

The results of the preceding code are:

```
b < c
a < c
b is between a and c
```

The simplest data structure is the **list**. A Python list is a set of comma-separated values (or items) between square brackets. You can use a `for` or `for each` loop to iterate over a list. There are many methods supported by a list. For example, you can use the `list.append()` method to append an element to a list. The following code shows how to create lists and loop over them:

```
animals = ["cat", "dog", "pig"]
nums = []
for animal in animals:
    print ("Animal: ", animal)
for i in range(2, 5):
    nums.append(i)
print (nums)
```

The result of the preceding code is:

```
Animal:  cat
Animal:  dog
Animal:  pig
[2, 3, 4]
```

Python also supports the `while` loop. The following example shows how to create a list from a string using the `str.split()` method, create a second list, and then use the `while` loop to pop an element from the second list and add it to the first list:

```
s1 = "a b c d e f"
l1 = s1.split(' ')
l2 = ['g','h','i','j','k','l']
while len(l1) <= 10:
    x = l2.pop()
    l1.append(x)
    l1
```

Here are the results:

```
['a', 'b', 'c', 'd', 'e', 'f', 'l']
['a', 'b', 'c', 'd', 'e', 'f', 'l', 'k']
['a', 'b', 'c', 'd', 'e', 'f', 'l', 'k', 'j']
['a', 'b', 'c', 'd', 'e', 'f', 'l', 'k', 'j', 'i']
['a', 'b', 'c', 'd', 'e', 'f', 'l', 'k', 'j', 'i', 'h']
```

The last data structure presented in this introduction section is the **dictionary**. A dictionary is a set of the key/value pairs. You can see an example of a dictionary in the following code:

```
states = {
    "Oregon": "OR",
    "Florida": "FL",
    "Michigan": "MI"}
for state, abbrev in list(states.items()):
    print("{} is abbreviated {}.".format(state, abbrev))
```

The result of the previous code is:

```
Oregon is abbreviated OR.
Florida is abbreviated FL.
Michigan is abbreviated MI.
```

I mentioned that in Python you can also use object-oriented paradigms. You can define a **class** with multiple methods, and then instantiate **objects** of that class. The instantiation operation creates an empty object. You might want to create objects with instances customized to a specific initial state. You can use a special method named __init__(), which is automatically invoked by the class instantiation. You can refer to an instance of the class itself with the `self` keyword. The following is an example of a class with two objects instantiated from that class:

```
class CityList(object):
    def __init__(self, cities):
```

```
        self.cities = cities
    def print_cities(self):
        for line in self.cities:
            print(line)
EU_Cities = CityList(["Berlin",
                      "Paris",
                      "Rome"])
US_Cities = CityList(["New York",
                      "Seattle",
                      "Chicago"])
EU_Cities.print_cities()
US_Cities.print_cities()
```

And here is the result:

```
Berlin
Paris
Rome
New York
Seattle
Chicago
```

Going deeper into object-oriented programming with Python is beyond the scope of this book. You will learn more about the data science tasks instead—data manipulation, creating graphs, and using advanced analytical methods to get some information from your data.

Working with data

You might need more advanced data structures for analyzing SQL Server data, which comes in tabular format. In Python, there is also the **data frame** object, like in R. It is defined in the `pandas` library. You can communicate with SQL Server through the pandas data frames. But before getting there, you need first to learn about **arrays** and other objects from the `numpy` library.

In this section, you will learn about the objects from the two of the most important Python libraries, numpy and pandas, including:

- Numpy arrays
- Aggregating data
- Pandas Series and data frames
- Retrieving data from arrays and data frames
- Combining data frames

Using the NumPy data structures and methods

The term **NumPy** is short for **Numerical Python**; the library name is numpy. The library provides arrays with much more efficient storage and faster work than basic lists and dictionaries. Unlike basic lists, numpy arrays must have elements of a single data type. The following code imports the numpy package with the alias np. Then it checks the version of the library. Then the code creates two one-dimensional arrays from two lists, one with an implicit element data type integer, and one with an explicit float data type:

```
import numpy as np
np.__version__
np.array([1, 2, 3, 4])
np.array([1, 2, 3, 4], dtype = "float32")
```

You can create multi-dimensional arrays as well. The following code creates three arrays with three rows and five columns, one filled with zeros, one with ones, and one with the number pi. Note the functions used for populating arrays:

```
np.zeros((3, 5), dtype = int)
np.ones((3, 5), dtype = int)
np.full((3, 5), 3.14)
```

For the sake of brevity, I am showing only the last array here:

```
array([[ 3.14,   3.14,   3.14,   3.14,   3.14],
       [ 3.14,   3.14,   3.14,   3.14,   3.14],
       [ 3.14,   3.14,   3.14,   3.14,   3.14]])
```

There are many additional functions that will help you in populating your arrays. The following code creates four different arrays. The first line creates a linear sequence of numbers between 0 and 20 with step 2 returning every second number. Note that the upper bound 20 is not included in the array. The second line creates uniformly distributed numbers between 0 and 1. The third line creates 10 numbers between standard normal distribution with mean 0 and standard deviation 1. The third line creates a 3 by using the 3 matrix of uniformly distributed integral numbers between 0 and 9:

```
np.arange(0, 20, 2)
np.random.random((1, 10))
np.random.normal(0, 1, (1, 10))
np.random.randint(0, 10, (3, 3))
```

Again, for the sake of brevity, I am showing only the last result here:

```
array([[0, 1, 7],
       [5, 9, 4],
       [5, 5, 6]])
```

Arrays have many attributes. We will check all of them. The following code shows an example of how to get the dimensionality and the shape of an array. The result shows you that you created a two-dimensional array with three rows and four columns:

```
arr1 = np.random.randint(0, 12, size = (3, 4))
arr1.ndim
arr1.shape
```

You can access array elements and their position with zero-based indexes. You can also use negative indexes, meaning counting elements backwards. The following code illustrates this:

```
arr1
arr1[1, 2]
arr1[0, -1]
```

The result of the preceding code is:

```
array([[ 6,  8,  8, 10],
       [ 1,  6,  7,  7],
       [ 8,  1,  5,  9]])
7
10
```

First, the code lists the array created in the previous example, the two-dimensional array with three rows and four columns with random integers. Then the code reads the third element of the second row. Then the code retrieves the last element from the first row.

Besides retrieving a single element, you can also slice an array. In the next example, the first line retrieves the second row of the array `arr1`, and the second line the second column:

```
arr1[1, :]
arr1[:, 1]
```

Here are the results of the preceding code:

```
array([1, 6, 7, 7])
array([8, 6, 1])
```

You can concatenate or stack the arrays. The following code creates three arrays, and then concatenates the first two arrays along the rows, and the first and the third along the columns:

```
a1 = np.array([[1, 2, 3],
               [4, 5, 6]])
a2 = np.array([[7, 8, 9],
               [10, 11, 12]])
a3 = np.array([[10],
               [11]])
np.concatenate([a1, a2], axis = 0)
np.concatenate([a1, a3], axis = 1)
```

Here is the result:

```
array([[ 1,  2,  3],
       [ 4,  5,  6],
       [ 7,  8,  9],
       [10, 11, 12]])
array([[ 1,  2,  3, 10],
       [ 4,  5,  6, 11]])
```

You can also use the np.vstack() and np.hstack() functions to stack the arrays vertically or horizontally, over the first or over the second axis. The following code produces the same result as the previous code, which uses the np.concatenate() function:

```
np.vstack([a1, a2])
np.hstack([a1, a3])
```

You can imagine that you can do this stacking only with conformable arrays. The following two lines would produce errors:

```
np.vstack([a1, a3])
np.hstack([a1, a2])
```

In order to perform some calculations on array elements, you could use mathematical functions from the default Python engine, and operate in loops, element by element. However, the numpy library also includes vectorized versions of the functions, which operate on vectors and matrices as a whole, and are much faster than the basic ones. The following code creates a 3 by 3 array of numbers between 0 and 8, shows the array, and then calculates the sinus of each element using a numpy vectorized function:

```
x = np.arange(0, 9).reshape((3, 3))
x
np.sin(x)
```

And here is the result:

```
array([[0, 1, 2],
       [3, 4, 5],
       [6, 7, 8]])
array([[ 0.        ,  0.84147098,  0.90929743],
       [ 0.14112001, -0.7568025 , -0.95892427],
       [-0.2794155 ,  0.6569866 ,  0.98935825]])
```

Numpy also includes vectorized aggregate functions. You can use them for a quick overview of the data in an array, using the descriptive statistics calculations. The following code initializes an array of five sequential numbers:

```
x = np.arange(1,6)
x
```

Here is the array:

```
array([1, 2, 3, 4, 5])
```

Now you can calculate the sum and the product of the elements, the minimum and the maximum, the mean, and the standard deviation:

```
np.sum(x), np.prod(x)
np.min(x), np.max(x)
np.mean(x), np.std(x)
```

Here are the results:

```
(15, 120)
 (1, 5)
(3.0, 1.4142135623730951)
```

In addition, you can also calculate running aggregates, like a running sum in the following code:

```
np.add.accumulate(x)
```

The running sum result is here:

array([1,   3,   6, 10, 15], dtype=int32)

There are many more operations on arrays available in the numpy module. However, I am switching to the next topic of data science on this Python learning tour, to the `pandas` library.

Organizing data with pandas

The `pandas` library is built on the top of the `numpy` library. Therefore, in order to use pandas, you need to import `numpy` first. The `pandas` library introduces many additional data structures and functions. Let's start our pandas tour with the panda `Series` object. This is a one-dimensional array, like a numpy array; however, you can define an explicitly named index, and refer to those names to retrieve the data, not just to the positional index. Therefore, a pandas `Series` object already looks like a tuple in the relational model, or a row in a table. The following code imports both packages, `numpy` and `pandas`. Then it defines a simple pandas Series, without an explicit index. The Series looks like a simple single-dimensional array, and you can refer to elements through the positional index:

```
import numpy as np
import pandas as pd
ser1 = pd.Series([1, 2, 3, 4])
ser1[1:3]
```

Here are the results. I retrieved the second and the third element, position 1 and 2, with a zero-based positional index, as shown here:

```
1     2
2     3
```

Now I will create a Series with an explicitly named index, as shown in the following code:

```
ser1 = pd.Series([1, 2, 3, 4],
                  index = ['a', 'b', 'c', 'd'])
ser1['b':'c']
```

As you can see from the last example, you can refer to elements using the names of the index, which serve as column names in a SQL Server row. And here is the result:

```
b    2
c    3
```

You can create a Series from the dictionary object as well, as the following code shows:

```
dict1 = {'a': 1,
         'b': 2,
         'c': 3,
         'd': 4}
ser1 = pd.Series(dict1)
```

Imagine you have multiple Series with the same structure stacked vertically. This is the pandas `DataFrame` object. It looks and behaves like the R data frame. You use the pandas `DataFrame` object to store and analyze tabular data from relational sources, or to export the result to the tabular destinations, like SQL Server. The following code creates two dictionaries, then a pandas `Series` from each one, and then a pandas `DataFrame` from both Series:

```
age_dict = {'John': 35, 'Mick': 75, 'Diane': 42}
age = pd.Series(age_dict)
weight_dict = {'John': 88.3, 'Mick': 72.7, 'Diane': 57.1}
weight = pd.Series(weight_dict)
people = pd.DataFrame({'age': age, 'weight': weight})
people
```

The resulting data frame is:

	age	weight
Diane	42	57.1
John	35	88.3
Mick	75	72.7

You can see that the Series were joined by the common index values. The result looks like a table and is therefore suitable for exchanging data and results with relational systems.

You can do a lot of manipulations with a data frame. For the beginning, I am extracting some meta-data, and creating a projection by extracting a single column, as shown in the following code:

```
people.index
people.columns
people['age']
```

Here are the results:

```
Index(['Diane', 'John', 'Mick'], dtype='object')
Index(['age', 'weight'], dtype='object')
Diane    42
John     35
Mick     75
```

You can add a calculated column to a data frame. For example, the following code adds a column to the `people` data frame I am using here:

```
people['WeightDivAge'] = people['weight'] / people['age']
people
```

The result is:

```
        age   weight   WeightDivAge
Diane   42    57.1     1.359524
John    35    88.3     2.522857
Mick    75    72.7     0.969333
```

You can transform columns to rows with the `T` function of the pandas `DataFrame`, as shown in the following code:

```
people.T
```

You can see the transformed data frame from the result:

```
                    Diane        John        Mick
age             42.000000   35.000000   75.000000
weight          57.100000   88.300000   72.700000
WeightDivAge     1.359524    2.522857    0.969333
```

You can refer to the elements of a data frame by position or by column and index names. A data frame is still a matrix and not a relational table, so the zero-based positional index is also accessible. You can even use expressions in order to filter a data frame. Here are some examples:

```
people.iloc[0:2, 0:2]
people.loc['Diane':'John', 'age':'weight']
people.loc[people.age > 40, ['age', 'WeightDivAge']]
```

The results of the previous operations are:

```
        age   weight
Diane   42    57.1
John    35    88.3
        age   weight
```

```
Diane    42    57.1
John     35    88.3
         age   WeightDivAge
Diane    42       1.359524
Mick     75       0.969333
```

From many other operations possible with data frames, let me just expose the joins. You can join two data frames with the `pd.merge()` method. The following code creates two data frames and joins them using the same index:

```
df1 = pd.DataFrame({'Person': ['Mary', 'Dejan', 'William', 'Milos'],
                    'BirthYear': [1978, 1962, 1993, 1982]})
df2 = pd.DataFrame({'Person': ['Mary', 'Milos', 'Dejan', 'William'],
                    'Group': ['Accounting', 'Development', 'Training',
'Training']})
pd.merge(df1, df2)
```

Here is the result:

```
    BirthYear    Person        Group
0        1978      Mary   Accounting
1        1962     Dejan     Training
2        1993   William     Training
3        1982     Milos  Development
```

Note you could always use an explicit key name, or even different key names, one from the left and one from the right data frame involved in the join, as long as the key values match. Here is an example of using an explicit key name:

```
pd.merge(df1, df2, on = 'Person')
```

The result is, of course, the same as the previous one. This was a one-to-one join. You can also do one-to-many joins, as the following example shows:

```
df3 = pd.DataFrame({'Group': ['Accounting', 'Development', 'Training'],
                    'Supervisor': ['Carol', 'Pepe', 'Shasta']})
pd.merge(df2, df3)
```

The joined result is:

```
         Group    Person Supervisor
0   Accounting      Mary      Carol
1  Development     Milos       Pepe
2     Training     Dejan     Shasta
3     Training   William     Shasta
```

Finally, you can also perform many-to-many joins, as the last example in this section shows:

```
df4 = pd.DataFrame({'Group': ['Accounting', 'Accounting',
                              'Development', 'Development',
                              'Training'],
                   'Skills': ['math', 'spreadheets',
                              'coding', 'architecture',
                              'presentation']})
pd.merge(df2, df4)
```

The result of this example is:

```
        Group   Person        Skills
0   Accounting     Mary          math
1   Accounting     Mary   spreadheets
2  Development    Milos        coding
3  Development    Milos  architecture
4     Training    Dejan  presentation
5     Training  William  presentation
```

I guess this chapter was quite terse so far, and also exhaustive. Unfortunately, all of this knowledge is needed to get to the data frames, which were our target from the beginning of the chapter. Therefore, it is finally time to do some more interesting things, namely analyze the data.

Data science with Python

In a real-life data science project, the work is spread over time like your effort with this chapter. A lot of work is put in during the first part of the allocated time, with the fun coming at the end. It is time to do some more advanced analysis on your data. You will learn about visualizations, data mining, and machine learning, and using Python with SQL Server. You will use some of the most advanced Python libraries, including matplotlib and seaborn for visualizations, scikit-learn for machine learning, and scalable revoscalepy, and `MicrosoftML` libraries provided by Microsoft.

This section introduces data science tasks with Python, including:

- Visualizations with matplotlib
- Enhancing graphs with seaborn
- Machine learning with scikit-learn
- Using SQL Server data in Python
- Executing Python in SQL Server

Creating graphs

You will learn how to do graphs with two Python libraries: `matplotlib` and `seaborn`. Matplotlib is a mature, well-tested, and cross-platform graphics engine. In order to work with it, you need to import it. However, you need also to import an interface to it. Matplotlib is the whole library, and `matplotlib.pyplot` is a module in matplotlib. Pyplot is the interface to the underlying plotting library that knows how to automatically create the figure and axes and other necessary elements to create the desired plot. Seaborn is a visualization library built on matplotlib, adding additional enhanced graphing options, and makes working with pandas data frames easy.

Anyway, without further talking, let's start developing. First, let's import all the necessary packages for this section, using the following code:

```
import numpy as np
import pandas as pd
import matplotlib as mpl
import matplotlib.pyplot as plt
import seaborn as sns
```

The next step is to create sample data. An array of 100 evenly distributed numbers between 0 and 10 is the data for the independent variable, and then the following code creates two dependent variables, one as the **sinus** of the independent one, and the second as the natural logarithm of the independent one:

```
x = np.linspace(0.01, 10, 100)
y = np.sin(x)
z = np.log(x)
```

The following code defines the style to use for the graph and then plots two lines, one for each function. The `plt.show()` command is needed to show the graph interactively:

```
plt.style.use('classic')
plt.plot(x, y)
plt.plot(x, z)
plt.show()
```

If you execute the previous code in Visual Studio 2017, you should get a pop-up window with the desired graph. I am not showing the graph yet; before showing it, I want to make some enhancements and besides showing it also save it to a file. The following code uses the `plt.figure()` function to create an object that will store the graph. Then for each function it defines the line style, line width, line color, and label. The `plt.axis()` line redefines the axes range. The next three lines define the axes titles and the title of the graph, and define the font size for the text. The `plt.legend()` line draws the legend. The last two lines show the graph interactively and save it to a file:

```
f = plt.figure()
plt.plot(x, y, color = 'blue', linestyle = 'solid',
        linewidth = 4, label = 'sin')
plt.plot(x, z, color = 'red', linestyle = 'dashdot',
        linewidth = 4, label = 'log')
plt.axis([-1, 11, -2, 3.5])
plt.xlabel("X", fontsize = 16)
plt.ylabel("sin(x) & log(x)", fontsize = 16)
plt.title("Enhanced Line Plot", fontsize = 25)
plt.legend(fontsize = 16)
plt.show()
f.savefig('C:\\SQL2017DevGuide\\B08539_15_04.png')
```

Here is the result of the previous code—the first nice graph:

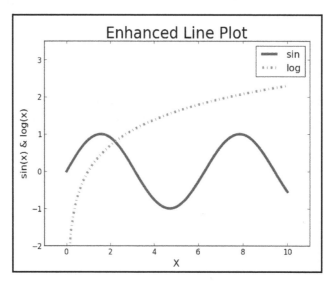

Line chart

If you are interested in which graphical formats are supported, use the following code:

```
f.canvas.get_supported_filetypes()
```

You will find out that all of the most popular formats are supported.

Now it's time to switch to some more realistic examples. First, let's import the target mail data from a CSV file in a pandas DataFrame and get some basic info about it:

```
TM = pd.read_csv("C:\SQL2017DevGuide\Chapter15_TM.csv")
# N of rows and cols
print (TM.shape)
# First 10 rows
print (TM.head(10))
# Some statistics
TM.mean()
TM.max()
```

The next graph you can create is a **scatterplot**. The following code plots YearlyIncome over Age. Note that the code creates a smaller data frame with the first hundred rows only, in order to get a less cluttered graph for the demo. Again, for the sake of brevity, I am not showing this graph:

```
TM1 = TM.head(100)
plt.scatter(TM1['Age'], TM1['YearlyIncome'])
plt.xlabel("Age", fontsize = 16)
plt.ylabel("YearlyIncome", fontsize = 16)
plt.title("YearlyIncome over Age", fontsize = 25)
plt.show()
```

For categorical variables, you usually create bar charts for a quick overview of the distribution. You can do it with the countplot() function from the seaborn package. Let's try to plot counts for the BikeBuyer variable in the classes of the Education variable, with the help of the following code:

```
sns.countplot(x="Education", hue="BikeBuyer", data=TM);
plt.show()
```

If you executed the previous code, you will have noticed that the Education variable is not sorted correctly. Similarly to R, you also need to inform Python about the intrinsic order of a categorical or nominal variable. The following code defines that the Education variable is categorical and then shows the categories:

```
TM['Education'] = TM['Education'].astype('category')
TM['Education']
```

In the next step, the code defines the correct order, as shown here:

```
TM['Education'].cat.reorder_categories(
    ["Partial High School",
     "High School","Partial College",
     "Bachelors", "Graduate Degree"], inplace=True)
TM['Education']
Now it is time to create the bar chart again. This time, I am also saving
it to a file, and showing it in the book.
f = plt.figure()
sns.countplot(x="Education", hue="BikeBuyer", data=TM);
plt.show()
f.savefig('C:\\SQL2017DevGuide\\B08539_15_05.png')
```

So, here is the resulting bar chart:

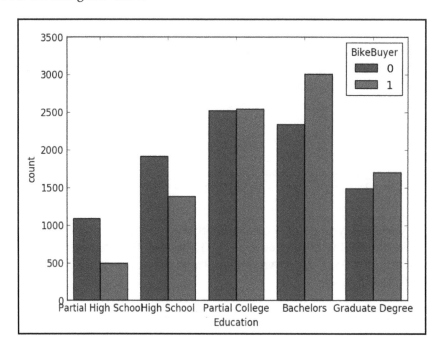

Bar chart

You can also do a chart with small sub-charts, the trellis chart, with the `FacetGrid()` function. Note that the following code uses the `set()` function to set the `font_scale` for all text in the graph at once:

```
sns.set(font_scale = 3)
grid = sns.FacetGrid(TM, row = 'HouseOwnerFlag', col = 'BikeBuyer',
```

```
                        margin_titles = True, size = 10)
grid.map(plt.hist, 'YearlyIncome',
        bins = np.linspace(0, np.max(TM['YearlyIncome']), 7))
plt.show()
```

The following figure shows the result:

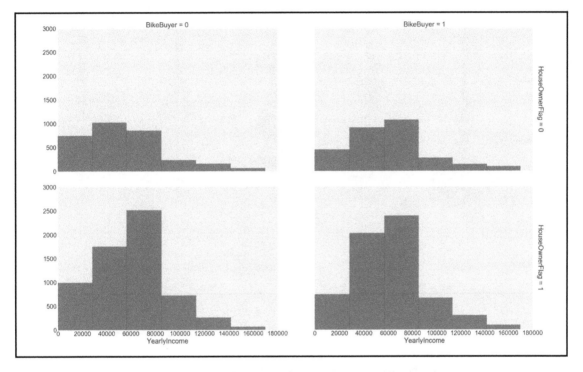

Trellis chart

Finally, let me also show you a nice `violinplot`, similar to the one created with the `ggplot` library in R in `Chapter 14`, *Data Exploration and Predictive Modeling with R* in SQL Server R. The code analyzes the distribution of the income in classes of education:

```
sns.violinplot(x = 'Education', y = 'YearlyIncome',
              data = TM, kind = 'box', size = 8)
plt.show()
```

Here is the resultant graph:

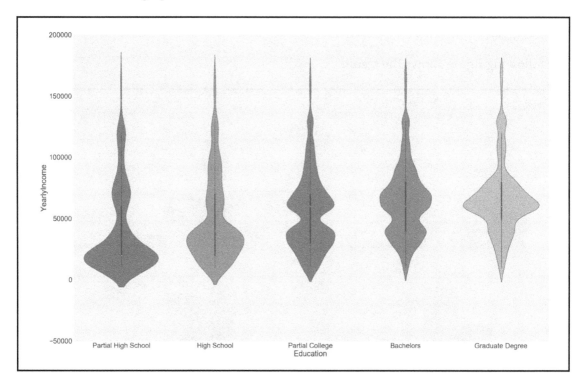

Violin plot

Performing advanced analytics

You can find many different libraries for statistics, data mining, and machine learning in Python. Probably the best known one is the `scikit-learn` package. It provides most of the commonly used algorithms, and also tools for data preparation and model evaluation.

In scikit-learn, you work with data in a tabular representation by using pandas data frames. The **input table** (actually a two-dimensional array, not a table in the relational sense) has columns used to train the model. Columns, or attributes, represent some features, and therefore this table is also called the **features matrix**. There is no prescribed naming convention; however, in most of the Python code you will note that this features matrix is stored in variable X.

If you have a directed or supervised algorithm, then you also need the **target variable**. This is represented as a vector, or one-dimensional **target array**. Commonly, this target array is stored in variable y.

Without further hesitation, let's create some mining models. First, the following code imports all necessary libraries for this section:

```
import numpy as np
import pandas as pd
import matplotlib as mpl
import matplotlib.pyplot as plt
import seaborn as sns
from sklearn.model_selection import train_test_split
from sklearn.metrics import accuracy_score
from sklearn.linear_model import LinearRegression
from sklearn.naive_bayes import GaussianNB
from sklearn.mixture import GaussianMixture
```

Next, let's re-read the target mail data from the CSV file, using the following code:

```
TM = pd.read_csv("C:\SQL2017DevGuide\Chapter15_TM.csv")
```

The next step is to prepare the features matrix and the target array. The following code also checks the shape of both:

```
X = TM[['TotalChildren', 'NumberChildrenAtHome',
        'HouseOwnerFlag', 'NumberCarsOwned',
        'YearlyIncome', 'Age']]
X.shape
y = TM['BikeBuyer']
y.shape
```

The first model will be a supervised one, using the Naïve Bayes classification. For testing the accuracy of the model, you need to split the data into the training and the test set. You can use the train_test_split() function from the scikit-learn library for this task:

```
Xtrain, Xtest, ytrain, ytest = train_test_split(
    X, y, random_state = 0, train_size = 0.7)
```

Note that the previous code puts 70% of the data into the training set and 30% into the test set.

The next step is to initialize and train the model with the training data set, as shown in the following code:

```
model = GaussianNB()
model.fit(Xtrain, ytrain)
```

That's it. The model is prepared and trained. You can start using it for making predictions. You can use the test set for predictions, and for checking the accuracy of the model. In the previous chapter, Chapter 14, *Data Exploration and Predictive Modeling with R* in SQL Server R, you learned about the classification matrix. You can derive many measures out of it. A very well-known measure is the **accuracy**. The accuracy is the proportion of the total number of predictions that were correct, defined as the sum of true positive and true negative predictions with the total number of cases predicted. The following code uses the test set for the predictions and then measures the accuracy:

```
ymodel = model.predict(Xtest)
accuracy_score(ytest, ymodel)
```

You can see that you can do quite advanced analyses with just a few lines of code. Let's make another model, this time an undirected one, using the clustering algorithm. For this one, you don't need training and test sets, and also not the target array. The only thing you need to prepare is the features matrix, as shown in the following code:

```
X = TM[['TotalChildren', 'NumberChildrenAtHome',
        'HouseOwnerFlag', 'NumberCarsOwned',
        'YearlyIncome', 'Age', 'BikeBuyer']]
```

Again, you need to initialize and fit the model. Note that the following code tries to group cases in two clusters:

```
model = GaussianMixture(n_components = 2, covariance_type = 'full')
model.fit(X)
```

The predict() function for the clustering model creates the cluster information for each case in the form of a resulting vector. The following code creates this vector and shows it:

```
ymodel = model.predict(X)
ymodel
```

You can add the cluster information to the input feature matrix, as shown in the following code:

```
X['Cluster'] = ymodel
X.head()
```

Now you need to understand the clusters. You can get this understanding graphically. The following code shows how you can use the seaborn `lmplot()` function to create a scatterplot showing the cluster membership of the cases spread over income and age:

```
sns.set(font_scale = 3)
lm = sns.lmplot(x = 'YearlyIncome', y = 'Age',
                hue = 'Cluster',  markers = ['o', 'x'],
                palette = ["orange", "blue"], scatter_kws={"s": 200},
                data = X, fit_reg = False,
                sharex = False, legend = True)
axes = lm.axes
axes[0,0].set_xlim(0, 190000)
plt.show(lm)
```

The following figure shows the result. You can see that in cluster **0** there are older people with less income, while cluster **1** consists of younger people, with not so distinctively higher income only:

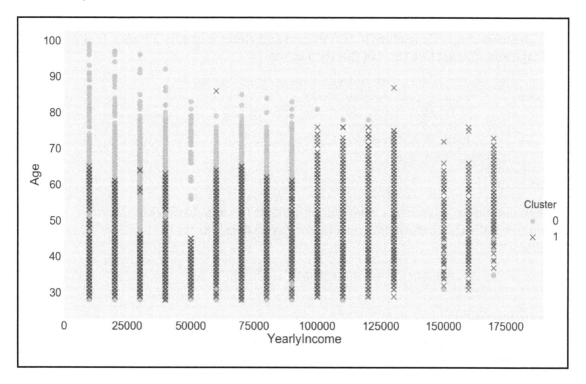

Understanding clusters

Using Python in SQL Server

In the last section of this chapter, you are going to learn how to use Python with SQL Server and in SQL Server. You can use two scalable libraries, the `revoscalepy` and `MicrosoftML` libraries, which correspond to equivalent R libraries. You can also read SQL Server data by using ODBC. You can use the `pyodbc` package for this task. The following code imports all the necessary libraries for this section:

```python
import numpy as np
import pandas as pd
import pyodbc;
from revoscalepy import rx_lin_mod, rx_predict, rx_summary
```

Now it is time to read SQL Server data. Note that like for R, I also used the ODBC Data Sources tool to create a system DSN called **AWDW** in advance. It points to my `AdventureWorksDW2014` demo database. For the connection, I use the same RUser SQL Server login I created for R. Of course, I created a database user in the `AdventureWorksDW2014` database for this user, and gave the user permission to read the data. The following code reads SQL Server data and stores it in a data frame. It also checks the shape and the first five rows of this data frame:

```python
con = pyodbc.connect('DSN=AWDW;UID=RUser;PWD=Pa$$w0rd')
query = """SELECT CustomerKey, Age,
             YearlyIncome, TotalChildren,
             NumberCarsOwned
          FROM dbo.vTargetMail;"""
TM = pd.read_sql(query, con)
TM.head(5)
TM.shape
```

You can use the `rx_summary()` revoscalepy scalable function to quickly get some descriptive statistics for the data. The following code does this for the `NumberCarsOwned` variable:

```python
summary = rx_summary("NumberCarsOwned", TM)
print(summary)
```

Here are the results:

Name	Mean	StdDev	Min	Max	ValidObs
NumberCarsOwned	1.502705	1.138394	0.0	4.0	18484.0

The next step is initializing and training a linear regression model, using number of cars owned as the target variable, and income, age, and number of children as input variables. Please note the syntax of the `rx_lin_mod()` function—it actually uses R syntax for the function parameters. This syntax might be simpler for you if you already use R; however, it might look a bit weird to pure Python developers:

```
linmod = rx_lin_mod(
    "NumberCarsOwned ~ YearlyIncome + Age + TotalChildren",
    data = TM)
```

Finally, the following code makes and shows the predictions:

```
predmod = rx_predict(linmod, data = TM, output_data = TM)
predmod.head(10)
```

Now you need to switch to SSMS. You will use Python inside T-SQL code. If you did not configure your SQL Server to allow external scripts, you have to do it now, with the help of the following code:

```
USE master;
EXEC sys.sp_configure 'show advanced options', 1;
RECONFIGURE WITH OVERRIDE;
EXEC sys.sp_configure 'external scripts enabled', 1;
RECONFIGURE WITH OVERRIDE;
GO
-- Restart SQL Server
-- Check the configuration
EXEC sys.sp_configure;
GO
```

You can immediately check whether you can run Python code with the `sys.sp_execute_external_script` procedure. The following code returns a 1 x 1 table, with value 1 in the single cell:

```
EXECUTE sys.sp_execute_external_script
@language =N'Python',
@script=N'
OutputDataSet = InputDataSet
print("Input data is: \n", InputDataSet)
',
@input_data_1 = N'SELECT 1 as col';
```

The following code creates the `RUser` login and database user used earlier for reading SQL Server data in Python. It also gives this user the permission to read the data:

```
CREATE LOGIN RUser WITH PASSWORD=N'Pa$$w0rd';
GO
USE AdventureWorksDW2014;
GO
CREATE USER RUser FOR LOGIN RUser;
ALTER ROLE db_datareader ADD MEMBER RUser;
GO
```

And finally, here is the big code that runs Python to create the same linear regression model as before, however this time within SQL Server. In the result, you get the actual data with the predicted number of cars:

```
USE AdventureWorksDW2014;
EXECUTE sys.sp_execute_external_script
@language =N'Python',
@script=N'
from revoscalepy import rx_lin_mod, rx_predict
import pandas as pd
linmod = rx_lin_mod(
    "NumberCarsOwned ~ YearlyIncome + Age + TotalChildren",
    data = InputDataSet)
predmod = rx_predict(linmod, data = InputDataSet, output_data =
InputDataSet)
print(linmod)
OutputDataSet = predmod
',
@input_data_1 = N'
SELECT CustomerKey, CAST(Age AS INT) AS Age,
  CAST(YearlyIncome AS INT) AS YearlyIncome,
  TotalChildren, NumberCarsOwned
FROM dbo.vTargetMail;'
WITH RESULT SETS ((
 "CustomerKey" INT NOT NULL,
 "Age" INT NOT NULL,
 "YearlyIncome" INT NOT NULL,
 "TotalChildren" INT NOT NULL,
 "NumberCarsOwned" INT NOT NULL,
 "NumberCarsOwned_Pred" FLOAT NULL));
GO
```

Before finishing this section, let me point out casts in the input SELECT statement. In comparison to SQL Server, Python supports a limited number of data types. Some conversions between SQL Server data types can be done implicitly, others must be done manually. You can read the details about possible implicit conversions at `https://docs.microsoft.com/en-us/sql/advanced-analytics/python/python-libraries-and-data-types`.

Summary

In this chapter, you learned the basics of the Python language. You can use it together with R or instead of R for advanced analyses of SQL Server and other data. You learned about the most popular Python libraries used for data science applications. Now, it is up to you to select the language of your choice.

In the next chapter, you will learn about graph support in SQL Server 2017.

16
Graph Database

In the recent years, the data landscape has changed significantly: massively structured and unstructured data is being generated from various sources. Applications and services are being developed with agile methodologies more frequently than ever, the data changes being fast and significant. Scalability requirements are also very important. Relational database management systems are not designed to handle all these challenges. Therefore, enterprises use NoSQL database solutions, which are more appropriate for new data requirements.

Graph databases belong to the NoSQL databases family. They have only existed for a few years and are used for storing and querying highly connected data, usually connected with many-to-many relations. SQL Server 2017 offers graph database capabilities in a feature called **SQL Graph**.

This chapter is divided into the following three sections:

- Introduction to graph theory and graph databases
- SQL Graph in SQL Server 2017
- Limitations in the current version

The first section starts with a brief introduction to graph theory. After a comparison between relational and graph tables, you will see examples and use cases for graph databases, and which solutions are available on the database market.

In the second section, you will see how SQL Server 2017 supports graph databases. You will learn how to create node and edge tables, how they are different from *normal* tables, and what the indexing recommendations are for them. Most of the time, you will traverse through graph structure; you will also learn how to do this in this section, with examples of usage of the new MATCH clause. At the end of the section, you can find an overview of built-in functions that deal with automatically generated columns in graph tables.

In the third section, you will see what is still missing in SQL Server 2017 and what would be nice to have in the set of graph capabilities in future versions.

Introduction to graph databases

As mentioned in this chapter's introduction, relational databases do not provide a good enough answer for the actual software development and data challenges. In today's world, you need to be fast; faster than the others. This means that data is created, updated, and changed faster than ever. Relational databases are inert and are not designed to handle fast changes and meet new business requirements as well as agile development. Handling changes in relational databases is too expensive and too slow. Achieving scalability and elasticity is also a huge challenge for relational databases. Nowadays, changes occur frequently, and data modeling is a huge challenge: you only partly know the necessary requirements and you have less time for development and deployment than ever. Furthermore, relational databases are not suitable for processing highly related and nested data or hierarchical application objects.

To handle tremendous volumes of data as well as a variety of data and to achieve scalability, in recent years, companies have started to use NoSQL-based database solutions. They usually belong to one of the following four categories:

- **Key-value store**: It is the simplest and most flexible NoSQL model. Every item in the database is stored as a key, together with its value. It is very performant, easy to scale out, and good for high availability. Examples are: Redis, Berkeley DB, and Aerospike.
- **Document store**: It stores a complex data structure for each key (document). Documents can contain many different key-value pairs, key-array pairs, or even nested documents. Examples are: Micosoft Azure DocumentDB, MongoDB, ElasticSearch, and CouchDB.

- **Wide-column store**: It stores tables as sections of columns of data rather than as rows. It can be described as a two-dimensional key-value store. Multiple columns are supported, but you can have different columns in each row. Examples are: Cassandra and HBase.
- **Graph databases**: They are the most complex NoSQL systems and store both entities and relations between them. Examples are: Neo4J, Azure Cosmos DB, OrientDB, FlockDB, DSE Graph, and so on.

Before starting with graph databases, let's have a very brief introduction to graph theory.

What is a graph?

Graphs are studied in graph theory, a part of discrete mathematics. A graph data structure consists of a finite set of two types of objects:

- `nodes` or vertices
- `edges` or lines, which are related pairs of nodes

The formal, mathematical definition for a graph is just this: **G = (V, E)**. This means a graph is an ordered pair of a finite set of vertices and a finite set of edges.

If all edges within a graph are bidirectional, the graph is undirected. A simple, undirected graph is shown as follows:

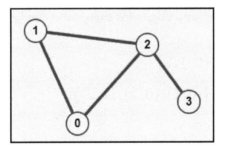

Simple undirected graph

This graph consists of four nodes and four edges. The set of nodes and edges can be represented with a formula similar to the following:

$$V = \{0, 1, 2, 3\}$$

$$E = \{\{0, 1\}, \{0, 2\}, \{1, 2\}, \{2, 3\}\}$$

Curly braces mean unordered pairs (it is possible to travel from one node to another in both directions). *{0,2}* is the same as *{2,0}*.

In case of a directed graph (digraph), edges can go only in one way:

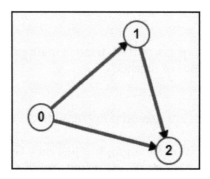

A simple directed graph

This graph consists of three nodes and three edges, but edges represent relation in one direction only. The set of nodes and edges for this graph can be represented with a formula similar to the following:

$$V = \{0, 1, 2\}$$

$$E = \{(0, 1), (0, 2), (1, 2)\}$$

Nodes and edges can have names and properties. A graph model that supports properties is an extension of the graphs from the graph theory, and this is called the **property graph model**. Both nodes and edges can have names (labels for nodes and types for relationships), as shown in the following figure:

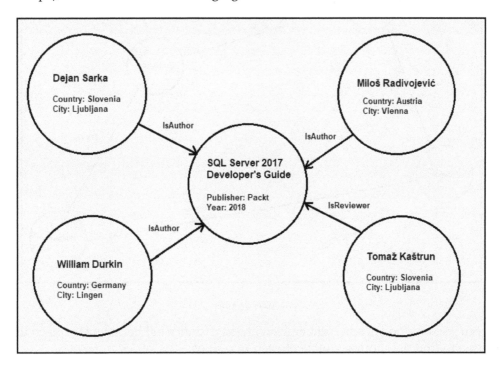

A simple property graph data model

This is a digraph, and you can see four nodes representing four instances of the `Person` entity and a node representing the `Book` entity with their names (or labels), and additional key/value pairs of properties. There are two different edge types representing two relations between the persons and the book entity. All edges are directed.

A graph model can be extended by assigning a weight to edges. Such a graph is called a **weighted graph**, and usually represents structures where relations between nodes have numerical values, such as the length of a road network.

The following figure shows a simple weighted graph:

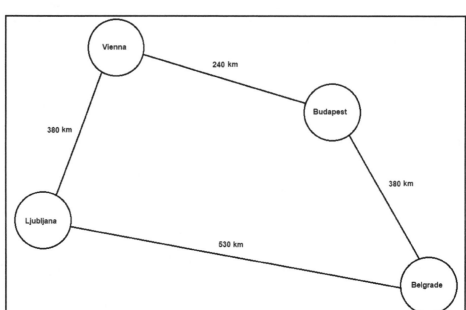

A simple weighted graph

As you can see, four nodes represent cities with the distance in kilometers between them. It can be used to find the shortest route between two cities.

Graphs are useful for representing real-world data. There are many useful operations and analyses that can be applied.

Graph theory in the real world

Graphs are useful for representing real-world data. Many practical problems can be represented by graphs. Therefore, they are becoming increasingly significant as they are applied to other areas of mathematics, science, and technology.

Your first association with the usage of graph theory is most probably social networks—sets of people or groups of people with some pattern of contact or interactions between them, such as Facebook, Twitter, Instagram, LinkedIn, and so on. Here are small graphs illustrating a few users of the first two social networks:

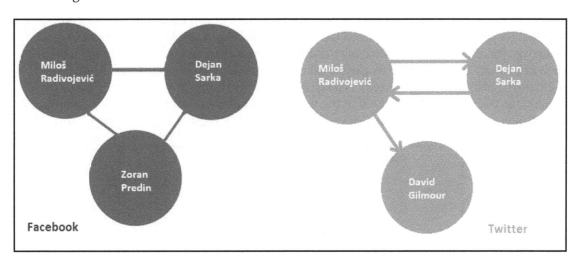

A simple weighted graph

The graph on the left side is undirected and represents connected users as *friends* from a **Facebook** point of view, while the graph that illustrates **Twitter** is a digraph and shows that **Miloš Radivojević** follows the official account of **David Gilmour**, but unfortunately, he does not follow him back. Graph theory in social networking is used to implement requests such as friend(s) finder, friends of friends, to find degrees of connectedness, homophily, small-world effects, and to analyze many aspects of relationships between people and people and products or services. Results of such analyses are used by recommendation engines. It is also used to model many to many relations, such as relationships between actors, directors, producers, and movies, for instance, in the IMDb database.

In a computer network, the transmission of data is based on the routing protocol, which selects the best routes between any two nodes or devices. Graph theory is used in computer networking to find the best or least costly path between two nodes (shortest path algorithm).

In information networks, the link structure of a website can be represented by a directed graph, with web pages as nodes and links between them as edges. Web crawlers run graph search algorithms on the web and traverse through web page networks. The **Google search engine** uses a graph in the *PageRank algorithm* to rank resulted pages.

There are several biological and medical domains where graph theory techniques are applied: identifying drug targets, and determining the role of proteins and genes of an unknown function. It is being actively used for the modeling of bio-molecular networks, such as protein interaction networks, metabolic networks, as well as transcriptional regulatory networks. Graph theory is also one of the most important factors in generations of genome assembly software. One of the typical examples of usage of graphs is the usage of *de Bruijn graphs* in the assembly of genomes from DNA sequencing:

Assembly of genomes using de Bruijn graph

Graph theory is also used to study molecules in chemistry and physics. **Chemical graph theory (CGT)** is a branch of mathematical chemistry which deals with non-trivial applications of graph theory to solve molecular problems.

Finding the shortest path between two points or best possible routes in road networks is one of the oldest problems where graphs are used. Graph theory reduces transport networks to a collection of nodes (cities and road intersections) and edges (roads and rail lines) with the distance between two nodes as weights to help find the optimal route or the list of points that are reachable from the starting point. It is being actively used in airline information systems to optimize flight connections from a distance and cost point of view.

There are many other areas where graph theory is applied: fraud detection, recommendation engines, garbage collectors in programming languages (finding unreachable data), model checking (all possible states and checking if the code is OK), checking mathematical conjunctions, solving puzzles and games, identity and access management, Internet of Things (for modeling the connection between system components and IoT devices), and so on.

Now, as you have learned about graphs and graph theory, let's proceed to graph databases.

What is a graph database?

Simply put, a graph database is a database that is built on top of a graph data structure. Graph databases store nodes and edges between nodes. Each node and edge is uniquely identified and may contain properties (for example, name, country, age, and so on). An edge also has a label that defines the relationship between two nodes.

Graph databases exhibit the same schema flexibility, which is a huge advantage, given that current schemas are liable to change: you can add new nodes without affecting existing ones. This flexibility makes them appropriate for agile development. They are very good for retrieving highly related data. Queries in graph databases are intuitive and similar to the human brain.

When should you use graph databases?

Most of the things that graph databases can do can also be achieved using a relational database. However, a graph database can make it easier to express certain kinds of queries. In addition to this, they may perform better. You should consider using graph database capabilities when your applications:

- Use hierarchical data
- Have to manage complex many-to-many relationships
- Analyze highly related data and relationships
- Use intensively nested data

Graph databases have been in existence for a few years. The actual SQL: 2016 standard does not define graph databases. However, several years ago, different vendors started to deliver database solutions with graph capabilities. In the following section, you will see a short overview of actual graph databases on the market.

Graph databases market

Nowadays, you can find several commercial and open source graph databases on the market. There are also some specific graph-based solutions that are not truly graph databases and are specialized to handle specific relationship problems, usually developed by large companies to solve their own problems. Here is an overview of the leading graph database providers on the market.

Neo4j

Neo4j is probably the most popular graph database. It is developed by Neo4j, and it is a native graph database: Neo4j is built from the ground up to be a graph database. It's the product of the company Neo Technology, with the Community Edition under the GPL license. For highly available and scalable Neo4j Clusters, you need the Enterprise Edition. Neo4j is ACID compliant. It's Java-based, but has bindings for other languages, including Ruby and Python.

Neo4j supports its own Cypher query language, as well as Gremlin. Cypher supports advanced graph analytical queries such as transitive closure, shortest path, and PageRank.

> You can find more information about the Neo4j graph database here: https://neo4j.com.

Azure Cosmos DB

Azure Cosmos DB is a scalable, globally distributed NoSQL database service from Microsoft. This is an *all-inclusive solution* and allows you to store and manipulate with key-value, graph, column-family, and document data in one service.

For querying graphs, **Azure Cosmos DB** supports the Gremlin graph traversal language.

> You can find more information about the Cosmos DB graph database here:
> `https://azure.microsoft.com/de-de/services/cosmos-db/`.

OrientDB

OrientDB is an open source NoSQL database management system written in Java. It is a multi-model database, supporting graph, document, key/value, and object models, but the relationships are managed in graph databases with direct connections between records. It supports schema-less, schema-full, and schema-mixed modes. It has a strong security profiling system based on users and roles, and supports querying with Gremlin analog with SQL, extended for graph traversal.

> You can find more information about the OrientDB graph database here:
> `http://orientdb.com`.

FlockDB

FlockDB is an open source, distributed, fault-tolerant graph database created by Twitter to store and analyze relationships between users, for example, followings and favorites. It is designed for rapid set operations and very large adjacency lists (20,000 writes and 100,000 reads/second), and it is not intended for graph traversal operations. Since it is still in the process of being packaged for use outside of Twitter, the code is still very rough and hence there is no stable release available yet.

You can find more information about the FlockDB database here: `https:/ /github.com/twitter-archive/flockdb`.

DSE Graph

DSE Graph is a part of the always-on DataStax Enterprise data platform of DataStax, Inc. According to the vendor, the DSE Graph is the first graph database powerful enough to scale to massive datasets while offering advanced integrated tools capable of deep analytical queries. It is built on the architecture of Apache Cassandra and can handle billions of items and their relationships, spanning hundreds of machines across multiple datacenters with no single point of failure. It is used by more than 500 customers in 50 plus countries. Recently, the DataStax Managed Cloud has been added to support a fully-managed service for the DSE data platform.

You can find more information about the DSE Graph here: `https://www. datastax.com/products/datastax-enterprise-graph`.

Amazon Neptune

The new graph database Amazon Neptune is offered as an AWS cloud solution. It supports open graph APIs for Gremlin and SPARQL, and provides high performance for both graph models and their query languages. It also supports read replicas, point-in-time recovery, continuous backup to Amazon S3, and replication across **Availability Zones** (**AZ**). It's optimized for processing graph queries and supports up to 15 low latency read replicas across three Availability Zones to scale read capacity and execute several graph queries per second. Neptune continuously backs up data to Amazon S3, and transparently recovers from physical storage failures.

You can find more information about **Amazon Neptune** here: `https:// aws.amazon.com/neptune/`.

AllegroGraph

AllegroGraph is a scalable semantic graph database, which turns complex data into actionable business insights. It can store data and meta data as triples; you can query these triples through various query APIs like SPARQL (the standard W3C query language) and Prolog.

> You can find more information about the AllegroGraph here: `https://franz.com/agraph/allegrograph/`.

Graph features in SQL Server 2017

Prior to SQL Server 2017, relationships in graph structures were represented by junction tables. SQL Server 2017 supports graph databases by bringing graph extensions called `SQL Graph` features. `SQL Graph` and graph extensions are part of the SQL Server database engine. You don't need to install separate services; as soon as you install SQL Server, you can use SQL graph capabilities in all SQL Server editions.

In SQL Server 2017, you can create two types of graph objects, node and edge tables, and use the new `MATCH` clause to traverse through the graph. Node and edge tables are *normal* tables with some special columns and attributes. A graph is a collection of node and edge tables, and all tables within a database belong to the same graph. Since node and edge tables are SQL Server tables, you are allowed to create regular relationships between the tables.

To support the creation and alteration of graph tables, the `CREATE/ALTER TABLE` Transact-SQL statements have been extended in SQL Server 2017.

Node tables

A node table represents an entity in a graph schema. It must have properties (at least one column). All you need is to finish your `CREATE TABLE` statement with the `AS NODE` extension to indicate that the table represents a graph node. The following statements create and populate a node table in SQL Server 2017:

```
CREATE TABLE dbo.TwitterUser(
UserId BIGINT NOT NULL,
UserName NVARCHAR(100) NOT NULL
```

```
) AS NODE
GO
INSERT INTO dbo.TwitterUser VALUES(1, '@MilosSQL'),(2, '@DejanSarka'),(3,
'@sql_williamd'),(4, '@tomaz_tsql'),(5, '@WienerSportklub'),(6,
'@nkolimpija');
```

With the exception of the AS NODE extension, this code is a typical Transact-SQL code, and you did not enter any graph attributes. However, when you look at the table content, you'll find more data than you have inserted:

```
SELECT * FROM dbo.TwitterUser;
```

Here is the table content:

$node_id_5D10F4EF7513480493EE8EE678AAB355	UserName	UserId
{"type":"node","schema":"dbo","table":"TwitterUser","id":0}	@MilosSQL	1
{"type":"node","schema":"dbo","table":"TwitterUser","id":1}	@DejanSarka	2
{"type":"node","schema":"dbo","table":"TwitterUser","id":2}	@sql_williamd	3
{"type":"node","schema":"dbo","table":"TwitterUser","id":3}	@tomaz_tsql	4
{"type":"node","schema":"dbo","table":"TwitterUser","id":4}	@WienerSportklub	5
{"type":"node","schema":"dbo","table":"TwitterUser","id":5}	@nkolimpija	6

In the result set, you can see another column, which was not specified in the CREATE TABLE statement. This column is automatically created by the system and uniquely identifies a node in the database. The column contains a JSON conforming string. Its name is long and consists of two parts: the word $node_id and a unique hexadecimal string. However, you can access it by specifying the $node_id only (without a hex part or the name) as in the following code:

```
SELECT $node_id, UserId, UserName FROM dbo.TwitterUser;
```

As you can see, the JSON value contains the schema and table name and an incremental number. Moreover, when you query the sys.columns catalog view for a node table, you can see another automatically generated column. Use this code, shown as follows, to find all columns in the dbo.TwitterUser table:

```
SELECT name, column_id, system_type_id, is_hidden, graph_type_desc
FROM sys.columns WHERE object_id = OBJECT_ID('dbo.TwitterUser');
```

You can see the fourth column with the name `graph_id<some_hex_string>` in the output, as shown in the following code:

```
name                                    column_id  system_type_id  is_hidden  graph_type_desc
-------------------------------------   ---------  --------------  ---------  ----------------
graph_id_4519EEB1CC8B4541A969BABD82594E35      1         127            1          GRAPH_ID
$node_id_5D10F4EF7513480493EE8EE678AAB355      2         231            0          GRAPH_ID_COMPUTED
UserId                                         3         127            0          NULL
UserName                                       4         231            0          NULL
```

This column is hidden and thus not shown in the result set when you query the table if you specify `SELECT *` to indicate that you want to return all columns. Moreover, it cannot be accessed at all, even if you specify its full name, as shown in the following code:

```
SELECT graph_id_4519EEB1CC8B4541A969BABD82594E35, $node_id, UserId,
UserName FROM dbo.TwitterUser;
```

Instead of rows, you will see the following error message:

```
Msg 13908, Level 16, State 1, Line 17
Cannot access internal graph column
'graph_id_id_4519EEB1CC8B4541A969BABD82594E35'.
```

This column contains an internally generated `bigint` value, and it is also part of the `$node_id` column. The value of the `$node_id` column is automatically generated and represents a combination of the `object_id` of the node table and the value in the `graph_id` column.

> You can use the `NODE_ID_FROM_PARTS` function to see how this value is automatically generated. You will learn about functions later in this chapter.

Of course, you can see graph tables and columns in **SQL Server Management Studio** (**SSMS**) too. They are grouped in the new `Graph Tables` folder:

Graph node table in SQL Server Management Studio

It is recommended to create a unique constraint or index on the `$node_id` column at the time of creating the node table; if one is not created, a default unique, non-clustered index is automatically created and cannot be removed. Use the following code to recreate and refill the table by creating your own constraints:

```
DROP TABLE IF EXISTS dbo.TwitterUser;
GO
CREATE TABLE dbo.TwitterUser(
UserId BIGINT NOT NULL,
```

```
UserName NVARCHAR(100) NOT NULL,
CONSTRAINT PK_TwitterUser PRIMARY KEY CLUSTERED(UserId),
CONSTRAINT UQ_TwitterUser UNIQUE($node_id)
) AS NODE
GO
INSERT INTO dbo.TwitterUser VALUES(1, '@MilosSQL'),(2, '@DejanSarka'),(3,
'@sql_williamd'),(4, '@tomaz_tsql'),(5, '@WienerSportklub'),(6,
'@nkolimpija');
GO
```

A node table is a normal table with extended columns and properties. With a node table, you can perform standard table actions, such as creating indexes, foreign keys, and constraints. There are limitations, but you will learn more about them later in this chapter.

Edge tables

Relationships in SQL Server 2017 are represented with edge tables. To create an edge table, use the extended CREATE TABLE statement. Unlike node tables, an edge table can be created without a single property. In this example, you will create the dbo.Follows edge table, which should represent who is followed by whom from the set of users created in the previous section. Assume that the users follow the other users according to the following table:

User	Follows
@MilosSQL	@DejanSarka, @sql_williamd, @tomaz_tsql, @WienerSportklub
@DejanSarka	@MilosSQL, @sql_williamd, @tomaz_tsql, @nkolimpija
@sql_williamd	@DejanSarka, @tomaz_tsql
@tomaz_tsql	@MilosSQL, @DejanSarka, @sql_williamd
@WienerSportklub	@MilosSQL
@nkolimpija	@DejanSarka

In a relational world, this relation would be represented with a junction table, as in the following example:

```
CREATE TABLE dbo.UserFollows(
    UserId BIGINT NOT NULL,
    FollowingUserId BIGINT NOT NULL,
CONSTRAINT PK_UserFollows PRIMARY KEY CLUSTERED(
    UserId ASC,
    FollowingUserId ASC)
);
```

Use the following code to create foreign keys in this junction table, to ensure data integrity:

```
ALTER TABLE dbo.UserFollows  WITH CHECK ADD CONSTRAINT
FK_UserFollows_TwitterUser1 FOREIGN KEY(UserId) REFERENCES dbo.TwitterUser
(UserId);
ALTER TABLE dbo.UserFollows CHECK CONSTRAINT FK_UserFollows_TwitterUser1;
GO
ALTER TABLE dbo.UserFollows  WITH CHECK ADD CONSTRAINT
FK_UserFollows_TwitterUser2 FOREIGN KEY(FollowingUserId) REFERENCES
dbo.TwitterUser (UserId);
ALTER TABLE dbo.UserFollows CHECK CONSTRAINT FK_UserFollows_TwitterUser2;
GO
```

And here is the INSERT statement that implements the relation from the previous table:

```
INSERT INTO dbo.UserFollows VALUES
(1,2),(1,3),(1,4),(1,5),(2,1),(2,3),(2,4),(2,6),(3,2),(3,4),(4,1),(4,2),(4,
3),(5,1);
```

To create an edge table in SQL Server 2017, you can use the following statement:

```
CREATE TABLE dbo.Follows AS EDGE;
```

As you can see, you did not specify anything but the table name! Similar to node tables, whenever an edge table is created, three visible implicit columns are automatically generated:

- $edge_id: This column uniquely identifies a given edge in the database (along to the $node_id column of a node table)
- $from_id : It stores the $node_id of the node, from where the edge originates
- $from_id : It stores the $node_id of the node, at which the edge terminates

In addition to these three, there are five more hidden columns, as shown in the upcoming screenshot. Now, you will enter the same relations that you previously inserted into the relational table, but this time into the edge table. Entries in edge tables connect two nodes. An edge table enables users to model many-to-many relationships in the graph. Unlike a normal table, in an edge table, you need to refer to the `$node_id` keys rather than to natural business keys. Use the following statement to populate the edge table by using the entries in the relational table:

```
INSERT INTO dbo.Follows
SELECT u1.$node_id, u2.$node_id
FROM dbo.UserFollows t
INNER JOIN dbo.TwitterUser u1 ON t.UserId = u1.UserId
INNER JOIN dbo.TwitterUser u2 ON t.FollowingUserId = u2.UserId;
```

Now, use a simple `SELECT` statement to check the content of the edge table:

```
SELECT * FROM dbo.Follows;
```

Here is the result:

Content of an edge table

In analog to node tables, you can also use short names for the automatically generated columns in an edge table. The following statement also returns the output shown in the preceding screenshot:

```
SELECT $edge_id, $from_id, $to_id FROM dbo.Follows;
```

Here is what this edge table looks like in SSMS:

Graph edge table in SQL Server Management Studio

You can also see that an edge table without properties has eight automatically generated columns. It is also recommended that you create an index on the $from_id and $to_id columns for faster lookups in the direction of the edge, especially in a typical OLTP workload:

```
CREATE CLUSTERED INDEX ixcl ON dbo.Follows($from_id, $to_id);
```

In the first release, converting an existing relational table into a node or edge table is not supported. There are many restrictions and limitations in edge tables. You will see them later in the *SQL Graph limitations* section.

The MATCH clause

SQL Server 2017 added the new MATCH clause to support traversing through graphs by specifying search conditions. Here is the syntax of the MATCH clause:

```
MATCH (<graph_search_pattern>)

<graph_search_pattern>::=
    {<node_alias> {
                    { <-( <edge_alias> )- }
                    | { -( <edge_alias> )-> }
                  <node_alias>
                  }
    }
    [ { AND } { ( <graph_search_pattern> ) } ]
    [ ,...n ]
```

A typical query using the MATCH clause looks like this:

```
FROM node1, edge, node2
WHERE MATCH node1-(edge)->node2
```

You can see that the names of the involved tables are separated by a comma in the FROM clause, the same as in old-style JOIN statements. In the MATCH clause, you start from one node, write the edge table or alias in parentheses, and finally reach the other node table. To indicate the direction of the relation between the nodes, you can use a single dash (-), and dash and greater-than (->) characters. A single dash stays near the node table that is referenced in the $from_id edge column, and a dash and greater-than character represents the relation with the $to_id edge column. You can also use an arrow pointing in the other direction to point from node2 to node1:

```
FROM node1, edge, node2
WHERE MATCH node1-(edge)->node2
```

You can also use aliases for table names (sometimes, you must) as in the following example:

```
FROM node1 n1, edge 2, node2 n2
WHERE MATCH n1-(e)->n2
```

The node names inside MATCH can be repeated. In other words, a node can be traversed an arbitrary number of times in the same query. This part of the query is correct:

```
FROM node1, edge1, node2, edge2, node3
WHERE MATCH node1-(edge1)->node2 AND MATCH node1<-(edge2)-node3
```

However, an edge table name cannot be repeated inside the MATCH clause, and this pseudo-code won't work:

```
FROM node1, edge1, node2, node3
WHERE MATCH node1-(edge1)->node2 AND MATCH node1<-(edge1)-node3
```

In this case, you need to create another instance of the edge table:

```
FROM node1, edge1 AS e1, node2, node3, edge1 AS e2
WHERE MATCH node1-(e1)->node2 AND MATCH node1<-(e2)-node3
```

You saw that the MATCH clause can be combined with other expressions. However, only the AND operator is supported; you cannot use OR and NOT operators in the WHERE clause when you use MATCH.

This will be clear when you see the MATCH clause in action against the graph tables created and populated in the next section.

Basic MATCH queries

You will start with a very simple but common query—finding all users followed by a given user. In the relational approach, the following code returns all users followed by the user with the username @MilosSQL:

```
SELECT t2.UserName
FROM dbo.TwitterUser t1
INNER JOIN dbo.UserFollows uf ON t1.UserId = uf.UserId
INNER JOIN dbo.TwitterUser t2  ON t2.UserId = uf.FollowingUserId
WHERE t1.UserName = '@MilosSQL';
```

The resulting list contains four usernames:

```
UserName
----------------------
@DejanSarka
@sql_williamd
@tomaz_tsql
@WienerSportklub
```

The same result can be achieved by using the new MATCH clause, as in the following code:

```
SELECT t2.UserName
FROM dbo.TwitterUser t1, dbo.TwitterUser t2, dbo.Follows
WHERE MATCH (t1-(Follows)->t2) AND t1.UserName = '@MilosSQL';
```

You can see that the dbo.TwitterUser node table is referenced twice, and the edge table once. One instance of the node table represents followers, the other users who follow @MilosSQL. The MATCH filter contains the following statement:

```
MATCH (t1-(Follows)->t2)
```

It specifies that an element of the set t1 is in relation (follows) an element in the set t2. The MATCH clause is combined with another non-graph predicate by using the AND operator. And what about the execution plans for both queries? As you can see in the following figure, they are identical:

Execution plans for relational and graph queries

So, there is no difference from a performance point of view, but a query that uses the MATCH clause is more intuitive than one that uses JOINs.

To get the list of users who follow the user @MilosSQL, you can use one of the following two logically equivalent statements:

```
SELECT t2.UserName
FROM dbo.TwitterUser t1, dbo.TwitterUser t2, dbo.Follows
WHERE MATCH (t1<-(Follows)-t2) AND t1.UserName = '@MilosSQL';

SELECT t1.UserName
FROM dbo.TwitterUser t1, dbo.TwitterUser t2, dbo.Follows
WHERE MATCH (t1-(Follows)->t2) AND t2.UserName = '@MilosSQL';
```

In both cases, the result will look like the one shown in the following list:

```
UserName
-------------------
@DejanSarka
@tomaz_tsql
@WienerSportklub
```

In the first case, you have simply changed the arrow direction and left all the other sections untouched. The second query references the other instance of the node table in the WHERE clause. In both cases, the given user is on the right side of the relationship (the one who is followed), and both of them are intuitive and simpler than the relational counterpart.

To get all followers of *MilosSQL's*, you can use the following query:

```
SELECT DISTINCT t3.UserName
FROM dbo.TwitterUser t1, dbo.TwitterUser t2, dbo.Follows f1,
dbo.TwitterUser t3, dbo.Follows f2
WHERE MATCH (t1-(f1)->t2-(f2)->t3) AND t1.UserName = '@MilosSQL';
```

Since you have specified two levels in graph traversing, you would need three instances of the node and two instances of the edge table. The MATCH statement is a bit more complex, but still single lined and intuitive. Here is the result of the previous query:

```
UserName
-------------------
@DejanSarka
@MilosSQL
@nkolimpija
@sql_williamd
@tomaz_tsql
```

The same query with relational tables looks more complex and error-prone, as shown in the following code:

```
SELECT DISTINCT u3.UserName
FROM dbo.TwitterUser u1
INNER JOIN dbo.UserFollows  f ON u1.UserId = f.UserId
INNER JOIN dbo.TwitterUser u2 ON f.FollowingUserId = u2.UserId
INNER JOIN dbo.UserFollows f2 ON u2.UserId = f2.UserId
INNER JOIN dbo.TwitterUser u3 ON f2.FollowingUserId = u3.UserId
WHERE u1.UserName = '@MilosSQL';
```

As in the previous example, the execution plans are still the same; the benefit of graph queries are mainly readability and their intuitive nature.

As mentioned earlier, the MATCH clause cannot be combined with other expressions using OR and NOT in the WHERE clause. Therefore, the following code won't work:

```
SELECT t2.UserName
FROM dbo.TwitterUser t1, dbo.TwitterUser t2, dbo.Follows
WHERE  MATCH (t1-(Follows)->t2) OR t1.UserName = '@MilosSQL';
```

Instead of the list of followers, you will get an error message:

```
Msg 13905, Level 16, State 1, Line 3
A MATCH clause may not be directly combined with other expressions using OR
or NOT.
```

Advanced MATCH queries

In this section, you will see the power of the MATCH clause in more detail. Queries will be issued in a SQL Server 2017 instance of the **Internet Movie Database** (**IMDb**). The entirety of IMDb's datasets are available in TSV format at `https://datasets.imdbws.com`. Here is a sample data model of this graph database:

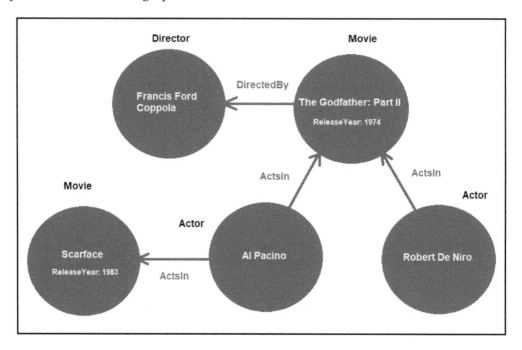

Simplified data model of the IMDb graph database

For the purpose of this example, I have created three node and two edge tables. Here is the code to create tables and indexes:

```
CREATE SCHEMA graph
GO
--node table Movie
CREATE TABLE graph.Movie(
Id INT NOT NULL,
Name NVARCHAR(300) NOT NULL,
ReleaseYear INT NULL,
CONSTRAINT PK_Movie PRIMARY KEY CLUSTERED (Id ASC),
CONSTRAINT UQ_Movie UNIQUE NONCLUSTERED ($node_id)
) AS NODE
GO
```

```
--node table Actor
CREATE TABLE graph.Actor(
Id INT NOT NULL,
Name NVARCHAR(150) NOT NULL,
CONSTRAINT PK_Actor PRIMARY KEY CLUSTERED (Id ASC),
CONSTRAINT UQ_Actor UNIQUE NONCLUSTERED ($node_id)
) AS NODE
GO

--node table Director
CREATE TABLE graph.Director(
Id INT NOT NULL,
Name NVARCHAR(150) NOT NULL,
CONSTRAINT PK_Director PRIMARY KEY CLUSTERED (Id ASC),
CONSTRAINT UQ_Director UNIQUE NONCLUSTERED ($node_id)
) AS NODE
GO

--edge table ActsIn
CREATE TABLE graph.ActsIn AS EDGE;
GO
CREATE CLUSTERED INDEX IX2 ON graph.ActsIn($from_id, $to_id);
GO
CREATE INDEX IX3 ON graph.ActsIn($to_id, $from_id);
GO

--edge table DirectedBy
CREATE TABLE graph.DirectedBy AS EDGE;
GO
CREATE CLUSTERED INDEX IX2 ON graph.DirectedBy($from_id, $to_id);
GO
CREATE INDEX IX3 ON graph.DirectedBy($to_id, $from_id);
GO
```

To populate the Movie table, you need to download and unzip the title.basics.tsv.gz file from the previously mentioned address. After that, you need to import data from the data.tsv file. In this example database, I have imported only titles categorized as *Movies* (not TV movies, series, and so on).

You should repeat the same procedure for the Director and Actor tables. In this case, you need to download and unzip the name.basics.tsv.gz file. Both directors and actors are located in this file; use the primaryProfession column to check whether a person is an actor or a director. Finally, in the files title.crew.tsv.gz and title.principals.tsv.gz, you can find relations between actors, directors, writers, other crew members, and movies.

After the data import, my graph tables have the following number of rows:

```
TableName                                        RowCnt
---------------------------------------------    ------------
graph.Movie                                      436323
graph.Actor                                      3228397
graph.Director                                   676655
graph.ActsIn                                     1797978
graph.DirectedBy                                 437241
```

Now, you can use the MATCH clause to intuitively answer common and simple business questions. For instance, the following query returns the 10 most recently produced movies directed by Martin Scorsese:

```
SELECT TOP (10) Movie.Name AS MovieName,  Movie.ReleaseYear
FROM graph.Movie, graph.DirectedBy, graph.Director
WHERE
    Director.Name = 'Martin Scorsese'
    AND MATCH (Movie-(DirectedBy)->Director)
ORDER BY ReleaseYear DESC;
```

The preceding query generates the following result:

```
MovieName                                        ReleaseYear
---------------------------------------------    -----------
The Irishman                                     2018
Silence                                          2016
The 50 Year Argument                             2014
The Wolf of Wall Street                          2013
Hugo                                             2011
George Harrison: Living in the Material World    2011
A Letter to Elia                                 2010
Shutter Island                                   2010
Public Speaking                                  2010
```

With the following sample and intuitive query, you can find Martin Scorsese's favorite actors:

```
SELECT TOP (5) Actor.Name AS ActorName,  COUNT(*) AS Cnt
FROM graph.Movie, graph.DirectedBy, graph.Director, graph.Actor,
graph.ActsIn
WHERE
    Director.Name = 'Martin Scorsese'
    AND MATCH (Movie-(DirectedBy)->Director)
    AND MATCH (Actor-(ActsIn)->Movie)
GROUP BY Actor.Name ORDER BY Cnt DESC;
```

The preceding query generates the following result:

ActorName	Cnt
Robert De Niro	9
Mardik Martin	6
Leonardo DiCaprio	5
Harvey Keitel	4
Joe Pesci	3

Or you can check for Robert De Niro's favorite directors:

```
SELECT TOP (5) Director.Name AS DirectorName, COUNT(*) AS Cnt
FROM graph.Movie, graph.DirectedBy, graph.Director, graph.Actor,
graph.ActsIn
WHERE
    Actor.Name = 'Robert De Niro'
    AND MATCH (Movie-(DirectedBy)->Director)
    AND MATCH (Actor-(ActsIn)->Movie)
GROUP BY  Director.Name ORDER BY Cnt DESC;
```

The preceding query generates the following result:

DirectorName	Cnt
Martin Scorsese	9
Barry Levinson	3
Brian De Palma	3
Paul Weitz	3
David O. Russell	2

Finally, here are actors that act in the same movies as Robert De Niro:

```
SELECT TOP (5) a2.Name AS ActorName,  COUNT(*) AS Cnt
FROM graph.Movie, graph.ActsIn, graph.Actor a1, graph.Actor a2
WHERE
    a1.Name = 'Robert De Niro'
    AND MATCH (a1-(ActsIn)->Movie)
    AND MATCH (a2-(ActsIn)->Movie)
    AND a2.Name <> 'Robert De Niro'
GROUP BY a2.Name ORDER BY Cnt DESC;
```

Instead of the list, you will get an error message:

```
Msg 13903, Level 16, State 1, Line 48
Edge table 'ActsIn' used in more than one MATCH pattern.
```

Node tables can be repeated in the MATCH clause (a node can be traversed any number of times), but edge tables cannot. Therefore, you need to add another instance of the edge table in the FROM clause:

```
SELECT TOP (5) a2.Name AS ActorName,  COUNT(*) AS Cnt
FROM graph.Movie, graph.ActsIn, graph.ActsIn ActsIn2, graph.Actor a1,
graph.Actor a2
WHERE
 a1.Name = 'Robert De Niro'
 AND MATCH (a1-(ActsIn)->Movie)
 AND MATCH (a2-(ActsIn2)->Movie)
 AND a2.Name <> 'Robert De Niro'
GROUP BY a2.Name ORDER BY Cnt DESC;
```

Now, the query produces the result:

ActorName	cnt
Joe Pesci	5
Al Pacino	4
Harvey Keitel	4
Arnon Milchan	3
Ben Stiller	3

For the final query in this section, you will create a list of movies with Robert de Niro and Al Pacino:

```
SELECT Movie.Name AS MovieName, Movie.ReleaseYear
FROM graph.Movie, graph.ActsIn, graph.Actor, graph.ActsIn ActsIn2,
graph.Actor Actor2
WHERE
    Actor.Name = 'Robert De Niro'
    AND Actor2.Name = 'Al Pacino'
    AND MATCH (Movie<-(ActsIn)-Actor)
    AND MATCH (Movie<-(ActsIn2)-Actor2)
ORDER BY ReleaseYear;
```

Here are the movies:

MovieName	ReleaseYear
The Godfather: Part II	1974
Heat	1995
Righteous Kill	2008
The Irishman	2018

You can see that queries are very simple and intuitive and look less complex than their relational counterparts with multiple JOIN operators.

SQL Graph system functions

SQL Server 2017 brings six new built-in functions to deal with automatically generated columns in node and edge tables. These are used to extract information from the generated columns or to show how they are generated.

The OBJECT_ID_FROM_NODE_ID function

This function extracts the `object_id` from a given `node_id`. The following code returns the `object_id` for the `dbo.TwitterUser` node table:

```
SELECT
OBJECT_ID_FROM_NODE_ID('{"type":"node","schema":"dbo","table":"TwitterUser"
,"id":0}');
```

It parses the input string, extracts the schema and table name, and returns the `object_id` if all these criteria are fulfilled:

- The input string is a JSON conforming string
- A node table exists with the extracted table name in the extracted schema
- The key id has a `bigint` value (a `node_id` with this value does not need to exist in the node table)

The following code will still return the correct `object_id`, even though there is no entry in the node table with the value 567890 for the `graph_id` column:

```
SELECT
OBJECT_ID_FROM_NODE_ID('{"type":"node","schema":"dbo","table":"TwitterUser"
,"id":567890}');
```

If the input string is not JSON conforming or NULL, the function returns NULL, as shown in the following code:

```
SELECT OBJECT_ID_FROM_NODE_ID('abc');
SELECT OBJECT_ID_FROM_NODE_ID('');
SELECT OBJECT_ID_FROM_NODE_ID(NULL);
```

Here is the output for the previous calls:

```
-----------
NULL

-----------
NULL

-----------
NULL
```

The function returns an exception if you provide a non-string input, as in the following example:

```
SELECT OBJECT_ID_FROM_NODE_ID(1);
```

Here is the output:

```
Msg 8116, Level 16, State 1, Line 16
Argument data type int is invalid for argument 1 of object_id_from_node_id
function.
```

The GRAPH_ID_FROM_NODE_ID function

This function is similar to the previous one; it returns a `graph_id` for a given `node_id`. The following code returns the `graph_id` for the `dbo.TwitterUser` node table:

```
SELECT
GRAPH_ID_FROM_NODE_ID('{"type":"node","schema":"dbo","table":"TwitterUser",
"id":0}');
```

The return value is 0, as shown in the following output:

```
--------------------
0
```

It does parse the input string in the same way as the `OBJECT_ID_FROM_NODE_ID` function and does not validate whether an entry with the returned `graph_id` exists in the given node table. Therefore, the following code will return a value, even though there is no entry with a value of 567890 for the `graph_id` in the node table:

```
SELECT
GRAPH_ID_FROM_NODE_ID('{"type":"node","schema":"dbo","table":"TwitterUser",
"id":567890}');
```

Here is the output:

```
------------
567890
```

The function returns NULL values and exceptions analogous to the
`OBJECT_ID_FROM_NODE_ID` function.

The NODE_ID_FROM_PARTS function

This function does an activity which is inverse to one of the previous functions. It generates
a JSON conforming string for a given `node_id` from an `object_id`, with the help of the
following code:

```
SELECT NODE_ID_FROM_PARTS(OBJECT_ID('dbo.TwitterUser'), 0);
```

It returns the JSON value that corresponds to the value for the first row in the
`dbo.TwitterUser` node table, as shown in the following code:

```
-------------------------------------------------------------
{"type":"node","schema":"dbo","table":"TwitterUser","id":0}
```

The function return NULL if a given `object_id` does not belong to a node table, as shown in
the following code:

```
SELECT NODE_ID_FROM_PARTS(58, 0);
```

Here is the output:

```
----------
NULL
```

The function returns NULL if a given `object_id` does not belong to a node table.

The OBJECT_ID_FROM_EDGE_ID function

This function behaves the same as the `OBJECT_ID_FROM_NODE_ID` function and returns the
`object_id` from a given `edge_id` rather than from a `node_id`. The following code returns
the `object_id` for the `dbo.Follows` edge table:

```
SELECT
OBJECT_ID_FROM_EDGE_ID('{"type":"edge","schema":"dbo","table":"Follows","id
":1}');
```

Here is the result:

```
-----------
1014294673
```

The GRAPH_ID_FROM_EDGE_ID function

This function behaves the same as the GRAPH_ID_FROM_NODE_ID function and returns the graph_id from a given edge_id rather than from a node_id. The following code returns the graph_id for the dbo.Follows edge table:

```
SELECT
GRAPH_ID_FROM_EDGE_ID('{"type":"edge","schema":"dbo","table":"Follows","id"
:1}');
```

Here is the result:

```
-----------
1014294673
```

The EDGE_ID_FROM_PARTS function

Finally, the EDGE_ID_FROM_PARTS function is analogous to the NODE_ID_FROM_PARTS function and constructs the edge_id from a given object_id and graph_id, as shown in the following code:

```
SELECT EDGE_ID_FROM_PARTS(OBJECT_ID('dbo.Follows'), 1);
```

It returns the JSON value that corresponds to the value in the first row in the dbo.Follows edge table, as shown in the following code:

```
-----------------------------------------------------------
{"type":"edge","schema":"dbo","table":"Follows","id":1}
```

SQL Graph limitations

The SQL Graph feature is new in SQL Server 2017 and has many limitations. In this review, you will see general limitations for graph tables and missing validation features in edge tables.

General limitations

You saw that creating node and edge tables in SQL Server 2017 is very straightforward. However, there are certain limitations for both table types in this version. Nodes and edge tables cannot be created as memory-optimized, system-versioned temporal tables or temporary tables. Table variables cannot be declared as node or edge tables. Automatically generated $from\_id$ and to_id columns in an edge table cannot be updated; you can insert a new edge and remove the existing one. Finally, cross database queries on graph objects are not supported.

It is usual that the first implementation of a new feature has certain limitations. It is also usual that most of them are removed in the next release. We have a good reason to hope that this will be the case with these limitations.

Validation issues in edge tables

In SQL Server 2017, it is not possible to define constraints on the edge table to restrict it from connecting any two types of nodes. That is, an edge can connect any two nodes in the graph, regardless of their types. Therefore, you can have relational duplicates in the table and thus, for instance, let the user follow him/herself. In a relational table, you can create a constraint and prevent this, as shown in the following code:

```
ALTER TABLE dbo.UserFollows ADD CONSTRAINT CHK_UserFollows CHECK (UserId <>
FollowingUserId);
```

Now, when you try to insert an entry that violates the constraints, as shown in the following code:

```
INSERT INTO dbo.UserFollows VALUES (1, 1);
```

You will be welcomed with the following error message:

```
Msg 547, Level 16, State 0, Line 10
The INSERT statement conflicted with the CHECK constraint
"CHK_UserFollows". The conflict occurred in database "SqlGraphDb", table
"dbo.UserFollows".
The statement has been terminated.
```

However, in an edge table, you cannot create such constraints on automatically created columns, and thus this insert would be possible. To prevent this integrity issue, you have to use **triggers**. The following trigger implements this:

```
CREATE TRIGGER dbo.TG1 ON dbo.Follows
    FOR INSERT, UPDATE
AS
BEGIN
    IF EXISTS(SELECT 1 FROM inserted WHERE inserted.$from_id =
inserted.$to_id)
    BEGIN
        RAISERROR('User cannot follow himself!',16,1);
        ROLLBACK TRAN;
    END
END
```

Now, the INSERT statement that indicates that the user follows him/herself should not work:

```
INSERT INTO dbo.Follows
VALUES('{"type":"node","schema":"dbo","table":"TwitterUser","id":0}','{"typ
e":"node","schema":"dbo","table":"TwitterUser","id":0}');
```

Indeed, when you execute the statement, you will get an error message informing you that the transaction has been aborted, as shown in the following code:

```
Msg 50000, Level 16, State 1, Procedure TG1, Line 7 [Batch Start Line 11]
User cannot follow himself!
Msg 3609, Level 16, State 1, Line 12
The transaction ended in the trigger. The batch has been aborted.
```

Referencing a non-existing node

In addition to the previous issue, you can also insert a relation into an edge table that uses node_ids that don't exist at all. For instance, in the table used in this chapter, there are no nodes with the ID of 45 and 65, and thus the next statement should not work:

```
INSERT INTO dbo.Follows
VALUES('{"type":"node","schema":"dbo","table":"TwitterUser","id":45}','{"ty
pe":"node","schema":"dbo","table":"TwitterUser","id":65}');
```

However, the result of the previous statement does not look like an error message, as shown in the following code:

```
(1 row affected)
```

As you might guess, to prevent this, you can use a trigger. The following code creates a trigger that does not allow you to reference a non-existing node in an edge table:

```
CREATE TRIGGER dbo.TG2 ON dbo.Follows
    FOR INSERT, UPDATE
AS
BEGIN
    IF NOT EXISTS(SELECT 1 FROM inserted
            INNER JOIN dbo.TwitterUser tu ON inserted.$from_id = tu.$node_id
            INNER JOIN dbo.TwitterUser tu2 ON inserted.$to_id = tu2.$node_id
            )
    BEGIN
        RAISERROR('At least one node does not exist!',16,1);
        ROLLBACK TRAN;
    END
END
```

Now, you can try to insert a relation for non-existing nodes:

```
INSERT INTO dbo.Follows
VALUES('{"type":"node","schema":"dbo","table":"TwitterUser","id":87}','{"ty
pe":"node","schema":"dbo","table":"TwitterUser","id":94}');
```

As you expected, you'll get an error:

```
Msg 50000, Level 16, State 1, Procedure TG2, Line 10 [Batch Start Line 0]
At least one node does not exist!
Msg 3609, Level 16, State 1, Line 1
The transaction ended in the trigger. The batch has been aborted.
```

If you specify a non-existing node table, the INSERT will fail:

```
INSERT INTO dbo.Follows
VALUES('{"type":"node","schema":"dbo","table":"Table7","id":87}','{"type":"
node","schema":"dbo","table":"TwitterUser","id":94}');
```

The preceding INSERT statement fails with the following error message:

```
Msg 515, Level 16, State 2, Line 1
Cannot insert the value NULL into column
'from_obj_id_CAD229E5EB9443328A3F0291CEEF166C', table
'SqlGraphDb.dbo.Follows'; column does not allow nulls. INSERT fails.
The statement has been terminated.
```

This issue is prevented by design and you don't need to use a trigger.

Duplicates in an edge table

As mentioned in the first subsection, in an edge table, you can connect any two nodes in the graph, regardless of their types. Therefore, you can have **relational duplicates** in the table. In relational tables, this is usually prevented by creating a primary key, as in the dbo.UserFollows relational table:

```
CONSTRAINT PK_UserFollows PRIMARY KEY CLUSTERED(
    UserId ASC,
    FollowingUserId ASC)
);
```

The primary key constraint will not let you enter the same pair of values for UserId and FollowingUserId again, but in the dbo.Follows edge table, this will be possible. The following statement will not fail:

```
INSERT INTO dbo.Follows
VALUES('{"type":"node","schema":"dbo","table":"TwitterUser","id":0}','{"typ
e":"node","schema":"dbo","table":"TwitterUser","id":1}');
```

When you check the content of the edge table, using the following code:

```
SELECT * FROM dbo.Follows;
```

You can see two entries with the same node_id, as shown in the following screenshot:

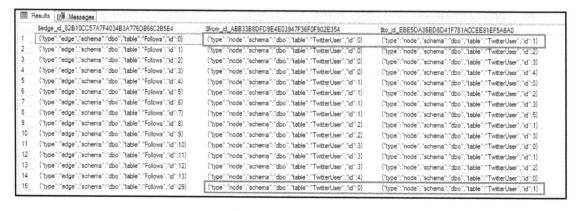

Duplicate entries in an edge table

You can see that the edge entries with IDs of 0 and 29 reference the same nodes. Of course, this problem will be solved with another trigger, but before that, you have to delete the last entry in this table by using the following statement:

```
DELETE FROM dbo.Follows WHERE
$edge_id='{"type":"edge","schema":"dbo","table":"Follows","id":29}';
```

Clearly, you might use another ID in the DELETE statement, when you try to execute this code on your machine.

Now, you can create a trigger to prevent duplicates in the edge table:

```
CREATE TRIGGER dbo.TG3 ON dbo.Follows
    FOR INSERT, UPDATE
AS
BEGIN
    IF (( SELECT COUNT(*) FROM inserted INNER JOIN dbo.Follows f ON
inserted.$from_id = f.$from_id AND inserted.$to_id = f.$to_id  ) >0)
    BEGIN
        RAISERROR('Duplicates not allowed!',16,1);
        ROLLBACK TRAN;
    END
END
```

Again, try the same INSERT statement using the following code:

```
INSERT INTO dbo.Follows
VALUES('{"type":"node","schema":"dbo","table":"TwitterUser","id":0}','{"typ
e":"node","schema":"dbo","table":"TwitterUser","id":1}');
```

This time, the INSERT statement failed, as you expected. Here is the error message:

```
Msg 50000, Level 16, State 1, Procedure TG3, Line 7 [Batch Start Line 11]
Duplicates not allowed!
Msg 3609, Level 16, State 1, Line 12
The transaction ended in the trigger. The batch has been aborted.
```

Deleting parent records with children

As mentioned earlier, you cannot create constraints by using automatically created columns in node and edge tables, and thus it is not possible to create foreign keys between these tables by using these columns. This means that you can delete a node, even if it is referenced in an edge table. For instance, the following code should work: the entry from the dbo.TwitterUser table with the UserId = 5 (@WienerSportklub) should be removed from the table, and two identical SELECT statements should return two different result sets, as shown in the following code:

```
BEGIN TRAN
    SELECT t2.UserName
    FROM dbo.TwitterUser t1, dbo.TwitterUser t2, dbo.Follows
    WHERE MATCH (t1-(Follows)->t2) AND t1.UserName = '@MilosSQL';

    DELETE dbo.TwitterUser WHERE UserId = 5;

    SELECT t2.UserName
    FROM dbo.TwitterUser t1, dbo.TwitterUser t2, dbo.Follows
    WHERE MATCH (t1-(Follows)->t2) AND t1.UserName = '@MilosSQL';
ROLLBACK
```

When you execute it, however, you will see the following error message:

```
Msg 547, Level 16, State 0, Line 250
The DELETE statement conflicted with the REFERENCE constraint
"FK_UserFollows_TwitterUser1". The conflict occurred in database
"ASQLGraph", table "dbo.UserFollows", column 'UserId'.
The statement has been terminated.
```

The entry in the node table is protected by the junction table that you created at the beginning of the section in order to compare graph and *normal* tables. However, when you remove the foreign key, the code will work, as shown in the following code:

```
BEGIN TRAN
    SELECT t2.UserName
    FROM dbo.TwitterUser t1, dbo.TwitterUser t2, dbo.Follows
    WHERE MATCH (t1-(Follows)->t2) AND t1.UserName = '@MilosSQL';

    ALTER TABLE dbo.UserFollows DROP CONSTRAINT
FK_UserFollows_TwitterUser1;
    ALTER TABLE dbo.UserFollows DROP CONSTRAINT
FK_UserFollows_TwitterUser2;

    DELETE dbo.TwitterUser WHERE UserId = 5;
```

```
    SELECT t2.UserName
    FROM dbo.TwitterUser t1, dbo.TwitterUser t2, dbo.Follows
    WHERE MATCH (t1-(Follows)->t2) AND t1.UserName = '@MilosSQL';
ROLLBACK
```

Now, the code is executed, and here is the output:

UserName

@DejanSarka
@sql_williamd
@tomaz_tsql
@WienerSportklub

UserName

@DejanSarka
@sql_williamd
@tomaz_tsql
NULL

You can see NULL in the second result set, since the entry is removed from the node table, but still exists in the edge table. To prevent this serious integrity issue, you will use a trigger, as shown in the following code:

```
CREATE TRIGGER dbo.TG4 ON dbo.TwitterUser
    FOR DELETE
AS
BEGIN
    IF (
        EXISTS(SELECT 1 FROM deleted INNER JOIN dbo.Follows f ON f.$from_id
= deleted.$node_id)
        OR
        EXISTS(SELECT 1 FROM deleted INNER JOIN dbo.Follows f ON f.$to_id =
deleted.$node_id)
    )
    BEGIN
        RAISERROR('Node cannot be deleted if it is referenced in an edge
table',16,1);
        ROLLBACK TRAN;
    END
END
```

Now, execute the previous code:

```
BEGIN TRAN
    SELECT t2.UserName
    FROM dbo.TwitterUser t1, dbo.TwitterUser t2, dbo.Follows
```

```
        WHERE MATCH (t1-(Follows)->t2) AND t1.UserName = '@MilosSQL';

        ALTER TABLE dbo.UserFollows DROP CONSTRAINT
FK_UserFollows_TwitterUser1;
        ALTER TABLE dbo.UserFollows DROP CONSTRAINT
FK_UserFollows_TwitterUser2;

        DELETE dbo.TwitterUser WHERE UserId = 5;

        SELECT t2.UserName
        FROM dbo.TwitterUser t1, dbo.TwitterUser t2, dbo.Follows
        WHERE MATCH (t1-(Follows)->t2) AND t1.UserName = '@MilosSQL';
ROLLBACK
```

The entry in the node table is now protected, as shown in the following code:

```
Msg 50000, Level 16, State 1, Procedure TG4, Line 11 [Batch Start Line 264]
Node cannot be deleted if it is referenced in an edge table
Msg 3609, Level 16, State 1, Line 271
The transaction ended in the trigger. The batch has been aborted.
```

Again, you had to create a trigger to protect data integrity. In relation tables, you can implement data integrity very easily and intuitively by using constraints and foreign keys. Sometimes, I get the impression that people who blame relational databases and are constantly look for speed often forget about the benefits of data integrity in the relational world!

Limitations of the MATCH clause

Some very useful and important graph-specific functions and methods are not supported in SQL Server 2017's SQL Graph:

- Transitive closure
- Shortest path between two nodes
- Polymorphism
- PageRank

A feature called **transitive closure**, usually present in graph databases, is not available in the SQL Graph feature of SQL Server 2017, an extension or superset of a binary relation so that whenever (a,b) and (b,c) are in the extension, (a,c) is also in the extension. This is a very useful feature that gives you all paths between two nodes or answers questions such as *May I fly from Linz (Austria) to Stavanger (Norway)?* or *How can I reach Liverpool from Belgrade?* Unfortunately, SQL Graph's MATCH clause does not support transitive closure and you need to use Transact-SQL solutions that include loops, cursors, or (inefficient) recursive common table expressions.

In Cypher (Neo4j's graph language), you can use the filter expression MATCH path = Belgrade -[*]-> Liverpool to get all paths from Belgrade to Liverpool.

A special case of transitive closure is the **shortest path** functionality, which is used to find the shortest path between two nodes. This is a common requirement in most of the graph database solutions, but is missing in the SQL Graph.

In Cypher, you can use the following query to get the shortest paths from Belgrade to Liverpool:
MATCH (c1:City {name: "Belgrade"}), (c2:City {name: "Liverpool"}), path = shortestpath((c1)-[:FLIGHT*]->(c2)) RETURN path

Polymorphism is the ability to find all nodes connected to a given node. Since SQL Graph does not support polymorphism, Microsoft recommends writing recursive queries with the UNION clause over a known set of node and edge types. However, this solution does not scale and can only be used for a small set of nodes.

PageRank gives us a measure of the importance of a node within a graph structure. It analyzes nodes that are in relation to a single node and calculates their importance or popularity. This is a complex algorithm, but answers simple questions such a *What is the most searched page?* or *Who are the most influential Twitter users?*

There are huge limitations in graph capabilities in SQL Server 2017, and without them, I cannot imagine a significant use of the SQL Graph feature in serious projects.

Summary

In this chapter, you learned how to create and manipulate with graph database objects in SQL Server 2017. You are now familiar with node and edge tables, and the new MATCH clause.

Microsoft's decision to support graph capabilities as an integrated part of SQL Server 2017 is very good, and you can start to consider graphs in your future database solutions. However, the current scope of graph capabilities is not good enough for serious database solutions. Some very important features are missing and workarounds that use recursive queries are not a good starting point for graph adventures.

The main reason for missing features is the missing time between two SQL Server versions, and Microsoft uses this to roll out new technologies in a nice, incremental manner, so we can expect to see significant extensions and improvements in graph capabilities in the next version.

In the last chapter of this book, you will learn how to install and manage SQL Server 2017 on Windows containers and Linux.

17

Containers and SQL on Linux

The introduction of virtualization provided a boost in the possible implementation scenarios for a range of different IT systems. As virtualization technology has matured, it has increased the flexibility of IT departments, allowing them to speed up deployments of new systems and separate logical services from physical infrastructure, leading to the ability to react to business changes at a much greater pace than even a few decades ago.

The classic virtualization strategy was to implement virtual machines—an entire operating system hosted on *big-iron* in the background. This simple but effective system was the first major step towards encapsulating IT services into logical, mobile units that no longer relied on a permanent connection to a specific piece of hardware. The rise of VMWare, Hyper-V, Xen Server, and other virtual machine hosting environments brought about major advances in software virtualization technologies. The largest implementations of virtualized (software-based) infrastructure can be witnessed in the globally available and global-scale *Cloud* offerings from Microsoft, Amazon, Google, and so on. These cloud providers rely heavily on virtualization technologies to provide customers with their computing capacity.

As powerful and flexible as virtualization is, when viewed as service hosting solutions Virtual Machines have a non-trivial overhead associated with them. Namely, each Virtual Machine is an *entire server* in an encapsulated unit; this includes hardware configurations, operating systems, and applications. As mobile and flexible as they are, these moving parts all require care and attention in the form of patches and general maintenance, which can result in a rather overwhelming amount of work when the number of machines is scaled to hundreds or thousands (or even millions, in the case of the aforementioned cloud suppliers).

Containerization and containers were designed to help counteract this administrative overhead by encapsulating applications into a more efficient subset of code and infrastructure modules. The aim of containers is to increase the portability of the packaged application by removing as many dependencies on the hosting environment as possible, while at the same time trying to keep the administration (patching and maintenance) of the contained modules/applications to a minimum.

In this chapter, we will look at how Microsoft has implemented containers in the Windows operating system and how SQL Server 2017 leverages this native container support. We will also investigate how it is now possible to host SQL Server natively on Linux, allowing the implementation of SQL Server to no longer be constrained by the operating system that it runs on.

Containers

Containers are a fantastic technology when it comes to allowing more portability of applications or services across operating systems and physical or virtual infrastructure. The idea of containers is to provide an abstraction layer between an application/service and the underlying operating system, similar to the abstraction layer provided by hypervisors between an operating system and the underlying hardware. This new abstraction layer is intended to allow an application and all ancillary files to be packaged together in a lightweight and portable *container* that can easily be moved from one host to another. An application that is placed into a container is therefore more (or even completely) separated from the infrastructure that it is running on top of. There are no requirements to ensure that the infrastructure is regularly patched or even held on a certain patch level. There are no dependencies between the container and the infrastructure that hosts the container.

Comparison of Virtual Machines and containers

In the preceding figure, we see the difference in the logical structure of a Virtual Machine on a host machine (on the left) and an application/service hosted inside a container (on the right). The subtle but important difference is that a Virtual Machine requires the operating system, the binaries, and application data to be packaged together into a logical unit. A container separates the operating system and the application/binaries. This makes a container a *lighter* logical object to control, because the operating system is no longer a requirement for the container. This spares us from needing to patch and update/administer the operating system for each and every container. We can also note that all containers on a host effectively *share* some resources found in the host and the container service. It is possible to isolate the separate containers even further by running the containers as Hyper-V containers. This is a special type of container that utilizes the Hyper-V features inside Windows to further isolate containers and their resources from one-another.

Containerization is not particularly new in the IT world (it has existed in one form or another since around since 2000). However, SQL Server 2017 is now supported when run inside a container on Windows, Linux, or macOS (yes, the operating system running the container service is pretty much irrelevant). However, this is not to say that the container contents are Windows, Linux, or MacOS; rather the operating system hosting the container service can be one of those three. This is a scenario distinct from the official support for installing and running SQL Server on Linux, which is also supported from SQL Server 2017 onward.

There are a few questions we ask ourselves when we hear that SQL Server can now be hosted inside a container:

- How does SQL Server work inside a container?
- What performance difference can we expect with SQL Server in a container versus on a Virtual Machine or physical host?
- What benefit(s) do we get from using containers with SQL Server?

The next section will provide guidance on all three points so that you can see the benefits and drawbacks of using containers, and identify where they can assist you as a developer. We will begin by taking the first steps to create a SQL Server 2017 instance inside a container and discover how containers work.

Installing the container service

Our prerequisites for using containers are Windows Server 2016 and a current-generation hardware platform that supports virtualization (any Intel/AMD processor from approximately 2005 onward with Intel VT-x or AMD-V technology).

It is possible to host containers inside a Virtual Machine, so feel free to try out this chapter on a Virtual Machine running Windows Server 2016.

The very first step is to activate the Container Services feature on the Windows Server machine that should host the container service. The Container Services feature inside Windows provides the interface between the operating system and the containers that are hosted on the server, and it is a requirement for natively hosting containers in Windows servers.

This is easily done using PowerShell (running using elevated privileges) with two simple commands:

```
Install-Module -Name DockerMsftProvider
Install-Package -Name docker -ProviderName DockerMsftProvider
```

This will download and install the Microsoft provider for Docker from the Microsoft Package Repository. Docker is just one of many container hosting services that are available to use on Windows. However, Microsoft integrated the Docker technology directly into the Windows kernel, allowing for a seamless implementation of containers in Windows using their technology stack.

Microsoft officially provides modules and features for the operating system using the online .NET package management directory powered called **NuGet** (like apt-get for readers who use Linux). This automatically provides dependency resolution and downloads all packages/modules required to make containers work on the current Windows installation:

```
PS C:\Users\Administrator> Install-Module -Name DockerMsftProvider -Force

NuGet provider is required to continue
PowerShellGet requires NuGet provider version '2.8.5.201' or newer to interact with
NuGet-based repositories. The NuGet provider must be available in 'C:\Program
Files\PackageManagement\ProviderAssemblies' or
'C:\Users\Administrator\AppData\Local\PackageManagement\ProviderAssemblies'. You can
also install the NuGet provider by running 'Install-PackageProvider -Name NuGet
-MinimumVersion 2.8.5.201 -Force'. Do you want PowerShellGet to install and import the
NuGet provider now?
[Y] Yes  [N] No  [S] Suspend  [?] Help (default is "Y"): Y
PS C:\Users\Administrator> Install-Package -Name docker -ProviderName DockerMsftProvider

Name                  Version        Source          Summary
----                  -------        ------          -------
Docker                17.06.2-ee-6   DockerDefault   Contains Docker EE for u

PS C:\Users\Administrator> _
```

Installing Docker using PowerShell

A server restart is usually required here, because a low-level reconfiguration of the Windows kernel has been made.

Once the server has been restarted, the container service should be running and available. The first check to ensure that the Docker service is running is to issue the command:

```
Administrator: Windows PowerShell
Windows PowerShell
Copyright (C) 2016 Microsoft Corporation. All rights reserved.

PS C:\Users\Administrator> docker version
Client:
 Version:       17.06.2-ee-6
 API version:   1.30
 Go version:    go1.8.3
 Git commit:    e75fdb8
 Built:         Mon Nov 27 22:46:09 2017
 OS/Arch:       windows/amd64

Server:
 Version:       17.06.2-ee-6
 API version:   1.30 (minimum version 1.24)
 Go version:    go1.8.3
 Git commit:    e75fdb8
 Built:         Mon Nov 27 22:55:16 2017
 OS/Arch:       windows/amd64
 Experimental:  false
PS C:\Users\Administrator> _
```

Docker version

Creating our first container

Now that Docker is installed and working, we can investigate what containers we would like to deploy on this machine. The first port of call is Docker Hub (the official Docker repository), which contains several pre-created container images.

By running the `docker search microsoft/mssql` command, we request a list of images with the terms `microsoft` and `mssql` associated with them. The list of available images is constantly changing, with official images from Microsoft and unofficial/privately created images from other Dockers:

Docker search

To create our first container on our test machine, we will issue a `docker pull` command and download the official SQL Server Express Edition image:

```
docker pull microsoft/mssql-server-windows-express
```

When we run the preceding command, the output is as follows:

docker pull

Please note that here we have a list of GUID-style IDs with download progress reports. This clearly demonstrates the functionality behind Docker images. As mentioned at the beginning of the chapter, Docker packages together applications and binaries so they're portable. To further reduce overhead on a container host, images reuse portions of the data on multiple images on the same host. If we were to install five containers, each running the same version of SQL Server, Docker would be able to use a form of memory de-duplication to reuse the SQL Server binaries on these five containers while only having to download and host one set of those binaries. Equally, this reuse of data and binaries allows Docker to rapidly copy and deploy images on the same host. This very technology is what we, as developers, will want to use to rapidly spin up a SQL Server instance for testing purposes, and then we can dispose of the instance immediately after the tests have been carried out.

This approach to service usage is already widespread in other areas of IT and software development (web servers being the simplest service that this approach supports). The container in this situation is the perfect unit of control to allow the database engine to be managed and approached as a simpler service offering, like a web server. As with many of the recent advancements in technologies around SQL Server for high availability and system deployments, we receive these container benefits through the innovations made to implement the Azure services in the cloud. This technology trickle-down has been communicated by Microsoft over the last few years in most of their products and services with the *Mobile First, Cloud First* strategy.

Once the image has been downloaded and extracted, we can request a list of images available in the Docker host with this command:

```
PS C:\Users\Administrator> docker images
REPOSITORY                            TAG       IMAGE ID        CREATED
microsoft/mssql-server-windows-express  latest    1986b8a8f950    6 weeks ago
PS C:\Users\Administrator> _
```

Docker images

We can now create our first container using this newly downloaded and provisioned image:

```
docker run -d -p 12345:1433 --env ACCEPT_EULA=Y --env sa_password=P4ssw0rd!
--name MySQLContainer microsoft/mssql-server-windows-express
```

Let's deconstruct this command to understand the different portions of it:

```
docker run -d
```

This tells Docker that we wish to start a container in *detached* mode (run as a background service):

```
-p 12345:1433
```

This maps the port on the host machine (`12345`) to the port inside the Docker container (`1433`, the default SQL Server port). This is done to allow network access to SQL Server inside the container. The native container services inside Windows allow for maximum flexibility on the networking side. However, for simplicity, the Windows Container Service will implement a **Virtual Network Interface Card** (**vNIC**) and use **Network Address Translation** (**NAT**) to forward network traffic from the physical host to the container.

> Container Networking is beyond the scope of this chapter and is also being extended at a rapid pace. For further details, please visit the MSDN documentation on Windows Container Networking:
> `https://docs.microsoft.com/en-gb/virtualization/`
> `windowscontainers/manage-containers/container-networking`

Defining environment variables inside a container:

```
--env ACCEPT_EULA --env sa_password=P$ssw0rd!
```

Two *environment* variables are defined. These are variables that are specifically passed into the container and not actually processed by Docker. In this case, we are informing the SQL Server image that we are accepting the licensing terms and conditions (as required when installing SQL Server) and providing the `sa` password:

```
--name MySQLContainer microsoft/mssql-server-windows-express
```

We assign a name to the container for future administration reference and supply the image that we want to use to base the container on.

Once the container has been created, we can show the status of the container with this command:

Here, we see an overview of the container, including network port assignment and which image was used to create the container.

To be able to connect to our SQL Server in the container, we need to know the *real* IP address that it has been assigned—`0.0.0.0` is not an address we can communicate with.

We can investigate the container to find out the externally accessible IP address:

```
        "IPAddress": "",
        "IPPrefixLen": 0,
        "IPv6Gateway": "",
        "MacAddress": "",
        "Networks": {
            "nat": {
                "IPAMConfig": null,
                "Links": null,
                "Aliases": null,
                "NetworkID": "7875ce9196e7ad91efff616035c577defcf9e5286da5fdd756b9288e37c4579e",
                "EndpointID": "fec99e72bb285d3272ce2ac49f2e47a2bb53ff4d96b6228ad72b98861737f2d3",
                "Gateway": "172.31.80.1",
                "IPAddress": "172.31.93.58",
                "IPPrefixLen": 16,
                "IPv6Gateway": "",
                "GlobalIPv6Address": "",
                "GlobalIPv6PrefixLen": 0,
                "MacAddress": "00:15:5d:da:a0:fb",
                "DriverOpts": null
            }
        }
    }
}
]
PS C:\Users\Administrator> _
```

Docker inspect

Now that we have a *public* **IP Address**, we can connect to the server using **SQL Server Management Studio** (**SSMS**). The server is no different from a normal SQL Server instance when connecting in SSMS:

Docker instance in SSMS

Data persistence with Docker

We have been able to spin up an instance of SQL Server inside a container. We have seen that a rapid deployment is possible once the image and supporting files are available on the container host system. The general idea behind containers is that they can be quickly created and destroyed at will, allowing for rapid deployments and short-lived instances of applications (great for testing/development). Once we have these files available, creating and destroying an instance of SQL Server is almost instantaneous and we can begin treating our database service just like a simple web server—a stateless relational database processing service. However, just because the database engine now enjoys rapid deployment, we must consider the second part of the RDBMS equation: the data.

The data inside a database is very much not stateless. It is the very antithesis of stateless, in that the database is supposed to persist our data and data changes. We must therefore consider how this new technology can be used to allow deployment agility and continue to host our databases without data loss. To achieve this, we must instruct Docker to either attach an existing database or to restore a database from a network share. Either will need to be configured as an action *after* the container has been deployed. In an automated deployment pipeline, this sort of preparation step before testing/development can begin is normal in software development outside the SQL Server space and may be familiar to some readers. The idea behind this approach is that an automated deployment has a preparation phase, then the deployment/testing phase, and a final tear-down phase.

The simplest way to allow a database to be accessed and remain usable after the container has been destroyed is to map a folder from the container host into the container itself. We need a folder on our host machine that will store the data and log files, and this will be mapped into the container at creation time (this example will create a new container on a different port and map C:Databases on the host filesystem to C:Databases in the container):

```
docker run -d -p 12346:1433 -v C:Databases:C:Databases --env ACCEPT_EULA=Y
--env sa_password=P4ssw0rd! --name MySQLContainer2 microsoft/mssql-server-
windows-express
```

Upon creation of the container, we are then able to connect to the instance and create a database using the new persistent storage location:

```
USE [master];
GO

CREATE DATABASE [MyContainerDB]
ON PRIMARY
(NAME = N'MyContainerDB', FILENAME = N'C:\DatabasesMyContainerDB.mdf')
LOG ON
```

```
(NAME = N'MyContainerDB_log', FILENAME =
N'C:\DatabasesMyContainerDB_log.ldf')
GO

USE [MyContainerDB];
GO

CREATE TABLE dbo.MyTestTable
(Id INT);
GO

INSERT INTO dbo.MyTestTable
(Id)
SELECT TOP 10 object_id FROM sys.objects
GO

SELECT * FROM dbo.MyTestTable;
```

Assuming that our test/development work is complete and we wish to keep the database for further processing but no longer need the container, we can destroy the container and be sure that the database files remain intact:

```
docker stop MySQLContainer2
docker rm MySQLContainer2
docker ps
```

The output of the preceding code is as follows:

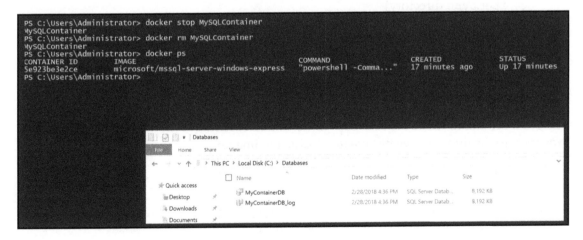

Destroying the Docker container

We then see that the files remain on C: Databases and can be re-attached to another instance for further use. This is extremely important in those cases where the database is still needed after a container has been destroyed (for example, when an automated test has been run and the database is needed for further testing/development purposes).

We also have the option of building a custom image for our containers for cases when we need to do some more configuration before working with the container. We have something called a **dockerfile**. It stores a set of commands that the Docker system can execute in sequence to first take an image and then process customized commands, before completing the build process of the image. This will allow us to include more complicated setup/preparation steps (such as adding or creating databases, users, instance configurations, and so on) that are required in our build process.

The dockerfile is a text file with no extension and contains a specific set of commands. In the following example, we will include the steps to create an image, create a directory for a user database, and attach the previously created MyContainerDB to the SQL Server instance we are starting up. However, this attach can easily be replaced with any other conceivable command (whether specifically for SQL Server or for the underlying operating system).

The contents of the dockerfile are as follows:

- FROM microsoft/mssql-server-windows-express
- The FROM statement defines which base image should be used
- Run PowerShell Command (the new-item -path c: -name Databases - itemtype directory)

The RUN statement tells Docker that we wish to run a specific command, in this case, a Powershell command to create a directory:

```
COPY MyContainerDB.mdf C:\Databases
COPY MyContainerDB_log.ldf C:\Databases
```

The COPY command tells Docker to copy the two database files from the root of the Docker execution to the directory we just created inside the image:

```
ENV sa_password=P$ssw0rd!
ENV ACCEPT_EULA=Y
ENV
attach_dbs="[{'dbName':'MyContainerDB','dbFiles':['C:\Databases\MyContainer
DB.mdf','C:\Databases\MyContainerDB_log.ldf']}]"
```

The three ENV commands are environment-specific commands that the SQL Server image requires to set the sa password, accept the EULA, and attach the newly copied files as a database on the container instance.

We build the image using `docker build` and name it with -t [imagename]. The . tells Docker to use the dockerfile in the current directory for customization:

```
docker build -t testimage
```

The output of the preceding code is as follows:

```
PS C:\Databases> docker build -t testimage .
Sending build context to Docker daemon  16.78MB
Step 1/7 : FROM microsoft/mssql-server-windows-express
 ---> 1986b8a8f950
Step 2/7 : RUN powershell -Command ('new-item -path c:\ -name Databases -itemtype directory')
 ---> Running in 9145748c86c1


    Directory: C:\


Mode                LastWriteTime         Length Name
----                -------------         ------ ----
d-----         3/5/2018   5:54 PM                Databases


 ---> 60476cc23aba
Removing intermediate container 9145748c86c1
Step 3/7 : COPY MyContainerDB.mdf C:\\Databases
 ---> 011ece420550
Removing intermediate container 4727f0b862d6
Step 4/7 : COPY MyContainerDB_log.ldf C:\\Databases
 ---> c85f79e0d0b3
Removing intermediate container b058819075c5
Step 5/7 : ENV sa_password P$ssw0rd!
 ---> Running in 0ea5e7707e7f
 ---> 148786b2982f
Removing intermediate container 0ea5e7707e7f
Step 6/7 : ENV ACCEPT_EULA Y
 ---> Running in ea28bc466e45
 ---> 18e06e420fcb
Removing intermediate container ea28bc466e45
Step 7/7 : ENV attach_dbs "[{'dbName':'MyContainerDB','dbFiles':['C:\\Databases\\MyContainerDB.mdf','C:\\Databases\\MyContainerDB_log
df']}]"
 ---> Running in d64ea53e4c53
 ---> 909e0aa0c537
Removing intermediate container d64ea53e4c53
Successfully built 909e0aa0c537
Successfully tagged testimage:latest
PS C:\Databases> _
```

Docker custom image creation

We are then able to create a container using the new image, then retrieve the IP address, connect to the instance, and see our attached database:

```
docker run -d -p 12346:1433 --name testcontainer testimage
```

The following screenshot shows the execution of the preceding code:

Custom image deployment

This provides us with maximum flexibility when deploying our images and containers. We are able to pull the official release version of SQL Server from Microsoft, alter the contents to meet our requirements, and deploy containers based on this modified base image.

From a developer's standpoint, using containers with SQL Servers allows us to be more flexible with our development process—we are no longer required to involve the DBA or SysOps team if we want to spin up a new instance. This allows us to test new versions and new features without the traditionally drawn-out process of requesting an instance; at the same time we incorporate business-specific configuration changes on top of standardized images supplied by Microsoft. A repeatable deployment process is possible with a minimal overhead.

SQL Server on Linux

Microsoft was openly hostile towards Linux for many years, with former CEO Steve Ballmer famously saying, *Linux is a cancer*. This hostility was understandable, when we consider that Windows was its main source of income for Microsoft and Linux was the direct.

Over the last few years, Microsoft has diversified its product palette, especially their cloud services. Then, in 2014, Microsoft open sourced the .NET Framework, something that couldn't have been expected during Steve Ballmer's tenure. Even with this development, the announcement that SQL Server would run on Linux came as a shock and seemingly out of nowhere.

The idea behind this move is to allow anyone to install and use SQL Server, regardless of the operating system that is being used. This is already being offered with containers, in that the container process can run on Linux or Windows, interchangeably. Where SQL Server on Linux differs is that the SQL Server instance is installed as a service, rather than as a virtual machine or container.

A *full-fat* operating system allows for full control over all parameters of the system, it also enables a company to use existing knowledge and skills to run the entire stack. Naturally, a traditional rival to Microsoft in this space has been Oracle, which has been able to run on Linux for a long time. This move by Microsoft will allow companies that have used Oracle in the past to be able to consider SQL Server as an alternative. The pricing of SQL Server is certainly very competitive when both products are compared—the removal of the operating system hurdle will now allow companies to ask the question: is SQL Server a product we can use?

How SQL Server works on Linux

Knowing that SQL Server was built to run on Windows means that there must have been some changes made to the architecture to support Linux. SQL Server was originally designed to control its resource requirements largely on its own—CPU scheduling, Memory Management, and Storage Access were controlled for the most part by the **SQL Server Operating System** (**SOS**). This deep control allows SQL Server to circumvent many operating system overheads and ensure that database engine activities perform at the highest performance levels while ensuring secure system access is adhered to. Naturally a system that was built over decades on one platform will tend towards using certain access methods of the operating system to achieve these goals. Some of this access on Windows is extremely low level in the operating system and creates dependencies on certain system level functionalities.

A move to allow a different operating system means that the symbiosis between SQL Server and Windows needed a separation layer to deal with these specialized system calls.

Microsoft Research had already invested a great deal of time into the virtualization space and had a project named *Drawbridge* which was designed to allow application sandboxing, where an application runs in a virtualized process and is provided with access to the Windows functionality via an abstraction layer. The work done in this project was then combined into a new project called the **SQL Platform Abstraction Layer** (**SQLPAL**). This abstraction layer was built to align operating-system-specific code together with all other operations and allow a platform-agnostic coding approach with the SQL Server engine code. The stated goal within Microsoft was to provide a full SQL Server experience on Linux with security and performance levels comparable to the current Windows version of SQL Server.

This change will also affect the Windows variant of SQL Server, in that all previous operating-system-specific calls that went directly to Windows are now directed through the SQLPAL, to avoid any future re-engineering requirements for the SQL on Linux variants. Through forcing the SQLPAL association and processing, any performance or security concerns are addressed centrally and affect all variants of SQL Server from this point onward. The advantage here is that SQL on Linux cannot be pushed along as a *second class citizen*, but rather it enjoys the benefits of improvements across the board.

The goals of the SQL on Linux project were publicly stated as follows:

- Quality and security must be the same for SQL Server on Windows
- To provide identical functionality, performance, and scale
- Support application compatibility on both platforms
- To ensure that fixes and updates are supplied for both platforms at the same time
- To provide a path to support future SQL Server services on Linux (for example Integration Services)

These goals basically mean re-engineering the aforementioned dependencies on Windows and pushing these calls into the SQLPAL. The efforts in this area span tens of millions of lines of code in the SQL Server codebase, covering three main areas:

- Win32 (`user32.dll`)
- The NT Kernel (`nrdll.dll`)
- Windows Application libraries (for example MSXML)

The first two areas are more common Windows kernel functionalities; the third section is where the main work in re-engineering will be found. This area covers features such as XML support (parsing XML and so on) as well as more core functionality within SQL Server such as SQLCLR (the common language runtime integration), COM and VDI interfaces for backups, Microsoft Distributed Transaction Coordinator as well as the SQL Server Agent integrations with the Windows Event Log, SMTP, and shell execution.

These features are all core to SQL Server and cannot be simply removed from the SQL Server with any Linux release—otherwise, a greatly crippled variant would be delivered and the goals of full support on any platform would not be met.

Limitations of SQL Server on Linux

As this re-engineering is such a mammoth task, not all features of the SQLOS and SQLPAL are combined. This means that, for SQL Server 2017, there is a list of features in SQL Server that are not supported. The clear plan at Microsoft is to make sure that these features are introduced into future releases of SQL Server, with the ultimate goal of feature parity between SQL Server running on both operating systems:

- Database Engine:
    - Transactional replication
    - Merge replication
    - Stretch DB
    - Polybase
    - Distributed query with third-party connections
    - System extended stored procedures (XP_CMDSHELL, and so on)
    - Filetable, FILESTREAM
    - CLR assemblies with the EXTERNAL_ACCESS or UNSAFE permission set
    - Buffer Pool Extension
- High availability:
    - Database mirroring
- SQL Server Agent:
    - Subsystems: CmdExec, PowerShell, Queue Reader, SSIS, SSAS, and SSRS
    - Alerts
    - Log Reader Agent
    - Change Data Capture
    - Managed Backup
- Security:
    - Extensible Key Management
    - AD Authentication for Linked Servers
    - AD Authentication for **Availability Groups** (**AGs**)
    - Third party AD tools (Centrify, Vintela, and Powerbroker)

- Services:
  - SQL Server Browser
  - SQL Server R services
  - StreamInsight
  - Analysis Services
  - Reporting Services
  - Data Quality Services
  - Master Data Services
  - **Distributed Transaction Coordinator** (DTC)

This list is, of course, rather long and includes some important candidates that may cause SQL Server on Linux to be a non-starter for many in its current incarnation. However, the list doesn't include some *first-class* features, such as In-Memory OLTP or Availability Groups, meaning that these features are supported with SQL Server on Linux.

As with recent releases of SQL Server, we can also expect that these, currently missing, features will quickly be included in the product so that a current *show-stopper* for a SQL Server on Linux deployment can expect to be removed from the missing-feature list in the foreseeable future.

Installing SQL Server on Linux

The first step we need to take before installing SQL Server on Linux is to understand that although the feature is titled *SQL Server on Linux*, there is a selection of supported Linux distributions. At the time of writing this book, the supported distributions were:

- Red Hat Enterprise Linux (version 7.3 or 7.4)
- SUSE Linux Enterprise Server (v12 SP2)
- Ubuntu 16.04

If you are knowledgeable about Linux, you will probably know that these listed distributions being supported means that other distributions will be able to host SQL Server. This is the case on a technical level, as the operating systems that are variants based on one of the supported distributions should pose no problems. However, Microsoft has limited resources to be able to provide enterprise level support for multiple Linux distributions and therefore focused their efforts on distributions found by the majority of customers/potential customers.

For this chapter, we will be using Ubuntu to perform the installation and demos. The main difference between the distributions as far as installing SQL Server are the commands to download and install SQL Server.

Further details on specific distributions can be found on MSDN: `https://docs.microsoft.com/en-us/sql/linux/sql-server-linux-setup#platforms`.

Once our Ubuntu server has been downloaded, installed and prepared for our first use we need to download and install the SQL Server binaries.

The first thing to do is to download and associate the PGP key from Microsoft so that our system can trust the applications that are published by Microsoft:

```
wget -qO- https://packages.microsoft.com/keys/microsoft.asc
sudo apt-key add -
```

The next step is to register the official Microsoft repository (all on one line):

```
sudo add-apt-repository "$(wget -qO-
https://packages.microsoft.com/config/ubuntu/16.04/mssql-server-2017.list)"
```

This now allows our Ubuntu machine to access the official package repository of Microsoft, containing all the necessary files and dependencies to be able to download and install SQL Server onto the Linux machine:

```
sudo apt-get update
sudo apt-get install -y mssql-server
```

The following screenshot shows the installation of SQL Server on Linux:

Installing SQL Server on Linux

We see that the installation of SQL Server on Linux is a much easier prospect than on Windows. Effectively, a single line is needed once the Microsoft repository has been registered in the operating system.

Our final step to complete the installation is to configure the instance for use:

```
sudo /opt/mssql/bin/mssql-conf setup
```

The following screenshot shows the output of the preceding code:

```
sql@ubuntu:~$ sudo /opt/mssql/bin/mssql-conf setup
Choose an edition of SQL Server:
  1) Evaluation (free, no production use rights, 180-day limit)
  2) Developer (free, no production use rights)
  3) Express (free)
  4) Web (PAID)
  5) Standard (PAID)
  6) Enterprise (PAID)
  7) Enterprise Core (PAID)
  8) I bought a license through a retail sales channel and have a product key to enter.

Details about editions can be found at
https://go.microsoft.com/fwlink/?LinkId=852748&clcid=0x409

Use of PAID editions of this software requires separate licensing through a
Microsoft Volume Licensing program.
By choosing a PAID edition, you are verifying that you have the appropriate
number of licenses in place to install and run this software.

Enter your edition(1-8): _
```

Configuring SQL Server

The first configuration step is deciding the edition we want to use. Although Linux operating system distributions are available without licensing costs, SQL Server on Linux remains a commercially available product and does require a license. The preceding screenshot named *Custom image deployment* shows the editions that are available, with notations about each edition's usage and cost.

```
Enter the SQL Server system administrator password:
Confirm the SQL Server system administrator password:
Configuring SQL Server...

Created symlink from /etc/systemd/system/multi-user.target.wants/mssql-server.service to /lib/systemd/system/mssql-server.service.
Setup has completed successfully. SQL Server is now starting.
sql@ubuntu:~$
```

Final configuration step

The last step is to assign the `sa` password to the instance.

At this point, the SQL Server is installed, configured, and potentially ready for use. A quick test to verify that the service is running correctly at a service level will confirm this:

```
systemctl status mssql-server
```

The result preceding code is as shown in the following screenshot:

```
sql@ubuntu:~$ systemctl status mssql-server
• mssql-server.service - Microsoft SQL Server Database Engine
   Loaded: loaded (/lib/systemd/system/mssql-server.service; enabled; vendor preset: enabled)
   Active: active (running) since Mon 2018-03-05 04:58:58 PST; 4min 56s ago
     Docs: https://docs.microsoft.com/en-us/sql/linux
 Main PID: 2533 (sqlservr)
   CGroup: /system.slice/mssql-server.service
           ├─2533 /opt/mssql/bin/sqlservr
           └─2553 /opt/mssql/bin/sqlservr
```

SQL Server service status

Our SQL Server is now ready for action. However, Linux does not natively provide local connectivity and tooling to access SQL Server. We can either connect using SSMS from a remote machine (which works out of the box, provided the firewall is open to the SQL Server port) as with any SQL Server, or download and install tools inside Linux.

To add the Linux SQL tooling, we must add another repository and then install the Unix ODBC developer package:

```
sudo add-apt-repository "$(wget -qO-
https://packages.microsoft.com/config/ubuntu/16.04/prod.list)"
sudo apt-get update
sudo apt-get install -y mssql-tools unixodbc-dev
```

This package provides SQLCMD and bcp to Linux machine. These are simplified tools that have existed for as long as SQL Server has existed. They are command-line interfaces for SQL Server and will allow us to connect to SQL Server and issue commands or export data. At the time of writing, there was no cross-platform support for SSMS and no such support is on the roadmap. SQL Server Operations Studio is the cross-platform tool of choice supplied by Microsoft and can be installed on Windows, macOS, or Linux (the supported distributions already mentioned in this chapter).

When we install the SQLCMD tool onto a Windows machine, the path to SQLCMD is registered for the user (allowing us to directly call SQLCMD regardless of the current folder location on the command prompt). To achieve the same "ease of use" using the Linux tools, we need to register the paths to the tools into our user session. We are registering the path of the tools 'bin' folder into the bash profile, so that we can directly call 'sqlcmd' without having to specify the full path to the command each time we wish to use it. This is done by entering the following three lines of commands/code:

```
echo 'export PATH="$PATH:/opt/mssql-tools/bin"' >> ~/.bash_profile
echo 'export PATH="$PATH:/opt/mssql-tools/bin"' >> ~/.bashrc
source ~/.bashrc
```

We can then connect to the instance using sqlcmd as we usually would on a Windows installation, by calling 'sqlcmd' without the full path to the mssql-tools/bin folder:

```
sqlcmd -S localhost -U SA -P '<YourPassword>'
SELECT name FROM sys.databases
GO
```

The execution of the preceding code is as shown in the following screenshot:

Connecting to SQL on Linux with sqlcmd

At this point, we have a *regular* SQL Server that can be queried and used just as any other SQL Server. From the outside, it is not even apparent that the server is running on Linux (just like the container variant of SQL Server). The programming experience and application connectivity are exactly the same as a SQL Server hosted on Windows. This is in keeping with the goal of transparency from a programming standpoint. It shouldn't matter to an application developer or a user where the SQL Server is hosted; a database is a database.

A further *magic* functionality around SQL Server on Linux is the process of installing patches and updates for SQL Server. Because the Linux operating system and filesystem separate processes from files, it is possible to upgrade files when they are in use (unlike in Windows). This functionality allows files to be updated without the dreaded Windows reboot. When it's time to apply an update to a SQL Server on Linux, we are able to continue using the package manager, pull down updated binaries, and apply them to the server:

```
sudo apt-get update
sudo apt-get install mssql-server
```

This command will update the installed instance to the latest version available in the official Microsoft repository previously registered to the Linux operating system. No system or user databases are affected by this action (just as with an update of a Windows hosted SQL Server instance).

It is equally simple to downgrade an instance (within a major version). You issue an install and provide the desired version number:

```
sudo apt-get install mssql-server=<version_number>
sudo systemctl start mssql-server
```

This will allow a seamless rollback from a particular build to a previous build, which is much simpler than a downgrade on a Windows-hosted SQL Server.

Summary

In this chapter, we got an overview of how SQL Server can be hosted in a container environment (natively on Windows), allowing us to easily deploy new instances of SQL Server with effectively a single line of code. This lightweight virtualization technology fits well into a development scenario and encourages us to experiment with new versions of SQL Server without the traditional overhead of enterprise IT workflows for deploying new servers.

We also saw how simple it is to install SQL Server on Linux, which is, in fact, even simpler than installing SQL Server on Windows. A single repository command can download the desired release of SQL Server and deploy it into a Linux installation. Depending on the internet connection, we can potentially spin up an instance of SQL Server in minutes rather than multiples of that time when working with Windows (including server restarts to register services).

At this point, we are able to see that the tight relationship between SQL Server and the operating system hosting it has been loosened. The flexibility afforded by this change has begun to allow changes in how developers are able to interact with SQL Server. The ability to rapidly deploy a new instance of SQL Server at a moment's notice on a new version of SQL Server allows for more experimentation and a move towards a more agile development strategy.

Equally, being able to run SQL Server on a Windows machine or a Linux machine (or inside a container) means that there is no longer a requirement to deploy a certain operating system. Companies that were previously married to a certain operating system that didn't support SQL Server (Linux) are now able to evaluate whether the fantastically wide feature set of SQL Server is a potential candidate to replace their current RDBMS system. Some of the competing offerings are priced well above the SQL Server licensing and could potentially be good candidates for a move towards the Microsoft product. The operating system question is widely unimportant at this stage, meaning companies can leverage their in-house skills to administer a server hosting environment.

A fluid transition between hosting operating systems and hosting environments (whether on-premise, private cloud, or public cloud) means that an application is also no longer tied to a specific supplier or a third party; rather, it permits a company to utilize the best supplier for a particular use case at any time. The message from Microsoft is now clear: choose the right platform to host the best-in-class RDBMS.

The main takeaway from this chapter should be: For developers, the host for SQL Server should be irrelevant - we don't want or have to care where our database is hosted, we just need to have a unified access to the data. SQL Server hosted inside a container or on a Linux operating system is (almost) identical to what we already know and love about a SQL Server from a year ago. This is exactly how it should be and we can expect this story to develop in the future until full parity of features is implemented.

Other Books You May Enjoy

If you enjoyed this book, you may be interested in these other books by Packt:

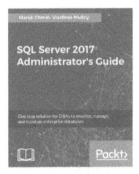

SQL Server 2017 Administrator's Guide
Marek Chmel, Vladimír Mužný

ISBN: 978-1-78646-254-1

- Learn about the new features of SQL Server 2017 and how to implement them
- Build a stable and fast SQL Server environment
- Fix performance issues by optimizing queries and making use of indexes
- Perform a health check of an existing troublesome database environment
- Design and use an optimal database management strategy
- Implement efficient backup and recovery techniques in-line with security policies
- Combine SQL Server 2017 and Azure and manage your solution by various automation techniques Perform data migration, cluster upgradation and server consolidation

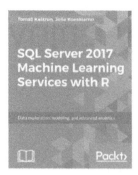

SQL Server 2017 Machine Learning Services with R
Tomaž Kaštrun, Julie Koesmarno

ISBN: 978-1-78728-357-2

- Get an overview of SQL Server 2017 Machine Learning Services with R
- Manage SQL Server Machine Learning Services from installation to configuration and maintenance
- Handle and operationalize R code
- Explore RevoScaleR R algorithms and create predictive models
- Deploy, manage, and monitor database solutions with R
- Extend R with SQL Server 2017 features
- Explore the power of R for database administrators

Leave a review - let other readers know what you think

Please share your thoughts on this book with others by leaving a review on the site that you bought it from. If you purchased the book from Amazon, please leave us an honest review on this book's Amazon page. This is vital so that other potential readers can see and use your unbiased opinion to make purchasing decisions, we can understand what our customers think about our products, and our authors can see your feedback on the title that they have worked with Packt to create. It will only take a few minutes of your time, but is valuable to other potential customers, our authors, and Packt. Thank you!

Index

9 781788 476195